BARRON'S

AP*

UNITED STATES HISTORY

2ND EDITION

Eugene V. Resnick, M.A.
Midwood High School
Brooklyn, New York

BARRON'S

*AP is a registered trademark of the College Board, which was not involved in the production of, and does not endorse, this product.

About the Author

Eugene V. Resnick has taught in the Social Studies Department at Midwood High School in Brooklyn, New York, for 22 years; he has taught AP United States History for 14 of those years. He received a Master's degree in American History from Brooklyn College.

Acknowledgments

Several colleagues and friends provided valuable assistance, advice, and support in completing this project. I would like to extend my gratitude to Joseph Peters, Jeffrey Paris, Sharone David, Noah Burg, Amber Reed, Katie Nekiunas, Daniel Impellizeri, Danielle Shapiro, and Miles Pittman. In addition, I would like to thank the many students who have taken my Advanced Placement United States History class; I have learned much from them. Finally, many thanks to the staff at Barron's Educational Series. I am indebted to Aaron Murray for his excellent copy-editing work, and to the two outstanding editors who have guided me through the entire process—Pat Hunter and Peter Mavrikis. This book is dedicated to my aunt, Estelle Holt, an intellectual and historian par excellence, and to the memory of my parents, Sid and Arlene Resnick.

All inquiries should be addressed to:

Barron's Educational Series, Inc.
250 Wireless Boulevard
Hauppauge, New York 11788
www.barronseduc.com

ISBN: 978-1-4380-0269-9 (book)
ISBN: 978-1-4380-7380-4 (book/CD-ROM package)

Library of Congress Control Number: 2014941404

PRINTED IN THE UNITED STATES OF AMERICA
9 8 7 6 5 4 3 2 1

10%
POST-CONSUMER WASTE
Paper contains a minimum of 10% post-consumer waste (PCW). Paper used in this book was derived from certified, sustainable forestlands.

CONTENTS

As you review the content in this book and work toward earning that **5** on your AP US HISTORY exam, here are five things that you **MUST** know above everything else.

Barron's **Essential** **5**

1
Thinking like a historian. The questions on the AP U.S. History exam are all built around historical thinking skills. The College Board has identified nine skills that are central to the exam and to the broader field of history. The first five skills—Historical Causation, Patterns of Continuity and Change over Time, Periodization, Comparison, and Contextualization—encourage you to develop the habits of mind required for a critical examination of the past. The other four skills—Historical Argumentation, Appropriate Use of Relevant Historical Evidence, Interpretation, and Synthesis—focus on constructing and evaluating historical arguments about the past. These skills encourage students to go beyond memorization and to engage with the past in complex and sophisticated ways.

2
Reading documents. Documents are the building blocks of history and are central to the AP exam. All of the multiple-choice questions and the short-answer questions are built around primary or secondary documents. In addition, the document-based essay question asks you to analyze a series of documents as you construct a response to the question. Focus on how documents relate to the question and on how documents often relate to one another. Remember that historical documents contain a point of view. You should be able to read a diary entry, a newspaper article, a speech, or an argument by a historian and ascertain the point of view and intent of the author.

3
Growth and conflict in American history. The rapid growth of the United States—territorially, economically, and demographically—is unprecedented in world history. On the one hand, this growth decimated Native American cultures; on the other, the nation has provided a haven for immigrants. The territorial growth of the country—inspired by the spirit of "manifest destiny"—intensified the debate over slavery in the antebellum period. The series of compromises over expansion eventually unraveled and helped bring about the Civil War. The economic and territorial growth of the United States continued in the period following the Spanish-American War, as the United States joined the other imperialist powers of the world. Be familiar with the causes of American expansion as well as the profound impacts.

4
The changing nature of the American experiment in democracy. The United States had made major contributions to the literature and the practice of modern representative government. However, be aware that democracy did not emerge fully formed with the birth of the nation. Americans have struggled over the meaning of democracy throughout American history. Abigail Adams encouraged her husband, John, to "remember the ladies" at the time of the creation of the United States. Slavery and the "Jim Crow" system excluded African Americans from the American experiment in democracy. The civil rights movement struggled to fully include African Americans in the democratic system. These conflicts over the meaning of democracy are crucial to understanding the evolution of the United States.

5
The dynamic nature of history. Traditional historians saw history as unidirectional—emanating from the minds and priorities of the elites in society. More recently, historians have seen events as part of a more dynamic process. Social and cultural historians have explored "history from below." As you study, look for such connections and interactions in history. For instance, while it is important to remember that President Lyndon Johnson endorsed and pushed for passage of the 1964 Civil Rights Act, you should be able to connect that with the growth of the grassroots civil rights movement, with the violent backlash against the movement, with shifts within the major political parties, and with the dynamics of the Cold War. Historical events do not occur in isolation of one another. Therefore, memorizing discreet events in American history is not sufficient for success on the AP exam.

Introduction: Preparing for the Redesigned Advanced Placement U.S. History Exam

Congratulations on taking the Advanced Placement course in United States History. If taken seriously, the class and the exam will develop your critical thinking skills and your ability to understand the world in nuanced ways. The class and the exam ask more of you than merely memorizing facts. You will be asked to think through problems, to engage in debates, to organize your thinking, to develop your communication skills, and to take thoughtful stands on important issues.

This book is designed to prepare students for the major changes that are being made in the AP United States History program. Starting in 2014–2015, the College Board is implementing a new curriculum framework for the Advanced Placement United States history course. This new curriculum is designed to prepare students for a redesigned AP United States History exam that will be offered for the first time in May 2015.

The new curriculum framework represents a significant change in the way United States history is organized and taught. The redesigned curriculum identifies nine periods in United States history. Within each period, the framework uses a thematic rather than a strictly chronological approach. Each of the nine periods is broken down into three "Key Concepts," and several supporting concepts and historical developments. These key concepts (identified with numbers), supporting concepts (identified with Roman numerals), and historical developments (identified with letters) form the structure of each of the nine periods in this book.

In addition to creating a new outline of the content of United States history, the College Board has also identified specific skills and themes that students must show proficiency in to earn high scores on the AP exam. The skills and themes in the new framework reflect the College Board's desire to align the AP curriculum and exam with history courses at the university level.

The redesigned exam should not be a cause for alarm. The changes introduced by the College Board better align the goals of the Advanced Placement course with college-level history. There is less of a necessity to memorize hundreds of seemingly unrelated facts and more of an emphasis on developing the historical thinking skills that will deepen your understanding and appreciation of history. Yes, you still must be familiar with a wide variety of developments in United States history. However, the exam will focus on your ability to use this historical content in analyzing and developing arguments, in making connections across time, in understanding the broader context of particular developments, in assessing causation, in challenging interpretations, and in developing new ones. The redesigned course and exam will push you toward greater intellectual growth and will help you think in new and sophisticated ways about the world we live in.

USING THIS BOOK TO HELP YOU PREPARE FOR THE REDESIGNED EXAM

This book has been revised with the explicit aim of helping you succeed on the redesigned AP United States History exam. You will find in the following chapter descriptions of the historical thinking skills and thematic learning objectives that are central to the redesigned exam. We will also provide examples of how these skills and themes apply to the content of American history. These descriptions are followed by a detailed description of the new exam. Each of the four sections of the redesigned exam will be explored, along with tips, strategies, and approaches for achieving high scores on the exam.

Next, the book contains nine chapters of historical content, corresponding to the breakdown of U.S. history in the redesigned concept outline. In addition to describing each of the points of the College Board's concept outline, these chapters provide you with a wealth of illustrative examples. This additional content is designed to illustrate and bring to life the points of the outline. Although the multiple-choice questions on the redesigned exam will be based on the main points and developments of the concept outline, the written sections of the exam invite you to draw on the wealth of American history. This book has condensed the vast content of American history into the illustrative examples that are most relevant to the points in the concept outline and will be most useful to you as you prepare for the AP exam.

Each of the nine content chapters concludes with a "Subject to Debate" section. These sections are designed to call your attention to important debates in regard to historical interpretation. Often, essays can be strengthened by a discussion of how historians have addressed a question. For example, the exam might ask, "To what degree was Reconstruction successful in improving conditions for African Americans?" The student should discuss his or her view of the period, but could also discuss the nature of the historical debate over interpretations of the period. The student might write: "Historians have held dramatically different views of the period. Many southern historians in the late nineteenth and early twentieth century looked at the Reconstruction period as a bitter failure. They were dismissive of any attempts to extend basic rights to African Americans. However, since the Civil Rights era of the 1950s and 1960s, historians have reexamined the record of the period and acknowledged its successes as well as its shortcomings." In this way, the student is recognizing the contentious nature of historical interpretation. Students should be prepared to not only recognize these ongoing debates about the past, but to also participate in them.

Finally, the book contains two practice exams, with two additional exams contained on a CD-ROM (if you purchased a copy of this book with the accompanying CD-ROM). It is suggested that you time yourself as you take these exams. In this way, you will get used to the pacing required for the actual Advanced Placement exam. The exams are followed by explanations to the multiple-choice questions. Please consult these explanations if the material in the question is not clear to you.

Good luck as you prepare for the AP exam.

Historic Thinking Skills and Thematic Learning Objectives

1

In the redesigned Advanced Placement United States History Curriculum Framework, the College Board identifies Historical Thinking Skills and Thematic Learning Objectives that shape the new curriculum framework and the new exam. These skills and themes are central to all the questions on the redesigned exam. The skills transcend American history and are important in the practice of history in any region or topic. The skills outlined by the College Board reflect the skills used by professional historians in their day-to-day work. The themes are windows to help students see continuities and enduring debates and challenges in United States history.

Below, these skills and themes are described and discussed; it is crucial to be familiar with them during the AP course and, of course, as you prepare for the AP exam.

HISTORICAL THINKING SKILLS

In redesigning the Advanced Placement United States History curriculum and exam, the College Board is making explicit nine specific skills that are commonly used by those who participate in the field of historical study. These nine skills are grouped into four skill type categories. The skills outlined by the College Board for the AP United States History exam are the same as those used on the AP World History exam, since its redesign as of the 2011–2012 academic year, and on the redesigned European History exam, which is to go into effect in 2015–2016. Therefore, familiarity with these skills can aid you in other AP history courses you may take. These skills are at the heart of the practice of history—in college, in graduate school, and in the field. At least one of these skills will be built into every question on the Advanced Placement exam. Therefore, an understanding of these skills is essential to success on the AP exam.

Skill Type I: Chronological Reasoning

SKILL 1: HISTORICAL CAUSATION

This skill involves thinking about the causes and effects of historical events. It requires students to see that events in history do not happen in a vacuum—that they are connected to and influenced by previous events in history. Students should be able to distinguish and compare causes and effects and to analyze both long-term and short-term causes of events. Further, historical events generally have multiple causes—rarely is there a direct linear relationship between one event and another. Students, therefore, should be able to evaluate the relationship of multiple causes and effects.

This skill also requires students to assess historical contingency. Historical contingency presumes that each event in history depends on a whole array of events and circumstances—that each event is contingent on this universe of previous conditions. If one or more of the antecedent conditions were absent, perhaps a historical event would have occurred differently or not at all. This skill requires students to interrogate and dissect the myths of inevitability that have shaped many people's thinking about the past. The events that led the United States to expand to it borders, for example, were contingent on earlier events—expansion was not simply the "manifest destiny" of the American nation.

Thinking about historical contingency requires students to distinguish among coincidence, causation, and correlation in looking at different events. Perhaps two events happening around the time are not related to one another in any significant way—they are merely coincidental. Perhaps one can be seen as the cause of the other. Or perhaps the two events are related, but one cannot clearly be seen as the cause of the other. Teasing out the relationship of events in history is key to historical interpretation and key to critiquing existing interpretations of causality.

SKILL 2: PATTERNS OF CONTINUITY AND CHANGE

Recognizing patterns of continuity and change requires students to see patterns and trends in history and at the same time to see that not all events can fit neatly into existing patterns. Students of history can readily see change over time—that our predecessors functioned with different technologies, lived under different laws, participated in different cultural pursuits. This skill requires students to understand these changes over time, but also to see continuities as well. Students must be able to evaluate and analyze these patterns, and to connect patterns of continuity and change with larger historical processes and themes.

Let us look at a specific occurrence in history to explore the skill of continuity and change. The implementation of restrictive quotas on immigrants in the 1920s can certainly be seen in light of continuities with earlier episodes of vocal nativist sentiment. One can explore thematic continuities between the anti-immigrant sentiment that led to the Emergency Quota Act of 1921 and the earlier "Know-Nothing" Party of the 1840s or the movement preceding the Chinese Exclusion Act of 1882. At the same time one can look at and evaluate the actions of prominent nativist writers and activists of the first decades of the twentieth century, such as Madison Grant. One can also look at the broader context of the Emergency Quota Act of 1921, including World War I and the Red Scare (see more on Contextualization, page 5). In this way, the student can also note discontinuities with earlier nativist movements. Finally, the student might be asked to weigh continuities and change over time, and cite evidence, to best understand the implementation of immigration restrictions in the 1920s.

SKILL 3: PERIODIZATION

A sophisticated understanding of history involves the ability to organize historical events into discrete periods. Students should be able to explain the ways that historical events and processes can be organized into blocks of time, and should also be able to evaluate competing strategies and models for organizing these historical periods. This process of periodization requires that historians evaluate historical events and processes and determine which ones are most significant—which ones can be considered turning points, signaling the beginning of different direction in the development of the country. This allows historians to create an overall narrative to make sense of the flow of history. Of course, different historians can come to different conclusions about the important turning points in history, and, consequently, about the periodization of American history.

With its redesigned Advanced Placement curriculum, the College Board has divided the history of North America and the United States into nine discrete periods. In order to familiarize students with this periodization, this book follows the breakdown of the College Board by utilizing the same nine periods. However, students should be prepared to question and challenge any particular breakdown. For instance, many historical narratives, including the College Board's, mark the 1890s as the beginning of the period of United States imperialism. The arguments for such a beginning point are persuasive—the U.S. annexation of Hawaii and the Spanish-American War (both in 1898) open an era of U.S. military and imperial efforts throughout the Americas and Asia. However, one could see continuities between the earlier Mexican-American War (1846–1848), a war that involved an expansion of American hegemony over foreign-held lands, and the Spanish-American War. The beginning and ending periods are not, therefore, self-evident; they are determined by the judgment and the point of view of the historian.

Skill Type II: Comparison and Contextualization

SKILL 4: COMPARISON

Students should be able to look at two or more different historic developments or processes and note similarities and differences. They should also be able to compare different perspectives on a particular process or development. This skill is often presented in history class as the directive to "compare and contrast."

The Advanced Placement exam might ask students to compare developments or processes across time and place. The developments might be from different societies or from within the same society. A sophisticated analysis might compare different developments and processes across more than one variable—such as across time and across space. In any case, a successful comparison will demonstrate the ability to describe, compare, and evaluate different historical developments or processes.

There is a wide variety of comparison-based questions that students might encounter on the AP exam: How similar and how different were the antebellum reform movements and the Progressive–era reform movements, or how does the anti-imperialism movement of the early twentieth century compare to the antiwar movement of the 1960s and 1970s? Students might be asked to compare thematic developments in different time periods, such as how ideas and debates around gender in the 1920s compare to those in the 1950s.

SKILL 5: CONTEXTUALIZATION

This skill requires students to look at historical events and processes and to be able to evaluate how they connect with other things happening at the same time. The context of a particular event can be regional, national, or global. In addition, students should be able to explain and evaluate how a phenomenon, event, or process connects to similar processes across space and time.

Contextualization deepens our understanding of how and why particular events and developments occur. In trying to understand why, for example, the civil rights movement occurred in the 1950s and 1960s, it is important to go beyond the stories of the individuals and organizations involved. Although finding continuities with earlier movements of African-American resistance might lead to fruitful insights, it is also important to understand what is happening contemporaneously in the South, in the United States, and even in the world. Students could look at the context of economic changes in the South in the post–World War II period or the experiences of African-American veterans to help understand the origins of the movement. More broadly, an understanding of the origins of the movement might lead one to examine changes in the Democratic Party as it moved the ideology of its base in the white South. Students could also look at the context of America in the Cold War to understand why calls for civil rights fell on receptive ears; many leaders found it difficult to accuse the Soviet Union of denying democracy to peoples within its orbit while the United States practiced Jim Crow segregation. These layers of context help students of history to more fully understand a particular event or phenomenon.

Skill Type III: Crafting Historical Arguments for Historical Evidence

SKILL 6: HISTORICAL ARGUMENTATION

A basic skill in the field of history is the construction of an argument. Students should be able to frame a question about the past, then develop an argument. A convincing argument contains a compelling and comprehensive thesis and draws on relevant evidence. In addition, students should understand that historians have been addressing major interpretative questions for generations. In constructing an argument, a student, therefore, is entering and interacting with a community of scholars.

This skill has three discrete parts. First, students should be able to analyze historical arguments. This requires students to explain how commonly accepted historical arguments are constructed from available evidence. Second, students should be able to construct compelling interpretations of the past through analyzing evidence. Finally, students should be able to construct persuasive arguments after evaluating and synthesizing conflicting historical evidence.

The skill of constructing a historical argument often operates in conjunction with course themes that involve students being able to transcend several periods of time and use other skills. For instance, in conjunction with the theme of peopling, students might be asked to construct an argument about the reasons for territorial expansion in the decades before the Civil War. This requires students to use the skill of historical causation in conjunction with the skill of argumentation to construct a coherent thesis. Students will have to include evidence from different periods of time, developing a sophisticated analysis of a variety of factors. Evidence might be found in the following: the Puritan belief in establishing a "city set upon a hill"; political ideas about the superiority of republican ideals; the evolution of American ideas about American Indians; and the economic, technological, and demographic changes that affected America in the first half of the nineteenth century.

SKILL 7: APPROPRIATE USE OF RELEVANT HISTORICAL EVIDENCE

Evidence is a basic building block in the study of history. Students must be able to carefully describe and evaluate evidence about the past from a variety of different sources. Historical evidence can include written documents, artifacts, oral traditions, works of music and art, and other primary sources. This skill requires students to understand the content of a piece of evidence, but also to go beyond the content and investigate the purpose, point of view, argument, limitations, format, authorship, and intended audience of different sources. In addition, students must be able to make supportable inferences and draw reasonable conclusions from analyzing and evaluating historical evidence.

A sophisticated use of evidence is central to writing responses to the document-based question. Documentary evidence will also be central to the multiple-choice questions and the short-answer question. Students should be proficient in "reading" a variety of sources, including documents from the point of view of traditionally underrepresented groups and cultures. For example, in understanding the impact of Protestant missionary work in nineteenth-century Irish-Catholic immigrant neighborhoods, students might be asked to look at different types of evidence—from the point of view of the Protestant missionaries as well as from the point of view of Irish immigrants. The exam might also invite students to analyze historical evidence beyond the written word; students might have to evaluate archeological evidence or geographical analyses. In addition, students should be prepared to examine popular culture in gaining an understanding of a period, such as the 1950s or 1960s. Finally, not all relevant evidence will be from an American point of view; in examining the role of the United States in the world, it is important to be able to understand the evidence of non-American actors.

Skill Type IV: Historical Interpretation and Synthesis

SKILL 8: INTERPRETATION

Students of history will confront a wide variety of interpretations of the past. This skill requires students to, first, analyze diverse historical interpretations. Second, students must evaluate how a historical interpretation is shaped both by the perspective of the historian and by the time and context in which the historian wrote.

This skill encourages students to be familiar with the historiography of various historical topics, such as the historiography of American imperialism. If students examine the work of various historians of American imperialism, they will see that interpretations change over time and are influenced by the social setting in which the historians wrote. For instance, historians writing during the World War II era might see American interventions abroad in a positive, even heroic, light, while historians writing a generation later, during the aftermath of the Vietnam War, might see American interventions abroad as misguided impositions of American economic priorities on weaker nations. Of course, the era in which historians live and write does not determine the content of their interpretation. Many factors shape historical interpretations. Historians writing during the same period can come up with widely divergent interpretations of events in the past.

As students come to understand the diversity of interpretations, they will learn to create their own interpretations of the past. When interpreting events students should be cognizant of "presentism"—a mode of historical analysis in which the writer anachronistically introduces contemporary perspectives into interpretations and depictions of the past.

SKILL 9: SYNTHESIS

This final skill involves the ability to use all of the other historical thinking skills in developing meaningful and compelling new understandings of the past. Students must be able to combine and make sense of a variety of types of evidence from primary and secondary sources. In addition, students should be able to apply understandings and insights about the past to other contexts and circumstances, including the present.

The practice of creating syntheses of historical narratives is fraught with difficulties. Traditional narratives of the past often leave out certain perspectives. Students should examine, for instance, whether interpretations of industrialization in the Gilded Age include evidence from the perspectives of working people or women, or whether interpretations of the World War II home front include the perspectives of women or African Americans. As they attempt to create new syntheses, students should be prepared to challenge traditional narratives and ask what voices and perspectives might be missing.

THEMATIC LEARNING OBJECTIVES

The redesigned Advanced Placement curriculum highlights seven themes that will be dealt with throughout the Advanced Placement course and that will be reflected on the questions on the Advanced Placement exam. Within each of the seven themes are several specific thematic learning objectives. All of the questions on the exam are designed to assess your proficiency in one or more of these thematic learning objectives.

Below is a list of the seven themes in the redesigned Advanced Placement curriculum followed by a description of each theme and a description of the learning objectives for each theme. There are five to eight specific learning objectives for each theme. Familiarity with the thematic learning objectives is crucial for success on the Advanced Placement exam.

The seven themes are

Identity
Work, Exchange, and Technology
Peopling
Politics and Power
America and the World
Environment and Geography—Physical and Human
Ideas, Beliefs, and Culture

Identity

This theme encourages students to analyze both the identity of the American people as a national entity, as well as to explore the ways that various groups of individuals have sought to define their identity within the broader American culture. This theme requires students to understand that identity changes over time and that participants themselves in these various groups play an important role in reshaping and redefining identity. Groups have sought to define themselves along lines of gender, class, race, and ethnicity.

Specifically, the College Board asks students to address two overarching questions: First, what changes have occurred in the debates around national identity over time? Second, how have identities around gender, class, ethnicity, region, race, and other factors changed in different eras? In regard to these two questions, the College Board has identified eight specific aspects of identity in American history—three related to national history and five related to group identity.

In regard to national identity, students should be able to

1. Analyze how competing ideas of national identity found voice in the various political institutions and cultural values from the late colonial period to the period preceding the Civil War.

2. Assess the evolution of national identity, as expressed through popular notions of progress and national destiny in the nineteenth century, looking at the impact of westward expansion, the Civil War, and industrialization.

3. Analyze the impact of a series of international crises—from the Spanish-American War through the Cold War—on debates about national identity in the twentieth century.

In regard to group identity, students should be able to

4. Explain how the interactions of European colonizers, Africans, and American Indians in the colonial era shaped ideas of group identity and autonomy.

5. Analyze the development of regional identities in the United States from the colonial period through the nineteenth century.

6. Analyze the development of racial and ethnic identities within the United States and how migration patterns—both into the United States and within the United States— have influenced conflicts over assimilation and distinctiveness.

7. Analyze how the economic, social, and cultural changes that have occurred in the United States from the late nineteenth century to the present have altered class identity and gender roles.

8. Explain the role of the African–American civil rights struggle and other social movements in the growth of identity-based politics during the twentieth century.

Work, Exchange, and Technology

This theme expands on the traditional theme in American history curricula of "economic history." The theme looks broadly at the development of the American economy, from the colonial period through the present. The College Board identifies agriculture, commerce, and manufacturing as the basis of the American economy. To understand the evolution of the American economy, the College Board identifies three overarching questions that students should be prepared to address. First, what role have changes in markets, transportation, and technology had in the shaping of the American economy? Second, how have labor systems changed over time and how have these changes affected American society? Third, how has the role of the American government in the economy changed over time, and how have these changes affected politics, society, the economy, and the environment? For each of these broad questions, the College Board has identified a total of eight specific learning objectives related to the theme of Work, Exchange, and Technology that students should be familiar with.

In regard to the question of changes in markets, transportation, and technology, students should be able to

1. Explain the impact of European contact on the Atlantic World—specifically how the exchange of commodities, people, diseases, and ideas shaped colonial-era societies in North America.

2. Analyze how the economy in North America, both on the national level and on the regional level, from the colonial period to the end of the Civil War, was shaped by innovations in markets, transportation, and technology.

3. Explain how the integration of the U.S. economy into the world economy since the Gilded Age, as well as changes in transportation and technology, have influenced U.S. society.

In regard to the question of different labor systems, students should be able to

4. Explain the development of the variety of labor systems that have characterized the American economy from the colonial period through the nineteenth century—indentured servitude, slavery, free labor, and sharecropping.
5. Explain the role of industrialization since the late nineteenth century in reshaping labor and in reshaping the lives of the working class.

In regard to debates over the role of the government in the economy, students should be able to

6. Explain how economic policies have evolved from the late eighteenth century through the twentieth century, and how these policy changes grew out of debates around market capitalism, corporate power, and the role of the government.
7. Compare movements that have advocated for economic change—such as the union movement, the Populist movement, and the Progressive movement—since the period of industrialization in the late nineteenth century.
8. Explain the changing role of the federal government in regard to regulating economic life from the end of the nineteenth century to the present.

Peopling

The theme of *peopling* covers migration into the United States, out of the United States, and within the United States. Further, this theme recognizes the impact that the adjustments of borders have had on the people who did not migrate. Migrants bring with them ideas, beliefs, technologies, gender roles, and traditions. This theme explores the ways in which people adapt to new settings and how these adaptations have shaped American society. This theme addresses two overarching questions. First, students should be prepared to explain why people have migrated—to, from, and within North America. Second, students should be able to analyze how these migrations have affected American life.

In regard to reasons for migrating, the College Board has identified three specific learning objectives. Students should be able to

1. Explain the movements of people within the Americas in the era before European contact, and explain the movements of people to and within the Americas in the era of European colonization.
2. Explain how the large-scale migrations of people into the United States in the nineteenth and twentieth centuries changed the ethnic and social composition of the population.
3. Analyze migrations within the United States; understand the causes and effects, for example, of urbanization and westward expansion in the nineteenth and early twentieth centuries, the Great Migration in the first half of the twentieth century, and the movement to the suburbs and to the "sun belt" in the second half of the twentieth century.

In regard to the impact of migrations in United States society, there are four learning objectives for students to review. Students should be able to

4. Analyze the impact of European contact on the peoples of the Americas, specifically in regard to disease, warfare, and displacement.

5. Explain the impacts of migrations, both forced and free, within the United States in the nineteenth century—specifically in regard to regional development, cultural diversity, and political and social conflicts.

6. Analyze the impacts on American society of the large-scale internal and international migrations from the mid-nineteenth century to the mid-twentieth century; be familiar with the role of these migrations in regard to urbanization, culture, the labor movement, and reform movements.

7. Explain the changes that have occurred in regard to the debates over immigration from the early twentieth century through the present.

Politics and Power

This theme expands on the traditional theme of political history, which has been at the center of standard American history curricula for decades. The theme of politics and power in the redesigned Advanced Placement curricula goes well beyond the traditional focus on elections, presidents, parties, and policies. This theme invites students to explore the interactions between power, on the one hand, and popular participation, on the other. Attempts have been made to limit participation by certain groups throughout American history; likewise, reform movements have attempted to expand avenues for participation in the political process. This theme also examines the debates about the proper role of government in society. Students should be familiar with changes in the relationship between the three branches of government and between the national government and the state governments. Finally, this theme invites students to explore the ongoing tensions between liberty and authority in American history.

In regard to the competition for power and influence in society, both in colonial North America and in the United States, students should be able to

1. Analyze the interactions among different societies and social groups in colonial North America; be familiar with the factors that led to either competition, cooperation, or conflict.

2. Explain how the different political party systems arose from the founding of the Republic through the end of the twentieth century; be familiar with how and why these political alignments have changed over time.

3. Explain the role of reform movements in terms of creating change to both state institutions and to U.S. society; be familiar with specific reform and activist groups including the reform movements of the antebellum period, the civil rights movement, and socially conservative movements.

4. Analyze changes in the role of the federal government in the political, social, and economic life of the United States; be familiar with how and why the New Deal, the Great Society, and the modern conservative movement attempted to change the role of the federal government.

In terms of the debates around which sets of values should guide the American political system, students should be able to

5. Analyze the arguments over the meaning and interpretation of the Constitution, and how these arguments have affected American politics since 1787.

6. Analyze debates over the role of the United States in the world in the nineteenth and early twentieth centuries; be familiar with how debates over political values (such as democracy and freedom) shaped debates over the extension of American ideals abroad.
7. Analyze how debates over civil rights and civil liberties have shaped political life and institutions in the twentieth century and early twenty-first century.

America and the World

Traditional United States history curricula have certainly focused on the diplomatic and military history of the United States. Such traditional history courses have focused almost exclusively on the decisions made by leaders and on the impact of those decisions. The redesigned Advanced Placement curriculum, however, goes beyond this traditional approach by looking at the United States in a global context and looking at a wide range of factors that have shaped the role of the United States in the world. The primary focus is no longer on the diplomatic and military decisions of American political leaders. The redesigned curriculum asks students to address two broad questions in regard to the theme, America and the World. First, students should be able to look at events in the United States and place them in a global context. The College Board is specifically distancing itself from an older school of historical thought that sees the United States as exceptional—immune, to a large degree, from the currents that affect the rest of the world. Second, students should be able to look at the broad array of factors and motives that have shaped specific decisions in regard to American military, economic, and diplomatic interventions abroad. Here the College Board is placing foreign policy into the broader context of American social, economic, and political history.

In regard to placing events in North American and United States history into the context of contemporary global developments, students should be able to

1. Explain how the origins and patterns of development in colonial North America were shaped by competition between the major imperial powers of the day and by the exchange of commodities across the Atlantic.
2. Explain how the intellectual currents of the Atlantic World influenced belief systems and independence movements through the early nineteenth century.
3. Explain how American society in the late 1800s was shaped by connections with global economic, labor, and migration systems.
4. Explain how domestic social changes in the United States in the twentieth century were shaped by American involvement in global conflicts.

In terms of understanding the array of factors that have influenced decisions about American military, diplomatic, and economic interventions abroad, students should be able to

5. Analyze the factors that influenced the economic, military, and diplomatic actions that resulted in the expansion of American territory and power in the years between the American Revolution and the Civil War.
6. Analyze the domestic debates that took place in the late nineteenth and early twentieth centuries in regard to American imperialism.
7. Analyze the motives and stated goals of policy-makers in regard to American involvement in major international conflicts; these conflicts include the Spanish-American War, the two World Wars, and the Cold War. In addition, explain how the role of the United States in the world has changed as a result of these conflicts.

8. Explain the factors, such as economic globalization and terrorism, that have influenced U.S. foreign policy goals since the middle of the twentieth century in regard to the developing world.

Environment and Geography—Physical and Human

The inclusion of this theme represents a coming together of two traditionally discrete disciplines—history and geography. In the last decade, geographers have become increasingly interested in the historic patterns of the human imprint on the physical world and historians have become increasingly interested in the degree to which the physical environment has shaped human patterns of behavior over time. The redesigned curriculum framework recognizes this development. It focuses on two major questions within the environment and geography theme. The first focuses on interactions. Specifically, how have interactions between the physical environment and different North American groups shaped their institutions and values? This question focuses on the period from before contact between Europeans and American Indians through the U.S. Civil War. The second question focuses on impact and policies. What impact did economic change and demographic shifts have on the environment, and subsequently on debates about the use and regulation of the environment and natural resources? This question covers American history from the colonial period to the present.

In regard to understanding how interactions with the environment shaped the values and institutions of different groups living in North America, students should be able to

1. Explain how the natural environment of North America was transformed by the introduction of new plants, animals, and technologies during the colonial period; in addition, analyze how the introduction of these new plants, animals, and technologies altered interactions among different groups of people.
2. Explain how the natural environment shaped the development of regional identities, institutions, and conflicts, from the period before European contact through the period of American independence.
3. Analyze how environmental factors affected major conflicts, such as the American Revolution and the Civil War; in addition, analyze the role of environmental factors in the formation of regional economic and political identities in the 1800s.

In regard to understanding the impact of economic growth and demographic shifts on the environment and natural resources, and the ensuing debates about use and regulation, students should be able to

4. Analyze how the search for and economic use of natural resources affected political and social developments from the colonial period through Reconstruction.
5. Explain how debates emerged around policies concerning the environment and the use of natural resources; also, explain how the terms of these debates changed from the late nineteenth century to the present era.

Ideas, Beliefs, and Culture

In traditional history courses, cultural history often occupied a marginal place, relegated to the random song or poem introduced as a precursor to the more "serious" history. Over the last generation, historians have worked to integrate cultural, religious, moral, and intellectual history into the mainstream of historical study. The College Board's redesigned curriculum framework recognizes this shift in the Ideas, Beliefs, and Culture theme. The theme explores the roles that ideas, beliefs, social mores, and creative expressions have played in the ongoing development of the United States. Part of understanding the identity of the United States is understanding the development of aesthetic, religious, scientific, and philosophical principles. In addition, students should be prepared to examine how these principles have affected individual and group actions. Beliefs and value systems do not exist in isolation—they intersect with ideas about community and economics, and with movements for social change. This theme raises two broad questions on which to focus—how have moral, philosophical, and cultural values changed over time in American history (from the pre-contact period through the current period), and how have those changes affected American history?

In regard to how moral, philosophical, and cultural values have changed, students should be able to

1. Compare the cultural values and attitudes of the various European, African, and American Indian groups that interacted in the colonial era; also, explain how contact with one another affected intergroup relationships and conflicts.
2. Analyze the emerging conceptions of national identity and democratic ideals in early United States history; also, analyze how these conceptions shaped value systems, gender roles, and cultural movements from the founding of the United States through the 1800s.
3. Explain the impact of the Civil War and industrialization on cultural values and artistic expression.

In regard to how changing moral, philosophical, and cultural values affected U.S. history, students should be able to

4. Analyze the relationship between changing values and beliefs on the one hand and the emerging political, cultural, and social world of the colonial era and early republic on the other; special attention should be paid to the role of religious ideas, Enlightenment beliefs, and republican thought.
5. Analyze how groups and individuals employed philosophical, moral, and scientific ideas to either defend or challenge the dominant economic and social order in the nineteenth and twentieth centuries.
6. Analyze the role of cultural and artistic expressions in movements for social and political change, from the 1800s through the current period.
7. Explain how the emergence of "modernity" in American culture and the growth of popular culture have affected politics and society throughout the twentieth century.

Navigating the Redesigned Advanced Placement U.S. History Exam

2

The redesigned AP United States History exam being introduced by the College Board in May 2015 represents a major departure from the structure and approach of the exam as it has existed in the past. The questions in the redesigned exam are focused explicitly on assessing students' achievement of the thematic learning objectives and on their use of the historical thinking skills. Familiarity with these themes and skills, discussed in the previous chapter, is essential to success on the exam.

The redesigned exam will have two sections; each section will have two parts. Section I will consist of the multiple-choice and the short-answer questions. Part A of Section I will consist of 55 multiple-choice questions. Students will have 55 minutes to complete this part; it will account for 40 percent of the total exam grade. Part B will consist of four short-answer questions. Students will have 45 minutes for this part; it will account for 20 percent of the total exam grade. Section II will consist of the free-response section. Part A of Section II will consist of a document-based question. Students will have 60 minutes for this part; it will account for 25 percent of the total exam grade. Part B will require students to complete one of two long essay questions. Students will have 35 minutes for this part; it will account for 15 percent of the total exam grade. The exam is 3 hours and 15 minutes long; students will have 100 minutes for the multiple-choice and short-answer section and 95 minutes for the free-response section.

In terms of content, the questions will focus on the points in the concept outline in the College Board's AP United States History Curriculum Framework. These points are described in this book within each of the nine chronological periods. The "Key Concepts" of each period are numbered one through three (for example, in Period 4, you will find "Key Concept 4.1," "Key Concept 4.2," and "Key Concept 4.3"). Under each key concept, you will find several supporting concepts, identified with Roman numerals. Finally, under each supporting concept, you will find several historical developments, identified with capital letters. Multiple-choice questions on the AP exam will be based on the points in the concept outline; however, the written portions of the exam invite you to introduce illustrative examples from history to add depth and insight to your responses. As you respond to the short-answer and essay questions, you will have flexibility to introduce illustrative examples that you think are appropriate and compelling.

The approximate breakdown of time periods for exam questions is as follows. About 5 percent of the exam will deal with Period 1—1491–1607. This represents an increased focus on the period before the first British settlements in North America. Approximately 45 percent of the exam will focus on the four periods between the founding of the Jamestown colony

(1607) and the period of the Civil War and Reconstruction. An additional 45 percent will focus of the three periods beginning with the economic developments following the Civil War and ending in 1980. The final 5 percent will focus on the period of 1980 to the present; again this represents an increased focus on the recent past. Note: There will be no long essay question or document-based question that will focus exclusively on the first period (1491–1607) or the last period (1980–present).

MULTIPLE-CHOICE QUESTIONS

Section I, Part A of the exam consists of 55 multiple-choice questions. You will have 55 minutes to complete this part of the exam; 40 percent of your grade on the exam is based on this section. The multiple-choice questions will focus on your ability to reason about different types of historical evidence. In a departure from the previous format of the exam, each question will refer to a primary source, secondary source, a historian's argument, or a historical problem. Questions will be organized in sets of 2–6, with each set referring to specific stimulus material. Each multiple-choice question will have four choices.

All of the multiple-choice questions will require you to show proficiency in one or more of the thematic learning objectives and will require you to apply one or more of the historical thinking skills. The questions will require you to reason about the stimulus material. The stimulus material could be graphs or charts, maps, paintings or political cartoons, historical interpretations, letters or diary entries—virtually any primary or secondary source. The multiple-choice questions will ask you to draw on the stimulus material as well as your knowledge of the concepts and historical developments in the College Board's curriculum framework. As indicated above, these concepts and developments are all described in this book. Events and topics beyond the key concepts, supporting concepts, and historical developments (the numbered and lettered entries in this book) will not appear in multiple-choice questions, unless they are introduced and explained in the stimulus material.

Bring a watch with you and try to work at a steady pace. You have about a minute for each question. This means that you cannot get hung up on difficult questions. If the answer doesn't immediately come to you, make a notation in the test book and come back to it if you have time. Make sure you leave yourself time to get to all the questions.

Sample Multiple-Choice Questions:

The following is a sample set of multiple-choice questions. In this case, students are presented with a political cartoon and then four questions related to the cartoon.

QUESTIONS 1–4 REFER TO THE FOLLOWING QUOTATION:

—Thomas Nast, "This Is a White Man's Government,"
Harper's Weekly, September 5, 1868

1. The political cartoon shown above makes the point that

    (A) northern capitalists benefit as much from the institution of slavery as southern plantation owners do.
    (B) Reconstruction was brought to an unfortunate end by a coalition of forces in the North and South.
    (C) African Americans were incapable of effectively participating in the political process.
    (D) nativist politicians were unfairly presenting Irish Americans as ignorant and brutish.

2. Which of the following would most likely support the perspective of the cartoon?

    (A) Radical Republicans
    (B) Southern Democrats
    (C) Working-class Irish immigrants
    (D) Northern opponents of the Civil War

3. The sentiments expressed in the cartoon most directly contributed to which of the following?

    (A) The compromise ending Reconstruction
    (B) The rise of the Ku Klux Klan in the South
    (C) The enactment of segregation laws in southern states
    (D) The passage of the Fifteenth Amendment

4. The ideas expressed in the cartoon most directly reflect which of the following continuities in United States history?

    (A) Debates about immigration policy
    (B) Debates about the regulation of big business
    (C) Debates about access to voting rights
    (D) Debates about nullification and secession

Answers and Explanations to Sample Multiple-Choice Questions

1. **(B)** This evocative political cartoon requires you to read a whole host of clues before you can understand its meaning. The man on the left is an Irish immigrant; the "5 Points" on his hat refers to the Irish neighborhood in New York City. Note his almost ape-like face. This was typical of representations of Irish immigrants as drawn by nativist cartoonists. The man in the middle has "C.S.A." on his belt buckle—Confederate States of America. His knife says "Lost Cause"—an allusion to the southern nostalgia for the noble fight the South put up in the Civil War. The man on the right has "Capital" written on the object he is holding; he is a northern capitalist, ready to use money to purchase votes. These three sinister forces are working together in the Democratic Party to deny African Americans the right to vote. Note the ballot box strewn on the ground in the lower right hand corner of the cartoon. Nast intended the cartoon as a warning about the dangers of a Democratic victory in the upcoming presidential election. The cartoon does not allude to the slave system or cotton production (A). The cartoon is drawn sympathetically toward African Americans; there is no allusion that the man on the ground is ignorant or debased (D). It is true that Irish immigrants were presented as ignorant, but the cartoonist is not critiquing that. In fact, he himself is presenting an Irish immigrant in an unflattering manner (E).

2. **(A)** The sentiment in the cartoon is that of the Radical Republicans. In the years after the Civil War, they grew alarmed at the assertiveness of the old plantation-owning class and the supporters of secession. This cartoon, published in the weeks before the 1868 presidential election, was intended to warn voters of the dangers of a victory by the Democratic Party. The cartoon depicts working-class Irish immigrants (C) in a stereotypically brutish manner; they would be unlikely to support the overall point of the cartoon. The cartoon is meant as a critique of the Democratic Party's agenda in the South (B); they would certainly not support the sentiment of the cartoon. Northern opponents of the Civil War (D), a war that undid the system of slavery, were unlikely to embrace the cause of suffrage for African Americans.

3. **(D)** The sentiments expressed in the cartoon most directly contributed to the passage of the Fifteenth Amendment. The Fifteenth Amendment states that the vote may not be denied to someone based on "race, color, or previous condition of servitude." Voting

rights for African Americans was a key element of the Reconstruction program of the radical Republicans. The cartoon shows empathy for African Americans, being pushed to the ground and having the vote denied them. The other choices all reflect the point of view of white southern opponents of Reconstruction. The compromise in 1877 that allowed Republican Rutherford B. Hayes to assume the White House also led to the end of Reconstruction, allowing Democrats in the South to reestablish power (A). One factor in pushing African Americans from meaningful participation in the political process was the rise of the Ku Klux Klan in the South (B). After Reconstruction southern states enacted segregation laws (D), further solidifying the second-class status of African Americans.

4. **(C)** The ideas expressed in the cartoon most directly reflect debates about access to voting. The Constitution left voting procedures up to each state. This lack of a federal mandate on voting opened the door to an ongoing debate about access to the ballot box. Initially, many states had property qualifications for voting. By the 1820s and 1830s, however, most states had eliminated them. Access to voting for African Americans has been an ongoing source of debate and struggle. Though the Fifteenth Amendment barred racial discrimination in voting, southern states devised strategies to suppress the African-American vote. These debates led to passage of the Voting Rights Act in 1965, removing many impediments to African Americans voting.

Short-Answer Questions

Section I, Part B of the exam will consist of four short-answer questions. You will have 45 minutes to complete this part of the exam; 20 percent of your grade on the exam is based on this section. Each short-answer question will have three parts, with each part given a grade of 0–1. Therefore, the maximum grade for each of the short-answer questions is 3. At least two of the questions will have some degree of internal choice, so you will be able to focus on what you know best. Each question will focus on one or more thematic learning objectives. These questions will include some sort of source material. You will be required to apply one or more historical thinking skills in responding to the source material—primary documents, historians' arguments, secondary sources, or general propositions about U.S. history. In each of these questions you will be asked to identify and analyze historical evidence relevant to the task at hand. The following is an example of a short-answer question:

QUESTION 1 IS BASED ON THE FOLLOWING TWO PASSAGES:

"I shall show how wrong they are in fact, with great harm to their own souls. For the Creator of every being has not so despised these peoples of the New World that he willed them to lack reason and made them like brute animals, so that they should be called barbarians, savages, wild men, and brutes, as they [Sepúlveda et al.] think or imagine. On the contrary, they [the Indians] are of such gentleness and decency that they are, more than the other nations of the entire world, supremely fitted and prepared to abandon the worship of idols and to accept, province by province and people by people, the word of God and the preaching of the truth. . . .

"Long before they had heard the word Spaniard they had properly organized states, wisely ordered by excellent laws, religion, and custom. They cultivated friendship and, bound together in common fellowship, lived in populous cities in which they wisely administered the affairs of both peace and war justly and equitably, truly governed by laws that at very many points surpass ours, and could have won the admiration of the sages of Athens. . . ."

—Bartolomé de Las Casas, *A Short Account of the Destruction of the Indies*, 1542

"War against these barbarians can be justified not only on the basis of their paganism but even more so because of their abominable licentiousness, their prodigious sacrifice of human victims, the extreme harm that they inflicted on innocent persons, their horrible banquets of human flesh, and the impious cult of their idols. Since the evangelical law of the New Testament is more perfect and more gentle than the Mosaic law of the Old Testament (for the latter was a law of fear and the former is a law of grace, gentleness, and clemency), so also [since the birth of Christ] wars are now waged with more mercy and clemency. Their purpose is not so much to punish as to correct evils. What is more appropriate and beneficial for these barbarians than to become subject to the rule of those whose wisdom, virtue, and religion have converted them from barbarians into civilized men (insofar as they are capable of becoming so), from being torpid and licentious to becoming upright and moral, from being impious servants of the Devil to becoming believers in the true God? They have already begun to receive the Christian religion, thanks to the prudent diligence of the Emperor Charles, an excellent and religious prince. They have already been provided with teachers learned in both the sciences and letters and, what is more important, with teachers of religion and good customs."

—Juan Ginés de Sepúlveda, *The Second Democrates*, 1547

1. Use the two passages above and your knowledge of United States history to answer parts A, B, and C.

    (A) Explain how Bartolomé de Las Casas and Juan Ginés de Sepúlveda disagree with each other.

    (B) Provide evidence from history to explain the context of the debate between Bartolomé de Las Casas and Juan Ginés de Sepúlveda.

    (C) Explain the impact that the debate had on Spanish policies in the Americas.

Explanation and Discussion of Sample Short-Answer Question

This question is based on two primary sources from the period of the Spanish conquest and settlement of areas of the Americas in the 1500s. The redesigned AP curriculum puts additional emphasis on the period of European colonization of the New World before the settlement of Jamestown by the English, so be prepared to answer questions relevant to the first period of the outline of United States history—1491–1607. This question revolves around a debate that occurred in the 1500s, primarily by the two men cited in the question, called the Valladolid debate (named after the city in which the two men debated face-to-face). The question focuses on the following thematic learning objectives: Peopling, #1 and Ideas, Beliefs, and Culture, #1. (Each of the themes is followed by specific, numbered, learning objectives; see previous chapter.) It requires you to use the historic thinking skills of Comparison, Contextualization, and Appropriate Use of Relevant Historical Evidence.

Part A of the question requires students to note that the debate centers on the Spanish treatment of native peoples in the New World and more broadly on the colonization of the Americas. The Dominican Friar Bartolomé de Las Casas argued that the Indians were free men in the natural order and deserved the same treatment as others; before the arrival of the Spaniards, he argued, "they had properly organized states, wisely ordered by excellent laws, religion, and custom." Opposing him was fellow Dominican Juan Ginés de Sepúlveda, who insisted that the Indians, because of their barbaric state, should be punished and therefore reduced to slavery. Such treatment, he argued, was in keeping with Catholic theology and natural law. He asserted that they were less than human and that they required Spanish masters in order to become civilized. Las Casas maintained that they were fully human and that forcefully subjugating them was unjustifiable.

Part B asks students to provide evidence to explain the context of this debate. The debate occurred in the context of Spanish conquest and settlement of the New World. More specifically, the context of Spanish treatment of the native peoples of the Americas must be discussed. Evidence could include a discussion of the forced conversion of native peoples to Christianity, the importance of the extraction of gold and silver, and the harsh details of the *encomienda* system. Part C asks students to explain the impact of the debate. Students should discuss how the debate led to limited changes. King Charles V of Spain created the position of Protector of the Indians to oversee the treatment of native peoples and appointed Las Casas to the position. There were limits placed on the *encomienda* system with the *repartimiento* system—essentially replacing actual slavery with slave-like forced labor by the Indians. The change, however limited, had one major effect on subsequent history—it led to a growth of the African slave trade, as African slavery gradually replaced Indian slavery.

Document-Based Question

Section II, Part A of the redesigned AP exam will consist of one document-based question. You will have 60 minutes to complete this part of the exam; 25 percent of your grade on the exam is based on the document-based question. The DBQ will assess your ability to assess, analyze, and synthesize a wide variety of types of historical evidence and to construct a coherent essay. Your response to the document-based question will be judged on your ability to formulate a thesis and to support it with relevant evidence. The documents can include written materials, charts, graphs, cartoons, and pictures. The documents will be carefully chosen to allow you to explore the interactions and complexities of the topic at hand.

Each DBQ will be based around a particular historical thinking skill, such as continuity and change over time or historical causation. In addition, every DBQ will also assess four additional thinking skills—argumentation, use of evidence, contextualization, and synthesis.

INTEGRATE THE DOCUMENTS INTO YOUR RESPONSE

As you develop your skill in constructing responses to the document-based question, it is important to work on integrating documents into your overall response. You are on the wrong track when the paragraphs of your essay begin as follows: "According to Document 1 . . ." or "As Document 3 indicates . . ." This is the making of a very low-scoring essay—one that merely describes the content of the documents rather than illustrating the targeted historical thinking skill. Try to begin paragraphs with your ideas. Then, within the paragraph mention the appropriate document or documents that illustrate that paragraph's idea. For example, in an essay comparing the temperance movement with the abolitionist movement in the pre–Civil War period, you might have a paragraph that leads with the following sentence: "Both the temperance movement and the abolitionist movement drew on middle-class Protestant fears of licentiousness; both stressed the importance of individuals possessing self-control." Within the paragraph, you might discuss an image of an out-of-control slave owner violently whipping a defenseless slave, as well as a newspaper article describing an out-of-control drunkard. By contrast, a weak lead to a paragraph in this essay might read like the following: "Document 3 shows a slave-owner whipping a slave. This image made people oppose slavery. . . ." The paragraph is not addressing the historical learning skill of comparison.

NOTICE CONNECTIONS BETWEEN DOCUMENTS

Often in document-based questions, two or more of the documents "talk to one another." That is, one responds to something in another one. One document might amplify an earlier one, or, more likely, offer a different perspective. In a document-based question on southern and northern home-front issues during the Civil War, one document might defend the New York City draft riot as a justified response to the "$300 rule" in the draft law; the next document might condemn the rioters as misguided and racist. Your job is to let the documents communicate with each other. Bring out the tensions implicit in these two documents. Begin a paragraph with these tensions: "New Yorkers had markedly different reactions to the draft riot. . . ." Do your best to make sense of the tensions between documents; don't simply avoid the documents that don't immediately conform to your thesis.

AUDIENCE, PURPOSE, CONTEXT, AND POINT OF VIEW

Higher scoring essays need to go beyond simply analyzing a source and fitting it into an argument (see rubric on page 23). Try to situate a document in its time and place, noting its intended audience, purpose, historical context, and the author's point of view. Do not take every document at face value. Note the origins and dates of particular documents as you use them, and take that knowledge into consideration. A report about the corruption and inefficiencies of Reconstruction governments in the South should be questioned if it was written by a former Confederate official. His purpose might be to discredit Reconstruction governments rather than merely describe their functioning.

OUTSIDE EVIDENCE

A strong response must have significant outside evidence. You cannot get the highest score on a document-based question by only citing evidence in the documents themselves (see rubric on page 23). You must introduce relevant outside information and evidence. A document-based question looking at changes in the civil rights movement from the 1950s to the 1960s might provide you with a reading from a Black Panther platform in 1967, illustrating a more militant direction for the movement in the 1960s. Outside evidence could include a speech by Malcolm X or by Stokely Carmichael.

Scoring Rubric for the Document-Based Question

The maximum score you can receive for the document-based question is 7. This grade is based on the following rubric:

- Thesis (Skills assessed: Argumentation and targeted skill)—0–1 point.

The thesis or your essay will be assessed on your proficiency in argumentation and the specific historical thinking skill addressed in the question. In other words, you must develop an argument around a specific historical thinking skill, such as historic causation or continuity and change over time. To receive the maximum score, 1 point, your thesis must directly address all parts of the question. You must do more than restate the question.

- Analysis of historical evidence and outside examples in support of thesis (Skills assessed: Use of historical evidence, argumentation, and targeted skill)—0–4 points.

Three of the four points in this part of the rubric assess your use of the historical evidence provided in the documents. To earn 1 point, you must offer a plausible analysis of the content of a majority of the documents, explicitly using this analysis to support the stated thesis or a relevant argument. To reach 2 points, you must, in addition to meeting the criteria for 1 point, also offer plausible analysis of at least one of the following for the *majority* of the documents: intended audience, purpose, historical context, and/or the author's point of view. To earn 3 points, you must perform the tasks necessary for 2 points, but apply them to *all,* or *all but one,* of the documents, rather than a majority.

The fourth point in this element of the rubric is based on your use of outside examples. To earn the 1 point, you must offer plausible analysis of historical examples beyond/outside the documents to support your stated thesis or argument.

- Contextualization (Skill assessed: Contextualization)—0–1 point

This element of the rubric assesses your ability to place your essay in a broader context. To earn the 1 point, you must accurately and explicitly connect historical phenomena relevant to the argument to broader historical events and/or processes.

- Synthesis (Skill assessed: Synthesis)—0–1 point

To earn 1 point you are required to tie up the elements of your essay—argument, analysis of documents, use of evidence, and contextualization—and then go beyond the immediate question at hand in one of three ways. First, you may appropriately extend or modify your thesis or argument. Second, you may note and effectively account for disparate and sometimes contradictory evidence from primary sources and/or secondary works in crafting your argument. Or third, you may appropriately connect the topic of the question to other historical periods, geographical areas, contexts, or circumstances.

The following is an example of a document-based question:

1. Compare the mobilization efforts by local, state, and federal authorities in the United States in preparation for World War I with mobilization efforts in preparation for World War II.

Document 1

Source: Announcement, The War Industries Board, June 6, 1918, reprinted in the *New York Times*, June 7, 1918.

Be it Resolved, by the War Industries Board, That the following agreement reached as a result of several conferences between a committee of the board and the American Iron and Steel Institute, be and the same is hereby ratified, confirmed, and approved, to become effective at once:

Whereas, A careful study of the sources of supply in connection with the present and rapidly increasing direct and indirect war requirements for iron and steel products has convinced the War Industries Board of the necessity for (1) a strict conservation of the available supply of iron and steel products, on the one hand, and (2) the expansion of existing sources and the development of new sources of supply of iron and steel products, on the other hand; and

Whereas, the producers iron and of iron and steel products in the main concur in this conclusion reached by the said board, and have expressed their willingness to cooperate wholeheartedly with the said board. . . .

Source: Poster, United States Food Administration, L.N. Britton (artist), 1917.

Source: "Another Tar and Feather Party Is Staged," *Ashland* [Wisconsin] *Daily Press*, April 11, 1918.

Adolph Anton, residing at 1100 Sixth Avenue West, was taken from his home at about nine o'clock last night by a party of five or six who came to the house in an auto, carried to a spot on the Beaser Avenue road known as the Chequamego Ice Company's farm, and given a coat of tar and feathers for alleged pro-German sentiments. He was then released and told to beat it for home. Stark naked and covered with a profuse coat of tar and feathers, he walked the distance to his home, about a mile.

Source: Poster, Milwaukee Country (Wisconsin) Council of Defense, 1917.

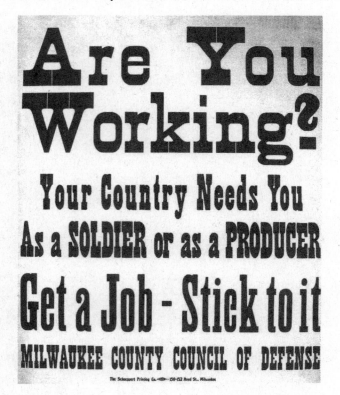

Source: Portion of the amendment to Section 3 of the Espionage Act of June 15, 1917, United States, *Statutes at Large*, Washington, DC, 1918.

SECTION 3. Whoever, when the United States is at war, shall willfully make or convey false reports or false statements with intent to interfere with the operation or success of the military or naval forces of the United States, or to promote the success of its enemies, or shall willfully make or convey false reports, or false statements, . . . or incite insubordination, disloyalty, mutiny, or refusal of duty, in the military or naval forces of the United States, or shall willfully obstruct . . . the recruiting or enlistment service of the United States, or . . . shall willfully utter, print, write, or publish any disloyal, profane, scurrilous, or abusive language about the form of government of the United States, or the Constitution of the United States, or the military or naval forces of the United States . . . or shall willfully display the flag of any foreign enemy, or shall willfully . . . urge, incite, or advocate any curtailment of production . . . or advocate, teach, defend, or suggest the doing of any of the acts or things in this section enumerated and whoever shall by word or act support or favor the cause of any country with which the United States is at war or by word or act oppose the cause of the United States therein, shall be punished by a fine of not more than $10,000 or imprisonment for not more than twenty years, or both. . . .

Source: Printing Office for the Office of Price Administration, 1943.

Source: Lt. Gen. J.L. DeWitt's letter of transmittal to the Chief of Staff, U.S. Army, June 5, 1943.

1. I transmit herewith my final report on the evacuation of Japanese from the Pacific Coast.

2. The evacuation was impelled by military necessity. The security of the Pacific Coast continues to require the exclusion of Japanese from the area now prohibited to them and will so continue as long as that military necessity exists. The surprise attack at Pearl Harbor by the enemy crippled a major portion of the Pacific Fleet and exposed the West Coast to an attack which could not have been substantially impeded by defensive fleet operations. More than 115,000 persons of Japanese ancestry resided along the coast and were significantly concentrated near many highly sensitive installations essential to the war effort. Intelligence services records reflected the existence of hundreds of Japanese organizations in California, Washington, Oregon and Arizona which, prior to December 7, 1941, were actively engaged in advancing Japanese war aims. These records also disclosed that thousands of American-born Japanese had gone to Japan to receive their education and indoctrination there and had become rabidly pro-Japanese and then had returned to the United States. Emperor-worshipping

ceremonies were commonly held and millions of dollars had flowed into the Japanese imperial war chest from the contributions freely made by Japanese here. The continued presence of a large, unassimilated, tightly knit and racial group, bound to an enemy nation by strong ties of race, culture, custom and religion along a frontier vulnerable to attack constituted a menace which had to be dealt with. Their loyalties were unknown and time was of the essence.

Document 8

Source: "We Can Do It!," by J. Howard Miller, produced by Westinghouse for the War Production Board, 1943.

Document 9

Source: Al Waxman, editor of the *Eastside Journal*, June 1943.

At Twelfth and Central I came upon a scene that will long live in my memory. Police were swinging clubs and servicemen were fighting with civilians. Wholesale arrests were being made by the officers.

Four boys came out of a pool hall. They were wearing the zoot-suits that have become the symbol of a fighting flag. Police ordered them into arrest cars. One refused. He asked: "Why am I being arrested?" The police officer answered with three swift blows of the night-stick across the boy's head and he went down. As he sprawled, he was kicked in the face. Police had difficulty loading his body into the vehicle because he was one-legged and wore a wooden limb. Maybe the officer didn't know he was attacking a cripple.

At the next corner a Mexican mother cried out, "Don't take my boy, he did nothing. He's only fifteen years old. Don't take him." She was struck across the jaw with a night-stick and almost dropped the two and a half year old baby that was clinging in her arms. . . .

Rushing back to the east side to make sure that things were quiet here, I came upon a band of servicemen making a systematic tour of East First Street. They had just come out of a cocktail bar where four men were nursing bruises. Three autos loaded with Los Angeles policemen were on the scene but the soldiers were not molested. Farther down the street the men stopped a streetcar, forcing the motorman to open the door and proceeded to inspect the clothing of the male passengers. "We're looking for zoot-suits to burn," they shouted. Again the police did not interfere. . . . Half a block away . . . I pleaded with the men of the local police substation to put a stop to these activities. "It is a matter for the military police," they said.

Answering the Document-Based Question

This document-based question asks you to compare the mobilization efforts of World War I with those of World War II. As you look at the documents, several themes should emerge. One theme that quickly emerges is that in both World War I and World War II, the role of the federal government grew. We can see this in the conservation efforts in both wars. In World War I, we see this in Document 2, a poster from the Food Administration urging a change in diet to prevent shortages of certain commodities (meat, sugar, and fat) for the war effort. In World War II, we see a similar effort at conservation in Document 6; commuters are urged to carpool so as to save fuel for the war effort.

In addition to conservation, we can see that in both wars, authorities put a good deal of effort into filling defense-industry plants with workers. For World War I, we see this in Document 4—a general plea to the public to get a job, either in industry or in the military. For World War II, we see this effort in Document 8, urging women to take industrial jobs, assuring them that they could handle such jobs. The World War II efforts to find employees are alluded to in Document 9 as well. This document describes one of the "zoot suit riots" that occurred in Los Angeles and elsewhere during the war. These anti-Mexican riots occurred after the federal government instituted the Bracero program, allowing thousands of Mexicans to legally enter the United States as temporary guest workers.

Another theme that emerges in the comparison is the treatment of different ethnicities. In World War I, we see violence against German Americans in Document 3. This document should remind students of the rise in xenophobia and anti-German violence during World War I. In World War II, in addition to the violence against Mexicans in the "zoot suit riots" (Document 9), we see discrimination against Japanese Americans with their relocation into the interior of the United States. In both wars, ugly expressions of ethnic hatred seemed to be unleashed by the war.

The final area of comparison to examine is the limits placed on civil liberties in both conflicts. In World War I, the government passed the Espionage and Sedition Acts, limiting free-speech rights. These acts are referenced in Document 7, an excerpt from the Espionage Act. During World War II, the government limited the civil liberties of the entire population of West Coast Japanese Americans by issuing Executive Order 9066, calling for the internment of people of Japanese descent in a series of camps. In both wars, the government expanded its power to limit civil liberties. Students can judge the merits of each action, noting similarities and differences.

Long Essay Questions

Section II, Part B of the exam will give students a choice between two comparable long essay questions. You will have 35 minutes to complete this part of the exam; 15 percent of your grade on the exam is based on the long essay. Since you have choice in deciding which of the two questions to write about, you have the opportunity to demonstrate what you know best. The long essay will be assessed on your use of specific historic thinking skills in explaining and analyzing important issues as defined by the thematic learning objectives. The long essay will require you to develop a thesis or argument and to support your thesis with an analysis of specific and relevant historical evidence.

Scoring Rubric for the Long Essay Question

The maximum score you can receive for the long essay question is 6. This grade is based on the following rubric:

- Thesis (Skills assessed: Argumentation and targeted skill): 0–1 point.

To receive the 1 point for this element of the rubric, you must state a thesis that directly addresses all parts of the question. The thesis must do more than restate the question. Your thesis must address the thinking skill specified in the question.

- Support for argument (Skills assessed: Argumentation and Use of historical evidence): 0–2 points.

To receive 1 point, you must support your thesis with specific evidence. To receive 2 points, you must also clearly and consistently state how the evidence you have introduced supports the thesis or argument, and establishes clear linkages between the evidence and the thesis or argument.

- Application of targeted historical thinking skill: 0–2 points.

This element of the rubric is determined by the specific historical thinking skill cited in the question. These skills can include Continuity and Change Over Time, Comparison, Causation, or Periodization.

For Continuity and Change Over Time questions, you will receive 1 point for describing historical continuity *and* change over time. For the additional point you must also analyze specific examples that illustrate continuity *and* change over time.

For Comparison questions, you will receive 1 point for describing similarities *and* differences among historical developments. For the additional point, you must also provide examples, and do one of the following, depending on the prompt: Either analyze the reasons for the similarities *and/or* differences among historical developments, or analyze the relative importance of the historical developments.

For Causation questions, you will receive 1 point for describing causes *and/or* effects of a historical development. For the additional point, you must also analyze specific examples that illustrate causes *and/or* effects of a historical development.

For Periodization questions, you will receive 1 point for describing the ways in which the historical development discussed in the prompt was different from *or* similar to developments that came before *and/or* afterward. For the additional point, you must analyze the extent to which the historical development discussed in the prompt was different from *and* similar to developments that came before *and/or* afterward, providing specific examples to illustrate the analysis.

■ Synthesis: 0–1 point.

To earn 1 point in this final element of the rubric requires that you tie up the elements of your essay—argument, use of evidence, and contextualization—and then go beyond the immediate question at hand in one of three ways. First, you may appropriately extend or modify your thesis or argument. Second, you may use an additional appropriate category of analysis beyond that called for in the prompt; categories can include political, economic, social, cultural, geographical, race/ethnicity or gender. Or third, you may appropriately connect the topic of the question to other historical periods, geographical areas, contexts, or circumstances.

The following are examples of long essay questions:

Questions 1–2: These questions ask students to analyze long-term and short-term causation in regard to American military conflicts. Students must develop an argument and support that argument with appropriate evidence. *Historical Thinking Skill: Patterns of Continuity and Change over Time. Thematic Learning Objectives: Work, Exchange, and Technology, #7 (for question 1) and #6 and #8 (for question 2).*

1. How did the levels of success of organized labor in the United States change from the 1880s to the 1930s?

2. How did the relationship between major corporations and the federal government change from the 1880s to the 1930s?

Explanation and Discussion of Sample Long Answer Question

Both questions invite students to examine continuity and change over time from the Gilded Age of the late 1800s to the era of the Great Depression and New Deal of the 1930s. In both cases, students are invited to describe the changes that occurred and to give examples to illustrate those changes. Also, in both cases, strong essays should place these historic changes in the context of times.

In regard to question 1, the key change to note in terms of the level of success of organized labor from the Gilded Age to the age of the New Deal was that organized labor was far stronger by the end of the period. Students could compare the defeats by organized labor in the Homestead Strike and the Pullman Strike in the 1890s with the remarkable growth of the C.I.O. in the 1930s. The more difficult task is to determine why. A major factor in understanding the change involves government policies toward unions. In the Gilded Age, government was generally on the side of management. Students could cite ample evidence for this—the use of the Sherman Antitrust Act against unions, the Supreme Court decision in regard to the Pullman Strike and Eugene V. Debs, the use of federal troops. During the New Deal era, President Franklin Roosevelt pushed for legislation that recognized the right of organized labor to collective bargaining. Students could cite section 7A of NIRA or the Wagner Act. Students could look at other factors to explain the change over time, such as the changing nature of work, immigration patterns, economic trends, political realignment, and changing intellectual currents. Now, to develop a thesis statement, below are two possible thesis statements, a weak one and a strong one:

Weak thesis: "Organized labor was more successful in the 1930s than in the 1890s because workers were determined and unified."

Strong thesis: "Though both the 1890s and the 1930s were periods of economic downturns, organized labor was far more successful in the 1930s than in the 1890s; this was largely the result of a shift in government policies, as the pro-business ideology of the "robber baron" era gave way to the demand-side ideology of the New Deal era."

In regard to question 2, again the changes from the Gilded Age to the era of the New Deal are striking. The government generally let major corporations have a free hand in conducting business. The laissez-faire ideology of the late nineteenth century dominated mainstream political thinking. This ideology was supported by Social Darwinism, by the sociological writings of William Graham Sumner, and even by the dime novels of Horatio Alger, Jr. Students could cite Supreme Court cases that made regulation exceedingly difficult, such as *Santa Clara County v. Union Pacific Railway*, which established the concept of "corporate personhood." Both the Sherman Antitrust Act and the Interstate Commerce Commission were circumvented by big business. By the 1930s, the ideology of laissez-faire no longer resonated as it had a generation earlier. The realities of the Great Depression and the pragmatism of Franklin Roosevelt made possible a far more active federal government in regard to major corporations. Students could cite the Securities and Exchange Act, the National Industrial Recovery Act, or the Glass-Steagall Act in illustrating this shift. Now, let us put these ideas together to develop a thesis statement.

Weak thesis: "In the 1890s the government was friendly to big business, but in the 1930s the government was hostile to big business."

Strong thesis: "The administration of President Franklin Roosevelt, shaped by the progressive crusades of the early twentieth century, by his battles against corrupt political machines and, most importantly, by the economic devastation of the 1930s, abandoned the laissez-faire, pro-business ideology of the Gilded Age, and implemented a sweeping series of reforms that dramatically increased the role of the federal government in regulating big business."

Period 1: 1491–1607 The Meeting of Three Peoples

3

TIMELINE

1492	Christopher Columbus (Italian, sailing for Spain) arrives in the New World, beginning era of European colonization of the Americas
1498	Vasco da Gama (Portugal) sails to India
1517	Martin Luther challenges Roman Catholic beliefs and practices; initiates Protestant Reformation
1521	Spanish forces, led by Hernan Cortes, defeat the Mexica people, led by Montezuma
1530	John Calvin breaks with the Catholic Church
1532	Spanish forces, led by Francisco Pizarro, defeat the Inca people
1542	Bartolomé de Las Casas writes *A Short Account of the Destruction of the Indies*
1549	The *repartimiento* reforms begin to replace the *encomienda* system
1587	Founding of the "lost" British colony of Roanoke
1588	British defeat of the Spanish Armada
1597	Juanillo's Revolt in Florida
1598	Acoma Pueblo Massacre in New Mexico

INTRODUCTION

The meeting of three peoples—American Indians, Europeans, and West Africans—on land held by American Indians on the North American continent created a new world.

A remarkable series of events, occurring between the 1200s and the 1500s, led to a broad transformation of much of the world, bringing peoples together from far-flung corners of the globe. The local and regional systems of an earlier era gave way to a global system. This reordering of the world created great wealth for some and utter destruction for others, as peoples from three regions—the Americas, Europe, and Africa—encountered one another. Out of these encounters developed new settlements and colonies in the New World.

KEY CONCEPT 1.1 PRE-CONTACT NORTH AMERICA

A wide variety of social, political, and economic structures had developed among the native peoples in North America in the period before the arrival of Europeans. These structures grew, in part, out of the interactions among native peoples and between native peoples and the environment.

I. Adaptations to Diverse Environments

As settlers migrated across North America over time, they developed a great diversity of complex social structures. These settlers both adapted to the environment and transformed it.

A. SOCIETIES OF THE WEST

Maize (corn) cultivation was common in many areas from present-day Mexico into the American Southwest. The cultivation of maize fostered economic development and social diversification among the peoples of this region. Farther north, societies in the Northwest and in areas of California also experienced economic development and social diversification, developing a mix of foraging and hunting.

The Pueblo People of the Southwest

The Pueblo people lived in areas that are part of the current southwestern United States. The Pueblo were named by the Spanish because many lived in small towns, or *pueblos*. Ancestral Pueblo culture developed around the year 900 AD in the area that is today known as the Four-Corners region of the Southwest—the area where Utah, Colorado, Arizona, and New Mexico meet. These early Pueblos, sometimes called the Anasazi people, became increasingly dependent on the cultivation of maize. These settled communities developed complex, technologically advanced societies. Many lived in architecturally sophisticated structures, including structures in the Chaco Canyon of New Mexico, some of which contained hundreds of rooms.

Because of climatic change, including volcanic eruptions and severe drought in the thirteenth and fourteenth centuries, the Pueblo people began to disperse from the complex settlements around the Four-Corners region. This dispersal led to conflict with neighboring peoples. Some Pueblos united with Zunis and Hopis in western New Mexico. Some joined with settled communities in the Rio Grande valley. This movement, known as the Great Migration, led the Pueblo to abandon the sophisticated towns they had developed over hundreds of years of civilization and to join other groups in the Southwest. This development weakened Pueblo communities just on the eve of European contact.

Chinook People of the Pacific Northwest

In the Pacific Northwest, the Chinook people lived along the Columbia River in present-day Washington and Oregon. The Chinook people consisted of several groups, all speaking related languages. These groups practiced foraging, hunting, and fishing, and tended to live in settled communities. Chinook communities had a high degree of economic development and social stratification. A higher caste of Chinook people—shamans, warriors, and successful merchants—lived in relative isolation from Chinook commoners. Many Chinook people lived in longhouses, which contained up to fifty people.

B. SOCIETIES OF THE GREAT BASIN AND GREAT PLAINS

The peoples of the Great Basin and the western Great Plains tended to develop mobile lifestyles in response to the lack of natural resources.

The Shoshone, Piute, and Ute People of the Great Basin

The Great Basin refers to the 400,000-square-mile area between the Rocky Mountains and the Sierra Mountains. The area has a great deal of environmental diversity but is characterized by a pronounced lack of natural resources. This dearth of resources was especially severe after a rise in temperatures, approximately 5,000 years ago, created hot, arid conditions, leading to a series of droughts that struck the American West from approximately 900 to 1400 AD. Historians and archeologists refer to a "desert culture" that was common among most of the pre-contact American Indian tribes of the Great Basin. "Desert culture" was characterized by seasonable mobility, as hunters and foragers searched for food throughout the year. "Desert culture" peoples often developed basket making, whereas more sedentary groups often developed pottery. Three large groupings of native peoples of the Great Basin are the Shoshone people, the Piute people, and the Ute people.

American Indians of the Great Plains

The Great Plains refers to the vast stretch of land in the United States and Canada that stretches from the Mississippi River to the Rocky Mountains. The Plains Indians are the native groups most commonly stereotyped in images of Indians in American popular culture. The stereotype often involves Plains Indians riding horses, wearing feathered headdresses, and hunting buffalo. In the minds of many Americans who know this stereotype from movies and television shows, this image represents not just Plains Indians, but all American Indians. The stereotype has little validity even in regard to Plains Indians. Although many Plains Indian groups, especially those of the western Great Plains, did depend on the buffalo for survival, it was not until European contact that horses were introduced into Plains Indian cultures. Before that, many American Indian cultures of the Great Plains, such as the Sioux, the Blackfoot, the Arapaho, and the Cheyenne, hunted for buffalo by foot, maintaining a mobile lifestyle. Some American Indian groups of the Great Plains, especially the eastern Great Plains closer to the Mississippi River (such as the Osage, the Wichita, and the Omaha) developed more sedentary, agrarian lifestyles.

C. SOCIETIES OF THE EAST

Along the Atlantic seaboard, many societies developed a mix of agricultural and hunter-gatherer economies. These economic developments fostered the development of permanent settlements.

The Algonquian Peoples

The Algonquian language group included hundreds of American Indian tribes along the east coast of the present-day United States and in the interior of the continent, around the St. Lawrence River and the Great Lakes. The Atlantic coast Algonquians hunted, fished, and grew corn. In northern New England and the upper Great Lakes region, the colder climate tended to make agriculture impractical, forcing Algonquians in these areas to rely on hunting and fishing.

The Iroquois Great League of Peace

In present-day New York State, groups of Iroquoian-speaking peoples formed a confederation made up of the Mohawks, Oneidas, Onondagas, Cayugas, and Senecas. (Later, in 1720, a sixth group, the Tuscaroras, joined the Iroquois League). The founding of the League dates back to perhaps the fifteenth century (although some oral traditions assert an earlier founding date). The League formed in order to end infighting among the groups. Over time, the cohesion of the five nations grew and the Iroquois League became one of the most powerful forces in the pre-contact Northeast.

The Iroquois lived in settled, permanent villages. They relied on farming, gathering, hunting, and fishing for their sustenance, but the majority of their food came from farming. Their three most important crops were corn, beans, and squash, called the three sisters of crops and common to many agrarian American Indian societies. The Iroquois are, traditionally, a matrilineal society—inheritance and descent pass through the mother's line.

KEY CONCEPT 1.2 EXPLORATION AND THE COLUMBIAN EXCHANGE

In the late 1400s and 1500s, European overseas exploration and settlement resulted in a series of interactions and adaptations among societies called the Columbian Exchange.

I. Contact, Conquest, and Transformations

European exploration, settlement, and conquest in the New World in the fifteenth and sixteenth centuries ushered in momentous demographic and social changes in Europe, Africa, and the Americas.

A. THE SPANISH AND PORTUGUESE MODEL

The first explorers and settlers in the New World were sponsored by Spain and Portugal. Their presence in the New World led to deadly epidemics that decimated native populations. Over time, a racially mixed population developed in the Americas. This society was characterized by caste distinctions that grew out of the intermixture of Spanish settlers, African slaves, and American Indians.

Portugal and Spain Lead the Way

Portugal, with the encouragement and guidance of Prince Henry the Navigator, embarked on a search for new trade routes to Asia that would bypass the Italian city-states that controlled Mediterranean trade. Portuguese explorers moved down the coast of Africa with the goal of rounding the Cape of Good Hope and crossing the Indian Ocean to arrive at India and China. Bartolomeu Dias sailed around the Cape of Good Hope in 1488 and Vasca da Gama reached India by 1498.

Spain also sought new trade routes. The Italian sailor Christopher Columbus convinced the Spanish monarchs, Isabella and Ferdinand, to fund a venture west, across the Atlantic, to reach the East. Columbus argued that the diameter of the earth was smaller than cartographers believed and that a venture in a westerly direction was both possible and feasible. (Most educated Europeans, including Columbus, believed the earth was round.) Columbus's three ships, the *Nina*, the *Pinta*, and the *Santa Maria*, set sail in 1492, and, six weeks later, reached a Caribbean island that he named San Salvador. Columbus assumed that he had reached the East Indies, and he named the Taino people he encountered, "Indians." The misnomer stuck. Columbus made two more voyages but never fully realized that he had voyaged to an entirely new continent. Others who followed in his footsteps made that realization, paving the way for a century of exploration, conquest, and riches.

Disease and Death

The peoples of the New World, having evolved and adapted separately from the peoples of the Old World, had no immunities to many of the germs and the infectious diseases that were inadvertently brought to the New World by explorers and settlers. These diseases included bubonic plague, cholera, scarlet fever, and, most important, smallpox. It is estimated that between 50 and 90 percent of the native peoples of the Americas died between 1500 and 1650.

> ## THE IMPACT OF DISEASE
>
> Remember that the main cause of the massive die-off of American Indians in the 1600s was disease, not warfare. Warfare was brutal, but it could not have affected the large number of people that disease did.

Spanish and Portuguese Ambitions

Spain was able to secure a dominant role in the New World following the Treaty of Tordesillas (1494) between Spain and Portugal. The treaty settled the competing claims of the two countries to the newly explored lands outside of Europe. The treaty drew a longitudinal line through the Atlantic Ocean and South America. Portugal was granted lands to the east of the line, including Brazil in the Western Hemisphere and Africa. Spain was granted the rest of the lands of the Americas. Spanish explorers made those claims real by establishing settlements throughout Central and South America. Spanish explorers even made it as far north as California and New Mexico, the area around the Mississippi River, and Florida. Ponce de Leon reached Florida in 1513. Spaniards later established the first permanent European settlement in what would become the United States at St. Augustine, Florida (1585).

The Conquistadores and the Defeat of Native Peoples

Within a generation of Columbus's first journey to the New World, Spanish forces wrested control of much of Central and South America from the native inhabitants, transforming the economic and social structures of the region, and devastating the native population.

The sixteenth century saw brutal fighting in the Americas as Spain extended its hegemony over much of Central and South America. One of the more brutal episodes of violence between the Spanish conquistadores and native peoples was the defeat of the Mexica people (also known as the Aztecs), led by Montezuma, by Spanish forces led by Hernan Cortes (1518–1521). The Incas of South America were defeated by Spanish forces led by Francisco Pizarro (1532).

B. SPAIN, PORTUGAL, AND THE AFRICAN SLAVE TRADE

Soon after European settlement in the Americas, a system of slavery developed. Spanish and Portuguese merchants worked with coastal West Africans to force other Africans into the slave system.

The Impact of the Slave Trade

Even before the settlement of the New World, Europeans began taking Africans from their villages and forcing them into slavery. Slavery has existed since ancient times, but the concept of slavery changed in the 1500s. Africans were thought of as slaves for life; it was not a temporary condition. Also, the children of slaves would now be considered slaves as well. This too was a break from tradition. African slaves were considered property, with no rights, as opposed to people who were enslaved for a period of time.

There are two main impacts of the slave trade on Africa from the 1500s onward. First, entire generations of strong, young people were kidnapped and taken out of the country. These would otherwise have become the leaders of their tribes or villages. Second, the introduction of European manufactured items undermined the traditional African economy.

C. THE "COLUMBIAN EXCHANGE"

One major impact of Spanish settlement in the New World was the introduction of new crops and livestock. These new organisms had a major impact on transforming the ecology of the New World and on the social, economic, and political development of the New World. Further, these new organisms had long-term effects on native settlement patterns.

The "Columbian Exchange" Transforms the Americas

Historians refer to the introduction of new products on each side of the Atlantic as the "Columbian Exchange." The Europeans introduced to the New World: horses, goats, cows, chickens, coffee, lettuce, and wheat, to name just a few. By far, the most important organisms brought from Europe to the New World were germs, which caused widespread disease and death (see page 37).

D. SPANISH EXPLOITATION OF NEW WORLD RESOURCES

Spaniards first turned to the labor of native Indians in a system known as the *encomienda*. This exploitative system was used in plantation agriculture and in the extraction of precious metals. Over time, native labor was replaced by African slavery.

Silver and the *Encomienda*

Upon gaining control of much of the Americas, Spain created a system to extract gold and silver and ship it to Spain. Spain soon became the wealthiest country in Europe with the influx of New World precious metals. Spain developed the *encomienda* system in order to exploit the labor of native peoples. In this system, the initial Spanish settlers were granted tracts of land and the right to extract labor from local inhabitants. In many ways, this system of New World colonization resembled Old World feudalism. Acting as feudal lords, the *encomenderos* had a free hand to run their holdings, as long as a percentage of gold and silver was sent back to the monarchy.

The *encomienda* system led to brutal exploitation. Spurred by Spanish critics such as Bartolomé de Las Casas, the crown issued a series of reform to the governance of Spain's New World colonies known as the *repartimiento* (1549). Treatment of native peoples did not improve appreciably, but control of Spanish America came to be exercised more directly by the crown (see Period 2).

II. Europe and the Age of Exploration and Conquest

European expansion into the New World was fueled by a variety of factors. In time, the impact of conquest and settlement in the New World was felt in the Old World. Expansion in the Americas resulted in increased competition among the nations of Europe as well as the promotion of empire building.

A. FACTORS CONTRIBUTING TO EUROPEAN EXPLORATION AND CONQUEST

A variety of factors help to explain why the age of exploration and conquest took place when it did. These factors include a desire for new sources of wealth, competition for power and status, and a push among Christian sects for new converts. Several important changes in Europe set the groundwork for exploration and conquest.

The Crusades and the Revival of Trade

The series of religious wars known as the Crusades shook the stability of European feudal society and whet the appetites of Europeans for foreign trade goods. The wars, with the goal of securing Christian control of the "Holy Land," occurred primarily in the twelfth and thirteenth centuries. The relatively self-sufficient manorial world of feudal Europe began its long demise during this period, as trade routes and regional and international economic activity shifted power and priorities. Europeans became interested in circumventing the Italian city-states and finding new trade routes with the East.

The Black Death and the Decline of Feudalism

The Black Death, probably caused by a pandemic outbreak of bubonic plague in the fourteenth century, reduced the European population by anywhere from 30 to 60 percent and also played a role in weakening the feudal system.

The Impact of the Renaissance

The Renaissance spirit of curiosity about the world inspired people to explore and map new areas. Universities and scholarly books—also infused with the spirit of Renaissance humanism—spread these new discoveries.

The Protestant Reformation and the Catholic Counter-reformation

Religious movements in the sixteenth century renewed many people's religious zeal and their desire to spread their gospels. The most important religious movement was the Protestant Reformation. Theologians Martin Luther and John Calvin both led breaks with Rome over church practices and beliefs. Both believed that the church had drifted from its spiritual mission. The Catholic Church's abuse of the practice of selling indulgences—or remissions of sin—was especially galling to Luther.

In England, King Henry VIII also led a break with Rome, but his break was more political than theological. The event that precipitated the break was the Pope's refusal to grant Henry a divorce. Some English Protestants, the Puritans, believed that the English Protestant Reformation did not go far enough. Motivated by Calvinist thinking, the Puritans argued for a complete reformation in England (see Period 2 for more on the Puritans).

The Catholic Church itself underwent a reform in the sixteenth century. This counter-reformation focused on a renewed sense of spirituality within the Catholic Church. Out of this movement came the Jesuits, a Catholic order devoted to spreading their gospel throughout the world.

Technological Advances and a Revolution in Navigation

A series of technological developments encouraged exploration. Johannes Gutenberg's printing press (developed in the 1440s) helped spread information and stimulated interest in new discoveries. The compass, the astrolabe, the quadrant, and the hourglass all aided navigation, helping sailors plot direction, determine speed, and assess latitude. *Portulanos*, detailed maps, also helped navigators. Portugal developed a quick, sturdy sailing ship called the caravel.

B. THE IMPACT OF EXPLORATION AND CONQUEST ON EUROPE

The introduction of new sources of wealth in the form of precious metals transformed the European economy and helped facilitate the ongoing transition from feudalism to capitalism. In addition, new crops and livestock contributed to population growth in Europe.

The Impact of the "Columbian Exchange" on Europe

A variety of new crops and livestock that were native to the Americas were introduced to Europe in the 1500s. The list of organisms brought by Europeans back to the Old World included turkeys, corn, potato, sweet potato, cacao (cocoa), and tomatoes. These foods, over time, revolutionized culinary traditions in Europe and supplemented the meager diets of the European peasantry. In addition, Spanish sailors brought syphilis back to Europe with them—the result of sexual encounters with women in the New World. Tobacco was introduced and created a craze among Europeans.

The Economic Impact of Conquest

It is assumed that since conquest brought so much hardship to American Indians as well as to Africans, it must surely have brought improvements to the status of Europeans. However, that, for the most part, was not the case. The position of ordinary Spaniards declined during the age of exploration and conquest; in many ways, ordinary Spaniards did not recover from this period until the nineteenth century. For one, the influx of silver and gold into Spain set off a wave of inflation in the 1500s that made many ordinary items considerably more expensive. Second, taxes went up in Spain, more than fivefold in the 1500s, so that the monarchy could pay for the military expenditures necessary to secure its New World empire. Third, Spain went into debt as it borrowed more and more from European banks to maintain its empire. The interest on this debt also depressed the Spanish economy.

C. TECHNOLOGICAL ADVANCES AND NEW ECONOMIC STRUCTURES

New forms of technology and new business models facilitated extensive changes in both the economy of Europe and the economy of the Americas.

The Joint-stock Company

The joint-stock company model was developed in Europe in the 1500s and became an important engine for exploration and colonization in the New World. In a joint-stock company, shareholders own a portion of the company in proportion to the number of shares they own. The joint-stock company model was embraced by many of the European nations embarking on risky expeditions of exploration, colonization, and trade because the risks involved would be spread out among multiple investors. Another advantage of the joint-stock company is the concept of limited liability; the shareholders can be held liable for company debts, but their liability is limited to the face value of their shareholding.

KEY CONCEPT 1.3 CHANGING WORLDVIEWS IN THE AGE OF EXPANSION AND CONTACT

The changes that were ushered in by the age of exploration and conquest included changes in the worldviews of those involved.

I. Changing European Worldviews

In the age of exploration and conquest, the worldview of Europeans began to change. They began to see the relationships that had developed between themselves and nonwhite people in a new light.

A. DEBATES AROUND PERCEPTIONS OF AMERICAN INDIANS

Most Europeans had little or no knowledge of people who were different from themselves before the age of exploration. Initially, Spanish and Portuguese explorers did not know what to make of the people they encountered in the Americas. Over time debates occurred around how civilized these peoples were compared with Europeans ideals.

Debates over Spain's Actions in the New World

As reports of the actions of the Spanish *conquistadores* and officials in the *encomienda* system reached Spain, a heated debate ensued about Spanish behavior in the New World. The priest Bartolomé de Las Casas roundly criticized Spanish actions as being among "the most unpardonable offences committed against God and mankind." His book, *A Short Account of the Destruction of the Indies* (written in 1542; published in 1552), chronicled atrocities against native peoples in the New World. He has been criticized as paving the way for the enslavement of Africans, in order to replace American Indian laborers. He did advocate such a transition, but later came to believe that all forms of slavery were morally wrong.

Las Casas was challenged by another Spanish theologian, Juan Gines de Sepulveda. Sepulveda defended the treatment that the Spaniards meted out to the native peoples of the Americas. He asserted that American Indians were beings of an inferior order. Because they could not be expected to perform duties beyond manual labor, he argued that they were "natural slaves." He followed in the footsteps of philosophers and theologians who argued for the existence of "natural law." He insisted that the battles of conquest in the New World were "just wars." His justifications for taking native peoples' lands and for destroying their culture—including the assertion that it was in their best interests—would resonate with Spanish policymakers in the coming centuries.

B. THE DEVELOPMENT OF THE BELIEF IN WHITE SUPERIORITY

As Europeans solidified their control over the New World and brought more American Indians and Africans under their control, a set of racist ideas developed to justify the continued subjugation of non-white people.

Race in the New World

The various European powers developed racist ideas to justify their conquest of American Indians and their enslavement of Africans. These racist ideas often grew out of earlier notions of race that had existed in Europe. For the Spaniards, for instance, these included traditional notions about "pure blood" (*limpieza de sangre*). In Spain, this description was used for those without Jewish or Muslim ancestry. The idea that "pure blood" was superior shaped Spanish understandings of race in the New World. As miscegenation—the mixing of races—occurred in the New World, Spaniards erected an elaborate hierarchy of racial classes. The degree of "pure blood" determined one's place in this hierarchy. Indians and Africans were at the bottom. This model drew on traditional Spanish beliefs and adapted them to a New World setting. The model was useful to the Spanish because it justified their position at the top of the hierarchy and the continued subjugation of those at the bottom.

II. Cultural Resistance by American Indians and Africans

In the face of enslavement, subjugation, and defeat, Africans and American Indians attempted to maintain a sense of political and cultural autonomy.

A. AMERICAN INDIAN RESISTANCE TO EUROPEAN CULTURE

A clash of cultures occurred in the Americas of the 1500s. As Europeans attempted to impose their ideas about culture, propriety, gender roles, family structure, religion, and the natural world, native peoples developed strategies for resistance and contestation.

Resistance and Adaptation in New Spain

The responses of American Indians to the catastrophe of conquest were varied. Some fled from the invading Spaniards, abandoning their ancestral homelands. These migrations led to population pressures and conflicts elsewhere in the Americas. Some made accommodations with the Spanish, adopting Christianity and adapting it to fit their needs and circumstances. Some native peoples adopted Catholicism whole cloth, while others incorporated certain Spanish spiritual beliefs into traditional religious practices.

Violent Resistance

Native people engaged in violent resistance as well as more passive cultural resistance. The Guale people lived near the Spanish mission in St. Augustine—one of four missions in Spanish Florida in the sixteenth century. As missionaries tried to bring Guale Indians into the mission system, a revolt, known as Juanillo's Revolt, occurred in 1597, resulting in the deaths of several missionaries.

Juan de Onate and the Pueblo People

In the western reaches of Spain's New World empire, a violent confrontation occurred among the Pueblo people in modern-day New Mexico. The Spanish *conquistador,* Juan de Onate, and his soldiers had, in the 1590s, occupied land held by the Acoma Pueblo people. In 1598, the Acoma people resisted an order by the Spaniards to hand over certain supplies that the Acoma needed to survive the upcoming winter. They attacked the Spanish occupiers, killing fifteen Spaniards, including the nephew of Onate. Onate responded by firing cannons from a mesa above the Acoma people, killing over 800 native people. The survivors were put on trial by the Spanish, whose punishments included the cutting off of one foot for males over the age of twenty-five. As many as eighty men had one of their feet cut off. The remaining 500 Acoma people were enslaved by the Spaniards.

B. CULTURAL ADAPTATION BY AFRICANS

As Africans were brought into the slavery system, they developed forms of cultural resistance that attempted, against great odds, to preserve traditional cultural patterns and to maintain a sense of autonomy.

Maroon Communities

Maroons were Africans who escaped from slavery in the New World and established independent communities. These communities existed throughout the New World, with many in the Caribbean and Brazil. Often these communities were formed by slaves who were the first generation brought out of Africa. These Maroons, with memories of Africa, were in the best position to preserve African traditions in the New World. These traditions included the use of medicinal herbs, often combined with special drumming and dancing as part of healing rituals. Other African healing traditions and rites have survived through the centuries through the descendants of these original Maroons. One of the most significant Maroon communities was Palmares, established in Brazil in the early 1600s. It had more than 30,000 residents and remained an independent community until it was conquered by the Portuguese in 1694. When the English took over Jamaica from the Spanish in 1655, many enslaved Africans fled into the interior and joined communities of Arawak Indians. Over time, the Maroons came to control large areas of the Jamaican interior.

SUBJECT TO DEBATE

Most American history textbooks provide vivid accounts of the brutality of the Spanish conquistadores toward American Indians. That the Spaniards were often cruel to the native peoples of the Americas is not in question; however, recently historians have begun to question the extent of Spanish brutality. The term, "Black Legend," was coined by a Spanish historian in 1914 to describe the anti-Spanish propaganda written by English, Italian, Dutch, or other European writers. Although English sources, say, from the 1500s onward should not be discounted, it would be prudent for the student to take into account the origin of these sources. English writers might have been trying to demonize Spanish behavior in order to portray British behavior in the New World in a more favorable light. The British portrayed themselves as altruistic, bringing God and civilization to the inhabitants of the New World, while the Spanish were portrayed as greedy and cruel. Of course, the historical record demonstrates that the British committed their share of atrocities in the New World, probably comparable to those committed in New Spain. The controversy provides us with a cautionary lesson: Look carefully at the source of documents as you use them to write about the past. The documents in the document-based question on the Advanced Placement exam clearly indicate their source. Do not ignore this information.

Practice Multiple-Choice Questions

> **Directions:** Pick the letter that best answers the following questions.

QUESTIONS 1–3 REFER TO THE FOLLOWING PASSAGE:

"The gold and silver mined with forced labor in Mexico and what is now Bolivia constituted a windfall that could have been used to develop Spanish agriculture, industry, and commerce. It could have helped the country catch up with northwestern Europe's more developed economies. . . .

"But Spain [in the 1500s] was in the grip of a tiny ruling class of royalty, Catholic Church hierarchy, and landed aristocracy. Two to three per cent of the population owned 97 per cent of the land in Castile, Spain's heartland. The great landowners had no incentive to modernize Spain. They just wanted to raise more sheep and sell more wool. The environmental degradation that overgrazing vast numbers of sheep entailed seems to have bothered the ruling class no more than the cutting of forests for timber to build ships and provide charcoal to smelt domestic Spanish silver ore. And so, what if the wool went to Holland to be manufactured into cloth rather than being processed in Spain itself.

"Meanwhile, successes in the New World swelled the Spanish monarchy's ambitions in the Old. The bonanza of bullion from the Americas encouraged Spain's rulers to build up the army into Europe's largest military force, setting off an arms race that forced rivals to multiply their armed forces as well. Spain hired German, Italian, and Irish mercenaries, building and buying a vast fleet of heavily armed ships. Hegemonic wars against the French, Dutch, and English followed. . . .

"The most lasting and far-reaching effect of the increase of money in circulation was to set off a long wave of inflation that spread throughout Western Europe. To be sure, deficit spending on unproductive armies, navies, and wars as well as debasement of coinage by monarchs in search of additional royal revenue contributed to the run-up in prices."

—A. Kent MacDougall, University of California, Berkeley, March 1992.

1. Which of the following best describes a central point of A. Kent MacDougall's argument?

   (A) During the age of exploration and conquest, a growing divide developed in Spain between the Catholic church and the monarchy over the treatment of American Indians.
   (B) The large-scale migration of Spanish peasants to the New World left Spain with a scarcity of workers and a depressed economy.
   (C) Spanish conquest of the New World led Spain to focus its military and diplomatic efforts toward subduing resistance in the New World and removing itself from the conflicts of Europe.
   (D) The successes of Spanish conquest in the New World did not result in a general economic improvement in Spain itself.

2. The description of Spanish actions by A. Kent MacDougall, excerpted on page 44, contributes to an understanding of which of the following developments beyond the 1500s?

   (A) The industrial growth of Spain in the seventeenth century
   (B) The growing gap between the wealthy and the poor in the seventeenth century
   (C) Spanish military domination over its European rivals in the seventeenth century
   (D) The success of independence movements in Spanish America in the seventeenth century

3. Concerns raised in Spain in the 1540s about "forced labor in Mexico and what is now Bolivia," mentioned in the first paragraph of A. Kent MacDougall's article, led to which of the following changes?

   (A) Limits being placed on the *encomienda* system and a shift toward African slavery
   (B) The growth of the Spanish abolitionist movement and a royal decree ending slavery in the New World
   (C) A shift in Spanish economic activities in the New World from export-oriented activities toward production for local consumption
   (D) The establishment of a line of demarcation in Spanish-held territories in the New World between areas for American Indians and areas for Spanish colonists

Answers and Explanations to Multiple-Choice Questions:

1. **(D)** The successes of Spanish conquest in the New World did not result in a general economic improvement in Spain itself. The article focuses on the shortsightedness of the wealthy class and the impact of ongoing warfare. The elite class in Spain did not try to improve infrastructure or develop new forms of processing and manufacturing.

2. **(B)** The article is attempting to account for a curious outcome. With all the gold and silver coming into Spain in the 1500s, why did the standard of living for most Spaniards decline from the 1500s until, according to the article, the late 1800s. MacDougall argues that the wealth was squandered rather than reinvested. Further, taxes and inflation both increased, putting the peasantry in a deeper hole. The author states, in another part of the article excerpted on page 44, "Super-exploitation of labor on the periphery of the world capitalist economy leads to increased exploitation of workers at the core."

3. **(A)** The article focuses on the impact of Spanish colonization on Spain itself, rather than on the Americas. However, it does allude to "forced labor in Mexico and what is now Bolivia." The super-exploitation of indigenous peoples by the Spaniards was raised in the 1540s by the Dominican Friar Bartolomé de las Casas. He described the brutality of slavery under the *encomienda* system. He asserted that Indians were free people in the natural order and deserved the same treatment as others. His also suggested replacing Indian labor with African labor. In the coming decades, Spain shifted toward a reliance on African slavery for labor in its New World Empire.

Period 2: 1607–1754 Patterns of Empire and Resistance

4

TIMELINE

1588	England defeats the Spanish Armada
1607	Jamestown colony founded
1609	Henry Hudson explores area that will become New York
1609–1610	"Starving time" in Virginia
1619	House of Burgesses established
1620	Founding of Plymouth colony
	Mayflower compact signed
1622	Attack on Jamestown by local Algonquin Indians
1624	New Amsterdam founded by the Dutch
1630	Founding of Massachusetts Bay colony
1630–1640	"Great Migration" of Puritans from England to Massachusetts
1632	Founding of Georgia colony
1636	Founding of Rhode Island colony
1638	Anne Hutchinson banned from Massachusetts
1639	The Fundamental Orders of Connecticut are adopted
1649	Act of Religious Toleration passed in Maryland
1662	The Half-Way Covenant
1663	Founding of Carolina colony
1675	King Philip's War
1676	Bacon's Rebellion
1679	New Hampshire colony separated from Massachusetts
1680	Pueblo Revolt (Pope's Rebellion)
1681	Founding of the Pennsylvania colony
1686	Creation of the Dominion of New England
1688	The Glorious Revolution
1689	New Englanders topple the Dominion of New England
1692	Salem witch trials
1711	Founding of North Carolina colony
1733	Molasses Act
1735	Zenger trial
1739	Stono Rebellion
1741	Arrests and executions in the supposed "Negro Plot" in New York City
	Jonathan Edwards's sermon, "Sinners in the Hands of an Angry God"

INTRODUCTION

Throughout the seventeenth century and the first half of the eighteenth century, the major European imperial powers and different groups of American Indians maneuvered and fought for control of the North American continent. Out of these conflicts, native societies experienced dramatic changes and distinctive colonial societies emerged.

England was eager to duplicate the stunning success of the Spanish in the New World. England emerged as the most powerful nation on the global stage after defeating the Spanish Armada in 1588. It then set its sights on North America. England, Spain, Holland, and France all made attempts to establish control over different areas of North America. These efforts led to different patterns of colonization and different types of interactions with American Indian groups.

Once established, the thirteen British colonies developed along different, but parallel, paths. We see distinct patterns of development in the three regions of colonial America. The southern colonies—Virginia, South Carolina, North Carolina, and Georgia—all moved toward an economy dominated by the institution of slavery. The New England colonies of Massachusetts, Rhode Island, Connecticut, and New Hampshire all experienced economic transformations that cast into doubt the pious ideals of the founding generation of Puritan settlers. The middle colonies of New York, New Jersey, Pennsylvania, and Delaware saw the development of economic and ethnic diversity as immigrants from Europe began to fill up these colonies. However, the thirteen colonies were united by shared experiences as much as they were separated by different patterns of development. All lived under the British crown and practiced some form of Protestantism; all maneuvered within mercantilist trade rules; all pushed back and fought with American Indians; and all were exposed to new philosophical and religious ideas. We begin to see, in the eighteenth century, a pattern of development in North America distinct from Great Britain. These distinctions begin to lay the groundwork for the political break that followed the intellectual break from the British.

KEY CONCEPT 2.1
PATTERNS OF COLONIZATION

In the seventeenth century, European empires competed for control of North America. These colonial powers had different priorities and goals. As they sought to exert control over different parts of North America, they established distinct patterns of settlement and colonization.

I. Competing Models of Colonization

The Spanish, French, Dutch, and British developed different patterns for colonizing the New World. These different patterns reflected the different economic and social goals, cultural assumptions, and traditions and folkways of these major powers.

A. SPAIN'S NEW WORLD COLONIES

Spain maintained tight control over its colonial empire in the New World. Spanish colonizers focused on converting American Indians to Christianity and on exploiting the labor of the native population.

The Evolution of Spanish America

The basis of Spain's New World empire was the exploitation of the labor of native peoples. By 1550, Spain abandoned the *encomienda* system. Under this system, the initial Spanish settlers in the Americas were granted tracts of land and the right to extract labor from local inhabitants. This system led to brutal treatment of Indians. The worst excesses of Spanish behavior were chronicled by the Dominican priest, Bartolomé de Las Casas (see period 1). The Spanish government replaced the *encomienda* system with the *repartimiento* system—banning outright slavery and mandating that Indians be paid wages. However, Spain's empire remained highly exploitative of native labor. Colonial authorities could still require that local people work for Spanish landlords. The work of Indians was supplemented by African slave labor.

By 1650, approximately 350,000 Spaniards had migrated to the New World. This population was supplemented by between 250,000–300,000 Africans. Indians were still the majority in Spanish America, but their population, by 1570, was reduced by approximately 90 percent from what it had been in 1492. Intermarriage was common in Spain's New World colonies. A complex social hierarchy resulted from the mixing of peoples of different backgrounds.

Spain's New World empire was tightly controlled by the crown, especially after the *repartimiento* system was established. In the sixteenth and seventeenth centuries, administration of the empire was divided between two administrative units. The northern portion of the empire, called the Viceroyalty of New Spain, was headquartered in Mexico City. The southern portion of the empire was called the Viceroyalty of Peru, consisting of Spanish holdings in South America and headquartered in Lima. New Spain attempted to extend its reach into modern-day Florida and New Mexico, but failed to establish a strong presence in the northern reaches of its holdings.

Most Indians lived removed from Spanish colonists—remaining in their own communities, under the authority of native leaders and speaking their own languages. Spanish priests were, however, aggressive in leaving the imprint of Catholicism on native communities. Priests converted communities en masse; Spanish efforts at conversion seemed amazingly successful. However, the Catholicism that was practiced in native communities was different from what Catholic priests had originally intended. Indians often accepted Jesus as one among many Gods and interwove Catholic practices with traditional Indian spiritual practices. At the same time, local ideas and expectations frequently reshaped Catholic practices. Catholic priests realized they had to accept certain adaptations in order to better reach native peoples.

B. FRENCH AND DUTCH COLONIES

Both France and Holland established colonies in North America, but they differed markedly from the Spanish and British models. Few French or Dutch actually settled in the New World. Rather, the French and Dutch colonies served as trading outposts. They both used trade and intermarriage to acquire furs and other valuable goods for export to Europe.

France's New World Empire

France's North American territory was vast on paper, but was thinly populated. It stretched from the mouth of the St. Lawrence River in Quebec, encompassed the Great Lakes region and the Ohio River Valley, and included the vast Great Plains region of what would later become the United States and the port of New Orleans. The first permanent French settlements were Port Royal (1605), in what would later become Nova Scotia, and Quebec (1608), founded by Samuel de Champlain. In 1642, French traders established a small settlement at what would later become Montreal. It was not until the latter part of the seventeenth century that the French established settlements at New Orleans and in the southern Great Lakes region.

French–American Indian Diplomacy

Because the French had relatively few actual colonists in the New World, they had to rely on diplomacy with American Indian groups more than the Spanish or the British did. French officers in the New World learned native languages and became well versed in American Indian diplomatic protocol, including smoking the long-stemmed calumet ("peace pipe") and giving and receiving gifts, including wampum belts. French officers and agents often married Indian wives as part of their efforts at maintaining good relations with native peoples. Despite these efforts, American Indians maintained actual control of the heart of the North American continent. In these areas, French agents had to adjust to Indian ways to maintain France's presence. The Osages, for example, south of the Missouri River, accepted some French agents into their kinship networks. This European accommodation of American Indian ways was extremely rare among Spanish and British colonists.

The Dutch Presence in the Americas

The Dutch presence in the New World dates from the 1590s. Like the French, the first Dutch colonies in the New World functioned more as trading outposts rather than as populated settlements. The Dutch established forts and small settlements in Guyana in 1590, followed by a string of island settlements in the Caribbean in the early 1600s. Dutch efforts at colonization were often stymied by rival European powers. In Tobago, for example, the Dutch attempted to build settlements four different times in the seventeenth century, with each settlement destroyed by either the French, the Spanish, or the British. Later in the seventeenth century, the Dutch obtained control of the colony in Suriname, in South America. The British had established a colony there in the 1650s. It was captured by a Dutch expedition in 1667 and was formally transferred to the Dutch as part of the Treaty of Breda, following the Second Anglo-Dutch War, 1665–1667. In the treaty, the Dutch formally relinquished control of New Amsterdam (see below). The Dutch continued focusing on sugar production in Suriname, relying on African slave labor.

Dutch New Amsterdam

In the early 1600s, the Dutch set their sights on North America. The Dutch Republic commissioned an expedition by English explorer Henry Hudson to North America. The project was funded by the Dutch East India Company, which instructed Hudson to search for a Northwest Passage to Asia. Hudson sailed into the Delaware River and then to Manhattan Island, present-day New York City, and up the river that would later bear his name. He sailed as far north as present-day Albany before turning back. Hudson never found a Northwest Passage, but his reports of abundant fur, timber, and fertile lands generated further interest among Dutch merchants to exploit these lands. After several more journeys of exploration and repeated attempts to find a Northwest Passage, the Dutch Republic chartered the Dutch West India Company to develop colonies in North America. The Dutch claimed a vast stretch of land from the Delaware River in the south to Cape Cod in the north. The Dutch later redrew the northern boundary of New Netherlands (to Connecticut) in order to accommodate the expansion of British New England.

The administrative seat and the most important settlement of New Netherlands was New Amsterdam. A settlement was established in 1624 on what is now Governor's Island, in New York Harbor. The following year, a fort was built at the tip of Manhattan, and settlement began around Fort Amsterdam. Legend has it that in 1626 Peter Minuit, the company director general of New Amsterdam, purchased the island of Manhattan for goods estimated to be worth $24. Almost all aspects of this transaction are in doubt—the value of the goods, the intentions of the American Indians, and even the legitimacy of the unnamed native people to "sell" the island. However, the myth of the "$24 Deal" has persisted.

The Economy of New Amsterdam

Like the English companies that funded moneymaking ventures to the New World, the Dutch West Indian Company did not see immediate profits. The colony floundered. Few Dutch settlers came. The company tried to induce immigrants with generous land grants along the Hudson River. Slowly, settlers began to arrive—an amalgam of Europeans of diverse national and religious backgrounds (the colony even attracted some Jewish settlers). The Dutch also brought African slaves to New Amsterdam.

The colony began to thrive under the leadership of the heavy-handed Peter Stuyvesant, who was hired by the company in 1647. The colony became a center for the thriving trade in beaver furs and a growing commercial town. However, soon the restored English king Charles II set his sights on the "Dutch wedge," which divided England's holdings in North America. The king sent a fleet of warships to New Amsterdam. Stuyvesant surrendered in 1664 without a fight. Charles II granted the colony to his brother James, the Duke of York, who rechristened it New York. Formal transfer to the British occurred in 1667, as part of the settlement following the Second Anglo-Dutch War.

C. BRITISH COLONIAL PATTERNS

Of the European empires that sought to establish colonies in the New World, the English pattern differed markedly from the Spanish, Dutch, and French. Whereas their European competitors sent relatively few colonists to the New World, the English sent substantial numbers of individuals to the new colonies.

The Founding of Jamestown

The first settlers to Jamestown arrived in 1607. Investors in England formed a joint-stock company, the Virginia Company, to fund the expedition. King James I chartered the company and territory in the New World. The Jamestown colony nearly collapsed during its first few years of existence. The colonists were not prepared to establish a community, grow crops, and sustain themselves. They were mostly male gentlemen, unaccustomed to working with their hands. These early settlers hoped to find gold and silver and to

GEOGRAPHY AND SOCIETY

The "starving time" for the Virginia colony illustrates the idea that geography and biology cannot always determine the outcomes of human events. One would have expected the Puritans in bitter-cold New England to die off in large numbers, while the Virginians, in a mild climate, thrived. The opposite occurred, showing that planning and organization often trump geography and biology.

quickly duplicate the Spanish successes in Central and South America. They did not find precious metals, nor did they plant crops. Their store of food diminished quickly and by 1608, only 38 of the original 144 colonists were still alive. By 1610, things had not improved; only 60 settlers, out of 500 who had come over, were still alive. Many had perished during the "starving time" winter of 1609–1610.

Jamestown and Its American Indian Neighbors

Relations with local American Indians also deteriorated rapidly during the early years of the Jamestown colony. The local Algonquian people were led by their chief Powhatan, who was the father of Pocahontas. Powhatan's people traded corn with the settlers at first, but when the American Indians could not supply a sufficient amount of corn for their English neighbors, the English initiated raids on Powhatan's people. These skirmishes occurred for years, until the American Indians organized an assault on Jamestown in 1622. The raid did not dislodge the Jamestown settlement, but it worsened relations between the English settlers and the local American Indians.. In many ways, the incidents in Jamestown foretell the history of relations between the American Indians of North America and the white settlers from Europe. Whites consistently encroached on American Indian lands and consistently defeated them in the violent encounters that resulted.

II. The Development of Slavery in the British New World

Slavery developed in British North America in response to economic, demographic, and geographic conditions. Slavery was part of English colonial North America from the earliest years. In 1619, twenty Africans arrived in Virginia, probably as slaves. However, slavery did not become central to the Southern economy until later in the seventeenth century.

A. RACIAL ATTITUDES IN THE BRITISH COLONIAL WORLD

Spanish, French, and Dutch colonies, which had fewer female colonists, were relatively accepting of intermarriages with native peoples, and unions with Africans were fairly common in the Spanish colonies. In contrast, the British colonies attracted both male and female colonists and did not tolerate intermarriage. In this context, as in New Spain, a rigid hierarchy developed in the British colonies.

The Origins of Racial Hierarchies

The racial hierarchy that developed within the British colonial world followed a long tradition in English thought of making divisions within humanity. These divisions—between civilized and barbaric, between Christian and heathen, between English and non-English—shaped English understandings of the world. Historians continue to debate whether racism against Africans developed as a result of the enslavement of Africans, or whether racist notions predated and allowed for the enslavement of Africans (see "Subject to Debate," page 74).

B. LABOR SHORTAGES AND THE DEVELOPMENT OF BRITISH SLAVERY

The persistent problem of the wealthy planters in the British New World was attracting enough settlers to do the difficult work of the cultivation and processing of staple crops. New immigrants were enticed to come to the New World with the offer of 50 acres, called a headright, upon arrival. But this still required a potential settler to scrape together the fare for passage to the New World—approximately a year's income for an agrarian worker in England.

Indentured Servitude

After failing to enslave the native population, wealthy Virginians settled on indentured servitude as a means of bringing laborers to the New World. Under this system, a potential immigrant in England would agree to sign a contract to work as an indentured servant for a certain number of years in the New World (usually four to seven) in exchange for free passage. An agent would then sell this contract to a planter in the New World. The system accomplished its goal, allowing for tens of thousands of impoverished English men and women to migrate to the New World, but the system also created an entire underclass of mistreated workers.

Bacon's Rebellion and the Development of Slavery In Virginia

In the latter half of the seventeenth century, Virginia planters began to experience problems with the system of indentured servitude. Upon the end of their indenture, these men and women were generally not integrated into Virginia society. Many moved from the fertile tidewater region of Virginia into the hilly piedmont region. This inland region was also where many American Indians had settled after being dislocated by the initial wave of English settlers. The former indentured servants grew resentful of the taxes they were required to pay the Virginia government, and at their lack of representation in the House of Burgesses. Things grew worse for them as violence intensified on the frontier between these hardscrabble farmers and the nearby American Indians.

> ## THE SHIFT TO SLAVERY
> Remember, historians view Bacon's Rebellion as a key event in the shift from indentured servitude to slavery as the main form of labor in the South.

In 1676, these frontier tensions erupted into a full-scale rebellion, known as Bacon's Rebellion. Nathaniel Bacon, a lower-level planter, championed the cause of the frontier farmers and became their leader. Governor William Berkeley refused to offer help in fighting the American Indians. Many of the wealthy grandees engaged in a profitable trade with American Indians and, therefore, did not want war waged against them. When colonial authorities refused to aid the frontier farmers, Bacon led a group of them into Jamestown, burning the homes of the elite planters and even the capital building. During the rebellion, Bacon himself died of disease, and the rebellion was soon put down.

The rebellion proved to be an important turning point in colonial history, as the elite planters turned increasingly to African slaves as their primary labor force. African slavery allowed the planters to emphasize a commonality of interests between themselves and the frontier farmers. Although the position of these frontier farmers did not appreciably improve, they could at least take solace in the fact that they were among the free Virginians and members of the race they were told was superior.

The African Slave Trade

The African slave trade became a thriving business in the eighteenth century. European traders set up operations in coastal towns and encouraged Africans to venture into the interior to kidnap members of other ethnic groups. The slave trade not only resulted in the kidnapping of individuals, it also exacerbated ethnic tensions and served to destabilize the region. The victims of the slave trade were from a variety of cultural and linguistic groups. These Africans—mostly young and mostly male, with men outnumbering women, two to one—were brought to coastal ports where they were sold to European slave traders. They were next transported to the New World in horrid conditions. This grueling, and often deadly, part of the journey is known as the Middle Passage. The most famous account of the middle passage by an African is contained in the narrative of Olaudah Equiano. This African slave trade is one of the legs of the Atlantic trade (also known as the triangle trade) that evolved during the colonial period.

C. SLAVERY, RACE, AND VIOLENCE AGAINST NATIVE PEOPLES

Slavery, as it developed in British North America, differed from earlier slave systems in some fundamental ways. British notions of racial hierarchy reinforced the idea that slavery would be a permanent condition. The British system of slavery changed African gender and kinship patterns. Further, the British notion of racial hierarchy led to increasing violent conflicts with native peoples.

The Nature of Slavery in British North America

Historians note that slavery evolved in the British colonies. Some contend that the few slaves present in colonial Virginia in the early seventeenth century were treated in a manner similar to other "unfree" people, such as indentured servants. Over the course of the seventeenth century, rules about slavery hardened in colonial Virginia. In 1640, an indentured servant of African descent, John Casor, was declared by a civil court to be a slave for life. The case represents an important turning point in the shift toward permanent enslavement. Later, in 1662, the Virginia legislature passed a law stating that the child of a slave woman would inherit its mother's status—that is, would be a slave for life. This principle, called in Latin *partus sequitur ventrum*, broke with traditional English common law; previously, the child would inherit its father's status, meaning the child of a white man and an enslaved woman would be considered a free person. This principle had a major impact on the dynamics on slavery in the British colonial system. In effect, it sanctioned the rape of slave women by their white owners.

Even the language that English settlers used to describe Africans changed by the end of the century. Early in the seventeenth century, English accounts of African slaves in Virginia usually describe them as "Negroes." By the end of the century, they are more frequently referred to as "black," a color with clear negative overtones for English people at the time. Colonists began to identify themselves as "white"—a color that denoted purity and beauty. After 1660, laws in Virginia made it clear that slavery was a permanent and inherited status. By the end of the century, white Virginians came to see "blacks" and "slaves" as nearly synonymous terms.

Racial Hierarchy and American Indians

The attitudes of British colonists toward American Indians changed over the course of the seventeenth century, just as their attitude toward enslaved Africans did. Earlier in the century, the primary goal of the British settlers in regard to native peoples was peace. The early British settlements were precarious and the importance of maintaining peace with their American Indian neighbors was acute. In this situation, British settlers made efforts to understand their neighbors and to figure out ways to coexist. As the century progressed, and as the settlements became growing colonies, the colonists' primary desire was no longer to maintain the peace, it was for American Indian land. As the British colonists expanded their land holdings, violent conflicts with American Indians inevitably ensued. This can be seen in King Philip's War in 1675 (see page 68). In the context of these clashes, the British colonists increasingly saw the American Indians as savages. "Savagery" became not just a description of American Indian behavior, but a trait of their race. This racial hierarchy of superior and inferior people hardened as the seventeenth century progressed and justified, in the minds of the British, the continued exploitation of American Indian lands.

D. RESISTANCE TO SLAVERY

Slaves resisted brutality, humiliations, and grueling work in a number of ways. Resistance was both overt and covert.

The main fear of slave owners was overt resistance in the form of violent rebellion. Such rebellion was uncommon. Since slave owners and white authorities had the law behind them, and a monopoly on weaponry, outright rebellion was tantamount to suicide. Yet, attempts at rebellion did occur. The most famous slave rebellion of the colonial period was the Stono, South Carolina, rebellion in 1739. The rebellion, initiated by 20 slaves who obtained weapons by attacking a country store, led to the deaths of 20 slave owners and the plundering of half a dozen plantations. But the rebellion was quickly put down, and the participants beheaded with their heads placed on mileposts along the road. Lesser forms of resistance, however, occurred on a daily basis, from working slowly to breaking tools. Also, slaves resisted by retaining cultural connections to Africa, maintaining traditional names and practices.

III. Geography and Regional Development in British North America

Although the colonists who settled British North America had much in common, the varied geographic and environmental characteristics of the New World did much to shape the particularities of the colonies along the Atlantic seaboard. We see distinct regional commonalities among the New England colonies, the middle colonies, the Chesapeake colonies, and the lower South and West Indian colonies.

A. THE NEW ENGLAND COLONIES

The first colonists of the New England region were driven more by religious reasons than economic gain. These settlers were devout Puritans. This religious motivation helps explain the unique patterns of development in New England.

Origins of Puritanism

The roots of Puritanism can be found in the Protestant Reformation of the first half of the sixteenth century. Martin Luther and John Calvin both broke with the Catholic Church for theological reasons. Both argued that the Catholic Church had strayed from its spiritual mission. The Protestant Reformation took hold in much of Northern Europe, but not, initially, in England. In the 1530s, King Henry VIII of England initiated his own break with the Catholic Church. His break, however, was not over theological differences with Rome, but over political control. Henry wanted control of the vast holdings of the church in England

and the power to appoint members of the church hierarchy, as well as the power to annul his marriage. Because Henry's break with Rome was not theological in nature, he did not question, nor did he change, traditional Roman Catholic religious practices. This "halfway reformation" upset many true Protestants in England. Those who sought a full reformation in England, who wanted the Church of England to be "purified" of Catholic practices, came to be known as Puritans. Some Puritans went even further and argued for a complete separation from the Church of England.

> ## THE RELIGIOUS SCHISMS OF EUROPE
>
> Though the Protestant Reformation occurred in Europe, it cannot be ignored by students of American history. The religious divisions of Europe profoundly impacted colonial America and the United States.

Puritan Beliefs and Practices

The Puritans took their inspiration from Calvinism. Calvinist doctrine taught that individual salvation was subject to a divine plan, rather than to the actions of individuals. This doctrine of predestination left true believers in a state of anxiety, since it was impossible to know God's will. To lessen this sense of anxiety, Puritans lived lives of strict piety, framed by prayer, righteous living, and hard work. Calvinism held that everyone had a "calling"—work on earth that God intended the individual to do. Being diligent at one's "calling," therefore, was central to Puritanism.

The Puritans also put a great value on community. Puritans believed it was God's wish that members of the community take care of one another, and watch that members don't go astray. Individual malfeasance could result in divine punishment for the entire community.

Finally, the Puritan approach to humanity and to God was markedly dour, even dark. The Puritans put a great deal of emphasis on "original sin" (stemming from Eve, and then Adam, violating God's injunction not to eat the forbidden fruit in the Garden of Eden) and saw humanity as tainted with this inheritance. Further, the Puritans' vision of God was closer to the vengeful, jealous God that is in much of the Old Testament, rather than the loving God that is in many of the New Testament books.

> ## PLYMOUTH AND NEW ENGLAND
>
> The Pilgrims of Plymouth would remain largely on the margins of New England society. The Massachusetts Bay Colony founded a decade later would prove to be far more successful. One reason for the centrality of Plymouth in historical accounts is that it was the first New England colony.

Plymouth and the Mayflower Compact

A group of English separatists, known to history as the "Pilgrims," fled England in 1608 to find a more hospitable religious climate in Holland. Holland, by this time, was tolerant of different beliefs and had a strong Calvinist presence, and seemed like the ideal location for this group of English Calvinists. Although the Pilgrims did not suffer religious persecution in Holland,

Pilgrim leaders became concerned about the material temptations of Holland. These leaders came to believe that the challenges of establishing a settlement in the New World would steel the congregants for the rigors of religious piety. William Bradford and the leadership of the separatist community got permission from the king to settle in the land granted to the Virginia Company. They formed a joint-stock company to fund the expedition. Slightly over one hundred separatists set sail on the *Mayflower* in 1620, arriving on Cape Cod eleven weeks later. They quickly realized that they were well north of their targeted area, and did not have legal authority to settle. To provide a sense of legitimacy they drew up and signed the Mayflower Compact, calling for orderly government based on the consent of the governed. The colony of Plymouth struggled the first year. By 1630, it achieved a small degree of success, but it failed to attract large numbers of mainline Puritans.

> ## CHURCH AND STATE
>
> Students of American history often make a profound mistake about church and state in colonial Massachusetts. They hear in history class, "The Puritans came to America to freely practice their religion." From this they conclude that the origins of religious freedom can be found in Massachusetts. This is absolutely incorrect. The Puritans (with the exception of Roger Williams) established theocratic governments.

Massachusetts Bay Colony— "A City upon a Hill"

In 1629 King Charles I granted a charter to the Massachusetts Bay Company to establish a colony in the northern part of British North America. The charter did not specify the exact location of the company's headquarters, allowing the governance of the Massachusetts Bay Company to be located in the colony instead of in England. This gave the colony a high degree of autonomy. The leader of the Massachusetts Bay Colony was John Winthrop. Before their ship, the *Arbella*, landed in present-day Salem in 1630, Winthrop gave a sermon that is considered one of the more important in American history. He stressed the importance of the colonists' mission. They should think of their colony as being "a city upon a hill," for, he insisted, "The eyes of all people are upon us."

> ## "A CITY UPON A HILL"
>
> The phrase is from Winthrop's sermon "A Model of Christian Charity." The sermon is very important and gives an excellent description of the Puritan mission in the New World.

The "Great Migration" and the Growth of New England

Like their fellow New Englanders in Plymouth, the settlers of the Massachusetts Bay Colony, centered in present-day Boston, had a difficult first year. However, unlike the Pilgrim settlement in Plymouth, Winthrop's colony was soon thriving. By 1640, a "great migration" of more than 20,000 settlers had come to Massachusetts Bay Colony. The settlers arriving in Massachusetts Bay were middling sorts—farmers, carpenters, textile workers—not the aristocratic settlers of Jamestown. Although the Jamestown settlers were primarily men, families came to Massachusetts Bay Colony. The settlers in Massachusetts were eager to build permanent, cohesive communities, and they were willing to labor; they were not looking for quick riches.

Massachusetts Bay Colony burgeoned with ten new towns in the first decade after 1630 and more than 130 by the end of the century.

> ## GREAT MIGRATIONS
>
> Avoid confusing the seventeenth-century "Great Migration" of the Puritans to New England with the twentieth-century "Great Migration" of African Americans from the rural South to the urban North and West.

New Hampshire

Some Puritans moved north to the area that would become New Hampshire. These settlers were predated by small fishing villages founded by the English in the 1620s. Massachusetts soon claimed the region, and a 1641 agreement gave it jurisdiction over New Hampshire. A royal decree separated the two colonies in 1679.

Roger Williams and the Founding of Rhode Island

Puritan society encouraged the intensive study of scripture. At the same time, the Puritan hierarchy enforced a rigid conformity to its own religious doctrine. This combination of a promotion of learning but insistence on conformity led to inevitable conflicts in New England. Roger Williams was a devout Puritan minister who became an important dissenter in Massachusetts. Williams was increasingly concerned about the mistreatment of American Indians by the Puritans (see below). He was also critical of the involvement of the church in matters of civil governance. He was worried that the concerns of civil government would distract ministers from godly matters. He fled to the Narragansett Bay area in 1636, and founded the colony of Rhode Island. One of the distinguishing characteristics of Rhode Island was the separation of church and state in its governance.

The Banishment of Anne Hutchinson

Another important theological dispute in Puritan New England involved Anne Hutchinson. Hutchinson was a deep religious thinker and had the temerity to hold meetings in her house to discuss theological matters with both men and women. In many ways, she took Puritan thought to its logical extreme, arguing that ministers were not needed to interpret and convey the teachings of the Bible; rather God could communicate directly to true believers. Further, she accused Puritan leaders of backsliding on the idea that salvation was determined solely by God's divine plan, not by the actions of individuals. In 1638, John Winthrop and other Puritan leaders tried, excommunicated, and banished Hutchinson and her family.

The Founding of Connecticut

Some settlers to the growing Massachusetts Bay Colony sought to rid themselves of the heavy-handed rule of the colony's governor, John Winthrop. The Reverend Thomas Hooker argued with Winthrop over who should be admitted to church membership. Hooker argued for the less rigorous requirement of basing membership on living a godly life. Winthrop, however, insisted that new members be able to demonstrate to church leaders that they had

had a conversion experience. Hooker led a group to the Connecticut River valley in 1636, where they founded the town of Hartford, well away from the reach of Winthrop. Other towns formed along the Connecticut River, combining with Hartford to form the colony of Connecticut. The Fundamental Orders of Connecticut were adopted in 1639. In 1662, the town of New Haven merged into the Connecticut colony.

B. THE CHESAPEAKE REGION AND THE MIDDLE COLONIES

The most diverse colonies in British North America—in regard to religion, ethnicity, and social class—were the middle colonies. The middle colonies developed a thriving export economy based on the cultivation of cereal crops. Farther south, the colonies of the Chesapeake region and North Carolina came to rely on labor-intensive tobacco, using the labor of indentured servants and slaves.

Slavery in the Eighteenth-century Upper South

Slavery existed in all the English colonies of North America, but grew most dramatically in the southern colonies in the last quarter of the seventeenth and the eighteenth century. The five southern colonies of Virginia, Maryland, South Carolina, North Carolina, and Georgia became the most populous region of the thirteen colonies—far surpassing both the New England colonies and the middle colonies. The main factor in this dramatic increase was the increase in the number of slaves in the South.

The upper South—consisting of the Chesapeake Bay colonies of Virginia and Maryland—was the most populous part of the South, containing 90 percent of the white population and 80 percent of the black population of the South. The main crop of the upper South was tobacco. Tobacco had been introduced by the Spanish to Europe in the 1500s, but it remained a scarce luxury there. John Rolfe first planted tobacco in Virginia in 1612, and the first shipments of it were sent to England in 1617. With its addictive properties, tobacco soon became hugely popular in Europe and hugely profitable in the Chesapeake Bay region. By 1700, the American colonies were exporting more than 35 million pounds of tobacco a year.

AGRICULTURE, NORTH VERSUS SOUTH

From the beginning, the northern and southern colonies developed different patterns of agriculture. The southern colonies focused on a few staple crops, grown for export. The northern colonies focused on smaller scale agriculture, and a variety of crops.

Maryland

Economically, the colony of Maryland bore similarities to Virginia. Like Virginia, it focused on the cultivation of tobacco as an export crop, and it used indentured servitude and slavery to work the tobacco fields.

Maryland was the first proprietary colony established by England in North America. The crown was moving away from the model of granting charters to joint-stock companies. It hoped that the proprietor (owner) of a colony would be more accountable to the monarch. The proprietor of Maryland was to be George Calvert, Lord Baltimore. Calvert was Catholic and hoped to create a refuge for Catholics in the New World. He was granted a charter by King Charles I, but died weeks before the colony was to be established. His son, Cecelius Calvert, became the actual proprietor of Maryland. Almost immediately, Protestants outnumbered Catholics, but Catholicism continued to be tolerated in Maryland.

North Carolina

The roots of North Carolina can be found in the Carolina colony. In 1711, the northern part of Carolina separated and formed North Carolina. The economy of North Carolina more closely resembled that of the Chesapeake colonies than the sugar economy of Barbados (see page 61).

Pennsylvania

In 1681, King Charles II granted an enormous piece of land (25,000 square miles) to William Penn to settle a debt that the king had owed to Penn's father. William Penn and the king were on friendly terms, despite the fact that Penn had become a devout Quaker and was often at odds with the official Church of England. Charles was no doubt pleased to see the establishment of a colony to draw the dissenting Quakers out of England. The king named the colony after William Penn's father, much to the embarrassment of Penn, the younger.

New Jersey and Delaware

New Jersey and Delaware were both initially established by the Dutch. After Dutch New Netherlands came into the hands of the British in 1664, the Duke of York gave the land adjacent to New York, between the Hudson and Delaware Rivers to two friends, Sir George Carteret and Lord Berkeley of Stratton, who established the colony of New Jersey.

Delaware was first settled by the Dutch in 1631, but all the initial settlers were soon killed in a dispute with American Indians. In 1638, Sweden established a trading post and colony in Delaware at Fort Christina (present-day Wilmington). In 1651, the Dutch established a fort in the Swedish colony; Holland took over the colony and incorporated it into its North American holdings, New Netherlands, in 1655. When the Dutch were ousted by the British in 1664, the Duke of York granted Delaware to his friend William Penn, who incorporated it into his Pennsylvania land grant. In 1704 Pennsylvania's Lower Counties, as Delaware was referred to, developed their own representative body and effectively became independent of Pennsylvania.

NEW AMSTERDAM AND NEW YORK

There are commonalities between colonial New Amsterdam and modern New York City. In both, commerce plays a more important role than religion. Also both are incredibly diverse ethnically and racially.

New York

New Amsterdam came into English hands in 1664, and was rechristened New York. New York continued to function as a commercial port, similar to Boston or Philadelphia. One factor that distinguished New York from similar northern port cities was the central position that slavery played in the local economy. By mid-century, New York had a larger slave population greater than North Carolina's (but less than the other southern colonies). On the eve of the American Revolution, New York City's 3,000 slaves accounted for 14 percent of the population.

The "Negro Plot of 1741"

The tensions in New York between whites and enslaved African Americans came to the surface in a series of events in 1741. A series of unexplained fires in the city led authorities to believe that a slave conspiracy was afoot. Over 150 African Americans were arrested, along with 20 whites. At least 20 people were executed, more than following the Salem witch trials. Historians have debated the extent of the plot, or whether there even was a plot.

C. THE LOWER SOUTH AND THE COLONIES OF THE WEST INDIES

The colonies of the Deep South—Carolina and Georgia—as well as British colonies in the West Indies, all shared certain characteristics that set them apart from the rest of British colonial America. These colonies had longer growing seasons and came to depend on export staple crops and the slave labor system. The population of the Deep South was considerably less than that of the upper South, but the ratio of blacks to whites was significantly different. In many cases, enslaved Africans made up the majority of the population. In South Carolina by the mid-eighteenth century, there were approximately twice as many black slaves as there were whites.

Sugar and Slavery in the West Indies

Barbados was the most profitable colony in England's New World empire. Barbados developed an economy based on agriculture and slavery, like the colonies of the Chesapeake region. However, the Barbados model was significantly different.

Barbados was settled by English colonists in the 1630s and soon became very successful. The source of wealth for the planters of Barbados was sugarcane. Sugarcane received high prices in England. By the end of the seventeenth century, the English colonies of the Caribbean were exporting nearly 50 million pounds of sugar per year. Sugarcane favored wealthy planters, because only they could afford the initial investment needed in a sugar growing and processing operation. Unlike Virginia, there was no small-scale yeoman-farmer class in Barbados. The wealthy sugar planters of Barbados were, on average, four times as wealthy as the tobacco planters of Virginia. In addition, the slave population of Barbados was much larger than that of Virginia. By the end of the seventeenth century, slaves made up 75 percent of the population of Barbados, compared to less than 25 percent in Virginia. The average sugar grower in Barbados owned 115 slaves, far more than average plantations in Virginia. Plantation work in Barbados was brutal—long hours of intense labor under the hot sun. Slaves were much less likely to form families in Barbados than they were in Virginia, with men outnumbering women two to one on the island.

Carolina

The initial settlers of the colony of Carolina were mostly planters who had migrated from Barbados. They brought with them the system of slavery that had developed on Barbados, making the economy of Carolina resemble that of Barbados more than that of Virginia. Carolina was established in 1663 by King Charles II. Charles II was restored to the throne in 1660 and sought to reward eight noblemen who helped him regain the thrown by granting them a charter for the lands below Virginia. The proprietors of Carolina successfully recruited additional wealthy slave-owning English settlers in Barbados to resettle in Carolina. These early Carolinians looked to reproduce the export-oriented plantation economy of Barbados, but they could not find a crop nearly as profitable as sugar to grow in the Carolinas. By the late 1600s, they began making money growing and exporting rice. South Carolina, made a royal colony in 1719, continued to replicate the economic conditions of Barbados with thousands of slaves controlled by a relatively small number of elite planters.

Georgia

The last of the original thirteen colonies to be established was Georgia. Britain became increasingly concerned about competition from other European nations in regard to New World land claims. Britain wanted to establish a buffer between South Carolina and Spanish-held Florida. Toward this end, Britain granted a charter to James Oglethorpe to establish the colony of Georgia in 1732. Oglethorpe was a philanthropist and hoped to establish a paternalistic colony for England's "deserving poor," including imprisoned debtors. Oglethorpe did not grant his charges any element of representative government. He did mandate military service for all males. The royal plan seems to have been to have the poor of Georgia protect the wealthy planters of South Carolina from Spanish encroachment. Oglethorpe's plans did not come to fruition. Few "deserving poor" met Oglethorpe's requirements. Instead, Carolinians in search of new land moved into Georgia, and brought slavery with them. In 1752, Oglethorpe gave up on his project and ceded control of the colony to the crown.

KEY CONCEPT 2.2
CONFLICT IN NORTH AMERICA—AMONG COLONIZERS AND BETWEEN THE COLONIZERS AND THE COLONIZED

In the seventeenth and eighteenth centuries, conflict intensified in North America between rival European empires and between North American colonists and American Indians.

I. Economic Growth Fuels Expansion and Conflict

A major source of conflict in colonial North America was competition over resources—notably land and furs.

A. EUROPEAN CONFLICTS AND NORTH AMERICAN POLITICAL INSTABILITY

The political situation in North America grew increasingly unstable in the seventeenth and eighteenth centuries. Old rivalries in Europe among the French, Dutch, British, and Spanish spilled over to the New World, and in the process drew different American Indian groups into these conflicts. The introduction of European guns into conflicts among American Indians altered the political and military landscape of North America.

The Beaver Wars

An especially brutal series of events, illustrating the destabilizing influence of trade and European firepower on American Indian relations, occurred in the mid-seventeenth century. The Beaver Wars occurred as competition in the fur trade (as the name of the war implies) led to violent conflict. Both the Dutch and the French had established trading posts to obtain furs from American Indian groups in exchange for a variety of goods, including firearms. French traders established a series of trading posts along the St. Lawrence River in the early 1600s, and had aligned themselves with Algonquian-speaking tribes. The Dutch had established a trading post at present-day Albany in 1614, at the edge of territory controlled by the Iroquois people, and had developed an alliance and profitable trade with the Iroquois Confederacy. By 1645 long simmering tensions between the Dutch-allied Iroquois and the French-allied Algonquian-speaking tribes of the Great Lakes region, notably the Huron, exploded into open warfare. The Iroquois people hoped to expand their trading network, but the Huron stood in their way.

War broke out in the 1640s, as it had in the previous century, but with the introduction of European firearms, and French soldiers, the Beaver Wars turned increasingly violent. After the Dutch were eliminated from New Netherlands in 1664, the English allied themselves with the Iroquois Confederacy in its ongoing battles with the French and their American Indian allies. Finally, the Beaver Wars ended in 1701, with the Great Peace of Montreal. The Iroquois were able to expand their territory and influence; the Huron suffered disaster (see below). The Iroquois also realized that they held the balance of power between the British and the French. The wars, the pressures of the fur trade, and the introduction of European firearms all contributed to a realignment of American Indian alliances and a reorganization of the societies.

Chickasaw Wars

European conflicts were again carried out, with American Indian allies, in the interior of North America in the early eighteenth century. The Chickasaw Wars involved the Chickasaw people, aligned with the British, and the Choctaw and Illini people, allied with the French. France was eager to establish control of the Mississippi River; they were concerned about threats from the British colonies to the east and American Indian groups that resisted French hegemony in the Mississippi River valley. When the Chickasaw refused to cooperate with French plans and continued to maintain trade with the British, France waged a war. A series of campaigns occurred between 1636 and 1639. Ultimately, the Chickasaw were able to hold their ground. However, they suffered huge losses and existed in an increasingly unstable political environment following the war.

B. THE EVOLUTION OF COLONIAL ECONOMIES

The colonies of the competing European powers became less interested in old European conflicts and more interested in their own economic development. New World colonies tended to focus on growing and obtaining goods that could be traded with Europeans. As economies grew, New World colonies consistently had to grapple with the problem of an insufficiently large labor force.

Tobacco, Indigo, Rice, Sugar, and Slavery in the South and the West Indies

By the eighteenth century, the economic status of most of the North American colonies improved, as the different colonies focused on crops and economic activities that were suited for the local climate and geography, and that could be marketed to European nations. After several years of economic uncertainty, Virginians came to settle on the cultivation, processing, and export of tobacco. John Rolfe brought seeds of a particular variety of tobacco that proved to be very popular in Europe. Tobacco became the most important crop for the Chesapeake region, accounting for nearly three-fourths of Chesapeake exports by 1750, and nearly one-third of all exports from British North America. The colonies of the lower South specialized in indigo and rice. These two crops made up nearly two-thirds of exports from the lower South by 1750. All told, the southern colonies supplied 90 percent of exports from British North America. However, the most profitable of all the British New World colonies were the sugar-growing islands of the West Indies. Throughout the South and the West Indies, agricultural work was performed primarily by slave labor.

The Fur Trade in the North American Interior

Initially, a lucrative fur trade drew French, Dutch, and English traders and colonists to the interiors of the North American continent—specifically the broad swath of land stretching north from the Ohio River toward the St. Lawrence River and the Great Lakes. This fur trade led Europeans to reach accommodations with American Indian groups, in contrast to the agricultural settlements along the Atlantic Coast, where relations with American Indians were characterized by extermination and removal. The increased trade in furs often destabilized American Indian communities by pushing native peoples to extend their traditional territory in search of more furs. This territorial expansion inevitably exacerbated conflict with neighboring Indian groups. We see an increase in the intensity of warfare in the seventeenth and eighteenth centuries, as American Indian groups, allied with and armed by competing European powers, fought for territory and trading privileges (see above).

Wheat, Indentured Servants, and Redemptioners in the Middle Colonies

By the eighteenth century, settlers in the middle colonies of Pennsylvania and New York, many of them German and Scots-Irish immigrants, developed the cultivation of wheat and other cereal crops for export to Europe. Whereas the southern colonies used the slave system to solve the problem of finding laborers in the New World, the middle colonies tended to rely on indentured servants and "redemptioners." Redemptioners were transported to the New World by sea captains; they promised to pay for their passage once they arrived in the New World, by either borrowing money from a friend or relative already in the New World, or by selling themselves into servitude. Redemptioners were at a distinct disadvantage as compared to indentured servants. Indentured servants generally worked out the details of their indenture back in Europe; they could negotiate and refuse unreasonable offers. Redemptioners, on the other hand—tired, ill-fed, frequently sick, stuck in an unsanitary ship in a New World harbor—were in no position to negotiate effectively with potential masters. Over time, however, the difficulties of servitude paid off for large numbers of Pennsylvanians. The standard of living for typical Pennsylvania farmers was higher than in any other comparable agricultural region in the eighteenth-century world.

Fish and Lumber in New England

The New England countryside did not lend itself to growing profitable export crops. New England farmers tended to grow a variety of crops for local consumption. Many New Englanders engaged in fishing in order to participate in the Atlantic trade. Salted fish made up a third of total exports from New England to Europe. Livestock and timber accounted for another third of New England exports. New England towns grew as commercial centers, engaged in an Atlantic exchange with Europe, the West Indies, and Africa. The population of New England was the most homogenously English of any of Great Britain's New World holdings. The colony grew through extensive waves of Puritan migrations in the seventeenth century and by natural reproduction throughout the colonial period. New England women tended to have many children and the mortality rate was relatively low.

C. TENSIONS BETWEEN GREAT BRITAIN AND NORTH AMERICAN COLONISTS

Over time, the priorities of the European powers and those of colonists in North America began to diverge. Mercantilist principles guided British policies in the New World. However, New World colonists began to chafe at imperial policies and developed a set of priorities often at odds with the imperialist powers. Colonists grew increasingly dissatisfied over a number of issues.

Mercantilism

England's ambitions in the New World were shaped by mercantilism—a set of economic and political ideas that shaped colonial policy for the major powers in the early modern world. Mercantilism holds that only a limited amount of wealth exists in the world. Nations increase their power by increasing their share of the world's wealth. Nations therefore try to maximize the amount of precious metals they hold. One way of acquiring precious metals is to maintain a favorable balance of trade, with the value of exports exceeding the value of imports. Mercantilist theory suggests that governments should advance these goals by maintaining colonies so as to have a steady and inexpensive source for raw materials. The theory also holds that the colonies should not develop manufacturing but should purchase manufactured goods from the ruling country. England imposed several navigation laws (see below) on the American colonies to make sure the colonies fulfilled their role. But some of these laws were difficult to enforce, and the thirteen colonies began to develop an economy independent of England.

> ## MERCANTILISM VERSUS CAPITALISM
>
> Be prepared to distinguish the economic ideas that shaped mercantilism from those that shaped capitalism. Mercantilism, for example, involved extensive government regulation of trade and economic activities; modern capitalism puts much more emphasis on free trade.

Navigation Acts and Mercantilism

From the 1650s until the American Revolution, England passed a number of Navigation Acts. The goal of the acts, in conformity to mercantilist principles, was to define the colonies as suppliers of raw materials to England and as markets for English manufactured items. Toward this end, England developed a list of "enumerated goods"—goods from the colonies that could only be shipped to England. These included goods that were essential for shipping, such as tar, pitch, and masts. Also, Britain insisted that profitable staple crops from the southern slave colonies, such as rice, tobacco, sugar, and indigo, could only be shipped to England. These goods were then sold within England, and at a considerable profit, to other countries. The enumeration of these goods was a double-edged sword; the colonies could not always get the highest price for their goods, but they had a consistent market for them. Several of the Navigation Acts—such as the Wool Act (1699), the Hat Act (1732), and the Iron Act (1750)—prohibited the colonies from manufacturing these items. In this way, England gave an advantage to manufacturers in England itself.

"Salutary Neglect" and the Growth of Smuggling

The Navigation Acts existed on paper, but were difficult to enforce. The lax enforcement of parliamentary laws in regard to the North American colonies is often referred to as "salutary neglect." The policy of "salutary neglect" allowed the North American colonies to thrive economically. Colonists routinely smuggled banned goods into and out of the thirteen colonies. For example, the Molasses Act (1733) placed a prohibitive import tax on sugar from non-English colonies into North America. Boston merchants routinely flouted this law, shipping illegal sugar to supply Massachusetts rum distilleries. However, "salutary neglect" allowed the colonies to develop a unique set of cultural and political practices that later made independence from Britain a viable option.

II. The Impact of Conflicts Between Europeans and American Indians

As European colonies grew and began to expand into the interior of the North American continent, clashes between Europeans and American Indians increased. These economic and social clashes caused changes in both European and American Indian communities.

A. CONTACT, TRADE, DISEASE, AND DEMOGRAPHIC CHANGES

The expansion of European colonial effort in the New World dramatically altered traditional patterns of American Indian peoples. Patterns of trade as well as disease reshaped American Indian communities. Many American Indian communities were devastated by disease, while others managed to maintain sustainable population levels. To some degree, the choices made by American Indians themselves played an important role in the outcome of increased contact with European colonists.

The Catawba—Contact, Trade, and Cultural Adaptation

In the face of conquest and encroachment by European settlers, American Indian groups were often left with stark choices—work for the settlers, move inland, resist, or join other American Indian groups. The Catawba people of the American Southeast attempted to ensure their survival by making themselves useful to the encroaching settlers. They had extensive contact with the towns of colonial South Carolina as traveling peddlers, selling goods to European settlers such as pottery, baskets, and moccasins. Sustained contact with settlers altered Catawba culture in significant ways. The nature of basket making and pottery changed, as Catawba artisans altered ancient practices to meet heightened demand. By the 1750s, the introduction of alcohol as a form of payment for goods led to drunkenness and increased brawls and instability within the Catawba community. The Catawba had generally amicable relations with colonists, but prolonged contact slowly eroded traditional cultural ways.

Contact and War in Colonial New England

Contact between American Indians and British colonists was more violent in New England, just as it had been in Virginia. The intensity of the clashes in New England led to major demographic changes in New England, as American Indians died in large numbers, with survivors moving farther into the interior of the region. The Puritan project of building an ideal community did not preclude them from forcing American Indian populations off land the Puritans hoped to settle. The interactions between the English settlers and native populations mirrored the violent clashes that occurred in Virginia. The most violent episode in the first years of settlement was the Pequot War of 1634–1638. The colonies of Massachusetts Bay and Plymouth worked in alliance with each other and with the Narragansett and the Mohegan peoples to defeat the Pequots. Later, additional warfare would virtually eliminate a cohesive native presence from New England.

Contact, Disease, and the Collapse of the Huron

Early in the seventeenth century, the Huron people, who lived in Ontario, made contact with French explorer Samuel de Champlain. In 1609, the Huron made an alliance with the French. By the 1630s, increased contact with French settlers, including Jesuit priests, proved to be disastrous for the Huron. It is estimated that the Huron numbered between 20,000 and 40,000 at the time of European contact. As contact increased after 1634, major epidemics of measles and smallpox afflicted the Huron people, resulting in the deaths of half to two-thirds of the Huron population.

B. SPANISH AND BRITISH PATTERNS OF COLONIAL INTERACTIONS

The Spanish and the English established different patterns of domination and accommodation in regard to American Indian communities. To a large degree, these divergent patterns reflected the cultural norms of each colonizing power as well as the power dynamics that developed between the colonizers and the colonized. Spanish colonial efforts were more ready to make some accommodations to American Indian cultural ways, while English efforts often resulted in more complete destruction of American Indian communities.

Pueblo Revolt

By the second half of the seventeenth century, Pueblo Indians in New Mexico had grown increasingly resentful of Spanish rule. The Spanish *encomienda* system undermined the traditional economy of the Pueblos, forcing Pueblos to labor in mines and fields. In addition, the Spanish outlawed traditional Pueblo religious practices. In 1680, these grievances came to the surface in the Pueblo Revolt, also known as Pope's Rebellion. The rebellion was centered in Santa Fe and resulted in attacks on Spanish Franciscan priests as well as on ordinary Spaniards. More than 300 Spaniards were killed. Spanish residents fled, but returned later in the decade. As a result of the uprising, Spanish authorities appointed a public defender to protect native rights and agreed to allow the Pueblo to continue their cultural practices. Also, each Pueblo family was granted land. The outcome of this rebellion was markedly different from conflicts between English settlers and native peoples. Such conflicts usually resulted in removal or eradication.

THE SPANISH COLONIAL EXPERIENCE

Students often ignore developments in New Spain. Be familiar with Spanish colonization, especially in the areas that would eventually become the United States. Contrary to traditional accounts, the American West was not an empty region before the period of "Manifest Destiny."

"Praying Indians" in Puritan New England

Whereas the Pueblo Indians managed to pressure Spanish colonizers to make some accommodations with Pueblo culture, the native peoples of New England were less able to maintain traditional cultural patterns in the face of English colonization efforts. Some New England Indian groups mounted armed resistance to encroachments by the English; these efforts, in the Pequot War (1637) and King Philip's War (1675–1678), ended tragically for the native peoples. Others made efforts to coexist with the Puritan settlers of New England. Some American Indians converted to Christianity and settled on farms. Puritan missionaries established "praying towns" for these "praying Indians." By the 1670s, there were fourteen of these "praying towns" in New England. "Praying Indians" were still seen as second-class citizens by the Puritans. Puritans insisted that the converted Christian Indians wear European-style clothing and that they completely abandon their spiritual traditions (in contrast with French Jesuit missionaries in Canada, who accepted that native peoples might combine elements of Catholicism with their traditional beliefs). In the end, the "praying towns" tended to impose English practices on the Indians rather than allowing native people to retain some elements of their traditional ways.

C. EUROPEAN CONTACT AND CHANGES IN WARFARE

Warfare became increasingly intense in the colonial era as Europeans introduced firearms, making rivalries and conflicts among American Indian groups far more deadly.

Warfare in the Great Lakes Region

This dynamic is evident in the Beaver Wars between the Iroquois Confederacy, backed by Dutch and English allies, and several American Indian groups supported by the French. The Huron people, who suffered major population collapse as a result of smallpox and measles epidemics in the 1630s and 1640s, faced further disaster at the hands of the Iroquois. In 1649, an Iroquois war party of about 1000 warriors, armed by their Dutch allies, destroyed the Huron mission villages in Ontario, killing approximately 300 people. Iroquois warriors also killed several Jesuits. The Huron ended up fleeing from the Iroquois to an island in Georgian Bay, Ontario, where large numbers died because of harsh conditions and lack of food. Eventually, many Huron resettled to Quebec and others to the upper Lake Michigan region. The intensity of the new form of warfare that was unleashed by European contact completely upended traditional methods of resolving conflicts for many American Indian groups. In the end, entire communities were often destroyed or relocated.

KEY CONCEPT 2.3
THE ATLANTIC WORLD—PATTERNS OF EMPIRE AND TRADE

Colonial societies experienced profound changes from their founding in the seventeenth century into the eighteenth century. Increasing cultural, political, and economic exchanges within the "Atlantic World" reshaped the worldviews and the prerogatives of New World colonists.

I. The "Atlantic World" in the Seventeenth and Eighteenth Centuries

Interactions among Europeans, Africans, and American Indians dramatically reshaped the "Atlantic World." These interactions included an increase in trade, as well as a sharing of religious, philosophical, and economic ideas. Ultimately, these interactions led to a tremendous growth in colonial economies, new forms of social interactions, and an increase in the use of slave labor.

A. THE ATLANTIC ECONOMY

The 1700s witnessed the growth of an Atlantic economy—one characterized by an increased exchange of goods and the development of an increasingly profitable African slave trade.

Traditionally labeled the "triangle trade," this complex trading network brought manufactured items from England to both Africa and to the Americas. These items included firearms, shoes, furniture, ceramics, and many other items. From Africa, kidnapped Africans were forced into the international slave trade. Africans were taken from interior regions, usually by members of coastal African groups. Once brought to port towns, European traders exchanged manufactured items for human cargo. Then, these Africans were forced to endure the brutal Middle Passage—the journey in cramped quarters to the New World. The colonies of the Americas produced a wide variety of raw materials. Caribbean sugar, for instance, was shipped both to New England and to Europe.

B. THE ANGLICIZATION OF THE BRITISH NORTH AMERICA

The imprint of Great Britain on its North American colonies cannot be overstated. Many ideas and structures—from self-government to legal codes, from commerce to print culture, from religious toleration to Enlightenment thought—made their way from Great Britain and found fertile soil in the New World.

Religious Toleration

The idea of religious toleration—of allowing religious groups outside of the official or established religion to practice freely—has European roots and New World manifestations. In both the Old World and the New World, the concept was the subject of much debate and contestation. The concept has a long history in Europe. The Edict of Nantes (1598) allowed Calvinist Protestants (known as Huguenots) to practice their religion in predominantly Catholic France. Several Enlightenment thinkers advocated religious toleration. Baruch Spinoza, a Dutch philosopher from a Portuguese Jewish family, embraced the idea of religious toleration in the mid-1600s. In 1689, amid concerns of a Catholic ascendency to the throne in England, John Locke wrote "A Letter Concerning Toleration," urging toleration of different Christian sects. Later, the French philosopher, Voltaire, wrote "A Treatise on Toleration" (1763) echoing Locke's sentiments but extending them to all faiths—including Islam and Judaism.

In colonial America, while religious orthodoxy shaped New England life, the idea of religious toleration emerged, haltingly, in several colonies. The 1649, Maryland passed the Act of Religious Toleration, guaranteeing rights to Christians of all denominations (although forbidding non-religious practices). In Dutch New Amsterdam, several residents wrote the Flushing Remonstrance in 1657, requesting that Peter Stuyvesant lift his ban on Quaker worship in the colony. Both documents are seen as early expressions of religious tolerance—an idea that would later come to fruition in the First Amendment of the United States Constitution, guaranteeing freedom of religion.

Quakerism and the "Holy Experiment"

Another British export that took hold in North America was Quakerism—the guiding set of beliefs in the founding of Pennsylvania. Quakerism developed in the religious ferment of seventeenth-century England. Its approach to religion, and indeed to life, was radically non-hierarchical. In a society characterized by social titles and rules of deference, Quakers saw one another as equals in the eyes of God. They addressed one another as "friend" (hence the formal name of Quakerism, "the Religious Society of Friends"). They avoided the practice of the "lower sorts" bowing or removing their hat to their "betters"; Quakers shook hands with one another. Quakers did not have sermons; they attended "meetings" in which each congregant could speak if moved. Penn wanted to establish a "holy experiment" in the New World to put Quakerism's egalitarian values into practice. Penn initiated friendly relations with local native groups. Pennsylvania's Quakers practiced religious toleration and frowned upon slavery (although it did exist in colonial Pennsylvania). Pennsylvania thrived in the seventeenth century, and its largest city, Philadelphia, surpassed New York as a commercial center.

> ## DEFERENCE AND EGALITARIANISM
>
> Deference—the ritualistic display of submission by common people toward those of a "superior" class—was standard social practice in the European and colonial American world of the seventeenth and eighteenth centuries. The egalitarian spirit of Quakerism would come to shape social norms in the early United States.

John Locke and the Principle of Self-government

An important Enlightenment thinker who shaped ideas about self-government in colonial North America was the seventeenth-century thinker and writer, John Locke. Locke broke with an earlier Enlightenment thinker Thomas Hobbes. Hobbes emphasized the selfish, "nasty," and "brutish" nature of humanity, and concluded that humans need ironfisted rulers to keep them in line. Locke shared with Hobbes the notion of the self-interested nature of humans, but he was much more optimistic about the ability of humans to use reason and to make sound decisions about governance. His thinking deeply influenced the British and the colonial idea of the legitimacy of self-government (see more on John Locke in period 3).

Representative Government in Virginia: The House of Burgesses

Virginians organized the first representative legislative body in British North America, the House of Burgesses, in 1619. The company saw the need for some sort of body to govern the inhabitants of the colony and created this representative assembly. All free adult men could vote for representatives. The body continued to exist after King James I revoked the Virginia Company's charter in 1624. Over time, the House of Burgesses became less powerful and more exclusive, as smaller planters were barred from voting.

C. EVOLVING ATTITUDES IN REGARD TO RACE IN COLONIAL NORTH AMERICA

British colonists developed distinctively different ideas about race than Spanish and French colonists. The experiences and predispositions of French colonists led them to see the concept of race in more fluid terms, whereas the British developed rigid racial categories. In the British colonies, sanctioned relationships between British settlers and either American Indians or Africans were rare, but a variety of interracial coupling created new communities in the French and Spanish colonial worlds.

The Metis of the French Colonies

In many French settlements in the interior of the North American continent, French women were few and far between. In these frontier communities, a certain intermingling of French and American Indian lifeways and people occurred. Detroit, for instance combined French elements and American Indian elements. The layout of the village resembled a French village, but many of the buildings were covered by bark, in the style of local American Indians. Clothing among French colonists also included European and native elements; European shirts and Indian shoes, for example. In addition, intermarriage with American Indians was not uncommon in these French colonies. The children of these marriages were known as Metis—an old French word for "mixed" or "mixed-blood." In the Metis communities, American Indian women often played important roles, in contrast to traditional French family structures. These women served as cultural mediators and were an important part of the fur trade as brokers. These Metis communities, combining Catholic practices and indigenous spiritual practices, continued to exist after the French officially withdrew from North America.

Spanish America and the *Casta* System

Despite traditional notions of the superiority of "pure blood" among Spaniards, a great deal more intermixing occurred in the Spanish colonial world than in the English. In Spain's New World colonies, Spaniards were always greatly outnumbered by native peoples. Further, men greatly outnumbered women. In these circumstances, intermarriage was common. The Spanish used the term *casta* to describe the variety of mixed race people in the new world. The *casta* system included *peninsulares* (born in Spain) and *creoles* (children born in the New World of Spanish parents) at the top of the social structure. These groups usually consisted of only 1 or 2 percent of the population. Just below them in social status were *mestizos*, the children of Spanish men and Indian women. *Mestizos* comprised about 4 to 5 percent of the population of Spain's New World empire. Below them were *mulattos* (children of Spanish men and African women), followed by American Indians and Africans at the bottom of the social pyramid. The Spaniards developed even finer gradations, based on the specific percentage of each background an individual possessed.

II. Tensions Between Great Britain and Its North American Colonies

We begin to see the tensions that characterized the pre-Revolutionary period as early as the first half of the eighteenth century. Great Britain faced a series of challenges as it sought to maintain firm control of its colonial empire. As Great Britain attempted to exert greater control over the colonies, the colonies began to chafe at the erosion of the autonomy they had come to enjoy living on the edge of the British Empire.

A. SIMILARITIES AMONG THE BRITISH COLONIES

The regional differences that characterized the founding and the development of the colonies in the 1600s began to wane as the North American colonies began to develop similar legal structures and governing institutions. The colonies all had the shared experience of being part of the British imperial system

From Charter Colony to Royal Colony

King James I revoked the charter of the Virginia Company in 1624 and made Virginia a royal colony, under the control of a governor appointed by the king. King James was alarmed at the level of violence directed against the American Indians, the high mortality rate among the colonists, and the general level of mismanagement in the colony. Ultimately, almost all the colonies—charter colonies and proprietary colonies—were taken over directly by the crown and became royal colonies.

B. FROM DOMINION TO SALUTARY NEGLECT

From the late seventeenth century through the middle of the eighteenth century, the British approach to governing its North American colonies changed dramatically. In the 1680s, the British attempted to exert greater control over the colonies, enforce mercantilist rules and integrate many of them into a single administrative unit. Because of colonial resistance, these efforts failed. By the early 1700s, the British embarked on a policy of "salutary neglect" that allowed the colonies to develop without excessive oversight.

The Dominion of New England

King Philip's War was highly destructive to Puritan New England, but it led to even more challenges to the underpinnings of the Puritan experiment. In the aftermath of the fighting, King Charles II sent an agent to New England to investigate the practices of the New Englanders. Charles II became increasingly resentful of the New Englanders, especially in light of the fact that Puritans had pronounced a death sentence on his father, Charles I, during the English Civil War. The agent found ample evidence of New Englanders not living in conformity with English law. In 1686, royal officials revoked the charters of all the colonies north of Maryland and formed one massive colony called the Dominion of New England. This new colony was ruled directly by a royal appointee, Sir Edmund Andros. The governance of New England was no longer based on Puritan beliefs and values. It was a devastating blow to the Puritan movement.

The Glorious Revolution and the Restoration of Colonial Charters

The Dominion of New England did not last long. Events in England again had a major impact on events in British North America. A crisis developed involving religion and succession to the throne. After King Charles II died, his brother James II became king (1685). James had previously converted to Catholicism. Many Protestants in England were troubled by this, but were calmed by the fact that James's daughter, Mary, the heir apparent, was Protestant, having married William of Orange. However, in 1688, James's wife bore a male child—a new heir apparent and a Catholic. If James's son assumed the throne, England would have a Catholic king and perhaps more Catholic monarchs in successive generations. Protestant parliamentarians would not stand for this. They rose up in the Glorious Revolution (1688), inviting the

Dutch William of Orange and his wife, Mary, to become England's monarchs. King James II was deposed in this bloodless revolution. The Glorious Revolution empowered Parliament and ended absolute monarchy in England. It also led to the establishment of the English Bill of Rights. The turmoil in England inspired New Englanders to arrest Andros and to topple the Dominion of New England in 1689. Soon, individual royal charters were issued by the crown to the New England colonies.

Salutary Neglect

The policy of "salutary neglect" is in part the result of circumstances—the difficulty of enforcing laws in a sprawling empire, thousands of miles from the mother country—and in part intentional. The policy is often attributed to Prime Minister Robert Walpole (1721–1742) because he urged the crown to not excessively interfere with the profitable trade generated by the North American colonies. However, the realities of distance in the age of sailing ships made enforcement of navigation acts difficult.

C. THE ENLIGHTENMENT, SELF-GOVERNMENT, AND RESISTANCE IN BRITISH NORTH AMERICA

In the context of salutary neglect, the British colonies developed ideas, beliefs, and practices that both set them apart from Great Britain, and provided them with a language and a world-view with which to resist British imperial control. Some of the ideas had roots in Great Britain. These developments included the advancement of self-government, changing ideas of liberty, a diversity of new religious ideas and movements, Enlightenment ideas, and a growing suspicion of corruption in the political system.

Self-Government in British North America

One of the results of salutary neglect was the development of a high degree of self-government in colonial America. The British did not have the ability or the will to install a comprehensive bureaucracy in the colonies (as they later would in India). Rather, most of the thirteen colonies followed a different form of political development. Whether the colonies were first ruled by a corporation or a proprietor, they eventually all came under the supervision of the crown. The king appointed a governor to rule over each colony (sometimes one governor ruled over two colonies). But in all cases, some sort of colonial legislature existed. These legislatures dealt with local matters (not trade regulations, for example), including the power to tax the inhabitants of the colony. Governors came to depend on funding from this tax revenue to run the colony. So, in many instances, the colonial legislatures were able to exercise a good deal of leverage over the royal governors. This "power of the purse" instilled in many colonists a sense of their ability to govern themselves.

The Zenger Trial and the Evolution of the Concept of Freedom of the Press

The colonists also came to value a free press. By the time of the American Revolution, more than forty weekly newspapers existed in colonial America. An important precedent for freedom of the press in America occurred in 1735. A New York City newspaper publisher, John Peter

DEMOCRACY IN COLONIAL AMERICA

It is tempting to argue in an essay that American democracy can be found in the history of the colonial period. Be cautious: One can easily find many undemocratic features of colonial life, from theocracy in New England to slavery throughout the colonies.

Zenger, was arrested and charged with seditious libel for printing articles critical of the governor. His lawyer successfully argued that he had the right to print such articles because they were truthful. The jury acquitted Zenger. In the wake of the case, more newspaper printers were willing to print articles critical of royal authorities.

The Great Awakening

In the face of declining church membership, a diminishing of religious zeal, and the rise of Enlightenment philosophy and deism, Christian leaders sought to take action. By the 1730s, we see several charismatic ministers attempting to infuse a new passion into religious practice. These ministers, and their followers, were part of a religious resurgence known as the Great Awakening. The leaders of the movement took a more emotional, and less cerebral, approach to religion. In Massachusetts, the Puritan minister Jonathan Edwards delivered his most famous sermon, "Sinners in the Hands of an Angry God" to a mesmerized audience. The most well-known Great Awakening preacher was George Whitefield. Whitefield was an English minister who visited America seven times and held large revival meetings. He gave dozens of sermons in various locales in the 1740s, bringing huge audiences to a state of religious ecstasy. Other itinerant preachers brought an emotional religious message to thousands of Americans. The Great Awakening's core message was that anyone could be saved, and that people could make choices in their lives that would affect their afterlife. This was in stark contrast with traditional Puritan ideas of "original sin" and predestination. In this, the Great Awakening was more egalitarian and democratic.

Deism and the Enlightenment

In the 1700s, many educated colonists moved away from the rigid doctrines of Puritanism and other faiths and adopted a form of worship that is known as *deism*. In a deist cosmology, God is seen as a distant entity. Deists did not see God intervening in the day-to-day affairs of humanity. God had created the world and had also created a series of natural laws to govern it. In their beliefs, deists were aligned with the Enlightenment ethos, including the aspiration to understand the earth's natural laws. Deists saw God as a great clockmaker—the earth is like a clock, which God created, but it is the mechanisms of the clock, rather than God's interventions, that move the hour and the minute hands.

SUBJECT TO DEBATE

There are several important historiographical questions surrounding the English settlement of North America. Historians have questioned traditional accounts contrasting English and Spanish colonization. In such accounts, the Spanish are portrayed as brutal, almost to the point of being sadistic, in their treatment of the native populations of Central and South America. Traditional accounts of English settlement of North America have deemphasized warfare with American Indians and focused more on theological issues among the Puritans and the economic development of the colonies. More recently, historians have questioned the veracity of some of the more graphic descriptions of Spanish actions in the Americas, and have shed new light on the history of violence by the English against native peoples.

Another question that has engaged historians is the comparison between the New England and the Chesapeake colonies in the seventeenth century. Historical accounts have looked for differences between the northern and southern regions—examining such differences almost from the first day of settlement. To some degree historians can be faulted for reading the more recent past (the Civil War) into the more distant past (the colonies in the 1600s) and concluding that the bloodshed of the 1860s was rooted in seventeenth-century patterns of development. It is open to interpretation whether the differences between the regions are more important than the commonalities.

Historians continue to debate several important issues in regard to the development of slavery. Historical work has examined the relationship between racism and slavery. Did African slavery develop because of preconceived notions of racial hierarchies, or did these notions of superior and inferior races develop over time to justify the continued enslavement of hundreds of thousands, and finally, millions of Americans?

In addition, historians have debated whether the thirteen colonies' ties to Great Britain were beneficial or not to the colonies. On the one hand, mercantilist rules restricted colonial economic activity. The economic activity that was permitted was designed to benefit Great Britain more than it did the colonies. To support the argument that mercantilist rules hampered colonial economic development, historians have cited many colonists complaining of being "oppressed" and reduced to the status of "slaves." Other historians note that many of the mercantilist rules were simply ignored by the colonists.

Practice Multiple-Choice Questions:

Directions: Pick the letter that best answers the following questions.

QUESTIONS 1–2 REFER TO THE FOLLOWING PASSAGE:

"There is little doubt that Puritanism was closer to medieval theory than the material goals and values of a growing middle class that was becoming prominent in England and western Europe after the fifteenth century. While the Puritan never thought of his religion in economic terms, he did emphasize the fact that man could serve God not by withdrawing from the world, but rather by following an occupation or calling that served the world.

"In spite of the proximity of certain Puritan values to the rising capitalistic ethic, Puritanism was more medieval than modern in its economic theory and practice. The idea of unrestrained economic individualism would have seemed a dangerous notion to any self-respecting Puritan. The statute books and court records of seventeenth-century Massachusetts abound in examples of price and wage controls instituted by the government of the colony. The Puritans, furthermore, always looked upon wealth as a gift from God given in the form of a trust; and they emphasized not only the benefits that accrued from work and wealth, but also their duties and responsibilities. In 1639, for example, one of the richest merchants in the colony was fined by the General Court (the highest legislative body) for excessive profiteering, despite the fact that there was no statute against the practice. The Puritans could never separate religion and business, and they often reiterated the medieval conception of the 'just price.'

"In the long run, however, the Puritan ethic, when divorced from its religious background, did serve to quicken and stimulate the spirit of capitalism. The limitations placed by the Puritans on the individual and the freedom of movement within society were subordinated as the time went on in favor of the enterprising and driving individual who possessed the ability and ambition to rise through his own exertions."

—Gerald N. Grob and Robert N. Beck, *American Ideas*, 1963, p.63

1. In the second paragraph, the authors discuss the 1639 legal proceedings against "one of the richest merchants in the colony," in order to show that

   (A) impoverished New Englanders used the legal system to vent class frustrations against the wealthy.
   (B) political corruption was common in Puritan New England.
   (C) Puritan magistrates were evenhanded in that they prosecuted anyone—rich or poor—who expressed heretical religious views.
   (D) the Puritans attempted to enforce economic values that emphasized communal notions of fairness over free-market individualism.

2. Which of the following reflects the main point that Gerald N. Grob and Robert N. Beck are making in the passage above?

   (A) Puritan restraints on economic activity prevented the economy of New England from growing, leading it to fall behind the South and the middle colonies during the colonial period.
   (B) The economy of Puritan New England came to resemble the feudal economy of medieval Europe, dominated by large estates passed on from father to son over several generations.
   (C) The economy of New England only began to thrive when non-Puritan immigrants began to move into New England after the 1640s.
   (D) As the seventeenth century progressed, the decline of Puritan orthodoxy, combined with Puritan patterns of work, allowed for the emergence of a market-oriented economy.

Answers and Explanations to Multiple-Choice Questions

1. **(D)** The mention of the arrest of "one of the richest merchants in the colony" by the authors of the above secondary source is meant the illustrate Puritan attempts to enforce economic values that emphasized communal notions of fairness over free-market individualism. Puritan communities passed a series of laws enforcing "fair prices" and "fair wages." This notion of a moral economy precedes capitalist individualism, dating back to the Middle Ages. The existence of such laws does not only help us understand the Puritan notion of an ideal community; these laws also demonstrate that some members of the community were moving away from the ideal. After all, why would such laws be needed if everyone observed the guidelines of a moral economy? The authors are pointing to a shift toward a more individualistic, market economy.

2. **(D)** The reading raises one of the interesting contradictions of Puritanism. The religion emphasized a rejection of worldly temptations and a rigid asceticism. Yet, its injunction to carry out one's calling—the work that God has intended you to do on earth—with dedication and vigor often led to material success. The reading is arguing that once the white hot zeal of Puritanism declined in New England, the road toward economic success was wide open.

Period 3: 1754–1800
The Crisis of Empire, Revolution, and Nation-Building

5

TIMELINE

1754	Beginning of French and Indian War
1763	Treaty of Paris ends French and Indian War
	Proclamation Act
1764	March of the Paxton Boys
	Sugar Act
	First Committee of Correspondence established in Boston
1765	Stamp Act
	Stamp Act Congress
1766	Declaratory Act
1767	Townshend Revenue Acts
1770	Boston Massacre
1772	*Gaspee* Affair
1773	Tea Act
	Boston Tea Party
1774	Coercive (Intolerable) Acts
	First Continental Congress
1775	Fighting at Lexington and Concord
	Second Continental Congress
1776	Publication of *Common Sense* by Thomas Paine
	Declaration of Independence
1777	Articles of Confederation
1778	Battle of Saratoga
	France enters the war on the side of the colonists
1781	Articles of Confederation ratified by states
1783	Treaty of Paris ends the American Revolution
1784	First Land Ordinance
	Treaty of Fort Stanwix
1785	Second Land Ordinance
1786	Shays' Rebellion
	Annapolis meeting to revise Articles of Confederation
1787	Northwest Ordinance
	Constitutional Convention in Philadelphia

1788	Publication of *The Federalist*
	Ratification of the Constitution
	First federal elections
1789	Inauguration of George Washington
	Judiciary Act
	Beginning of French Revolution
	Publication of *The Interesting Narrative of the Life of Olaudah Equiano*
1791	Ratification of the Bill of Rights
	Alexander Hamilton issues "Report on Manufacturers"
	The Bank of the United States is approved
1793	War between Great Britain and France
	Washington Neutrality Proclamation
1794	Whiskey Rebellion
	Jay's Treaty
1795	Pinckney's Treaty
1796	Washington's Farewell Address
1798	XYZ Affair
	"Quasi-war" with France
	Alien and Sedition Acts
	Kentucky and Virginia Resolutions
1800	Election of Thomas Jefferson

INTRODUCTION

The attempt by Great Britain to restructure its North American empire following the French and Indian War and to assert greater control over its colonies led to intense colonial resistance and finally to revolution. The American Revolution produced a new American republic. The first decades of the United States were marked by a struggle over the new nation's social, political, and economic identity.

The American Revolution was a monumental event in the history of United States, as well as in world history. The American Revolution brought to the surface tensions that existed between the thirteen American colonies and the government of Great Britain. It also brought into existence a democratic republic. The democratic spirit that imbued the founding of the United States inspired movements for change—both within the United States and abroad. The American Revolution did not give birth to a perfect democracy. Americans have struggled with the meaning and extent of democracy for the more than 230 years since winning independence.

> ### CRITICAL CONDITION
>
> Think of a patient in critical condition when you see the label "critical period" to describe the decade of the 1780s. Just like a patient in critical condition, the existence of the United States was in question.

The decade of the 1780s was a trying one for the new American nation. The newborn United States fought and won the final stages of the American Revolution and then was faced with a series of threats from within and from abroad that threatened its very existence. By the end of the "critical period," the nation had shifted directions in regard to governing structure—rejecting the Articles of Confederation and adopting the Constitution.

The first dozen years after the ratification of the Constitution were key in the shaping of the United States political system. The government reformed in conformity with the Constitution. The Bill of Rights established important civil liberties. It was in this period that many of the American political system's traditions and precedents—collectively known as the "unwritten Constitution"—were established. We see the development of political parties and of the two-party system during these years. Further, we see continuing struggles over the new nation's identity.

KEY CONCEPT 3.1
CRISIS OF EMPIRE—FROM THE FRENCH AND
INDIAN WAR TO INDEPENDENCE

The French and Indian War (1754–1763) proved to be a turning point in the relationship between Great Britain and the thirteen colonies. Before the war, Britain's policy of "salutary neglect" allowed both Great Britain and the colonies to benefit under loosely enforced mercantilist rules (see Period 2). After the war, the British government enacted a series of measures that many colonists found objectionable, unleashing a resistance movement that resulted in the American War for Independence.

I. American Indian Alliances in the Second Half of the Eighteenth Century

American Indian nations were in an increasingly precarious position in the second half of the eighteenth century. In the 1750s, American colonists began to push beyond the Appalachian Mountains, challenging France's profitable fur trade in the areas around the Ohio River valley. American Indian tribes were forced to adjust alliances in the wake of the French and Indian War between Great Britain and France, and again after the American Revolution.

A. BRITISH EXPANSION AND THE DISRUPTION OF AMERICAN INDIAN ALLIANCES

In the 1740s and 1750s, British colonists began to venture from Virginia to settle beyond the Appalachian Mountains in the Ohio River valley, land claimed by France. France began building fortifications in the region, notably Fort Duquesne at present-day Pittsburgh. The British colonists built a makeshift fort of their own nearby, Fort Necessity. In 1754, skirmishes between the two groups led to the beginning of the French and Indian War, which forced a shift in American Indian alliances.

Expansion and the French and Indian War

The French and Indian War had complex origins. In part, it was a continuation of decades of Old World conflicts between Great Britain and France. However, the causes of the war can also be traced to the New World. Both Great Britain and France had extensive land claims in North America. France's land claims stretched from Quebec, Montreal, and Detroit in the north to New Orleans at the mouth of the Mississippi River in the south, and from the Appalachian Mountains in the east to the Rocky Mountains in the west. France claimed more land in the New World, but Great Britain had many more colonists.

There are three distinct phases of the French and Indian War. At first (1754–1756), the war was a local affair—a continuation of the skirmishes between British colonists and French forces. Most of the American Indian tribes sided with the French, who tended to be more accommodating than the British to native peoples. The scattered colonists attempted, unsuccessfully, to work with one another during this period. Colonial leaders met in Albany, New York (1754), in an attempt to organize an intercolonial government. Benjamin Franklin's proposed Albany Plan was rejected by the delegates. On the battlefield, the colonists were in retreat.

In the second phase (1756–1758), the British government, under Prime Minister William Pitt, took full charge of the war. Pitt alienated many colonists with his heavy-handed tactics, including forcing colonists into the army and seizing supplies from them. The colonists resisted these moves, putting the entire British effort at risk.

In the final phase (1758–1761), Pitt tried to work with colonial assemblies and also reinforced the war effort with more British troops. These moves proved successful.

In 1761, French forces surrendered at Montreal. Two years later, a formal peace treaty was signed.

B. AMERICAN INDIAN–WHITE CONFLICTS IN THE WAKE OF THE FRENCH AND INDIAN WAR

In the aftermath of the French and Indian War, American Indians in the areas newly won by Great Britain found themselves in an increasingly precarious position—on the one hand they wanted to maintain the lucrative fur trade with Europeans, while on the other, they hoped to resist encroachment by British colonists.

The Treaty of Paris (1763)

In the Treaty of Paris, France surrendered virtually its entire North American empire. It ceded to Great Britain all French territory in Canada and east of the Mississippi River and to Spain, all territory west of the Mississippi River. British North American colonists were pleased that the land beyond the Appalachians seemed ready for additional settlement.

Clashing Cultures in the Great Lakes Region

As the British made their presence felt in the lands formerly held by the French, the difference between the British and the French in their approach to American Indians became more evident. The French, for practical and cultural reasons, worked at developing harmonious relations with American Indian tribes. For instance, they negotiated with Indian leaders and participated in ceremonial exchanges of gifts with American Indian tribes. The British, on the other hand, had little patience for gift exchanges. British general Jeffrey Amherst saw gift exchanges as demeaning; why, he argued, should the British pay tribute to American

Indians? American Indians, on the other hand, saw in generous gift-giving an expression of dominance and protection.

In the uncertain world created by the defeat of the French, some American Indians attempted to foster a greater sense of unity and cultural resistance among the often-fractious tribes of the Great Lakes and Ohio Valley regions. In 1760 and 1761, a Delaware leader named Neolin offered American Indians an apocalyptic vision of a future that could transpire if American Indians did not change their ways. He encouraged American Indians to curb their contact with European fur traders, reduce the presence of guns, alcohol, and other European goods, and lessen infighting. His efforts set the stage for violent resistance.

> ## ONGOING INDIAN WARS
>
> The "Indian Wars" of the 1790s are part of an ongoing pattern of the United States breaking treaties, expanding west, and engaging in military conflicts with American Indians. The pattern stretches from the seventeenth century to the late-nineteenth century.

Pontiac's Rebellion

With the defeat of the French in the French and Indian War, American Indian groups that had been allied with the French found themselves in a precarious situation. The Ottawa tribe, for instance, in the northern Ohio region found itself without allies as British colonists set their sights on traditional Ottawa lands. After the war, British troops occupied the French-built forts. The Ottawa chief, Pontiac, and other American Indian leaders organized resistance to British troops stationed in areas near the Great Lakes. In the months after the 1763 signing of the Treaty of Paris, Indian warriors attacked British-held Fort Detroit. This attack was followed by attacks on six other forts and on colonial settlements along a swath of land from upstate New York to the area south of Lake Michigan. The attacks were initially successful; Pontiac and his allies captured several forts west of Detroit, with more than 400 British soldiers and 2,000 colonists killed or captured. Major General Jeffrey Amherst was replaced by the more capable Thomas Gage in August 1763. Bloodshed continued into 1764. Pontiac's Rebellion was finally broken by Gage in the fall of 1764, but smaller skirmishes continued until the American Revolution, when many American Indian groups sided with the British.

The Proclamation Act (1763)

In response to the outbreak of Pontiac's Rebellion, Great Britain issued the Proclamation Act (1763), which drew a line through the Appalachian Mountains. Great Britain ordered the colonists not to settle beyond the line. The British government did not want to provoke additional warfare with native peoples in the region. Colonists were disgruntled; they felt that they had made sacrifices during the French and Indian War and they were now eager to settle in these newly claimed lands.

C. AMERICAN INDIAN POLITICAL ALLIANCES FOLLOWING THE AMERICAN WAR FOR INDEPENDENCE

Following the American Revolution, thousands of settlers pushed beyond the Appalachian Mountains into the lands along the Ohio River valley. This was land that the British had tried to close to settlement following the French and Indian War. However, Great Britain had given up claims to all lands east of the Mississippi River in the Treaty of Paris (1783). Of course, the American Indians of the old Northwest had not been consulted, nor had they given up their claims to the lands north of the Ohio River, in present-day Ohio and Indiana.

Treaty of Fort Stanwix

In 1784, the Articles of Confederation government tried to solve the problem of American Indian land claims north of the Ohio River by working out the Treaty of Fort Stanwix. However, this treaty was negotiated with members of the Iroquois Confederacy—a group of American Indian nations that did not, for the most part, occupy the land in question. The main occupants of the region, the Shawnee, the Delaware, and the Miami, were not part of these negotiations and protested bitterly that their land had been ceded without their consent.

American Defeat at the Wabash River

The situation between American Indian and white settlers grew increasingly tense after 1790. White settlers were no longer content to settle in the area south of the Ohio River, in present-day Kentucky. They were pushing north into American Indian territory. A series of military conflicts ensued in the 1790s in the Ohio territory. American troops led by General Arthur St. Clair suffered a massive defeat at the mouth of the Wabash River in 1791. More than 900 U.S. troops were killed in this encounter, making it the United States' single most costly battle in the entire history of wars with American Indians.

II. From Resistance to Rebellion—Colonial Responses to British Policies

In the aftermath of the French and Indian War, the relationship between the British colonists and Great Britain changed, as the colonists began to unite and organize around a series of threats—actual and perceived—posed by changing British policies. This changing relationship fostered a resistance movement and finally an independence movement.

A SHIFT IN COLONIAL POLICY

Note the shift in British policy from the "salutary neglect" approach prior to the French and Indian War to the close supervision of the postwar period.

A. DEBT AND TAXATION FOLLOWING THE FRENCH AND INDIAN WAR

If British colonists celebrated the removal of the French from North America, their celebration was short-lived. Almost immediately, the British government attempted to confront an ongoing problem—the large debt that had accumulated during almost half a century of constant warfare. The British government believed its victory in the French and Indian War (1754–1763) had been especially beneficial to the colonists. In return, the British reasoned it was fair for the colonists to assume some of the costs of the war and of continued protection through increased taxation. New taxes and more rigorous enforcement of existing taxes generated intense resentment and resistance among many colonists.

The Sugar Act

The Sugar Act (1764) actually lowered the existing tax on molasses imported into North America from French colonies in the West Indies. However, along with lowering the tax, the act also sought to crack down on widespread smuggling. The act strengthened the admiralty courts system, shifting prosecutions of smuggling cases from local jury trials to British maritime courts.

The Stamp Act

The Stamp Act (1765) represented a departure from previous British colonial policy. Previous tax acts were aimed at regulating trade; this act was purely and simply designed to raise revenue. It was a direct tax on the colonists, rather than an indirect trade duty. The act imposed a tax on all sorts of printed matter in the colonies—court documents, books, almanacs, deeds. Of the acts following the French and Indian War, the Stamp Act provoked the most intense opposition (see below).

Quartering of British Troops

The British stationed troops in Boston, forcing local residents to house and feed British troops (1765). Often these troops were given part-time wages, forcing them to supplement their wages by finding work in Boston.

B. MOBILIZING RESISTANCE IN COLONIAL AMERICA

We tend to assume, erroneously, that the seeds of independence were planted in the minds of the British colonists from the moment of their arrival in the New World. Even in the decade before independence, most colonists considered themselves to be loyal subjects of the British monarch. It was only through a wrenching process that colonists began to resist British authority and finally to break with Great Britain altogether.

The Stamp Act Congress

The first significant, coordinated protests against British policies occurred in response to the Stamp Act (see above). In October 1765, delegates from nine of the colonies met in New York and drew up a document listing grievances, which went beyond the Stamp Act. The Declarations of the Stamp Act Congress asserted that only representatives elected by the colonists could enact taxes on the colonies. "No taxation without representation" became a rallying cry of opponents of British policies. The declarations followed on the heels of a series of proposals, written by Patrick Henry, called the Virginia Resolves. Not all of the resolves were passed by the Virginia assembly, but they were all written up and circulated throughout the colonies. The resolves, debated in June 1765, called for a degree of colonial self-government that went beyond more moderate proposals.

The British responded to the cry of "No taxation without representation!" with the theory of "virtual representation." The theory held that members of Parliament represented the entire British Empire. The colonists therefore were "virtually represented" by the members of Parliament.

Committees of Correspondence

In communities throughout the colonies, committees of correspondence were organized, starting in 1764. These committees of opponents of British policies initially spread information and coordinated actions. By the 1770s, they had become virtual shadow governments in the colonies, assuming powers and challenging the legitimacy of the legislative assemblies and royal governors.

Crowd Actions

The Stamp Act generated a variety of crowd actions in the colonies. In cities and towns throughout the colonies, Sons of Liberty groups harassed, and occasionally attacked, Stamp Act agents. There were several incidents of stores ransacked if the proprietor did not comply with boycotts of British goods. In Boston, the home of the lieutenant governor, Thomas Hutchinson, was ransacked. Finally, the Stamp Act itself was rescinded (1766), but a series of British moves and colonial responses in the coming years worsened the situation.

MOBS AND CROWDS

Be aware of the different implications of "mob actions" and "crowd actions." "Mob actions" imply random acts of violence committed by unthinking groups of people, while "crowd actions" imply acts taken with a particular goal in mind by groups of people with an articulated agenda. Social historians have, of late, tended to favor using the term "crowd actions."

The Townshend Acts

The Townshend Acts (1767), passed in the wake of the Stamp Act fiasco, imposed additional taxes on the colonists. Chancellor of the Exchequer Charles Townshend made sure these new taxes—on paint, paper, lead, tea—were "external" taxes, on imports, not "internal" sales taxes on items.

STANDING ARMIES

During the eighteenth and nineteenth centuries, suspicion of standing armies was part of the British and American political tradition. In the contemporary world, most people accept standing armies, even in peacetime.

The Boston Massacre

During the winter of 1770 a deadly incident in Boston reverberated throughout the colonies. In March, a disagreement between a British officer and a young wigmaker's apprentice escalated into a scuffle. Angry colonists heckled and threw stones at British troops. Finally, the British troops opened fire on the colonists, resulting in five deaths, including the death of an African American named Crispus Attucks. The incident reflected colonial resentment of the "standing army" stationed in Boston. In years to come, the incident would be repeatedly used as propaganda to illustrate the brutality of the British.

DEFENSIVE VERSUS OFFENSIVE WARS

It is easier to defend one's territory than it is to conquer another's territory. This is seen in the American Revolution and was one of the advantages of the Confederacy in the Civil War.

Gaspee Affair

In 1772, the *Gaspee* affair represented a shift toward more militant tactics by colonial protestors. A British revenue schooner, the *Gaspee*, ran aground in shallow waters near Warwick, Rhode Island. Local men boarded the ship, looted its contents, and finally torched it.

The Tea Act and the Boston Tea Party

In 1773, the British passed the Tea Act, which eliminated British tariffs from tea sold in the colonies by the British East India Company. This act actually lowered tea prices in Boston, but it angered many colonists who accused the British of doing special favors for a large company. The colonists responded by dumping cases of tea into the Boston harbor. The dumping of the tea in the water was more than a symbolic act; its value, adjusted for inflation, would be more than $1 million.

The Coercive/Intolerable Acts

The British passed a series of acts in 1774 in the wake of the Boston Tea Party that were called the Coercive Acts, or Intolerable Acts.

The Massachusetts Government Act brought the governance of Massachusetts under direct British control.

The Administration of Justice Act allowed British authorities to move trials from Massachusetts to Great Britain.

The Boston Port Act closed the port of Boston to trade until further notice.

The Quartering Act required Boston residents to house British troops upon their command.

A fifth act, the Quebec Act, was passed around the same time but was unrelated to the Boston Tea Party. The act let Catholics in Quebec freely practice their religion. Protestant Bostonians assumed that this was an attack on their faith.

C. THE WAR FOR INDEPENDENCE—FACTORS IN THE VICTORY OF THE PATRIOT CAUSE

The imperial crisis reached a boiling point by 1775. Fighting between the British army and rebellious colonists known as Patriots began at Lexington and Concord in 1775 and intensified after the Second Continental Congress declared independence in July 1776.

Lexington and Concord

In April 1775 fighting began between colonists and British troops in the Massachusetts towns of Lexington and Concord. Americans often call the first shot of this clash, "the shot heard round the world." The event symbolized a marked shift in the colonial situation from resistance to rebellion.

Factors in the Outcome of the War

Both sides had important advantages and disadvantages in the American Revolution. The British had a highly trained, professional army; they had the strongest navy in the world; and they had substantial financial resources. The British could also count on the support of a percentage of the colonial population that remained loyal to Great Britain. Great Britain offered freedom to slaves who joined the British side. The British also could count on a majority of American Indian tribes for support.

However, the British were fighting far from home. It was difficult to maintain supply lines over the course of a long war. Also, Great Britain had enemies, such as the French who wanted to see the British defeated. Finally, Britain's formal style of fighting was ill-suited for the wild and vast North American countryside.

The Patriot side had excellent leadership in General George Washington. In addition, Washington had support from talented European generals: the Marquis de Lafayette (French); Baron von Steuben (German); and Thaddeus Kosciusko and Casimir Pulaski (Polish). The Patriots had the advantage of simply having to defend their home territory; they did not have to attack Great Britain to emerge victorious. Finally, many Patriot soldiers believed deeply in the cause of independence. Patriot disadvantages included lack of financing and a lack of a strong central governing authority.

The Phases of the American Revolution

Historians point to three distinct phases of the American Revolution. The first phase (1775–1776) took place primarily in New England. In this phase, Great Britain did not quite grasp the depth of Patriot sentiment among many colonists. The British thought that the conflict was essentially brought on by a few hotheads in New England. After the British were defeated at the Battle of Bunker Hill (March 1776), they abandoned Boston and reevaluated their strategy.

The second phase (1776–1778) occurred primarily in the middle colonies. The British thought that if they could maintain control of New York, they could isolate rebellious New England. A massive British force drove George Washington and his troops out of New York City in the summer of 1776. However, British forces coming south from Canada suffered a major defeat at the Battle of Saratoga in October 1777. The battle made it evident that the British might be able to hold urban centers, like New York City, but it would be very difficult for the British to control the vast wilderness of North America. The battle also showed France that the rebellious colonists were a formidable force. Early in 1778, France formally recognized the United States and agreed to supply it with military assistance. France's motivation was its animosity toward Great Britain, not affinity with the ideals of the Declaration of Independence.

URBAN AND RURAL AREAS

Later in American history, the United States also came to realize that urban centers are easier to hold on to than rural areas. This lesson was shown in the Vietnam War.

The third phase (1778–1781) took place in the South. Great Britain hoped that it could rally loyalist sentiment in the South, where it was strongest, and hopefully tap into resentment among the slave population of the South. The southern strategy did not bear fruit despite British victories at Savannah, Georgia, and Charleston, South Carolina. In the North, fighting had reached a stalemate, despite the aid that turncoat Benedict Arnold supplied to the British (1780). By October 1781, a joint American-French campaign caught British General Cornwallis off guard. He surrendered at Yorktown, Virginia. Skirmishes continued between the two sides until the 1783 Treaty of Paris formally ended the American Revolution.

III. Foreign Policy of the New American Nation

Under the Articles of Confederation, Congress faced several foreign policy challenges during the Critical Period. The United States did not, for the most part, resolve these problems in a satisfactory way. To some degree the Articles of Confederation failed to unify the thirteen states and failed to allow the United States to speak with a strong, united voice. However, more significantly, the United States was a young, weak country. It would have been surprising if such a country could force world powers such as Great Britain or Spain to toe the line.

A. EUROPEAN CHALLENGES IN NORTH AMERICA

European powers, perhaps sensing the newly formed United States was on precarious footing, maintained a presence in North America in the years following American victory. The United States faced challenges to its borders in the West and South. In addition, it attempted to assert neutral trading rights.

Spain Challenges American Growth in the West

In 1763, as a result of the French and Indian War, Spain gained control of the Louisiana Territory, the vast swath of land to the west of the Mississippi River, as well as the river itself. Spain also controlled the city of New Orleans, where the Mississippi empties into the Gulf of Mexico. Spain grew increasingly alarmed by the number of American settlers pouring west. It suspected that the growing American population would soon begin to cross into the Louisiana Territory, and that eventually the United States would challenge Spain's claims to the region. To discourage American settlement, Spain closed the Mississippi to American shipping. John Jay pressured the Spanish minister to the United States, Don Diego de Gardoqui, to reopen the river, but to no avail. Jay did not perhaps push as hard as he might have; he was more interested in developing and expanding Atlantic trade than western trade.

B. ROLE OF THE UNITED STATES IN THE AFTERMATH OF THE FRENCH REVOLUTION

Despite America's intention to be independent of European affairs, events in Europe greatly impacted the newly formed United States. Just as Americans were ratifying the Constitution in 1789, the French Revolution was beginning. Americans were divided, and their debates about the French Revolution foreshadowed ongoing debates about the role of the United States in the world.

The Question of Alliances

The debates over the role of the United States took on greater significance after France and Great Britain went to war in 1793. Many Americans felt that the United States had an obligation to help France because France had helped the United States in the American Revolution and because a 1778 treaty committed the United States to help France if it were under attack. Others argued that the United States should stay out. After all, the treaty was made with a French government that no longer existed, and the French Revolution had devolved from a democratic movement into a bloodbath. King Louis XVI and thousands of his countrymen had been guillotined. Many of these neutrality-minded Americans also harbored warm feelings for the British system, despite the fact that the war with Great Britain had concluded a mere decade earlier. Already the two nations had resumed commercial ties.

C. THE STRUGGLE FOR NEUTRALITY IN THE 1790s

Despite attempts by the United States to remain neutral in regard to European affairs in the 1790s, the United States found itself drawn into foreign conflicts. The positions that the United States took in regard to ongoing conflicts between Great Britain and France contributed to rancorous debates between the pro-British Federalist Party and the pro-French Republican Party.

Washington and Neutrality

President Washington chose to remain neutral in the conflicts between Great Britain and France. He issued the 1793 Neutrality Act and in his Farewell Address he urged the United States to avoid "permanent alliances" with foreign powers. He did not want the newly independent nation, on precarious footing, to be drawn into the seemingly endless conflicts of Europe. His calls for neutrality have been invoked by isolationists throughout American history, including during debates about U.S. entrance into both World Wars.

PARTIES AND FOREIGN POLICY

Note that during the administration of the Federalist John Adams, United States relations with France were more strained; during the administrations of Democratic-Republican presidents in the early 1800s, United States relations with Great Britain were more strained.

Conflict with France and the XYZ Affair

Events during the administration of President John Adams challenged America's commitment to neutrality. In 1797, in retaliation for America's favorable treaty with Great Britain (Jay's Treaty; see below), France rescinded the 1778 alliance with the United States and allowed French privateers to seize American ships. After more than 300 ships were seized, President Adams sent a delegation of negotiators to Paris to attempt a peaceful solution. The delegation was not initially allowed to discuss the matter with the French foreign affairs minister Charles Talleyrand. Rather, three agents approached the American delegation and informed them that they could begin negotiations if they paid $250,000 and promised a $12 million loan to France. The three French agents were never named. When word of this interchange made its way into American papers, the three agents were referred to simply as X, Y, and Z. The XYZ affair incensed President Adams and many Americans. Congress allocated money for a military engagement against France. Warships were dispatched to the Caribbean and fought French ships in America's first undeclared war, labeled the Quasi-War (1798–1800) by historians. Americans were deeply divided by the military action.

KEY CONCEPT 3.2
THE GROWTH OF DEMOCRACY AND REPUBLICAN FORMS OF GOVERNMENT

The ideas that grew out of the American Revolution did not develop in a vacuum. Experiments in democratic and republican forms of government developed across the Atlantic World. These ideas were shaped by new religious, economic, and cultural ideas.

I. Ideas Shape Debates Around New Structures of Government

The American Revolution occurred in the midst of a fertile period in the history of ideas. A variety of schools of thought put forth contending new ideas about society, politics, religion, and governance. It was in this context that Americans debated the proper structure of government in the newly formed United States.

A. PROTESTANT EVANGELISM AND ENLIGHTENMENT PHILOSOPHY

The rise of Protestant evangelical movements, in the form of the Great Awakening (see Period 2), shaped the worldviews of many British colonists, inspiring them to see themselves as a chosen people, surrounded by the blessings of liberty. In addition, the ideas of the Enlightenment shaped American thinking about the ideal political system.

The Ideas of John Locke

John Locke's ideas (introduced in Period 2) were profoundly influential in America during the age of the revolution. Locke wrote *Two Treatises on Government* in the early 1690s to defend England's Glorious Revolution (1688). He identified the basis of a legitimate government in his *Second Treatise of Government* (1689). Locke argued that a ruler gains legitimacy through the consent of the governed. The basic responsibility of government is to protect the natural rights of the people; Locke identified the most basic of these rights as life, liberty, and property. If a government should fail to protect these basic rights, it is the right of the citizens to overthrow that government. Locke's theory of natural rights states that power to govern belongs to the people. Locke was one of the main intellectual influences in the writing of the Declaration of Independence. Locke's writings challenged Thomas Hobbes's defense of an absolutist monarchy and Sir Robert Filmer's assertion of the divine right of kings.

B. *COMMON SENSE*, THE DECLARATION OF INDEPENDENCE, AND REPUBLICAN SELF-GOVERNMENT

Theoretical debates about the proper form of government took on urgency in the North American colonies in the 1770s as the imperial crisis intensified. Enlightenment ideas informed the writings of Thomas Paine and shaped the content of the Declaration of Independence. American thinkers and revolutionaries embraced the ideas of republican self-government based on natural rights theory.

Divided Loyalties

By 1776, even though fighting had begun between the colonists and the British, independence was not a forgone conclusion. Some colonists, known as "Patriots," wanted independence; others, known as "Loyalists," wanted to retain ties to Great Britain. (Of course, many colonists did not choose either side in the conflict.) Both sides had good reasons for their stance—whether those reasons were economic or emotional.

The Olive Branch Petition

Some members of the Continental Congress still hoped for reconciliation. Congress sent the "Olive Branch Petition" to the British king in July 1775, affirming loyalty to the monarch and blaming the current problems on Parliament (King George III rejected the petition).

Common Sense

As the debate about independence ensued, Thomas Paine published a best-selling pamphlet called *Common Sense*. He suggested that the American colonies declare independence from

Great Britain. He wrote that he could not see a "single advantage" in "being connected with Great Britain." Relations between Great Britain and the colonies were strained at the time Paine wrote his pamphlet. Paine argued against the logic of the Olive Branch Petition, plainly and forcefully putting the blame on the king.

The Declaration of Independence

On July 4, 1776, the delegates to the Second Continental Congress formally ratified the Declaration of Independence. The body of the Declaration of Independence is a list of grievances against the king of Great Britain, but the eloquent preamble contains key elements of Locke's natural rights theory. It states, "all men are created equal" and "endowed by their Creator with certain unalienable right." The declaration goes on to assert that government gains its legitimacy from having "the consent of the governed." If a government violates people's natural rights, the people have the right "to alter or abolish it." These ideas have shaped democratic practices in the United States and beyond.

Visions of Republicanism

When the United States declared, and eventually won, its independence from Great Britain, it was not immediately clear what type of government it would embrace. There was widespread agreement that America would become a republic—a country in which sovereignty, or power, ultimately rested with the people rather than a monarch. This was a radical move for the time; there had been virtually no republics in the world since the Roman republic, two thousand years earlier.

> **REPUBLICANISM**
>
> The eighteenth-century ideology of republicanism is not synonymous with the ideas of the Democratic-Republicans, 1790s–1820s), nor with the ideas of the later Republican Party (1850s–present).

There was, however, disagreement about what was expected of citizens in a republic. For many Americans, republicanism implied a particular moral stance in the world. Republican citizens, in this formulation, were independent people who embodied civic virtue, putting the interests of the community above their own self-interest. Republican citizens led industrious, simple lives. This vision of republicanism dated back to the ancient Roman republic. In this understanding of republicanism, virtuous citizens had to be on the watch for decadent and corrupt leaders who pursued luxury and power at the expense of the common good.

At the same time, other Americans were developing a different set of ideas about republicanism. They argued that individuals pursuing their own self-interest were the ideal republican citizens. This understanding of republicanism drew inspiration from the economic ideas of Adam Smith. It put more of a focus on ambition and economic freedom, while the earlier understanding put more of an emphasis on public virtue and civic-mindedness. These competing visions of republicanism shaped many of the debates during the first decades of the United States.

C. STATE CONSTITUTIONS AND THE ARTICLES OF CONFEDERATION

The framers of the Articles of Confederation created a "firm league of friendship" among the states, rather than a strong, centralized nation. Before 1776 they had lived under a powerful, distant authority and they did not want to repeat that experience. Also, many of these early leaders were fiercely loyal to their states and did not want to see state power taken away.

State Constitutions

In May 1776, even before independence had been declared, the Second Continental Congress urged the states to draft constitutions. By 1778, ten states had drawn up constitutions, and Connecticut, Massachusetts, and Rhode Island updated their colonial charters. All the state constitutions affirmed the republican notion that government ultimately rests on the consent of the governed. Most of these constitutions reflected the older view of republicanism. That is, these constitutions tended to be based on the idea that governing units should be relatively small and that distant power could become tyrannical. Some states created some form of direct democracy. Many states strengthened the lower legislative house. The lower house would be more responsive to the will of the people, through more frequent elections. Some states established annual elections in the lower house. Pennsylvania and Georgia abolished the upper house altogether.

Pennsylvania created the most radical of the state constitutions. The older, elite leadership of the colony was marginalized after it came out strongly against independence in the summer of 1776. The power vacuum that resulted was filled by a pro-independence democratic-minded group of activists, including Thomas Paine and Benjamin Rush. These activists gave voice to the artisan and lower-class communities of Philadelphia rather than to the merchant elite class. The constitution that was drafted abolished property qualifications for voting and abolished the office of governor. This constitution was in effect until the 1790s. Although Pennsylvania created the most democratic constitution, many states included lists of individual liberties that government was not to abridge. Virginia's bill of rights inspired other states to follow suit.

The Articles of Confederation

The Articles of Confederation was written in 1776, just as the Declaration of Independence was being written and debated. The Articles of Confederation, however, lacks any of the philosophical grandeur of Thomas Jefferson's document. The Articles more or less put down on paper what had come to exist organically over the previous year, as the First and Second Continental Congresses began to assume more powers and responsibilities. The main concern at the time was carrying out the war against Great Britain. The document was edited and sent to the states for ratification in 1777. It took, however, an additional four years for all the states to ratify it. The issue of western land claims caused several states to initially reject the document.

Structure of Government under the Articles

The Articles called for a one-house, or unicameral, legislature, continuing the practice of the Second Continental Congress. This Congress would have delegations from each state. States could send anywhere from two to seven delegates, but each state delegation would get one vote. Decision-making in Congress was not easy. Routine decisions required just a simple majority or seven votes. Major decisions, however, required nine votes, allowing five states to block major legislation. Changes and amendments to the document itself required a unanimous vote in Congress and ratification by all the state legislatures. In retrospect, these decision-making requirements seem to be a recipe for dysfunction. At the time, however, many Americans were weary of distant authority and wanted to keep decision making close to home; they did not want to see a central government with a free hand to do as it pleased.

II. The Constitution, the Bill of Rights, and Debating the Balance Between Liberty and Order

As the limitations of the Articles of Confederation became more apparent, American political leaders drafted the Constitution, which was based on the principles of federalism and separation of powers. Debates over the Constitution led to the adoption of a Bill of Rights as Americans continued to debate the proper balance between liberty and order.

A. DIFFICULTIES AND UNREST DURING THE CRITICAL PERIOD

The Articles of Confederation may have appealed to those who feared arbitrary and distant authority, but during the period of their operation, often called the "Critical Period," the United States faced a series of domestic and international problems that led some to call for a stronger central government.

Raising Revenue

Under the Articles of Confederation, the national government's lack of broad powers was especially problematic in regard to raising revenue. This was an acute problem during wartime. The central government did not have the power to directly tax the people. The idea of being taxed only by local representatives carried over from the days of the Stamp Act. The central government depended on voluntary contributions from the states. Congress agreed that states would contribute revenue in proportion to their population, but states were often tardy or resistant.

Inflation, Debt, and the Rejection of the Impost

The United States faced serious economic problems during the 1780s. The Confederation government and the states printed millions of dollars worth of paper money, driving up inflation. In addition, the government borrowed millions of dollars during the war. After the war, the government had trouble paying off these debts.

Robert Morris, chosen by Congress to address these issues, proposed a 5 percent impost, or import tax, to raise revenues. Since this would require a change in the Articles themselves, all thirteen states had to be on board. Rhode Island and New York, which both had thriving ports, did not want to give up the revenue stream from state duties, so they rejected the proposed impost. This rejection demonstrated the difficulties Congress faced in passing important reforms.

Toward a New Framework for Governance

By 1786, many Americans, especially elite property owners, began to raise concerns about the stature of the United States on the world stage and the competency of such a weak central government. With these concerns in mind, a group of reformers got approval from Congress to meet in Annapolis, Maryland, in 1786 to discuss possible changes in the Articles of Confederation. A follow-up meeting was scheduled for the following May (1787) in Philadelphia. In between these meetings, Shays' Rebellion erupted in Massachusetts (August 1786–February 1787; see below). It was put down, but it added fuel to the impetus to reform the governing structure. By the time of the Philadelphia meeting, the delegates were ready to scrap the entire Articles of Confederation and write something new.

B. THE FRAMING OF THE CONSTITUTION

The delegates who had been chosen to work on changes to the Articles of Confederation quickly agreed at the Philadelphia meeting (1787) to get rid of the Articles altogether and to create a new framework for government. For four months, delegates met, argued, and wrote. These deliberations resulted in a series of compromises that formed the basis of the new Constitution.

The Great Compromise

The delegates at the Constitutional Convention agreed that a central government with far greater powers was needed, but several contentious issues occupied much of their attention. A major source of debate was how the various states should be represented in the new government. Bigger states expressed dissatisfaction with the one-vote-per-state system that existed under the Articles; they argued that larger states should have a larger voice in government. The delegates from these states rallied around the Virginia Plan, which would have created a bicameral legislature that pegged the number of representatives from each state to the population of the state. The small states feared that their voices would be drowned out in such a legislature. They countered with the New Jersey Plan, which called for a one-house legislature with each state getting one vote (similar to the existing Congress under the Articles of Confederation). After much wrangling, the delegates agreed on the Great Compromise, which created the basic structure of Congress as it now exists. The plan called for a House of Representatives, in which representation would be determined by the population of each state, and a Senate, in which each state would get two members.

The Three Branches of Government, Separation of Powers, and Checks and Balances

The framers of the Constitution created three separate branches of government. The legislative branch creates laws, the executive branch carries out laws, and the judicial branch interprets laws. The Consti-

> **MADISON AND THE CONSTITUTION**
>
> The basic structural elements of the Constitution—three branches of government, with a system of checks and balances—are explained and defended in James Madison's Federalist Number 51.

tution spells out the powers of each branch. The powers of Congress are enumerated in Article I. These include the power to levy taxes, to regulate trade, to coin money, to establish post offices, to declare war, to approve treaties. The framers of the Constitution wanted it to have the flexibility to deal with the needs of a changing society. Toward this goal they included the elastic clause, which stretched the powers of Congress by allowing it to "make all laws necessary and proper. . . ." However, the definition of "necessary and proper" soon became a matter of much debate. The powers of the president are included in Article II. These include the power to suggest legislation, to command the armed forces, and to nominate judges. The president is charged with carrying out the laws of the land. The powers of the judiciary, headed by the Supreme Court, are outlined in Article III.

The framers were very conscious of the problems of a government with limitless powers. After living under the British monarchy, they came to believe that a powerful government without checks was dangerous to liberty. Therefore, they created a governmental system with three separate branches, each with the ability to check the powers of the other two. The goal was to keep the three branches in balance. An example of this concept of checks and balances is the president's ability to veto (or reject) bills passed by Congress, or the Supreme Court's ability to strike down laws that it deems unconstitutional.

Federalism—the National Government and the States

Federalism refers to the evolving relationship between the national government and the states. The Constitution gave the national government considerably more power than the Articles of Confederation had. Under the Constitution, states would still hold on to certain powers (reserved powers), but an expanded national government would be given many new powers (delegated powers). These expanded national powers include the power to tax, borrow money, regulate commerce, and promote the "general welfare." At one point, Madison proposed granting Congress the power to strike down state laws, but this measure was rejected. The Constitution does make it clear that the national government is the "supreme law of the land."

C. ANTIFEDERALISTS, AND THE ADOPTION OF THE BILL OF RIGHTS

Once the Constitution was completed, it went to the states for ratification. Each state was to call a convention to vote for ratification, and only nine states were needed for approval. This was still not an easy process. Large numbers of Americans opposed the creation of a powerful central government. Public opinion in Virginia, Massachusetts, and New York was clearly against ratification. North Carolina and Rhode Island did not even convene conventions. Finally, all of the states voted to ratify the Constitution. Many opponents of the new Constitution came around to voting in the affirmative only after leading supporters of the document promised to add a Bill of Rights to the Constitution.

The Federalists

The supporters of the Constitution labeled themselves Federalists. Three important Federalist theorists were Alexander Hamilton, John Jay, and James Madison. As the New York convention was debating ratification, the three wrote a series of articles that were later published in book form—*The Federalist*. This highly influential political tract outlined the failures of the Articles of Confederation and the benefits of a powerful government, with checks and balances. In Federalist Number 10, Madison argued that a complex government, governing a large and diverse population was the best guarantee of liberty. With such a complex government, no one group could gain control and dominate others. This argument challenged the traditional republican notion that republics must be small in order to be democratic. In Federalist Number 51, he argued for a separation of powers within the government and a system of checks and balances. In this essay, Madison asserted that "ambition must be made to counteract ambition."

> ## FEDERALIST PAPERS
>
> Be familiar with the overall approach of the *Federalist Papers*, and especially the arguments in Federalist No. 10 and No. 51.

Antifederalism

Opponents of the new Constitution, Antifederalists, as they were called by their Federalist adversaries, worried that the new government would be controlled by members of the elite. They saw the document as favoring the creation of a powerful, aristocrat ruling class. Leading Antifederalists were Patrick Henry and George Mason. They argued that government officials in the national government would be, almost by definition, removed from the concerns, and the control, of ordinary people. They were distrustful of distant authority. The thirteen colonies had just emerged from under the thumb of the British Empire, so many colonists were eager to see power exercised locally. One of the Antifederalists' primary concerns was that individual rights were not adequately protected by the Constitution. They noted that the document did not contain a bill of rights.

> ## THE ANTIFEDERALISTS
>
> The Antifederalists have been saddled with an unfortunate name. They sound like naysayers. However, you should take their ideas seriously. They had a comprehensive view of the world. Just because they lost the fight over ratification, does not mean they should be dismissed. After all, their agitation led to the Bill of Rights.

Ratification

Delaware ratified the Constitution almost immediately, in late 1787. By May of the following year eight states had voted to ratify. New Hampshire provided the ninth, and deciding, vote in June 1788. Since the Constitution itself does not devote much attention to individual rights, Antifederalists insisted on the addition of a list of individual rights that the government would not be allowed to take away. Many Antifederalists in the various states refused to support ratification of the Constitution unless such a list was added. The Federalists promised to add such a list if the Antifederalists agreed to support ratification. This agreement led to the writing and ratification of the first ten amendments to the Constitution, known as the Bill of Rights. By May 1790, the final four states— Virginia (1788), New York (1788), North Carolina (1789), and Rhode Island (1790)—voted for ratification and joined the new union.

The Bill of Rights

During the debate over ratification of the Constitution, seven of the states that ratified the Constitution did so only under the condition that Congress would ratify a list of rights of the people. Antifederalists in these states feared that a sprawling, powerful government would step on individual liberties. As promised, one of the first acts of Congress was passage of the Bill of Rights—the first ten amendments to the Constitution. Much of the language in the Bill of Rights, written by James Madison, comes from the various states' constitutions.

The First through Fourth Amendments: Basic Rights of the People

The First Amendment contains the "establishment clause" prohibiting the establishment of an official religion in the United States. The remainder of the First Amendment deals with various forms of freedom of expression. The Second Amendment guarantees the right to bear arms. Some have argued that the language of the Second Amendment seems to link the right to bear arms to participation in militias; others have argued that it is an absolute individual right. The Third Amendment addressed a much-hated British practice—forcing colonial residents to house British soldiers. Americans would not be compelled to quarter soldiers. The Fourth Amendment guarantees a modicum of privacy from searches by government officials. People are protected in their "persons, houses, papers and effects" from "unreasonable searches and seizures." Authorities must first obtain a warrant, issued by a judge upon evidence of "probable cause."

The Fifth Through Eighth Amendments: Rights of the Accused

Several amendments in the Bill of Rights address protections people have when they are brought into the legal system. The logic of these amendments is that the legal system is powerful and well funded, and should therefore have checks placed upon it to protect the individual. The Fifth Amendment calls for grand jury indictments, prohibits authorities from trying a suspect twice for the same crime ("double jeopardy") and from forcing a suspect to testify against him or herself. The Fifth Amendment also prohibits the government from seizing someone's property, unless it is for a "public use" and the owner receives "just compensation." This power of the government to seize private property, with these stipulations, is known as "eminent domain." The Sixth Amendment guarantees suspects the right to a "speedy and public" trial, with a jury, conducted in the district the crime was committed it. Also, the suspect has a right to be informed of the charges against him or her, and has the right to question the witnesses against him or her. Finally suspects have the right to call friendly witnesses to the stand and the right to a lawyer. The Seventh Amendment guarantees people the right to a trial by jury even in civil cases (involving conflicts between two parties over monetary damages). The Eighth Amendment prevents the government from inflicting "cruel and unusual" punishments and prevents the setting of "excessive bail."

The Ninth and Tenth Amendments

The last two amendments of the Bill of Rights deal with limits and parameters of rights and powers in the government. The Ninth Amendment guarantees that additional rights, not mentioned in the Bill of Rights, shall be protected from government infringement. The Tenth Amendment deals with governmental powers. It puts forth that powers not delegated to the federal government shall be retained by the states and by the people.

The Right to Vote

The right to vote is absent from the Bill of Rights. The federal government left it to the states to formulate rules for voting. It was only later that voting would be seen as a fundamental right that needed the protection of constitutional amendments. The Fifteenth Amendment (1870) prohibited voting restrictions based on race, the Nineteenth Amendment (1920) prohibited restriction based on sex, and the Twenty-sixth Amendment (1971) lowered the voting age to 18.

D. POLICY DEBATES IN THE NEW NATION

A series of policy conflicts and disagreements emerged during the presidential administrations of George Washington and John Adams, reflecting a growing divide among the public. Around these divides coalesced two political groups, Federalists and Democratic-Republicans (more on political parties below). These policy conflicts centered around economic policy, foreign policy, and the relationship between the federal government and the states.

Hamilton's Economic Program

Washington's secretary of the treasury, Alexander Hamilton, proposed a series of economic measures meant to put the United States on sound economic footing. Central to his plans was a national bank, which would hold the government's tax revenues and act as a stabilizing force on the economy. Hamilton proposed a national bank that would be 20 percent publicly controlled and 80 percent privately controlled. Hamilton thought it was important to have wealthy investors financially and psychologically invested in the new government. The proposal to create a national bank became a source of disagreement between Hamilton and Secretary of State Thomas Jefferson. Jefferson argued that the Constitution did not permit Congress to create a national bank. It was not among the powers listed in the Constitution. Hamilton countered that the elastic clause, which lets Congress do what it considered "necessary and proper," implicitly allowed for the creation of a national bank. President Washington agreed and signed the bank law in 1791.

> ### INTERPRETING THE CONSTITUTION
> The debate over a national bank represents an ongoing debate in American history between strict and loose interpretations of the Constitution.

Dealing with Debt

Hamilton's economic program included two other significant parts. He proposed an elaborate and controversial plan to deal with the new nation's substantial debt. He insisted that debts carried over from the war years be paid back, or funded, at full value. Many of the debt certificates had been sold by their holders. The original holders had little faith that the government would ever make good on the actual loans. The certificates were changing hands at a fraction of their original value. Full funding meant a financial windfall for speculators who bought up the certificates. In addition, Hamilton insisted that the government assume, or agree to pay back, state debts incurred during the war. The proposal met with strenuous opposition from states that either did not have a large debt or had already paid back their debts. To accomplish the goals of "funding" and "assumption," Hamilton prodded the government to take out new loans by selling government bonds.

> ### FUNDING AND ASSUMPTION
> Be familiar with these two terms in regard to Hamilton's approach to paying off war-related debt.

Encouragement to Manufacturing

The final piece of Hamilton's financial program was to encourage manufacturing by imposing tariffs on foreign-made goods and subsidizing American industry (Congress adopted Hamilton's "Report on Manufactures," except for his recommendation of subsidies to industry). He believed industrial development would be key to a balanced and self-reliant economy. The nation, however, was not yet ready for developing its manufacturing sector; the War of 1812 brought the importance of manufacturing to light.

Washington and the "Unwritten Constitution"

Washington wisely chose capable and experienced men to run the new government's three departments—state, war, and the treasury. Washington chose Thomas Jefferson for the Department of State, Henry Knox for the Department of War, and Alexander Hamilton for the Treasury. He also chose Edmund Randolph as the nation's first attorney general, and John Jay for chief justice of the Supreme Court. Washington began meeting regularly with these men, seeking their input on important decisions. This practice of meeting regularly with a presidential cabinet was subsequently practiced by all American presidents. The cabinet is one of several traditions and customs that Washington established that have come to be known as the "unwritten constitution." Washington's decision to run for no more than two terms was also part of the "unwritten constitution," until Congress and the states ratified the Twenty-second Amendment (1951), following Franklin D. Roosevelt's four electoral victories, making this tradition part of the actual Constitution.

The Alien and Sedition Acts (1798)

In an atmosphere of animosity and distrust between the Federalists and the Democratic-Republicans, the Alien and Sedition Acts were passed by a Federalist-dominated Congress, in order to limit criticism from the opposition Democratic-Republican Party. The Alien and Sedition Acts actually comprised four acts. Three of the acts, dealing with immigrant and naturalization made it more difficult for aliens to achieve American citizenship. The fourth act was the Sedition Act, which made it a crime to defame the president or Congress. The broad wording of the Sedition Act was consistent with contemporary British sedition laws, but seemed to challenge the free speech guarantees of the recently ratified First Amendment. Jeffersonians were especially troubled by the expansion of federal power that the acts represented.

The Kentucky and Virginia Resolutions

Thomas Jefferson and James Madison were so opposed to the Alien and Sedition Acts that they proposed the idea of nullification in their Virginia and Kentucky Resolutions. These resolutions put forth the idea that a state had the right to nullify a law it found to be inconsistent with the Constitution. The idea of state nullification of a federal edict did not slow down the Alien and Sedition Acts, but it raised the issue of the relationship between the federal government and the states. These issues emerged on several occasions in the first half of the nineteenth century, and were part of the slavery debates that led to the Civil War.

> **STATE VERSUS FEDERAL POWER**
>
> The Virginia and Kentucky Resolutions were part of an ongoing debate over the respective powers of the federal and the state governments. The issue was largely settled by the Civil War, but it would continue to emerge in the postwar era.

III. The Ideas of the American Revolution—at Home and Abroad

The ideas of the American Revolution reverberated around the world. At home, an ongoing tension emerged between those who sought to expand democratic participation and those who sought to maintain traditional forms of inequality.

A. THE CALL FOR EGALITARIANISM

Although the primary goal of the American Revolution was gaining independence from Great Britain for the thirteen colonies, the rhetoric that was employed to justify the revolution inspired others to demand fundamental changes in society. Many called for the abolition of slavery and for greater political democracy in the new governing structures.

Moves to Abolish Slavery

Despite the language of equality in the Declaration of Independence and in many state constitutions, political leaders were reluctant to apply such language to enslaved African Americans. In several northern states, enslaved African Americans petitioned state legislatures to grant them their "natural rights," namely freedom. In 1779, petitions for emancipation in New Hampshire and Connecticut were rejected. In Massachusetts, seven free African Americans, including the brothers Paul and John Cuffe, refused to pay taxes on the ground that they did not vote and were, therefore, not represented. Their actions led to the extension of voting rights to tax-paying African Americans in Massachusetts. Slaves in Massachusetts sued for their freedom, initiating several legal cases that cited the language of the Massachusetts constitution, "all men are born free and equal." Several such cases were decided in favor of the slaves, effectively ending slavery in Massachusetts through judicial decisions.

Several other states slowly began to take action against slavery. Vermont, which was a sovereign entity from 1777 to 1791 (when it was admitted as the fourteenth state), outlawed slavery in its 1777 constitution, citing the language of the Declaration of Independence. In 1780, political leaders in Pennsylvania voted to end slavery by gradual emancipation. The law was not immediately beneficial to enslaved people in Pennsylvania. It stated that infants born on or after March 1, 1780, would be free, but only after they reached the age of 28. However, many slaves in Pennsylvania simply ran away, sometimes aided by sympathetic whites.

B. THE CONSTITUTION AND SLAVERY—COMPROMISE AND POSTPONEMENT

Though many voices noted the inconsistency of slavery and the ideals put forth in the nation's founding documents, slavery continued in the United States. The framers of the Constitution were, to some degree, uneasy with the institution. This uneasiness is reflected in the fact that the word "slavery" is not mentioned in the entire document. Slaves are referred to as "other persons." Although the framers of the Constitution did not mention the word slavery, they were willing to compromise on the issue and postpone any final decision about slavery to the future. This postponement led to decades of debate and conflict over the issue.

The "Three-Fifths Compromise"

Once it was established that representation in the House of Representatives would be based on population, the issue arose: Who would be counted in determining a state's population? Specifically, would a southern state be able to count its slave populations in the census? This was a major issue when one considered that for states such as South Carolina and Mississippi the slave population comprised more than 50 percent of the population. To count them in the census would more than double the size of their delegations in the House. Northern states objected on the grounds that slaves could not vote; in fact, they were considered property, not human beings. After much debate, a compromise was reached in which southern states could count three-fifths of their slave populations in the census. This "Three-Fifths Compromise" defied common sense, but it got the delegates through an impasse.

Tacit Approval of Slavery

Other sections of the Constitution seem to give tacit approval of the institution of slavery. The delegates voted to protect the international slave trade for 20 years, guaranteeing the flow of slaves into the country from Africa and the Caribbean for another generation. (The international slave trade was ended by Congress in 1808, the earliest date that the Constitution allowed.) Finally the Constitution provided for the return of fugitive slaves. (A mechanism for the return of fugitive slaves was contained in the Fugitive Slave Act of 1793; the process was strengthened with the Fugitive Slave Act of 1850.) Though slavery was not mentioned by name, the inclusion of regulations around slavery made clear that the Constitution recognized its existence.

C. THE IMPACT OF THE AMERICAN REVOLUTION ABROAD

The ideas of the American Revolution reverberated among many different peoples struggling against oppressive regimes.

Revolution in France

In 1789, a little over a decade after the thirteen colonies declared independence and a mere six years after the Treaty of Paris was signed, a revolution began in France. The French revolutionaries were inspired by some of the same Enlightenment ideas that had inspired revolutionaries in America, and were inspired by the American model itself. This first phase of the revolution was begun by the national legislature against the absolutist power of the king. This phase had widespread support in the United States. Soon, the revolution entered a more radical phrase. In 1783, the monarchy was completely abolished and the king and queen were publicly executed, the power of the church was limited, and, during a fever of revolutionary zeal, more than 40,000 suspected enemies of the revolution were executed. This reign of terror, carried out by the Jacobins' political club, peaked in 1793–1794. The leader of the Jacobins, Maximilien Robespierre, was executed in 1794 in the Thermidorian Reaction. The Directory, a body of five men, took power in 1795 and held power until 1799, when the French Revolution concluded. After that, Napoleon Bonaparte assumed power in a coup d'état. As the revolution took a turn in a more radical direction in 1793, Americans became increasingly divided about the events in France.

Rebellion in Haiti

In 1791, a revolution broke out in the western part of the island of Hispaniola. The revolution occurred in the French part of the island, called Saint Domingue. This French colony was primarily a sugar-producing slave society, made up of half a million African slaves, and 60,000 free people. Of the free people, about half were white and half were mixed-race people (*gens de couleur*). The mixed race population of Saint Domingue owned about a third of the slaves on the island, but were barred from participation in the political system. The revolution had three phases. First, the white colonists resisted French rule, inspired in part by the model of the American Revolution and in part by the recent French Revolution. Second, the mixed-race planters rebelled, challenging their second-class status. Finally, the slaves themselves rebelled. The slave rebellion, led by Toussaint L'Overture and aided by Spanish troops, occupied much of the country. The rebellion of slaves on Saint Domingue sent waves of fear among southern planters in the United States, especially after fleeing whites and mixed-race people brought stories of the rebellion to communities in the southern United States. Soon after L'Overture's death, Haiti established its independence (1804) as the first black republic in the Americas.

Independence Struggles in Latin America

Of all the revolutions that followed the American Revolution, those in Latin America are most similar to the American Revolution. After all, in both the British North American colonies and the Spanish South American colonies, colonists decided to break long-held ties with European powers. Also, both the North American and the South American struggles for independence involved deep divisions within the respective colonial societies; rebels and loyalists clashed on both continents. Both revolutionary struggles occurred in societies that included slavery. Starting in 1808, several nations in Spain's vast New World American empire—which extended from Mexico in the north to Argentina in the south; Peru in the west to Venezuela in the east—rebelled against Spanish rule. The revolutionaries were inspired by a combination of ideology, geopolitics, and material interests—just as their North American predecessors were.

KEY CONCEPT 3.3
CONFLICT AND THE DEVELOPMENT OF A MULTIETHNIC SOCIETY IN NORTH AMERICA

The closing decades of the seventeenth century witnessed increased migrations, competition for resources, and cooperative interactions. Intensified conflicts between peoples and nations led to shifting boundaries and changing policies. Individuals and groups asserted different visions of an emerging national identity.

I. Migrations Within North America

After the French and Indian War (1754–1763), British colonists were eager to migrate into the interior of the American continent. This process continued after the American Revolution. This migration led to interactions and competition between whites and American Indians, resulting in shifting alliance and cultural blending.

A. CONFLICT IN THE INTERIOR OF THE CONTINENT FOLLOWING THE FRENCH AND INDIAN WAR

Settlement of the interior of colonial America in the decades after the French and Indian War set the stage for ongoing tensions between the policies of ruling authorities—generally based in the cities along the Atlantic seaboard—and the poorer folk, remote from the commercial activity of the cosmopolitan centers.

Settling Beyond the Appalachians

After the French and Indian War, Americans were restless to push into the interior of the continent. The Proclamation Act (1763) attempted to halt colonists from settling beyond the Appalachian Mountains. Great Britain wanted to prevent future clashes between the colonists and American Indians. Great Britain did not want to incur the costs of additional warfare in the West, and it wanted to continue garnering profits from the valuable fur trade with American Indians. Colonists, however, were eager to venture forth; they pushed toward the foothills of the Appalachian in the interiors of the existing colonies, and they trickled beyond the Appalachians. After the American Revolution, the flow of Americans beyond the Appalachians increased dramatically. This movement, encouraged by government policies, displaced American Indians, setting the stage for a new series of battles over the interior of the United States. The movement was challenged by the continued presence of Spain and Great Britain along the borderlands of the newly formed United States.

The Scots-Irish

The middle colonies—Pennsylvania, New York, New Jersey, and Delaware—experienced remarkable growth in the eighteenth century. German, Scots-Irish (or Scotch-Irish), and other immigrants contributed to the growth of the colonies. The largest immigrant group in the eighteenth century was the Scots-Irish, which was a label created in America to describe Scottish and English Protestants who had colonized northern Ireland before immigrating to the United States. Difficult economic conditions in those regions propelled the migration. Immigrants from the southwestern German states were the second biggest group. These immigrants tended to be "middling sorts"—farmers, artisans, and laborers.

Economic Opportunity in Pennsylvania

The primary destination of the Scots-Irish was Pennsylvania. The availability of land and the need for workers brought immigrants to Pennsylvania, especially to Philadelphia. Farther south, slavery was the dominant form of labor; further north, the legacy of Puritanism still enforced a cultural homogeneity. New York City attracted immigrants, but farmers found the best land along the Hudson River taken up by large estates.

The Paxton Boys

By the 1720s, some farmers were settling beyond the crest of the Appalachian Mountains, in the "backcountry" of Pennsylvania, Virginia (the area that would later become West Virginia), and North Carolina. Small-scale farmers in Pennsylvania specialized in growing wheat and experienced a higher standard of living than their counterparts in Europe. These backcountry Scots-Irish farmers carried with them from Europe resentments toward British rule. In the aftermath of the French and Indian War and of Pontiac's Rebellion, a vigilante group of these Scots-Irish immigrants organized raids against American Indians on the Pennsylvania frontier. These raids included an attack on Conestoga Indians in 1763 that resulted in 20 deaths. After the attacks on the Conestoga, in January 1764, about 250 Paxton Boys marched to Philadelphia to present their grievances to the Pennsylvania legislature. Their "Apology" (or explanation), presented to the legislature, reflected bitterness toward the American Indians on the frontier of Pennsylvania, as well as resentment of the Quaker elite of the colony for maintaining a more lenient policy toward American Indians.

B. TENSIONS IN THE "BACKCOUNTRY"

As more people began to leave the more settled coastal towns of the United States and moved inland, tensions increased between elites and backcountry farmers. These tensions evolved along cultural and political lines.

Shays' Rebellion (1786–1787)

Tensions between coastal elites and struggling farmers in the interior can be seen most clearly in Massachusetts. Several of the problems associated with the "critical period" were evident in a farmers' rebellion in Massachusetts called Shays' Rebellion (1786–1787). Struggling farmers, many of whom were veterans of the American Revolution, in the western part of the state were troubled by several government actions. Taxes in Massachusetts, unlike some states, were stiff and had to be paid in hard currency (backed by gold or silver), not cheap paper currency. Unable to pay these taxes, many farmers were losing their farms to banks. The farmers petitioned the legislature to pass stay laws, which would have suspended creditors' right to foreclose on farms. This, along with petitions to lower taxes, was rejected by the Massachusetts legislature.

After being frustrated by the legislature, hundreds of Massachusetts farmers, led by Daniel Shays, protested and finally took up arms. They were responding to a perceived injustice as they had a decade earlier when under British rule. They closed down several courts and freed farmers from debtors' prison. Local militias did not try to stop the actions, which spread to more towns in Massachusetts. After several weeks, the governor and legislature took action, calling up nearly 4,000 armed men to suppress the rebellion. Concerns about the ability of the authorities to put down future uprisings were on the minds of the delegates to the Philadelphia convention, which convened just three months after Shays' Rebellion ended.

The Excise Tax and the Whiskey Rebellion (1794)

Another conflict between elites and western farmers occurred in Pennsylvania in 1794. To help raise revenues to pay for his ambitious plans, Hamilton proposed enacting new taxes. The most prominent, and controversial, of these taxes was an excise, or sales, tax on whiskey. This tax hit grain farmers especially hard. These hardscrabble farmers in remote rural areas were barely making ends meet. Distilling grain into whiskey allowed them to increase their meager profit. Transporting bushels of grain over primitive roads to population centers was prohibitively expensive; distilling it down to whiskey made it easier to transport.

The grain farmers of western Pennsylvania felt that they could not shoulder this substantial tax. In 1794, farmers took action. Fifty men gathered and marched to the home of the local tax collector. From there the gathering swelled to 7,000 men and marched to Pittsburgh. At this point, the federal government took action. Alexander Hamilton and George Washington had vivid memories of Shays' Rebellion, which occurred less than a decade earlier. Farmers in western Massachusetts had staged a violent rebellion for weeks before it was finally put down by local militias. They were determined that the current rebellion would not get out of control. Washington nationalized nearly 13,000 militiamen into the army and marched them himself to Pennsylvania to suppress

the rebellion and ensure that the laws of the land were followed. Washington's response to the rebellion had the desired effect. It established federal authority and made clear that a strong national government would not tolerate unlawful challenges to its authority.

C. SPANISH MISSIONS IN CALIFORNIA

Spain encouraged migration into the northern reaches of New Spain—present-day California—by expanding mission settlements. These missions offered opportunities to Spanish soldiers and settlers, while fostering a cultural blending of Spanish and Indian peoples.

The Expansion of the Mission System

In the last decades of the eighteenth century and into the nineteenth century, Spanish Catholics of the Franciscan order established a series of missions in California with the goal of spreading the Christian faith among local American Indians. A Catholic priest, Junipero Serra, was instrumental in establishing the first missions in California; ultimately twenty-one missions were founded. These missions were both religious and military outposts, and represented an attempt by Spain to maintain a presence along the northern borderlands. The goal of the missions was not only spiritual. The Spaniards extracted labor from the American Indians.

The missions had disastrous results for the American Indians of California. Disease ravaged American Indian populations; in 1806, a measles epidemic wiped out a quarter of the mission Indians in the San Francisco area. Further, missionaries often treated the local populations brutally, raping women and subjecting local populations to beatings and slavery-like working conditions. A revolt took place by American Indians at the Mission San Diego de Alcala in 1775, but the missions continued to exist into the early 1800s. By the 1830s, the Mexican government abandoned the mission project, selling mission lands to private individuals.

II. United States Policies Encourage Westward Migration

The United States pursued policies to encourage migration beyond the Appalachian Mountains. Central to this was developing a set of procedures that would allow for the incorporation of new territories into the United States. This process would both extend republican institutions and lead to increased conflict with American Indians.

A. ORGANIZING THE NORTHWEST TERRITORY

The Confederation Congress made important progress in incorporating the country's western lands by passing the Northwest Ordinance and establishing procedures and guidelines for the incorporation of new states.

The Northwest Territory

The Treaty of Paris set the boundary of the United States at the Mississippi River. There was debate about the status of the vast swath of land between the Appalachian Mountains and the Mississippi River. Some states insisted that western land claims from the colonial period should be honored. Virginia, for instance, claimed all of the land north of the Ohio River. New York claimed a huge portion of the West, including land that overlapped with Virginia's claim. Some states, such as New Jersey and Maryland, had no claims. Maryland insisted that it would not ratify the Articles until all states gave up their land claims and the western lands became part of a national domain. Congress persuaded the states with claims to do just that.

> ## SUCCESS IN THE WEST
>
> The most significant accomplishments of the Articles of Confederation government involved dealing with the complex problems associated with the lands to the west of the Appalachian Mountains.

Land Ordinances and the Northwest Ordinance

Once the western land came under the control of the national government, Congress set about passing a series of acts to clarify the status of these lands and to encourage their settlement. The Land Ordinance of 1784 called for the division of the west into ten states, with the guarantee of self-government. The following year, Congress passed the Land Ordinance of 1785, reducing the number of states from ten to between three and five, and calling for the area to be surveyed and divided into lots. A lot in every town was set aside for education; the rest were to be sold. In 1787, Congress passed the Northwest Ordinance, setting up a process by which areas could become territories, and then states. Once the population of a territory reached 60,000, it could write a constitution and apply for statehood. These states would be on equal footing with the original thirteen states; they would not have a second-class, colonial status. Also, the Northwest Ordinance banned slavery in the territory north of the Ohio River. These acts encouraged the steady and orderly flow of settlers into the West. This, however, proved disastrous for American Indians.

> ### LACK OF PROGRESS IN FOREIGN RELATIONS
>
> The United States failed to achieve important foreign policy goals during the Articles of Confederation period. This can be attributed to the weaknesses of the Articles or to the precarious position of a newly created nation.

B. AMERICAN INDIAN POLICY IN THE NEW NATION

The ratification of the Constitution did not bode well for Indians within the boundaries of the United States. The Constitution did not precisely define the relationship between the government and the American Indians. This failure set the stage for further bloody conflicts on the frontier.

The Battle of Fallen Timbers and the Treaty of Greenville

President Washington was determined to gain control of the region north of the Ohio River. He doubled the U.S. presence in Ohio and appointed General Anthony ("Mad Anthony") Wayne to lead American forces. At the Battle of Fallen Timbers (1794), American Indians were soundly defeated by superior American firepower. The following year, 1795, American Indians gave up claim to most of Ohio in the Treaty of Greenville. The treaty brought only a temporary peace. Within a generation, settlers would push farther into Ohio and Indiana; these incursions would become connected with the United States declaration of war against Britain in 1812.

C. SPAIN AND GREAT BRITAIN CHALLENGE AMERICAN GROWTH

The United States continued to have difficulties with the presence of European powers in North America. The British were reluctant to abandon North America and Spain persisted in challenging American use of the Mississippi River.

The British and American Indians

Americans became increasingly frustrated that the British seemed intent on thwarting the westward movement of Americans huddled along the eastern seaboard. British forces had not evacuated forts in the western part of the United States following the signing of the Treaty of Paris (1783). The British maintained a thriving fur trade with American Indian groups in the area of the West above the Ohio River. Further, the British provided the Shawnees, the Miamis, and the Delawares with weapons. The British insisted that they would not abandon their western presence until the United States repaid its war debts and allowed Loyalists to recover property that had been confiscated during the war. The United States minister to Great Britain pressed for a resolution of these issues but to no avail.

Conflicts with Great Britain and Jay's Treaty

There were several contentious issues between the United States and Great Britain in the 1790s. Once war broke out between France and Great Britain in 1793, United States ships maintained a brisk trade with both the French West Indies and with France itself. Great Britain was none too pleased with this development and began intercepting American ships (almost 300) in or near the West Indies. In addition, southern planters wanted reimbursement from the British for slaves that had fled to British lines during the American Revolution and were never returned. Also, western settlers were resentful of the continued presence of British forces in forts in the West. This last issue became significant in light of the increasingly bloody clashes between American forces and American Indians. Americans accused the British of aiding American Indians in order to maintain the profitable fur trade.

Washington sent John Jay, the chief justice of the Supreme Court, to Great Britain to seek redress of these grievances. Jay returned in 1795 with a treaty that was perceived as especially favorable to the British. The British did agree to withdraw from the West, but only after 18 months. The British would not compensate American shippers for lost cargoes, nor would they compensate American planters for lost slaves. In addition, American planters would be forced to repay debts to the British that dated from the colonial era. The one concession that Jay managed to wrest from the British was limited trading rights in the West Indies. Other issues would be addressed in the future by arbitration commissions.

Reactions to Jay's Treaty were decidedly mixed. Hamilton and his supporters saw the treaty as the best they could get at the moment. Supporters of Jefferson, especially from the South and the West, argued that their interests were sold out to the mercantile interests in New England. They saw the treaty as evidence of the pro-British sympathies of the Hamiltonians. An opponent of the treaty scrawled on a wall "Damn John Jay! Damn everyone who won't damn John Jay!"

Conflicts with Spain over the Mississippi River and Pinckney's Treaty

The United States had ongoing conflicts with Spain since the Treaty of Paris (1783) established the western boundary of the newly formed United States at the Mississippi River, adjacent to the Spanish-held Louisiana Territory. Spain repeatedly attempted to limit American shipping on the river. The United States was able to resolve this and other ongoing issues with Spain. Negotiations between the American diplomat Thomas Pinckney and Don Manuel de Godoy of Spain resulted in Pinckney's Treaty (1795; ratified in 1796). Spain agreed to allow for American shipping on the Mississippi River and it defined the border between the United States and Spanish held territory in western Florida. Spain's willingness to negotiate with the United States was motivated, in part, by the apparent friendship between the United States and Great Britain following Jay's Treaty.

III. Regional Identities Compete with National Identity

A variety of cultural expressions in the newly formed United States contributed to the forging of a national tendency. At the same time, regional identities persisted and held sway over many people.

A. THE DEVELOPMENT OF POLITICAL PARTIES

A series of policy differences in the newly formed United States led to the development of the first two political parties. These parties reflected regional as well as ideological differences.

Federalists and Democratic-Republicans

The first two political parties—the Federalists and the Democratic-Republicans—were able to both articulate profound differences around public policy, while at the same time facilitate a national debate on these issues. Federalists tended to be more pro-British, more critical of the French Revolution, more friendly to urban, commercial interests, and more ready to use the power of the federal government to influence economic activity. The leading theorist of the Federalists was Alexander Hamilton. The Democratic-Republicans tended to be more critical of the British, more supportive of the French Revolution, at least in its early stages, more critical of centralized authority and more favorable to agricultural interests. Jefferson was a leading theorist of the Democratic-Republicans.

B. DIVERGENT REGIONAL ATTITUDES TOWARD SLAVERY

After the American Revolution, attitudes around slavery became increasingly shaped by region, as slavery became more entrenched in the South and in adjacent western lands, while it began to disappear in the North.

The North Moves Toward a Free Labor System

Many northerners came to see unfree labor as inconsistent with the Democratic-Republican ideas of the American Revolution. Even indentured servitude disappeared from most states by 1800. In many northern states, slavery became less important to the economy. Vermont outlawed slavery altogether, Pennsylvania passed a gradual emancipation law, and other northern states began to follow suit. Many northern states passed gradual emancipation laws. Such laws did not free existing slaves; they provided for the freedom of the future children of slave women (often after serving their master for a certain number of years). Such an approach respected contemporary understandings of property rights. In the years after the American Revolution, free black communities developed in many northern states and in some of the states of the upper South, such as Virginia and Maryland.

The Growth of Slavery in the South

In the decades after the American Revolution, slavery became increasingly important in the South. Eli Whitney's invention of the cotton gin in 1793 set the stage for a remarkable growth in the production of cotton, in the growth of the southern economy, and in the increased reliance on slavery (see Period 4). Despite gradual emancipation in the North, voluntary emancipation throughout the United States, and the escape of many slaves during the chaos of the

American Revolution, the number of slaves in the United States grew from 500,000 in 1776 to 700,000 in 1790. With the ending of indentured servitude, the stark differences between the growing free labor ideology of the North and the expanding slave labor system of the South became more apparent. These diverging attitudes on slavery would come to shape many of the debates leading up to the Civil War.

C. EVOLVING IDEAS ON GENDER

The importance of women in the revolutionary struggle and Enlightenment ideas around equality set the stage for the evolution of ideas around gender. The ideal of "republican motherhood" emerged in the decades after the American Revolution.

"Republican Motherhood"

The arguments deployed by the Patriot cause in the American Revolution inspired many male and female writers to challenge traditional notions of gender and to put forth new ideas about the proper role of men and women in the new nation. The concept of "republican motherhood," drawing together a number of elements, asserted that women did indeed have civic responsibilities in the evolving culture of the new nation. The concept drew on Enlightenment thinkers, such as John Locke, who asserted, in his *Two Treatises on Government*, that women and men had more equal roles in marriage, challenging traditional notions of female subordination. Further, the experience of women participating in the struggle for independence, from organizing boycotts to aiding men on the battlefield, engendered a sense of egalitarianism among many women and men. Finally, the rhetoric of the revolutionary era railed against tyrannical rule. Many found analogies between the tyranny of king over subjects and the tyranny of husband over wife.

The concept of "republican motherhood" did not put forth an agenda of political equality between men and women. It only went so far as to assert that women did have a role to play in civic life. The main feature of this role was to raise civic-minded republican sons and to reform the morals and manners of men. It asserted that women were active agents in maintaining public virtue—a realm traditionally associated with men. The ideas of "republican motherhood" still confined women to a largely domestic role, but they did expand the possibilities for women to gain an education; after all, it was important for women to gain the literacy and knowledge to raise the next generation of republican leaders.

SUBJECT TO DEBATE

Along with the Civil War, the American Revolution is one of the most heatedly debated topics in the history field. The American Revolution gave birth to the United States, so the stakes in understanding and interpreting it seem especially high. One's understanding of the American Revolution is shaped by, and shapes, one's understanding of the United States itself.

Historians for generations have debated the reasons the thirteen colonies declared independence. Some historians have stressed economic grievances against the mother country—colonists declared independence to be free of British mercantilist rules. These historians have emphasized the colonial cry "No taxation without representation" as central to the struggle. This theory assumes a basic continuity, in regard to social values, between the colonial period and the national period.

Opposing historians have argued that economic issues were only part of the equation. They see a real break with the past—socially, culturally, and ideologically. Bernard Bailyn's *The Ideological Origins of the American Revolution* (1967) points to the development of a new set of ideas about politics and democracy that are profoundly important.

Historians influenced by the "New Left" look at class divisions within American society, not just divisions between the colonies and Great Britain. This approach sees a class conflict in colonial America. On the one side of the conflict are the colonial elites who tried to prevent the American Revolution from becoming revolutionary. They wanted to maintain the colonial social structure, but without the British overlords. On the other side were dockworkers, small-scale farmers, apprentices, slaves, free blacks, and other "lower sorts" who pushed for a real break with the hierarchies of the past. Their radical agenda was largely derailed by the delegates at the Constitutional Convention who put a lid on these revolutionary impulses.

There are several important questions that you should be aware of in regard to the Critical Period. The first important question is the nature of the Articles of Confederation. Because it lasted less than a decade, and because the Constitution has endured for more than 230 years, there is a tendency to elevate the historical standing of the Constitution and to denigrate the Articles of Confederation. This is to be expected, but we should be careful not to go too far. To admit to the effectiveness of the Constitution does not require us to ignore anything positive about the Articles. The thirteen colonies won the American Revolution during the Articles of Confederation period. Also, the Articles did an excellent job of dealing with the newly acquired western lands. It is true that the national government was weak under the Articles; but even this can be seen as a positive. The Articles, we can argue, effectively protected the traditional rights of the states. Historical debate should be fair to the much-maligned Articles.

The Constitutional Convention has been the subject of much debate in American history. Charles Beard, a Progressive-era historian, asserted that the men who wrote the Constitution were all men of means who wrote the document to protect their economic interests. This interpretation notes the undemocratic features of the Constitution (the electoral college and the method for selecting senators) and asserts that the document is essentially interested in protecting the economic interests of the propertied class at the expense of democracy. Some left-leaning historians see the ratification of the Constitution as a virtual coup d'état, checking the more revolutionary elements of the American Revolution. This view runs counter to mainstream thinking, which elevates the effectiveness of the Constitution, especially when contrasted with the ineffective Articles of Confederation.

HISTORICAL NEUTRALITY

Try to avoid using the words "us," "our," and "we," when discussing the United States. Refer to the United States in a neutral manner. Strong essays should be intellectually engaged, but not emotionally invested in a particular outcome or position. Such personal investment tends to undermine one's argument.

Practice Multiple-Choice Questions

Directions: Pick the letter that best answers the following questions.

QUESTIONS 1–3 REFER TO THE FOLLOWING IMAGE:

—Benjamin Franklin, "Magna Britannia: Her Colonies Reduc'D," 1767

1. The main point of the cartoon above is that

    (A) the thirteen British North American colonies should unite in order to better advance their grievances against Great Britain.
    (B) the North American colonists, in the aftermath of the French and Indian War, should develop a better system of defending themselves from attacks from Great Britain.
    (C) British policies in North America, notably enacting taxes, could have fatal effects on the British Empire.
    (D) the presence of a British standing army in North America will have a detrimental effect on the liberties and rights of the British colonists.

2. The primary intended audience for this cartoon was

    (A) members of Parliament in Great Britain.
    (B) Boston merchants and traders.
    (C) backcountry settlers in Pennsylvania.
    (D) members of the Sons of Liberty.

3. The sentiment reflected in the image above was also reflected in which of the following?

(A) Paul Revere's engraving, "Boston Massacre," 1770
(B) The Treaty of Fort Stanwix, 1768
(C) The "Olive Branch Petition," adopted by the Continental Congress in 1775
(D) Thomas Paine's pamphlet, *Common Sense*, 1776

Answers and Explanations to Multiple-Choice Questions

1. **(C)** In this cartoon, Benjamin Franklin is warning of an unfortunate future. He is predicting that British taxation policies, notably the Stamp Act, could have fatal effects on the British Empire. A dismembered Britannia has fallen from the globe and sits surrounded by her scattered limbs, identified as different North American colonies. In the background of the cartoon we see British ships sitting idle—an allusion to the importance of Britain's trade with America. On the ground sits a rejected olive branch. The banner across Britannia's body reads "Date Obolum Bellisario," an allusion to a Roman military hero who was reduced to beggary after being accused of treason.

2. **(A)** The primary intended audience for this cartoon was members of Parliament in Great Britain. Franklin was living in Great Britain at the time and spent a great deal of effort trying to pressure Parliament to rescind the Stamp Act. The cartoon shows a solidarity with Great Britain and reflects a hope that bridges could be mended between Great Britain and its North American colonies.

3. **(C)** The sentiment reflected in the image—that peace and reconciliation between Great Britain and the colonies was a desirable goal—was also reflected in the "Olive Branch Petition," adopted by the Continental Congress in 1775. Franklin himself had moved toward a more oppositional position by that point, but many colonists still held out hope in 1775 that a peaceful solution could be reached.

Period 4: 1800–1848
The Meaning of Democracy in an Era of Economic and Territorial Expansion

6

TIMELINE

1800	Election of Thomas Jefferson
1803	Louisiana Purchase
	Marbury v. Madison
1804	Reelection of Jefferson
1807	*Chesapeake* affair
	Embargo Act
1808	Election of James Madison
1810	*Fletcher v. Peck*
1811	Battle of Tippecanoe
1812	Beginning of War of 1812
	Reelection of Madison
1814	Hartford Convention
	Treaty of Ghent
1815	Battle of New Orleans
1816	Election of James Monroe
	Chartering of the Second Bank of the United States
1817	Construction of Erie Canal begins
1819	Panic of 1819
	Dartmouth College v. Woodward
	McCulloch v. Maryland
1820	Missouri Compromise
	Election of James Monroe
1821	Opening of the Lowell factories
	Cohen's v. Virginia
1822	Stephen Austin established first American settlement in Texas
1824	*Gibbons v. Ogden*
	Election of John Quincy Adams
1825	Opening of the Erie Canal
1827	Public school movement begins in Boston
1828	Passage of the "Tariff of Abominations"
	Election of Andrew Jackson
1829	Publication of *David Walker's Appeal to the Colored Citizens of the World*

1830	Opening of the Baltimore and Ohio Railroad
	Passage of the Indian Removal Act
	Founding of Mormonism
1831	William Lloyd Garrison begins publication of the *Liberator*
	Cherokee Nation v. Georgia
1832	Beginning of Nullification Crisis
	Jackson vetoes renewal of Second Bank of the United States
	Worcester v. Georgia
1833	Founding of the American Anti-slavery Society
1834	Whig Party organized
	First strike by the "Lowell girls"
1835	Publication of Alexis de Tocqueville's *Democracy in America*
1836	Congress passes the "gag rule"
	Jackson issues Specie Circular
	The Battle of the Alamo
	Texas independence
1837	Elijah Lovejoy murdered by proslavery mob
1838	"Trail of Tears"
1840	Election of William Henry Harrison of the Whig Party
	Formation of the Liberty Party
1841	John Tyler assumes presidency upon Harrison's death
	Brook Farm founded
1843	Dorothea Dix organizes movement for asylum reform
1844	Samuel Morse invents the telegraph
	James Polk elected president
	Texas annexation
1846	Creation of the Independent Treasury
	Resolution of dispute with Great Britain over Oregon Territory
	Beginning of Mexican War
1848	Seneca Falls Convention
	Treaty of Guadalupe Hidalgo ends Mexican War
	Gold found in California
1851	Herman Melville writes *Moby Dick*
1854	Ostend Manifesto

INTRODUCTION

The first half of the nineteenth century witnessed a series of economic, territorial, and demographic changes that led to struggles over the definition and limits of democratic government.

Growth and expansion were defining features of the United States in the decades between the 1800s and the Civil War. The economy was rapidly changing and growing, as an older semi-subsistence economy was giving way to a market economy with a national and even international reach. The market revolution affected different parts of the country differently. Reformers and intellectuals tried to make sense of these changes and entered into debates about the meaning and shape of democracy. The boundaries of the United States grew several times during this period, as the United States attempted to fulfill its professed "manifest destiny," and American Indians resisted and changed in the process. In the northern states, we begin to see the beginnings of industrialization, while slavery grew dramatically in the South on the strength of the cultivation of cotton. In some ways, the regions of the United States became more interlinked as local economies were drawn into national markets, but at the same time, the issue of free versus slave labor pushed the country further apart.

KEY CONCEPT 4.1
DEMOCRACY, REFORM, AND THE FORMATION
OF A NATIONAL CULTURE

The turn of the nineteenth century witnessed the unfolding of the world's first mass democracy and the beginning of a national culture. Americans debated the nature of its democracy and many worked to reform social institutions to match the nation's democratic ideals.

I. Power, Authority, and Rights in a Mass Democracy

Although the Constitution put down on paper the basic structure of governance in the United States, the specific roles of the different branches of government and the specific relationship between the federal government and the state governments needed to be defined and clarified. This process began to occur during the first half of the nineteenth century, amid much debate and contestation. In addition, this period witnessed debates around what rights and responsibilities individual citizens had.

A. POLITICAL AGENDAS AND THE EVOLUTION OF THE TWO-PARTY SYSTEM

Although many of the founders of the United States did not anticipate them, political parties developed in the 1790s and have been a feature of American political life ever since. These parties are often large tents that are built around a variety of interest groups and constituencies.

The First Two-Party System: The Democratic-Republicans and the Federalists

Usually, two primary parties compete for votes. In a winner-take-all system of voting, it is difficult for a third party candidate to gain traction. The first two-party system developed in the 1790s and pitted the Democratic-Republicans against the Federalists (see Period 3). The Federalists, coalescing around the agenda of Alexander Hamilton, embraced a broader national agenda, advocating the use of a national bank and import duties to promote commercial and manufacturing activities, while the Democratic-Republicans, following the lead of Thomas Jefferson, sought to limit the power of the national government and reserve greater authority on the state level. These two parties developed a strong antipathy toward each other, especially after the passage of the Alien and Sedition Acts in 1798, which seemed like thinly veiled attempts to silence and weaken the Democratic-Republicans. The passage of the acts seemed to backfire; the Democratic-Republicans gained strength and won the presidential election of 1800.

The Decline of the Federalist Party and the "Era of Good Feelings"

Despite fears of turmoil, power peacefully changed hands in 1800 from the Federalist Party to the Democratic-Republicans (known colloquially as the Republicans). Some of the political acrimony of the 1790s died down during the first decades of the nineteenth century. The Federalist Party lost support in the first decades of the nineteenth century as the agricultural areas of the country grew more rapidly than the commercial centers of the Northeast. The Federalists suffered a further blow because of their vigorous opposition to the popular War of 1812. The decline of the Federalist Party led to the "Era of Good Feelings" in the 1810s and 1820s—when only one major party competed for votes on the national level.

With the Federalist Party in its death throes, the Democratic-Republican Party candidate, James Monroe easily won the election of 1816. Four years later, the Federalists made even less of a challenge to Madison. Madison was a throwback to the eighteenth-century presidents. He was the last president to consistently wear the silk stockings, knee breeches, and powdered wigs of an earlier era. He also adopted Washington's practice of bringing men of differing ideological bents into his administration. Many of Madison's policies, such as promoting "internal improvements," seemed like pages out of the Federalist playbook.

The Federalist agenda also lived on in the Supreme Court. The Supreme Court, not subject to the whims of the electorate, kept alive many Federalist ideas. Also, the nation began to adopt manufacturing, just as Alexander Hamilton had hoped. Henry Clay's "American System" kept alive much of Hamilton's program.

The Second Two-Party System: The Democrats and the Whigs

A second two-party system developed in the 1830s out of the contentious issues of the era of President Andrew Jackson. The tense unity of the one-party "Era of Good Feelings" broke apart as the Jacksonian branch of the Democratic-Republicans became known simply as the Democratic Party and Jackson's opponents organized the Whig Party (1833). It is difficult to generalize about the type of constituents in each party. Northerners and southerners, for example, could be found in both parties. Many Whigs supported government programs aimed at economic modernization (based on the thinking of both Alexander Hamilton and Henry Clay). The language of the Democratic Party was more populist, arguing that high tariffs would "fatten" urban commercial interests. Issues, in general, tended to be less important in this period than they were in the formative years of the country or than they would become again during the lead-up to the Civil War. Both parties focused intently on winning elections and holding on to power.

> ## THE TWO-PARTY SYSTEM
> The United States has always had two principle political parties vying for power, except during the "Era of Good Feelings," when there was only one viable party, the Democratic-Republicans.

B. THE SUPREME COURT ASSERTS FEDERAL POWER AND THE POWER OF THE JUDICIARY

The Supreme Court, during the tenure of Chief Justice John Marshall (1801–1835) issued a series of decisions that extended the power of the federal government over state laws, while at the same time establishing the primacy of the judiciary in interpreting the meaning of the Constitution.

Marbury v. Madison (1803)

The most important decision of the Marshall Court was in the case of *Marbury v. Madison.* The important outcome of the case was that the principle of judicial review was established. The details of the decision have to do with the seating of judges that had been appointed in the last days of the John Adams administration. These judges had been appointed by Adams to fill slots created by an expended judiciary that grew out of the Judiciary Act of 1801. The act was passed in the final weeks of the Adams administration, and he worked feverishly to fill these seats before his term expired, thereby solidifying Federalist power in the court system for years to come. When Jefferson assumed office, not all the commissions had been formally delivered. Jefferson, angered at the eleventh-hour appointments, ordered his secretary of state, James Madison, to not deliver them. In this way, he could appoint his own judges.

One potential judge, William Marbury, sued to have his commission delivered. The Supreme Court ruled that Marbury was not entitled to his seat because the law he was basing his argument on—the Judiciary Act of 1789—was unconstitutional. Marshall established the Supreme Court's power to review laws and determine if they are consistent with the Constitution. Laws declared unconstitutional by the Court are immediately struck down. This power of judicial review has been the main function of the Supreme Court since then and has been instrumental in maintaining balance between the three branches of the government.

Other Marshall Court Decisions

Two important decisions strengthened federal power over state power.

McCulloch v. Maryland (1819) prohibited Maryland from taxing the Second Bank of the United States, a federal institution. *Gibbons v. Ogden* (1824) invalidated a monopoly on ferry transportation between New York and New Jersey that had been issued by New York, and asserted that only the federal government could regulate interstate trade. The Marshall Court affirmed the right of the Supreme Court to take appeals from state courts in the case of *Cohens v. Virginia* (1821). The case, which originated in the Virginia state court system, involved the ability of the state to prohibit the Cohen brothers from selling lottery tickets in Virginia. The Court upheld Virginia's right to forbid the sale of tickets.

The Supreme Court again revoked a state statute in the case of *Worcester v. Georgia* (1832). The case resulted in a judicial challenge to the national government's forced removal of the Cherokee people under the dictate of the Indian Removal Act (see page 142). Specifically, the decision struck down a Georgia statute that forbade non–American Indians from entering American Indian territory without first obtaining a license from the state. In a larger sense, the Court upheld the autonomy of American Indian communities. The Cherokees were "a distinct community, occupying its own territory," the Court asserted; "the laws of Georgia can have no force." The decision was largely ignored by the United States government as it pursued its Indian removal policy.

C. THE MARKET ECONOMY, THE ROLE OF THE GOVERNMENT, AND REGIONAL LOYALTIES

The growth of the market economy, often labeled the "market revolution" by historians, dramatically altered

> ## THE DEVELOPMENT OF A NATIONAL ECONOMY
>
> The market revolution linked cities and regions. We see the local economies of the eighteenth century giving way to a national, and even international, economic system.

many aspects of American society—drawing local economies into the national and international economy. Americans debated what role the government should play in this changing economy. Although the growth of the national economy was evident in the first half of the nineteenth century, regional economic and political loyalties persisted.

The Persistence of Regionalism

The market revolution affected different parts of the country differently. In the northern states, we begin to see the beginnings of industrialization, while slavery grew dramatically in the South on the strength of the cultivation of cotton. In some ways, the regions of the United States became more interlinked as local economies were transformed into national markets, but at the same time, the issue of free versus slave labor pushed the country further apart.

The Incorporation of America

Economic growth was facilitated by the changes in laws that made it much easier to create and expand a corporate entity. In the late 1700s and early 1800s, corporate charters were granted to groups of individuals, but mainly on a temporary basis, and mainly for a public-oriented purpose, such as building a bridge or a road. After 1810, states began rewriting corporate laws allowing for the chartering of business. Incorporation encouraged investment into the corporation and protected the individual investors from liability law.

The Supreme Court and the Market Economy

Supreme Court decision in the first half of the nineteenth century tended to uphold and define the rules of the growing market economy. The Supreme Court in the decision of *Trustees of Dartmouth College v. Woodward* (1819) granted corporations several rights they had not previously had. The case revolved around New Hampshire's attempt to rescind the charter that Dartmouth College had received from the king during the colonial period; the state wanted to turn Dartmouth into a state college. This decision and the decision in *Fletcher v. Peck* also upheld the sanctity of contracts. In *Fletcher v. Peck* (1810), the Supreme Court upheld a corrupt land deal between the state of Georgia and private individuals. The Court ruled that the deal might not have been in the public interest, but a contract should be upheld. In the following decades, the number of corporations, and investors, grew dramatically.

The Expansion of Banking

Banking and credit began to play an increasingly important role in economic expansion, especially after the panic of 1819. The panic of 1819 demonstrated the volatility of this new market economy. However, the remarkable growth afterward demonstrated the vitality of the new economy. The Second Bank of the United States, chartered in 1816, extended credit, as did many newly chartered state banks. These banks issued bank notes, which were the only paper currency in circulation at the time. The system of bank notes as currency was imperfect—values of notes from one state might be less in another state—but the ability of banks to put currency into the economy fueled economic growth.

D. SLAVERY AND SOUTHERN REGIONAL IDENTITY

In the first half of the nineteenth century, white southerners defended the institution of slavery vigorously. The defense of slavery became an element in the development of regional pride in the South.

Southern Defense of Slavery

As the abolitionist movement attacked the system of slavery (see below), southern public figures emerged to give a vigorous defense of the institution. Arguments took a variety of approaches. Some contrasted the factory system of the North with the slave system of the South, arguing that northern "wage-slaves" were not taken care of or fed and were fired when business was slow. The most well-known defender of slavery in the 1850s was George Fitzhugh. He was sharply critical of the pronouncements of northern defenders of the "free labor" ideology, insisting that the system masked a heartless approach to the world. Other southerners argued that slavery was sanctioned in the Bible. This movement went so far as to claim that slavery was a "positive good" for the slaves—that it provided them with skills, discipline, and "civilization."

> ## SHIFTING DEFENSE OF SLAVERY
> Between the era of Jefferson and the era of Fitzhugh, we can say that the defense of the slavery system shifted from slavery being a "necessary evil" to it being a "positive good."

II. Debates Around Extending the Reach of Democratic Ideals

Many Americans debated what a democracy should look like in the first half of the nineteenth century. Many reformers sought to expand the reach of democracy in this period, pushing for the abolition of slavery and the extension of women's rights. At the same time, the period witnessed an increase in racist sentiment, manifested in the spread of proslavery ideas, anti-immigrant ideas, anti-Indian ideas, and restrictions on the rights of free African Americans.

A. RELIGIOUS AND SECULAR REFORM

A series of reform movements and voluntary organizations grew in number and importance in the first half of the nineteenth century. These movements were influenced by the Second Great Awakening religious movement, as well as by European liberal ideas. The Romantic notion of human perfectibility was central to these movements.

The Second Great Awakening

In the first decades of the nineteenth century, American ministers sought to revive religious sentiment among the American people. The situation was similar to the first Great Awakening of a century earlier. At the turn of the nineteenth century, many ministers worried that Americans seemed more captivated by politics—forming and building a new nation—than by God and salvation. Many ordinary Americans also felt a yearning to get in touch with a more immediate religious experience. The result was the Second Great Awakening. The movement of large "camp meetings" began in Kentucky early in the 1800s, and soon spread to other states. It was especially strong in upstate New York and western Pennsylvania. The growing towns adjacent to the Erie Canal came to be known as the "burned over district" because of the intensity of the religious revival there.

The movement spoke to many of the farmers, merchants, and businessmen and women who were brought into the larger society by the "market revolution." The messages of the market and of the Great Second Awakening were similar. Market relations told the individual that success or failure was in his or her hands; hard work, dedication, and restraint would lead to economic success. The Second Great Awakening told the individual that salvation was also in his or her hands. Righteous living, self-control, and a strong moral compass would lead to salvation. This idea that one could determine his or her eternal life was very different from the old Puritan notion of predestination, which held that one's eternal life was planned out by God.

The Second Great Awakening not only encouraged individual redemption, but also societal reformation. Not only could one become perfect in the eyes of God, but one could work to perfect society as well. In this respect the Second Great Awakening acted as a springboard for a variety of reform movements.

Mormonism

The Church of the Latter-Day Saints, known as the Mormons, was founded in 1830 by Joseph Smith, Jr. in upstate New York, growing out of the Second Great Awakening. The group was met by hostility for its unorthodox teachings and practices. The most controversial practice was polygamy—allowing men to have multiple wives (long since renounced by the Mormon church). The group journeyed from New York to Ohio, then to Missouri, and finally to Illinois. In Illinois, Smith was killed by a mob (1844), and a new leader named Brigham Young led the majority of Mormons to Utah.

Reform Movements

Although reform movements have existed throughout most of American history, the antebellum period saw a dramatic upswing in reform activity. Reform movements have attempted to improve different aspects of American society, but have had varying degrees of success.

> ### PERIODS OF REFORM
>
> Be familiar with the three most prominent periods of reform in American history: The reform movements of the 1830s and 1840s, the progressive reform movement of the 1900s and 1910s, and the reform movements of the 1960s and 1970s that were inspired by the civil rights movement.

Temperance

The goal of the temperance movement was to limit or even ban the production, sale, and consumption of alcoholic beverages. Many temperance activists focused on individual self-control; they encouraged people to voluntarily take an oath to abstain from alcohol. Others sought to use the power of government to limit or eliminate the consumption of alcoholic beverages. The temperance movement was the biggest reform movement of the first half of the nineteenth century.

There were several reasons the temperance movement attracted a large following in the antebellum period. The temperance movement was especially popular among women. Many women were troubled by the large amount of alcohol their husbands drank. Alcohol was part of the fabric of daily life for many men. By 1830, the average man drank almost 10 gallons per year of hard liquor and about 30 gallons per year of beer, wine, and hard cider. In an era when pure water was difficult to come by, especially for urban working-class people, it made sense to drink alcoholic beverages. The alcohol killed dangerous bacteria. In addition, tavern owners were more than happy to cash men's paychecks on Friday evening, knowing that much of that money would stay in the tavern. Men not only came home with little money in their pockets, they came home drunk. Many men, in this drunken state, took out their frustrations on their wives and children. This acting out could take the form of verbal abuse and physical abuse. So it made sense for women to organize to stop liquor consumption.

In the pre-Civil War period, the American Temperance Union had some success. Maine became a "dry" state in 1851, completely banning the sale or manufacture of all alcoholic beverages. But alcohol consumption was on the rise throughout the 1800s, despite the efforts of the temperance movement.

The Asylum and Penitentiary Movement

In early America, the mentally ill were often treated as common criminals, spending years behind bars. In the 1840s, activists, including many women, spearheaded a movement to improve treatment for the mentally ill. One of the main organizers was Dorothea Dix. Her efforts led to the creation of the first generation of mental asylums in the United States.

Public Education

The campaign for free public education gained a large following in the 1840s. Horace Mann was among the most vocal advocates during this period. Mann was secretary of education in Massachusetts in the 1840s and 1850s, and served in the U.S. House of Representatives. The movement saw education as essential to democratic participation.

Seneca Falls Convention

A group of women challenged the cultural and legal restrictions on women in the antebellum period. Many of these women met in the Seneca Falls Convention (1848). The meeting is often considered the birth of the women's rights movement. The convention was organized by Lucretia Mott and Elizabeth Cady Stanton. The genesis of the convention was their exclusion from an abolitionist conference in London in 1840. Mott and Stanton began thinking not only about the abolition of slavery but also about the conditions of women in the United States. The convention issued a Declaration of Sentiments modeled after the Declaration of Independence. The document declared, "all men and women are created equal."

B. DEBATING THE FUTURE OF SLAVERY IN AMERICA

Slavery became an increasingly contentious issue in the United States in the first half of the nineteenth century. After the outlawing of the international slave trade in 1808, many states restricted the citizen possibilities of African Americans. The period witnessed a growing abolitionist movement as well as plans for emancipation, including colonization of Africa.

Abolitionism

The reform spirit of the Second Great Awakening inspired the modern abolition movement. Abolitionism was a minority opinion among northern whites in the antebellum period, but it had a major impact on America, opening up sectional divisions that contributed to the Civil War.

William Lloyd Garrison and "Immediate Emancipation"

In 1831, William Lloyd Garrison, a white abolitionist, began publication of *The Liberator*. Garrison quickly became the key figure in the movement for the immediate and uncompensated abolition of slavery. Antislavery sentiment existed before that, but most antislavery groups advocated a more gradual approach to ending slavery. That is, slave owners would keep their current slaves, but would not be able to enslave additional people. Slavery would therefore gradually end as the current slaves died. Additionally, most antislavery activists before Garrison advocated colonization (see below), Garrison broke with both of these approaches. He said all slaves should be immediately freed, that there should be no compensation to their owners, and that freed slaves were entitled to the same rights as white people.

American Colonization Society

The American Colonization Society was founded in 1817 with the goal of transporting African Americans to Africa. The motives of the founders of the organization varied. Some sympathized with African Americans and urged them to leave the United States to escape from the ingrained racism of white Americans. Other founders thought of African Americans as an inferior caste and wanted to rid America of them. Advocates of colonization believed that slaves either could not or should not receive treatment as equals in the United States. The society purchased land in Africa and began a colony they called Liberia. Between 1820 and the Civil War only about 12,000 African Americans went to Africa. About 7,000 were former slaves who were freed under the condition that they leave the United States; the rest were free African Americans who believed they had a better chance to succeed in Liberia. Most African Americans, free or slave, showed very little interest in leaving their country to live in Africa. Frederick Douglass, for example, was very critical of colonization proposals.

SUPPORT FOR COLONIZATION

The American Colonization Society was started by antislavery Quakers, but it also had the support of many southern slave-owners who wanted to rid the South of its free black population. Southern slave-owners saw this population as a threat.

Abolitionism and Electoral Politics

A group of abolitionists formed the Liberty Party in 1840. This minor third party put forth the idea that the Constitution was essentially an antislavery document and that the United States should live up to the ideals contained in the document. In this, the party differed from Garrison, who insisted that the Constitution protected slavery and, therefore, should be condemned. The Liberty Party hoped to influence public opinion through the electoral arena. Garrison, on the other hand, rejected participating in electoral politics.

Frederick Douglass

Starting in the 1840s, the towering figure in the abolitionist movement was Frederick Douglass. Douglass was born into slavery (1818) and escaped to the North in 1838. He had learned to read and write, and soon became a powerful speaker in the antislavery movement. Douglass remained an important figure before, during, and after the Civil War, until his death in 1895.

C. RESISTANCE TO THE EXPANSION OF DEMOCRATIC IDEALS

Although many reformers sought to promote and extend democratic ideals, many groups, individuals, and government reflected an anti-democratic ethos. The period witnessed a vigorous defense of the institution of slavery, rising xenophobia, public expressions of racism, and restrictive government policies in regard to American Indians.

Racism and Resistance to the Antislavery Movement

Slavery shaped southern views of race in distinct ways. Although many northerners subscribed to white supremacist views, white supremacist ideas were not central to the culture of the region because there were very few African Americans in the North (less than 1 percent of the population). In the South, however, white supremacy became central to southern white culture in the first half of the nineteenth century, especially after northern abolitionists began to press the cause of antislavery forcibly in the 1830s. Most white southerners held that African Americans were inferior beings. This view justified slavery, as an institution both necessary and proper. White supremacy and slavery allowed the main divide in the South to be race rather than class. It allowed even the poorest whites to feel that they were part of the superior caste and allowed them to feel like they had something in common with the wealthiest plantation owners.

The Lovejoy Incident

The abolitionist movement faced opposition in the North as well as from white southerners. A violent incident in 1837 sent a chill over the abolitionist movement. Elijah Lovejoy, an abolitionist newspaper publisher in Illinois, was killed by a proslavery mob. He had been the subject of harassment. Mobs had destroyed his printing press three times before they killed him.

Nativism

The first half of the nineteenth century witnessed a dramatic increase in immigration from Europe, as well as a strong xenophobic nativist movement. Nativism was both an emotional impulse as well as an organized movement. Many Americans thought that immigrants drank more than native-born Americans. They thought that the new immigrants, who were mostly non-Protestant, lacked the self-control of "proper," middle-class Protestant Americans. Maybe these new immigrants did not drink more than native-born Americans, but they probably drank more publicly. Middle-class people had their parlors to enjoy wine or scotch with their friends. Working-class immigrants drank at the local taverns—much more in the public eye.

III. Cultural Ferment in the Antebellum Period

Many Americans participated in the creation of a variety of cultural movements. Many Americans contributed to the development of a national culture, combining European elements with distinctly American elements. At the same time, groups of people in the United States developed cultural forms that reflected the particularities of their own experiences and world-views.

A. THE EMERGENCE OF A NATIONAL CULTURE

The aftermath of the War of 1812 saw not only an increase in nationalist sentiment, but also the development of a uniquely American culture. This culture borrowed elements of European culture, but also sought to create something uniquely American. Noah Webster, for instance, sought to codify a specifically American dictionary, separate from British English, when he published his *American Dictionary of the English Language* in 1828.

Hudson River School

The reverence for European cultural products combined with a desire to create a uniquely American form of expression can be seen in the landscape paintings that came to be labeled the Hudson River School of painting. The Hudson River School, which flourished from the 1820s to the 1870s, is best represented by three artists—Thomas Cole, Asher Durand, and Frederick Church. These artists were inspired by the European tradition of Romantic paintings of dramatic landscapes, often featuring the ruins of ancient castles or temples. The United States lacked such ancient ruins. In their place, these artists captured pristine wilderness. Many of the paintings hinted at the impending hand of civilization, about to spoil virgin landscapes. Many Hudson River painters shared Transcendentalist ideas about the glory of nature. Many of the works focused, of course, on the Hudson River, a waterway that generated new interest after the opening of the Erie Canal (1825). These paintings often emphasized emotional sentiment over accuracy.

The American Renaissance

The antebellum period experienced a renaissance in literature. Some of the greatest literature in American history comes out of the decades before the Civil War. In the early 1850s, this literary spirit reached its apogee. The literature of that period included Herman Melville's *Moby Dick*, the first edition of Walt Whitman's *Leaves of Grass*, Nathaniel Hawthorne's *The Scarlet Letter* and *The House of the Seven Gables*, and Thoreau's *Walden*. This literature is uniquely American, grappling with religious and existential questions raised by the legacy of the Puritans and focusing on the promise and the contradictions of America's experiment in building a democratic nation in the New World.

> ### THE IMPACT OF THOREAU
>
> Thoreau's book, *Walden; or, Life in the Woods* (1854), was influential in the back-to-the-land movement of the 1960s and 1970s.

B. SUB-CULTURES IN A GROWING NATION

While many artists and writers expressed nationalist themes and tried to foster a national culture in the first half of the nineteenth century, other groups sought to develop more particular cultural forms. These groups developed cultures that reflected the experiences of groups as diverse as American Indians, women, religious followers, and members of the rising middle class.

Gentility, Domesticity, and the Middle-Class Ideal

Many contemporary writers and historians note the emergence of a middle-class culture in the first half of the nineteenth century, built around the home, nostalgia and sentimentality, and a watered-down (non-Calvinist) Christian piety. This middle-class cultural ideal assigned to women a dependent role as the "weaker sex." In an increasingly market-oriented society, women were seen as outside of this rough-and-tumble world of money and politics. The qualities that were assigned to women were timidity and disdain for competition. This culture was manifested in sermons by Protestant ministers, seeking to broaden their appeal, and by female authors of fiction.

American Indian Cultural Developments

Many American Indians, in the face of warfare, disease, dispossession, and displacement, developed spiritual practices that both borrowed from traditional American Indian religious beliefs and adapted elements from their contemporary experiences, including exposure to Christianity. In the wake of the defeat and dispossession of the Iroquois Confederacy, a Seneca man named Handsome Lake developed a set of spiritual practices that came to be known as the "Longhouse Religion." Drawing on traditional and Quaker motifs, he denounced the factionalism that undermined American Indian resistance to white incursions and spoke out against alcohol consumption and the breakdown of the family. Though Handsome Lake met resistance from both Christian missionaries and from traditionalists, he offered many American Indians a sense of hope in the face of staggering setbacks.

C. THE CULTURES OF AFRICAN-AMERICAN COMMUNITIES—FREE AND SLAVE

African Americans developed cultural forms that emphasized maintaining dignity and autonomy in the face of enslavement and oppression. Both free communities and slave communities developed strategies and cultural patterns that both challenged their status and pointed toward a better future.

David Walker

An important early figure in the abolitionist movement was the African American David Walker. In 1829, he issued a pamphlet entitled *David Walker's Appeal to the Coloured Citizens of the World*. This radical tract called on people of African descent to resist slavery by any and every means. His praise of self-defense made Southerners furious.

The African Methodist Episcopal (AME) Church

Throughout American history, African Americans developed religious beliefs and practices that reflected their experiences in America. The African Methodist Church (AME) church reflected this tradition. The denomination was founded in Philadelphia in 1816, from several African–American Methodist churches, by Richard Allen. The founding of the AME reflected a desire on the part of the free African-American community to have greater autonomy and to tailor religious service to the needs and experiences of the African-American community. The AME borrowed many elements from the mainstream Methodist church; the founder of the Methodist movement, John Wesley, was an outspoken critic of the slave trade. However, in contrast to mainstream Methodism, the AME developed a distinctively racial theology.

Cultural Resistance to Slavery

Slaves were not passive as they endured slavery. Certainly, they learned that outright rebellion would almost certainly end in failure and death. However, slaves developed cultural practices that constituted more subtle forms of resistance—practices that sustained families and communities, and that attempted to carve out some degree of autonomy in the face of near total control. Slaves passed on fanciful stories from generation to generation that often had a pointed message. In the Br'er Rabbit stories, the weak often got the better of the strong. Music often sustained slave communities. Slaves, for instance, might make gourd fiddles, using a large gourd for the body and horsehair for the strings. The gourd fiddle, a hybrid of African and American instruments, was used to create music that combined African traditions with the traditions of the South and to provide a relief from the unremitting drudgery of slavery.

KEY CONCEPT 4.2
MARKETS, TECHNOLOGY, SETTLEMENT PATTERNS, AND POWER

A constellation of changes in technology and commerce brought about a series of transformations in American society. These changes affected patterns of settlement, family relations and gender norms, political power, regional identities, and the way Americans acquired goods.

I. Technological Innovations Transform Agriculture and Manufacturing

A series of technological innovations dramatically altered the American economy. These changes created regional, national, and international markets for goods. Old patterns of economic activity gave way to new patterns of production, distribution, and consumption, changing the nature of agriculture and manufacturing.

A. ADVANCES IN TECHNOLOGY

A series of technological innovations extended the market economy and brought efficiency to the production of goods. These innovations included the steam engine, interchangeable parts, canals, railroads, the telegraph, and machinery to produce textiles.

Improvements in Transportation

Improvements in transportation made possible production for faraway markets. By 1850, the eastern half of the United States was crisscrossed by a series of roads, canals, and railroads that, along with navigable rivers, moved goods from city to city and from the interior to the coast. These projects were often encouraged by the government and at least partially funded by it. The cost of moving a ton of freight from Buffalo to New York City dropped by approximately 90 percent with the development of the Erie Canal. The cost of moving a ton of wheat one mile went from about 30 to 70 cents by wagon in 1800 to about 1.2 cents by railroad in 1860.

Canals and Roads

The first set of improvements, which occurred in the years between the dawn of the nineteenth century and about 1830, included the expansion and improvement of roads and canals and the development of the steamboat. The construction of canals and roads, called at the time *internal improvements*, did much to expand trade, especially between the Midwest (then known as the West) and eastern cities. Most significant was the Erie Canal (completed in 1825), which connected the Hudson River to the Great Lakes, thus connecting New York City with the interior of the country. The most significant road project was the building of the National Road, also known as the Cumberland Road, stretching from Maryland into the Ohio River valley. Construction took place from 1811 to 1853. Soon, however, roads and canals were overshadowed by a quicker and more powerful means of transportation, the railroad.

Railroads

The first railroad tracks were laid in 1829 by the Baltimore and Ohio Railroad. By 1860, railroads connected the far reaches of the country east of the Mississippi River, and beyond. They sped up the movement of goods and expanded markets. The government encouraged this expansion of the railroad network by giving railroad companies wide swaths of land. The government gave railroad companies a total of 129 million acres in land grants. The railroad companies built rail lines and also sold land adjacent to the tracks. The price of land near railroad stops soared, bringing about $435 million into the pockets of the railroad companies. All of these transportation improvements dramatically increased the nation's economic activity.

Advances in Communication

The major advance in communications in the antebellum period was the telegraph. Samuel Morse developed and patented the telegraph, and sent the first message—"What hath God wrought?"—in 1844. The first telegraph line was from Washington, DC, to Baltimore. Telegraph messages were transmitted in a code of long and short electrical impulses called Morse code. By 1850, telegraph lines, usually built alongside railroad tracks, connected the country. The telegraph greatly facilitated the development of a national market of products and services. A clothing manufacturer in Massachusetts, or even Great Britain, could send his requirements to southern cotton growers in a matter of minutes. Previously, it could take weeks to send information across the sea, and days to send it across the country. Orders could be placed, materials could be ordered, information could be sent—all in minutes.

Slater Mill and the Development of the Factory System

Before the Civil War, America began to move toward the industrial mass production of goods. This trend continued with even greater energy after the Civil War. The first field to industrialize was the textile industry. As early as the 1790s, Samuel Slater built the first factory in the United States after smuggling plans out of Great Britain. This factory in Pawtucket, Rhode Island, and dozens that were built in the following years, spun thread and yarn. The spinning machines in Slater's mill were powered by the fast-flowing Blackstone River. Water, human, and animal power characterized industry in the pre–Civil War era.

B. WORKERS ARE DRAWN INTO NEW METHODS OF PRODUCTION

New methods of production drew men and women into a growing market economy and away from small-scale agricultural work.

The "Putting-out System"

In the first decades of the nineteenth century a system of manufacturing developed in which home-based workers performed piecework at home. In this "putting-out system," men and women would perform a task arranged by an agent and would be paid by the piece. Often, the task was a small part of a larger operation, such as repeatedly cutting leather forms, to be sewn elsewhere into shoes. This system was suited to small and rural communities. Often families might be simultaneously involved in semi-subsistence agriculture and in the putting-out system; the seasonal nature of farm work allows for additional work to be taken in at various times of the year. This system was something of a bridge between the craftwork of the eighteenth century and the industrial revolution of the late nineteenth century.

The Lowell System

Early elements of industrialization emerged in rural New England in the 1820s and 1830s. Extensive, water-powered textile factories opened along the Merrimack River in Lowell, Massachusetts, starting in 1821, and drew in young women from the New England countryside to operate the machines. It was thought that these women could be paid less and would only be temporary factory operatives. At some point, it was thought, they would get married and be replaced by new women who would be recruited to replace them. Also, the era of mass migration from Europe had not yet begun, so it was difficult to recruit male factory operatives, especially with farmland in the United States still reasonably priced. By 1830, eight mills employed more than 6,000 women.

The fathers of these young women were told by factory recruiters that their daughters would be working in a "factory in the garden"—a clean, bucolic setting, unlike the dirty and dangerous factory cities of Great Britain. The women tended to live in closely supervised boarding houses, and the work was also strictly monitored. Despite this scrutiny, both on the job and even at the boarding houses, the "Lowell girls" experienced a degree of freedom and autonomy unheard of for young women at the time. Many participated in producing a periodical called the *Lowell Offering*. They demonstrated their sense of solidarity and assertiveness by going on strike in 1834 and again in 1836, following announced wage cuts. The 1836 strike restored their original wages, but by the 1840s the farm women were being replaced by Irish immigrants who were in dire straits and were ready to work for lower wages.

II. The American System, Regional Specialization, and the Movement of People

The American economy developed rapidly in the first half of the nineteenth century, with different regions specializing in different economic activities. Most notably, cotton became "king" in the South, shaping the national and the international economy. Regional specialization also resulted in new settlement patterns.

A. THE GROWTH OF COTTON PRODUCTION

In the first half of the nineteenth century, cotton replaced other staple crops as the most profitable crop throughout the South. The profitability of southern cotton contributed to a dramatic growth in slavery in the first half of the nineteenth century and an expansion of the internal slave trade. Most of the cotton used in the mills in New England was grown by slave labor in the South. The invention of the cotton gin by Eli Whitney (1793) allowed for the rapid processing of cotton. That, combined with insatiable demand in the North and in Great Britain for cotton, led to more and more acres being put under cultivation. Cotton production connected the United States to the global economy.

Cotton and Slavery

Slavery become dominant in the South just as it was becoming unpopular in the eyes of the world. In 1807, Great Britain outlawed the international slave trade. The following year, the United States took the same step (the international slave trade had been protected by the Constitution until 1808). All of the northern states had voted to abolish slavery outright or gradually.

KING COTTON, NORTH AND SOUTH

Cotton was not only king in the South. The increase in cotton production benefitted many elements in the North as well as in the South. Cotton was bought and sold in New York City and processed into cloth in New England.

Some northerners, and even some white southerners, were critical of slavery, but slavery and cotton were the main engines behind American economic growth in the first half of the nineteenth century. By 1860, 58 percent of American exports consisted of cotton. Cotton production increased from about 700,000 bales in 1830 to nearly five million bales on the eve of the Civil War. Cotton was justifiably called "King Cotton." As cotton production increased, the number of slaves in the South also increased. In 1790, there were approximately 700,000 slaves in the United States; that figure climbed to 2 million by 1830, and 4 million by 1860.

Both the North and South were growing economically in the first decades of the nineteenth century. In many ways, the growth of each region reinforced the growth of the other. However, this symbiotic relationship would not persist. Political and ideological differences would emerge as America moved toward the midway point in the century. These differences would come to overshadow commonalities and would lead to the Civil War.

B. THE PROMISE AND THE LIMITS OF THE "AMERICAN SYSTEM"

Attempts by the government to create linkages between the regions of the country were of limited success. The market economy ended up creating stronger links between the North and the Midwest; the South became increasingly isolated from the rest of the country.

Henry Clay's "American System"

In the nationalist mood that followed the War of 1812, Henry Clay, a leading member of the House of Representatives, proposed a series of proposals to promote economic growth that he later called the "American System." First, Clay realized that America needed "internal improvements" in transportation in order to grow economically. At the beginning of the century, the transportation system in the United States was woefully lacking. At the time of the War of 1812, the military had difficulty moving materials and men because of the nation's inadequate transportation system. Second, Clay proposed putting high tariffs on imported goods. He believed that high tariffs on incoming manufactured goods would promote American manufacturing. High tariffs would make foreign goods more expensive to the consumer, and American-made goods would seem cheaper by comparison. Third, Clay proposed chartering a Second Bank of the United States in order to stabilize the economy and to make credit more readily available. These proposals were important steps taken by the government to usher in the market revolution. By the end of the Monroe Administration, Congress had rechartered the Bank of the United States and passed a protective tariff (both in 1816).

> ## HAMILTON AND CLAY
>
> Note the marked similarities between Hamilton's economic program and Clay's "American System." Both support a tariff, a central bank, and government encouragement for manufacturing. Contemporary Republicans often are pro-business; however, current pro-business policies favor low tariffs and deregulation of the economy—not supporting "internal improvements."

The Growing Isolation of the South

Despite Clay's attempt to foster unity among the regions of the country, the South became increasingly isolated from both the North and the Midwest. Roads and railroads connected the North and the Midwest, but tended to bypass the South. Further, patterns of migrations connected the North and the Midwest culturally. Farmers, artisans, and laborers living in the older cities and towns of New England, New York, or Pennsylvania were far more likely to venture toward Ohio or Illinois in the first half of the nineteenth century than they were toward South Carolina or Mississippi. These connections isolated the South culturally from the rest of the nation and would, over time, isolate it politically.

C. RESOURCES AND MIGRATIONS

The growing importance of a market economy in the first half of the nineteenth century depended, to a large degree, on the exploitation of both labor and natural resources. The government took steps to encourage the movement of peoples across the continent in order to better gain access to the continent's copious natural resources.

The Politics of Expansion

Efforts aimed at encouraging the movements of peoples included expanding the amount of land in North America under American control, the development of railroads to open these new lands to settlement, and forcibly removing American Indians from lands desired by white settlers. Northern politicians pushed for measures to provide homesteads for settlers on western lands in the decades before the Civil War, but southern politicians blocked them in an effort to keep this land open for possible expansion of the plantation system. It was not until during the Civil War that Congress was able to pass a homestead act.

III. The Impact of the Market Revolution

As the market revolution gained traction in the United States and drew more people and regions into its orbit, American society changed in significant ways. The United States experienced new migration patterns, new ideas about family and gender relations, and a shift in political power.

A. INTERNAL MIGRATIONS

Improvements in transportation, as well as a variety of social and economic factors, encouraged native-born white citizens to move into the West and settle new communities. New community and social ties replaced older family and local relationships.

The Movement to the West

The West grew rapidly in the antebellum period, especially after the War of 1812, as improvements in transportation—first roads and canals, and later railroads—opened new areas for settlement. More than 4 million Americans crossed the Appalachian Mountains between 1800 and 1840 to settle in the West. Most of these migrants to the West traveled in groups. New communities grew quickly, with migrants depending on one another to clear land, construct dwellings and barns, and create a sense of community on the frontier. Many southern planters moved into Alabama, Mississippi, Louisiana, Arkansas, and, later during this period, Texas. Many of these small-scale farmers hoped to recreate the Cotton Kingdom, complete with slave labor, on the less expensive lands of the West. From the upper South, many farmers moved into the southern portions of Ohio, Indiana, and Illinois. Finally, many New England and New York farm families settled in northern Ohio, Indiana, and Illinois, as well as Wisconsin and Michigan. Some migrants "squatted" on their new land, lacking legal title or deed. Others purchased land from either the federal government or from speculators. Over time, the regional distinctiveness of the original thirteen states left its imprint on newly settled areas. The towns and churches of the Northwest (the current upper Midwest) began to resemble New England, while the plantations and slave-labor system of the new lower South resembled the Old South.

> ### COMPETING MOTIVATIONS
>
> Be aware of the variety of motivations that drew people to the West: Some were small farmers inspired by the "free soil" ideal; some were drawn to Texas to find a place as slave-owning cotton growers; some were part of the Mormon exodus to Utah; some were gold seekers drawn to California.

Texas—from Settlement to Statehood

Foreign borders did not stop the flow of Americans to the West. Americans began settling in Texas as early as the 1820s. Mexico was eager to attract settlers to its northern frontier, in part to provide a buffer from incursions by American Indian groups. Led by Stephen Austin, settlers, mostly from the American South, were attracted to Texas because there was an abundance of affordable land that could be used for cotton cultivation. They had very little interest in conforming to the laws and customs of Mexico. They were confident that, somehow, United States control of Texas would follow them.

The Alamo and Texas Independence

Mexico allowed these settlers a degree of self-government in the 1820s, but tensions began to develop in the 1830s. The Texas settlers routinely flouted Mexican law—most notably in practicing slavery, which was banned in Mexico. The new president of Mexico, General Antonio Lopez de Santa Anna, sought to bring the Texans in line with Mexican law and custom. In 1835, the Texans rebelled. At first they suffered major setbacks. Almost 200 died at the Alamo in San Antonio, a former mission where the rebels had taken refuge. Weeks later, almost 400 rebels were killed by Mexican forces near the town of Goliad. The rebels, under the leadership of General Sam Houston, regrouped and emerged victorious. Texans fought for and won independence from Mexico, establishing the independent Lone Star Republic in 1836.

B. MIGRATIONS FROM EUROPE

Immigrants were drawn from Europe in the first half of the nineteenth century by the growing economy and the sense of opportunity in the United States. The majority of immigrants who arrived in the United States between 1800 and 1860 came from northern and western Europe. The two largest groups came from Ireland and from the Germanic states. Many immigrants stayed in the cities of the Northeast, while some ventured into the interior of the country.

Irish Immigration

The largest immigrant group into the United States during the antebellum period was from Ireland. Increased immigration from Ireland to the United States during the 1840s was primarily the result of crop failures that led to mass starvation. Blight afflicted the potato crop, which was a staple for Irish people. The potato blight was partly a natural phenomenon and partly the result of British policies. Great Britain controlled Ireland and used the best land to grow wheat and other crops for export, while potato farming was pushed to marginal land. The result was weak potato plants less able to withstand disease. It is estimated that a million Irish starved to death between 1845 and 1850, while another million left for America. Four-fifths of the Irish immigrants settled in port cities such as New York and Boston, and in other cities and towns of the Northeast.

German Immigration

The second-largest immigrant group during this period was the Germans. German immigrants into the United States tended to be better off than the Irish immigrants. Many were skilled craftsmen and entrepreneurs. Many German immigrants came to the United States to escape the political repression following the failed revolutions of 1848 in the Germanic states. German immigrants were more likely to have the resources to continue their journeys beyond their initial city of disembarkation (usually New York City). Many settled in the "German triangle" of western cities—Cincinnati, St. Louis, and Milwaukee.

C. THE SOUTHERN EXCEPTION

In many ways the South remained distinct from the rest of the country. Ideologically, politically, and culturally, the South developed a regional identity markedly different from the other regions of the country. The South was also distinct in its dependence on exports to the international market; by 1850, the South was supplying approximately half of the world's cotton; by 1860, three-quarters.

The Evolution of Slavery

The main source of the distinctiveness of the South was, as Alexis de Tocqueville noted in *Democracy in America* (1831), slavery. Slavery grew rapidly in the decades leading up to the Civil War. By 1850, nearly a third of the southern population was African American. In 1790, there were approximately 700,000 slaves in the South. By 1830, that figure had climbed to 2 million and by 1860, to 4 million. In Mississippi and South Carolina, African Americans were the majority of the population. In contrast, on the eve of the Civil War only about one northerner in seventy-six was African American. The presence of such a large African-American population in the South played an important role in shaping southern culture. This can be seen in language, food, music, and dialect. However, the most important consequence of the presence of a large slave population in the South was the commitment of white southerners to white supremacy. A belief in the racial inferiority of blacks mixed with fear and even hatred shaped the white southern view of African Americans. Although some white northerners also held racist notions of African Americans, the white supremacist outlook lacked the intensity it held in the South.

D. THE MARKET REVOLUTION'S IMPACT ON CLASS AND GENDER

The Market Revolution dramatically altered the nation's social fabric. The gap between the rich and the poor widened, while at the same time fostering the growth of an emerging middle class. Changes in the economy contributed to changed ideas about class, gender, and family. Society also experienced a widening separation between the private realm of the home and the public realm of work and politics.

Work and Power

The Market Revolution ushered in changes to American society that undermined older American notions of a self-governing citizenry and perceptions of a public composed of autonomous individuals whose rise and fall is determined by their own actions. With the growth of larger-scale manufacturing operations and increasingly powerful incorporated businesses, the ability of the individual to rise and become "his own man" was compromised. In this context, we see some working people, men and women, turning to the idea of forming unions in order to advance their goals. A labor union allowed workers in a firm to bargain collectively with their employer. The rise of the union movement signals a shift away from the face-to-face relationships that characterized workplace settings in the eighteenth century.

The "Cult of Domesticity"

Antebellum society witnessed a redefinition of women's "proper" role in society. The ideas of "republican motherhood," current in the decades after the American Revolution, gave way to a less public-minded conception of a middle-class woman's "place." Commentators in the first half of the nineteenth century tended to see women as intellectually inferior and insisted that their proper role was maintaining the house and caring for children. This "cult of domesticity" insisted that women keep a proper, Christian home—separate from the male sphere of politics, business, and competition. This ideal discouraged women from participating in public life. The laws of the country relegated women to a second-class status. Women could not vote or sit on juries. Women were not entitled to protection against physical abuse by their husbands. When women married, any property they owned became the property of their husbands. Under the legal doctrine of *femme covert*, wives had no independent legal or political standing.

E. POWER AND POLITICS ON THE NATIONAL AND REGIONAL LEVELS

A growing schism between northern and southern political leaders can be seen in the first half of the nineteenth century. Regional economic interests often trumped nationalist interests.

ADAMS'S POST-PRESIDENCY

Most presidents have rather dull retirements. John Quincy Adams did not. He is the only former president to serve in the House of Representatives. He became an outspoken critic of slavery. Other presidents with meaningful careers after their terms in office are William Howard Taft, who became chief justice of the Supreme Court, and Jimmy Carter, who has been active in Habitat for Humanity and issues of war and peace.

Political Divisions During the Jackson Administration

Many of the political divisions that characterized this period emerged in force during the administration of President Andrew Jackson. The years of his presidency (1829–1837), as well as the immediate aftermath, bear the name the Age of Jackson, or the Age of Jacksonian Democracy. Jackson and his supporters were bitter at the results of the election of 1824; they held on to the accusations of a "corrupt bargain" made by President John Quincy Adams with Henry Clay. In the election of 1828, Jackson's supporters painted John Quincy Adams as out-of-touch and elitist, while Adams's supporters portrayed Jackson as ill-tempered. Jackson's backwoods, populist appeal helped him win the election.

The election of 1828 is considered by many historians to be the first modern election. First, the electorate was much broader than in previous elections. In the 1820s most states reduced or removed property qualifications for voting so that most free males had the right to vote. Consequently, candidates had to campaign more aggressively and tailor their appeal to reach a broader audience. Related to the democratization of the voting process was an increased focus on character and personality.

The "Tariff of Abominations"

Tariff rates become an extremely contentious issue in the first half of the nineteenth century. A major controversy around tariff rates occurred during the administration of President Jackson and reflected the intensifying of regional tensions. The controversy originated with the Tariff of 1828, which revised tariff rates on a variety of imports. The act, known by its critics as the Tariff of Abominations, dramatically raised tariff rates on many items, and led to a general reduction in trade between the United States and Europe. This decline in trade hit South Carolina, which depended on cotton exports, especially hard. Congress lowered tariff rates slightly with the Tariff of 1832, but this did not satisfy many southern political leaders.

TARIFFS IN THE 1800s

Though tariff rates do not stir passionate debate today, they were one of the most divisive issues throughout the nineteenth century and into the twentieth century.

Destruction of the Second Bank of the United States

One of the fiercest battles of the Jackson presidency was over the Second Bank of the United States. Jackson revived the criticism of a national bank that had been part of the national discourse since Hamilton had first proposed such an institution in 1791. Despite the fact that the bank was performing its function admirably, Jackson insisted that it put too much power into the hands of a small elite. Jackson's political opponents thought that Jackson's animosity to the bank would hand them a political victory. These opponents brought the issue of rechartering the bank to Congress in 1832, four years before the bank's charter was to expire. They thought that a Jackson veto would weaken his chances for reelection. But Jackson's opponents miscalculated. Jackson did veto the rechartering of the bank. However, the angry class-based rhetoric in his veto message played well with the voters and he won reelection. Jackson, encouraged by his electoral success, was not satisfied to let the bank die its natural death upon its charter running out in 1836. He took actions to kill the "monster" bank immediately. He moved federal deposits from the Bank of the United States to state banks in Democratic-leaning states.

The Specie Circular and the Panic of 1837

Jackson's suspicion of bankers and credit led him to issue the Specie Circular (1836), mandating that government-held land be sold only for hard currency (gold or silver "specie"), not paper currency. The move resulted in a shortage of government funds. Both the destruction of the Second Bank of the United States and the Specie Circular contributed to the economic downturn known as the Panic of 1837.

Regional Divisions and the Slavery Question

The most divisive regional issue in the first half of the nineteenth century was slavery. The issue became especially divisive in the House of Representatives. Beginning in the 1830s, abolitionists agitated to have antislavery resolutions introduced and debated on the floor of the House. Representative John Quincy Adams (who was elected to the House after his tenure as president) was a key House figure in attempting to bring such resolutions to the floor. In response, southern politicians successfully pushed for a series of resolutions that would automatically "table" any such resolutions, preventing them from being read or debated. Such "gag rules" were in effect in the House from 1836 to 1844.

KEY CONCEPT 4.3
EXPANDING BOUNDARIES AND FOREIGN POLICY CONFLICTS

The Unites States pursued a foreign policy around the goals of expanding its boundaries, increasing trade, and isolating itself from European conflicts. These goals were pursued both through government actions and through private initiatives.

1. Trade and Dominance of the Western Hemisphere

During the first half of the nineteenth century, United States foreign policymakers aimed at promoting foreign trade, dominating the territory of North America, and establishing the United States as a global presence.

A. NEW MARKETS AND NEW LANDS

The desire of many Americans to establish new patterns of trade and to acquire new lands and open them up to settlement led to numerous economic, diplomatic, and military initiatives in both the Western Hemisphere and in Asia.

Trade and Territory

The desire of the United States to trade freely throughout the world, across both the Atlantic and Pacific Oceans led to a series of foreign policy actions in the first half of the nineteenth century. Early in the century, the United States struggled to establish favorable trading relationships across the Atlantic; these efforts led to the War of 1812. Later during this period, the United States took actions to open trade with Asia. As the American economy grew in the decades between the War of 1812 and the Civil War, many Americans continued the push farther and farther into the continent. This westward movement had ominous implications for neighboring nations and as well as for American Indian nations within the borders of the growing United States. Finally, the acquisition of additional territory enflamed sectional tensions, as the debate over the expansion of slavery intensified in the decade before the Civil War.

The Barbary Wars, 1801–1805

President Jefferson's first foreign policy crisis involved United States trade with the Middle East. Trade in the Mediterranean was controlled by four North African states—Morocco, Algiers, Tunis, and Tripoli, known as the Barbary states. These states demanded large payments from trading nations as "tribute." Nations that did not comply found their shipping subject to seizure and plundering by Barbary pirates. Merchants during the colonial era enjoyed the protection of Great Britain. When the United States became independent, Presidents Washington and Adams agreed to the terms set by the Barbary states. In 1801, Tripoli demanded a steep increase in payment from the United States. When Jefferson refused, Tripoli declared war on the United States. Jefferson sent warships to the region to engage in fighting and to protect American shipping. The move proved popular. The slogan "Millions for defense, but not a cent for tribute" became popular in America. In the end, the United States did not achieve a decisive victory, but it boosted America's profile on the world stage.

Continued Troubles with European Nations

The conflicts between Great Britain and France that occupied the Washington and Adams administrations reemerged during the administrations of Thomas Jefferson and James Madison. Both Presidents Jefferson and Madison attempted to continue the policy of neutrality that Washington had set forth while at the same time extending foreign trade, sometimes with nations at war with each other. In 1803, Napoleon declared war on Britain. At first, the United States benefited from trading with both warring partners. Soon, both countries tried to block American trade with the other. Great Britain was more aggressive in its efforts to stop American ships. British ships routinely stopped and boarded American ships, often seizing cargo. More irritating still for the Americans was the practice of seizing American seamen and pressing them into service in the British navy. Britain claimed that these men were deserters from the British navy, but most were not. This practice of impressments affected 6,000 American seamen between 1803 and 1812. The situation between the United States and Britain reached a crisis in 1807 when the British ship *Leopard* fired on the American ship *Chesapeake*. Three Americans were killed and four were abducted in the Chesapeake Affair.

"Peaceful Coercion" and Free Trade

As Great Britain continued to interfere with American shipping, Presidents Jefferson and Madison initially chose "peaceful coercion" over war. Jefferson passed the Embargo Act (1807), which cut off U.S. trade to all foreign ports. Jefferson thought that this would pressure the belligerent nations to agree to leave U.S. ships alone. However, the main effect of the embargo was to cripple America's mercantile sector. The embargo proved to be very unpopular, especially in New England, where trade was nearly at a standstill.

President Madison replaced the unpopular Embargo Act (1807) with the Non-intercourse Act of 1809, opening trade with all nations except for Great Britain and France. But this act proved to be almost as unpopular, as Great Britain and France had been two of America's biggest trading partners.

ECONOMIC INDEPENDENCE

The Embargo Act (1807), the Non-intercourse Act (1809), and the War of 1812 (1812–1815) all had the effect of creating demand for American-made goods. The acts proved to be a catalyst for American manufacturing and contributed to the United States becoming more economically self-sufficient.

Macon's Bill No. 2 (1810)

In an attempt to revive trade, Congress passed Macon's Bill No. 2 in 1810. The bill stipulated that if either Great Britain or France agreed to respect America's rights as a neutral nation at sea, the United States would prohibit trade with that nation's enemy. Napoleon agreed to this arrangement, and consequently, the United States cut trade to Britain in 1811. However, Napoleon did not honor his commitment and France continued to seize American ships. The cutting off of trade to Britain worsened relations and pushed the two nations to the edge of war.

War of 1812

Trade conflicts and pressure from the War Hawk congressmen pushed Madison to declare war against Great Britain in 1812. The vote on the war in Congress was divided along sectional lines. New England and some Middle Atlantic states opposed it; the South and West voted for it. The declaration of war occurred just as Britain was making assurances that it would stop interfering with American shipping.

The war lasted two and a half years. Britain achieved several stunning early victories in the war, defeating American forces at Fort Dearborn and Detroit. Madison managed to win reelection in the midst of the war, but the Federalists, who were critical of the war effort, made a strong showing. By 1813, the United States began to achieve some victories in battle. The United States burned the city of York (now Toronto), and won several battles at sea. At the Battle of Thames in Canada, American forces defeated British and American Indian forces and killed the American Indian leader Tecumseh. In one of the stunning episodes of the war, British forces seized and burned Washington, DC, in 1814. The United States achieved a major victory in New Orleans in early 1815, led by General Andrew Jackson. Jackson and his British adversaries had not realized that the United States had already signed a peace treaty, formally ending the war, weeks before in late 1814.

The Treaty of Ghent

The Treaty of Ghent (1814) ended the War of 1812. Britain had grown weary of war after fighting Napoleon for more than a decade and the United States for two years. The United States realized that it could not achieve a decisive victory over Great Britain. The treaty ended the war where it had begun. The two sides agreed to stop fighting, give back any territory seized in the war, and recognize the boundary between the United States and Canada that had been established before the war. The treaty did not mention the specific grievances the United States had against Britain—aid to American Indians, interfering with American shipping, or impressments of American seamen.

Acquiring New Territories: The Louisiana Purchase

President Thomas Jefferson's commitment to reducing the scope of the federal government would soon be tested when the United States was given the opportunity to purchase the vast swath of land beyond the Mississippi River known as the Louisiana Territory. The Louisiana Territory was long held by France until France ceded it to Spain in 1763 following the French and Indian War. France then regained the territory in 1801. The ambitious French leader Napoleon Bonaparte, in need of cash to fund war with Great Britain, was ready to sell the Louisiana Territory at a reasonable price. American negotiators quickly agreed to a price of $15 million.

Jefferson was at first reluctant to approve the deal because the Constitution did not allow for the acquisition of additional lands. Jefferson had long held a strict constructionist view of the Constitution, asserting that the government's power was limited to what was explicitly allowed for in the Constitution. But if Jefferson waited for a constitutional amendment specifically allowing Congress to acquire new lands, Napoleon could rescind his offer. So Jefferson violated his stated principle and quickly presented the offer to Congress, which assented and appropriated the money.

The purchase of the Louisiana Territory was arguably the most significant act of Jefferson's presidency. The purchase was important for two reasons. First, it doubled the size of the United States, adding the fertile Great Plains. This flat area west of the Mississippi would become the most important agricultural region in the United States. Second, the United States gained full control of the port of New Orleans. New Orleans is at the outlet of the mighty Mississippi River, which stretches from Minnesota down the spine of the United States. The impact of the Louisiana Purchase on economic growth was remarkable. Between the 1810s and the 1850s, the value of produce from the interior of the United States received at the port of New Orleans went up more than tenfold.

Annexation of Texas and Tensions with Mexico

After much debate and delay (see below), Texas was annexed by the United States in 1844. This move was an important catalyst for the Mexican-American War (1846–1848) between the United States and Mexico. The Mexican government was furious that Texas had become part of the United States. Meanwhile, President James Polk and American expansionists were eager to incorporate the remainder of Mexico's northern provinces into the United States.

"Fifty-four Forty or Fight:" Negotiating the Oregon Border

Both Great Britain and the United States made historic claims to the lands of the Pacific Northwest. In 1818, the two nations agreed on a "joint occupation" of the Oregon Country. In the 1830s and 1840s, adventurous Americans began traveling west along the Oregon Trail and settling in the lush valley of the Willamette River. In 1844 politicians pushed for sole U.S. ownership of the entire Oregon Country, the northern boundary of which was the north latitude line at 54°40'. "Fifty-four forty or fight" was the rallying call of those who wanted the United States to own the entire territory. Great Britain balked at giving up all the territory. In 1846, the Polk administration reached a compromise with Great Britain establishing the border at the 49th parallel. That line is the current boundary between the United States and Canada.

"Old China Trade"

The United States merchants opened a lucrative trade with China following the American Revolution. The Treaty of Paris (1783) freed American trade from British control. This trade, not officially sanctioned by the United States government, is known as the "Old China Trade." The trade, driven by the American demand for Chinese products, such as tea, porcelain, silk, and nankeen (a coarse cotton cloth), opened new markets to the United States, but also brought to the fore cultural differences between the United States and China. From the American perspective, trade was seen as a basic right and as a means to expand national and personal wealth; it was assumed that other countries would want to also expand their trade for similar reasons. In traditional Chinese thought, however, commerce was looked down upon. Of the four social classes that were described, in ascending order of importance, in Confucian thought—scholars, peasants, artisans, and merchants—merchants were the one class that was seen as superfluous, making profit without producing anything.

Chinese officials did allow trade with foreign countries, but they saw this trade through the lens of tradition—the trade existed by the largess of the emperor in return for tribute paid by states that acknowledged the superior position of China. Trade increased in the nineteenth century as the United States found that furs were in demand in China. These furs were obtained from American Indian groups along the Pacific Coast through the "maritime fur trade," from as far north as Alaska. This trade was carried in increasingly large clipper ships. This unofficial "Old China Trade" ended in 1844. Seeing the growing power of Great Britain in China, the United States worked out the Treaty of Wanghia with China, in which China extended to the United States the same trading privileges that had been extended to Great Britain.

B. MAINTAINING DOMINANCE OVER NORTH AMERICA

United States policies sought to extend dominance over the North American continent through military actions, judicial edicts, and diplomatic efforts.

Nationalist Sentiment and the Monroe Doctrine (1823)

America's newfound confidence on the international stage was evident in President Monroe's foreign policy address to Congress in 1823. The major purpose of the Monroe Doctrine was to limit European influence in the Western Hemisphere. President Monroe was alarmed at threats by the Holy Alliance of Russia, Prussia, and Austria to restore Spain's lost American colonies. He also opposed a decree by the Russian czar that claimed all the Pacific Northwest above the 51st parallel. Though both problems worked themselves out, Monroe issued a statement warning European nations to keep their hands off the Americas. The United States did not have the military might to enforce this pronouncement at the time, but it was an important statement of intent. The Monroe Doctrine and Washington's farewell address became cornerstones of America's isolationist foreign policy.

The Webster-Ashburton Treaty

The United States settled a dispute in 1842 with Great Britain over the border between Maine and British-ruled Canada. The treaty split the disputed territory and also settled a dispute over the border between the Minnesota territory and Canada.

II. Responses to Territorial Expansion and the Growth of National Power

Americans responded to the expansion of territory and of governmental power in a variety of ways, some championing these developments, some resisting them.

A. DEBATES OVER NEW TERRITORIES

As America expanded, public debates ensued over whether the new lands would be free or slave, and what lands would be reserved for American Indians.

The Wilmot Proviso

The issue of slavery in the new territories was one of the most divisive issues of the first half of the nineteenth century and was the catalyst that would eventually plunge the nation into civil war. Americans reached an uneasy truce on the issue with the passage of the Missouri Compromise in 1820 (see page 144). However, the issue came to the fore again as the United States gained additional territory following the Mexican-American War (1846–1848). Northern politicians tried, unsuccessfully, to ban slavery in territories that might be gained in the war by putting forth the Wilmot Proviso (1846). These politicians were not, for the most part, abolitionists, but they believed in the "free soil" ideal. They wanted additional land for white settlers to set up homesteads, without competition from the slave system. The proviso was passed by the House of Representatives, where politicians from the populous northern states dominated, but failed in the Senate.

> ## A DIVIDED CONGRESS
> In the antebellum period, the Senate tended to be friendlier to the slave system than the House. The southern states had more power in the Senate than they did in the population-based House.

"Indian Territory"

As part of the government's Indian removal policy, many American Indian tribes from east of the Mississippi River were relocated to a designated "Indian Territory" that existed within the boundaries of present-day Oklahoma. This establishment of the Indian Territory was part of the Indian Intercourse Act of 1834. Many American Indian groups resisted relocation to the Indian Territory through legal channels and through armed resistance. Once in the Indian Territory, conflicts ensued between American Indian groups indigenous to the area and those relocated there. Eventually this territory was reduced in size and finally it ceased to exist and was folded into the Oklahoma Territory in 1907.

B. STATES' RIGHTS AND NULLIFICATION

On different occasions during the first half of the nineteenth century, political leaders on the state level took steps to resist the assertion of federal power.

The Hartford Convention and Opposition to the War of 1812

The first major challenges to federal policy in the nineteenth century came not from the South but from Federalist politicians in New England. The War of 1812 was unpopular among some Americans, especially among New England merchants, who saw their trade with Great Britain disappear. As diplomats were negotiating the Treaty of Ghent in December 1814, Federalists from New England convened in Hartford, Connecticut, to express their displeasure with the war. Some of the more

> ## TALK OF SECESSION
> The Hartford Convention demonstrated that talk of secession was not restricted to southerners.

radical delegates suggested that New England secede from the union, but this proposal was rejected by the delegates at the convention. The Hartford Convention did pass a resolution calling for a two-thirds vote in Congress for future declarations of war.

John C. Calhoun and the Nullification Crisis

In the 1830s, debates over tariff rates pitted many southern politicians against federal policy. The high tariff rates established by the Tariff Act of 1828 (labeled the "Tariff of Abominations" by its detractors) especially angered southern politicians. By 1832, South Carolina politicians, led by Jackson's former vice president, John C. Calhoun, asserted the right of states to nullify federal legislation. Under this theory of nullification, a state could declare an objectionable law null and void within that state. In actuality, from the early nineteenth century until today, only the Supreme Court can strike down a law if it finds the law to be inconsistent with the

Constitution. Jackson was alarmed at this flaunting of federal authority and challenged the move. He pushed through Congress a bill, called the Force Bill (quickly nullified by the South Carolina legislature), which authorized military force against South Carolina for committing treason. At the same time, Congress revised tariff rates, providing relief for South Carolina. The Force Bill and the new tariff rates, passed by Congress on the same day, amounted to a face-saving compromise. But the issue of states' rights versus federal power would emerge again in the coming decades in regard to the issue of slavery.

C. CONTENTION BETWEEN WHITES AND AMERICAN INDIANS OVER WESTERN LANDS

White settlers and American Indians clashed on the frontier. The enthusiasm of land-hungry settlers was matched by the determination of native peoples to hold on to their traditional lands. These clashes led to wars and to federal efforts to control American Indian groups.

American Indians and the West

Westward settlers were continuing in the footsteps of early colonists—pushing into the interior of the continent and antagonizing American Indians in the process. In the early 1800s, white Americans were pouring into the Ohio River valley, which included the state of Ohio (1803) and the Indiana territory. Federal and state officials had extracted land agreements from American Indians for years. It was never clear if the American Indians who made the agreements had the authority to do so, nor was it clear that white settlers would live by these agreements. In 1809, the governor of the Indiana territory, William Henry Harrison, negotiated the Treaty of Fort Wayne. American Indians agreed to cede three million acres at a nominal fee. The most important regional American Indian leader at the time, Tecumseh, was not present for this agreement. He was on a trip recruiting American Indians to resist encroachments by white settlers. He and his brother, Tenskwatawa, "the Prophet," had been organizing a spiritual and political front, attempting to unite all the Indian nations east of the Mississippi River.

WAR HAWKS

The War Hawks tended to hail from western and southern states.

Battle of Tippecanoe and the War Hawks

Settlers in the Indiana territory persuaded Harrison to wage war against Tecumseh's confederation. The Battle of Tippecanoe (1811) ousted members of the confederacy and was perceived as an American victory. Western congressmen, who became known as the War Hawks, became convinced that Britain was encouraging and funding Tecumseh's confederation. Just as relations with Britain were deteriorating over trade issues, these War Hawks, led by Henry Clay of Kentucky and John C. Calhoun from South Carolina, were pushing for military action against the British. Such action, it was thought, would allow the United States to eliminate the American Indian threat and, perhaps, allow the United States to move into Canada. This pro-war sentiment in the West was one of the causes of the War of 1812.

Indian Removal Act (1830)

As the profitability of cotton production rose in the South in the first half of the nineteenth century, the value of land increased dramatically. Many whites wanted to push west and others wished to acquire land in the interior of the South. Much of the southern territory was the traditional lands of the "Five Civilized Tribes"—Cherokee, Chickasaw, Choctaw, Muscogee-Creek, and Seminole. As far back as the Jefferson administration, Federal policy had been to respect the rights of American Indians to inhabit this land. President Andrew Jackson, however, abandoned this policy and, in deference to market pressures and the call of white southerners to expand, adopted a policy of Indian removal. This policy applied to the American Indians of the South as well as the old Northwest, and, to a lesser degree, New England and New York. Jackson asserted that it was necessary for these American Indians to be removed to the areas of the United States beyond the Mississippi River. He said, perhaps disingenuously, that this was in the best interests of the Indians themselves, who were being subsumed by the encroachment of white settlers. He pushed for the Removal Act of 1830.

The "Trail of Tears"

The state of Georgia, with the support of President Jackson and then Jackson's successor, President Martin Van Buren, initiated the process of moving American Indians to the West despite the Supreme Court decision in *Worcester v. Georgia* (1832) declaring that American Indian tribes were subject to federal treaties not to the actions of states. The decision, in effect, voided Georgia's efforts to remove the Cherokee. President Jackson purportedly said, "John Marshall has made his decision. Now let him enforce it." By 1838, the Cherokees had exhausted their legal and political challenges to removal. Some cooperated with removal and ceded their lands. However, the majority, led by the Cherokee "principal chief," John Ross, adopted a policy of passive resistance to remain on their land. Federal troops were dispatched to enforce Georgia's removal policy. The resulting expulsion of 18,000 American Indians to the Oklahoma territory, labeled the Trail of Tears (1838), resulted in the deaths of approximately a quarter of the Indians on the journey.

American Indians and Florida

Americans, especially white southerners, had a long history of conflict with American Indians in Florida. Florida had long been Spanish territory. It was ceded to Great Britain in 1763 following the French and Indian War and was given back to Spain in the Treaty of Paris (1783) following the American Revolution. In the late 1700s and early 1800s, white southerners grew frustrated with the number of escaped slaves who made their way into Florida. These fugitives were often given protection by American Indians in Florida. This concern led to raids by southern whites into Florida, followed by counterraids by Seminoles and other American Indians on communities in Georgia and Alabama.

> ### CUBA AND THE UNITED STATES
>
> Cuba, ninety miles off the coast of Florida, has loomed large in American diplomatic history from the French and Indian War, through the Ostend Manifesto, the Spanish-American War, and the age of Fidel Castro.

These hostilities led to the first Seminole War, which began during the War of 1812 and continued to the end of the decade. A second Seminole War occurred in the 1830s. Florida had come into American hands as a result of the Adams–Onis Treaty (1819). By the 1830s, the Seminole were being pressured by the federal government to relocate to the West. In the Second Seminole War (1835–1842), Seminole warriors fought United States troops to a standstill in the Everglades. Many Seminoles remained defiant of government removal efforts even after the capture of the Seminole leader, Chief Osceola.

III. Debate over the Extension of Slavery

As the United States acquired new territories, Americans debated whether these new lands should allow slavery or not. Attempts at compromise were made in the first half of the nineteenth century, with mixed results.

A. A TEMPORARY TRUCE ON THE SLAVERY QUESTION

The Missouri Compromise (1820) created a temporary, uneasy truce over slavery in new territories. As the United States gained additional territories, this truce broke down.

The Missouri Compromise

The "Era of Good Feelings" (1816–1825) was not free of disagreements and sectional competition. The issue of slavery, which most politicians sought to avoid, emerged in 1820. Controversy arose between the slave-holding states and the free states in 1820 when Missouri applied for statehood as a slave state. At the time, there were eleven slave and eleven free states. The admission of Missouri would have upset that balance. A compromise was reached to maintain the balance between free and slave states by allowing for the admission of two new states—Missouri as a slave state and Maine as a free state. The Missouri Compromise also divided the remaining area of the Louisiana Territory at 36°30′ north latitude. Above that line, slavery was not permitted (except in Missouri); below the line, it was permitted. In the 1850s, as white Americans continued to expand into the territories of the West, debates over the slavery question would continue to roil the nation.

B. SLAVERY AND DEBATES OVER ITS FUTURE MOVE WEST

As cotton became increasingly profitable in the first half of the nineteenth century, growers often depleted the soil through overcultivation. As a result, cotton growers sought new lands in the new Southwest, intensifying sectional controversy over the extension of slavery.

Annexation of Texas and the Politics of Slavery

As early as the 1820s, white Americans began moving into the Mexican territory of Texas. Many of these settlers were southern whites who hoped to duplicate the plantation model from the Old South in Texas. The introduction of slavery into Texas caused friction with the government, contributing to the movement for Texas independence. After two years of fighting, Texas achieved independence, forming the Republic of Texas in 1836.

Many Texans were eager for their Lone Star Republic, as the Republic of Texas was known, to join the United States; one of the first official acts of the Texas president was to send a delegation to Washington to offer to join the United States. Democratic President Andrew Jackson, however, not wanting to add to sectional tensions by admitting a large slave state, blocked annexation. His successors likewise did not want to open the contentious debate that would accompany Texas annexation. The Democrat Martin Van Buren (1837–1841), and the Whig presidents William Henry Harrison (1841) and John Tyler (1841–1845) all avoided the issues.

The Election of 1844 and the Annexation of Texas

The election of 1844 put the issue of Texas annexation on the national agenda. Democratic candidate James K. Polk promised to push for Texas annexation as well as a resolution of a border dispute with Great Britain over Oregon, offering something to both southern and northern voters. By 1844, the Democrats were clearly emerging as more expansionistic and more proslavery than the Whigs. Polk defeated the incumbent president Tyler. Even before Polk took office, the outgoing President Tyler saw Polk's victory as a mandate for Texas annexation and pushed it through Congress. Texas joined the United States as the fifteenth slave state in 1844. The issues raised by the annexation of Texas would reemerge in the aftermath of the Mexican-American War and assume a prominent place in the political schisms of the 1850s.

SUBJECT TO DEBATE

Historians have debated the nature of the "Era of Good Feelings." Consensus historians—those who deemphasize divisions in American history and focus on national commonalities—look to the era as a golden age of cooperation and growth. Other historians have noted the beginnings of divisions over the issue of slavery. These divisions were evident in the debates over the Missouri Compromise. Other historians have focused on class divisions that began to emerge in the United States as the old master-apprentice system gave way to the wage-labor system that came to dominate the economy by the post–Civil War period.

The fortunes of the memory of Andrew Jackson have risen and fallen repeatedly in the nearly two centuries since his presidency. Jackson has been a frequent topic of free-response questions on the AP exam—an understanding of how he has been remembered will be useful in discussions of the period. Early on, in the latter part of the nineteenth century, he was scoffed at in historical literature. Historians of the era were from the elite classes of New England. To them, Jackson seemed boorish, arrogant, ignorant, and authoritarian. By the early twentieth century, Progressive-era historians influenced by Frederick Jackson Turner's frontier thesis looked more favorably upon Jackson. Turner saw the experience of the frontier as central to the shaping of the American character. The image of frontier pioneers became part of popular culture just as Americans were becoming more urban and more settled. Americans developed a sense of nostalgia for the pioneers, as is evident in the popularity of Laura Ingalls Wilder's *Little House on the Prairie* books. In this cultural moment, Jackson was rehabilitated. He was a man of the pioneer and brought that democratic, pioneer spirit with him to the White House.

More recently, the historical memory of Jackson has again taken a turn for the worse. From the 1960s onward, more recent historians have drawn unfavorable parallels between Jackson's expansionistic impulses and American foreign adventures abroad, from Vietnam to Iraq. Further, since the 1970s many Americans have become more attuned to the historical suffering of American Indians. In this context, the Indian Removal Act and the "Trail of Tears" began to loom large in the historical memory of the Jackson administration.

The economic and social transformations of the antebellum period have become important topics in historical work recently. Social historians have become more interested in the lives of workers, women, American Indians, families on the frontier, and slaves than in the policies and acts of presidents. These social historians, active in the field since the 1970s, have done much to topple the "great, white men" from their pedestals in the historical field. In place of laws, speeches, and treaties, social historians look at letters, diaries, census records, and court records to get a better sense of what life was like for ordinary Americans. This is not to say that political history is no longer relevant or important; it is, both in the history field at large and on the AP exam. However, do not ignore the advances made in the field of social history. Be aware of the important social groups of each era and the impact they had on history.

Historians have disagreed over the nature of the reform movements in the antebellum period. Some have focused on the democratic and egalitarian impulses of the movement. The women's rights movement and the abolitionist movement certainly were attempts to push America in a more democratic direction. However, other historians have focused on the more judgmental, restrictive nature of the reform movement. One can see some of the Puritan dogma still present in the antebellum period. The temperance movement reflects the more restrictive aspect of the movement. The push for public education can be seen in both lights. One the one hand, it embodies the democratic spirit of providing free education to all—a prerequisite for meaningful participation in the democratic process. At the same time, the lessons and the rote learning were meant to reinforce a rigid set of middle-class Protestant values.

History textbooks implicitly grapple with a major issue of interpretation—how should the expansion of the United States be discussed. Territorial expansion at the expense of indigenous people and neighboring nations would, when done elsewhere, generally win the disfavor of textbook writers. These books, for instance, might discuss the arrogance of Napoleon's actions or the brutality of Japanese expansion in Asia in the 1930s. By contrast, the era of Manifest Destiny is often shrouded in the language of idealism, democracy, adventure, and optimism. Perhaps this is understandable, but historical interpretation, to be taken seriously, should try to maintain fair and consistent criteria in evaluating parallel actions committed by different nations.

Practice Multiple-Choice Questions

Directions: Pick the letter that best answers the following questions.

QUESTIONS 1–3 REFER TO THE FOLLOWING PASSAGE:

"From whence originated the idea, that it was derogatory to a lady's dignity, or a blot upon the female character, to labor? and who was the first to say, sneeringly, 'Oh, she works for a living'? Surely, such ideas and expressions ought not to grow on republican soil. The time has been, when ladies of the first rank were accustomed to busy themselves in domestic employment.

"Homer tells us of princesses who used to draw water from the springs, and wash with their own hands the finest of the linen of their respective families. The famous Lucretia used to spin in the midst of her attendants; and the wife of Ulysses, after the siege of Troy, employed her self in weaving, until her husband returned to Ithaca. And in later times, the wife of George the Third of England, has been represented as spending a whole evening in hemming pocket-handkerchiefs, while her daughter Mary sat in the corner, darning stockings.

"Few American fortunes will support a woman who is above the calls of her family; and a man of sense, in choosing a companion to jog with him through all the up-hills and down-hills of life, would sooner choose one who had to work for a living, than one who thought it beneath her to soil her pretty hands with manual labor, although she possessed her thousands. To be able to earn one's own living by laboring with the

hands, should be reckoned among female accomplishments; and I hope the time is not far distant when none of my countrywomen will be ashamed to have it known that they are better versed in useful, than they are in ornamental accomplishments."
—"Dignity of Labor," the *Lowell* [Massachusetts] *Offering*, 1842

1. The essay from the *Lowell Offering*, quoted above, describes the physical labors performed by important women—princesses in the time of Homer, the Roman noblewoman Lucretia, the wife of Ulysses, and the daughter of King George III of Great Britain—in order to

   (A) demonstrate the long history of women being treated as second-class citizens.
   (B) assure poor women that hard work and dedication were the keys to advancement to a higher status.
   (C) differentiate the emerging American culture from the corrupt traditions of Europe.
   (D) convince middle-class men and women that they should not look down upon women performing physical work.

2. The contributors to the *Lowell Offering* were

   (A) New England abolitionists who participated in the Second Great Awakening.
   (B) "factory operatives" at the textile mills in Lowell, Massachusetts, during the early stages of American industrialization.
   (C) Transcendentalist writers who lived at the Brook Farm utopian community.
   (D) African-American women who gained their freedom following the gradual elimination of slavery in Massachusetts.

3. The reading from the *Lowell Offering* reflects which of the following historical developments?

   (A) The popularity of the "Arts and Crafts" movement, which sought to revive traditional artisan techniques
   (B) The cultural shift that allowed for women to replace men in offices, as typists, accountants, and receptionists
   (C) The increasing number of Americans who made their living producing goods for foreign markets rather than relying on semi-subsistence agriculture
   (D) The movement to encourage society to see women's work in the home as actual labor that contributed to the social good

Answers and Explanations to Multiple-Choice Questions

1. **(D)** The main point of the essay in the *Lowell Offering* is that there is dignity in productive work. The writer is citing the long history of important women performing physical tasks in order to convince middle-class men and women that there is nothing inappropriate about women working. Many members of the middle class subscribed to a set of cultural ideas known as the "cult of domesticity," which insisted that women keep a proper, Christian home—separate from the male sphere of politics, business, and competition. This ideal discouraged women from participating in public life.

2. **(B)** The contributors to the *Lowell Offering* were "factory operatives" at the textile mills in Lowell, Massachusetts, during the early stages of industry in the United States. Starting in 1821 a series of textile mills were built in Lowell, Massachusetts, drawing in young women from the New England countryside to operate the machines. It was thought that these women could be paid less and would only be temporary factory operatives. The era of mass migration from Europe had not yet begun, so it was difficult to recruit male factory operatives. By 1830, eight mills employed more than 6,000 women.

3. **(C)** The reading from the *Lowell Offering* reflects the increasing number of women, as well as men, who were making the transition from semi-subsistence agriculture to production for distant markets. This was a key aspect of the market revolution. Although much of this work was done in factories, many people performed piecework at home as part of the "putting-out system," in which men and women would perform a particular task as part of a larger operation—such as making shoes or small firearms.

Period 5: 1844–1877 Slavery, Civil War, and the Transformation of American Society

7

TIMELINE

1848	Treaty of Guadalupe Hidalgo ends the Mexican-American War
1850	Compromise of 1850
1852	Publication of *Uncle Tom's Cabin*, by Harriet Beecher Stowe
1856	Beginning of "Bleeding Kansas"
	The beating of Senator Charles Sumner
1857	*Dred Scott v. Sanford* decision
1859	John Brown's raid on Harper's Ferry arsenal
1860	Election of President Abraham Lincoln
	South Carolina secedes from the United States
1861	Inauguration of Lincoln
	Six more states, all from the Deep South, secede
	Fighting at Fort Sumter
	Four more states, from the upper South, secede
	First Confiscation Act
1862	Homestead Act
	Morrill Land Grant Act
	Second Confiscation Act
1863	The Emancipation Proclamation goes into effect
	The draft is introduced in the North
	New York City Draft Riots
	Prize cases
1864	Sherman's March to the Sea
1865	Freedman's Bureau is established
	Thirteenth Amendment is ratified
	Lincoln is assassinated
	Southern states begin to pass Black Codes
	Beginning of Great Sioux War
1866	Civil Rights Act passed
	Ku Klux Klan is formed
	Ex parte Milligan
1867	Reconstruction Acts passed; beginning of Congressional Reconstruction
	Tenure of Office Act

1868	Johnson is impeached
	Fourteenth Amendment is ratified
1870	Fifteenth Amendment is ratified
1875	Civil Rights Act
1876	Disputed election between Samuel J. Tilden (Democrat) and Rutherford B. Hayes (Republican)
	Custer's Last Stand
1877	Agreement ends Reconstruction; Hayes becomes president

INTRODUCTION

As the United States expanded its borders, its economy, and its population, regional tensions—most notably over slavery—led to a civil war. The war and its aftermath dramatically transformed American society.

The acquisition and settlement of new territories in the western half of the North American continent opened up a question that politicians had sought to avoid—should these new territories allow slavery? Most northern politicians were not abolitionists; indeed, abolitionism was a minority position in the North in 1850. However, the issue of the expansion of slavery became increasingly divisive in the 1850s. Some northerners adopted the free-soil ethos—the idea that lands out West should be open to small-scale farming, without competition from large-scale plantation agriculture using slave labor. By the end of the decade, more northerners were grappling with the moral issues around slavery. Positions became decidedly more entrenched on the eve of the Civil War.

The importance of the Civil War to American history cannot be overstated. The bloody war settled one of the most vexing issues in American history—the existence of slavery in an otherwise democratic country—and opened up space for broad debates about the substance of democracy in post–Civil War America.

KEY CONCEPT 5.1
THE UNITED STATES AND GLOBAL CONNECTIONS

The United States became more connected with the world during the period immediately before and after the Civil War. The United States pursued an expansionistic foreign policy within the Western Hemisphere while also becoming a primary destination for immigrants from other countries.

I. Territorial Expansion Shapes the National Debate

The drive for the United States to expand west had several causes. Many Americans came to believe that the economic growth and security of the United States depended on expansion. The drive to expand was also fueled by a set of beliefs around race and culture that saw non-whites in an inferior light. The desire for more territory resulted in war, new markets, the acquisition of territory stretching to the Pacific Ocean, and intense ideological conflicts.

A. "MANIFEST DESTINY": THE CAUSES AND EFFECTS OF WESTWARD EXPANSION

Many Americans came to believe that it was the "manifest destiny" of the United States to expand westward and extend its power in the Western Hemisphere. This idea was based on a belief in the cultural and racial superiority of white Americans. The idea of manifest destiny shaped much of the political debates of the era.

Manifest Destiny and the Movement West

Manifest destiny alluded to the political extension of United States territory, but it also referred to the movement of individuals to newly acquired lands. The term *manifest destiny* was coined in an 1845 newspaper article by John O'Sullivan. It captured the fervor of the westward expansion movement, implying that it was God's plan that the United States take over and settle the entire continent. Americans who did settle out West were probably driven more by economic factors, such as cheap land or precious metals, than they were by a desire to fulfill a divine plan. The spirit of manifest destiny embodied and reinforced contemporary notions of race. The movement west was seen as proof of the superiority of the so-called Anglo-Saxon race over the "savage tribes" of the West. The conquest of Mexico (see below) was seen as a victory by liberty-loving Protestants over tyrannical and anti-republican Catholics.

War with Mexico

The immediate cause of the Mexican-American War was a border dispute. Mexico and the United States disagreed over the southern border of the new United States territory of Texas. Texas had recently (1844) been annexed by the United States (see Period 4). Mexico said the border was at the Nueces River. The United States insisted it was at the Rio Grande, 150 miles to the south. In 1846, skirmishes in the disputed area led to war between Mexico and the United States.

Victory over Mexico on the Battlefield

The United States won several early battles in the war. One prong of the war, in the area of Mexico south of Texas, was led by General Zachary Taylor. United States forces also won victories in present-day California. However, Mexico was very reluctant to part with its northern provinces after having lost Texas. It took an attack on the Mexican capital, Mexico City, led by General Winfield Scott, to force the Mexican government to capitulate.

The Treaty of Guadalupe Hidalgo

In 1848, the Mexican government signed the Treaty of Guadalupe Hidalgo, giving up its claims to the disputed territory in Texas and agreeing to sell the provinces of California and New Mexico, known as the Mexican Cession, to the United States for $15 million. This territory includes present-day California, Nevada, Utah, and parts of Arizona, New Mexico, Colorado, and Wyoming.

Gadsden Purchase

The final land acquisition in what would become the continental United States was the Gadsden Purchase, acquired from Mexico in 1853, five years after the Mexican War. It added an additional area to the vast swath of land obtained by the United States following the war. The Gadsden Purchase was sought by the United States as a possible southern route for a transcontinental railroad.

Cuba and the Ostend Manifesto

For many expansionists, the manifest destiny of the United States did not stop at the Pacific. Southern expansionists hoped to extend their slavery empire farther south. Cuba, with its profitable sugar plantations, came into their sights in the 1850s. President Polk offered to purchase it from Spain. When Spain balked, some American adventurers tried to take it by force. American diplomats, sent by pro-southern president Franklin Pierce to Ostend, Belgium, again tried to secretly buy Cuba. Their goals, written up as the Ostend Manifesto (1854), provoked anger from northern politicians when the document was released to the press.

B. DEBATES OVER NEWLY ACQUIRED LANDS

The Mexican-American War resulted in the United States gaining a large part of northern Mexico. The debate over slavery became increasingly fractious in the wake of the American acquisition of the Mexican Cession.

The Aftermath of the Mexican-American War

The Treaty of Guadalupe Hidalgo (1848) following the Mexican-American War granted the United States a huge portion of Mexico for a mere $15 million. Very soon after, gold was discovered in California, leading to a rapid and substantial growth in the population. The question of whether the newly acquired territories would be admitted as free or slave states became a pressing issue in the years following the war. The Wilmot Proviso (introduced in 1846), banning slavery from the Mexican Cession, never became law (see Period 4).

Popular Sovereignty

Senator Lewis Cass proposed a compromise measure on the question of slavery in the newly acquired territories. He came up with the idea that the question of slavery should be left to the people of a particular territory. This idea became known as *popular sovereignty*, and though Congress failed to act on his idea, popular sovereignty became an important issue in the 1850s.

The Election of 1848

In the election of 1848, both the Whigs and the Democrats avoided taking strong stands on the issue of slavery. Cass was the Democratic candidate, but he lost to Whig candidate Zachary Taylor, one of the heroes of the Mexican-American War. In response to the marked silence on the part of the major parties on the slavery question, antislavery men in both parties founded the Free-Soil Party in 1848.

C. WESTWARD EXPANSION AND AMERICAN INDIANS

Economic activities and the desire for raw materials pushed Americans farther west, resulting in environmental transformations and settlement on lands taken from American Indians.

American Indians in California

In the aftermath of the Mexican-American War (1846–1848), the migration of white Americans to California had devastating effects on American Indians. The Indian population of California dropped from about 150,000 in 1848, on the eve of the gold rush, to less than 30,000 by the beginning of the Civil War (see more on the gold rush, page 154). California Indians were often portrayed as degenerate, primitive, and idle. Disease took the lives of thousands of American Indians, but systematic campaigns of extermination by white settlers against the native peoples of California contributed to what many historians label a genocide. The federal government greatly reduced the size of reservations set aside for American Indians in California in 1853. In addition, farmers were eager to exploit the labor of Indians. When the framers of the California constitution prohibited slavery, they had black slavery, not Indian slavery, in mind. As the 1850s progressed, thousands of Indians were either murdered or enslaved. The Yuki people of Round Valley in northern California were viciously targeted; their population fell from over 5,000 in 1854 to approximately 300 a decade later. Several Indian groups simply ceased to exist, with their people either killed or dispersed.

> ## "INDIAN WARS"
>
> Historians discuss the "Indian Wars" as occurring during the post–Civil War years, but violence between whites and American Indians had been happening since the early days of the Jamestown colony. The fighting had moved farther west, generally on the frontier of white settlements.

D. ECONOMIC EXPANSION BEYOND THE WESTERN HEMISPHERE: THE UNITED STATES AND ASIA

American economic interests included opening up trade to Asia. The United States initiated economic, cultural, and diplomatic ventures toward this end.

Opening Trade with Japan

With the growth of the economy and with the acquisition of West Coast ports, the United States became increasingly interested in trading with Japan. The Tokugawa shogunate (1600–1868) had virtually isolated Japan from Western countries since the seventeenth century. It had allowed for limited trade with the Netherlands and with China. The Tokugawa government repeatedly resisted, occasionally by force, attempts by Americans and Europeans to establish business and diplomatic ties. The United States was determined to alter this policy and open Japan to American trade. With a letter from President Millard Fillmore, Commodore Matthew C. Perry led a naval expedition to Japan. The first journey was in 1852–1853 and a second occurred in 1854. Perry, through vague threats and skillful diplomacy, was able to secure a treaty with Japan that opened Japan up to American trade.

II. Expansion, Migrations, and the End of Slavery

The United States experienced profound transformations in the middle decades of the nineteenth century as a result of westward expansion, new migration patterns, and the end of slavery. As the boundaries of the nation were reshaped, conflicts ensued over the cultural identity of the nation. Americans debated questions of citizenship and rights for various groups of United States inhabitants.

A. IMMIGRATION INTO THE UNITED STATES

Large numbers of immigrants entered the United States before the Civil War. Many of these groups lived in ethnic communities and retained the religions, languages, and customs of the "old world." In response, many Americans developed antagonistic feelings toward new immigrant groups and attempted to limit their rights and their cultural influence.

The Five Points

Large-scale immigration from Ireland in the antebellum period transformed American cities and contributed to a strong nativist movement (see more on the Irish migration in period 4). The largest destination for Irish immigrants in the United States was the Five Points neighborhood of New York City. It was one of the most desperate urban slums in the western world in the mid-nineteenth century, comparable to London's East End. The neighborhood was certainly the worst in the United States in terms of density, disease, infant and child mortality, unemployment, prostitution, and violent crime. At the same time, the neighborhood could be seen as the original American melting pot, combining elements of the African-American community (especially as slavery gradually ended in New York in the period up to 1827) and the Irish community. Irish immigrants and African Americans, and smaller numbers of other immigrant groups, worked side-by-side, lived in the same boarding houses, intermarried, and danced and sang together at dancehalls and saloons. Intermarriages were prevalent enough that the census added the category "mulatto" to the 1850 census. At the same time, tensions existed between the two groups. These tensions came to the surface in the draft riots during the Civil War (see page 156). This cultural race-mixing combined with bitter racism became an important element of American identity into the twentieth century.

> ### NATIVISM OVER TIME
>
> Anti-immigrant sentiment has surfaced several times in American history, usually targeting the most recent immigrant: Irish immigrants in the 1850s; Chinese immigrants in the 1880s; the "new immigrants" of eastern and southern Europe at the turn of the twentieth century; and Latino immigrants in the twenty-first century.

The "Know-Nothings" and the Rise of Nativism

The defining issue of the Know-Nothing party was opposition to immigration. The party was the political wing of a growing anti-Catholic, anti-Irish nativist movement that gained traction in the wake of the large-scale Irish immigration of the late 1840s and 1850s. The Know-Nothing Party (formally known as the American Party) emerged in the 1840s and, by the 1850s, achieved electoral success in several states, especially in the Northeast.

B. WESTERN MIGRATIONS

A variety of peoples—white, African American, Asian—were drawn to the West by economic opportunities or to escape religious persecution. The federal government created legislation designed to promote westward migration

The California Gold Rush

The Gold Rush began when gold was discovered at Sutter's Mill in Coloma, California, in 1848. That year, California became United States territory as a result of the Mexican War (see page 151). As word spread, thousands of people came to California to try to strike it rich. A large percentage of the 300,000 people who migrated to California came in 1849, thus their nickname "forty-niners." A few people did strike it rich. But very soon, the easily accessible gold was panned from riverbeds. To get access to gold beneath the surface, capital-intensive methods were required. This expensive machinery was beyond the reach of ordinary prospectors.

The Mormon Exodus

In 1847, the Church of the Latter-Day Saints, the religious group known as the Mormons, settled along the banks of the Great Salt Lake in Utah. The land at the time was Mexican territory. When the Mormons arrived, the Mexican War had already begun. After the United States victory in the war (1848), Utah and the remainder of the Mexican Cession territory became United States territory. The Mormons ended up in Utah after suffering persecution in more populated areas.

The Homestead Act

The government encouraged development of the West by passing the Homestead Act (1862), which provided free land in the region to settlers who were willing to farm it. The Homestead Act reflected the "free labor" ideal of the Republicans. With the absence of Democrats from Congress during the Civil War, the Republican Party was able to pass several pieces of legislation that reflected their vision of America. Hundreds of thousands of people applied for and were granted homesteads. Many of these homesteaders did not have extensive farming skills and went bankrupt. Increasingly, by the late 1800s, it became difficult for small farmers, even competent ones, to compete with large-scale agricultural operations.

C. EXPANSION AND CONFLICT ON THE FRONTIER

Western expansion led to conflicts on the frontier with American Indians and with Hispanics. As the boundaries of the United States changed and as migrants pushed west, conflicts ensued over the control of land. These conflicts played an important role in changing the cultures and lifeways of the groups involved. Finally, questions emerged about the legal status of these groups.

Expansion and Violence on the Frontier

The period between the 1850 and the turn of the twentieth century saw the last large-scale military conflicts between the United States and American Indian groups. These wars resulted in defeat for American Indians, as the last autonomous American Indian groups came under the control of the U.S. government. By the 1850s, settlers were pushing beyond the Mississippi River in large numbers. Many were headed to the West Coast, following the annexation of the lush agricultural lands of the Oregon territory (1848) and the discovery of gold in California (1848). However, the trails west went right through American Indian lands, creating tension and conflict.

The Treaty of Fort Laramie

In 1851, the United States government and more than ten thousand Plains Indians came together in Fort Laramie in Wyoming and came to an agreement that American Indians would provide a corridor for the passage of wagon trains to the West. In exchange, the United States government promised that the remainder of American Indian lands in the West would not be encroached upon.

The Great Sioux Uprising (1862)

White settlers refused to honor the Treaty of Fort Laramie. In 1862, Sioux Indians, led by Chief Little Crow, challenged white encroachments onto their lands. The Sioux ended up killing more than a thousand settlers before being defeated by the military.

The Sand Creek Massacre (1864)

In 1864, Colonel John M. Chivington led an American attack upon a Cheyenne village, killing 270, mostly women and children. Chivington ignored the villagers' surrender flags.

KEY CONCEPT 5.2
EXPANSION, REGIONAL DIVISIONS, AND CIVIL WAR

The debate over slavery intensified as America expanded its boundaries westward. This debate, coupled with regional divisions over economic, political, and cultural issues, contributed to the onset of the Civil War.

I. Increased Sectional Divisions in the 1840s and 1850s

Sectional divisions between the North and the South intensified in the decade leading up to the Civil War. These divisions resulted from the ideological debates around slavery, along with regional economic and demographic changes. The status of slavery in new territories brought these debates to the surface.

A. ECONOMIC DIFFERENCES BETWEEN THE NORTH AND THE SOUTH

The economies of the North and South were moving in different directions in the period leading up to the Civil War. The economy of the North was increasingly focused on a free-labor model, with manufacturing at its base; the economy of the South was increasingly dependent on a slave-labor, agricultural economy. The population of the North grew rapidly during this period while the South's population growth was slow.

B. ABOLITIONISM IN THE 1850s—STRATEGIES AND TACTICS

The abolitionist campaign became increasingly visible and vocal in the 1850s. Abolitionists debated the most effective strategies and tactics. Some abolitionists relied on the written word and forceful arguments against the institution of slavery. Others helped fugitive slaves make their way north. A small minority advocated using violence to achieve their goals.

The Fugitive Slave Act and Personal Liberty Laws

Many northerners grew alarmed at the enforcement of the Fugitive Slave Act. Previously, the majority of northerners could ignore the brutality of the slave system, but following 1850, slave catchers brought the system to the streets of northern cities. In response, many northern states passed "personal liberty laws" offering protection to fugitives. Many whites and free African Americans in northern cities even formed vigilance committees to prevent the slave catchers from carrying out their orders. The Supreme Court protected slave-catchers from state restrictions on their activities. In *Prigg v. Pennsylvania*, the Court overturned the abduction conviction of Edward Prigg, a slave-catcher, on the grounds that federal law—the Constitution itself and the Fugitive Slave Law of 1793—was superior to state law. This approach was reinforced by the decision in *Ableman v. Booth* (1859). In this case the Court overturned a Wisconsin Supreme Court ruling. The Wisconsin court had ruled that Sherman Booth, who had interfered with the carrying out of the 1850 Fugitive Slave Act, was not guilty; it declared the act itself unconstitutional. The United States Supreme Court reversed this decision, asserting the supremacy of federal court decisions over state courts.

Uncle Tom's Cabin

Sectional tensions were further enflamed by the publication in 1852 of the novel *Uncle Tom's Cabin*. The novel, written by Harriet Beecher Stowe of the antislavery Beecher family, depicted in graphic and sentimental detail, the brutality of slavery. For many northerners, slavery now had a human face. The novel outraged southern supporters of slavery, who attempted to ban it.

John Brown and the Raid on Harper's Ferry

In the fall of 1859, John Brown carried out a raid on an armory in Harper's Ferry, Virginia (now West Virginia) that pushed North–South relations to the breaking point. Brown, with ties to many of the leading abolitionists of the day, including Frederick Douglass, planned to recruit a small group of men to overtake the armory, and then to distribute the weapons inside to slaves. Brown believed that this would initiate a massive slave rebellion that would topple slavery. The men managed to overtake the armory, but were soon overwhelmed by reinforcements. Brown was tried and executed later in 1859.

Although the event did not accomplish its stated goal, its impact on history is undeniable. It convinced proslavery southerners that there was a conspiracy afoot among northerners to violently interfere with the institution of slavery. The truth of the matter was that Brown's raid was roundly condemned by most northern politicians, but the perception of a united front among northerners persisted in the mind of the South.

WAS JOHN BROWN INSANE?

Be careful about referring to John Brown as "crazy" or "wild" or "insane." There is not strong evidence to support such a claim. His lawyer claimed he was insane in court, but that was to prevent Brown from getting the death sentence. Brown protested his lawyer's tactics. It's safe to say that Brown was deeply religious and committed to the antislavery cause.

C. THE SOUTHERN RESPONSE TO THE SLAVERY QUESTION

In the decade before the Civil War, white southerners defended slavery as a "positive good." This defense of slavery was accompanied by racist stereotyping of African Americans. The defense of slavery went hand-in-hand with a defense of states' rights and with the theory of nullification.

Racism and the Defense of Slavery

In the first half of the nineteenth century, the defense of slavery shifted. From the revolutionary era into the nineteenth century, white southerners often defended slavery as a "necessary evil." Thomas Jefferson likened the institution to holding a "wolf by the ear," acknowledging that slavery was an evil, but asserting that its end would have dire consequences. John C.

Calhoun dismissed this older description of slavery as a "moral and political evil"; he labeled such views as "folly and delusion." By the middle of the nineteenth century, southern whites, influenced by writers such as George Fitzhugh, asserted that slavery was actually a "positive good" (see Period 4). By the 1850s, these arguments proliferated and shaped cultural and religious practices in the South.

Racist ideas were also reflected in the rise in popularity of minstrel shows. Minstrel shows have a long tradition in American history. They generally consisted of whites (and occasionally blacks) performing variety shows in blackface. The shows included skits, jokes, music, singing, and dancing. Minstrel shows presented racist caricatures of African Americans as lazy, shiftless, dim-witted, and happy-go-lucky. By the 1850s the culture of minstrelsy evolved and grew—many historians see this evolution as a conscious rebuttal to abolitionist agitation. Minstrelsy in the 1850s often featured the characters of homesick former slaves or ridiculous northern dandies. Representations of blacks became increasingly vicious— with black characters cooked or hunted or fished for. The shows were not restricted to the South—they reflected a broader sentiment among American whites in regard to race. Some white southerners actually objected to the shows because they brought the issues of race and slavery to the fore. The shows, however, remained popular throughout the country and reinforced political and social ideas about the position of African Americans in society.

By the 1840s and 1850s, southern slave-owners became increasingly interested in the religious practices of their slaves, often building churches on their plantations and mandating attendance. Christian views in the South evolved in this context. Ministers in the South might point out that the Hebrews owned slaves or that slavery was not condemned by Jesus. Further, these ministers often cited biblical passages about the importance of servants obeying their masters.

II. The Failure of Compromise and the Journey from Mistrust to Secession

Northern and southern politicians tried repeatedly to compromise on the issue of slavery in the new territories of the United States in the 1850s, but these attempts proved to be unsuccessful. Whatever trust existed between sectional leaders broke down by 1860. The rancorous election of 1860 resulted in the secession of the southern states.

A. ATTEMPTS AT COMPROMISE IN THE 1850s

From 1850 until the eve of the Civil War, political leaders in the North and the South, as well as the Supreme Court, put forth a variety of proposals and plans for resolving the issue of slavery in the territories. These included the Compromise of 1850, the Kansas–Nebraska Act (1854), and the *Dred Scott* decision (1857). However, none of these moves proved to be successful in regard to reducing sectional tensions.

California and the "Compromise" of 1850

In 1849, President Zachary Taylor urged California and New Mexico to apply for statehood. Both areas had antislavery majorities. California was quickly ready to apply for statehood. The population of California grew to more than 300,000 in the wake of the discovery of gold.

By 1850, California had enough people to form a state. Californians wrote up a constitution to submit to Congress in which slavery would be illegal. Southern senators objected to the admission of an additional free state. Senate negotiators, led by the aging Henry Clay, worked out a series of measures to resolve this extremely contentious problem. These measures became known as the Compromise of 1850. The most important elements of the compromise were the admittance

DIVISIVENESS IN CONGRESS

The lack of agreement on the 1850 "compromise" highlights the hardening of sectional tensions.

of California as a free state, which pleased northern politicians, and a more stringent Fugitive Slave Law, which pleased southern politicians. Other measures included allowing New Mexico and Utah to decide the question of slavery based on popular sovereignty, accepting a new boundary between Texas and Mexico, and banning the slave trade (but not slavery) in Washington, DC. Senate negotiators put forth these measures as an omnibus bill, but it soon became clear that neither antislavery senators from the North nor proslavery "fire-eaters" from the South would vote "yes" on the Omnibus Bill. Stephen Douglas, a Democratic senator from Illinois, proposed "unbundling" the legislative package and on voting each measure separately. The measures all passed, and President Millard Fillmore (who assumed the presidency in 1850 upon the death of President Zachary Taylor) signed them into law.

The Kansas–Nebraska Act

In 1854, Senator Stephen Douglas of Illinois introduced the Kansas–Nebraska Act to the Senate. Douglas, who owned significant tracts of land in Chicago, hoped that the first transcontinental railroad would have a more northern route, using Chicago as a hub. The act called for dividing the northern section of the Louisiana Purchase territory into two organized territories, Kansas and Nebraska. Any railroad construction would have to be carried out in organized territory. The most contentious part of the act was allowing for the possibility of slavery in the territories of Kansas and Nebraska—areas that had been closed to slavery by the Missouri Compromise (1820). The act mandated that the question of slavery in these territories be decided by popular sovereignty. Many northerners were angry at the act and at Douglas.

The Beating of Senator Charles Sumner

The growing tensions between North and South, and the inability to achieve compromise, were evident in a violent incident that occurred on the floor of the Senate in 1856. Senator Charles Sumner from Massachusetts had given a pointed antislavery speech, called "Crimes against Kansas," in which he singled out Senator Andrew P. Butler of South Carolina. Butler's nephew, a South Carolina representative named Preston Brooks, heard about the speech and came over to Sumner's desk in the Senate chamber and beat him repeatedly with a heavy cane. The injuries left Sumner incapacitated for four years. Northerners saw the beating as a further sign of southern barbarity; southerners made Brooks a hero.

The *Dred Scott* Decision

Northern and southern relations were further pushed apart by the Supreme Court decision in the case of *Dred Scott v. Sanford* (1857). The case involved the fate of a slave named Dred Scott. Scott was owned by a doctor serving in the United States Army. Scott and his wife, along with their owner, lived for a time in the state of Illinois and in the Wisconsin Territories, areas in which slavery had been banned by the Northwest Ordinance. Years after returning to Missouri, Scott sued for his and his wife's freedom on the grounds that they had lived for a time in free areas, and that made them free. The Supreme Court did not find Dred Scott's arguments persuasive. First, the Court ruled that Scott was still a slave and did not even have the right to initiate a lawsuit. Next, the Court ruled that Congress had overstepped its bounds in declaring the northern portion of the Louisiana Purchase territory off-limits to slavery. It therefore invalidated the Missouri Compromise of 1820. Finally, the decision declared that no African Americans, not even free men and women, were entitled to citizenship in the United States because they were, according to the Court, "beings of an inferior order." Northerners were astounded at the sweep of the decision. The decision seemed to argue that slavery was a national, rather than regional, institution, and that Congress could do little to stop it.

WAS SLAVERY BECOMING "NATIONAL"?

Antislavery politicians wondered if slavery was becoming a "national" rather than a "sectional" institution. They worried that the Supreme Court would hamper any attempts to stop the spread of slavery.

B. THE DEATH OF THE SECOND TWO-PARTY SYSTEM

Controversies over slavery weakened the second two-party system. As the Whigs collapsed, and the Democratic Party become stronger in the South and more explicitly proslavery, sectional parties emerged, notably the Republican Party, with strength in the North and in the Midwest.

Party Realignment

The Kansas-Nebraska Act became a lightning rod for sectional divisions. The Whigs became bitterly divided between proslavery "Cotton Whigs" and antislavery "Conscience Whigs." Meanwhile, the Democratic Party became increasingly a regional southern, proslavery party.

The Birth of the Republican Party

In 1854, the modern Republican Party was born. This party was made of many different factions—former members of the Know-Nothing Party, "Conscience Whigs," free-soilers, abolitionists, and former Democrats, to name a few. Though the party was critical of slavery, it did not advocate the abolition of slavery. Rather, it adopted the position that slavery should not be allowed to spread to the new territories.

REPUBLICANS, THEN AND NOW

The Republican Party, started in 1854, is the same party that exists today, however its politics have changed considerably. The party that was born in opposition to the spread of slavery now gets less than 10 percent of the African-American vote. Since the 1920s, it has been more conservative and pro-business than the Democratic Party.

The Election of 1856

The election of 1856 made clear that the stability of the Democrat–Whig two-party system was over. With the Whig Party dissolved, and the Know-Nothing Party divided over the slavery issue, the Republican Party emerged as a major party just two years after its birth.

The Democratic Party won the election by shrewdly picking a northern candidate who had southern sympathies, James Buchanan. It was clear after the election that a new two-party system was emerging, with the Democrats and the Republicans. Though these two parties have changed dramatically in the last century and a half, they remain the two main parties.

C. THE ELECTION OF 1860 AND SECESSION

The victory of Abraham Lincoln, espousing a free soil platform, in the presidential election of 1860 convinced many southern political leaders that they should take action to remove their states from the Union.

The Election of 1860

The election of 1860 demonstrated the fractured nature of the American political system on the eve of the Civil War. The Democratic Party divided between a northern wing and a southern wing. The northern Democrats, rallying around the idea of popular sovereignty, nominated Stephen Douglas for president, who carried only Missouri and part of New Jersey. The southern Democrats, who strongly endorsed slavery, carried the deep South. A third formation, the Constitutional Union, which endorsed maintaining the Union and avoided the slavery issue, won the upper South.

Lincoln and Slavery

The Republican Party chose Abraham Lincoln in 1860 as its standard bearer. Lincoln had served briefly as a Whig congressman from Illinois, speaking out against the war with Mexico. He ran for Senate in 1858, losing to Stephen Douglas, but impressing the public with his oratory skills. In seven debates in different parts of Illinois, Lincoln repeatedly asked Douglas whether he favored the spread of slavery. Douglas avoided the issue, putting forth popular sovereignty as a cure-all to the slavery question, and race-baiting Lincoln. Lincoln had been opposed to the institution of slavery his entire life, and had been an advocate of the American Colonization Society, but, as he ran for president, he indicated that he would not nor could not tamper with slavery where it already existed. He promised, however, to block its expansion to new territories in the West. Lincoln won 40 percent of the popular vote, but carried the electoral vote, winning virtually all the states of the North, as well as California and Oregon.

Even if Lincoln kept his promise to not interfere with slavery in the slave states, many southern slaveholders would still not have been satisfied. In many ways, slavery needed to grow in order to remain economically viable. Abraham Lincoln's electoral victory in 1860 alarmed southern defenders of slavery, to the point that leading political figures in the South were ready to secede. Even before Lincoln was inaugurated, seven southern states seceded.

The Onset of War

Once inaugurated, Lincoln made clear that he would not tolerate southern secession, but he also did not want to initiate a war with the breakaway states. The continued presence of United States troops at Fort Sumter, in the harbor of Charleston, South Carolina, proved to be the match that ignited the war. The leadership of the newly

WHAT HAPPENED TO THE "UNITED STATES"?

When textbooks discuss the Civil War, they often call the United States, "the Union." This is fine, but it is also fine to continue to use "the United States" in your essays. The United States did not disappear. Perhaps historians use "the Union" for the sake of clarity; however, the decision also has political overtones.

formed Confederate States of America decided that they would not tolerate the presence of the United States flag over Fort Sumter. Confederate president Jefferson Davis ordered soldiers to bombard the fort. This bombardment constituted the opening shots of the Civil War. Lincoln reacted resolutely. In April 1861, he issued a proclamation calling up 75,000 troops to "cause the laws to be duly executed." Soon, the United States and the seceded southern states, calling themselves the Confederate States of America, were at war.

KEY CONCEPT 5.3
CIVIL WAR, RECONSTRUCTION, AND THE ISSUES OF POWER AND CITIZENSHIP

The victory of the United States over the secessionist South in the Civil War and the federal reconstruction plans settled two major issues—slavery and secession. However, these events left other issues unsettled, including questions about the power of the federal government and the citizenship rights of different groups of Americans.

1. Union Victory in the Civil War

There are several key factors in understanding the Union victory over the Confederacy. The states that stayed with the Union had a larger population and a larger industrial capacity than the secessionist states. The decision to shift the focus of the war from union to emancipation also played a part in the Union victory in the Civil War.

A. MOBILIZING FOR WAR

Both the Union and the Confederacy had to mobilize their entire societies and economies in order to successfully wage war. Both sides also faced opposition on their home fronts.

Industrialization

The Civil War spurred rapid industrialization of the North. During the Civil War, the Union government required an enormous amount of war materials, from guns and bullets to boots and uniforms. Manufacturers rose to the occasion by rapidly modernizing production. These changes in production sped up the process of industrialization that was in its beginning stages before the war. Industrialization stimulated a long period of economic growth, turning the United States into a world economic power.

The Republican Agenda

With the Democrats absent from Congress, the Republicans had a free hand to implement legislation that would further their vision of the United States. Congress passed the Homestead Act in 1862, granting settlers up to 160 acres as an enticement for moving west. This act was part of the "free-labor, free-soil" ideal of the Republicans. A second act was the Morrill Land Grant Act, also passed in 1862, which promoted secondary public education. The federal government provided states with federal land on which they could build public colleges or sell the land to fund the building of public colleges.

New York City Draft Riot

President Lincoln had to deal with a great deal of resistance to the war within the borders of the loyal states. One of the most significant episodes of resistance to Union policies was a riot against the wartime draft in New York City in July 1863. Protests began initially against government draft offices. Protesters were particularly angry about a law that allowed those who were drafted to pay $300 to avoid serving. This substantial sum was well beyond most working-class men. In the subsequent days, the protests turned violent, and the target became the city's African-American population. At least 120 people were killed in the riots.

B. ISSUING THE EMANCIPATION PROCLAMATION

The issuing of the Emancipation Proclamation expanded the focus of the Civil War from preserving the Union to emancipating the slaves. This move proved to be decisive to northern victory; it opened up the possibility of large-scale enlistment by African Americans and it contributed to the Confederacy remaining isolated diplomatically.

Lincoln and Slavery

Perhaps Lincoln's greatest wartime achievement was playing a key role in the liberation of the slaves. Lincoln was partly motivated by the desire to keep Great Britain at bay during the war. Great Britain might aid the Confederacy to ensure the steady flow of southern

> **TOWARD EMANCIPATION**
>
> The evolution of Lincoln's thinking in regard to emancipation is a complex process. Historians cite a variety of circumstances—military, ideological, political, ethical—that entered into the equation. Certainly a complete understanding of the process cannot leave out the role of the slaves themselves in advancing the process.

cotton but it would not join the South to continue slavery. However, Lincoln did not achieve this historic goal on his own—abolitionists, Radical Republicans, and, of course, the slaves themselves all contributed to the effort to put the issue of liberation on the wartime agenda. Lincoln was able to usher in this historic event while guiding the country through a wrenching war. He was able to convince a reluctant country that ending slavery was consistent with the most basic American values.

At first, Lincoln was reluctant to take action against slavery, for fear of pushing the border states toward secession. When Congress passed the Confiscation Acts in 1861 and 1862, Lincoln was opposed (although he did not veto them). These acts were framed as military measures. The first declared that any slaves pressed into working for the Confederacy could be taken as "contraband of war," meaning "confiscated property." The second act allowed for the seizure of the slaves owned by Confederate officials.

> **CIVIL LIBERTIES DURING WARTIME**
>
> Before condemning Lincoln as being "authoritarian" or "heavy-handed" for suspending habeas corpus, keep the following in mind. In most civil wars in human history, it has been common for authorities to simply shoot enemy sympathizers; arresting them without due process is relatively humane for a civil war.

By the summer of 1862, Lincoln had come to believe that the time was right for moving forward in regard to emancipation. He waited until the Union had achieved a victory on the battlefield. The Battle of Antietam in September 1862 was enough of a Union victory to prompt the president to issue the Emancipation Proclamation on September 22, 1862. The edict ordered the freeing of all slaves in rebel-held territory as of January 1, 1863. The order significantly exempted slaves in the loyal border states, and even in Union-held areas of Confederate states. Of course, orders from the United States government did not hold any weight for Confederate leaders, so the Emancipation Proclamation did not actually free any slaves. However, the order clearly changed the goals and tenor of the war, and made clear that this was as much a war for the liberation of the slaves as it was a war to preserve the Union.

C. TURNING THE TIDE: FACTORS IN THE UNION VICTORY

The Confederacy demonstrated initiative and military skill early in the war, but a variety of factors contributed to the Union victory in a lengthy war. The North eventually found skilled leadership in its army and developed effective battlefield strategies. The material advantages of the North began to play a more important role as the war progressed. The Union decision to wage "total war" on the South's infrastructure and environment also played a part in Union victory.

Strengths and Weaknesses of the Two Sides

The Union side had some key advantages in the war. It had a far greater population than that of the rebellious southern states (22 million versus 6 million). It also had a far greater military capacity than the South, a more diverse economy, and an extensive railroad network. All of these advantages would become especially significant in a lengthy war. The Union had the capability to resupply its troops and to recruit reinforcements for fallen soldiers.

The Confederacy's biggest advantage was that it simply had to fight a defensive war. It did not have to invade and conquer the North in order to declare victory. The Union, on the other hand, had to fight an offensive war in southern territory. Another Confederate advantage was the South's rich military tradition. It had able generals and a cohort of military men to draw from.

Fighting the Civil War

The Union had a three-part strategy for the war. First, the navy would blockade southern ports. The intent of this plan, labeled the Anaconda Plan, was to prevent supplies from reaching the South. The second part was to divide Confederate territory in half by taking control of the Mississippi River. Finally, a contingent of troops would march on the Confederate capital of Richmond, Virginia, and achieve victory.

Lincoln and much of the northern populace expected that the war would be quick and victory would be easy. These illusions were shattered after the First Battle of Bull Run, in Virginia. Confederate troops successfully pushed back advancing United States troops. The Confederacy continued to hold the advantage on the battlefield for the remainder of 1861 and throughout 1862. President Lincoln went through several generals-in-chief to lead the Union army before, in 1864, settling on General Ulysses S. Grant. Union forces suffered defeats at the Second Battle of Bull Run, the Battle of Fredericksburg, and other encounters. The Battle of Antietam is considered a Union victory by historians, but a more aggressive Union general might have inflicted heavier damage. The early years also saw the first encounter between two ironclad ships, the Confederacy's *Merrimac* and the United States' first ironclad ship, the *Monitor*.

> ## MILITARY HISTORY
>
> The material in this section about the military aspects of the war is, more or less, the extent of what you need to know. For this and other wars, there might be a question about strategy, diplomacy, or "turning points," but there is rarely a question about the inner workings of a specific battle. The AP exam does not usually test on purely military history.

The fighting between the two ships resulted in a draw, but it pointed the way toward the future of naval battles.

An important turning point in the war was the Battle of Gettysburg (1863). The battle, in Pennsylvania, was the high-water mark for the Confederacy. After Gettysburg, the Confederacy was in retreat. Another important Union victory was at Vicksburg, Mississippi. With that victory, Union forces gained control of the Mississippi River, cutting the Confederacy in two. In 1864, General Sherman's "March to the Sea," broke the spirit of the South. Confederate general Robert E. Lee finally surrendered to General Grant at Appomattox Courthouse in Virginia (1865).

II. The Impact of the Civil War and Reconstruction on Government and Society

The impact of the Civil War on American society was profound. Broadly speaking, the war changed the relationship between the states and the federal government. Specifically, the war made it clear that the United States was indivisible; secession would not be allowed. Further, the war altered the relationship among the three branches of government. Perhaps most important, the Civil War ended the practice of slavery in the United States. However, many of the social and economic patterns of southern society remained unchanged.

A. FROM SLAVERY TO SHARE-CROPPING

The Civil War undid slavery and the ratification of the Thirteenth Amendment made certain that it would not reemerge. However, new economic patterns emerged —notably the sharecropping system—that would prove to be both exploitative and soil-intensive.

The Development of the Sharecropping System

Economically, most African Americans were still engaged in agricultural work. Immediately following the Civil War, plantation owners sought to hire gangs of African-American workers to labor under the supervision of a white overseer. African Americans chafed at this arrangement—with its stark resemblance to the slavery system. African Americans desired a plot of their own—"Forty acres and a mule." Some Radical Republicans urged the government to divide the former slave plantations and distribute the land to freedmen. This radical proposal did not gain sufficient support to become realty. Short of this, African Americans began to rent land. They would customarily pay "rent" with a portion of their yearly crop—usually half. This sharecropping system was somewhat of a compromise—African Americans did not have to work under the direct supervision of an overseer and white plantation owners generated cotton to be sold on the open market. After paying back loans for seed money and tools, sharecroppers were left with very little for basic necessities. The system created a cycle of debt, which prevented African Americans from acquiring money and owning land.

B. THE SHORT-TERM ACCOMPLISHMENTS OF RECONSTRUCTION

The Reconstruction period resulted in some short-term successes—bringing the Union back together, extending political and leadership opportunities to former slaves, and altering the relationship between the races in the South. The period also saw a shift in power from the early period of Reconstruction, dominated by the executive branch, to the latter period, dominated by Congress.

Approaches to Reconstruction

As the Civil War was coming to an end, President Lincoln and the Republican Party began to address several questions regarding the postwar world. These questions included: What accommodations would be made for the freed men and women of the South? How would the secessionist South be reintegrated into the United States? What punishments, if any, would be meted out to those who rebelled against the United States? Finally, who held responsibility for reuniting and reconstructing the country—the president or Congress? Did, as the president argued, the secessionist states still exist as political entities, simply awaiting new governing personnel, or had they committed "suicide." Many congressional Republicans argued that the states had ceased to exist, and therefore needed to be readmitted by Congress. The answers to these questions formed the basis of competing visions of what Reconstruction would entail.

Wartime Reconstruction

President Lincoln was eager to quickly restore the Union. An initial goal of his was restoring southern representation in Congress. In 1863 he announced his "ten percent" plan. Under this plan, if 10 percent of the 1860 vote count in a southern state took an oath of allegiance to the United States and promised to abide by emancipation, then that state could establish a new government and send representatives to Congress. This was a low bar for these states to comply with. In 1864, he vetoed the Wade–Davis Bill, which would have established much stricter standards for the southern states to meet. The bill would have required half of the voters in a state to sign a loyalty oath to the United States before Reconstruction could begin and would have guaranteed equal treatment before the law for former slaves. Finally, in 1865, in his Second Inaugural Address, Lincoln announced that he wanted to reunite the country "with malice toward none; with charity for all." This approach was consistent with Lincoln's broader goals of ending the war as soon as possible. Lincoln was assassinated less than a month after his second inauguration, so it is difficult to surmise how he would have negotiated the difficulties of the Reconstruction era.

Presidential Reconstruction

After President Lincoln's assassination, his vice president, Andrew Johnson, assumed power. Johnson had been tapped for the vice presidency by Lincoln because he did not vacate his seat in the Senate when his native Tennessee declared secession in 1861. Although Johnson had broken with the planter class in the South, it became clear that he had no affinity for the Republican Party, nor for emancipation and equality for African Americans. He continued with the lenient and rapid approach to Reconstruction that Lincoln had mapped out. Johnson quickly recognized the new southern state governments as legitimate after they repudiated secession and ratified the Thirteenth Amendment banning slavery. In the South, many members of the old slave owning class were now back in power. These men tried to replicate the conditions of the Old South, including passing a series of restrictive laws known as the Black Codes. Postwar conditions were so similar to prewar conditions that many northerners wondered if they had "won the war, but lost the peace."

Congress and the President Clash over Reconstruction

In 1866, tensions between the president and congressional Republicans intensified. President Andrew Johnson vetoed two measures passed by Congress—an extension of the Freedman's Bureau and a Civil Rights Act that was designed to overturn the Black Codes that the southern states had implemented. Congress ultimately overrode both vetoes. The biggest fight, however, was over the Fourteenth Amendment. This amendment made all people born in the United States citizens. In this, it undid the *Dred Scott* decision, which held that African Americans were not citizens of the United States. The amendment further guaranteed all citizens "equal protection of the laws," and prohibited states from denying any citizen "life, liberty, or property without due process of law." Although the amendment did not extend voting guarantees to African Americans, it did allow Congress to reduce the representation of states that withheld the vote from African-American males. In this section, the Constitution mentions the word "males" for the first time, much to the consternation of women who had hopes that the amendment would also extend voting privileges to them.

Radical Reconstruction

President Andrew Johnson tried to mobilize skeptical white voters against the Fourteenth Amendment in the 1866 mid-term elections. However, the strategy backfired. Republicans won a resounding victory in the 1866 elections and embarked on more sweeping measures. This phase of Reconstruction, known alternatively as Radical Reconstruction or Congressional Reconstruction, showed the potential of a biracial democracy in the United States while also showing the limits of federal resolve and the strength of white southern opposition.

Reconstruction Acts of 1867

Republicans were able to push through the Reconstruction Acts of 1867. These sweeping acts divided the South into five military districts. These areas could only rejoin the United States if they guaranteed basic rights to African Americans. The radicals were not able to fully carry out their program. They were not able to extend land ownership to African Americans, nor did they carry out mass arrests of former Confederates.

Civil Rights Act of 1867

The final congressional Reconstruction act was the Civil Rights Act of 1867. This act guaranteed equal treatment for African Americans in public accommodations, such as hotels and restaurants, and it prohibited the exclusion of African Americans from juries. The act was poorly enforced. Already, by 1867, northern Republicans were losing their enthusiasm for carrying out broad reforms in the South.

Impeachment of President Johnson

The clash between President Johnson and the congressional Republicans degenerated to such an extent by 1868 that the Republicans voted to impeach Johnson. The House charged the president with violating the Tenure of Office Act, an act the Republicans had passed to protect their ally, Secretary of War Edwin Stanton. The act prohibited the president from firing cabinet members without Senate approval. The act itself is of questionable legality, but Johnson fired Stanton anyway, initiating the impeachment trial. The Senate narrowly found Johnson not guilty, but the whole procedure rendered Johnson powerless to stop Congress's Reconstruction plans.

Reconstruction in Practice

The record of the Reconstruction governments in the South is still a subject of controversy, almost a century and a half later. White southerners at the time, and afterward, complained bitterly about the burdens imposed by the Reconstruction governments, and about their corruption and ineptitude. More recently, however, historians of the period have pointed out that corruption was less pronounced than it was in other parts of the country, and that these governments accomplished a great deal, against great odds.

The southern governments were composed of a variety of elements. Democrats still served in state legislatures, often in the minority, during the Reconstruction period. The Republicans were made up of several different groups. Southern whites who joined the Republicans were labeled "scalawags" by their Democratic opponents. Many southern white Republicans were former Whigs and sought to promote economic progress for the South. Many northerners came to the South to participate in Reconstruction. Some of these northern Republicans sought personal advancement in coming South; many were motivated by a desire to assist the former slaves in their adjustment to life as freed men and women. Southern Democrats labeled these northerners "carpetbaggers," implying that they hurriedly threw all their belongings in a bag and traveled south to make a quick fortune. Finally, many of the Republican legislators were African Americans. Only in South Carolina, and only briefly (1873), did African Americans control the majority of seats in even one legislative chamber. They were consistently in the minority. But that African Americans were elected to public office in the South at all was a major accomplishment. It was not until after the Civil Rights era that significant numbers of African Americans held public office again. Two African Americans were elected to the United States Senate—Hiram Revels and Blanche K. Bruce, and more than a dozen representatives were elected to the House of Representatives.

> ### "SCALAWAGS" AND "CARPETBAGGERS"
>
> If you use these terms in an essay, do so with caution. Remember, they are not neutral descriptions; they are disparaging terms to describe those who cooperated with Reconstruction. When you use them, at least use quotation marks. Or consider modifying them with the phrase "so-called."

The accomplishments of the Reconstruction included the establishment of schools for African Americans. The attainment of an education was a burning desire for many of the freed African-American men and women. Schools thrived in the period despite the costs involved and despite the personal risk incurred by participants. Important African-American institutions such as Howard University and Morehouse College were established during the Reconstruction period. In addition, the Reconstruction governments established hospitals that served the African-American community, rewrote constitutions, updated penal codes, and began the physical rebuilding of the war-torn South.

C. THE LONG-TERM FAILURES OF RECONSTRUCTION

The successes of the Reconstruction period proved to be short-lived. The Republican Party failed to establish itself as a viable political party in the South. Further, efforts at changing the culture and racial attitudes of the South proved elusive. Finally, a combination of resistance by white southerners and a lack of resolve on the part of northerners led to the end of the Reconstruction period.

The End of Reconstruction

Several factors contributed to the end of the Reconstruction period, after only a dozen years. Southern conservative Democrats, who called themselves "redeemers," aggressively sought to regain power, state by state. The "redeemers" were aided by networks of white terrorist organizations that used violence to silence African Americans and to intimidate them from participating in public life. Also, northern whites simply lost their zeal for reforming the South. By the 1870s, many whites in the North were more interested in the industrial development of the North than in the "race problem" in the South.

The Formal End of Reconstruction: The Election of 1876

The final nail in the coffin of Reconstruction was the disputed presidential election of 1876. The Democratic candidate Samuel J. Tilden won the majority of the popular vote, but neither he nor his Republican opponent, Rutherford B. Hayes, were able to claim enough electoral votes to be declared the winner. In three states—South Carolina, Louisiana, and Florida—the Democrats and the Republicans both claimed victory. A special electoral commission, with a Republican majority, declared Hayes the winner in the three contested states. Democrats protested, with some threatening to block Hayes's inauguration. Party leaders reached an informal compromise, known as the Compromise of 1877, which allowed Hayes to win the presidency. In return, the Republicans agreed to end Reconstruction, paving the way for rule by the Democratic Party in the South.

> ### THE ELECTORAL COLLEGE
>
> A working understanding of the electoral college is essential to comprehension of some close elections in American history, especially those in which the winner of the national popular vote did not end up winning the presidency. This occurred in 1824, 1876, 1888, and 2000.

III. Conflicts over Notions of Citizenship and American Identity

During the Reconstruction period, amendments to the Constitution reflected a changing notion of national purpose and identity. These changes led to debates among Americans over the rights for African Americans, women, and other groups.

A. THE PROMISE AND LIMITS OF CONSTITUTIONAL CHANGES

The Fourteenth and Fifteenth Amendments to the Constitution granted citizenship, equal protection of the laws, and voting rights to African Americans. In the years that followed, these rights were systematically attenuated by violence and political tactics. A system of segregation, with approval from the Supreme Court, became entrenched in the South.

The Fourteenth Amendment

The Fourteenth Amendment, adopted in 1868, was one of the Reconstruction Amendments. This complex amendment made all natural-born or naturalized people American citizens. Further, it stated that the "privileges and immunities" of citizens shall not be abridged by states. Also, it states that no citizens shall be derived of "life, liberty, or property without due process of law." The amendment was bitterly opposed by southern states, which were forced to approve it before they could regain representation in Congress. The law undid custom and the *Dred Scott* decision (1857; see above) by making African-Americans citizens on equal footing with whites, and providing a guarantee of equality before the law.

The Fifteenth Amendment

The Fifteenth Amendment, granting African-Americans voting rights, was ratified in 1869. The Fifteenth Amendment states that the vote may not be denied to someone based on "race, color, or previous condition of servitude." African-American women, of course, still could not vote. Women were not granted the right to vote until 1920. Voting rights for African Americans was a key element of the Reconstruction program of the radical Republicans.

Segregation in the South

A series of segregation laws were passed in the southern states in the years after Reconstruction came to an end. These laws came to be known as Jim Crow laws. The origins of the term can perhaps be attributed to a song-and-dance routine from the 1830s called "Jump Jim Crow," which included white actors in blackface caricaturing African Americans. Later in the century, "Jim Crow" became a pejorative term for African Americans; the laws that applied to African Americans, therefore, became known as Jim Crow laws. These laws segregated public facilities, such as railroad cars, bathrooms, and schools. They relegated African-Americans to second-class status in the South. These state and local laws first appeared in the South after Reconstruction ended (1877).

The *Slaughter-house* Cases and the Narrowing of the Fourteenth Amendment

The passage of Jim Crow laws in the South after Reconstruction was aided in part by a narrow interpretation of the Fourteenth Amendment by the Supreme Court. Advocates for civil rights for African Africans hoped that the Fourteenth Amendment (ratified in 1868) would prevent the implementation of Jim Crow laws. The amendment prevents states from making laws that limit the "privileges or immunities" of any United States citizens. However, the Supreme Court interpreted this broad language in such a narrow way that it allowed for the implementation of Jim Crow laws. Earlier, in the *Slaughter-house* cases (1873), the Court made a distinction between national citizenship and state citizenship. The case was not a civil rights case—it involved a suit by several New Orleans slaughter-houses that had been closed down by the state. The slaughter-houses asserted that their due process rights had been taken away in violation of the Fourteenth Amendment. The Court ruled that the Fourteenth Amendment applied to national citizenship rights, such as the right to vote in national elections and the right to travel between states. The Court said that the amendment did not apply to rights that derived from "state citizenship." Therefore, the Fourteenth Amendment would not be of use in prohibiting state Jim Crow laws. Later, in the case of *Plessy v. Ferguson* (1896), the Supreme Court specifically asserted that racial segregation did not violate the equal protection provision of the Fourteenth Amendment (see Period 6).

The Exclusion of African Americans from the Political Process

A series of actions effectively removed African Americans from the political process and relegated them to the status of second-class citizens. Literacy tests and poll taxes limited their ability to vote. Poor whites got around these rules with the "grandfather clause," guaranteeing a man the right to vote if he or his father or grandfather had the right to vote before the Civil War. In addition, the Democratic Party often held "whites only" primaries, thus legally excluding African Americans from the only election that really mattered in the solidly Democratic South. African Americans who spoke out against this were targets of violence and even murder. The Ku Klux Klan was first organized in 1866. Thousands of African Americans were killed by lynch mobs as the local authorities looked the other way.

B. THE WOMEN'S RIGHTS MOVEMENT AND THE CONSTITUTION

Although some elements within the women's rights movements welcomed the Reconstruction-era Constitutional amendments, other elements objected to their limited nature.

Debates over the Fifteenth Amendment

The proposal to ratify the Fifteenth Amendment generated a great deal of debate within the women's rights movement. Elizabeth Cady Stanton and Susan B. Anthony refused to support the Fifteenth Amendment because it did not extend the vote to women. Other feminists, led by Lucy Stone and her husband, Henry Blackwell, while disappointed with the wording of the Fifteenth Amendment, argued that it was important to support Reconstruction and the Republican Party. They asserted that women's suffrage could be accomplished on a state-by-state basis. These divisions led to the formation of rival organizations. Stanton and Anthony formed the National Woman's Suffrage Association (NWSA) in 1869. Stone, Blackwell, and others established the American Woman's Suffrage Association (AWSA), also in 1869. The AWSA and NWSA eventually reconciled and in 1890 merged to become the National American Woman's Suffrage Association (NAWSA).

C. THE RECONSTRUCTION ERA SOWS THE SEEDS OF TWENTIETH-CENTURY CIVIL RIGHTS PRINCIPLES

Though the Fourteenth and Fifteenth Amendments were largely sidestepped in the decades following Reconstruction, they established judicial principles that have come to fruition in twentieth-century civil rights decisions.

A "Second Reconstruction"

Reconstruction lasted only a decade; its accomplishments were limited and short-lived. However, in many respects the failures of Reconstruction in the nineteenth century set the stage for a "second reconstruction" in the twentieth. The democratic spirit of the Reconstruction period inspired civil rights activists throughout the twentieth century. The principles established in the Fourteenth Amendment were invoked in several important Supreme Court decisions in the twentieth century—most notably, *Brown v. Board of Education* (1954). In the Brown decision, the Court specifically cited the amendment's assertion that "no State shall . . . deny to any person . . . the equal protection of the laws." It used this wording as the basis for declaring segregated schools unconstitutional (see more in Period 8).

SUBJECT TO DEBATE

The events of the 1850s have assumed a central place in one of the most contentious historiographical discussions about American history: How should the coming of the Civil War be understood? Central to that question is the role of slavery in the coming of the Civil War. Partisan historians from the South and from the North have tended to blame the other side. Southern partisans blame the North for interfering with their "domestic institutions." Northern partisans blame the extreme language of the Dred Scott decision, the violence done to

Senator Sumner, and the strident defense of slavery as indicators of intransigence on the part of the South.

Many historians for decades after the war held that the war was an "irrepressible conflict." The phrase was actually coined before the war by Senator William H. Seward, discussing the possibility of a future conflict between the sections—one he saw as inevitable. The war was inevitable, the theory held, because of slavery. Slavery was both at the heart of the issue and was beyond compromise. The "irrepressible conflict" school has gotten more recent backing from contemporary historian Eric Foner. Foner focuses less on northern moral concerns about slavery, and more on the "free labor" ideology. The "free labor" ideology, which was a central part of the culture of the North, held that the lands out West should be for small-scale farming, without competition from slave labor.

Several historical schools have questioned the centrality of slavery in the conflict. Progressive historians Mary and Charles Beard, writing in the 1920s, argued that the conflict was actually between a capitalist industrial North and an agrarian, almost feudal, South. Other historians have blamed the conflict on "blundering politicians"—asserting that the politicians could have compromised on slavery and other issues. This school of thought gained adherents from the 1920s onward, but has been challenged more recently in the post–civil rights movement era.

For decades, the southern myth of the "lost cause" has influenced mainstream historical writing on the Civil War. The "lost cause" myth holds that the Confederate cause was a noble and honorable one. The South had a rich tradition of military skill and chivalry. The only reason the South lost the Civil War was because of the overwhelming forces of the North. The North had greater industrial capacity and a larger population to draw from. This understanding completely ignores the centrality of the slavery question. Even among northerners in the first half of the twentieth century, the question of slavery was left out of discussions of the war. It is only in the last third of the twentieth century that the history field has fully rejected the "lost cause" myth.

Traditional historical accounts of the Reconstruction period criticize the Republican Party for imposing crushing burdens on the South, for occupying it with troops, and for saddling it with inept and corrupt government. Recent historical accounts have moved away from this grim representation by emphasizing the real progress made by African Americans under Reconstruction. The short-lived gains made under Reconstruction helped to inspire civil rights activists throughout the late nineteenth and twentieth centuries.

Practice Multiple-Choice Questions

Directions: Pick the letter that best answers the following questions.

QUESTIONS 1–2 REFER TO THE FOLLOWING PASSAGE:

"It is the sentiment around which all their actions, all their arguments, circle, from which all their propositions radiate. They look upon it as being a moral, social, and political wrong; and while they contemplate it as such, they nevertheless have due regard for its actual existence among us, and the difficulties of getting rid of it in any satisfactory way and to all the constitutional obligations thrown about it. Yet, having a due regard for these, they desire a policy in regard to it that looks to its not creating any more danger. They insist that it should, as far as may be, *be treated* as a wrong; and one of the methods of treating it as a wrong is to *make provision that it shall grow no larger.*"

1. The above quotation describes the position on slavery of the

   (A) Democratic Party in 1860
   (B) Whig Party in 1836
   (C) Liberty Party in 1840
   (D) Republican Party in 1858

2. The logic of the quotation is most consistent with

   (A) George Fitzhugh's 1857 book, *Cannibal's All!*
   (B) the Wilmot Proviso, introduced in Congress in 1846, 1847, and 1848.
   (C) Frederick Douglass's 1852 oration commonly known as, "What to the slave is the 4th of July?"
   (D) "John Brown's Last Speech," read in court in 1859.

Answers and Explanations to Multiple-Choice Questions

1. **(D)** The quotation describes the position on slavery of the Republican Party in 1858. Lincoln is describing the policies of the Republican Party in one of his 1858 debates with Stephen Douglas during the run for Senate that year. Lincoln was a member of the Republican Party, even though he uses the word "they," rather than "we," to describe the Republicans. In this excerpt, Lincoln is outlining the position of the Republican Party on slavery at that moment—it was against the institution and opposed its spread to new territories. However, with "due regard for its actual existence among us," the party believed that slavery, where it already existed, was protected by the Constitution.

2. **(B)** The logic of the Republican position—opposition to the spread of slavery— was most consistent with the Wilmot Proviso. Following the Mexican-American War (1846–1848), Congressman David Wilmot and other northern politicians tried, unsuccessfully, to ban slavery in territories that might be gained in the war by putting forth the Wilmot Proviso (1846). The proviso was passed by the House of Representatives, where politicians from the populous northern states dominated, but failed in the Senate.

Period 6: 1865–1898 The Challenges of the Era of Industrialization

8

INTRODUCTION

The transformation of the United States from an essentially rural and agrarian society to an increasingly industrial and urban one brought about a host of economic, political, diplomatic, social, cultural, and environmental changes.

The United States economy expanded tremendously in the late 1800s as the country experienced an industrial revolution. Before the Civil War businesses generally served local or regional markets. After the war we see the development of businesses with a national, and even international, reach. The era of industrial expansion after the Reconstruction period is known as the "Gilded Age." Although the nation as a whole enjoyed an increase in its wealth, that wealth was not equally distributed. The owners of big businesses, labeled "robber barons" by their critics, enjoyed unparalleled wealth, whereas many of the workers lived in squalid conditions in working-class slums. The contrast between the mansions of Andrew Carnegie and Henry Frick along New York City's Fifth Avenue and the tenements depicted in Jacob Riis's *How the Other Half Lives* (1890) startled many Americans.

The era of rapid industrial and economic expansion in the late nineteenth century dramatically transformed American culture and society. Americans experienced new cultural products, new patterns of work and leisure, and new class and ethnic divisions. These new aspects of American life were most evident in America's growing cities. Cities became centers of industrial production and magnets for the large number of immigrants coming into the United States. At the same time, agriculture was becoming more mechanized, requiring fewer people in rural areas. New York retained its stature as the largest American city, with Chicago, Cleveland, Detroit, and other cities of the Midwest and the Northeast also growing rapidly.

In addition, during the decades between the end of the Civil War and the turn of the twentieth century, a series of important developments transformed the South and the West. White and African-American southerners both shaped the "new" South, as it left behind plantation slavery. Ultimately, white southerners were able to create a series of laws and customs that relegated African Americans to a second-class status. At the same time, government policies and economic opportunity encouraged waves of settlers to make their way west. The Midwest became a major agricultural region, and the center of a politicized and determined farmers' movement. As settlers ventured farther west, clashes ensued with American Indian groups who lived on coveted lands. These clashes led to the demise of autonomous American Indian groups within the United States borders.

KEY CONCEPT 6.1
THE RISE OF BIG BUSINESS: MIGRATIONS, URBANIZATION, REFORM, AND NATIONAL IDENTITY

The rise of big business in the last decades of the nineteenth century encouraged profound changes in American society. The United States experienced massive migrations, into and within the United States, and rapid urbanization. These developments led to efforts to reshape the American economy and the environment. The era saw renewed debates about national identity.

I. Industrialization in the "Gilded Age"

During the "Gilded Age," the United States experienced unprecedented changes in production, as large-scale industry and business consolidation replaced older forms of production. These changes were accompanied by innovations in technology, expanding international communications networks, and pro-business government policies. The age was marked by new forms of consumption and marketing.

A. TECHNOLOGICAL ADVANCES AND NEW BUSINESS MODELS

The government subsidized new transportation and communication systems during the Gilded Age. These new systems opened new markets in North America. At the same time, new structures of business and finance, aided by technological innovations, made possible the greater exploitation of natural and human resources.

The Rise of Major Industries

During the Gilded Age of the late 1800s, the era of small, local-oriented businesses began to give way to large corporations and trusts that came to dominate entire industries (see below). The three most important industries of the era were the railroad industry, the steel industry, and the oil industry.

Land Grants to Railroads

The federal government encouraged economic growth by subsidizing improvements in transportation and communications. Most importantly, the government encouraged the building of railroad lines. Railroads connected the far reaches of the country and sped up the movement of goods and expanded markets. The cost of goods came down and the standard of living of Americans rose. The government encouraged this expansion of the railroad network by giving railroad companies wide swaths of land through which new rail lines would be built. These generous land grants totaled more than 180 million acres, an area equal to the size of Texas. These land grants generated huge profits for railroad companies. The presence of railroad lines made the land on either side of the tracks more accessible and more valuable, bringing about $435 million into the pockets of the railroad companies.

The Telegraph and the Telephone

Advances in communication greatly facilitated the development of corporations with a national, and even international, reach. The telegraph network developed before the Civil War (see Period 4) continued to spread throughout the country and enabled the growth of national and international business. In 1876, Alexander Graham Bell was granted a patent for the telephone. Like many innovations, many individuals were working simultaneously developing the telephone. Within a year the Bell Telephone Company was established. By the end of 1880, almost 50,000 telephones were in use in the United States.

B. LOOKING ABROAD FOR NEW MARKETS AND RESOURCES

Both political and business leaders began to look abroad—to the Pacific, Asia, and Latin America—to gain greater access to foreign markets and resources.

Industry and Empire

The United States entered the scramble for overseas possessions a little after the major European powers began carving up Africa and Asia. Many Americans resisted the idea of the United States embarking on overseas expansion; after all, the United States was born in a war against a major imperial power. However, the growing industrial capacity of the United States and the desire for new markets led the United States to look abroad. The American acquisition of Hawaii and the Spanish-American War (both 1898) set the United States on the path of having a global presence. (The role of the United States as an imperialist power is discussed in detail in Period 7.)

C. ECONOMIC CONSOLIDATION

Consolidation, monopolies, trusts, and holding companies became defining features of the business landscape during the Gilded Age. At the same time, new theories, such as Social Darwinism, which defended this new business landscape, gained currency.

The "Robber Barons"

The men who controlled the major industries in the United States came to be known as "robber barons," a scornful title meant to call attention to their cutthroat business activities and their attempts to control the government. The biggest of these industries were the railroad industry, the steel industry, and the oil industry.

Andrew Carnegie and Vertical Integration (or Consolidation)

Andrew Carnegie came to dominate the steel industry by investing in all aspects of steel production, from mining to transportation to processing to distribution. This type of organization is called vertical integration.

Rockefeller and Horizontal Integration (or Consolidation)

Horizontal integration entails creating a monopoly, or near monopoly, in a particular industry. A common way that corporations gained monopoly control of an industry was by establishing trusts. A trust consisted of trustees from several companies involved in the same industry acting together rather than in competition with one another. John D. Rockefeller organized the most well-known trust in the oil processing industry.

Other "Robber Barons"

Carnegie and Rockefeller were the most well known "robber barons," but certainly not the only ones. Others include Collis P. Huntington, a railroad magnate, Mark Hanna, a coal and iron merchant who became a leading senator from Ohio, Philip Armour, a meat processing giant in Chicago, and Stephen Elkins, a magnate in mining, railroads, and politics. Financiers, such as J. P. Morgan, parlayed leverage attained through control of various industries, including several railroad companies, into dominance of the entire economy.

THE APPEAL OF SOCIAL DARWINISM

Social Darwinism, with its call for a laissez-faire approach to the economy, appealed to owners of large corporations, because it both justified their wealth and power and warned against any type of regulation or reform.

Social Darwinism

In this era of business consolidation, new theories gained currency to explain and justify this phenomenon. Social Darwinism was one attempt to defend the new social order. Social Darwinists sought to apply Charles Darwin's ideas about the natural world to social relations. The theory was popularized in the United States by William Graham Sumner. Sumner was attracted to Darwin's ideas about competition and "survival of the fittest." He argued against any attempt at government intervention into the economic and social spheres. Interference, he argued, would hinder the evolution of the human species. The inequalities of wealth that characterized the late 1800s were part of the process of "survival of the fittest." This hands-off approach to economic activities is known by the French phrase *laissez-faire*.

D. URBANIZATION—WEALTH AND POVERTY IN URBANIZING AMERICA

As America became increasingly urbanized, cities became divided between the wealthy, living lives of opulence and "conspicuous consumption," and those living in relative poverty.

A Divided City

The Gilded Age is characterized by a bifurcation, or division, of the city between working class districts and wealthy enclaves. Before the Civil War, different classes lived in close proximity to one another. An owner of a printing shop, for example, might live on the second and third stories of a building, above his street-level shop. His apprentices might live in his attic—owner and workers under one roof. However, in the second half of the century, the middle class and the wealthy moved from the industrial zones, away from the factories, the docks, and the slaughterhouses. In New York City, the wealthy moved uptown; elsewhere, they moved away from the urban core. In the bifurcated city, the working-class districts tended to become utterly squalid, while the wealthier areas had the nicest amenities—wider streets, large parks, and sunlight.

The Wealthy Class

The Gilded Age saw the growth of a well-to-do class that greatly surpassed previous wealthy classes in terms of money, cohesiveness, and power. These wealthy businessmen built gaudy mansions along New York's Fifth Avenue and on other cities' "gold coasts," and built equally sumptuous summer "cottages" in Newport, Rhode Island, and other exclusive spots. The social critic and economist Thorstein Veblen's book, *The Theory of the Leisure Class* (1899), coined the phrase "conspicuous consumption" to describe the lavish spending habits of the wealthy.

The Working Class and the Poor

At the other end of the social spectrum, often living just blocks or miles from the wealthy class, were the Gilded Age's "have-nots"—the working class and the poor. The densest neighborhood in the world in the late 1800s was the

> ### WAS JACOB RIIS A RACIST?
> Not exactly. But he reflected contemporary middle-class perceptions of different ethnic groups. His depictions could be read as condescending and sentimental.

Lower East Side of New York. Conditions there were typical of many similar districts in other cities—many people packed into small apartments in substandard tenement buildings, lack of ventilation and light, streets thick with horse dung, and lack of basic municipal services—sewer lines, running water, and garbage removal.

The conditions of the poor were chronicled in Jacob Riis's *How the Other Half Lives*. His photographs, often criticized for their condescension and stereotyping, did draw many people's attention to the plight of the poor.

The Middle Class

Although the contrasts between the very wealthy and the very poor were stark, there was a growing middle class in the late 1800s. Industry needed managers, accountants, and marketers. Further, there were more doctors, teachers, and lawyers in American society.

II. Schisms and Contestation in Industrializing America

Although many Americans hoped to create a unified industrialized nation, divisions opened up on a number of fronts, including migration, region, and class.

A. MIGRATIONS AND A DIVERSE WORKFORCE

Migrations from abroad and from within the United States created an expanded and more diverse industrial workforce. The growing labor force also resulted in lower wages and an increase in child labor.

The "New Immigration"

After 1880, immigration took on new importance in providing a steady stream of workers for American factories and in transforming American society. Immigrants, and internal migrants, flooded into the industrializing cities of the United States (and to a lesser degree Europe). These immigrants tended to come from the areas just beyond the industrial core of Europe and North America (an area bounded by Chicago, St. Louis, and Toronto in the west, and Berlin, Warsaw, and Milan in the east). The ring of agricultural areas beyond this core—primarily southern and eastern Europe, but also Scandinavia, Canada, the western plains of the United States, and northern Mexico—supplied the vast majority of immigrants as traditional economic patterns broke down in the face of capitalist development. This so-called new immigration was differentiated from the "old immigration" of northern and western Europeans. The large wave of immigrants who came to the United States between 1880 and 1920 was essential to the industrialization of the United States. An estimated 20 million people, from Russia, Italy, Poland, the Balkan region, and elsewhere immigrated to the United States, most settling in industrial cities such as New York, Pittsburgh, and Chicago.

The Declining Status of Work in the Age of Industrialization

Workers saw their position and status erode during this period, as cutthroat competition and mechanization of the work process pushed down wages and worsened working conditions. In addition, the increased reliance on child labor and the growing number of immigrants into the United States further eroded wages. The wealth generated by the rapid expansion of industry in the post–Civil War period was certainly not evenly distributed. However, workers' grievances during the Gilded Age went beyond low wages. Workers were alarmed at how the changing workplace eroded their sense of autonomy and control of the work process. This loss of control was both a blow to workers' sense of pride and their ability to control the pace and conditions of work. Many workers responded by forming and joining labor organizations, or unions, to advance their cause through collective bargaining, and, if all else failed, through striking.

B. CONFLICT AT THE WORK SITE

The Gilded Age witnessed a marked increase in the number and intensity of workplace conflicts between labor and management. Workers organized local and national unions and engaged in battles with management over wages and working conditions.

An Era of Pitched Workplace Battles

The fierce labor battles were almost exclusively won by management, with its near-monopoly on fire-power, the support of the government and the courts, and vast numbers of poor, working-class men willing to serve as strike-breakers. These battles often occurred in the wake of pay cuts announced during the economic downturns of the 1870s and of the 1890s.

The Knights of Labor

A significant early union was the Knights of Labor, founded in 1869. This union welcomed all members, regardless of race, sex, or level of skill. The Knights had a broad agenda that included not only improvements in wages and hours for their workers, but also social reforms such as an end to child labor and better safety rules. By 1886, the organization had approximately 800,000 members, but a series of circumstances, as well as organizational problems caused a sharp decline in the Knights' membership and influence by the 1890s. Ethnic, linguistic, and racial barriers among members of the Knights of Labor made united action more difficult. In addition, a centralized and autocratic governing structure within the Knights of Labor prevented new leadership from expanding the organization. Finally, government repression in the wake of the Haymarket bombing in Chicago (see below) weakened the organization.

The Great Railroad Strike of 1877

In 1877, The Baltimore and Ohio Railroad (B&O) announced a 10 percent pay cut for its workers. Wages had already been falling during the economic depression that followed the Panic of 1873. Railroad workers in West Virginia went on strike. Railroad workers down the line—in Pittsburg, Chicago, even San Francisco followed suit. At its height the Great Railroad Strike involved more than 100,000 railroad workers and more than half a million other workers. Violence erupted in nine states. President Rutherford B. Hayes called out federal troops, many recently withdrawn from enforcing Reconstruction policies in the South. Many observers thought a second civil war was unfolding.

> ### REASSIGNMENT OF TROOPS
> Many of the soldiers assigned to put down the Great Railroad Strike of 1877 had just been released from duty in the South, as Reconstruction ended earlier that year.

The Haymarket Incident (1886)

In 1886, a strike at the McCormick reaper works in Chicago turned violent. Unskilled workers at the McCormick works struck and were quickly replaced by "scab"—or replacement workers. The striking workers attacked several of the "scabs" on May 3, two days after a large May Day rally in Chicago for the eight-hour day. The police and Pinkerton guards opened fire on the strikers, killing or injuring six men. The strikers called for a rally on May 4 in Haymarket Square. Toward the end of the rally a bomb exploded in the midst of the police ranks. Several police were killed. The police responded by opening fire on the rally. Eight men were tried and convicted on scanty evidence; four were executed. At the time, many Americans shied away from the perceived violence of the labor movement. The popularity of the Knights of Labor was especially hard hit.

The American Federation of Labor (1886)

Born in the 1880s, the American Federation of Labor (AFL) also emerged during the Gilded Age. One of its founders and its first leader was a cigar maker named Samuel Gompers. The

AFL differed from the Knights of Labor in that it included only skilled workers, the "aristocracy of labor." It did not permit unskilled workers to join, nor did it allow African Americans or women to join. It was known as a craft union, in contrast to the Knights, which was an industrial union. Further, the AFL did not engage in any sort of political activities. It was known as a "bread and butter" union, in that its one goal was getting higher wages and better conditions for its members. It did not work for broader social reform. The AFL maintained a growing membership into the twentieth century.

The Homestead Strike (1892)

A momentous labor battle took place at Andrew Carnegie's steel works in Homestead, Pennsylvania in 1892. Though Carnegie had the reputation of being a friend of labor, he was determined to break the union—the Amalgamated Association of Iron and Steel Workers, a powerful craft union under the AFL umbrella. When the Amalgamated's contract expired in 1892, he announced that he would not renew it—in effect breaking the union. Carnegie traveled outside of the country in the summer of 1892 and left the plant under the charge of manager Henry Clay Frick, a notorious anti-union man. Frick built a fence around the plant, locked-out the workers, brought in "scabs," and hired Pinkerton guards to enforce his edicts. A battle ensued between the "Pinks" and the workers. The workers won a temporary victory, and took over the plant. But the governor then called in 8,000 National Guard troops to retake the plant. Frick was able to reopen the plant, without union workers, in a devastating blow for organized labor.

THE COURTS AND STRIKERS

During the Gilded Age, the courts generally sided with management over labor. *In re Debs* and *United States v. E.C. Knight Company* are two examples of Supreme Court cases that went against labor.

The Pullman Strike: Strife in a Company Town (1893)

The Pullman strike occurred during the economic downturn following the Panic of 1893. The Pullman Company, which built railroad cars, cut wages several times in 1893 and 1894. Pullman was also the name of the town in Illinois where the workers lived. The town was built by the Pullman Company in 1880 as a model company town. The housing was better than most working-class housing, but was also more costly. The town exemplified the two sides of company towns—on the one hand they provided decent housing, but on the other hand they allowed the company to have a great deal of control over their workers and to deny housing to "troublemakers" (such as pro-union workers). The company owned all the housing, and rent was taken directly out of wages. When wages were cut in 1893 and 1894, rents were not cut. Workers appealed to the American Railway Union, led by Eugene V. Debs, to come to their aid. In May 1894, three organizers were fired. Soon most of the 3,300 workers were on strike. ARU members across the nation voted to support the strike by refusing to handle trains that contained Pullman cars. Railroad traffic was brought to a standstill. Courts issued two injunctions against the strike. President Cleveland eventually called out federal troops to put down the strike. Violence immediately ensued, leading to the death of twenty-five strikers. The strike ended in defeat for the union, with

"COMPANY TOWNS"

Pullman, Illinois was one of many company towns built during the industrialization of America in the late nineteenth and early twentieth century. They shared certain features with Pullman: Slightly better living conditions in exchange for being under the control and watch of the company.

new workers hired by Pullman. In the wake of the incident, the Supreme Court, in *In re Debs* (1895), decided that the government was justified in stopping the strike.

C. THE LIMITED SUCCESS OF CALLS FOR A "NEW SOUTH"

Promoters of a "New South" encouraged industrialization in the South. Although some segments of the southern economy experienced industrialization, overall the South remained predominantly agrarian, with sharecropping and tenant farming dominating the region.

The New South

After the Civil War, several public figures in the South argued for a "New South." The most prominent of these spokesmen was Henry Grady, an Atlanta journalist. He argued for a mixed economy in the South that would include industrialization. He wanted to move away from the single-crop plantation agriculture of the "Old South." It was hoped that southern industrialists could join forces with northern businessmen and bankers. There were pockets of industrialization in the South, especially textile production.

However, for the most part, the promise of a "New South" proved to be hollow. For the remainder of the century and well into the twentieth century, the South remained mired in poverty and underdevelopment. African Americans continued to toil in the sharecropping system or as tenant farmers (see Period 5). Both systems involved African Americans working land that they did not own. In the sharecropping system, farmers would pay "rent" with a portion—or share—of their yearly crop. Tenant farming was a slight step up the social ladder from share-cropping. Generally tenant farmers rented land in cash from a landowner. Often the tenant farmer owned his own tools and only had to rent the land itself at a fixed rate.

III. The Movement Westward

A series of political and social conflicts occurred during the Gilded Age over changes that occurred in the West. These conflicts revolved around new systems of farming and transportation, westward migration, as well as economic instability.

A. CONTROL OF NATURAL RESOURCES IN THE WEST

In the late 1800s, private and public interests waged pitched battles over control of resources in the West. Conservationists and government agencies sought to extend public control over resources such as land and water, while corporate interests sought to allow these resources to be exploited in industrial and extractive processes.

Concern for Disappearing Wilderness

By the middle of the nineteenth century, some Americans were beginning to note the disappearance of wilderness and the toll that human activities were taking on the environment. Sportsmen were early advocates of environmental protection. In 1887, the sportsman, zoologist, and adventurer George Bird Grinnell and Theodore Roosevelt organized the Boone and Crockett Club—named after two prominent American backwoodsmen—to promote outdoor activities, but also to lobby for environmental protection. In addition, romanticism, a dominant intellectual and artistic movement in the mid-to-late nineteenth century, generated interest in untouched natural environments. Romantics worried about the corrupting influences of civilization and championed the restorative powers of nature. Paintings of the West by Albert Bierstadt, depicting awe-inspiring landscapes and hinting at the storm clouds of modern civilization on the horizon, generated interest in "unspoiled" landscapes.

John Muir and the Sierra Club

An early champion of preserving wilderness was John Muir. Muir, who was born in Scotland and raised in Wisconsin, began studying and exploring the natural environment. Early in his life he embraced the Transcendentalist movement. Later, he was one of the founders of the Sierra Club (1892), an organization dedicated to preserving wilderness and to monitoring the federal governments' oversight of protected lands.

Government Efforts to Protect the Environment

The efforts of John Muir and others pushed the government to take action to protect the environment. In 1871, Congress established an independent commission to investigate the decline in fish and aquatic populations in rivers, lakes, and coastal waters. The United States Fish Commission investigated fishing technologies, operated hatcheries, and oversaw the Alaskan fur seal industry. The Department of the Interior was also charged with expanding its responsibility to include overseeing federally held protected lands and parks. The Department of the Interior had been created before the Civil War in 1849. In the aftermath of the Mexican-American War, the amount of land under federal control grew tremendously; a cabinet level department was therefore created to bring together the functions of the Bureau of Indian Affairs and the General Land office, with other offices later brought under the control of the Department of the Interior. Initially the department had the conflicting tasks of protecting Indian rights and organizing the assessment and sale of federally-held land. After the Civil War, the department expanded its purview to include national parks and monuments. As concern about clear-cutting of forests grew, Congress appointed a special agent in the Department of Agriculture to assess the condition of forested land in the United States. This office grew into the Division of Forestry in 1871. The agency was later renamed the United States Forest Service in 1905, with Gifford Pinchot as the first chief forester.

> ## REMEMBERING THE CIVIL WAR
>
> The most popular subject for monuments in this era was the Civil War. Most monuments, however, forgot the main result of the Civil War—the abolition of slavery. In an age of Jim Crow laws and "scientific" racism, the cause of African Americans was jettisoned. In its place was a focus on heroism and shared sacrifice.

B. FARMERS RESPOND TO MECHANIZED AGRICULTURE

Farmers in the last decades of the nineteenth century found themselves drawn into the world of mechanized agriculture. In many cases, these farmers formed local and regional organizations in order to resist the power of railroads and corporate interests.

The Declining Position of American Farmers

During the post–Civil War period, Midwest farmers felt they were being squeezed from all sides. Railroad companies were overcharging farmers for carrying their produce to Chicago and other destinations. Also, the tight supply of currency in the United States was both making it difficult for farmers to pay off their debts and was driving down the commodity prices they received for their crops. Also, banks were foreclosing on farms. These problems led farmers to seek solutions through forming local and regional organizations to challenge corporate power. Some of their political agitation was carried out within the two-party system, but, significantly, they decided to also work outside of mainstream politics.

The Greenback Party

An early political formation that sought an expansion of the currency supply was the Greenback Party. Founded in 1878—during the economic downturn following the panic of 1873—the party advocated issuing paper money that was not backed by gold or silver. This was done briefly during the Civil War, and farmers received higher prices for their goods. The party received a million votes in the 1878 congressional elections. The party soon disbanded, but the call for expanding the money supply was taken up again following the panic of 1893.

> ## THIRD PARTIES IN AMERICAN HISTORY
>
> It is very difficult for a third-party candidate to win election in the American political system. The system favors the two main parties. So why join a third party? They often put issues on the national agenda, even if they don't win the election. This has been true from abolitionism to environmentalism.

The Grange and Granger Laws

The Grange was a farmers' organization that pushed for state laws to protect farmers' interests. In many Midwestern states, they were successful in passing laws that regulated railroad freight rates and made certain abusive practices illegal. These laws came to be known as Granger laws. Initially, the Supreme Court, in *Munn v. Illinois* (1877), upheld these laws, asserting that it was within the government's permissible powers to regulate private industry. Later, the court overruled itself. In *Wabash v. Illinois* (1886), the Court ruled that individual states could not regulate railroads because they cross state lines. This led to the federal government establishing the Interstate Commerce Commission to regulate railroads (1887).

Protecting Communal Lands of the Southwestern *Hispanos*

Clashes occurred in the 1880s and 1890s in the Southwest between recently arriving Anglo-Americans and long-time Mexican and American Indian occupants of the land. Much of the conflict occurred in northern New Mexico, which was federally administered land that the United States gained from Mexico following the Mexican-American War (1846–1848). For years Anglo-Americans had been migrating to this area and squatting on the land. The Homestead Act of 1862 gave these squatters a degree of legitimacy in the eyes of the federal government.

Large portions of these lands were lands used communally by the local *Hispano* population (the name given to people of colonial Spanish descent in what would become the United States). These Hispanos lived in villages and used the surrounding lands for grass, timber, water, and other resources. By the 1890s, the local Hispanos and American Indians lost more than 90 percent of their traditional lands and began organizing resistance. Attempts by the local population to regain their lands from federal authorities fell on deaf ears. The Surveyor of General Claims Office generally demanded that documentation of ownership be in English, however titles held by the Hispanos were in Spanish. Finally, groups such as Las Gorras Blancas (named after the white caps they wore) and Las Manos Negras (The Black Hands) organized resistance. This included raids on Anglo-held land, often cutting fences and burning property.

C. FARMERS AND THE POPULIST PARTY

The People's (Populist) Party was formed by activists to challenge the growth of corporate power over the agricultural sector. The party sought a radical redistribution of power in the United States and pushed for stronger government control of the economy.

Organizing the Populist Party

The call for the government to undo the "crime of '73"—to move away from a gold standard and again allow for the "free and unlimited coinage" of silver—became loud in the 1890s, especially after the panic of 1893. It became one of the main rallying cries of the Populist Party, which was born in 1892. The Populists were able to harness growing discontent following the panic of 1893 and gave a voice to a radical program for change that included increased democracy, a graduated income tax, and regulation of the railroads. This program was included in their Omaha Platform, written at their founding convention in 1892. The party did remarkably well in the presidential election later in 1892, garnering more than one million votes and twenty-two electoral votes. The party made solid gains in the midterm election of 1894, electing six senators and seven representatives from the farming regions in the South and the West. The Populists were perhaps the most successful third-party in the nineteenth century, but their popularity was short-lived.

> ### THE "HAYSEED" VERSUS THE POPULIST
>
> Farmers have been represented throughout history as slow and dim-witted. Their participation in the Grange, in farmer co-ops, and in the populist movement demonstrate a level of sophistication at odds with the image of the "hayseed." Avoid condescending stereotypes.

Coxey's Army

In 1894, "Coxey's Army," a group of disgruntled workers, many of whom were recently laid-off by railroad companies, marched from Ohio, through Pennsylvania, and onto Washington, DC, to demand that the government take action to address the economic crisis. There were similar "armies" of populist-inspired working-class men.

> ### WAS COXEY AHEAD OF HIS TIME?
>
> In 1894, the Coxeyites were ridiculed and ignored. However, a generation later, the New Deal consisted of exactly the types of programs Coxey and his men were pushing for. It shows that social movements influence government policies, but sometimes the process takes a while.

The Election of 1896 and the "Cross of Gold" Speech

The election of 1896 was significant in several ways. It resulted in the demise of the Populist Party and it helped to establish the identity of the major political parties in the twentieth century. The most contentious issue in the election was the amount of currency in circulation. William Jennings Bryan ran for president in 1896 on the ticket of the Democratic Party. He broke with the more conservative elements in the party and endorsed the call for the "free and unlimited coinage of silver." In his famous "Cross of Gold" speech, he promised not to let the American people be crucified "upon a cross of gold." He was also endorsed by the farmer-oriented Populist Party because of his support for the free coinage of silver. The Republican candidate William McKinley appealed to banking and business interests by promising to keep the country on the gold standard. McKinley's victory was devastating to the Populist Party, which had thrown its support to Bryan. The positions of the two parties shaped the political landscape well into the twentieth century. The Republican Party continued to be more aligned with pro-business interests, and the Democratic Party continued to present itself as the champion of the "little guy."

> **THE "CROSS OF GOLD" SPEECH**
>
> Be familiar with Bryan's speech; it appears frequently on the AP exam.

D. THE BATTLE TO PROTECT THE WILDERNESS

Conservationists and preservationists pushed for some degree of protection of unspoiled wilderness lands, through measures such as the establishment of national parks. Business interests often attempted to thwart these initiatives.

The Establishment of National Parks

After intense lobbying efforts, the government took several steps to conserve the wilderness of the West. In 1864, the federal government, for the first time, took action in setting aside land for preservation and recreation by establishing Yosemite Grant in the Yosemite Valley of the central Sierra Nevada Mountains in California. Eight years later, in 1872, the federal government created the first national park in the United States—Yellowstone Park, primarily in Wyoming. The government had a freer hand to set aside land in Wyoming than it did in California because Wyoming was not yet a state—it was federally held land. (Yosemite was later designated a national park, in 1890.)

Resistance by Business Interests to Protections of Public Lands

Business interests often tried to thwart attempts by the government and by advocates to protect public-held lands from exploitation. This occurred in the 1870s and 1880s in regard to foresting. The 1870 census report noted major deforestation in the Great Lakes region. Secretary of the Interior Carl Schurz called for measures that would restrict foresting activities in order to protect the supply of forested lands into the future. Business interests balked at such measures and pushed Congress to pass the Timber Cutting Act of 1878, further facilitating the cutting of timber on federal lands. It was another generation before the government took measures to conserve and manage forested lands by regulating cutting.

KEY CONCEPT 6.2
GENDER, RACE, ETHNICITY, AND CLASS IN AN INDUSTRIAL CULTURE

The United States witnessed the emergence of an industrial culture in the United States during the Gilded Age. This new culture offered both opportunities for and restrictions on women, immigrants, and minority groups.

I. Migrations, Inequalities, and Reform

During the Gilded Age, America experienced unprecedented migrations, both from abroad and within the United States. These migrations increased both urban and rural populations. As these migrations continued, inequalities along racial, gender, religious, and social class lines became more evident in the United States. These inequalities inspired a host of reform efforts to create a more egalitarian society.

A. MIGRATIONS AND DEMOGRAPHIC CHANGES

Increased migrations transformed many parts of the United States. Southern and eastern Europeans, as well as Asians, came into the United States in large numbers during the last decades of the nineteenth century. In addition, many African Americans moved within the South and out of the South altogether. These movements changed rural areas as well as urban areas.

The "Exoduster" Movement

As Reconstruction came to an end (see Period 5), many African Americans in the South realized that they were losing the few white political allies they had in their home states. The withdrawal of federal oversight in the South, accompanied by a rise in Ku Klux Klan violence and the enactment of the Jim Crow laws, solidified the status of African Americans as second-class citizens. In this atmosphere, some African Americans decided to abandon the South and head west. Starting in the late 1870s, a movement of approximately 40,000 African Americans—labeled the "Exoduster" movement—migrated from states along the western tier of the Confederacy, crossing the Mississippi River to settle in Kansas. Smaller numbers settled in Oklahoma and Colorado. Some "Exodusters" made it only as far as Missouri. African-American activists and white philanthropists established organizations, such as the Colored Relief Board and the Kansas Freedmen's Aid Society to help "Exodusters" make the journey to Kansas.

B. OPPORTUNITY AND INEQUALITY IN CITIES

Many migrants were drawn to American cities by increased opportunities. These cities began to show deep social and economic divisions along lines of class, race, ethnicity, and culture.

Working-class Culture and Urban Life

Though wages remained stagnant and even fell for working-class people during the Gilded Age, city life and a slightly shorter workday provided more opportunities for leisure-time activities for the masses of urban residents. The large number of working-class people entering cities transformed the culture of cities and changed the physical city itself.

The Saloon

The most popular leisure-time activity for working-class men was drinking in saloons. Saloons were often part social hall, part political club, and part community hub. The attacks on saloons, and on alcohol consumption in general, were seen as attacks on working-class immigrant culture as much as they were on drunkenness.

Newspapers

As printing costs went down and literacy went up, newspaper circulation increased dramatically in the Gilded Age. Large circulation papers, such as Joseph Pulitzer's *New York World* and William Randolph Hearst's *New York Journal*, in the latter decades of the nineteenth century, gained read-

> ### MUCKRAKING JOURNALISM VERSUS "YELLOW JOURNALISM"
> Don't confuse these two terms. Muckrakers were genuinely interested in exposing social ills. "Yellow journalism" was simply a technique to sell newspapers.

ership through exaggerated, sensationalistic coverage of events. This "yellow journalism" played a role in pushing public opinion toward support for the Spanish-American War (1898) (see Period 7).

The Health of the City and the Parks Movement

As cities became denser and more disease-ridden in the Gilded Age, reformers sought to provide more opportunities for working-class men, women, and children to enjoy outdoor recreation. Older notions of disease causation—that disease, for example, was divine punishment for sinful behavior—gave way to the idea that our environment played a significant role in our health. Later, doctors adopted the germ theory of disease causation, put forth by Robert Koch (who was active from the 1870s to the 1900s). Public parks were part of a strategy to provide an alternative to dirty streets and alleyways, as well as saloons, for people to recreate.

Frederick Law Olmsted and New York's Central Park

The most important park project of the nineteenth century was New York's Central Park (1858). The design competition was won by Frederick Law Olmsted and Calvert Vaux. The park embodies some of the contradictions of the parks movement. On the one hand, Olmsted sought to create a democratic meeting place where the city's different classes could congregate and enjoy the benefits of nature. On the other hand, working-class advocates wondered aloud why the park was built so far from the working-class districts of the city. Also, the rules and regulations of the park made the park seem, to some people, more about control than enjoyment.

Recreation and Spectator Sports

Park grounds soon became centers for a variety of recreation activities. Several of these activities went from being participatory activities to spectator sports. These include:

Baseball: Developed in 1845, baseball became the "national pastime" by the Gilded Age. The first truly professional team was the Cincinnati Red Stockings (1869).
Tennis: Lawn tennis was developed in Great Britain (1873) as a women's sport. It gained popularity in America among men and women during the Gilded Age.
Croquet: Croquet was a popular activity in public parks during the last third of the nineteenth century. It was often played by mixed-sex groups.

Cycling: "Wheeling"—bicycle riding—became very popular in the Gilded Age. The difficult "penny-farthing" bicycles, with their enormous front wheel, gave way to the modern design of the "safety bicycle" in the 1880s. Wheeling was especially popular among women, who enjoyed the freedom from male supervision that bicycle riding offered.

Football: College football games became popular in the Gilded Age. The first contest was between Rutgers and the College of New Jersey (Princeton) in 1869.

THE ROMANTICIZATION OF THE WEST

Be aware of the differences between the real history of the West and the romanticization of the West. "Buffalo Bill" Cody was romanticizing the West when people still had memories of the real West.

The Commercialization of Leisure

The growth of cities went hand in hand with the commercialization of leisure-time activities. The community-sponsored town fairs and dances of rural America were replaced by for-profit ventures in the city. The most successful large-scale amusement area was Brooklyn's Coney Island. Coney Island consisted of three main amusement parks, as well as a boardwalk, vaudeville theaters, and other assorted attractions. Other successful amusements included "Buffalo Bill" Cody's Wild West show (starting in 1883), which mythologized the "Old West," even before the "Indian Wars" of the actual West had ended. Circuses became popular in the Gilded Age. P.T. Barnum created the most popular circus of the era (1871), labeling it "the greatest show on earth."

C. ISSUE OF IDENTITY AND OPPORTUNITY FOR IMMIGRANTS

The economic growth of the Gilded Age presented immigrants, African Americans, and women with increased career opportunities, even as social prejudices were on the rise. Immigrants often grappled with issues of assimilation—how much would immigrants "Americanize" and how much would they seek to retain their native cultures.

The Persistence of Ethnicity in the Gilded Age City

The large number of immigrants pouring into the United States in the late 1800s dramatically altered the social geography of American cities (see Period 7). At the same time, the experience of moving to the United States remade the immigrants themselves. Immigrants from the small towns and rural areas of southern and eastern Europe had to adjust to life in urban America. Immigrants grappled with the pull of assimilation on one hand and the desire to maintain a sense of ethnic solidarity on the other. In New York, Chicago, and other large cities, foreign language papers emerged, such as the Yiddish-language *Jewish Daily Forward* and the Italian-language *Il Progresso Italo-Americano*. Neighborhoods in New York became increasingly defined by ethnicity, such as Little Italy and the Jewish Lower East Side. Immigrant groups established savings institutions, insurance programs, choruses, political organizations, and summer camps. The various ethnic enclaves of the gilded age city provided grocery stores so that immigrants could purchase foods reminiscent of their countries of origin. Some newcomers to the city did not intend to stay. Millions of immigrants, mostly young men, worked for part of the year in the United States and then spent part of the year in their home country. These young men were called "birds of passage" because of their seasonal migrations.

D. POWER AND REFORM IN URBAN AMERICA

The growing cities of the Gilded Age experienced changes in governance and movements for political reform. Political machines became increasingly powerful in urban America, sometimes providing social services to immigrant groups in exchange for political support. Settlement houses and self-help groups emerged in the last decades of the nineteenth century to help immigrants adapt to life in America.

Urban Politics and the Rise of Machine Politics

Politics in major cities came to be dominated by political machines. In the aftermath of the Civil War, political parties on the local level created smooth-running organizations whose main purpose was to achieve and maintain political power. Ideology was barely a concern in these bare-knuckled electoral contests. New York City was dominated by the Democratic Party machine, headquartered at Tammany Hall. The most famous Tammany chief was "Boss" William Marcy Tweed. Tweed and other political bosses earned a reputation for corruption. Tweed's complicated schemes included the building of a courthouse that involved millions of dollars in kickbacks to Tammany Hall. Tweed's nefarious doings were exposed by the press, most notably by cartoonist Thomas Nast. The Tammany Hall political machine was popular with German and Irish immigrants; under the Democratic Party, the city initiated massive municipal projects that provided jobs to thousands of immigrants.

> ## IMMIGRANTS AND POLITICAL MACHINES
> Don't be too quick to condemn political machines for exploiting immigrants. The relationship is complicated. Political machines were corrupt but they provided real benefits to immigrant communities.

The Campaign Against Prostitution

The issue of prostitution tapped into the concerns of a variety of constituencies. Religious-based activists saw it as sinful. Campaigners for gender equality saw a double standard in society's acceptance of male extramarital sexual activities (including with prostitutes). Public health advocates saw prostitution as a means of spreading venereal disease. Anti-poverty activists saw prostitution as reinforcing a cycle of poverty for working-class women. These forces united in pressuring local authorities to close "red-light" districts. Later, in the early twentieth century, progressive reformers successfully lobbied for the Mann Act (1910), which cracked down on the transport of women across state lines to engage in prostitution.

The Temperance Campaign

The movement to ban alcohol from American society was one of the largest reform movements in the nineteenth century. The Anti-Saloon League (founded in 1895) and the Women's Christian Temperance Union (founded in 1874) headed the temperance campaign in the early twentieth century. The temperance movement was especially popular among women. Many women, who had the responsibility of putting food on the table, were troubled by the fact that their husbands often drank away their paychecks. Another reason for the popularity of the temperance crusade was that it complemented the growing nativist, or anti-immigrant, movement. (See more on the temperance movement in Period 7).

II. Westward Migrations and American Indians

As settlers moved westward, American Indians were increasingly threatened. The reservation system, the destruction of the buffalo, military actions, and assimilationist policies worked to circumscribe American Indian options and culture.

A. MIGRATIONS WESTWARD

Economic opportunity and government policies drew more people westward after the Civil War. This movement of people put additional pressures on land held by American Indians and caused the federal government to violate treaties it had made with American Indian groups.

Settling the West

A variety of factors brought hundreds of thousands of settlers to the West in the period after the Civil War. Railroad companies were anxious to sell the land they had been granted in order to build rail lines. They relentlessly promoted land sales in the overcrowded cities of the East. In addition, the Homestead Act of 1862 (see Period 5) drew settlers to the West. By the late 1800s, a system of agricultural production and distribution developed, drawing western grain farmers into national and international markets. The populations of Minnesota, the Dakotas, Kansas, and Nebraska all grew dramatically between the end of the Civil War and 1900 (from 300,000 to 5 million). Immigrants from Scandinavia, Germany, Canada, and Great Britain mingled with native-born whites and African-American "Exodusters" (see above) in this multicultural West.

B. VIOLENCE ON THE FRONTIER

Increased migration to the West led to violence on the frontier. White settlers increasingly clashed with American Indians and Mexican Americans.

The End of Autonomous American Indian Groups

As more and more white settlers made their way to the West, American Indians felt their world narrowing. By the 1880s, the last autonomous American Indian groups were defeated in the "Indian Wars" and brought under U.S. control through a series of large-scale military conflicts. From the earliest encounters between white people and American Indians, white settlers had encroached upon American Indian lands and, using superior firepower, pushed American Indians farther into the interior of the continent. American attitudes and policies toward American Indians sometimes emphasized assimilation, sometimes removal, and sometimes extermination. All these approaches saw American Indians as a problem that needed to be rectified.

C. AMERICAN INDIAN RESISTANCE AND GOVERNMENT POLICIES

American Indians developed different strategies to respond to threats to their land. The United States government responded to this resistance with violence and with calls for assimilation.

The Growth of the Reservation System

After the Civil War, starting in 1867, the government attempted to solve the "Indian problem" through peaceful means, rather than through more warfare. The center of this policy was pushing American Indians onto reservations—confined areas that were set aside by the government. This policy made American Indians wards of the government until they learned "to walk on the white man's road." Often the lands set aside for reservations were incapable of sustaining crops, reducing the inhabitants to utter poverty. Many tribal groups resisted being put into reservations.

Destruction of the Buffalo

As railroads pushed west, the herds of the American bison (commonly known as the buffalo) were decimated. Railroad workers and passengers went on a killing spree, shooting buffalo for food and sport. Also, industrial uses for the hides of buffalo put pressure on their numbers. In a matter of decades, the buffalo herds on the Plains were virtually exterminated. This greatly weakened the Plains peoples that depended on the buffalo for spiritual and physical sustenance.

Treaty of Medicine Lodge (1867)

Southern Plains Indians signed a treaty with the government at Medicine Lodge, Kansas, in 1867, agreeing to move to a reservation in exchange for government protection of their land from white encroachment.

Helen Hunt Jackson and the Call for Reform

By the 1880s, white sympathizers of American Indians pushed for a change in government policy. A prominent reformer was Helen Hunt Jackson, whose 1882 book *A Century of Dishonor* chronicled the abuses of the United States government committed against American Indians. She sent a copy of the book to each member of Congress.

The Dawes Act

Efforts at reform resulted in shifts in American policy toward American Indians. The Dawes Act (1887) abandoned the reservation system and divided tribal lands into individually owned plots. The goal of the policy was for American Indians to assimilate into white culture. This reform proved to be as damaging to American Indians as the earlier reservation policy. The government eventually undid this destructive policy with the Indian Reorganization Act (1934), allowing autonomy for American Indian tribal lands.

The Ghost Dance Movement

In the midst of the apocalyptic losses suffered by American Indians in the 1870s and 1880s, some American Indians adopted a spiritual practice known as the Ghost Dance. The Ghost Dance movement was developed by an American Indian named Wokova. It drew on traditional American Indian rituals, and emphasized cooperation among tribes and clean living and honesty. It wasn't successful in stopping white incursions, but it led to a spiritual revival that had a profound effect on American Indian tribes into the twentieth century.

Massacre at Wounded Knee

The last battle of the "Indian Wars" was at Wounded Knee, South Dakota, in 1890. U.S. forces surrounded a group of Sioux Indians, and proceeded to open fire on them. In all, two to three hundred American Indians were killed.

KEY CONCEPT 6.3
THE POLITICS AND CULTURE OF THE "GILDED AGE"

New intellectual and cultural movements developed during the Gilded Age of the last decades of the nineteenth century. Americans also engaged in political debates over economic and social policies.

I. The Politics of the Gilded Age

Business and politics became increasingly linked during the Gilded Age. Several economic issues came to dominate national political debates—tariffs, currency, corporate expansion, and the role of government in economic affairs.

A. GOVERNMENT CORRUPTION, BIG BUSINESS, AND THE CALL FOR REFORM

Close ties—and charges of corruption—came to define the relationship between government and business in the Gilded Age. In response to charges of corruption, members of the public called for reform on the local, state, and national levels.

The Evolution of the Two-party System

Neither the Democrats nor the Republicans, the two main political parties from the Civil War to the present, were able to dominate national politics during the Gilded Age. The Republicans controlled the White House for most of the period from 1869 to the turn of the century (the one exception was the two nonconsecutive terms of President Grover Cleveland). However, the elections were extremely close, with no presidential candidate receiving a clear majority of the popular vote in any election between 1872 and 1896. Control of Congress was split. The Republicans controlled the Senate for most of the period, and the Democrats controlled the House. Only briefly, for three different two-year periods, did one of the parties control the White House and both houses of Congress.

In many ways, the Gilded Age saw the two main political parties, the Democrats and the Republican, become increasingly removed from the concerns of ordinary Americans. Both parties seemed more responsive to the priorities of the newly formed trusts and industrial giants than to the needs of farmers, workers, of the urban poor. Corruption permeated political life from the backrooms of local political clubhouses to the corridors of power in Washington, DC. A spate of reform movements developed to address this situation, most notably the People's Party, better known as the Populist Party, in the last decade of the nineteenth century.

Ideology Takes a Backseat

Neither of the two political parties took strong stands on most of the pressing issues of the day. Neither party showed a willingness to deal with any of the various problems associated with the industrial expansion of the age. Issues like child labor, the consolidation of industries, workplace safety, and abuses by railroad companies were either avoided or dealt with in a superficial fashion. Neither party did much to protect the rights of African Americans (especially after the end of Reconstruction) or American Indians. Neither party addressed the call of many women for the right to vote. The one issue that consistently divided the parties was the tariff (Democrats wanted lower tariff rates and Republicans wanted higher tariff rates).

Both parties seemed aligned with the priorities of big business. Owners of major companies openly curried favor with congressmen with contributions, gifts, and outright bribery.

Political leaders, even presidents, seemed to shrink in importance when compared with the towering industrial figures of the day. Cornelius Vanderbilt, John D. Rockefeller, and Andrew Carnegie are far more clearly imprinted on the national collective memory than the "forgotten presidents" of the Gilded Age.

Corruption and the Grant Administration

American political life was rife with corruption during the Gilded Age. This was true on the local level, as evidenced by the illegal schemes of "Boss" Tweed in New York, as well as on the national level. The administration of Ulysses S. Grant (1869–1877) was tainted by corruption. Historians assess Grant's ability as a president far below his abilities on the battlefield. The Republican president was not decisive on the issue of Reconstruction (see Period 5). In addition, he surrounded himself with incompetent and corrupt advisors and appointees. He rewarded friends, army contacts, and party loyalists with jobs that required political experience. Though Grant was not directly charged with corruption, key members of his administration, including his vice president, were.

> ### CORRUPTION AND THE HISTORY OF RECONSTRUCTION
>
> Corruption in American politics seemed everywhere during the Gilded Age. However, traditional histories tended to single out the state Reconstruction governments for "extravagance" and corruption. More recent histories of the period look at such claims with a critical eye.

Corruption and Civil Service Reform

Civil service reform became a major issue in the Gilded Age. The civil service is the workforce of government employees. Attempts were made to reform the civil service in the 1880s so that jobs would be allocated to the most qualified people rather than to friends and relatives of powerful politicians.

Mugwumps, Stalwarts, and Half-Breeds

The issue of civil service reform divided the Republican Party in the wake of the scandals of the Grant administration. Reform-minded Republicans, mainly from Massachusetts and New York, were nicknamed "Mugwumps" by their critics, after the Algonquin word for "chief." They wanted to move away from the corruption of the Grant years and create a merit-based civil service. Those most resistant to abandoning the spoils system were nicknamed "Stalwarts." Those loyal to the Republican leadership, but wanting some degree of reform were known at "Half-Breeds." Hayes, who won the disputed election of 1876, was not well liked by any of the factions and chose not to run for reelection in 1880.

The Pendleton Act

A series of events of the summer of 1881 made civil service reform a more pressing issue and led to passage of the Pendleton Act. The Republicans nominated James A. Garfield for president in 1880. He won the presidency, but was shot four months after his inauguration in 1881. Garfield died from the wound two months later. The assassin was no doubt unbalanced, but the reason he gave for his actions was that he was passed over for a government job, despite his work on the Garfield campaign. Congress finally passed the Pendleton Act in 1883 to set up a merit-based federal civil service, a professional career service that allots government jobs on the basis of a competitive exam. This system still covers most of the bureaucratic jobs in the federal government. Upper level, policy oriented positions are still rotated when new presidential administrations come into office.

The Politics of Tariff Rates

The rate of taxation on imported goods had long divided many Americans. Industrialists tended to encourage higher tariffs to keep out foreign competition. Farming interests tended to support a lower tariff rate. They sold cotton and wheat to Europe and benefitted from increased international trade; high tariffs impeded international trade. Republicans had pushed tariffs higher during the Civil War to fund the war effort. By the 1880s, the government was awash in money from the tariff, and tariff reformers argued that lowering the tariff would put more money into circulation and stimulate economic activity. President Chester Arthur also broke with Republican orthodoxy and looked into lowering the tariff. Tariff reform foundered in Congress; ultimately a small decrease in tariff rates was passed.

The tariff issue remained contentious during Democratic president Grover Cleveland's first administration. Many Democrats, including Cleveland, began to push for lower rates. These tariff reformers became increasingly critical of the power of trusts and large corporations in dominating the economy. They saw high tariff rates as benefiting these big business interests at the expense of consumers and small producers. In 1888, the Republican Party nominated Benjamin Harrison, grandson of President William Henry Harrison. Business interests poured money into the Harrison campaign. In 1890, Harrison signed into law the highest tariff in the nation's history. The tariff became the most divisive issue in national elections in the post–Civil War period.

> ### THE PANIC OF 1893
>
> This economic crisis was the worst in American history before the Great Depression of the 1930s.

The Currency Issue

The vibrant economic growth that characterized much of the Gilded Age came to a screeching halt in 1893 (see more on the Panic of 1893 in Period 7). Many observers, both contemporaries and historians, cite the inadequate amount of currency in circulation as one of the underlying weaknesses in the economy. The money supply in the Gilded Age did not have the ability to grow as the economy expanded. The United States used metallic money, as stipulated in the Mint Act of 1792. The act allowed for the "free and unlimited coinage" of gold and silver. Individuals could coin gold or silver at a fixed ratio (the amount of silver in a silver dollar was to weigh fifteen times as much as the amount of gold in a gold dollar). However, in 1873, Congress changed this policy, allowing only for the coinage of gold. The amount of gold being coined in the 1870s and 1880s could not keep up with the growing economy. This was especially hard on farmers as it depressed the prices they received for their goods, and made it difficult to repay loans. The situation was beneficial to bankers, who wanted a relatively stable currency so that money repaid on loans retained its value.

> ### CURRENCY AND INFLATION
>
> Be familiar with basic economic concepts involving the currency supply. An expansion of the currency supply increases inflation. This would tend to benefit farmers, but would hurt consumers.

Regulation Versus Laissez-faire

Critics of corporate power pushed the government to take steps to reign in these massive corporations. However, these efforts at regulation were often hampered by the courts and by lax enforcement. Take, for example, the case of railroad regulation. In 1886 the Supreme Court, in the *Wabash, St. Louis and Pacific Railway Company v. Illinois* case, limited the ability of states to regulate railroads, asserting that such regulations could not impose "direct" burdens on interstate commerce. In response, the federal government created the Interstate Commerce Commission (1887) to regulate railroads. However, the ICC was chronically underfunded and was, therefore, ineffective. A similar pattern can be seen in antitrust legislation. In 1890 the Sherman Antitrust Act was passed to break up trusts. The act, however, had limited usefulness. In the case of *United States v. E.C. Knight Company* (1895), the Supreme Court greatly limited the scope of the act by making a distinction between trade (which would be subject to the act) and manufacturing (which would not).

B. THE POLITICS OF RACISM AND DISCRIMINATION

Racist and nativist theories became prominent in the Gilded Age. These theories, along with the Supreme Court decision in the *Plessy v. Ferguson* case, justified discrimination, segregation, and even violence against African American and certain immigrant groups.

Segregation in the "New South"

Jim Crow laws segregated public facilities such as railroad cars, bathrooms, and schools. These laws relegated African Americans to second-class status in the South. State and local segregation laws first appeared in the South after Reconstruction ended (1877). Though the Fourteenth Amendment (1868) guaranteed all citizens equal protection of the laws, in the *Slaughterhouse* cases (1873), the Supreme Court had ruled that the Fourteenth Amendment applied only to national citizenship rights, such as the right to vote in national elections and the right to travel between states—not to rights derived from "state citizenship" (see Period 5). In this legal setting, Jim Crow laws proliferated throughout the South.

Plessy v. Ferguson and the "Separate but Equal" Doctrine

In the case of *Plessy v. Ferguson* (1896), the Supreme Court decided that racial segregation did not violate the equal protection provision of the Fourteenth Amendment. The case began when Homer Plessy was arrested for violating the 1890 Separate Car Act, a Louisiana law that required separate accommodations for black and white passengers on railroads. Plessy was born a free man and was an "octoroon" (someone of one-eighth African descent). Plessy was encouraged to challenge the law by the Comité des Citoyens (Committee of Citizens). The committee hoped to use Plessy's arrest as a test case. The decision was a setback for those who sought an end to the Jim Crow system of racial segregation in the South. Jim Crow laws, opponents argued, violated the Fourteenth Amendment because the laws relegated African Americans to inferior public accommodations and had the effect of making African Americans second class citizens. However, the Court disagreed. The decision stated that segregation was acceptable as long as the facilities for both races were of equal quality.

The Rise of Nativism and Chinese Exclusion Act

Immigration patterns changed during the years of the Gilded Age. The Irish and German immigrations of the pre–Civil War years were supplemented by waves of immigrants from southern and eastern Europe and from Asia. These new immigrant groups were seen, by some, as markedly different from the pre–Civil War groups, in terms of appearance, language, and customs. The label "new immigrants" was applied to these groups (see more on the "new immigrants" in Period 7). The "new immigrants" heightened fears among conservative, Protestant public figures, such as Henry Cabot Lodge and Madison Grant. These nativists feared that the Anglo-Saxon Americans were committing "race suicide" by allowing "inferior" races to enter America in large numbers. Chinese Americans were especially targeted by nativists. The 1882 Chinese Exclusion Act represents the only instance in which a particular national group has been explicitly excluded from entrance into the United States. Later, in the 1920s, the government imposed quotas on immigrants that greatly reduced the overall number of immigrants allowed into the United States.

II. Cultural and Intellectual Movements of the Gilded Age

During the Gilded Age, a variety of individuals and groups put forth ideas about the age they were living in. Some of these ideas justified the prevailing social structure of the day; others challenged it.

A. JUSTIFYING SUCCESS: THE BENEFITS AND OBLIGATIONS OF WEALTH

Several theories that justified the socioeconomic structure of the Gilded Age gained currency. At the same time, some argued that the wealthy had an obligation to help those less fortunate.

Andrew Carnegie and the "Gospel of Wealth"

Andrew Carnegie asserted, in an essay entitled "Wealth" (1899), that the wealthy have a duty to live responsible, modest lives and to give back to society. This "gospel of wealth" asserted that wealthy entrepreneurs should distribute their wealth so that it could be put to good use, rather than frivolously wasted. Carnegie ended up donating the majority of his fortune to charity and public-oriented projects. Carnegie believed in a laissez-faire approach to social problems. He did not want the government interfering in the social and economic spheres. That is, in part, why he urged his fellow millionaires to take action on behalf of the community. In this way, the government wouldn't have to.

Horatio Alger and the Myth of the Self-made Man

Horatio Alger wrote a series of "dime novels" that often featured a poor boy who achieves success in the world. His success is usually the result of a bit of luck and a bit of pluck—fortuitous circumstances as well as determination and perseverance. These "rags to riches" novels, such as "Ragged Dick," put forth the idea that anyone could make it in Gilded Age America; the reality, of course, was quite different.

B. CHALLENGES TO THE DOMINANT CORPORATE ETHIC

A variety of critics challenged the dominant corporate ethic of the day. Some of these critics offered utopian visions of the future, some questioned the logic of the capitalist system itself.

Henry George and the "Single Tax" on Land

Henry George was a thinker, economist, and politician who was critical of the persistence of poverty in a nation of such technological and industrial progress. In his book, *Progress and Poverty* (1879), he criticized the vast resources, especially land, controlled by wealthy elite. He argued for a "single tax" on land values, which he believed would create a more equitable society.

Socialism and Anarchism

Many Americans began to question the basic assumptions of capitalism and embraced alternative ideologies, such as anarchism and socialism. These radical ideas never gained the number of adherents in the United States that they did in Europe. Occasionally, conservative newspapers and politicians exaggerated the strength of these movements in the United States. Newspapers often conflated the labor movement in general with these "dangerous" movements in order to delegitimize or stigmatize the labor movement. Still, these movements had adherents in the United States. After the utter failure of the Pullman strike, Eugene V. Debs moved away from the labor movement and toward socialism. He was one of the founders of the Socialist Party of America in 1901.

Edward Bellamy's *Looking Backward, 2000–1887*

The most famous American socialist tract of the nineteenth century was Edward Bellamy's *Looking Backward, 2000–1887* (1888). This novel imagined a man who falls asleep in 1887 and awakens in 2000 to find a socialist utopia in which the inequities and poverty of the Gilded Age have been eradicated.

C. RETHINKING RACE AND GENDER IN THE GILDED AGE

Women and African-American activists challenged ingrained ideas around gender and race and offered a vision of political, social, and economic equality.

Challenging Notions of Domesticity

As the economic dislocations wrought by industrialization touched more and more families, many women became more politically engaged. Many women began to challenge the rigid gender expectations embodied in the "cult of domesticity" (see Period 4). In the 1880s and 1890s, women's clubs began to emerge in many towns and cities. These clubs investigated and advocated around issues of poverty, working conditions, and pollution. In 1890, women organized an umbrella organization—the General Federation of Women's Clubs. These clubs often used the rhetoric of domesticity to justify their activism outside the home. The organization used the term "maternalism" to describe the dual role of women as mothers and as social activists. Many women put their energy into the campaign to curb alcohol consumption in the United States. The Women's Christian Temperance Union, founded in 1874, became a mass organization, especially under the leadership of Frances Willard. Members of the WCTU later got involved in both the populist movement of the 1890s and the Progressive movement of the early twentieth century (see Period 7). Women continued to press for voting rights in the late 1800s. The National American Woman Suffrage Association formed in 1890, merging two earlier suffrage groups (see Period 5).

Challenging Jim Crow in the Gilded Age

After Reconstruction ended (1877), African Americans saw the meager gains of the Reconstruction era—in terms of political and economic rights—steadily erode. In the face of segregation and marginalization, African Americans did not remain idle. Ida B. Wells was one of the more radical voices for social justice in the Gilded Age. As a young woman, she sued the Chesapeake and Ohio Railroad for denying her a seat in the ladies' car. After three friends of hers were lynched, she began to write and campaign against the practice of lynching. Her journalism deconstructed many of the myths around lynching—most important, that lynchings were carried out in response to the crime of interracial rape. Another important gilded age activist was Booker T. Washington. Washington encouraged African Americans to gain training in vocational skills. Toward this end, he was selected to be the first leader of the Tuskegee Institute (1881). He argued that confrontation with whites would end badly for African Americans; he counseled cooperation with supportive whites and collective self-improvement. Later, his conciliatory approach was challenged by the more radical W.E.B. Du Bois (see Period 7).

SUBJECT TO DEBATE

There has been a major disconnect between the West of popular memory and the West of the historical record. Generations of western movies have presented a morality play between virtuous pioneers and conniving Indians. It is only in the last generation that the popular memory of the West has shifted. Movies such as *Dances with Wolves* (1990) have served as correctives. In your writing, try to avoid the stereotypes and clichés of the "cowboy and Indian" genre.

A central point of contention in interpretations of the Gilded Age is the place of the owners of big business. The image that has stuck is that of the bloated "robber baron." This image was promoted by many contemporaries during the Gilded Age. The accumulation of such wealth and power was unprecedented and seemed at odds with the ideal of the yeoman farmer or the urban artisan. Further, the lavish spending habits of these men—illustrated by the gaudy mansions of New York's Fifth Avenue—also seemed outside of the American tradition of thrift and humility. This image of greed and excess was kept alive by Progressive-era historians and is still part of the collective memory of the era. Recently, some historians have begun to question this representation of the Gilded Age. For one, even in the late nineteenth century, most of the big companies were incorporated and run by boards of directors. The age of an arbitrary proprietor, ordering his employees around, was an anachronism even in the late Gilded Age. Second, recent historical interpretations have noted the tremendous wealth generated during this period. Eventually, this rising-tide of wealth helped lift all boats. It is not by accident that so many "new immigrants" came to the United States—it truly was a land of opportunity at the turn of the twentieth century. In your essay writing, keep in mind the origins of the image of the "robber baron" and its usefulness in understanding the realities of the Gilded Age.

Historians have long debated the "revolt of the farmers" in the 1880s and 1890s. You should be familiar with the different poles in the debate. On the one hand, some historians have looked admiringly on the populist movement. These historians note the dire situation farmers found themselves in and see the movement as a reasonable response. This approach also looks approvingly at the legacy of the movement; some of its goals were taken up by the Progressive movement in the early decades of the twentieth century, and even by the New Dealers in the 1930s. Other historians paint the movement as an irrational, emotional rebellion against the modern world. These historians site the racism, anti-Semitism, anti-urbanism, and anti-immigrant sentiment evident in certain corners of the movement. In this light, the populist movement is a precursor of the Ku Klux Klan in the 1920s and McCarthyism in the 1950s.

Historians have debated the impact of "machine politics" in the nineteenth century. Starting in the Progressive era, historians wrote disparagingly about the corruption of the political bosses of the Gilded Age. In this narrative, these bosses undermined democracy until reformers rose up and cleaned up the political process. There is certainly truth to the narrative. However, reality is always more complicated. Social historians have recently examined the positive impact the political machines had on immigrant communities. The machines may have been corrupt but they were the only safety net and jobs-program for recently arrived immigrants. In some ways, the attacks on the political machines were attacks on the structure of the immigrant community. In your essay writing, it would be wise to exercise caution when talking about the political "bosses" of the Gilded Age.

Practice Multiple-Choice Questions

Directions: Pick the letter that best answers the following questions.

QUESTIONS 1–3 REFER TO THE FOLLOWING PASSAGE:

"Be it enacted by the Senate and House of Representatives of the United States of America in Congress assembled, That in all cases where any tribe or band of Indians has been, or shall hereafter be, located upon any reservation created for their use, either by treaty stipulation or by virtue of an act of Congress or executive order setting apart the same for their use, the President of the United States be, and he hereby is, authorized, whenever in his opinion any reservation or any part thereof of such Indians is advantageous for agricultural and grazing purposes, to cause said reservation, or any part thereof, to be surveyed, or resurveyed if necessary, and to allot the lands in said reservation in severalty to any Indian located thereon in quantities as follows: . . . "

—Dawes Severalty Act (excerpt), 1887

1. A primary goal of the Dawes Severalty Act (1887) was to

   (A) turn American Indians into property-owning, profit-oriented, individual farmers.
   (B) keep alive traditional practices and languages.
   (C) open up American Indian lands in Georgia, South Carolina, and Alabama to mining and cotton farming.
   (D) compensate American Indian tribes for lands that had been taken through fraudulent treaties.

2. An important impetus for the passage of the Dawes Severalty Act was

   (A) the Supreme Court decision in the case of *Worcester v. Georgia.*
   (B) a non-violent protest movement against existing policies led by Crazy Horse.
   (C) the success of the Freedman's Bureau in addressing the problems of African Americans in the South.
   (D) the depiction of mistreatment of American Indians in Helen Hunt Jackson's book, *A Century of Dishonor.*

3. Which of the following developments was similar to the Dawes Severalty Act in that they both had the same goal for the future of American Indians?

(A) The formation of the Ghost Dance movement
(B) The establishment of Indian Boarding Schools
(C) The passage of the Indian Reorganization Act
(D) The founding of the American Indian Movement

Answers and Explanations to Multiple-Choice Questions

1. **(A)** A primary goal of the Dawes Severalty Act (1887) was to turn American Indians into property-owning, profit-oriented, individual farmers. This was part of a push toward assimilation as a policy in regard to American Indians. Some reformers had come to believe that the reservation system was destructive to American Indians and that the best strategy forward was to encourage them to give up traditional ways. In addition, the seeming inability or unwillingness on the part of American Indians to adopt a mainstream American lifestyle was seen by many Americans as both unacceptable and uncivilized.

2. **(D)** An important impetus for the passage of the Dawes Severalty Act was the depiction of mistreatment of American Indians in Helen Hunt Jackson's 1881 book, *A Century of Dishonor*. Her book chronicled the abuses of the United States government committed against American Indians. She hoped to awaken the conscience of the American people, and their representatives, to the brutal mistreatment of American Indians. She sent a copy of the book to each member of Congress.

3. **(B)** American Indian boarding schools were boarding schools established in the late nineteenth and early twentieth centuries as a means of educating American Indian children according to the standards of mainstream white American culture. In this regard, they were similar to the Dawes Act in that both promoted assimilation as the solution to the "Indian problem." Children were forbidden to speak their native languages, were given European-American style haircuts, and we given new names to replace their traditional names.

Period 7: 1890–1945 Economic Dislocation and Reform in the Age of Empire and World War

9

1914	Federal Reserve Act
	Federal Trade Commission
	Clayton Antitrust Act
	Beginning of World War I
1914–1917	United States intervention in Mexico
1915	Release of D.W. Griffith's film *Birth of a Nation*
1916	Reelection of Woodrow Wilson
1917	Espionage Act
1918	Sedition Act
	Armistice ends World War I
1919	Eighteenth Amendment (prohibition) ratified
	Creation of the Comintern
1919–1920	Boston Police Strike
1920	Nineteenth Amendment (women's right to vote) ratified
	Deportation of Emma Goldman
	Schenck v. United States
	Seattle General Strike
	Height of the "Palmer raids"
	Election of Warren G. Harding
1921	Emergency Quota Act
	Beginning of the Teapot Dome Scandal
1924	National Origins Act
	Election of Calvin Coolidge
1925	Scopes trial
1927	Execution of Sacco and Vanzetti
1928	Kellogg–Briand Pact
	Election of Herbert Hoover
1929	Stock market crash
	The Great Depression begins
1930	Hawley-Smoot Tariff
1931	The Marx Brothers' movie *Duck Soup* is released
1932	Bonus March
	Reconstruction Finance Corporation established
	Franklin D. Roosevelt elected president
1933	The 100 Days
	"Bank holiday"
	Agricultural Adjustment Act (AAA)
	Glass–Steagall Act (Federal Depositors Insurance Corporation established)
	National Industrial Recovery Act (NIRA)
	Civilian Conservation Corps (CCC)
	Ratification of the Twenty-first Amendment (repeal of prohibition)

1934	Share Our Wealth clubs started by Huey Long
	Securities and Exchange Commission
	Clifford Odets writes the play *Waiting for Lefty*
1935	National Labor Relations Act (Wagner Act)
	Social Security Act
	Schechter decision strikes down NIRA
	Works Progress Administration
	First Neutrality Act
1936	Butler decision strikes down the AAA
	Roosevelt's "court packing" plan
	Roosevelt elected to a second term
	Charlie Chaplin's *Modern Times* is released
1936–1939	Spanish Civil War
1937	"Roosevelt Recession"
	Farm Security Administration
	Panay incident
	Quarantine Speech
1939	Cash-and-Carry Policy
	Nazi–Soviet Pact
	The movie *Mr. Smith Goes to Washington* is released
	John Steinbeck writes *The Grapes of Wrath*
1940	Selective Service Act
	Tripartite Pact
	Roosevelt elected to unprecedented third term
1941	Lend–Lease Act
	Japanese attack on Pearl Harbor
1942	Battle of Midway
1943	Teheran Conference
1944	*Korematsu v. United States*
	Bretton Woods Conference
1945	Battles of Iwo Jima and Okinawa
	Yalta Conference
	Potsdam Conference
	Dropping of the atomic bomb on Hiroshima and Nagasaki

INTRODUCTION

The United States faced a series of profound domestic and international challenges during this period. As the country became increasingly pluralistic, Americans debated how best to meet these challenges. These debates centered on the role of the government in the economic and social life of the country, and on the role of the United States on the global stage.

In response to the rapid industrialization, political corruption, and unplanned urbanization of the Gilded Age, the Progressive movement grew and developed an extensive slate of proposals for reform. The movement claimed many legislative victories, and ultimately influenced both the New Deal and twentieth-century liberalism.

After 1890, the United States began to play a more aggressive role on the world stage, intervening in Hawaii, Cuba, Panama, Mexico, and beyond, and acquiring possessions from Puerto Rico to the Philippines. These ventures raised the profile of the United States and established it as one of the world's major powers. When the Great War, later known as World War I, began in Europe in August 1914, most Americans were not eager to join the conflict. The war seemed to be a continuation of the age-old rivalries of the European nations. As the conflict dragged on, a number of factors pushed America toward intervention. The United States did not play a major role in World War I until the final year of the conflict, but the war ushered in some important changes in the United States. Culturally, the country became more jingoistic and conservative; the reform impulse of the Progressive era was pushed to the background. The war expanded the role of the federal government and it contributed to the Great Migration of African Americans. America's participation in the war strengthened its position on the world stage, even though the United States withdrew into isolationism in the years following the war.

During the 1920s, we see the development of some of the cultural divisions that have roiled Americans since. Many historians note the resurgence of traditional values in the United States in response to the unfolding of a more modern America. This tension between tradition and modernity has shaped much of the historical work on the 1920s. Not all the elements of the 1920s fit neatly into this model of tradition versus modernity. The experiment in the prohibition of alcohol comes to mind; its origins were both in the Progressive movement's push for government-sponsored social engineering, as well as in the religious crusade to eradicate "immoral" habits. Still, the tradition-versus-modernity model is a useful lens through which to examine the 1920s. The 1920s ended with the stock market crash that ushered in the Great Depression.

The Great Depression was the most devastating economic downturn in American history. It is one of several such downturns, which include the panics of 1819, 1837, 1857, 1873, and 1893. However, in none of these panics did the country reach the depths of despair realized during the Great Depression. A basic understanding of introductory economic concepts, such as supply and demand, Keynesianism, and the business cycle, will come in handy in assessing the causes and responses to the Great Depression. The most significant response to the Depression, the New Deal, helped to redefine the relationship between the government and the economy and helped launch the modern welfare state.

This period ends with World War II, a cataclysmic war that profoundly transformed the nations that participated in it, including the United States. World War II set in motion a series of demographic, political, and social trends that would shape American history for the remainder of the twentieth century. A large percentage of the millions of returning soldiers soon settled down, married, and had the children who would comprise the "baby boom" generation. The war brought the United States out of the Great Depression and set the country on a trajectory of sustained economic growth for a generation. Wartime experiences inspired both African Americans and women, setting the stage for the civil rights movement and the women's liberation movement. The United States did not retreat into an isolationist stance after the war, as it had after World War I. The wartime alliance of the United States and the Soviet Union would soon degenerate into a cold war.

KEY CONCEPT 7.1
RESPONSES TO ECONOMIC DISLOCATION AND UNCERTAINTY

The industrialization of the Gilded Age, and the accompanying trends of migrations and urbanization, dramatically transformed American society. The government, as well as social and political organizations, attempted to address the impact that these changes brought to American society.

I. Economic Growth and the Uncertainty of the Business Cycle

The consolidation of large corporations that began in the Gilded Age continued into the twentieth century. The growth and power of corporations transformed the social and economic life of the United States. These changes contributed to economic growth and urbanization, while at the same time contributing to economic instability and increasingly severe fluctuations in the business cycle.

A. A CORPORATE ECONOMY

Large corporations came to dominate the American economy. Improvements in technology and new manufacturing techniques led to increased production of consumer goods.

Toward Greater Consolidation

The Gilded Age saw the advent of the modern corporate economy, as mergers, holding companies, and trusts led to fewer entities controlling larger segments of the economy (see Period 6). This trend continued into the twentieth century, as the assembly line, mass production, and new management techniques contributed to a further consolidation of the economy. The production and consumption of consumer goods stoked the American economy for much of the 1920s. New products, such as automobiles and radios, captured the public's imagination, and new production techniques increased industrial output.

Henry Ford and Mass Production

The most important figure in the development of new production techniques was Henry Ford. In 1913 he opened a plant with a continuous conveyor belt. The belt moved the chassis of the car from worker to worker, so that each did a small task in the process of assembling the final product. This mass production technique reduced the price of his Model T car, and also dealt a blow to the skilled mechanics who had previously built automobiles. Unskilled assembly line workers gradually replaced skilled craft workers in American industry.

> ### THE DESKILLING OF THE LABOR PROCESS
>
> Mass production and assembly-line work weakened the position of workers in terms of bargaining for better wages and conditions.

Scientific Management

An important aspect of mass production was the scientific management techniques developed by Frederick Winslow Taylor. Taylor carefully watched workers, noted the most efficient techniques, and wrote down in exacting detail how a particular task was to be done. Work became more efficient, but also more monotonous. Many workers, especially those with a degree of skill, resisted the loss of control and autonomy that scientific management techniques entailed.

Advertising and Mass Consumption

If the quality of work deteriorated for factory workers in the 1920s, the availability of consumer goods to average workers greatly increased. Cars, radios, toasters, health and beauty aids, and other consumer goods filled showrooms and stores. The advertising industry also changed a great deal in the 1920s. Advertising and public relations men tapped into the ideas of Freudian psychology and emerging ideas around crowd psychology. Many ads in this period attempted to reach the public on a subconscious level, rather than presenting products and services in a straightforward manner. The public relations pioneer Edward Bernays, a nephew of Sigmund Freud, was a key figure in the shift in marketing toward elaborate corporate advertising campaigns. Easy credit and layaway plans also helped move merchandise.

B. THE TRANSITION TOWARD AN URBAN, INDUSTRIAL ECONOMY

The forces of change that began in the Gilded Age continued to transform the United States in the twentieth century. America continued the transition from a rural, agrarian society to an urban, industrial one. The new society offered new opportunities to women and to migrants—both from abroad and from within the United States.

New Opportunities for Women

From the late 1800s into the twentieth century, urbanization and industrialization provided new opportunities for women in the workforce. The most common occupation for women in the mid-nineteenth century was in domestic service; in the late nineteenth century more women were working in factories and by the first decades of the twentieth century, office work became their primary occupation.

WOMEN AND PUBLIC LIFE

When traditional history texts discuss women and gender, they often discuss fashion and appearance. In your writing, try to avoid limiting your discussions of gender to these topics.

New opportunities for women were not confined to the workplace. The "new" woman of the 1920s was engaged in public issues. She participated in the political struggles of the Progressive movement and gained a new sense of confidence in public issues, especially after women achieved the right to vote in 1920. These economic and political changes for women were reflected in changing ideas around gender. The new image of women during the 1920s was symbolized by the popularity of the flappers and their style of dress. Flappers were independent-minded young women of the 1920s who openly defied Victorian moral codes about "proper" lady-like behavior. The typical flapper of the 1920s was characterized by a short haircut, called a bob, and shorter dresses. Women of the 1920s moved away from the heavy, matronly dresses of the Victorian era.

C. ECONOMIC INSTABILITY AND THE CALL FOR GREATER FEDERAL REGULATION

The United States economy continued to grow in the late 1800s and early 1900s. However, fluctuations in the business cycle became increasingly common and increasingly severe. From the Panic of 1893 to the Great Depression, these economic downturns led to calls for greater federal regulation of the economy.

The Panic of 1893

Throughout American history, the business activity has moved in cycles. In the nineteenth century, the economy experienced several downturns, often labeled economic "panics." Notable panics had occurred earlier in 1819, 1837, 1857, and 1873. As the economy became more consolidated in the Gilded Age, with fewer corporations controlling larger and larger segments of the economy, the potential for more severe downturns intensified. After all, if a few large corporations experience downturns, the potential for a large-scale disruption to the economy was more likely. Such a scenario played out in 1893.

The Panic of 1893 began as the Philadelphia and Reading Railroad went bankrupt, followed by other railroads, as well as banks that had lent them money. The stock market followed suit as Wall Street panicked. Millions of workers were unemployed by 1894.

Causes of the Great Depression

The Panic of 1893 paled in comparison to the economic downturn of the 1930s. Although on the surface the economy of the 1920s seemed strong, there were structural weaknesses that became more apparent as the decade progressed. The precise reasons for the Great Depression are still debated by historians, but the following explanations are frequently mentioned.

Overproduction and Under-consumption

Industrial production greatly expanded in the 1920s. New products, such as automobiles and radios, captured the public's imagination, and new production techniques, such as the assembly line and "scientific management," increased industrial output. For much of the 1920s, the public, induced by easy credit and seductive advertising, was able to absorb this increased industrial output, but by 1927 manufacturers noticed that warehouse inventories were on the rise. Consumption just could not keep up with production. A weak labor movement in the twenties led to stagnant wages. Ordinary Americans did not share in the economic expansion of the 1920s. The gap between the wealthy and the poor grew. During the 1920s, income for the top 1 percent of the population increased by nearly 75 percent, while the bottom 90 percent of the population saw their income rise by less than 10 percent. By the late 1920s, manufacturers made the logical decision of beginning layoffs, worsening a bad situation.

Problems on the Farm

Throughout the 1920s, the agricultural sector lagged behind the rest of the economy. Farmers had put more acres under cultivation during World War I to meet increased demand for agricultural goods. By the twenties, Europe was back on its feet, yet American farmers did not cut back on production. Mechanization and expansion left the farmers of the 1920s in a cycle of debt, overproduction, and falling commodity prices. Increased tariff rates and an isolationist foreign policy further reduced the international market for American agricultural goods.

An Inflated Stock Market

Investing in the stock market is always something of a gamble, but in the 1920s people gambled recklessly with other people's money. In the 1920s, people increasingly bought stocks on margin, paying only 10 percent of the purchase price upfront with the promise of paying the remainder in the future. This practice worked as long as stock prices rose, which they did throughout most of the 1920s. By the late 1920s, however, serious investors began to see that stock prices were reaching new heights as the actual earnings of major corporations were declining. This discrepancy between the price per share and the actual earnings of corporations led investors to begin selling stocks, which stimulated a panic. On October 29, 1929, "Black Tuesday," the stock market crashed, destroying many individuals' investments.

> ## SPECULATION AND THE STOCK MARKET
>
> Many accounts of the economy in the 1920s fault the speculative practices of the stock market. Try to avoid an overemphasis on the speculative nature of the 1920s stock market. Speculation is, of course, at the heart of the stock market, then and now.

II. Progressive Era Reform

The Progressive movement was a response to the economic instability, social inequality, and political corruption that had begun during the Gilded Age and continued into the twentieth century. Progressive reformers called for greater government intervention in the economy, as well as increased democratization of the political process, social justice, and conservation of natural resources.

A. THE PROGRESSIVE MOVEMENT

The Progressive movement developed in the late 1890s and in the first decades of the twentieth century. Reformers and journalists addressed a host of issues associated with an industrial society. Progressive-era reformers tended to be largely urban and middle class; many were women. They worked on reform on the local, state, and national levels.

The Making of the Progressive Movement

The Progressive movement was essentially a middle-class response to the excesses of rapid industrialization, political corruption, and unplanned urbanization. Not only were the primary activists in the movement middle-class college graduates, but also the tone and tenor of the movement was decidedly middle class. Progressivism existed at the grass-roots level as well as in the corridors of power. Two influential presidents, Theodore Roosevelt and Woodrow Wilson, took on the progressive mantle. The movement was more an amalgam of interests, ideas, groups, and individuals, rather than a tight-knit cohort of activists with a cohesive ideology and a clearly articulated vision of the future. The movement was a bundle of contradictions. It championed reforms to benefit the working class, but looked at the actual working class with a mix of paternalism and suspicion. The movement challenged women's exclusion from the political process but largely accepted the prevailing social views of African Americans. To some degree progressivism challenged the abuses of unbridled capitalism; but, at the same time, many industrialists embraced progressive legislation in order to rationalize the freewheeling nature of the capitalist system.

Women and the Progressive Movement

A large percentage of progressive activists were women. The Progressive movement provided a means for women to become engaged in public issues in an era when the vote was still restricted to men in most states. Women often framed their participation in the movement as "social housekeeping." In this way, it did not seem like such a radical break from the traditional domestic activities that women were expected to find fulfillment in. Prominent women in the Progressive movement included: Florence Kelly, an activist for the reform of factories and chief factory inspector for Illinois (1893); Frances Perkins, head of the New York Consumers' League (1910) and, later, secretary of labor under President Franklin Roosevelt (1933–1945); and Jane Addams, founder of Hull House in Chicago (1897).

Jane Addams and the Settlement House Movement

The settlement house movement was the most visible example of an alliance between middle-class reformers and working-class men and women. Settlement houses were established to aid immigrants, especially immigrant women. By 1911, more than 400 settlement houses existed in the United States, usually run by women. Jane Addams founded and ran Hull House in Chicago; she is considered one of the founders of the field of social work in the United States. Addams wrote two autobiographical volumes, including *Twenty Years at Hull House* (1910), and was awarded the Nobel Peace Prize in 1931.

Scientific Management and the Quest for Efficiency

Many Progressive reformers embraced the goals of expertise and efficiency. Progressives tended to believe that expert management in the workplace and in government would benefit society as a whole. This system of expert managers would replace systems based on cronyism, nepotism, and favoritism. Many progressives looked favorably to the "scientific management" techniques developed by Frederick Winslow Taylor. Work tended to become monotonous under rigid scientific management, but also, no doubt, more efficient (see more on Frederick Winslow Taylor above). The movement held the optimistic belief that experts, with the backing of the government, could address a variety of social ills, using scientific and rational criteria. Many of these ideas are articulated in Walter Lippmann's book, *Drift and Mastery* (1914).

Pragmatism

Progressives gravitated toward the pragmatist philosophical ideas of William James and John Dewey. Pragmatists questioned the philosophical quest for eternal truths. Rather, they argued, the value of an idea lay in its ability to positively impact the world. Experimentation was central to the pragmatists' work. Dewey put this idea into practice in an experimental school he started in Chicago. The school put much more of an emphasis on the process of learning and on student participation than on the content of the curriculum.

Reform Darwinism

Progressive activists rejected the ethos of social Darwinism, which applied Charles Darwin's ideas about the natural world to the world of human interactions (see Period 6). Progressives embraced the Darwinian idea of evolution, but thought that the evolution of human society to its highest ideals required active intervention and cooperation, rather than a laissez-faire approach. This call to active intervention in the evolution of the social order is called reform Darwinism.

Muckrakers and the Birth of Investigative Journalism

Progressives believed in the power of the newly developed mass print media to shed light on social ills and to inspire action. The practitioners of this new investigative form of journalism were known as muckrakers. *McClure's, Harper's, Cosmopolitan*, and several other magazines became staples of middle-class homes by the turn of the twentieth century, and readers were increasingly drawn to articles detailing the corruption and scandal of the modern world. Many of these muckrakers saw themselves on a mission to shine a light on the sordid business and political practices of the day. Important muckrakers include Upton Sinclair, Ida Tarbell, Lincoln Steffens, and Frank Norris (all of them are discussed below in the context of the topics they wrote about).

Progressives and Municipal Reform

Progressive activists were alarmed at the inefficiency and corruption of municipal government. The political machines that developed in large American cities in the nineteenth century continued to dominate cities in the early twentieth century. The most famous nineteenth-century political machine was the Democratic Party machine in New York City—headquartered in Tammany Hall and dominated by "Boss" William Marcy Tweed (see Period 6).

The Galveston Flood and the Commission Form of Government

The issue of municipal inefficiency and corruption came to the fore in the aftermath of a devastating hurricane and flood that struck Galveston, Texas, in 1900. Upwards of 8,000 people died in the disaster. The ineffective response by the city government in Galveston convinced local leaders to create commissions to spearhead the cleanup and rebuilding of the city. This commission form of government soon spread from Galveston to other cities. In this form of government, voters elect a group of commissioners who run the city and head various departments, such as public works, fire, and sanitation. In this way, city officials are not beholden to the largess and patronage of powerful political bosses.

The inefficiencies of urban governance were highlighted in Lincoln Steffens's 1904 muckraking book *The Shame of the Cities*. The book is a collection of pieces he had written for *McClure's* magazine.

Progressivism and Moral Reform

The progressive zeal to attack social ills led many to campaign against "sin" and "vice." These middle-class reformers were more than ready to impose their notions of proper behavior on the society as a whole. Reformers tackled excessive drinking, prostitution, rowdy behavior, and cheap entertainment in their attempt to "civilize" the urban environment.

The Temperance Campaign and the Eighteenth Amendment

The movement to ban alcohol from American society had been one of the largest reform movements in the nineteenth century, and it gained new enthusiasts among progressives who sought to harness the power of the government to change social behavior. (See more on the temperance movement in Period 6.)

The final victory for the temperance movement came as the United States entered World War I. The movement successfully equated the prohibition of alcohol with the quest to bring democracy to the world. The United States would purify the world of undemocratic forces and purify its citizens of corrupting alcohol. Also, with wartime shortages of grain, it made sense to ban grain-based alcoholic beverages. The anti-German sentiment that developed during World War I also played a role because many American breweries had German names. All these factors led to the ratification of the Eighteenth Amendment, which banned alcohol production, sales, and transportation as of January 1, 1920.

B. PROGRESSIVE REFORM ON THE NATIONAL LEVEL

The Progressive movement had a profound impact on national politics. Progressives pushed for federal legislation to expand democratic participation and to protect both the economy and the environment from abuses.

Progressivism and Industrial Capitalism

During the Gilded Age of the late nineteenth century, America's industrial output grew exponentially, with virtually no government regulation. Industrialists and their allies championed laissez-faire economics—the idea that government should stay out of economic activities. By the early twentieth century, many Americans came to believe that unregulated industry could be harmful to individuals and communities, and even to the health of industrial capitalism itself. If people lost confidence in the products of the industrial system, sales would suffer.

The Jungle and the Meat-packing Industry

A public outcry about the conditions of the meat processing industry was generated by Upton Sinclair's 1906 novel, *The Jungle*, which vividly depicted the horrible conditions in the meat-packing industry. The novel takes place in Chicago and follows a Lithuanian immigrant family through the stockyards of Chicago. The novel, based on extensive research by Sinclair, brought to light the unsanitary and dangerous conditions of the meat packing industry. The socialist message of the book was largely ignored by the public but the depiction of meat processing was not. The public uproar that followed publication of the book led Congress to pass the Meat Inspection Act (1906) and the Pure Food and Drug Act (also 1906), which established the Food and Drug Administration.

The History of the Standard Oil Company

The Standard Oil Company, a giant trust assembled by John D. Rockefeller, had come to dominate the petroleum-processing industry by the end of the nineteenth century (see period 6). Ida Tarbell detailed the rise of Standard Oil in a series of articles in *McClure's Magazine* and then in the book, *The History of the Standard Oil Company* (1904). Her research exposed the ruthlessness of John D. Rockefeller's oil company. Her book contributed to the government breaking up the Standard Oil Trust in 1911.

The Triangle Factory Fire

The Progressive movement was spurred to take action after a tragic fire swept through the Triangle Shirtwaist Factory in 1911. The factory, which produced women's blouses (then known as "shirtwaists"), was located in the upper floors of a factory building in the Greenwich Village section of New York City. The employees were mostly young women, many of whom were recent Italian or Jewish immigrants. A fire began in one of the scrap bins and soon spread. The workers discovered that one of the entrances was blocked by the flames and another was locked (perhaps to keep the workers in, or to keep union organizers out). Some escaped by elevator, some by a fire escape before it collapsed. Ultimately 146 workers died. The tragedy led to the creation of fire safety laws in New York and led to the rapid growth of the International Ladies Garment Workers' Union.

Regulating Workplace Practices—*Muller v. Oregon* and the "Brandeis Brief"

Progressives tackled the dual issues of long working hours and child labor. In the late-nineteenth century, workdays of twelve hours or more were not uncommon, and child labor had become a common practice in large factories. The movement to reform the workplace suffered a setback in 1905 when the Supreme Court shot down a New York State law restricting hours for bakers in the case of *Lochner v. New York*. The court cited the sanctity of private contracts between employers and employees. However, the Progressive movement achieved a major boost in another Supreme Court decision just three years later, *Muller v. Oregon* (1908). That decision upheld an Oregon law limiting the number of hours women could work. This case cited the supposed physical limitations of women and the threat to their health that long workdays posed. The case specifically cited women's role as child bearers. The case is significant because of the brief written by future Supreme Court justice Louis Brandeis. On behalf of the state of Oregon, Brandeis prepared a brief citing copious scientific, psychological, and sociological studies to bolster the case for limiting women's hours of work. This type of legal argument has come to be known as a "Brandeis brief." The use of non-legal information in legal matters would become increasingly common in the twentieth century, including in the *Brown v. Board of Education of Topeka* case (1954).

MULLER AND THE PROGRESSIVE AGENDA

The *Muller* decision represented a major victory for the Progressive movement. The decision also reflected differing attitudes about gender within the movement. Although many progressives challenged traditional understandings of gender, this decision reinforced traditional notions of female frailty.

Challenging Child Labor

Evocative photographs of children in workplace settings by photographers such as Lewis Hine, brought the issue of child labor to public attention. The Progressive movement had a short-lived success in regard to the issue of child labor. In 1916 Congress passed the Keating-Owen Child Labor Act. Realizing that local factory rules were under the domain of state law, Congress addressed the issue of child labor by prohibiting the sale in interstate commerce of goods produced by factories that employed children under fourteen. Congress used its power to regulate interstate commerce. Less than a year later, in the case of *Hammer v. Dagenhart* (1917), the Supreme Court shot down the act. The Court asserted that the goods being regulated were not inherently "immoral," as prostitution or liquor might be. Therefore, what was being addressed by the law was manufacturing practices, and manufacturing practices were subject to state, not federal, law. Child labor was not effectively addressed until federal fair-labor standards were established during the New Deal era of the 1930s.

Progressivism in the White House

The Progressive movement was primarily a grassroots movement of thousands of activists, but in the early-twentieth century, progressivism entered the discourse of the national political parties. President Theodore Roosevelt, a Republican, embraced many progressive reforms, but his handpicked successor, President William H. Taft, proved to be a disappointment to the Progressive movement. The divisions within the Republican Party over Taft led to the electoral victory in 1912 of the Democrat Woodrow Wilson. The pervasiveness of the progressive ideology crossed party lines, and Wilson implemented some important progressive reforms.

Theodore Roosevelt and the Square Deal

Theodore Roosevelt assumed the presidency following the assassination of William McKinley (1901) and quickly began to move the Republican Party and the nation itself in a progressive direction. His domestic agenda was known as the "Square Deal." He championed the cause of conservation of natural resources and came to be known as "the trust-buster."

Roosevelt and the Regulation of Business

Roosevelt's "Square Deal" approach to public issues is reflected in his handling of the anthracite coal strike in 1902. Roosevelt called representatives from both management and labor to the White House. He even threatened to take over the mines if owners did not negotiate in good faith. Ultimately, the miners received a 10 percent wage increase, but not union recognition. Roosevelt also pushed for important consumer protections in the wake of the publication of *The Jungle*. Also, Roosevelt pushed for stronger regulation of the powerful railroad industry. The power of the railroad industry was the subject of Frank Norris's novel, *The Octopus: A California Story* (1901). Roosevelt strengthened the Interstate Commerce Commission (created in 1887) with the Elkins Act (1903), which targeted the railroad practice of granting rebates to favored customers, and the Hepburn Act (1906), which gave the commission greater latitude to set railroad rates.

Roosevelt as "Trust Buster"

Roosevelt saw the concentration of economic power in a few hands as potentially dangerous to the economy as a whole. Though the Sherman Antitrust Act (1890) was passed to limit monopolistic practices, the act was not enforced with a great deal of enthusiasm. Roosevelt made a point of using the act to pursue "bad trusts"—ones that interfered with commerce—not necessarily the biggest trusts. One of his first targets was the Northern Securities Company, a railroad holding company. His efforts were challenged in court. In *Northern Securities Co. v. United States* (1904), the Supreme Court upheld the power of the government to break up Northern Securities under the Sherman Antitrust Act. The case was a victory for Roosevelt. His efforts at challenging monopolies earned him the nickname "trust buster."

Roosevelt and Conservation

President Roosevelt became increasingly concerned with the rapid destruction of much of the nation's pristine wilderness. Logging and mining operations were taking a toll on forested areas starting in the late 1800s. He therefore embraced the cause of environmental conservation. This view endorses using natural resources in a responsible way so that these resources continue to exist for future generations. This view can be contrasted with the views of environmental preservationists. Preservationists want society to have a hands-off approach in regard to the remaining relatively untouched natural areas. An early preservationist was John Muir, one of the founders of the Sierra Club (1892). Both conservationists and preservationists were concerned about the rapid disappearance of natural areas in the United States. But the two positions clashed in controversies such as the destruction of the Hetch Hetchy valley in Yosemite National Park in California. In pursuit of his conservationist agenda, Roosevelt set aside millions of acres as protected areas. These include six national parks. In keeping with the progressive reliance on expertise, he appointed the scientifically trained Gifford Pinchot to effectively head government conservation efforts.

The Administration of William Howard Taft

After Roosevelt's nearly two terms in office, he picked his secretary of war, William Howard Taft, to succeed him. Taft readily won the nomination of the Republican Party and defeated the Democratic candidate, William Jennings Bryan, in the election in 1908.

Progressives were repeatedly disappointed by Taft. Taft was not an adroit politician and failed to develop a base of support. He agreed to higher tariff rates by signing the Payne-Aldrich Tariff into law (1909), despite the progressive goal of lowering tariff rates to reduce consumer prices. He also ended up firing Gifford Pinchot as chief of the United States Forest Service, after Pinchot's clashes with Taft's development-minded secretary of the interior, Richard Ballinger. Taft did pursue antitrust suits, even though his public rhetoric did not emphasize this. He initiated ninety antitrust cases, including a major case against U.S. Steel.

Taft, Roosevelt, and the Election of 1912

Theodore Roosevelt came to regret his decision to throw his support behind President Taft. After 1910, a wide rift developed within the Republican Party between Taft and Roosevelt. By 1912, this rift became a civil war within the party. Roosevelt and his supporters walked out of the Republican Party nominating convention in 1912 after the party nominated Taft to run for re-election. Roosevelt and his loyalists founded the Progressive Party (more commonly known by its nickname, the Bull Moose party), and nominated Roosevelt to run as a third-party candidate in the general election. The election was further complicated by the candidacy of Eugene V. Debs of the Socialist Party (see below). The split within the Republican Party allowed the Democratic Party candidate, Woodrow Wilson, to win the presidency. He won the majority of the electoral votes, despite winning only 41 percent of the popular vote, to Roosevelt's 27 percent, Taft's 23 percent, and Debs's 6 percent.

Progressivism and Woodrow Wilson

Woodrow Wilson was an anomaly in the White House. He was only the second Democrat to serve since Andrew Johnson (1865–1869). Republicans had repeatedly "waved the bloody shirt"—alluded to the role of the Democratic Party in secession and the Civil War—and won several close presidential elections during the Gilded Age. Wilson was also the first southerner elected to the White House since 1844 (he was from Virginia). Wilson was an historian and a scholar. He had been the governor of New Jersey and the president of Princeton University before assuming the presidency. Wilson had established a track record as a progressive reformer when he entered the White House.

Wilson and the Federal Reserve Act

President Wilson grew increasingly suspicious of the banking industry. He argued that it was inflexible and in the service of the stock market more than in the service of the American public. To rectify this situation he pushed for passage of the Federal Reserve Act, which created the Federal Reserve Bank in 1913. The Federal Reserve Bank is a partly privately controlled and partly publicly controlled national bank. One of its main functions is to regulate economic growth. Its policies can expand or contract the currency supply. If the economy is sluggish, the Fed will attempt to stimulate economic growth. If inflation occurs, the Fed will attempt to slow down economic activity by expanding the currency supply. An important mechanism for regulating economic growth is raising or lowering the interest rate at which the Fed loans money to other banks. Other banks follow suit, raising or lowering the interest rates at which they loan money to the public. For example, by lowering interest rates the Fed stimulates economic activity by making it more attractive for people to make major purchases.

Regulation of Business

President Wilson was a strong supporter of small business and took a dim view of the growing power of big business. He readily took on the mantle of regulation of big business that had been central to the agenda of the Progressive movement from its inception. Progressives had become increasingly alarmed at the power of unregulated business during the era of rapid industrialization in the late nineteenth century. In 1890, the Sherman Antitrust Act had been passed, but was used with limited success. Wilson strengthened the antitrust powers of the federal government with the Clayton Antitrust Act (1914). A key difference in the new act is that it specifically exempted labor unions from being targeted by antitrust actions. The Sherman Act had often been used to break up strikes.

President Wilson also pushed for the creation of the Federal Trade Commission (1914) to regulate business practices. One of the many regulatory responsibilities of the commission is reducing the power of trusts and guarding against "unfair trade practices."

The Democratization of America

The reform of municipal government was part of a larger effort by progressive activists to make local, state, and national government more responsive to the popular will. Perhaps the most important reform to come out of the Progressive era was the Nineteenth Amendment to the Constitution, which gave women the right to vote.

The Referendum, the Recall, and the Initiative

Reformers hoped that by expanding democracy, the power of political machines would be lessened. In states across the United States, progressives proposed, and often implemented, reforms to expand democracy. The referendum was a Progressive era reform that allowed people to vote directly on proposed legislation. A proposed referendum item would appear on the ballot on election day. Voters would either vote "yes" or "no" on the referendum. Several states still have the referendum. The recall empowered the people of a city or state to remove an elected official before his or her term ended. Several states still have the recall. In 2003 Californians recalled Governor Gray Davis and replaced him with Arnold Schwarzenegger. The initiative allowed citizens to introduce a bill to the local or state legislature by petition.

Direct Primaries

In the nineteenth century, party machines generally picked the candidates who would run in the general election. This practice removed a key element of the electoral process from public participation. The Progressive movement pushed for the adoption of direct primaries, which empowered voters to choose party candidates to run for elected public office. Wisconsin was the first state to adopt a direct primary in 1903. Most other states also adopted direct primaries by 1916.

Direct Election of Senators

Progressives pushed for the Seventeenth Amendment (1913), which called for the direct election of senators. Previously, senators were chosen by state legislatures.

PROGRESSIVE-ERA AMENDMENTS

Four important amendments to the Constitution came out of the Progressive era: the Sixteenth Amendment allows for a federal income tax; the Seventeenth Amendment provides for the direct election of senators; the Eighteenth Amendment called for prohibition; and the Nineteenth Amendment extended the vote to women.

The Australian Ballot

In the nineteenth century, political machines routinely printed ballots with their candidates on them. Voters would then deposit these ballots in voting boxes, allowing anyone who was interested to see which ballot a voter deposited. This system allowed for voter intimidation. In 1888, Massachusetts adopted a secret ballot, which was already in use in Australia. These ballots, printed by the state instead of the parties and filled out by voters in curtained booths, became the norm in America by 1910.

III. The New Deal and Debates over a Limited Welfare State

A series of developments led to the creation of a limited welfare state in the 1930s. The most important development was the ongoing economic dislocation caused by the Great Depression. Reformers at all levels of government advocated moving beyond the dictates of laissez-faire capitalism.

A. THE CREATION OF A NEW DEAL

During the depths of the Great Depression, President Franklin Roosevelt pushed for a series of reforms to address both the causes and the effects of the economic crisis of the 1930s. Roosevelt and his advisors drew on progressive ideas in the creation of the New Deal. The focus of the New Deal was three-pronged—extend relief to the poor, stimulate economic recovery, and create long-term reform of the American economy.

The Election of Franklin D. Roosevelt and the New Deal

In 1932, Franklin Delano Roosevelt offered the public a marked contrast to President Herbert Hoover. Roosevelt was from a wealthy New York family. He was a distant cousin of Theodore

Roosevelt. In 1928, Roosevelt won the governorship in New York and introduced a number of innovative programs to help New Yorkers as the Great Depression deepened. Though Roosevelt was from a wealthy background, he was able to convey to the public a sense of empathy and warmth. Further, his openness to experimentation allowed for a more flexible response to the Depression than Hoover's more ideological approach. Roosevelt won the election of 1932 easily, garnering 57 percent of the popular vote and 472 out of 529 electoral votes.

Roosevelt took the federal government in a new direction by asserting that it should take some responsibility for the welfare of the people. The Roosevelt administration developed a series of programs that are known as the New Deal. Previously, churches, settlement houses, and other private charities helped people in times of need. However, the levels of poverty and unemployment during the Great Depression were unprecedented. Roosevelt believed that the government needed to take action. The New Deal provided relief to individuals through a variety of agencies.

The First New Deal

The Roosevelt administration developed a remarkable array of programs during its first Hundred Days in 1933, and in the months immediately following. These programs, which comprise the first New Deal, reflected Roosevelt's willingness to experiment and the scope of problems that faced the nation. Below are some of the more important programs.

> ## THE NEWNESS OF THE NEW DEAL
>
> The extension of the federal government into the economic lives of individuals represented a marked departure from the traditional role of the government.

Glass-Steagall Act (1933)

One of the most pressing problems that President Roosevelt faced was the instability of the banking industry. Many people had lost confidence in the banking system, and withdrew their money in fear that their bank might fold. With thousands of people withdrawing their money at the same time, many banks actually did close, turning collective fears into a self-fulfilling prophecy. The Federal Deposit Insurance Corporation, created by the Glass-Steagall Act, insures deposits so that if a bank does fold, people would not lose their savings.

National Industrial Recovery Act (1933)

The National Industrial Recovery Act called for representatives from labor and competing corporations to draw up a set of codes. These codes were designed to eliminate discount selling, shorten hours for workers, and establish minimum wage levels. The idea was that cutthroat competition hurt the economy and pushed workers' wages, and their ability to purchase goods, down.

Agricultural Adjustment Act (1933)

The Roosevelt administration took the counterintuitive measure of paying farmers to *not* grow crops. The goal of the Agricultural Adjustment Act was to reduce production in order to bolster sagging commodity prices and strengthen the agricultural sector. Commodity prices did increase, but the AAA had an unintended negative effect. Landowners often evicted tenant farmers and sharecroppers in order to take land out of cultivation. This hurt many of the nation's poorest farmers, including many African-American farmers.

Tennessee Valley Authority (1933)

This innovative program, which is still in existence, was the federal government's first experiment in regional planning. The TVA built dams, generated electricity, manufactured fertilizer, provided technical assistance to farmers, and fostered economic development in the Tennessee Valley.

Federal Emergency Relief Act (1933)

This agency was created to distribute more than $500 million to state and local governments, who would, in turn, distribute aid to the poor. FERA was intended to provide temporary relief for people in need.

Civilian Conservation Corps (1933)

President Roosevelt created the Civilian Conservation Corps (CCC) to provide outdoor work for young men between the ages of 18 and 24. CCC projects included soil conservation, flood control, trail and road building, and forest projects. During the 1930s, approximately 2.75 million men worked on CCC projects.

Securities and Exchange Commission (1934)

Many individuals had lost confidence in the stock market after the 1929 crash, which was partly caused by unsound practices. The Securities and Exchange Commission was created to oversee stock market operations by monitoring transactions, licensing brokers, limiting buying on margin, and prohibiting insider trading.

B. CRITICS OF THE NEW DEAL

President Roosevelt had to negotiate the New Deal through the tumultuous political currents of the 1930s. A variety of social and political movements emerged, each offering different solutions to the economic crisis. To some degree these movements hindered the New Deal; to some degree they influenced it. From the left, union activists, radicals, and populist leaders pushed for more extensive reforms. From the right, conservatives—in the media, in Congress, and on the Supreme Court—attempted to limit the scope and influence of the New Deal. The left's critique of the New Deal ultimately led to a second set of reforms, which went beyond the scope of the programs of Roosevelt's first year in office.

The Growth of the Communist Party

Although the Communist Party never attracted a large following in the United States, it did gain new members and it exerted influence beyond its numbers in the 1930s. Some Americans were impressed with the achievements of the Soviet Union, and some simply felt that the capitalist system was not working. The Communist Party attracted members by adopting the "Popular Front" strategy (put into effect by the Comintern from 1934 to 1939); the strategy called for the Communist Party to drop talk of an impending revolution and to cooperate with a spectrum of anti-fascist groups and governments, including President Roosevelt's New Deal administration.

Populist Opposition to the New Deal

Although President Roosevelt could count on tacit support from the Communist Party, other voices on the left criticized the New Deal as being overly cautious. Upton Sinclair (author of *The Jungle*) ran for governor of California in 1934 under the banner "End Poverty in California," proposing sweeping, somewhat socialistic solutions. Francis Townsend, also from California, proposed a tax to generate enough money to give everyone over sixty a monthly stipend. The most serious threat to Roosevelt from the left came from Huey Long, the flamboyant populist governor, and then senator, from Louisiana. His Share Our Wealth Society, begun in 1934, proposed breaking up the fortunes of the rich and distributing them to everyone else. His slogan was "Every Man a King." He talked of running against Roosevelt in 1936, but was assassinated in 1935.

The Growth of Organized Labor

President Roosevelt encouraged union membership in order to increase the purchasing powers of workers. Organized labor, in turn, pushed Roosevelt to adopt more extensive reform measures. Section 7A of the National Industrial Recovery Act (1933) and the Wagner Act (1935) legalized union membership in the United States. Union membership, which had been falling in the 1920s and early 1930s, rose from 3 million in 1933 to 10.5 million by 1941. By the end of World War II, 36 percent of nonagricultural American workers were in unions.

The Congress of Industrial Organizations

The drive to organize workers in the 1930s led to tensions within the labor movement. The fifty-year old American Federation of Labor (AFL), a coalition of craft unions, had never shown much interest in organizing unskilled assembly line workers. Labor leaders such as John L. Lewis of the United Mine Workers wanted the AFL to do more organizing in this growing sector of the labor force. In 1935, he and other leaders from primarily unskilled unions organized the Committee for Industrial Organization within the AFL. The Committee's task of organizing basic industries met the ire of AFL leadership, which ordered the Committee to disband in 1936, and then, when it refused, expelled the Committee unions in 1937. In 1938, the Committee reconstituted itself as the independent Congress of Industrial Organizations. It grew rapidly, surpassing the AFL by 1941—the CIO had about 5 million members compared to the AFL's 4.6 million.

> ### THE CIO AND THE AFL
>
> The CIO started out as the Committee for Industrial Organization within the AFL in 1935. In 1938 it became the independent Congress of Industrial Organizations. In 1955, it merged with the AFL to form the AFL-CIO.

The Sit-down Strike

Although unions were legal in America, employers were still under no compulsion to accept union demands. A wave of strikes ensued in the late 1930s. A new, militant tactic that CIO unions engaged in was the sit-down strike, in which workers stopped work and refused to leave the shop floor, thus preventing the employer from reopening with replacement workers (or "scabs" in the parlance of the labor movement). The most famous sit-down strike took place at the General Motors plant in Flint, Michigan, in the winter of 1936–37.

Conservative Critics Denounce "Creeping Socialism"

Some conservative critics saw the New Deal as socialism in disguise. The New Deal, they argued, had pushed the government too far into new realms. Roosevelt's "court packing" scheme (see below) seemed especially heavy-handed to many Americans. The most prominent group on the right was the American Liberty League (founded in 1934), which consisted primarily of conservative businessmen. The group supported conservative politicians of both parties, and promoted the "open shop"—a business in which the employees are not required to join a union. Father Charles Coughlin, using his popular national radio show, attacked Roosevelt as being a communist and a dictator. Coughlin had initially supported Roosevelt in 1932, but grew increasingly critical of the New Deal, adding anti-Semitic and even fascistic elements to his broadcast.

The Second New Deal

By 1935, President Roosevelt was facing several problems. The economy improved slightly between 1933, when Roosevelt took office, and 1935. Average weekly earnings increased for workers, and unemployment dropped from about 25 percent to 20 percent. But with more than 10 million people out of work, Roosevelt could not claim that the New Deal had resolved the nation's economic woes. In addition, the Supreme Court had declared key New Deal legislation unconstitutional. In *A.L.A. Schechter Poultry Corp. v. United States* (1935), the Court ended the National Industrial Recovery Act, asserting that the codes of the National Recovery Administration violated the constitutional separation of powers by delegating legislative powers to the executive branch. Several months later, the Court declared the Agricultural Adjustment Act unconstitutional in the *United States v. Butler* decision (1936). The Court held that taxes enacted by the AAA amounted to statutory regulations; such actions, therefore, fell under state powers, not federal powers.

THE SUPREME COURT AND POLITICS

Throughout history, note the connections between Supreme Court decisions and contemporary political currents. The justices are products of their society; they don't make their decisions in a vacuum.

With mounting pressure from a variety of populist and leftwing forces, and with a presidential election looming in 1936, Roosevelt introduced a second set of programs that are known as the second New Deal. This second phase of the New Deal was less about involvement with the different sectors of the economy, and more about providing assistance and support to the working class.

Works Progress Administration (1935)

The Works Progress Administration (WPA) was a massive initiative that created jobs for millions of unemployed men and women. The jobs ranged from construction work to theatrical productions to writing guidebooks about each of the states. Earlier jobs programs, such as the Civilian Conservation Corps, were piecemeal compared with the immense WPA.

Social Security Act (1935)

Social Security is perhaps the initiative that has had the largest long-term impact on American society. The Social Security Act was designed to help the unemployed, the elderly, and the disabled. The most important element of the plan was retirement benefits, funded by taxes on workers and employers, which workers collected after they turned sixty-five.

The Wagner Act (1935)

The Wagner Act encouraged the formation of unions. The act established the National Labor Relations Board, which is still in existence, to oversee union elections and to arbitrate conflicts between workers and owners. It also prohibited owners from taking punitive actions against workers who sought to organize unions. The act led to a tremendous increase in union activity.

The Second New Deal and the Supreme Court

President Roosevelt feared that the Supreme Court would invalidate key elements of this second New Deal, as it had in earlier New Deal acts. In 1937 he proposed a bill to alter the composition of the Supreme Court by allowing him to appoint six additional justices. This "court-packing" bill generated a great deal of opposition. Congress rejected this plan, but the Court became friendlier to the president anyway. Over the next few years some of the more conservative justices retired and Roosevelt was able to appoint seven new justices, including the liberal Hugo Black.

The Rollback of the New Deal

In late 1937 and 1938, Roosevelt took the New Deal in a new direction that, many historians believe, hurt the economy. By 1937, the economy was showing signs of improvement. Unemployment was going down and banks and businesses were showing signs of stability. Roosevelt took the advice of some of the more conservative members of his cabinet and cut back on spending with the goal of balancing the budget.

The "Roosevelt Recession"

President Roosevelt's move to cut spending on New Deal programs contributed to a further downturn in economic activity in 1938 known as the "Roosevelt recession." Later in 1938, Roosevelt shifted direction again and increased government spending. The economy did show signs of growth, but the real boost to the economy came in 1939 as the United States began producing armaments and supplies for World War II.

Keynesian Economics

When President Roosevelt cut back spending to balance the budget in the middle of the Great Depression, he was rejecting the advice of the economist John Maynard Keynes. Keynes's most important book, *General Theory of Employment, Interest and Money* (1936), argued that deficit spending by the government was acceptable, and even desirable, as a means of increasing overall demand and stimulating economic activity. This idea of using the tools of the government—the Federal Reserve Bank, and spending and taxation polices—to influence economic activity is known as Keynesian economics.

KEYNES AND GOVERNMENT POLICY

Be familiar with Keynesian economics. His theories have influenced government policy in the twentieth century, especially during Democratic administrations. Republicans have focused on cutting spending.

C. THE LEGACY OF THE NEW DEAL

The New Deal did not solve the economic crisis of the 1930s, but it did profoundly change the United States. It left a legacy of agencies and laws aimed at economic security and it ushered in a major political realignment, as a new coalition of ethnic groups, African Americans, and working-class communities identified with the goals of the Democratic Party.

Political Realignment

> ### HOOVER'S ECONOMIC POLICIES
> Hoover's approach to the economy and his rhetoric set a template for Republican economic policy for much of the twentieth century.

The 1930s witnessed the emergence of the political and ideological alignment that has existed, to some extent, to the present. President Herbert Hoover's generally conservative laissez-faire approach has been echoed in the policies of Republican president Ronald Reagan and both Presidents Bush, while President Roosevelt's generally liberal interventionist approach inspired Democratic president Lyndon Johnson's "Great Society." Today, Democratic leaders debate how closely their party should be associated with New Deal liberalism, while Republicans brand their opponents "tax and spend" liberals. The debates of the 1930s are still part of the political culture.

The Depression and Affected Groups

Different sectors of society were affected by the Great Depression and the New Deal differently. Although the 1930s was certainly a dismal time economically, some groups in the United States were able to put forth agendas for change and to achieve gains.

African Americans

African Americans, in a vulnerable position in American society before the Great Depression, were especially hard hit by the economic difficulties of the 1930s. Many New Deal programs ignored African Americans, such as the Agricultural Adjustment Act, which did not help tenant farmers. Roosevelt was leery of losing the support of the southern wing of the Democratic Party, so he did not push for civil rights legislation. Neither did he endorse federal anti-lynching legislation (which Congress never passed).

> ### SLOW STEPS TOWARD CIVIL RIGHTS
> We can see Roosevelt and the Democratic Party just beginning to shift toward support for civil rights in the 1930s. This was a major shift for a party that in the 1860s pushed the southern states to secede in order to defend slavery.

Despite President Roosevelt's reluctance to take the lead in civil rights legislation, African Americans switched their allegiance from the party of Lincoln (the Republicans) to the Democratic Party. There are several reasons for this historic shift. First Lady Eleanor Roosevelt and Interior Secretary Harold Ickes did champion civil rights causes. The most dramatic gesture by Eleanor Roosevelt was organizing a concert by Marian Anderson in 1935 on the steps of the Lincoln Memorial after she was blocked by the Daughters of the American Revolution from performing at their concert hall. Also, the president met periodically with a group of African-American advisors called the "Black Cabinet." In 1941 Roosevelt issued an executive order banning discrimination in government jobs. Finally, African Americans believed that Roosevelt, despite his shortcomings, was attempting to improve conditions for poor and working-class people.

The "Scottsboro Boys" Case

The racial biases of the justice system were demonstrated in the highly publicized "Scottsboro Boys" case (1931–1935). Nine African-American youths were convicted of rape in Alabama on flimsy evidence. In 1932, the Supreme Court reversed most of the convictions on the grounds that the defendants' due process rights had been violated because they were denied effective counsel. The cases were then sent back to state court for retrial. The defendants were again found guilty, even after one of the alleged victims admitted fabricating her story. Charges were later dropped for four out of the nine defendants.

Women

Women suffered a double burden during the Depression—on the one hand, they were responsible for putting food on the table during difficult times, while on the other hand, they were frequently scorned if they "took a job away from a man" by working outside the home. Further, New Deal programs tended to slight women; the Civilian Conservation Corps (1933)—a New Deal program that sent young men from urban areas to work on federal lands—excluded women, and the National Industrial Recovery Act (1933) set lower wage levels for women than for men. Nonetheless, individual women such as Frances Perkins, the first female cabinet member (secretary of labor) and Eleanor Roosevelt, one of the most active and public first ladies in American history, opened doors for women. Despite criticism, more women were working outside the home in 1940 than in 1930.

American Indians

New Deal legislation profoundly affected American Indians. The Indian Reorganization Act (1934) largely undid the 1887 Dawes Act. The Dawes Act had attempted to "Americanize" American Indians by breaking up reservations and dividing the land into small plots for individual American Indians. The Indian Reorganization Act reversed this policy by restoring tribal ownership of reservation lands and recognizing the legitimacy of tribal governments. The act also extended loans to American Indian groups for economic development.

KEY CONCEPT 7.2
THE STRESSES OF MODERNITY

In many ways, the first decades of the twentieth century ushered in key elements of the modern world. New forms of communications and travel helped create a modern, mass culture. As the reach of this new culture extended to more and more Americans, a series of culture clashes ensued. These culture clashes were exacerbated by large-scale migrations, world wars, and economic crises.

I. New Technologies and the Making of Modernity

New technologies were a double-edged sword for American society in the early twentieth century. On the one hand, standards of living improved, but on the other hand, divergent reactions to these changes resulted in political and cultural conflict.

A. THE IMPACT OF NEW TECHNOLOGIES

Technological advances in the first decades of the twentieth century improved standards of living, increased personal mobility, and created better systems of communications.

Radio and the Development of Mass Culture

Radio grew from being virtually nonexistent at the beginning of the 1920s to becoming an extremely popular medium by the end of it. The medium was begun by amateurs who sent out music or sermons to the few scattered people who had "wireless receivers." Soon, Westinghouse and other corporations saw the potential to reach the masses with radio. By 1923, there were almost 600 licensed radio stations. Early successful programs included *The Amos 'n' Andy Show* (1928), a holdover from "blackface" minstrel shows of the nineteenth century.

The Rise of the Motion Picture Industry

Movie attendance achieved staggering levels in the 1920s. By the end of the decade, three-fourths of the American people (roughly 90 million) were going to the movies every week. The first "talkie," *The Jazz Singer*, came out in 1927.

MOVIES IN THE PRE-TELEVISION ERA

Movies would never draw as large a percentage of the public as they did in the 1930s and 1940s. Some thought that television would destroy the movie industry. The predictions did not come true, but television certainly made deep cuts into the movie industry's audience.

The Impact of the Automobile

Americans embraced the automobile more rapidly and more thoroughly than people in other nations did. By the end of the 1920s, Americans owned 80 percent of the world's automobiles. Approximately 23 million cars were on the road. Automobiles became increasingly affordable. When the Model T was first introduced in 1908, an average American worker had to work approximately 20 months to earn enough money to purchase an automobile. By 1924, a Ford car cost about the equivalent of two to three months' salary.

The automobile changed American society in profound ways. The proliferation of the automobile industry—using mass production techniques developed early in the twentieth century by Henry Ford—stimulated the growth of the steel, chemical, oil, and glass production industries, employing nearly four million Americans. The automobile led to a reshaping of demographic patterns, as more Americans began to settle in suburban communities (see more on the rise of suburbs in Period 8). Although automobiles reduced rural isolation, they also contributed to urban sprawl. Cities that developed in the twentieth century, such as Los Angeles or Houston, were built around the automobile, spread out over wide geographic areas.

B. MODERNITY AND CULTURE CLASHES

Modernity—embodied in new technologies, mass culture, and changing demographics—engendered a number of political and cultural conflicts. A host of conflicts—rural versus urban, Christian fundamentalism versus scientific modernism, native-born versus immigrant—pitted Americans against one another. These included conflicts around race, immigration reform, control of the work place, and morality.

The Persistence of White Supremacy

Since the end of the Reconstruction period (1877), southern states had passed a series of Jim Crow laws, segregating African Americans from whites in public facilities. Further, voting laws and intimidation had virtually excluded African Americans from voting, despite passage of the Fifteenth Amendment (1870). Violence by the Ku Klux Klan and others had become the backdrop to life in the South for African Americans.

African-American activists attempted to put the issue of race and racism on the national agenda. W.E.B. Du Bois was a militant civil rights activist who wrote about the injustices carried out against African Americans in the South. He was one of the founders of the National Association for the Advancement of Colored People (NAACP). The NAACP was formed in 1909. The leadership of the organization had first met in 1905 on the Canadian side of Niagara Falls where they formed the Niagara movement. Du Bois's call for full political equality and civil rights for African Americans was in marked contrast to the more conciliatory approach of Booker T. Washington (see Period 6). A third important figure in the African community was Marcus Garvey. He is best known for urging African Americans to return to their ancestral homelands in Africa. Not many African Americans made the journey, but Garvey was very influential in instilling a sense of pride among many African Americans; in this he is seen as an important figure in the black nationalist movement.

However, white progressives turned a blind eye toward the plight of African Americans. Progressive president Woodrow Wilson was, in fact, an outspoken racist. He ordered the segregation of government offices, including post offices throughout the country. His advocacy of white supremacy went even further than contemporary social attitudes. He praised the racist film, *Birth of a Nation* (1916) by D.W. Griffith, with its positive portrayal of the Ku Klux Klan during the Reconstruction period.

The Resurgence of the Ku Klux Klan

The original Ku Klux Klan, a violent, racist group with its roots in the immediate aftermath of the Civil War, had died out by the 1870s. By the 1920s, however, the organization was a genuine mass movement. By 1925, it grew to 3 million members, by its own estimate. The Klan was devoted to white supremacy and "100 percent Americanism."

Racial Violence

As the Great Migration led to many African Americans making the journey from the rural South to the urban North (see below), racial violence ensued in many cities. There were at least twenty-five significant race riots in 1919 alone. This racial antagonism was, in part, an offshoot of the reactionary political backlash against progressivism following World War I. In July, a riot against African Americans occurred in Washington, DC, and an even more violent riot in Chicago left thirty-eight people dead and more than 500 injured. Racial violence also occurred in the South, including at Longview, Texas, and Elaine, Arkansas.

The Bible Versus Science

During the 1920s, a large number of Americans, especially in the South, adopted a fundamentalist, literalist approach to the Bible and to religion. The Scopes trial of 1925 illustrated the conflict between

A THIRD GREAT AWAKENING

Some historians refer to the rise of fundamentalism in the 1920s as a "third great awakening."

Protestant fundamentalism and modern science. The Scopes trial involved the teaching of evolution in public schools. John Scopes, a Tennessee biology teacher, was arrested for violating the Butler Act, a state law forbidding the teaching of evolution. The case turned into a national spectacle, with the famous lawyer Clarence Darrow representing Scopes and William Jennings Bryan representing the state. It is one of several important events that highlighted cultural divisions in the 1920s.

Anti-Immigrant Sentiment

Nativism, or opposition to immigration, rose sharply in the years after World War I. A large wave of immigrants from southern and eastern Europe had arrived in the United States between 1880 and 1920. There are several reasons nativists resented this new wave of immigration. Some nativists focused on the fact that most of the new immigrants were not Protestant. Poles and Italians tended to be Catholic, Russians and Greeks tended to be Eastern Orthodox, and Jews came from several countries in eastern Europe. The cacophony of languages heard on the streets of New York or Chicago repelled many nativists. Some Americans were anti-European after the trauma of World War I. Some nativists associated immigrants with either radical movements or drunkenness. Finally, working-class people feared that low-wage immigrant laborers would take jobs from native-born American workers.

Rural and Urban Responses to Prohibition

The movement to ban alcohol from American society was one of the largest movements in the nineteenth and early twentieth centuries. It finally achieved success in 1919 when prohibition became national policy with the ratification of the Eighteenth Amendment to the Constitution. The amendment called for a ban on the manufacture, sale, and transportation of alcoholic beverages. However, the victory of the movement proved to be hollow. Although per capita consumption of alcohol dropped dramatically in the early 1920s, it increased as the decade progressed, possibly approaching pre-Prohibition levels by 1925. Further, the amount of lawlessness in America went up as bootleggers, speakeasies, and organized crime filled the gap left by the death of the legitimate alcoholic beverage industry. Criminal activity became so widespread that Congress ratified the Twenty-first Amendment (1933), which repealed Prohibition.

C. NEW CULTURAL FORMS IN THE MODERN WORLD

The social and economic transformations that roiled America in the first decades of the twentieth century contributed to a variety of new cultural expressions. On the one hand, new technologies helped usher in a national, mass-media oriented culture. On the other hand, the experiences of particular groups—based around race, ethnicity, and region—produced a variety of other cultural expressions.

Movies and the Development of Mass Media

The movie industry, which had entered the "talkie" era in the late 1920s, thrived during the Great Depression (between 60 percent and 90 percent of the American public went to the movies every week). Escapist musicals such as *Gold Diggers of 1933* and *42nd Street* (1933), with lavish sets and spectacular numbers, proved popular. In *The Wizard of Oz* (1939), Dorothy, played by Judy Garland, escapes a Kansas farm, shown in black-and-white, and is transported, along with the audience, to the magical land of Oz, shot in Technicolor. The Marx Brothers produced and starred in anarchic comedies, such as *Monkey Business* (1931) and *Duck Soup* (1933), which mocked authority figures and the pretensions of the wealthy. Charlie Chaplin's comedy *Modern Times* (1936) satirized the entire capitalist system, from the drudgery of assembly line work to the corruption of the law enforcement system. Some movies attempted to grapple with the wrenching public issues of the time. *The Grapes of Wrath* (1940), the film version of John Steinbeck's novel, chronicled the conditions of dust bowl farmers fleeing to California, while Frank Capra's *Mr. Smith Goes to Washington* (1939) depicted the triumph of a decent, "everyman" politician.

The Cultural Impact of Radio

Radio, which had become a popular medium in the 1920s, continued its popularity in the 1930s. Americans listened to weekly serials such as *The Shadow* and *The Lone Ranger*, comedians such as Jack Benny and George Burns, and soap operas. In addition, big band swing music became very popular. Americans listened to big bands led by Duke Ellington, Tommy Dorsey, and Glenn Miller. Radio and movies tended to create a more homogenous culture in the United States in the 1930s.

The Harlem Renaissance

The Great Migration of African Americans from the rural South to the urban North (see below) contributed to the Harlem Renaissance, a literary, artistic, and intellectual movement centered in the African-American neighborhood of Harlem, in New York City. A key goal of the movement was to increase pride in African-American culture by celebrating African-American life and forging a new cultural identity among African-American people. Contributions included the poetry of Langston Hughes, Claude McKay, and Countee Cullen and the jazz music of Louis Armstrong, Duke Ellington, and Bessie Smith. Langston Hughes's poems include "Harlem," "The Negro Speaks of Rivers," and "I, Too, Sing America." He wrote an essay that became a manifesto for Harlem Renaissance writers and artists entitled "The Negro Artist and the Racial Mountain." Duke Ellington is perhaps the most important figure in twentieth-century jazz. Some of his most important compositions are "Mood Indigo," "Don't Get Around Much Anymore," and "Take the A Train."

The "Lost Generation" Writers of the 1920s

The "Lost Generation" literary movement expressed a general disillusionment with society, commenting on everything from the narrowness of small town life to the rampant materialism of American society. Several writers were troubled by the destruction and seeming meaninglessness of World War I. *The Great Gatsby* (1925) by F. Scott Fitzgerald exposed the shallowness of the lives of the wealthy and privileged of the era. Sinclair Lewis's novels, such as *Main Street* (1920) and *Babbitt* (1924), mocked the narrowness of the middle class. Ernest Hemingway's *A Farewell to Arms* (1929) critiqued the glorification of war.

Literature of the 1930s

Pearl Buck's *The Good Earth* (1931), a story of peasants in China, Steinbeck's tale of the Dust Bowl, *The Grapes of Wrath* (1939), and Margaret Mitchell's account of the Old South, *Gone With the Wind* (1936) have endured as classics of 1930s literature. Several novels of the 1930s reflected the influence of the Communist Party on American culture. Anti-fascist novels included *It Can't Happen Here* (1935) by Sinclair Lewis. Proletarian literature included the novel *The Disinherited* (1933) by Jack Conroy and the play *Waiting for Lefty* (1935) by Clifford Odets.

II. The Conservative Backlash of the 1910s and 1920s

The years during and immediately following World War I saw a backlash against the experimentation of the Progressive era and a rise in patriotism and xenophobia. This conservative backlash, coupled with the large number of "new" immigrants in the United States, resulted in the implementation of a rigid system of quotas that greatly reduced the number of immigrants allowed in the United States.

A. CIVIL LIBERTIES DURING WARTIME

A repressive atmosphere arose around World War I, as Congress passed legislation curbing free speech.

CIVIL LIBERTIES IN COMPARISON

The debate over civil liberties during wartime is an ongoing issue. Be prepared to compare restrictions on civil liberties in the context of the "Quasi-war" with France, the Civil War, World War I, World War II, and even the current war on terrorism.

The Espionage and Sedition Acts

Despite the hopes of many progressives, World War I ushered in a repressive atmosphere that stymied progressive reform and led to the curtailment of civil liberties. The Espionage and Sedition Acts were passed during World War I to put limits on public expressions of antiwar sentiment. The Espionage Act (1917), along with the Sedition Act (1918), made it a crime to interfere with the draft or with the sale of war bonds, or to say anything "disloyal" in regard to the war effort.

The Espionage Act was upheld by the Supreme Court in the decision in *Schenck v. United States* (1919). Charles Schenck and other members of the Socialist Party had been arrested for printing and distributing flyers opposing the war and urging young men to resist the draft. The Supreme Court argued that freedom of speech is not absolute and that the government is justified in limiting certain forms of speech during wartime. The court argued that certain utterances pose a "clear and present danger." By analogy the court reasoned that one is not allowed to falsely shout "Fire!" in a crowded theater.

B. THE CRUSADE AGAINST ORGANIZED LABOR AND DISSENT

The first "Red Scare" occurred in the immediate aftermath of World War I, as labor conflicts and the increased visibility of radical movements led to an atmosphere of repression against radicals and immigrants.

The Strike-wave of 1919

When World War I ended, the government disbanded the agencies that it had created to regulate economic activity during the war. Workers, for instance, no longer had the protections of the National War Labor Policies Board. In addition, inflation was no longer kept in check by the government. In 1919, prices rose nearly 75 percent. In these conditions, workers across

America organized and fought to protect wartime gains. The year 1919 saw the biggest strike wave in American history. There were more than 4,500 strikes, involving four million workers. The biggest strike was the Seattle General Strike in February. The radical Industrial Workers of the World and the more moderate American Federation of Labor worked together to virtually close down Seattle. In September, more than 340,000 steelworkers went on strike. Late in 1919 and into 1920, the police force in Boston went on strike. In all three of the strikes, and in countless others, the workers were defeated. In many cases, management was able to paint the striking workers as would-be Bolsheviks. It was not until the New Deal era of the 1930s that the labor movement was able to regain momentum.

The "Red Scare"

The backlash against the strike wave of 1919, combined with the virulent strain of patriotism unleashed by World War I, set the groundwork for the Red Scare of the late 1910s and early 1920s, a crusade against suspected communists, anarchists, labor leaders, and other radicals. The Red Scare was a grassroots movement of ordinary Americans as well as a government-orchestrated campaign. The movement can be traced to the successful Bolshevik revolution in Russia that brought the Communist Party to power and led to the establishment of the Soviet Union. In 1919, the Bolsheviks created the Comintern, an international organization of Communist Party leaders determined to duplicate the success of the Bolsheviks in other countries. Conservative Americans took the pronouncements of the Comintern at face value, even though the Communist movement in the United States was extremely small.

In December 1919, the Russian-born anarchist and activist Emma Goldman was deported by the Justice Department. In January 1920, Attorney General A. Mitchell Palmer began a broad hunt for suspected radicals. Palmer's Justice Department carried out unwarranted raids, known as "Palmer Raids," of suspected radicals' homes. Six thousand alleged radicals were identified by Palmer's men. Although Palmer did not uncover the makings of an uprising, he did end up deporting more than 500 non-citizens. The movement spread to the local level as radical newspapers were shut down, libraries were purged of radical books, and elected officials were removed from office. The Supreme Court decision in *Schenck v. United States*, which established the "clear and present danger" guideline for limiting free speech, gave cover to such excesses. Soon, Americans began to question the aggressive tactics of Palmer, but suspicions of "reds" persisted throughout the 1920s.

The Trial of Sacco and Vanzetti

The repressive atmosphere of the Red Scare era can be seen in the trial of Nicola Sacco and Bartolomeo Vanzetti. Their trial for robbery and murder illustrated the intolerance that many Americans had toward immigrants and toward radicals in the 1920s. The two men were accused of robbing and killing a payroll clerk in Massachusetts in 1920. The evidence against them was sketchy but the judge was openly hostile to the two men, who were not only immigrants but also anarchists. After they were found guilty, many Americans protested the verdict and wondered if an immigrant, especially with radical ideas, could get a fair trial in the United States. Despite protests the two men were executed in 1927.

C. IMMIGRATION RESTRICTIONS IN THE 1920s

Congress passed restrictive immigration quota acts in the 1920s, responding to a rise in xenophobia in America in the late 1910s and 1920s. At the same time, Congress continued to allow open immigration from nations in the Western Hemisphere, notably Mexico.

The Quota System

The nativist sentiment that characterized the postwar period led to passage of legislation that greatly reduced the number of immigrants allowed into the United States. The Emergency Quota Act (1921) and the National Origins Act (1924) set quotas for new immigrants based on nationality. The first act set the quota for each nationality at 3 percent of the total number of that nationality that was present in the United States in 1910. The second act reduced the percentage to 2 percent and moved the year back to 1890. This had the effect of setting very low quotas for many of the "new immigrants"—from eastern and southern Europe.

III. Migrations During the World Wars and in the Interwar Years

The two world wars were catalysts for movements of people within the United States and from within the Western Hemisphere, as job opportunities in war-related industries spurred migrations. The economic dislocations of the 1930s also caused internal movements of people.

A. WAR, OPPORTUNITY, AND THE AFRICAN-AMERICAN COMMUNITY

Economic opportunities caused by industrialization and World War I caused many African Americans to embark on a "Great Migration" out of the rural South. Segregation and racial violence also contributed to this migration.

The Great Migration

The needs of industry for labor during World War I led to the Great Migration of African Americans out of the South, which lasted from the 1910s until the onset of the Great Depression (a second wave of the migration occurred during and after World War II). There are several important reasons for the migration of African Americans from the rural South to the urban North. A basic factor was the mistreatment that African Americans received in the South. White southerners created a series of Jim Crow laws that separated African Americans from whites in schools, busses, trains, and other facilities. A rigid system of segregation persisted in the South well into the twentieth century and constantly reminded African Americans of their second-class citizenship. In addition, African Americans were excluded from the political system in the South. A series of obstacles, such as literacy tests and poll taxes, limited their ability to vote.

The main factor that drew African Americans north was jobs. By the turn of the twentieth century the industrial revolution was in full swing in northern cities such as New York and Chicago. Factories using new mass production techniques were able, at first, to fill the jobs with local people and European immigrants. But World War I created a labor crisis for these factories. Factories were producing goods around the clock. Even before the United States entered the war in 1917, American factories were producing war goods for Great Britain. After entering the war, demand for these goods increased. In addition, European immigration to the United States dropped significantly because of the war. Also millions of potential factory hands were pressed into the U.S. military. Factory agents from the North frequently made recruiting trips to the South, offering immediate employment and free passage to the North.

B. DEPRESSION, WAR, AND INTERNAL MIGRATIONS

Large numbers of people moved within the United States because of the economic dislocations caused by the Great Depression. In addition, wartime job opportunities also led to migrations during both of the world wars.

The Migration from the Dust Bowl to California

From 1934 to 1937, parts of Texas, Oklahoma, and surrounding areas of the Great Plains suffered from a major drought. The area became known as the "Dust Bowl." The Dust Bowl was caused by unsustainable over-farming coupled with a devastating drought. The natural grass cover of the region had been removed in the years leading up to the Dust Bowl, as wheat farmers increased the number of acres under cultivation. With this natural root system gone, the fertile topsoil simply blew away when drought struck from 1934 to 1937. The government, through the Soil Conservation Service, encouraged farmers to replant trees and grass and purchased land to be kept out of cultivation.

The Dust Bowl prompted some significant cultural responses, such as the album *Dust Bowl Ballads* by the folk singer Woody Guthrie (1940) and the novel *The Grapes of Wrath* (1939) by John Steinbeck. These cultural responses chronicled the plight of Dust Bowl refugees, including the "Okies" who fled from Oklahoma.

C. MEXICO AND MIGRATIONS

The United States put forth ambivalent policies in regard to Mexican migration in the 1930s and 1940s. During this period, many Mexicans migrated into the United States, drawn by economic opportunities.

Mexican Americans and the Great Depression

Many Mexicans had moved to the southwest United States in the 1920s to work in agriculture. These Mexican Americans saw their wages plummet in the 1930s, and New Deal programs did little to help. For instance, the CCC and the WPA excluded migrant farm workers by requiring a permanent address. Many Mexicans returned to their homeland. The Mexican-American population decreased by almost 40 percent during the Great Depression.

Mexicans and World War II

The administration of Franklin Roosevelt initiated the *bracero* program in 1942 to bring into the United States temporary contract workers from Mexico. The Mexican government pushed the United States to guarantee that these temporary workers would not be drafted. More than 200,000 Mexicans participated in the program, and it is estimated at least that amount came into the United States as undocumented workers.

Mexicans and Mexican Americans were the object of discrimination, harassment, and violence during World War II. In California, whites frequently targeted Mexican Americans for violent attacks. These white teenagers and servicemen especially targeted Latinos wearing colorful "zoot-suits," then in style among Latinos and African Americans. A serious "zoot-suit riot" occurred in Los Angeles in 1943.

KEY CONCEPT 7.3
THE UNITED STATES ON THE WORLD STAGE

A series of conflicts from the 1890s to the 1940s forced the United States to reconsider its values and priorities. These conflicts revolved around resources, power, territories, and ideologies. During this period, the United States emerged as a dominant player on the world stage in terms of its military, political, cultural, and economic position.

I. The United States in the Age of Imperialism

Many Americans pushed for the United States to become part of the imperialist push to acquire overseas possessions. These territorial ambitions led the United States to acquire new territories in the Western Hemisphere and the Pacific.

A. THE MOTIVE OF AMERICAN IMPERIALISM

A variety of motivations led America to pursue overseas possessions. These factors included economic motives, competition with the imperialist nations of Europe, and racial theories. America began to reach beyond the North American continent as the perception grew that the western frontier was closed.

INTERROGATE SOURCES

In a DBQ about the causes of American imperialism, be careful to note the source of a document. The pronouncements of a president or a senator might not explain actual motivation. Often a public rationale for an event is different from the actual rationale. Look carefully, for instance, at President McKinley's assertion that the war in the Philippines was motivated by a desire to "civilize" the Filipino people.

Reasons for Overseas Imperialism

The United States entered the overseas imperialism scramble a little after the major European powers began carving up Africa and Asia. Many Americans resisted the idea of the United States embarking on overseas expansion; after all, the United States was born in a war against a major imperial power. However, several factors led United States political leaders to engage in overseas expansion.

IMPERIALISM VERSUS COLONIALISM

The two terms are not always interchangeable. Colonialism usually implies the effort of one country to establish a settlement in another land; imperialism usually implies the effort to rule territory that is already occupied and organized.

Alfred Thayer Mahan and the Importance of Naval Power

Alfred Thayer Mahan stressed the importance of naval power in achieving and maintaining influence on the world stage. This idea might seem commonplace, but the United States throughout the nineteenth century was more focused on domestic issues and expansion over the American continent. He pushed for the United States to develop a strong navy, maintain military bases and coaling stations throughout the world, and administer an overseas empire. These ideas were central to his book, *The Influence of Sea Power Upon History, 1660–1783* (1890).

Industrialization and the Depression of 1893

Contributing to the push for imperialism was the unprecedented growth of American industry. Some policy makers thought that imperialism would become necessary if the United States were to become the world's predominant industrial power. Imperial holdings would provide American industry with important raw materials. Also, the people in these new American possessions could provide a market for the growing output of consumer products that American industry was turning out. The desire for new markets intensified with the onset of the panic of 1893. This economic downturn left Americans unable to absorb additional consumer items. The economy did not begin to improve until 1896.

"The White Man's Burden"

Imperialist ventures were motivated by a particular cultural set of ideas that created a racial hierarchy. Mainstream thinking in the United States in the late 1800s posited the superiority of the descendants of the Anglo-Saxon people, and the inferiority of the non-white peoples of the world. This racist notion was widely held, but it led to divergent impulses. Some white Americans felt it was the duty of the "civilized" peoples of the world to uplift the less fortunate; others felt that the inferior races would simply disappear in a struggle for the "survival of the fittest." The push to uplift the peoples of the world was made clear in Rudyard Kipling's famous poem, "The White Man's Burden" (1899). Josiah Strong, a Protestant clergyman, echoed Kipling's sentiment. He argued that the "Anglo-Saxon" race had a responsibility to "civilize and Christianize" the world.

The racial hierarchy implicit in "The White Man's Burden" was starkly displayed at the World's Fair in Chicago in 1893, as a sideshow of the "exotic" people's of the world was presented to fairgoers. These displays of "natives" were contrasted with the industry and progress of the advanced civilizations. The obvious implication was that the advances of civilization must be made available to the rest of the world. Frederick Douglass attended the fair and, with Ida B. Wells, wrote a scathing critique of the racist assumptions of the fair.

CONSENSUS IN CONFLICT IN THE PAST

Students often assume that the unpleasant ideas of earlier eras—such as slavery or racism—were simply accepted by all of society. However, it is important to recognize that these ideas were not universally accepted. In regard to both slavery and to notions of white supremacy, important voices challenged the mainstream thinking of the day.

Christian Missionaries

Christian missionary work went hand-in-hand with American expansion. Missionaries were eager to spread the Christian gospel and introduce new populations to Christianity. Many of these missionaries targeted China's large population.

Hawaii

American missionaries arrived in Hawaii as early as the 1820s. Later in the century, American businessmen established massive sugar plantations, undermining the local economy. Discord between the American businessmen and the ruler of the island, Queen Liliuokalani, emerged after 1891. The pineapple grower Sanford Dole urged the United States to intervene. American businessmen staged a coup in 1893, toppling Queen Liliuokalani. U.S forces immediately protected a new provisional government, led by Dole. The provisional government hoped for U.S. annexation of the islands, but that did not occur until 1898.

B. THE SPANISH-AMERICAN WAR AND ITS AFTERMATH

The Spanish-American War was a turning point in terms of America's role in the world beyond North America. As a result of the war, the United States acquired island territories, became more involved in the Caribbean and Latin America, acquired the Philippines after a protracted struggle, and became increasingly involved in Asia.

United States Interest in Cuba

In the 1890s, Spain was still in control of Cuba, but a Cuban independence movement was trying to break its ties to Spain. The Spanish governor of Cuba, Valeriano Weyler, used brutal tactics to suppress the rebellion. Thousands of Cubans were crowded into concentration camps. By 1898, approximately a quarter of Cuba's rural population (approximately 300,000 people) had died as a result of starvation and disease.

Many Americans wanted the United States in intervene on Cuba's side in its struggle against Spanish rule. Some Americans saw parallels between the Cuban struggle for independence from Spain and America's struggle for independence from Great Britain. Also, some American businessmen were angered by the interruption of the sugar harvest by the fighting between Cuban rebels and Spanish forces.

"Yellow Journalism" and the Call to War

Events in Cuba were brought to the attention of ordinary Americans through mass-produced and mass-distributed newspapers. Industrialization and increased literacy set the groundwork for America's first mass media. To attract customers, newspapers began printing bold, sensationalistic headlines, often disregarding accepted journalistic practices and even the truth. This sensationalistic journalism came to known as "yellow journalism." News organizations used these techniques of exaggeration and innuendo to build support for war with Spain. These newspapers breathlessly followed events in Cuba, with lurid accounts of Spanish wrongdoing and condemnations of "Butcher" Weyler—the Spanish governor.

The Sinking of the *Maine*

The event that led directly to the Spanish-American War was the destruction of a United States warship, the USS *Maine*, in the harbor of Havana, Cuba. Many in the United States thought that the destruction of the ship was the work of Spain, especially after American newspapers bluntly accused Spain of the crime, despite the scarcity of evidence.

The Spanish-American War

The Spanish-American War was brief. American forces landed in Cuba on June 22, 1898, and Spain surrendered on July 17. Fighting in the Philippines—also held by Spain—lasted just days, as Admiral George Dewey led American forces in taking the capital city of Manila. Theodore Roosevelt led a charge up San Juan Hill in a key battle for Cuba. The colorful

Roosevelt and his men—known as the "Rough Riders"—made headlines in American papers, and elevated Roosevelt's status in the political realm.

The Treaty of Paris

The United States and Spain negotiated the Treaty of Paris (1898) following the war. In the treaty, Spain agreed to cede the Philippines, Puerto Rico, and Guam to the United States; the United States agreed to pay Spain $20 million for these possessions.

Cuba and the Platt Amendment

Cuba gained its independence following the Spanish American War, but in many ways, Cuba became independent in name only. The United States wanted to ensure that American economic interests would not be challenged by a future Cuban administration. The United States, therefore, insisted that the Platt Amendment be inserted into the Cuban Constitution. This amendment allowed the United States to militarily intervene in Cuban affairs if it saw fit. The amendment limited the Cuban government's ability to conduct its foreign policy and to manage its debts. Also, the amendment allowed the United States to lease a naval base at Guantanamo Bay. Americans troops intervened in Cuba three times between 1902 and 1920.

War in the Philippines

Many Filipinos were surprised and disappointed to learn that the United States decided to hold on to the Philippines as a colony after the Spanish-American War. They had seen the United States as a liberating force that would help rid the nation of Spanish rule and usher in independence. This was not the intent of the United States. Following the ratification of the Treaty of Paris, a bitter, three-year-long war, known as the Philippine-American War, ensued that was far more lengthy and deadly than the Spanish-American War itself (Filipino forces continued to resist American control for another decade). Filipino forces were led by Emilio Aguinaldo. The war cost American forces 4,000 lives. Estimates vary in regard to the number of Filipino casualties; historians estimate 20,000 to 30,000 Filipinos died in the conflict and perhaps another 200,000 (and possibly more) civilians died. The United States held on to the Philippines until after World War II (1946).

> ### A TALE OF TWO WARS
>
> In writing about American imperialism, don't forget about the war in the Philippines. It lasted longer (three years) and resulted in more casualties (more than 4,000 American deaths; possibly 200,000 or more Filipino deaths) than the better-known Spanish-American War (four months; fewer than 400 American deaths; fewer than 15,000 combined Cuban and Spanish deaths).

China and the Open Door Policy

The bitter conflict in the Philippines was in many ways designed to provide the United States a stepping-stone to an even greater prize—trade with China. China's large population and natural resources made it a target for the imperialist nations. The major powers of Europe had previously begun carving up China. Britain, Japan, Germany, Russia, and France each proclaimed a "sphere of influence"—a port city and surrounding territory—in which other foreign nations would be excluded. The United States asserted that all of China should be open to trade with all nations. The United States secretary of state, John Hay, wrote a series of notes to the major powers asserting an "open door" policy for China. The United States claimed to be concerned for the territorial integrity of China, but was more interested in gaining a foothold in trade with China. The "open door" policy was begrudgingly accepted by the major powers.

The Boxer Rebellion

Christian missionaries had come to China in large numbers, but met with little success there. The number of converts was small, and the presence of the missionaries inspired militant anti-foreign secret societies. The most well known of these societies was the Boxers, or the Society of Righteous and Harmonious Fists. The Boxers led a rebellion that resulted in the death of more than 30,000 Chinese converts as well as 250 foreign nuns. The United States participated in a multination force to rescue westerners held hostage by the Boxers (1900).

Theodore Roosevelt and the "Big Stick"

In September 1901, President McKinley was shot at the Pan-American Exposition in Buffalo, New York, by the anarchist Leon Czolgosz and soon died from the wound, just six months into his second term as president. His vice president, Theodore Roosevelt, became president. (See more on Roosevelt's domestic agenda above.) Roosevelt was an adventurer, an expansionist, and a hero of the Spanish-American War. His foreign policy approach is neatly summed up in his famous adage that the United States should "speak softly, but carry a big stick" when dealing with other nations (Roosevelt had borrowed the phrase from an African proverb). The "big stick" implied the threat of military force. He envisioned the United States acting as the world's policeman, punishing wrongdoers. He asserted that the "civilized nations" had a duty to police the "backward" countries of the world. He claimed that the United States had the right to militarily intervene in the nations of Latin America. This assertion of American might is known as the Roosevelt Corollary to the Monroe Doctrine. In 1902, he sternly warned Germany to stay out of the Americas after Venezuela failed to repay a loan to Germany and Germany threatened military intervention.

FOREIGN POLICY AND ECONOMIC PRIORITIES

Often in American history, economic priorities drive foreign policy decisions. A Central American canal was a major priority for American commercial and industrial interests at the beginning of the twentieth century.

Panama and the Panama Canal

Roosevelt's aggressive approach to Latin America is clearly evident in regard to Panama. With the acquisition of Pacific territories and with an increased interest in trade with China, American policy-makers became interested in a shortcut to the Pacific. Merchant ships and naval ships had to travel around the southern tip of South America to reach the Pacific Ocean. The building of a canal through Panama, therefore, became a major goal of Roosevelt.

Before 1903 Panama was a region of Columbia. American investors picked the narrow piece of land as an ideal location for a canal to facilitate shipping between the Atlantic and Pacific Oceans. When Columbia refused the U.S. offer of $10 million to build a canal, American investors, with the backing of President Roosevelt and the United States military, instigated a "rebellion" in Panama against Columbia. Panama became an independent country and immediately reached a deal with the United States to build a canal. President Roosevelt boasted that he "took Panama."

Roosevelt, Diplomacy, and the Nobel Peace Prize

President Roosevelt was interested in establishing the United States as a major player in world diplomacy. Toward this end, he acted as a mediator between France and Germany in their conflict over Morocco (1905). Roosevelt was also interested in maintaining a balance of power among the other world powers. That same year, Roosevelt offered to mediate an end to the Russo-Japanese War (1904–1905). A peace conference was held in Portsmouth, New Hampshire, with Roosevelt presiding. Despite Roosevelt's aggressive actions in Latin America, he was granted the Nobel Peace Prize (1906) for his other diplomatic efforts.

> ### THE NOBEL PRIZE
> Three other United States presidents have won the Nobel Peace Prize: Woodrow Wilson in 1919; Jimmy Carter in 2002; and Barack Obama in 2009.

The "Gentleman's Agreement"

In 1907, the diplomatic gains that Roosevelt had achieved with Japan were threatened by discriminatory legislation passed in California, restricting the rights of "Orientals." Roosevelt quietly worked out a "Gentleman's Agreement" with Japan, in which Japan agreed to limit immigration to the United States and Roosevelt agreed to pressure officials in California to end discriminatory practices.

President Taft and "Dollar Diplomacy"

President William Howard Taft (1909–1913) continued to pursue an aggressive foreign policy, but he put more emphasis on expanding and securing American commercial interests than on pursuing the global strategic goals that Roosevelt had championed. Taft's foreign policy has come to be known as "dollar diplomacy." He sent troops to Nicaragua and the Dominican Republic to coerce them into signing commercial treaties with the United States. In general, he tried to substitute "dollars for bullets" in pursuing American interests. He failed to stem revolution in Mexico in 1911.

President Wilson's Foreign Policy

President Wilson's initial focus as president was on domestic concerns. However, his administration became increasingly drawn into foreign policy matters, from problems in the Americas to war in Europe. Wilson was driven by both a desire to secure American economic interests abroad and by a strong moral compass; often these impulses clashed with each other.

> ### LACK OF VOLUNTEERS
> The tepid response to President Wilson's call to volunteer reflects the mixed feelings Americans had about the war.

Wilson immediately signaled a break with his Republican predecessors by appointing the anti-imperialist William Jennings Bryan to be secretary of state. Bryan sought peaceful accommodations of differences with many nations, but he and Wilson were not above flexing America's military muscle in the Americas. Wilson authorized the occupation of Nicaragua by American marines to suppress a rebellion against the American-backed president of the country. He sent troops to Haiti in 1915 and to the Dominican Republic in 1916 to ensure that American business interests were not challenged.

Wilson and the Mexican Revolution

President Wilson became enmeshed in the convulsions of the Mexican Revolution, which lasted through the 1910s. The revolution began with the ousting of an autocratic leader in 1910. The revolution soon degenerated into a civil war that left nearly a million Mexicans dead. In 1914, Wilson challenged the legitimacy of the new Mexican leader, General Victoriano Huerta. He sent 800 marines to Mexico. Huerta fled the country, and a new government, more amenable to American interests, came to power. This new government was challenged by an uprising led by the rebel leader Francisco "Pancho" Villa. Villa successfully intercepted a train carrying American gold and led a raid into American territory that left eighteen Americans dead. Wilson authorized more than 12,000 troops to invade Mexico to capture Villa. Villa eluded the American forces, and the United States, in early 1917, began preparations for World War I.

C. DEBATE OVER THE ROLE OF THE UNITED STATES IN THE WORLD

As America became increasingly involved in world affairs, debates ensued in the United States about the country's proper role. These debates pitted imperialists against anti-imperialists and, later, interventionists against isolationists.

Imperialism and National Identity

As the dust settled following the Spanish-American War, the American public realized that the Treaty of Paris would grant the United States ongoing control of several lands beyond America's existing borders. The United States had recently annexed Hawaii (1898). The Treaty of Paris (1898) would give the United States control over Puerto Rico, Guam, and the Philippines. Although Cuba was technically independent, the Platt Amendment made it a U.S. protectorate. To many Americans, these acquisitions were markedly different from earlier acquisitions; these new islands were densely populated and were far away from the settled parts of the United States, unlike the Louisiana Purchase (1803) or the Mexican Cession (1848). Perhaps the distinction amounted to splitting hairs, but critics did surmise one additional key difference. The earlier territorial gains of the United States were intended to absorb American citizens and to eventually achieve statehood and equal footing with the existing states. There was no expectation, on the other hand, that the Philippines would absorb large numbers of American citizens. The United States would, indefinitely, rule *over* a foreign population, much as Great Britain had ruled over the Thirteen Colonies.

The American Anti-Imperialist League

In 1898, as the Treaty of Paris was debated in the Senate, a group of critics of American imperialism formed the American Anti-Imperialist League. The league was a coalition of conservative Democrats (known at the time as "Bourbon Democrats") as well as more progressive elements. The league included the American author Mark Twain, who became increasingly radical as he grew older. He was the vice president of the league from 1901 to 1910, and wrote some of the league's more scathing condemnations of imperialism.

The league suffered a major schism in 1900, as the more conservative members rejected the candidacy of Democrat William Jennings Bryan, while the more progressive elements embraced it. Jennings was an anti-imperialist, but many of his other positions, especially his criticism of the gold standard, alienated many of the conservative "Bourbon Democrats." The Republican William McKinley won reelection, continuing an aggressive foreign policy.

The debate over imperialism—over whether the United States Constitution permitted the American government to make rules for peoples who were not represented by lawmakers— nearly imperiled ratification of the Treaty of Paris. Democratic opponents of imperialism rallied against the treaty, which barely achieved the necessary two-thirds majority in 1899.

Does the Constitution Follow the Flag?

The question of whether Constitutional provisions applied to people in the new American territories continued in the courts after the ratification of the Treaty of Paris. Expansionists argued that the Constitution did not necessarily follow the flag; anti-imperialists insisted that it should. The Supreme Court settled this issue in a series of cases in 1901 that have come to be known as the Insular cases ("insular" means island-related). The Court agreed with expansionists that democracy and imperialism are not incompatible, and that the imperial power need not grant its colonial subjects constitutional rights. The decisions were based on the racist assumption that the colonial subjects were of an inferior race, and the colonial power had the responsibility to uplift these peoples before granting them autonomy.

II. The United States and World War I

As World War I began in Europe, Americans began to debate the proper role of the United States in the world. The aftermath of the war led to debates about how the United States could best pursue its interests in the world.

A. THE UNITED STATES ENTERS WORLD WAR I

The United States initially proclaimed neutrality in World War I. A variety of factors including President Woodrow Wilson's call to make the world "safe for democracy," led the United States to enter the conflict.

The Onset of War

Historians cite several factors that created an unstable—even dangerous—situation in pre-war Europe. History teachers often graphically represent these factors as sticks of dynamite; the sticks, in such a drawing, are labeled "nationalism," "imperialism," "militarism," and "the alliance system." By the end of the nineteenth century, one can certainly see a rise in nationalism among the European powers. The nations of Europe began to see themselves as actors in a Darwinian struggle to be the "fittest." Inexpensive newspapers and rising literacy rates allowed for the dissemination of patriotic sentiments to an entire nation. This sense of nationalism was fueled by a competition to imperialize the remaining independent areas of Asia and Africa. A scramble occurred among the major powers, setting the stage for tensions and conflict. The situation was made more dangerous by an ominous arms build-up among the European nations, especially the rival nations of Great Britain and Germany. The two nations built larger and larger warships, including Great Britain's HMS *Dreadnought*, which ushered in an era of similarly massive "dreadnought" battle ships. Finally, the situation was made more volatile by a series of alliances that guaranteed that any conflict between two belligerents would soon degenerate into a broad conflagration as mutual defense treaties would drag more nations into the conflict.

If the long-term causes of World War I are presented as sticks of dynamite, then the spark that ignited them is the assassination of the heir to the throne of the Austro-Hungarian empire, Archduke Franz Ferdinand. The archduke was assassinated by a Pan-Slavic nationalist while visiting the city of Sarajevo, in Bosnia, part of Austria-Hungary. The assassination resulted in Austria-Hungary declaring war on Serbia. The alliance system brought Germany into the conflict on the side of Austria-Hungary, while Russia, and then France and Great Britain, were brought into the conflict on the opposing side. As the war began Russia, France, and Great Britain comprised the Triple Entente (later known as the Allied Powers); Austria-Hungary, Germany, and Italy were known at the Triple Alliance (later known as the Central Powers). (Italy switched sides in 1915.) The conflict would last four years and result in the deaths of an astounding 8.5 million soldiers.

United States Neutrality

The United States initially assumed that it could stay neutral in World War I. Several factors kept the United States neutral in the war for its first three years. The United States, from the time of Washington's farewell address, had attempted to stay aloof from the ongoing conflicts of Europe. That had not always been easy. The United States got into wars with Great Britain at the beginning of the nineteenth century (1812) and with Spain at the end of it (1898). These wars, however, were both fought in the Americas (and Asia, in the case of the Spanish-American War), not in Europe. Isolationism in regard to European affairs remained strong. Neutrality also allowed the United States to trade with both sides in the conflict.

> ## UNDERSTANDING NEUTRALITY
>
> Be familiar with the variety of social, economic, political, and historical factors that contributed to United States neutrality during the first years of the World War I.

Immigration Patterns and Public Opinion Around World War I

Immigration patterns did not immediately predispose the United States toward support for either side in World War I. The United States was home to millions of people who were from the belligerent nations on both sides of the conflict. On the one hand, German and Irish immigrants tended to favor the Triple Alliance, which came to be known as the Central Powers. Germans favored their motherland; the Irish had a longstanding resentment of the British. On the other hand, America had ties to Great Britain. Despite the two wars that they had fought (the American Revolution and the War of 1812), the United States and Great Britain shared a language and strong cultural ties.

> ## WORLD WAR I AND MODERN ADVERTISING
>
> The campaign organized by the Committee on Public Information to garner American support for the war effort could be considered one of the first major national advertising campaigns in United States history.

Progressives and the War

Progressives, such as John Dewey, were initially very leery about American involvement in the war. They predicted that participation in a major war would distract the nation from domestic reform and would unleash a jingoistic fervor that would result in a conservative shift in the United States.

From Neutrality to Intervention

Although several factors initially kept America out of World War I, important developments propelled the United States toward intervention. President Wilson emphasized the principle of freedom of the seas. Wilson indicated that the United States would trade and sell weaponry to either side in the conflict, but Great Britain had effectively blockaded Germany. Trade therefore shifted to Great Britain as the war progressed. Between the start of the war in 1914 and 1917, U.S. trade with Britain increased by 300 percent, while trade with Germany shrank to almost nothing.

Germany responded by warning that United States ships in the waters off Great Britain would be subject to attack by U-boats, or submarines. The sinking of the British ocean liner *Lusitania* infuriated many Americans (128 Americans were among the dead). Germany, however, wanted to keep the United States out of the war and agreed in the Sussex Pledge (1916) to make no surprise submarine attacks on U.S. ships. The United States took advantage of this pledge and traded extensively with Great Britain, much to the consternation of Germany.

President Woodrow Wilson and the War

As the war dragged on in Europe, public opinion began to shift toward the Allied Powers of Great Britain, France, and Russia. This was partly brought about by wartime news coverage, which tended to present Germany and the Central Powers as aggressive, and even barbaric, in their execution of the war. Also, the Allied Powers seemed to be more clearly the democratic side of the war after czarist Russia was no longer part of the alliance. (The czar was toppled in February 1917, and Russia later withdrew from the war.) Wilson's approach to the conflict changed rapidly. During his bid for reelection in 1916, Wilson's campaign repeatedly reminded voters that "he kept us out of war." But, after his reelection, Wilson became increasingly convinced that United States participation in World War I was necessary to make the world "safe for democracy."

Wilson's shift to a pro-war stance divided Americans. Some joined Wilson on his intellectual journey; they too began to think of participation in the war as an idealistic crusade to create a new world order based on peace and autonomy. However, many opposed the drive for war. The government went to great lengths to alter public opinion in regard to the war. The United States finally entered the war in 1917.

The Zimmermann Note and Unrestricted German Submarine Warfare

Many Americans moved toward a pro-war position after the secret "Zimmermann note" became public. The intercepted telegram from German foreign secretary Arthur Zimmermann indicated that Germany would help Mexico regain territory it had lost to the United States if Mexico joined the war on Germany's side. Americans took this as a threat to their territory.

Finally, in early 1917, Germany announced that it would rescind the Sussex Pledge and that it would resume unrestricted submarine warfare against Great Britain and its allies, including the United States. In February and March of 1917, hundreds of American ships had been sunk by German submarine attacks. This proved to be the final straw for the United States. In April 1917, the United States declared war on Germany.

B. THE UNITED STATES, WORLD WAR I, AND THE POSTWAR WORLD

The United States played an important role during the final year of World War I. Following the war, President Woodrow Wilson was active in the negotiations around a peace treaty. His involvement was important in proposals to create the League of Nations. American entrance into the League, however, caused strenuous debates in the United States.

American Participation in World War I

The United States entered the war late in the game. It did provide the Allies—Great Britain and France—with much needed support. France and Great Britain had been at war for nearly three years when the United States joined the conflict. The two million soldiers of the American Expeditionary Force that the United States provided proved to be crucial in the Allied victory. By the time the United States had entered the war, it had bogged down in a brutal stalemate. Both sides had dug themselves into trenches, separated by a strip of "no-man's land." One side might attempt a frontal attack on the other, but as soon as the soldiers were ordered out of their trench they would be subjected to machine gun fire, barbed wire, and poison gas attacks. Perhaps one or the other side would capture a few miles of desolate land, only to be subsequently pushed back. The five-month-long Battle of the Somme (1916), for example, resulted in more than a million casualties, and no substantial gains for either side.

Wilson's Fourteen Points

President Wilson was determined to shape the structure of the postwar world. He felt strongly that the causes of war should be identified, addressed, and alleviated.

Wilson put forth a document, known as the Fourteen Points (1918), that emphasized international cooperation. He envisioned a world order based on freedom of the seas, removal of barriers to trade, self-determination for European people, and an international organization to resolve conflicts. These ideas were rejected by the victorious European powers except for the creation of the League of Nations.

United States Rejection of the Treaty of Versailles

Ironically the United States did not end up joining the League of Nations. This international body was the one component of President Wilson's Fourteen Points document that was embraced by the victorious European nations. The United States would have had to approve the Treaty of Versailles in order to join the League. Despite Wilson's enthusiasm for passage of the treaty, some senators wanted to isolate the United States from world affairs and opposed membership in the league. These isolationists announced that they would vote to reject the treaty. Some senators took a middle position; they would agree to vote to approve the treaty, if the Senate put certain conditions on American participation in the League of Nations. Wilson refused to compromise with these senators and urged his allies in the Senate to reject any conditions. Without these senators in the middle, the Treaty of Versailles was rejected by the Senate. In many ways, the debates around the Treaty of Versailles and the victory of isolationist sentiment shaped American foreign policy for the next decade.

C. AMERICAN FOREIGN POLICY IN THE INTERWAR YEARS

America largely maintained a position of neutrality in the interwar years. It did, however, play an increasingly large role in international treaties and investment. The United States engaged in military interventions, mostly in the Western Hemisphere, with the goal of advancing its vision of international order.

> ### POLITICS AND LITERATURE
>
> Some of the antiwar novels written in the wake of World War I, such as *All Quiet on the Western Front* (1929) by the German writer Erich Maria Remarque and *A Farewell to Arms* (1929) by Ernest Hemingway, added fuel to the isolationist sentiment of the 1930s.

The Politics of Isolationism in the 1920s

Isolationist sentiment ran high in the United States. Many Americans were disillusioned about World War I while others had grown resentful of the wave of "new immigrants" who had come to America. The United States remained outside the League of Nations (see page 244 for the rejection of the Treaty of Versailles).

> ### TARIFF RATES IN HISTORY
>
> Debates about tariff rates have existed throughout American history, from Alexander Hamilton's "Report on Manufactures" (1791) to the passage of the North America Free Trade Agreement (1994). Tariff rates were passionately debated in the nineteenth century.

Higher Tariff Rates

The isolationist Republican presidents of the 1920s enacted higher tariffs to keep out foreign goods. In 1922, the Fordney-McCumber Act dramatically raised tariff rates. In 1930, in the midst of the Great Depression, isolationist legislators pushed through the Smoot-Hawley Tariff Act, which increased tariffs to their second highest rate in United States history, exceeded only by the "Tariff of Abominations" (1828).

> ### TARIFFS IN THE 1920s
>
> Tariffs in the 1920s were at their highest rate in American history other than in the period following the "Tariff of Abominations." Raising tariff rates during the 1920s was exactly what the country didn't need. The United States needed to trade more with Europe in order to sell excess goods. Tariffs closed off trade with Europe.

Washington Conference

The presidents of the 1920s attempted to isolate the United States from world affairs, and reduce spending on war munitions. President Harding successfully pressed for a reduction of naval power among Britain, France, Japan, Italy, and the United States at the Washington Disarmament Conference in 1921.

The Kellogg-Briand Pact

The United States was one of sixty-three nations to sign the Kellogg-Briand Pact, renouncing war in principle. The pact was unenforceable, negotiated outside of the League of Nations, and, ultimately, meaningless.

The Challenges of Isolationism in the 1930s

The United States existed in an increasingly dangerous world in the 1930s, creating new debates around the isolationist stance that had shaped foreign policy in the 1920s. The Fascist Party, led by Benito Mussolini, had taken power in Italy in 1922. The Nazi Party, led by Adolf Hitler, came to power in Germany in 1933. A civil war in Spain led to the rise of a government run by the dictator Francisco Franco in 1939. In Japan, militaristic leaders set Japan on an aggressive course. These dictatorial governments all took aggressive actions in the 1930s. Japan attacked China in 1931. Germany occupied the demilitarized Rhineland in 1936, annexed Austria in 1937, and occupied Czechoslovakia in 1939. Italy conquered Ethiopia in 1936. The League of Nations protested and Great Britain and France objected, but it was not until Germany attacked Poland in September 1939, that Hitler was seriously challenged. Great Britain and France declared war on Germany, beginning World War II. Germany, Italy, and Japan formed the Axis Powers with the signing of the Tripartite Pact (1940).

> ## EUROPE IN THE 1930s
>
> Even though it is not American history, the events in Europe in the 1930s should be familiar to you. Often, events abroad have an impact on the United States—fighting between France and Britain at the turn of the nineteenth century; European imperialism in the late nineteenth century, the World Wars, and the Cold War to name just a few.

The Continued Pull of Isolationism

As events degenerated into war in Europe, a debate occurred in the United States about America's role. Isolationists argued strongly that the United States should stay out of world affairs. Many of these isolationists looked back to World War I as a lesson in the futility of getting involved in European affairs. America lost over 100,000 men in World War I for no apparent reason, they argued. World War I hadn't made the world safe for democracy. Almost as soon as the war ended, antidemocratic forces emerged and set Europe once again on the path toward war. In addition, the Senate's Nye Committee (1934–1937) uncovered evidence that certain American corporations had profited greatly from World War I. Americans wondered if the so-called merchants of death had pushed the country into World War I.

The Argument for Intervention

Many Americans, on the other hand, believed that it would be a mistake for the United States to isolate itself from world affairs on the eve of World War II. They mocked the idea that the Atlantic Ocean would indefinitely protect the United States from dangerous trends in Europe. Interventionists believed that the United States could no longer stand apart. Airplanes and submarines could bring the war to the United States very quickly. If Britain were defeated, there would be nothing standing between Hitler and America. Interventionists believed that the Atlantic Ocean would not be a barrier for Hitler; rather it would be a means for him to bring his war machine farther west to the United States. Also, many interventionists believed that the war in Europe was different from earlier European quarrels over territory or national pride. They believed that if Hitler and Mussolini were successful, civilization itself would be threatened. They were convinced that the Axis Powers were determined to defeat democratic forces all over the world.

President Franklin Roosevelt Proceeds with Caution

President Franklin Roosevelt was cautious in his responses to the conflict in Europe. He was sympathetic to the countries defending themselves against fascism, but he knew he couldn't commit the United States to an interventionist position without the support of the public. Early on, in 1937, Roosevelt recognized that a European war could engulf people far from Europe. He was not ready to commit the United States to intervene, but he didn't pretend that the United States could isolate itself from the affairs of Europe.

The Onset of World War II—from "Cash-and-Carry" to Pearl Harbor

The question of the role of the United States grew more intense in 1939 as World War II formally began. The war started after Germany attacked Poland. Britain and France quickly declared war on Germany. Soon after, Roosevelt pushed for legislation allowing the United States to send armaments to Britain with the condition that Britain pay for the weapons first and transport them in their own ships. The policy of cash-and-carry allowed the United States to support Britain without the risk of U.S. ships being destroyed.

By mid-1940, the American public began to shift toward a more interventionist stance. The situation in Europe grew dire. Americans were shaken by the defeat of France at the hands of the Nazis in June 1940. They saw how one of the democratic powers was easily defeated by the Nazi war machine. Would Britain fall next? Would the United States be the next target? By 1941, 70 percent of the American people were ready to directly help Britain, even if it meant risking getting involved in World War II. In 1940, Roosevelt pushed for the enactment of the Selective Service Act, calling for compulsory military service for males between 21 and 35. With this shift in public opinion and with his victory in the presidential election of 1940, Roosevelt was ready to take more direct action. In March 1941, Congress approved his Lend-Lease Act, which allowed the United States to ship armaments to Britain in American ships. Though officially neutral, the United States was moving steadily toward intervening on the side of Britain.

The public was not unified in its support of intervention. Isolationists such as the renowned aviator Charles Lindbergh continued to argue against any U.S. steps toward helping Britain. He was a leader of the America First Committee, and, historians argue, a Nazi sympathizer. Even as late as 1941, it was clear that many Americans still had major reservations about America entering World War II. Debates about intervention ended abruptly on December 7, 1941. Japanese planes attacked the U.S. base at Pearl Harbor, Hawaii. Almost immediately the United States entered World War II. With American involvement in World War II, the isolationist position was largely silenced.

III. The United States and World War II

World War II had a major impact on the United States, both domestically and internationally. Domestically, the mobilization for the war transformed American society. Internationally, the war led to America playing a preeminent role in the world.

A. MOBILIZING FOR WORLD WAR II

The massive efforts by the United States to mobilize society for war led to the end of the Great Depression. The efforts to supply troops for the armed forces and to produce war-related materials led to opportunities for women and minorities to improve their position in society. In many ways, World War II required the participation of the entire American public, not simply members of the military. These efforts created a sense of unity and common cause in the country.

Rationing and Recycling

During the war, there were shortages of key items because of the needs of the military. Starting in 1942, the Office of Price Administration began rationing key commodities to civilians, such as gasoline and tires. Next, the government began rationing food—sugar, meat, coffee, lard, butter, and many other items. Families were given ration books, and would use ration stamps, along with cash, when they purchased these items. In addition, children organized Tin Can Clubs to collect scrap metal to be melted down to produce weapons and ammunition.

Funding the War Effort

The Roosevelt administration paid for the war effort through the sale of war bonds and increases in taxes. The government went into massive debt during the war, with the debt rising by a factor of six between 1940 and 1949. The experience of World War II demonstrates that massive government spending, and ensuing deficits, can play a significant role in stimulating a sluggish economy.

War Production

If the United States were to become the "arsenal for democracy," as President Roosevelt promised in a speech in 1940, it would have to dramatically and rapidly step up the production of war-related materials. In 1942, Roosevelt created the War Production Board, and later the Office of War Mobilization, to oversee the conversion from civilian industry to war production. Almost overnight, the persistent unemployment of the 1930s ended. After the United States entered the war in December 1941, the country faced the opposite problem—labor shortages. With millions of men and women in the armed forces, the Roosevelt administration took several important steps to ensure a sufficient supply of factory workers. To ensure uninterrupted production, labor unions agreed to refrain from striking during the war. This promise was kept, with the exception of a few strikes in the coal industry.

> ## WORLD WAR I AND THE NEW DEAL
>
> Although the constellation of wartime agencies were disbanded after the war, a similar set of agencies was created by President Franklin Roosevelt, as part of his New Deal during the Great Depression.

"Rosie the Riveter"

The government also made a concerted effort to recruit women to participate in the war effort. Women were needed because factories were working around the clock producing military goods, and much of the male work force was in the military. Many recruiting posters were produced by the government, usually through the Office of War Information, showing women in industrial settings. The fictional "Rosie the Riveter" character was often featured in this public relations campaign. Female workers were presented in a positive light—helping the nation as well as the men in combat abroad. Such a campaign was needed because prewar societal mores discouraged women from doing industrial work. During the Great Depression of the 1930s, women were encouraged to leave the job market so that there would be enough jobs available for male "bread winners." The World War II recruiting campaign was successful. By 1945, one third of the work force was female.

Staffing the Army

The Roosevelt administration began a push to enlarge the size of the army even before the attack on Pearl Harbor brought the United States into the war. The Selective Service Act was passed in September 1940, creating the first peacetime draft in American history. By the summer of 1941, almost a million and a half men were in the armed forces. In the course of the war, more than 15 million men and women would serve in the military. Many women served as nurses. In addition, more than 150,000 women served in the Women's Army Auxiliary Corps (later, the Women's Army Corps) and in the WAVES, the women's unit of the Navy.

B. WORLD WAR II AND AMERICAN VALUES

A series of debates and decisions during World War II—including the decisions related to the internment of Japanese Americans and to the dropping of the atomic bomb, as well as debates over race and segregation—raised fundamental questions about American values.

The Japanese Relocation

In 1942 President Roosevelt issued Executive Order 9066, authorizing the government to remove more than 100,000 Japanese Americans from West Coast states and relocate them to camps in Arizona. The order applied to both Issei (Japanese Americans who had emigrated from Japan) and Nisei (native-born Japanese Americans). Most of their property was confiscated by the government. In *Korematsu v. United States* (1944), the Supreme Court ruled that the relocation was acceptable on the grounds of national security. Much later, in 1988, the U.S. government publicly apologized to the surviving victims and extended $20,000 in reparations to each one. The Korematsu decision is one of several rulings by the Supreme Court that have curtailed civil liberties in times of war. The court upheld restrictions on free speech during World War I in the *Schenck v. United States* decision (1919).

> ## CIVIL LIBERTIES DURING WARTIME
>
> The Korematsu case is often on the AP exam. Be prepared to discuss it in the context of the broader question of civil liberties during wartime.

The Decision to Drop the Atomic Bomb and Japanese Surrender

In July 1945, President Harry S. Truman learned that the United States had successfully tested an atomic bomb and that more bombs were ready to be used. The United States had been working on this awesomely deadly weapon since 1940. The top-secret research program was known as the Manhattan Project. The project involved research labs at different sites. The facility at Los Alamos, New Mexico, headed by physicist J. Robert Oppenheimer, was charged with the construction of the bomb.

The United States used this new weapon twice on Japan. On August 6, 1945, the United States dropped an atomic bomb on Hiroshima; on August 9 a second bomb was dropped on Nagasaki. Soon after, Japan surrendered, thus ending World War II. At the time, the decision to drop the atomic bomb did not generate much public debate. The atomic bombing swiftly ended a bloody conflict that had consumed 50 million lives. But in the decades since the war, some Americans have raised questions about the decision. Critics argue that it was morally wrong for the United States to have targeted civilian populations and that the Japanese were ready to surrender anyway. Others stand by the decision to drop the bomb. Virtually every Japanese city was involved in some way in military production. Further, it is not clear that the Japanese were on the verge of surrendering. Some members of the Japanese military argued against surrendering even after the second bomb was dropped.

World War II and the Status of African Americans in American Society

During World War II, a series of changes occurred that led to a reevaluation of attitudes and practices around race. African Americans mounted a frontal challenge to the system of Jim Crow segregation, both through their participation in the armed forces and in war-related industries. In many ways, this challenge continued into the postwar world. It also put the issues of race and segregation on the national agenda.

African Americans in the Armed Forces

African Americans participated in the war effort in unprecedented numbers. The National Association for the Advancement of Colored People encouraged African Americans to take part in the "Double V" campaign—promoting victory against fascism abroad and victory against racism at home. Ultimately, 125,000 African Americans served overseas during World War II. The most famous segregated African-American units were the Tuskegee Airmen and the 761st Tank Battalion. African-American effectiveness on the battlefield encouraged President Truman to later (1948) desegregate the armed services with Executive Order 9981.

African Americans and War Production

Initially, many war industries were reluctant to hire African Americans. An important African–American labor leader, A. Phillip Randolph, the president of the Brotherhood of Sleeping Car Porters, planned a public demonstration in Washington, DC, in 1941 to protest discrimination in war-related industries. When the Roosevelt administration heard of these plans, it worked out a bargain. Roosevelt issued Executive Order 8802, banning discrimination in war-related industries, and Randolph called off the march.

African Americans joined millions of other Americans in moving toward industrial centers. The Great Migration that began in World War I continued, with African Americans moving to the West Coast in addition to moving to northern industrial cities.

C. THE ALLIED VICTORY OVER THE AXIS POWERS IN WORLD WAR II

The United States played an important role in the Allied victory over the Axis powers. American leaders participated in joint political and military efforts with the other Allied countries. In addition, American industrial production and advances in technology and science played an important role in the war effort. Finally, the commitment of large sections of the American public to victory and to the advancement of democratic ideals helped the overall war effort.

War in the Pacific Theater

Through the first year of the war, the United States sent more of its troops to the Pacific theater than to Europe. Even though the defeat of Hitler was a top priority for the United States, it was Japan that had directly attacked the United States. The United States suffered several setbacks at the hands of the Japanese military in the first few months of the war. Japan took over the Philippines at the end of December 1941. By May 1942, Japan controlled a massive empire, and had Australia in its sights.

The Battles of Coral Sea and Midway

The United States turned the tide of the war in the Pacific in two naval battles in 1942. In May the United States stopped a Japanese fleet as it was headed to New Guinea in the Battle of the Coral Sea. In June, the United States achieved a victory over the Japanese fleet in the Battle of Midway. After the Battle of Midway, the United States slowly began to push Japanese forces back toward the Japanese home islands.

TURNING POINTS IN WAR

Although extensive knowledge of battles is not required for the AP exam, be aware of key turning points in wars, such as the Battle of Saratoga in the American Revolution and the capture of Vicksburg and the Battle of Gettysburg in the Civil War.

"Island Hopping"

By the end of 1943, the United States began employing a strategy called "leapfrogging" (also known as "island hopping") in regard to defeating Japan in the Pacific. The basic idea of leapfrogging was that the United States and its allies would avoid attacking some of the most heavily fortified islands in the Pacific. Instead, it would focus on islands that were important in the drive toward the Japanese home islands, but that were not as well defended. The United States then hoped to isolate the Japanese-held islands that it had leapfrogged over by blockading supply ships. The Japanese forces on these islands would, according to strategy, "wither on the vine."

War in Europe

Before June 1944, most of the fighting against Germany was carried out by the Soviet Union in eastern Europe. Joseph Stalin, the leader of the Soviet Union, had been urging the United States and Britain to open a second western front in Europe against Germany. At a meeting in Tehran, Iran (more on the Tehran Conference below), in November 1943, President Franklin Roosevelt and British leader Winston Churchill assured Stalin that they would open up a second European front.

The Washington and Casablanca Conferences

In June 1942, Roosevelt and Churchill met in Washington, DC, to discuss strategy. In January 1943, they met again in Casablanca, Morocco. Stalin did not attend either meeting, but he let it be known that he hoped the allies would soon open up a major second front in Europe. The brunt of the fighting against Hitler's forces was carried out by the Red Army. Nearly 90 percent of German casualties came at the hands of Soviet troops. At both meetings, Churchill opposed the idea of immediately invading France; the British did not want to prematurely initiate a repeat of the trench warfare of World War I. Churchill and Roosevelt agreed to open a front in North Africa, followed by an attack on "the soft under-belly" of the Axis—Italy.

Fighting in North Africa

The first offensive involving American troops against Nazi-occupied areas occurred in North Africa in November 1942. American forces, led by General Dwight D. Eisenhower, landed in Morocco and Algeria and pushed back the forces of the French Vichy government, which collaborated with the Nazis. Americans also fought German troops in Tunisia and Libya. By May 1943, North Africa was in Allied hands.

The "Soft-Underbelly" of the Axis

Approximately a quarter of a million Allied forces landed in Sicily in June 1943. The allies captured Sicily by August, which led to the Italian king dismissing Mussolini as prime minister. A new Italian government left the Axis and eventually joined the Allies. Germany, however, was not ready to accept Allied-occupation of Italy. Hitler sent reinforcements into Italy. After further fighting, the Allies finally marched into Rome in June 1944.

D-Day

In June 1944, Allied troops landed on the beaches of Normandy, France, and began pushing Hitler's forces back toward Germany. By August 1944, Allied forces had liberated Paris from Nazi occupation.

V-E Day

Hitler made a last attempt to stop the Allied assault in the winter of 1944–1945. German forces drove through Allied lines into Belgium in the Battle of the Bulge before being stopped by Allied forces. American and British troops approached Germany from the west as Soviet troops approached from the east. By April 1945, Soviet troops were on the outskirts of Berlin. On April 30, Hitler committed suicide, and on May 7, 1945, Germany surrendered, ending the war in Europe.

The Holocaust

As the war in Europe was ending, the Allies became aware of the full extent of the barbaric crimes against civilians committed by the Nazis during the war. The Holocaust was the systematic murder of 6 million European Jews and other "undesirables" by the Nazis. In 1939, Hitler and other leading Nazis developed the "final solution of the Jewish question," a plan to eliminate the Jewish population. After the Germans took over most of continental Europe, this plan went from being the scheming of a madman to a horrible, deadly reality. The plan also included other groups such as gypsies and homosexuals. Nazis rounded up Jews first into crowded urban areas called ghettos, then moved them to concentration or labor camps, and finally to death camps, where gas chambers and incineration ovens were built to carry out the "final solution."

Victory in the Pacific

By February 1945, American forces had taken most of Japan's empire from Japanese control. Two small heavily fortified islands stood between American forces and the Japanese home islands—Iwo Jima and Okinawa. Capturing these two islands proved to be an onerous task for American forces. The battle for Iwo Jima lasted six weeks in February and March 1945.

Approximately 7,000 Americans died in the battle. The battle of Okinawa was even more deadly. The island of Okinawa was to be a staging area for an attack on the Japanese home islands. Fighting there lasted from early April until mid-June 1945. The United States mobilized 300,000 troops for the battle. Approximately 12,000 American troops died, while Japan lost approximately 140,000 troops. After these bloody battles, Japan's sphere of control was reduced to its home islands. At that point, the United States decided to unleash the newly developed atomic bomb, finally bringing Japan to surrender.

D. THE UNITED STATES AND THE POSTWAR WORLD

The United States played an important role in the Allied victory in World War II and in shaping the postwar world through peace conferences and settlements. With Europe and Asia ravaged from the war, the United States emerged from World War II as the dominant power in the world.

> ### AMERICAN ENGAGEMENT
> Note the marked difference between American disengagement following World War I and American engagement following World War II.

Teheran Conference

Stalin, Churchill, and Roosevelt, met in Tehran, Iran, in November 1943. The Allies agreed that the D-Day invasion would coincide with a major Soviet offensive. Also, Stalin pledged that the Soviet Union would join the war in Asia following the defeat of Germany. The Allies agreed in theory to forming an international peacekeeping organization.

Bretton Woods Conference

In 1944, forty-four nations met at Bretton Woods, New Hampshire, to discuss the basis of the global economy following the war. The International Monetary Fund was established at this meeting.

Yalta Conference

The Yalta Conference, held in 1945, was the most significant, and last, meeting of Churchill, Stalin, and Roosevelt. At Yalta, a coastal city in Ukraine, the "big three" agreed to divide Germany into four military zones of occupation (the fourth zone would be occupied by France). Also, Stalin agreed to allow free elections in Poland in the future, with a Soviet-dominated interim government immediately following the war. Also at the meeting, secret agreements were made allowing for Soviet control of Outer Mongolia, the Kurile Islands, and part of Sakhalin Island, as well as Soviet railroad rights in Manchuria. In exchange, Stalin reaffirmed his commitment to help the United States defeat Japan following the surrender of Germany. Critics later faulted Roosevelt and Churchill for "abandoning" Poland and the rest of Eastern Europe to communist forces. But there was little the United States and Britain could do to dislodge the Red Army from Eastern Europe, short of starting a third world war.

Potsdam Conference

In 1945, at this final meeting of the United States, the Soviet Union, and Britain, Stalin, President Truman in place of Roosevelt, who died in April 1945, and British Prime Minister Clement Atlee in place of Churchill, hammered out the details of the administration of occupied Germany. These details included the process of "denazification" of Germany, which led to the Nuremberg War Crimes Trials. The victorious nations set up this international tribunal to try leading Nazis for waging aggressive war and for committing crimes against humanity. At these trials, about thirty American judges participated. The chief justice of the U.S. Supreme Court was a chief lawyer for the prosecution. Many of the Nazis defended themselves by claiming that they were merely following orders.

SUBJECT TO DEBATE

History textbooks can take one of several approaches to discuss American imperialism. You should be familiar with these approaches in order to write about events and documents from this period within a broader intellectual framework.

James Loewen, in his survey of American history textbooks, identifies three approaches to talking about American imperialism. Critics of American imperialism often discuss the United States as if it were a "colossus," imposing its will on the world. This "American colossus" approach asserts that any talk of spreading democracy around the world is cynical window-dressing to hide the actual motives of American imperialism: economic exploitation. A competing view acknowledges that economic motives drive foreign policy, but is not troubled by that fact. This hard-nosed "realpolitik" approach holds that America must expand if it wants to maintain the standard of living that Americans have come to appreciate. A third view, which Loewen calls the "international good guy" approach, ignores economic motives altogether. It asserts that American motives in the world are altruistic and noble. This view takes the words of public figures at face value.[1]

These approaches are useful when confronted with a document such as President Wilson's call for intervention in World War I. You should be able to interrogate his claims that we are entering the war to "make the world safe for democracy." You should be able to discuss the intent of such a document, rather than simply recounting information contained within it as fact.

For much of the twentieth century, the Progressive movement was treated quite favorably by historians. Historians generally accepted the self-descriptions of the Progressive movement—that it was a movement devoted to eliminating corruption, inefficiencies, inequalities of wealth, and unhealthy working and living conditions. It would be hard to find fault with such a movement, especially because a large percentage of historians would probably consider themselves progressive and would probably share many of the same ideas about society that members of the Progressive movement did. However, by the 1960s we begin to see questions being raised about the movement.

Some historians argued the Progressive movement did not pose a serious challenge to the profitability of business. They contend that much of the impetus to reform business either originated with the business community or was shaped by it. Members of the business community were interested in reigning in the worst elements of the business world. The example of the meat packing industry demonstrates this point well. After the publication of *The Jungle*, the public's confidence in the entire industry declined. Industry leaders wanted to reform their world—rationalize and standardize it—so that people would continue to buy meat. Rather than resisting reform, industry leaders initiated it in order to save their industry.

A second avenue of criticism of the movement had to do with the attitude of the Progressive movement toward the poor. This critique painted the Progressive movement as elitist

1 James Loewen, *Lies My Teacher Told Me: Everything Your American History Textbook Got Wrong* (New York: New Press, 1995).

and condescending toward the working class it was trying to help. The movement was ready to impose its idea of proper behavior on others. This is most evident in the prohibition movement—in which middle-class activists told working-class people that they shouldn't drink. The crusade against "immoral" behavior—gambling, prostitution, smoking—also raises this issue of elitism. The nature of reform movements in general continues to divide historians.

World War I often gets relegated to the backseat in standard history curricula—with World War II much more prominent. Perception of World War II is of a war imbued with a sense of mission—it was a "good fight" carried out by the "greatest generation." On the mall in Washington, DC, a new large World War II memorial occupies a prominent place between the Washington Monument and the Lincoln Memorial. The World War I monument, by contrast, is a modest gazebo tucked away to the side of the mall. It is not even a national monument—it commemorates local residents who perished in the conflict. One reason World War I has gotten ignored is that there isn't a clearly identifiable "evil" that the United States was trying to stop. The history of World War I does not read like a morality play.

That said, it would be unwise for a student preparing for the AP exam to ignore World War I. There are several crucial questions to consider. For instance, how do we account for the fact that the American political landscape changed completely from the beginning of the war to the end of the war? In 1914, on the eve of the war, the Progressive movement was enjoying its heyday; in 1919, as the war ended, America had become violently conservative. The "Red Scare" was paving the way for the rise of the Ku Klux Klan, restrictions on immigration, and attacks on secularism. Students should be cognizant of the role that war plays in changing the political climate.

The decade of the 1920s poses problems for historians in the "consensus" tradition. Consensus history asserts that there is a broad consensus among Americans around basic ideas and feelings. According to consensus historians, Americans share a belief in democracy and individual liberties; they believe that hard work leads to advancement; they believe in God, but do not try to impose their beliefs on others or on society as a whole; and they are a tolerant, welcoming people. Consensus history gained traction in the 1950s; this broad set of ideas set America apart from the Soviet Union—an essentially different system developed by people from an essentially different background. True, consensus historians acknowledge, there have been conflicts, but they have not been over essential values. Take the labor battles of the Gilded Age. Consensus historians would argue that these disagreements do not represent fundamental differences. The strikers were not revolutionaries; they simply wanted a fair share of the pie, just like all Americans.

Consensus historians have a great deal of difficulty explaining the 1920s. Here is a decade in which the Ku Klux Klan claimed to have 3 million members in a country of 100 million people. Even if the membership figures are inflated, the Ku Klux Klan was a huge organization. Three million Americans joined a violent, racist, intolerant, anti-Semitic organization. In addition, there were many cases of German American residents being beaten in their homes by mobs of Americans in the early 1920s. These violent episodes challenge the assumptions of the consensus historians. Some historians have tried to minimize the importance of these facts or stress the fun of the "jazz age." Others have seen the reactionary impulses of the decade as responses to rapid social change. However, the undercurrent of intolerance and violence in the 1920s is difficult to fit into the traditional consensus model of American history.

Historians have debated the legacy of President Herbert Hoover in recent years. History textbooks tend to give Hoover a bad name. He is presented as aloof and rigid in the face of economic disaster. Hoover is remembered for what he didn't do (provide direct relief to the poor) rather than what he did do.

Hoover's legacy in historical work tells us a great deal about historical writing. Many historians have come to lionize Hoover's successor, President Franklin Roosevelt. Roosevelt both saved the country from the worst ravages of the Great Depression at home and from the fascist menace abroad. In the process, he created the modern liberal welfare state. This adoration of Roosevelt has influenced historical writing about Hoover. Hoover, in this context, has become the anti-Roosevelt, representing the negative side of the coin. Hoover is lumped in with the other two Republican presidents of the 1920s, Harding and Coolidge. However, a brief look at the record would indicate that Hoover was not the incompetent that he is often been portrayed as. He was an exceptionally competent administrator, running the successful Food Administration during World War I. When the depression hit, he did not sit idly by. He implemented the far-reaching Reconstruction Finance Corporation, which provided needed funds to key components of the economy. Later he implemented public works programs. Even his handling of the Bonus March is not as heavy-handed as usually portrayed; the most aggressive acts were carried out by General Douglas MacArthur, without the permission of Hoover.

The nature of the New Deal has been a subject of much debate among historians, as it was among contemporaries. Conservative critics in the 1930s railed against "creeping socialism." Liberals championed the expansion of the state to help society cope with economic dislocation. Radicals asserted that the New Deal was essentially a conservative scheme to prop up capitalism. Historians often have in mind contemporary debates about government intervention in the economy when they are looking at the New Deal.

Historians have tried to understand the intellectual and political origins of the New Deal. Some look to the reform impulses of the Populist and Progressive movements of the late 1800s and early 1900s. They see continuities between the reform programs of Presidents Theodore Roosevelt and Woodrow Wilson and the reform impulses of the New Deal. They note that many New Dealers were active in the Progressive era. Some historians see more of a break between earlier reform efforts and the New Deal. The progressives were mostly middle-class men and women, imposing their values on society. The New Deal, some argue, was driven more by working-class concerns.

Was the New Deal successful or not? Some historians have noted that the New Deal did not solve the problems of the Depression. They see the creation of a bloated government bureaucracy that was too large and impersonal to address the concerns of ordinary people. These historians note that the Depression ended only when the United States began producing materials for World War II. Other historians, more sympathetic to Roosevelt and the New Deal, argue that the New Deal restored hope among the American people and prevented more widespread suffering. Defenders of the New Deal also note that organized labor made great strides because of New Deal legislation. These debates parallel contemporary debates about the efficacy of government efforts at solving social and economic problems.

Two of the most heated historical questions involving the World War II era both have to do with issues of morality, justice, and war. Historians have recently had heated debates over both the Holocaust and the dropping of the atomic bomb on Japan. Some historians have insisted that the United States could have done more to save European Jews. These historians cite prewar immigration restrictions that prevented Jewish refugees from coming into the

United States. In 1939, the State Department did not allow the passenger ship St. Louis to dock in Florida. The ship was carrying more than a thousand Jewish refugees seeking asylum. The ship was forced to return to Antwerp, where most of the Jews aboard ended up dying in concentration camps. This question has resonated in the contemporary world as Americans have debated how much their country should intervene in human rights crises abroad, such as in Kosovo or Darfur.

The debate over the dropping of the atomic bomb has also generated a great deal of controversy in the historical world. In 1994, the Smithsonian Museum announced plans for an exhibit to open the following year to commemorate the fiftieth anniversary of the dropping of the atomic bomb on Hiroshima and Nagasaki. When the floor plans and the text of the proposed exhibit were released to the public, there was a firestorm of controversy. Veterans groups and conservative historians accused the Smithsonian of "revisionism" by portraying the United States in a bad light. The plans revealed a balanced exhibit, but it was not the heroic exhibit that critics had hoped for. The text asked troubling questions, such as whether Japan was actually ready to surrender. The exhibit also showed scenes of death and destruction, which one would expect at an exhibit about a nuclear explosion. Ultimately, the entire exhibit was scrapped. The museum ended up displaying the Enola Gay (the plane that dropped the bomb on Hiroshima), but it left out any context or thought-provoking questions.

Practice Multiple-Choice Questions

Directions: Pick the letter that best answers the following questions.

QUESTIONS 1–2 REFER TO THE FOLLOWING IMAGE:

1. The point of view of the cartoon above is that

    (A) Christian missionaries were overly concerned with gaining converts in other lands while they ignored poverty at home.

    (B) open immigration policies were undermining the economic stability of the United States.

    (C) the United States should look beyond its borders and become an imperialist power.

    (D) the widening gap between the wealthy and the poor was creating a potentially revolutionary situation in the United States.

2. A reader who supported the sentiment of the cartoon above would most likely have been in support of which of the following?

    (A) The Chinese Exclusion Act

    (B) The Spanish-American War

    (C) The Supreme Court decision in the Insular Cases

    (D) The settlement house movement

Answers and Explanations to Multiple-Choice Questions

1. **(A)** The central figure, with the telescope, represents a Protestant missionary worker. In the cartoon, the missionary worker is looking abroad to see which lands would be fruitful for missionary work. He seems to be ignoring the people in need right at his feet. The cartoon is not critical of immigration policies (B); the people at his feet are not shown to be recent immigrants. In any case, they are presented in a sympathetic light. The cartoon does not allude to imperialist ventures (C), nor to the constitutional rights of people in American colonies (D).

2. **(D)** Supporters of the point of view of the cartoon would also support the work of the settlement house movement, because the settlement house movement was addressing the issue that the cartoonist asserted was being ignored by Protestant missionaries—poverty at home. Settlement houses were established to aid immigrants, especially immigrant women. By the 1910s more than 400 settlement houses existed in the United States, usually run by women. Jane Addams ran Hull House in Chicago.

Period 8: 1945–1980 Redefining Democracy in the Era of Cold War and Liberal Ascendency

10

TIMELINE

1944	G.I. Bill is passed
1946	*Baby and Child Care* by Dr. Benjamin Spock is published
	Largest strike wave in United States history
1947	Publication of the "X Article" ("Sources of Soviet Conduct") by George Kennan
	Truman Doctrine (containment) is announced
	$400 million in military aid to Greece and Turkey
	House Un-American Affairs Committee begins investigations of Hollywood
	Taft-Hartley Act
1948	Beginning of the Berlin Blockade
	President Truman issues order desegregating the military
	President Truman wins election
1949	Formation of North Atlantic Treaty Organization (NATO)
1950	Senator Joseph McCarthy gains public spotlight on the issue of anticommunism
	NSC-68 is adopted
	Beginning of Korean War
	Passage of McCarran Internal Security Act
1951	Truman fires General Douglas MacArthur
	United States tests world's first hydrogen bomb
1952	Execution of Julius and Ethel Rosenberg
	Army–McCarthy hearings
	Dwight D. Eisenhower wins presidential election
1954	Interstate Highway Act
	Brown v. Board of Education of Topeka
1955	Creation of Warsaw Pact
1956	Rosa Parks arrested for not giving up her seat; Montgomery Bus Boycott
	Reelection of Eisenhower
1957	Soviet launch of the *Sputnik* satellite
	Founding of the Southern Christian Leadership Conference
	Crisis in Little Rock, Arkansas, over school desegregation
	On the Road by Jack Kerouac is published

1960	Soviet Union shoots down U-2 spy plane
	Lunch-counter sit-in movement begins
	Founding of the Student Non-Violent Coordinating Committee
1961	Bay of Pigs invasion in Cuba
1961	The Freedom Rides begin
1962	Cuban Missile Crisis
1963	Campaign to desegregate Birmingham, Alabama
	Assassination of President John F. Kennedy
	March on Washington, DC; Martin Luther King, Jr., delivers his "I Have a Dream" speech
1964	Civil Rights Acts passed
	"Freedom Summer" voter registration drive in Mississippi; killing of Michael Schwerner, James Chaney, and Andrew Goodman
	Gulf of Tonkin Resolution
1965	Voting Rights Act
	Malcolm X is assassinated
	March from Selma, Alabama, to Montgomery, Alabama
1966	Founding of the Black Panthers
1967	"Summer of Love"
	Rioting in Detroit, Newark, and other cities
1968	Assassination of Martin Luther King, Jr.
	Assassination of Robert F. Kennedy
	Violence at the Democratic Convention in Chicago
	Election of Richard Nixon
	Founding of the American Indian movement
1969	Woodstock Festival
	Stonewall Riot in New York City; birth of the gay liberation movement
	Apollo 11 lands on the moon
1970	President Nixon widens the Vietnam War into Cambodia
	Four students killed by the National Guard at Kent State protest
1971	Publication of the Pentagon Papers in the *New York Times*
1972	Arrest of burglars at the Watergate Complex
	Reelection of Richard Nixon
1973	Congressional hearings on Watergate
1974	Nixon resigns presidency; Gerald Ford assumes the presidency
	Ford grants Nixon a complete pardon
1976	Election of Jimmy Carter
1977	Supreme Court decision in *Bakke v. University of California*
1978	Panama Canal Treaty
	Camp David Accords
1979	Three Mile Island nuclear accident

INTRODUCTION

In the post–World War II period, the United States assumed a position of global leadership and experienced unprecedented prosperity. At the same time, the country grappled with domestic and international issues as it sought to define itself and struggled with living up to its stated values.

The Cold War began after World War II, when two former allies, the United States and the Soviet Union, emerged as rival superpowers. The perceived threat of communist aggression presented several challenges to the United States. The United States changed in many ways as a result of the Cold War. The country became much more engaged in the affairs of the world and assumed a leading role in the opposition to communism. In addition, the nation changed domestically. New programs were initiated during the Cold War. Some of these programs helped allay people's concerns about the threat of communism, while some initiatives might have added to people's fears.

In many ways, World War II was a watershed in American society. The postwar world was almost indistinguishable from the prewar world. A more modern, more affluent society emerged in the postwar era—one unimaginable in the depth of the Great Depression.

> ## LIBERALISM
>
> Note that liberalism has meant different things at different times. In the nineteenth century, liberalism implied unfettered individual rights; since the New Deal, liberalism has meant support for government programs to rectify social ills.

This period also witnessed the high tide of American liberalism, with the election of the youthful John F. Kennedy, a series of progressive decisions by the Warren Court, the implementation of President Johnson's "Great Society" programs, and the successful passage of landmark civil rights legislation.

Finally, the 1960s and 1970s saw the unraveling of the liberal agenda as the war in Vietnam sucked valuable resources from social programs and urban rioting highlighted the limits of the federal government's ability to address the problems of the African-American underclass. These years saw violence in the streets of American cities, a widening and eventual abandonment of the war in Vietnam, assassinations of major public figures, a nation-wide energy crisis, and a major political scandal that brought down a sitting president. The roots of a resurgent conservative movement can be seen toward the end of this period.

KEY CONCEPT 8.1
THE UNITED STATES AND THE COLD WAR

The United States emerged as the pre-eminent power in the post–World War II world, engaged in a cold war with the Soviet Union. It attempted to maintain a leadership position in an increasingly uncertain and unstable world. This new role for the United States had profound domestic and international consequences.

I. Containment, Economic Stability, and Collective Security

After World War II, the United States adopted a policy of containment, attempting to limit the influence of the Soviet Union and communism in the world. Toward this end, the United States sought to build a system of international security as well as a stable global economy.

A. FORGING A NEW FOREIGN POLICY IN THE POSTWAR WORLD

After World War II, the United States pursued a foreign policy that emphasized collective security and the establishment of a multinational economic framework. The goal of this new foreign policy was to bolster non-communist states in the Cold War era.

Origins of the Cold War

Tensions existed between the United States and the Soviet Union from the time of the Russian Revolution (1917). However, historians tend to date the beginning of the Cold War from the close of World War II. The United States believed that the Soviet Union was intent upon extending its control over Europe. As the war ended, the Soviet Union left its Red Army troops in the nations of Eastern Europe. These nations became satellites of the Soviet Union. The Soviet Union indicated that it would allow free elections in Poland. But even there, the Soviet Union imposed its will and installed a puppet regime. The United States was worried that the Soviet Union would try to push into Western Europe. The leader of the Soviet Union, Joseph Stalin, insisted that he only wanted to have friendly nations on the border of the Soviet Union. After numerous attacks from western powers, from Napoleon to Hitler, the Soviet Union was wary of the West.

CONTAINMENT

A sophisticated essay might draw comparisons between Truman's policy of the containment of communism in the 1940s and 1950s and Lincoln's policy of the containment of slavery in the 1860s. The position of the Republican Party, starting in 1854, was to contain slavery within its then-present borders.

Containment and the Truman Doctrine

In order to block any further aggression by the Soviet Union, Truman issued the Truman Doctrine (1947), in which he said that the goal of the United States would be to contain communism. The containment approach to the Soviet Union had been spelled out in an article entitled "Sources of Soviet Conduct," published in *Foreign Affairs* (1947). The article was also known as "X Article" because it was published using the pseudonym "X." Later it was learned that the author was George Kennan, a diplomat who had served in the United States embassy in Moscow (1944–1946). Containment remained the cornerstone of American foreign policy for decades to come.

Military Aid to Greece and Turkey

As part of the policy of containment, the United States extended military aid to Greece and Turkey in 1947. The aid was successful. It helped the Greek monarchy put down a communist-influenced rebel movement. Further, the move quieted Republican criticism of Truman and improved Truman's standing in public opinion polls; he won reelection the following year. The United States demonstrated that it was committed to a policy of containment.

POSTWAR POLICIES

Be prepared to compare United States foreign policy following each of the two world wars. After World War I, the United States retreated into isolationism; after World War II, the United States maintained its involvement in world affairs with the containment policy.

The Marshall Plan

The United States further demonstrated its commitment to global engagement with the massive Marshall Plan. The plan, developed by Secretary of State George Marshall, allocated almost $13 billion for war-torn Europe to rebuild. A total of seventeen nations received aid between 1948 and 1951, with West Germany, France, and Britain receiving the bulk of it. The plan stabilized the capitalist economies of Western Europe and contributed to remarkable growth, as the standard of living in the countries improved. The goal was to provide a viable alternative to Soviet-style communism; ultimately, the plan was successful in creating a strong Western Europe, allied with American interests.

The Berlin Blockade and the Berlin Airlift

In 1948, the United States decided to challenge the Soviet blockade of West Berlin. West Berlin was part of West Germany (an American ally), but it was completely within the territory of East Germany (a Soviet ally). In 1948, the Soviet Union decided it would prevent any food or other supplies from entering West Berlin. The goal was for the Soviet Union to take over West Berlin and make it part of East Germany. The United States did not stand by idly when it learned of the Berlin blockade. President Truman decided to send thousands of planes, filled with supplies, into West Berlin in an action known as the Berlin Airlift. The Berlin Airlift prevented West Berlin from starving and prevented the Soviet Union from taking over the city.

The Formation of NATO (1949)

The United States demonstrated its commitment to protect Western Europe when it participated in the founding of the North Atlantic Treaty Organization (NATO) in 1949. The members of NATO vowed to collectively resist any aggressive actions by the Soviet Union. This marked the first time that the United States joined a peacetime alliance.

B. CARRYING OUT THE POLICY OF CONTAINMENT

In the 1950s and 1960s, the United States pursued the policy of containment in several different ways, including direct military engagements in Korea and Vietnam, a robust nuclear weapons program, and the pursuit of a space race.

NSC-68 (1950)

A National Security Council Paper, known as NSC-68, called for a more aggressive defense policy for the United States. It recommended raising taxes and devoting more money to military spending. The document largely shaped United States foreign policy during the Cold War through the 1960s.

The Cold War in Asia

The initial conflicts of the Cold War occurred in Europe, but by the late 1940s, American policy makers became increasingly concerned about events in Asia. The United States' Cold War policies had mixed results in Asia. The United States successfully ushered Japan toward democracy and economic self-sufficiency. The United States also granted independence to the Philippines in 1946. But China proved to be a difficult problem for President Truman.

Communism in China

China had been roiled by an ongoing civil war. The conflict abated during the Japanese occupation of World War II, but began again after the war. The United States had allied itself with the Nationalist side, led by Jiang Jieshi (Chiang Kai-shek). However, it became increasingly clear that the opposition Communist Party, led by Mao Zedong, was amassing a huge following among the poor rural population of China. Mao's forces won in 1949 and the People's Republic of China was established. The news that China, the most populous nation in the world, had become communist shocked many Americans. Republicans accused Truman of "losing" China, although in reality there was not much that could have been done to prevent the eventual outcome.

The Korean War (1950–1953)

The next hotspot in the Cold War was Korea. Korea had been divided at the 38th parallel after World War II, with the United States administering the southern half and the Soviet Union administering the northern half (similar to the division of Germany). In 1948, this arrangement was formalized with the creation of two nations, North Korea, a communist country, and South Korea, an American ally. In June 1950, North Korean troops, using Soviet equipment, invaded South Korea. President Truman decided to commit troops to support South Korea, and managed to secure United Nations sponsorship. United Nations forces, led by U.S. General Douglas MacArthur, pushed the North Korean troops back to the thirty-eighth parallel and then marched into North Korea. When the U.N. troops got within 40 miles of the border between North Korea and China, China sent 150,000 troops over the Yalu River to push back the U.N. forces. After intense fighting the two sides settled into positions on either side of the thirty-eighth parallel.

The Firing of General MacArthur

During the Korean War, General Douglas MacArthur made it clear that he thought the United States could successfully invade China and roll back communism there. Truman was convinced that initiating a wider war, so soon after World War II, would be disastrous. MacArthur made public pronouncements about strategy, arguing that, "There is no substitute for victory." Truman fired MacArthur for insubordination and other unauthorized activities.

Armistice in Korea

The Korean War ended as it began—with North Korea and South Korea divided at the thirty-eighth parallel. By 1953, an armistice was reached accepting a divided Korea, although a formal treaty ending the war was never signed.

President Eisenhower, the "New Look" in Foreign Policy, and "Massive Retaliation"

Faced with the competing priorities of balancing the budget on the one hand and continuing the policy of containment on the other, President Dwight Eisenhower pursued a policy labeled the "New Look." The policy emphasized the development of strategic nuclear weapons as a deterrent to potential threats from the Soviet Union. The increased reliance on nuclear weaponry was accompanied by a shift away from maintaining costly ground forces. A strong nuclear arsenal, Defense Secretary Charles Wilson argued, would provide the United States with "bigger bang for the buck."

Central to the strategy of increasing the American arsenal of nuclear weapons was the idea of "massive retaliation." The idea was put forth by Secretary of State John Foster Dulles in a 1954 speech. The idea of "massive retaliation" is that the United States would maintain a large nuclear arsenal so that it would be able to massively retaliate against aggressive moves by the Soviet Union. The threat of massive retaliation was designed to deter conventional as well as nuclear strikes by the Soviet Union. Dulles also put forth the idea of "brinksmanship"—the Soviet Union needed to be aware that the United States was willing to "go to the brink" of war with its nuclear arsenal. As the Soviet Union developed a similarly powerful nuclear force, the ensuing nuclear standoff between the Soviet Union and the United States came to be known as "mutually assured destruction."

The Launching of *Sputnik*

Starting in the late 1950s, the Cold War expanded to a race for supremacy in terms of exploration of outer space. The space race began in earnest with the 1957 launching of the Soviet unmanned satellite *Sputnik* into space. The launch caught many Americans off guard and led to several important domestic developments.

Sputnik alarmed United States government officials because they realized that the same type of rocket that launched the satellite could also be used to quickly deliver atomic weapons to any location on earth.

The Space Race

After the launch of *Sputnik*, the United States created the National Aeronautics and Space Administration (NASA) in 1958 to carry out the nation's space program. In 1961, President John F. Kennedy announced the goal of landing a man on the moon before the close of the 1960s. The budget for NASA grew under Kennedy. The goal was accomplished in 1969, when the United States was the first nation to successfully land men on the moon.

UNDERSTANDING NASA

Be aware of the different, and often competing, goals of NASA. On the one hand, it was created to engage in scientific research for the benefit of humanity; on the other hand, it helped further the military goals of the United States during the Cold War.

Espionage and the U2 Incident (1960)

The United States began an extensive program of spying on the military capabilities of the Soviet Union. At first the United States denied the program, but after a U2 plane was shot down over Soviet territory in 1960, Eisenhower admitted the program existed and defended its goals. These actions all demonstrated that the United States would take a more active role in challenging the Soviet Union.

Cuban Missile Crisis

The Cuban Missile Crisis occurred in 1962 when a United States U-2 spy plane discovered that Cuba was preparing bases for Soviet nuclear missiles to be installed. President Kennedy felt that these missiles, in such close proximity to the United States, amounted to an unacceptable provocation and demanded that Soviet Premier Nikita Khrushchev halt the operation and dismantle the bases. Khrushchev insisted on the right of the Soviet Union to install the missiles. For about a week, the world stood on the brink of nuclear war. Finally a deal was reached in which the Soviet Union would abandon its Cuban missile program and the United States agreed to honor the sovereignty of Cuba. Quietly, the United States also agreed to remove missiles from Turkey.

The War in Vietnam

Vietnam is a small country hugging the edge of the Indochina peninsula in Southeast Asia. From the mid-nineteenth to the mid-twentieth centuries it was a colony of France. It was occupied by Japan during World War II. After the war many Vietnamese hoped to finally be free of foreign control, but France reoccupied it. A resistance movement, led by Ho Chi Minh, intensified in the 1950s. In 1954, French forces were defeated at the Vietnamese town of Dien Bien Phu, and France withdrew from the region, leaving Vietnam divided at the 17th parallel between a communist-controlled North Vietnam, led by Ho Chi Minh, and a Western-allied South Vietnam. A rebel movement, known as the Vietcong, continued to press its cause in South Vietnam. American observers came to the conclusion that without outside help the government of South Vietnam could very likely fall to communist rebels.

The "Domino Theory"

American involvement in Vietnam was influenced by a belief in the "domino theory." The domino theory asserts that when a nation adopts a communist form of government, its neighbors are likely to become communist as well. The theory presumes that communism is imposed on a country from the outside—that it does not develop as a result of internal conditions.

The United States Sends Advisors to Vietnam

United States interest in Vietnam began in the 1950s when it sent military advisors and assistance to the government of South Vietnam after Vietnam was divided in 1954. The United States feared that South Vietnam would become a communist nation, as North Vietnam had.

The Gulf of Tonkin Resolution

The United States became heavily involved in the Vietnam War after Congress gave President Lyndon Johnson broad latitude to pursue "conventional" military actions in Southeast Asia with the Tonkin Gulf Resolution (1964). In August 1964, Johnson announced that American destroyers had been fired upon in the Gulf of Tonkin, off the coast of North Vietnam. Later, reports questioned the accuracy of the announcement, but the incident led Congress to effectively give Johnson a "blank check" to engage in military operations in Vietnam without a formal declaration of war. The Gulf of Tonkin Resolution can be considered the beginning of the war in Vietnam.

The Tet Offensive

In January 1968 the Vietcong and North Vietnamese forces launched the Tet Offensive, a major attack on South Vietnamese, U.S., and allied forces. This offensive left 1,600 American troops dead, while the North Vietnamese and the Vietcong suffered more than 40,000 deaths. The offensive was defeated, but it demonstrated the ability of the Vietnamese to organize a coordinated strike and to push deep into South Vietnamese territory.

The My Lai Massacre

In 1968, a company of American troops killed nearly every inhabitant of the Vietnamese village of My Lai, despite finding no enemy forces there. The U.S. Army covered up the massacre for more than a year. In 1971, the commander of the company, Lieutenant William Calley, was tried in a U.S. military court for the massacre. The incident led many Americans to further question the morality of the war in Vietnam.

"Vietnamization" of the Vietnam War

Nixon assured the American people that he had a plan for "peace with honor" in the Vietnam War when he ran for president in 1968. However, victory proved elusive for the United States in Vietnam. Nixon widened the war to Cambodia in 1970. Starting in 1969 Nixon began the policy known as Vietnamization. This involved replacing American troops with South Vietnamese troops. However, all the measures that Nixon took would not lead to American victory. The United States pulled out of Vietnam in 1973. By 1975, South Vietnam was defeated. Vietnam was then reunited as a communist country.

C. THE COLD WAR—FROM CONFRONTATION TO DÉTENTE

At times the Cold War involved military confrontations—both direct and indirect—while at other times it involved mutual coexistence or détente.

Eisenhower and Khrushchev Pursue Coexistence

After the death of Soviet leader Joseph Stalin in 1953 and the emergence of the more moderate Nikita Khrushchev, Eisenhower held out hope for a warming of relations with the Soviet Union and a reduction in the threat of nuclear war. Eisenhower met with Khrushchev at a summit in Geneva, but no substantive agreements came out of the meeting. The launching of *Sputnik* (see page 267) and the first Soviet test of an intercontinental ballistic missile (ICBM), both in 1957, pushed the two nations farther apart. However, a new round of meetings, between Khrushchev and Vice President Richard Nixon, occurred in 1959. Nixon's trip to the Soviet Union included his famous "kitchen debate" with Khrushchev. The two, while visiting an American model home display at an international exhibition in Moscow, debated the merits of communism versus capitalism. The exchange highlighted differences between the countries, but did not derail progress in nuclear talks. The following year, the two countries were on the verge of signing a nuclear test ban. Khrushchev and Eisenhower had scheduled a summit in Paris to finalize the treaty; however, just before they met, the American U-2 spy plane was shot down (see page 267), scuttling any potential agreement.

U.S.-Soviet Relations Under Kennedy

Kennedy made attempts to ease tensions between the Soviet Union and the United States. In the wake of the Cuban Missile Crisis, a Partial Test Ban Treaty was signed by the United States, the Soviet Union, and Britain in 1963. The ban exempted underground nuclear tests.

Détente with China and the Soviet Union

President Richard Nixon's policy of détente represented a thawing in the Cold War and an improvement of relations with the Soviet Union. In 1971, Nixon initiated an agreement with the Soviet Union whereby the Soviet Union accepted the independence of West Berlin and the United States recognized East Germany. Also the Strategic Arms Limitation Talks (SALT) led to two arms control agreements in 1972. Tensions still existed but détente led to discussions between the two sides, limited arms agreements, and cultural exchanges. In 1972, Nixon visited China, making it the first time an American president visited the People's Republic of China. The visit was an important step in normalizing relations with the communist government of China.

> ## THE LEGACY OF PRESIDENT NIXON
>
> Although Nixon is most vividly remembered for the continued war in Vietnam and the Watergate scandal, there is not a consensus among historians in regard to Nixon's legacy. Many cite his foreign policy accomplishments alongside his scandalous downfall.

II. The United States Confronts the Complexities of the Cold War

During the Cold War, the United States focused on containing the expansion of communism. However, a series of foreign policy issues complicated the focus on containing communism. These complications included decolonization, regional conflicts, shifting alignments, and global economic and environmental transformations.

A. DECOLONIZATION, NATIONALISM, AND ALLEGIANCES IN THE COLD WAR ERA

In the post–World War II period, nationalist movements developed in many colonized countries in Asia, Africa, and the Middle East, setting off a wave of decolonization struggles. Both of the major powers in the Cold War struggle attempted to gain the allegiance of these newly independent countries. However, many of these countries remained non-aligned.

Iran and the CIA

During the Cold War, the United States engaged in a number of covert operations designed to oust regimes (often democratically elected) that were deemed insufficiently friendly to American interests. An early covert operation occurred in Iran in 1953. Earlier, in 1951, the left-leaning, reform-minded Mohammad Mosaddegh was elected prime minister of Iran. Mosaddegh nationalized oil fields and refineries, angering Western oil interests. In addition, he challenged the power of Iran's hereditary ruler, Shah Mohammed Reva Pahlavi, who was close to the Iranian elite and to Western oil interests. President Eisenhower, stressing the importance of having regimes friendly to American interests in the oil-rich Middle East, authorized the CIA, with the support British M16 agents, to instigate a coup against Mosaddegh. The Iranian army captured Mosaddegh and restored the Shah's power. Although the United States accomplished its goal of establishing a friendly regime in Iran, the events of 1953 came back to haunt the United States a generation later in the aftermath of the 1979 Iranian Revolution (see Period 9).

B. THE COLD WAR IN LATIN AMERICA

During the Cold War, the United States supported a variety of non-communist regimes in Latin America. These regimes had varying levels of commitment to democratic practices.

Regime Change in Guatemala

In Guatemala, the United States orchestrated the ouster of the democratically elected government of Jacobo Arbenz (1954). Arbenz, who had been elected the president in 1951, was a reform-minded leader who began a land reform program in Guatemala. He moved to nationalize some of the vast land-holdings of the American-owned corporation, the United Fruit Company, growers of Chiquita Bananas. He intended to nationalize lands that were not under cultivation and distribute these lands to poverty-stricken peasants. He offered to buy the land from United Fruit Company at the value the company had declared the land for tax purposes, but the company refused. The CIA then organized a plan to topple the Arbenz government. It trained and armed an opposition army that toppled Arbenz and installed a military dictatorship in its place. The bitter feelings left in the wake of the coup contributed to civil war in Guatemala that lasted into the 1990s.

Hostilities with Cuba

Events in Cuba occupied much of President Kennedy's brief tenure as president, as Cuba became a hotspot in the Cold War in 1959. Cuba had been run as a military dictatorship with close ties with the United States from 1933 to 1959. In 1959, Fidel Castro led a successful guerilla movement to topple

> ### CUBA AND FLORIDA
>
> Hostilities toward Cuba have persisted from the 1960s until today, despite the fact that the United States has normalized relations with other communist nations (China and Vietnam). One reason for the continued hostility is that both major political parties fear alienating Cuban Americans in Florida and losing that state in the presidential election.

the dictatorship. By 1960, the relationship between the United States and Cuba grew hostile, while the relationship between the Soviet Union and Cuba grew friendly. In the final months of the Eisenhower administration, advisors planned for the United States to train, arm, and aid a group of Cuban exiles opposed to the communist government of Fidel Castro.

Kennedy adopted the plan and green-lighted its implementation in 1961. The exiles landed at the Bay of Pigs in Cuba in April 1961, but were quickly captured by Cuban forces. The Bay of Pigs incident was the first of several attempts to oust the communist regime from Cuba.

C. THE COLD WAR IN THE MIDDLE EAST

United States policy in the Middle East during the Cold War was driven by several, sometimes conflicting, priorities. Ideological, military, and economic concerns shaped American policy in the Middle East. After several oil crises, the United States attempted to create a policy in regard to its energy future.

The Energy Crisis

In 1973, the Arab oil-producing nations of OPEC—the Organization of Petroleum Exporting Countries—cut off exports to the United States and increased the price of oil. These moves were largely in retaliation for United States supporting Israel in the 1973 Yom Kippur War between Israel and its Arab neighbors.

The Energy Crisis and the Limits of Growth

Starting with the OPEC oil embargo in 1973, fuel prices rose dramatically in the 1970s. America had to confront a stark reality—there were limits to the amount of fossil fuels, particularly petroleum, available in the world, and much of it came from the volatile Middle East. Until the 1970s, Americans assumed that petroleum was a cheap, inexhaustible commodity. The 1970s saw a dramatic spike in petroleum prices and long lines at gas pumps.

Toward a National Energy Policy

While many policy makers were trying to find alternative sources of power to Middle East petroleum, some were looking for ways the United States could reduce its consumption of energy. Americans are by far the largest consumers of energy, consuming nearly twice the amount as the average resident of the United Kingdom or France. Starting as early as the 1950s, the United States increased reliance on nuclear power. Nuclear power, however, did not achieve the level of energy generation that planners had hoped for. Amid concerns about cost overruns and the safety of nuclear energy, only about half of the planned 253 generators were ever built. Currently, nearly 20 percent of electricity is generated by nuclear power in the United States. A National Maximum Speed Law was enacted in 1974 (since repealed). President Jimmy Carter, through the newly created Department of Energy (1977), encouraged conservation measures, such as turning down thermostats and turning off lights when not in use. He also encouraged investment in renewable sources of energy, such as solar power. Americans, however, were remarkably resistant to adopting conservation measures.

III. Debates over Carrying Out the Cold War

There were major debates and disagreements in the United States about appropriate activities in terms of pursuing international and domestic goals during the Cold War. Americans continued to debate the proper balance between liberty and order. In addition, some Americans questioned the growing power of the federal government.

A. CONTAINMENT AND THE DOMESTIC RED SCARE

Though there was consensus between the major parties in regard to the policy of containment, Americans debated the increasingly aggressive methods of the federal and state governments in terms of identifying and applying sanctions to suspected communists in the United States.

The Strike Wave of 1946 and the Taft-Hartley Act (1947)

Immediately following World War II, the United States experienced the largest strike wave in its history, as five million workers walked off their jobs. Unions, which had refrained from striking during the war, feared that the gains they had made during the war would be taken away. The strike wave was largely successful, boosting wages for factory workers and allowing them to partake in the consumer culture of the era.

The Taft-Hartley Act (1947) was a law passed over President Truman's veto designed to monitor and restrict the activities of organized labor. The law was

AN ASSAULT ON ORGANIZED LABOR

Organized labor saw the Taft-Hartley Act as an unreasonable attack on the union movement. It labeled it a "slave labor" law and the "Tuff-Heartless" Act.

passed by a conservative Republican-dominated Congress that had been elected in 1946. The law imposed restrictions on unions that made it more difficult to strike. It allowed states to pass "right to work" laws, banning union shops (a union shop is a workplace in which all the workers are required to join the union after a majority had voted to do so). The law also required union leaders to pledge that they were not members of the Communist Party.

Federal Employee Loyalty and Security Program (1947)

This program barred communists and fascists from serving in federal government positions. This loyalty program was created by President Truman with Executive Order 9835. It also allowed for investigations into the political affiliations of current employees.

Employees had to promise to uphold the Constitution and promise that they were not members of the Communist Party or other "subversive" organizations.

The McCarran Internal Security Act (1950)

This restrictive act mandated that communist groups in the United States register with the government. It also allowed for the arrest of suspected security risks during national emergencies. Truman saw this act as a grave threat to civil liberties and vetoed it. However, Congress passed it over his veto.

Senator Joseph McCarthy

The most prominent elected figure in the anticommunist movement of the 1950s was Senator Joseph McCarthy, a Republican from Wisconsin. McCarthy rose to national prominence in 1950 when he announced that he had a list of 205 "known communists" who were working in the State Department. He later reduced that figure to 57, but he encouraged a mindset where people began to suspect those around them of being communists. This and similar claims, mostly baseless, created a name for McCarthy and set the stage for a host of measures to halt this perceived threat. The anticommunist movement of the 1950s is often referred to as McCarthyism because Senator McCarthy was so closely identified with it.

The Attack on Hollywood

Senate and House anticommunists put a great deal of effort in investigating the movie and television industry, fearing that communists would subtly get their message out through the media. In 1947, a group of prominent directors and writers, subsequently known as the "Hollywood 10," was summoned to testify in Washington. They refused, citing their First Amendment rights to freedom of speech and assembly. These ten and others who refused to cooperate were "blacklisted" in the 1950s, unable to find work in Hollywood.

The Threat of Nuclear War

Although the fear of communist plots might have been overstated, the threat of nuclear war was a constant presence in American life during the Cold War. Both nations invested large sums of money into nuclear weapons programs. Americans were never sure whether a conventional conflict, such as the Korean War, would turn into a nuclear war. Many Americans built bomb shelters in their basement or backyard. Local authorities established civil defense programs to build bomb shelters in public buildings and prepare the public for a nuclear emergency.

"Duck and Cover"

The government took a series of actions in regard to the threat of nuclear war. One action taken by the government was air raid drills in public schools. When an alarm sounded, students would either be ushered to a fallout shelter in the basement of the school or would be ordered to "duck and cover" under their desks.

The Rosenberg Case

When the United States learned that the Soviet Union had built and tested a nuclear bomb, many Americans were convinced that communists in the United States, loyal to the Soviet Union, had provided the Soviets with essential information about the bomb. Ethel and Julius Rosenberg were an American couple who were accused of passing secrets of the nuclear bomb to the Soviet Union. The Rosenbergs, who were members of the Communist Party, insisted on their innocence but were sent to the electric chair in 1953. Evidence has emerged since the end of the Cold War that suggests that Julius had been involved in some sort of espionage on behalf of the Soviet Union.

The Smith Act and the Communist Party

Government prosecutors used the World War II–era Smith Act to arrest leading members of the Communist Party in several states on the grounds that they "conspired" to "organize" and "advocate" the overthrow of the government by force. Between 1949 and 1957, more than 140 communists were arrested including the leader of the party, Eugene Dennis.

The Fall of McCarthyism

Eventually, critics began to assert that some of the harshest anticommunist measures violated people's constitutional right to freedom of speech. Criticism became more common after the conclusion of hostilities in the Korean War (1953). Finally Senator McCarthy himself went too far, accusing members of the military establishment of being members of the Communist Party. The Senate voted to censure him in 1954, ending the worst excesses of what many people referred to as a witch-hunt. In the case of *Yates v. United States* (1957), the Supreme Court overturned the convictions of members of the Communist Party under the Smith Act.

B. DEBATES OVER THE VIETNAM WAR

Americans generally supported the containment policy as it was deployed in the Korean War. However, the Vietnam War generated a sizable antiwar movement. The movement used a variety of tactics as the war escalated.

A LACK OF CONSENSUS

Note the evolution of popular sentiment in regard to Vietnam and the factors that contributed to antiwar sentiment among many Americans.

Erosion of Support for the Vietnam War

As the Vietnam War dragged on through the latter half of the 1960s, many Americans began to see the war as unwinnable—a quagmire from which the United States could not extricate itself. Americans began to grow impatient with the war effort and many began to question the wisdom and the morality of the war. There were several factors that led to this questioning of the Vietnam War.

The Draft

Starting in 1964, the Selective Service System began drafting young men to serve in the armed forces. In 1965, the monthly totals of draftees doubled. The draft made the Vietnam War much more of an immediate concern for millions of young men and contributed to the number of young people participating in the antiwar movement.

A "Living Room War"

The Vietnam War was the first American war to occur in an age when the vast majority of Americans owned television sets (90 percent by 1960). Americans were able to see uncensored images of warfare in their living rooms for the first time. Many were shocked at what they saw. A report by Morley Safer in 1965 showed Marines evacuating Vietnamese civilians from their homes and then setting their village on fire.

More disturbing images followed and contributed to public opinion questioning the wisdom and justness of the war.

THE MEDIA AND WAR

During the Vietnam War, Americans saw uncensored images of the horrors of war. This contributed to antiwar sentiment among many Americans. Later, during the Iraq War (2003–2013), the government kept tight reins on media coverage. If reporters wanted access to the military, they had to agree to be embedded with a unit. The military would then have great control over what was reported. President George W. Bush had taken a lesson from the Vietnam War.

A Working-class War

In many ways, the war in Vietnam was a working-class war. Eighty percent of the troops in Vietnam were working class and poor. Middle-class youths often managed to get college deferments or had connections to get a stateside (in the United States) position in the National Guard. In 1967, Martin Luther King, Jr., gave a speech entitled "Beyond Vietnam," condemning the war and its impact on American society.

OLD LEFT VERSUS NEW LEFT

The "old left" of the 1930s focused on workers and workplace issues. The "new left" of the 1960s focused on "participatory democracy" and cultural and social, as well as economic and political, issues. The new left developed on college campuses rather than in factories.

The Unraveling of the Vietnam War

By 1968, the war in Vietnam seemed increasingly unwinnable. The Vietcong and North Vietnamese forces launched the Tet Offensive in January (see page 269), shocking the American public. Further, extensive, uncensored media coverage of the war left many Americans questioning its morality and propriety. By 1969, the horrific violence of the 1968 My Lai Massacre (see page 269) became known to the American public, further eroding faith in the war effort. Opponents of the war became increasingly vocal as the decade wore on.

The Antiwar Movement

The antiwar movement can be traced back to the early 1960s as small peace groups questioned the purpose of the armed advisors that were sent to Vietnam. An important antiwar group on college campuses was Students for a Democratic Society, founded in 1960 (see more below). By the late 1960s, several important antiwar groups had emerged out of the growing protest movement. The National Mobilization Committee to End the War in Vietnam was formed in 1967 to organize large national protests against the war.

Vietnam Veterans Against the War

Another significant antiwar group was the Vietnam Veterans Against the War. Born in 1967, the organization harnessed the frustrations of returning veterans of the conflict. Many front-line soldiers grew to question the tactics, and even the purpose, of the war. There were several incidents of "fragging" in Vietnam—soldiers attacking and even killing commanding officers.

The Shootings at Kent State and Jackson State

The antiwar movement was stunned when four students were killed at Kent State University in Ohio in May 1970 during a demonstration against President Nixon's decision to invade Cambodia. National Guardsmen opened fire on the demonstrators, killing four and wounding ten. A week later, two African-American students were shot and killed by state police at Jackson State University in Mississippi. By the beginning of the school year in September 1970, college campuses were considerably quieter.

Publication of the *Pentagon Papers*

Many of the suspicions of the antiwar movement were borne out with the publication of the *Pentagon Papers*, a secret study of the Vietnam War written by the Pentagon. The study revealed official deception and secrecy. It was leaked to the press by Daniel Ellsberg, a Pentagon official critical of the direction the Vietnam War was taking. The Nixon administration tried to block the *New York Times* and the *Washington Post* from publishing the papers. Initially, the Nixon administration obtained an injunction against publication, but the Supreme Court, in the case of *New York Times v. United States* (1971), overruled the injunction and upheld the right of the newspapers to publish the information.

> ## THE GOVERNMENT AND A FREE PRESS
> The publication of the *Pentagon Papers* helped to clarify free speech issues in regard to the government's ability to squelch embarrassing information. The Supreme Court upheld the rights of the press.

C. THE "MILITARY-INDUSTRIAL COMPLEX," THE ARMS RACE, AND THE POWER OF THE EXECUTIVE

A series of debates occurred during the Cold War about the power of the president to carry out foreign and military policies. In addition, many Americans became increasingly concerned about the power of the "military-industrial complex." Finally, debates occurred around the expansion of America's nuclear arsenal.

The "Military-Industrial Complex"

The term "military-industrial complex" was popularized after it was used in President Eisenhower's "Farewell Address." The term implies a close-knit relationship between government officials, leaders of the military, and corporate interests, especially those involved in the production of goods and services used by the military. The implication is that important decisions about policy—including decisions about military interventions—are made, in part, to advance the interests of the military-industrial complex.

Challenging America's Nuclear Policy

Starting in the 1950s and 1960s, many Americans began challenging the country's military priorities. In the 1960s, many Americans began to protest against military actions in Vietnam (see below). Even before that, there were those who grew critical of America's nuclear weapons policy. It became evident that the United States had developed enough nuclear weapons to destroy the world several times over. The policy of "massive retaliation" implied, to many people, a dangerous readiness to use nuclear weapons. With both the United States and Soviet Union possessing such powerful nuclear arsenals, policy makers accepted the policy of mutually assured destruction, or MAD. For some policy makers, MAD created a powerful deterrent to the use of nuclear weapons; to critics, it seemed to represent a dangerous precipice on which the world was perched. The 1964 dark comedy, *Dr. Strangelove or: How I Learned to Stop Worrying and Love the Bomb,* directed by Stanley Kubrick, depicted MAD policy gone terribly wrong. Critics of nuclear proliferation formed the Committee for a SANE Nuclear Policy in 1957 to challenge the ongoing nuclear tests being conducted by the Eisenhower administration. In 1961, the newly formed Women's Strike for Peace organized more than 50,000 women in sixty cities to march for peace.

KEY CONCEPT 8.2
THE HIGH TIDE OF LIBERALISM

Liberalism—an approach to politics that embraced anticommunism abroad and an activist federal government at home—reached its highpoint in the mid-1960s. Liberalism generated a wide variety of political and cultural responses in the United States.

I. The Civil Rights Movement

An influential civil rights movement emerged in the years following World War II. Civil rights activists sought to press America to fulfill the promises of the Reconstruction-era. The movement achieved some marked political and legal successes in regard to ending segregation. However, progress toward achieving full racial equality in the United States proved to be a more daunting task.

A. STRATEGIES AND TACTICS OF THE CIVIL RIGHTS MOVEMENT

After World War II, civil rights activists used a variety of strategies and tactics, including legal challenges, civil disobedience, non-violent protests, and direct action, to press for an end to racial discrimination.

The Civil Rights Movement in the 1950s

One of the most significant reform movements in American history blossomed in the 1950s—the civil rights movement. The movement challenged the legal basis of the segregation of African Americans in the United States, but it also challenged the pervasive racism of American society. This racism justified the existence of slavery and the persistence of Jim Crow segregation. The movement forced America to examine its most cherished institutions and also to reevaluate its patterns of thought.

World War II and the Origins of the Civil Rights Movement

World War II was a transformative experience for many African-American men and women. Many returning soldiers felt a sense of empowerment and engagement that they had not previously felt. These veterans had taken part in the NAACP's "Double V" campaign during the war—victory against fascism abroad and victory against racism at home. The injustices of American life seemed especially reprehensible to men who had just risked their lives serving their country. In addition, the migration of many African-American men and women from the familiar patterns of rural southern life to the new challenges of urban, industrial America whetted their appetite for change and justice. This was the generation that would become the leaders of the civil rights movement in the decades after the war.

Rosa Parks and the Montgomery Bus Boycott (1955–1956)

Rosa Parks was a civil rights activist who refused to give up her seat to a white person on a Montgomery, Alabama, city bus in 1955. She was arrested for this action. Her arrest led to the Montgomery bus boycott, which lasted about a year (1955–1956). The boycott led to the bus company ending its policy of making African Americans give up their seats to whites.

Martin Luther King, Jr., and Nonviolent Civil Disobedience

The Montgomery bus boycott was led by a young reverend, Dr. Martin Luther King, Jr., from Atlanta, Georgia. King's leadership during the boycott made him a well-known figure. He soon became the central figure in the civil rights movement of the 1950s and 1960s. King advocated the tactic of civil disobedience to directly challenge unjust practices.

The Civil Rights Movement in the 1960s

The civil rights movement continued into the 1960s. As the 1960s began, a younger generation of activists began to play a prominent role in the movement. Over time, rifts developed between the older, church-based leadership of the movement and a younger cadre of activists.

The Lunch-counter Sit-ins (1960)

In 1960, students in Tennessee and North Carolina began a campaign of sit-ins at lunch counters to protest segregation. The sit-ins occurred as some members of the movement grew frustrated with simply protesting and pushed the movement to take direct action to challenge and defy racist practices. The lunch counter sit-ins began in 1960 in Greensboro, North Carolina, when four African-American students challenged the "whites only" policy of Woolworth's lunch counter and sat at the counter. The lunch counter sit-ins spread to other cities, including Nashville, Tennessee. They put the practice of segregation on the front pages of newspapers and eventually pressured companies to end the practice.

The Freedom Rides (1961)

The Freedom Rides occurred in 1961. The previous year, the Supreme Court had ruled that state laws separating the races on interstate transportation facilities were unconstitutional.

Still, states maintained Jim Crow segregation codes that separated African American from white passengers. In 1961, the Congress on Racial Equality (CORE) organized a series of bus rides through the South, with African-American passengers riding alongside white passengers, to challenge these local codes. The Freedom Rides met a great deal of resistance in the South. In Alabama, a mob slashed the tires of one bus and then firebombed it. President Kennedy finally sent federal marshals to Alabama to protect the Freedom Riders and to enforce federal law.

"Bull" Connor and the Birmingham Campaign (1963)

Martin Luther King, Jr., and the Southern Christian Leadership Conference decided to launch a major campaign in Birmingham, Alabama, to protest racial segregation in the spring of 1963. The campaign proved to be a turning point in the push for federal legislation. The public safety commissioner of Birmingham, Eugene "Bull" Connor, would not tolerate public demonstrations. He used fire hoses, police dogs, and brutal force to put down the campaign. The campaign included a children's march, sometimes called the "children's crusade," in May 1963. Connor used violent tactics to break up the children's march. Images of police brutality brought the Birmingham campaign to the attention of the nation and helped to bring public sympathy to the side of the civil rights movement. During the Birmingham campaign, King was arrested and wrote his famous "Letter from Birmingham Jail," a response to a call by white clergy members to allow the legal system to address the issue of racial injustice. King insisted that the black community had waited long enough for change to happen. The Birmingham campaign paved the way for the passage of the Civil Rights Act, a year later.

The March on Washington (1963)

In 1963, the civil rights movement held one of the biggest demonstrations in American history in Washington, DC. More than 200,000 people gathered to march, sing, and hear speeches, including Martin Luther King, Jr.'s, "I Have a Dream Speech." Some of the tensions that divided the civil rights movement in the years to come were evident at the March on Washington. The leader of the Student Nonviolent Coordinating Committee, John Lewis, was told by some of the older organizers of the event to tone down his fiery rhetoric. The original draft of his speech, which urged the movement to march "through the heart of Dixie the way Sherman did . . . and burn Jim Crow to the ground," anticipated the Black Power movement of the coming years.

The Selma to Montgomery March (1965)

With passage of the Civil Rights Act, the movement focused on voting rights. A major march, from Selma, Alabama, to Montgomery, Alabama, was scheduled for March 1965. As the marchers crossed a bridge over the Alabama River, county and state police blocked their path and, after ordering them to turn back, attacked them with clubs and tear gas. The incident, known as "Bloody Sunday," was broadcast on national television and aroused indignation among many Americans. The march was finally held later in the month. "Bloody Sunday" and the Selma to Montgomery march raised awareness of the issue of voting rights.

B. GOVERNMENT RESPONSES TO CIVIL RIGHTS ACTIVISM

The three branches of the federal government made several important policy shifts in regard to race from the 1940s through the 1960s. These shifts included the desegregation of the armed forces, the issuance of the decision in the case of *Brown v. Board of Education*, and the passage of the Civil Rights Act of 1964. These measures, prompted in large part by civil rights activism, were intended to promote greater racial justice.

Truman and Civil Rights

President Truman, the Democratic president from Missouri who took office when President Franklin Roosevelt died in 1945, was an early supporter of civil rights. He created the Committee on Civil Rights in 1946 and he pushed Congress to enact the committee's recommendations in 1948. In 1948 Truman issued an executive order to ban segregation in the military, but he failed to implement it until the Korean War (when the military needed additional personnel). Truman was motivated to take these steps both out of personal conviction and in response to actions by civil rights activists. Truman felt that he could not go too far because he would lose the support of southern Democrats.

A Favorable Supreme Court

Early civil rights activists pressed their cause in a number of ways, but a very promising one was to bring the issue of segregation in front of the Supreme Court. The movement realized that the Supreme Court in 1954 was far more liberal than the Supreme Court of 1896, which had issued the infamous *Plessy v. Ferguson* decision. In 1953, the Supreme Court got a new, more liberal chief justice, Earl Warren, appointed by President Dwight Eisenhower. The NAACP and its lead lawyer Thurgood Marshall thought the time was right.

The Case of *Brown v. Board of Education of Topeka* (1954)

The case of *Brown v. Board of Education of Topeka* was actually several cases looked at simultaneously by the Court. The Brown in the case was the Reverend Oliver Brown, whose eight-year-old daughter had to go to an African-American school more than a mile from her house rather than attend a white school nearby. The Court heard a variety of types of evidence in the case, including studies on the psychological impact of segregation on young people. The Court ruled unanimously that segregation in public schools was unfair and had to end. The Brown decision set in motion a major upheaval in American society. It gave great encouragement to the civil rights movement, which believed that the federal government was in favor of civil rights.

Kennedy, Johnson, and the Politics of Civil Rights

The Democratic Party for years had walked a thin line in regard to civil rights for African Americans. On the one hand, many Democratic leaders since the Franklin Roosevelt administration believed that extending civil rights to African Americans was the correct and just thing to do, but on the other hand, the party did not want to alienate its southern wing. As the civil rights movement put the issue on the national agenda and as violence by white southerners put the issue on the nightly news, Democratic leaders had to react. In June 1963, the same month that civil rights leader Medgar Evers was murdered in front

THE GRASSROOTS AND THE GOVERNMENT

The civil rights movement vividly illustrates the complex relationship between the grassroots movement and government policy. The movement pushed the government to take action; support from the government emboldened the movement.

of his house in Jackson, Mississippi, President Kennedy made a national address in which he called civil rights a "moral issue" and pledged to support civil rights legislation. After Kennedy's assassination in November 1963, President Lyndon Johnson took up the cause of civil rights legislation with vigor, pressuring reluctant Democratic legislators to support it.

Civil Rights Act (1964)

The Civil Rights Act was passed by Congress and signed by President Johnson in the summer of 1964. The act was intended to end discrimination based on race and sex. The Civil Rights Act guaranteed equal access for all Americans to public accommodations, public education, and voting. Another section banned discrimination in employment based on race or sex.

The Voting Rights Act (1965)

The Voting Rights Act, passed in August 1965, authorized the federal government to oversee voter registration in counties with low African-American registration. The act also outlawed literacy tests and poll taxes—means of preventing African Americans from voting. By 1968, the number of southern African-American voters jumped from 1 million to more than 3 million. In many ways, the Civil Rights Act and the Voting Rights Act were the culmination of the civil rights movement.

C. CHALLENGES FOR THE CIVIL RIGHTS MOVEMENT

A series of challenges confronted the civil rights movement as the 1960s progressed. White resistance to desegregation grew more intense and slowed the progress of the movement. In addition, a series of debates occurred within the movement in the mid-1960s over philosophy and tactics.

"Massive Resistance"—in Little Rock Crisis and Beyond

The civil rights movement generated a violent backlash from many southern whites. These people vowed to engage in "massive resistance" against efforts toward integration. An example of the backlash was evident in the reaction of white southerners to segregation in Little Rock, Arkansas, in 1957 and 1958. The conflict in Little Rock began when local authorities had decided to allow nine African-American students to enroll in Central High School at the beginning of the school year in 1957. Governor Orville Faubus refused to cooperate with the plan, leading to mob action and violence outside of the high school. Faubus initially mobilized the National Guard to block the African-American students from entering the school; later he removed all state authorities, leaving local police to deal with a combustible situation. The violence and the national news coverage of the flaunting of federal authority convinced Eisenhower to send federal troops. Although Eisenhower took decisive action in Little Rock, his administration was otherwise very reluctant to take action in regard to civil rights for African Americans.

> ### STATE AND FEDERAL POWER
>
> The crisis in Little Rock brought to the fore the issue of the relationship of federal power to state power. This was a central issue in the Civil War. When President Eisenhower sent troops to Little Rock, Governor Faubus used language that was purposely evocative of the Reconstruction period. The reaction of Faubus brings to mind William Faulkner's quotation: "The past is not dead. In fact, it's not even past."

From "Freedom Now!" to "Black Power!"

As the civil rights movement achieved success in ending legal segregation (*de jure* segregation) and removing barriers to voting, pervasive problems continued to plague the African-American community. Patterns of segregation enforced by custom, rather than law (*de facto* segregation) persisted. Also, the bitter realities of poverty, substandard housing, and lack of decent jobs continued to plague large sections of the African-American community. A younger generation of activists continued to push the movement in a more militant direction and to demand power, not just rights. A central rallying cry of the movement, "Freedom now!," was, after 1964, often replaced by the call for "Black power!"

The Assassination of King (1968)

Martin Luther King, Jr., was killed by an assassin on April 4, 1968, in Memphis, Tennessee. The assassination of King was both a source of national mourning and an indicator of the end of the civil rights movement. The movement had accomplished much, but was unable to provide a solution for many of the problems facing the African-American community. As the 1960s wound down, rioting engulfed many African-American neighborhoods, highlighting the continued frustrations of the black community.

II. The Civil Rights Movement Inspires Other Movements to Challenge Inequalities

The visibility and successes of the civil rights movement inspired other movements for social change. These movements, focused on gender, sexuality, and ethnicity, addressed a host of inequalities and issues of identity.

A. MOVEMENTS FOR WOMEN'S RIGHTS AND GAY LIBERATION

Activists began to challenge ingrained assumptions around gender. Movements developed in the 1960s to push for greater social and economic equality for women and for gays and lesbians.

The Women's Liberation Movement

In the 1960s, a women's liberation movement developed, challenging inequities in the job market, representations of women in the media, violence against women, and an ingrained set of social values. Many women looked at the circumstances of their own lives and saw connections to the larger society, giving rise to the motto, "the personal is political." Many women were inspired by Betty Friedan's 1963 book, *The Feminine Mystique*, which challenged the traditional options in life offered to middle-class women. Friedan later was one of several women to found the National Organization for Women (1966), the leading liberal organization supporting women's rights. The movement gave birth to the nationally circulated magazine, *Ms.*, founded by Gloria Steinem, Letty Cottin Pogrebin, and others. Many women in the movement had come out of New Left activist organizations (see below), empowered to fight for a better world, but frustrated at the treatment women received in these organizations.

Protest at the Miss America Pageant

Many Americans heard about the women's liberation movement for the first time from news reports of a protest at the 1968 Miss America pageant. The pageant exemplified, to the protesters, society's attitude toward women. Women were forced to wear skimpy outfits and give vacuous answers to questions, in order to win male approval.

Title IX (1972)

An important success of the women's liberation movement was passage of Title IX of the Educational Amendments of 1972. Title IX banned sex discrimination in all aspects of education, such as faculty hiring and admissions. It has had a major impact on funding for female sports activities at the high school and college level.

The Gay Liberation Movement

The gay liberation movement was born in 1969 when patrons at the Stonewall Inn, a gay bar in New York's Greenwich Village, resisted a raid by the police and fought back. The event brought a series of grievances into the open. Gay men and women had suffered discrimination in many walks of life, including in government civil service jobs. Many gays attempted to avoid such discrimination by concealing their sexual identity and remaining "in the closet."

B. LATINOS, AMERICAN INDIANS, AND ASIAN AMERICANS PRESS FOR JUSTICE

In the wake of the civil rights movement, different ethnic groups, including Latinos, American Indians, and Asian Americans, pushed for a redress of past injustices as well as economic and social equality.

The American Indian Movement

The example set by the civil rights movement also inspired a movement to fight for justice for American Indians. The American Indian movement was founded in 1968. The following year, the movement made headlines when several dozen activists seized control of Alcatraz Island, in the San Francisco Bay, claiming that the former prison belonged to the first inhabitants of the area—American Indians. The movement won greater autonomy over tribal lands and affairs.

Cesar Chavez and the United Farms Workers

Cesar Chavez and Delores Huerta founded the United Farm Workers in 1962 to protect the interests of migrant farmers, including many Mexican Americans. The UFW organized a nationwide boycott of grapes to pressure farm owners to pay their workers a decent wage. The boycott did result in a wage increase in 1970.

C. AFFLUENCE AND POVERTY

The post–World War II period was marked by a growing middle class and the perception of overall affluence. However, writers and activists raised awareness of the persistence of poverty among large sectors of the population. These efforts resulted in efforts to address the issue of poverty in America.

Abundance in Postwar America

Perhaps the most remarkable development of the postwar years was the unprecedented growth of the economy and the rising living standard for millions of Americans. The gross domestic product of the country—the total value of goods and services produced in the United States in a year—rose dramatically between 1945 and 1960, from $200 billion to $500 billion. Such growth is unprecedented in American society. In this period we see a dramatic rise in the middle class, as millions of Americans from working-class backgrounds were able to achieve many of the markers of middle-class life—home and car ownership, a college education, and a comfortable income.

The Other America

Large pockets of poverty persisted despite the growth of the postwar economy. Many Americans, including President John F. Kennedy, were made aware of the existence of pervasive poverty alongside the affluence of American society by Michael Harrington's book *The Other America: Poverty in the United States* (1962). Harrington, a writer and Socialist activist, noted that 40 to 50 million Americans lived in poverty, many in decaying urban slums and many in isolated rural towns. He noted that many of the technological developments associated with economic growth, such as mechanization of agriculture and automation of factory work, resulted in job displacement and bitter poverty. Harrington's work shaped the domestic agendas of President Kennedy and President Lyndon Johnson.

III. Liberalism, the Federal Government, and the Supreme Court

Liberal ideals shaped federal policies and several key Supreme Court decisions in the 1960s and 1970s. This liberal agenda came under attack from groups and individuals on the left who insisted that the steps being taken were insufficient to create a truly just and equitable world. The gains of liberalism would come under attack from a resurgent conservative movement that showed signs of life in the 1960s and 1970s, but did not come into fruition until the last decades of the twentieth century.

> ### FEDERAL PROGRAMS
>
> Note the continuities between the New Deal of the 1930s and the Great Society of the 1960s. Both expanded the role of the federal government in the lives of ordinary Americans. Both met with only limited success.

A. THE GREAT SOCIETY

President Lyndon Johnson's Great Society programs represented the highpoint of the liberal agenda. Johnson spearheaded a series of programs that sought to end racial discrimination, alleviate poverty, and address other social issues.

President Lyndon Johnson's Agenda

Lyndon Johnson took office upon the assassination of President Kennedy. Johnson, a Texas Democrat, proved to be a remarkably effective president, passing a host of domestic programs that rivaled the New Deal in scope. However, his administration took a tragic turn, as Johnson's hopes for a "Great Society" were damaged by a costly and unpopular war in Vietnam.

The "Great Society"

A major goal of President Johnson's Great Society program was to end poverty in the United States. Great Society programs include the development of Medicare and Medicaid, welfare programs, and public housing. Johnson created the Office of Economic Opportunity, which oversaw many of the Great Society initiatives. These programs have had limited success.

The cycle of poverty proved to be too difficult to break in a short period of time. Further, the war in Vietnam became increasingly costly, diverting billions of dollars that could have been used for antipoverty programs. Part of the Great Society included reforming the restrictive immigration policies that had been put in effect in the 1920s. The Immigration Act of 1965 continued to limit the number of immigrants in the United States, but it eliminated the quota system, based on "national origins" (see more on immigration reform below).

B. FEDERAL POWER AND THE SUPREME COURT

A series of important Supreme Court decisions from the 1950s to the 1970s expanded democracy and individual freedoms. These decisions, coupled with the expansion of federal power during the era of the Great Society, unintentionally fueled a conservative movement that sought to defend traditional notions of morality and limit the role of the state.

The Warren Court

Earl Warren was the chief justice of the Supreme Court from 1953 to 1969. The Court under his leadership moved in a decidedly liberal direction. The first case

> ## CHIEF JUSTICES
>
> The AP exam does not require you to know all the chief justices of the Supreme Court, but you should be familiar with John Marshall (1801–1835) and Earl Warren (1953–1969). Both courts maintained a consistent ideological approach that is evident in the respective decisions of each.

Warren dealt with as chief justice was the landmark Brown case. Through the 1960s, the Warren court continued to protect the rights of minorities, reinforced the separation of church and state, established an individual's right to privacy, and protected the rights of people accused of crimes. Liberals have generally welcomed Warren Court decisions, while conservatives have accused him of practicing judicial activism.

Expanding the Rights of the Accused

Two important decisions expanded the rights of people accused of crimes. In *Gideon v. Wainwright* (1963), the Supreme Court ruled that the states must provide court appointed attorneys to impoverished defendants. Previously this stipulation only applied to federal court procedures. In *Miranda v. Arizona* (1966) the Court ruled that arrested people must be read basic rights, now known as *Miranda rights*, including the right to remain silent and the right to have a lawyer.

The Right to Privacy

Although the right to privacy is not specifically mentioned in the Constitution, the Warren Court asserted that the right is implicit in it. In *Griswold v. Connecticut* (1965) the Court ruled that laws forbidding the use of birth control devices were unconstitutional. The right to privacy would become important in the case of *Roe v. Wade* (1973), which insisted that states allow abortions during the first two trimesters of pregnancy.

Free Speech

In *Tinker v. Des Moines* (1969), the Supreme Court ruled that a school board prohibition against students wearing black armbands in protest of the war in Vietnam was unconstitutional. The Court ruled that students in school had the right to free speech, including symbolic speech, as long as their actions did not interfere with the educational process.

In *Brandenberg v. Ohio* (1969), the Court ruled that the government cannot restrict inflammatory speech unless that speech is likely to directly incite imminent unlawful action. The case revolved around an incendiary interview with a Ku Klux Klan leader. Local authorities arrested him under a criminal syndicalism statute. The decision set the precedent of protecting anti-government and provocative speech.

Freedom of the Press

In *New York Times v. Sullivan* (1964), the Supreme Court overturned a lower court libel award of $500,000 to L.B. Sullivan, a city commissioner in Montgomery, Alabama. Sullivan had sued the *New York Times* for running an ad calling attention to the violence being committed in the South against civil-rights demonstrators. Sullivan contended that the ad libeled him, even if it did not mention him by name. White southern officials frequently used plaintiff-friendly libel laws to curb reporting of civil rights issues. The Court found such laws were detrimental to a free press. The Court set a higher standard for libel—insisting that public officials must show that a publication exhibited "actual malice" in order to prove libel. Specifically, a public official filing suit must show that a publication knew a statement was false and/or recklessly disregarded the truth. The *Sullivan* decision has been the Court's most forceful defense of press freedom.

Reapportionment and "One-person, One-vote"

In *Baker v. Carr* (1966), the Supreme Court ruled that states must periodically redraw legislative districts so that districts have roughly equal numbers of people. Previously, Tennessee had not redrawn its legislative districts for more than sixty years. Urban areas such as Memphis had grown much faster than rural districts. Without reapportionment, urban areas would be underrepresented, violating the principle of "one-person, one-vote."

Prayer in Public Schools and the Separation of Church and State

In *Engel v. Vitale* (1962), the Supreme Court ruled that the Regents' Prayer, a state-mandated prayer that was recited by public school children in New York State, was unconstitutional because it violated the doctrine of separation of church and state.

> **CHURCH AND STATE IN AMERICAN HISTORY**
>
> Disagreements over the relationship between church and state have occurred throughout American history from Roger Williams and the founding of Rhode Island in the 1630s to recent controversies about the teaching of evolution in public schools.

C. THE NEW LEFT AND THE BLACK POWER MOVEMENT

Individuals and groups on the left criticized the liberal agenda of the 1960s for doing too little to significantly challenge the economic and racial inequalities at home and for pursuing an immoral foreign policy.

Students for a Democratic Society and the Rise of the New Left

The most significant organization in the antiwar movement of the 1960s was Students for a Democratic Society (SDS), with chapters at major college campuses across the country.

The name was coined in 1960, with SDS developing out of an earlier organization. SDS held its first national convention at Port Huron, Michigan. At this convention the organization adopted a guiding manifesto, known as the Port Huron Statement, which became an important document in the development of the New Left. The document, written by Tom Hayden, stressed participatory democracy and direct action. The label "New Left" applies to activist organizations of the 1960s that broke with the worker-oriented, top-down movement that developed in the 1930s. SDS continued to grow throughout the 1960s, but disbanded in 1969 after intense factional infighting.

Malcolm X

By the mid-1960s, many African-American activists were attempting to push civil rights activism in a more militant, confrontational direction. Malcolm X was a central figure in the more militant turn the civil rights movement took. Between 1952 and 1964 he was a member and then a leader of the Nation of Islam, an African-American group that shares certain practices with mainstream Islam, but differs from mainstream Islam in several important respects. The organization advocated that African Americans organize among themselves, separate from whites. After making a pilgrimage to Mecca in 1964 and seeing Muslims of different races interacting as equals, Malcolm X revised his views about black separatism. He was killed by assassins from the Nation of Islam in 1965, but his words continued to inspire the movement through the remainder of the 1960s.

The Black Panthers

The Black Panthers Party was formed in 1966. The Panthers took up the call for a "Black Power" movement, embracing self-defense and militant rhetoric. Initially, the Back Panthers focused on community organizing; however, their activities grew increasingly confrontational.

KEY CONCEPT 8.3
POSTWAR SOCIETY

The United States experienced a series of demographic, economic, and technological changes in the decades following World War II. These changes profoundly impacted American society, politics, and the environment.

I. The Promise and Perils of Postwar Society

Many Americans were optimistic about the rapid economic and social changes that were occurring in society in the period after World War II. At the same time, some Americans challenged many of the assumptions of postwar society.

A. THE GROWTH OF SUBURBIA AND THE MIDDLE CLASS

The postwar period witnessed the growth of the middle class and demographic shifts toward the suburbs and toward the "sun belt." A variety of factors stimulated these trends, including strong economic growth, federal spending, a "baby boom," the expansion of higher education, and new technological developments.

The G.I. Bill

The federal government helped returning veterans adjust to the peacetime economy with the Servicemen's Readjustment Act (1944), more commonly known as the G.I. Bill. The act provided low-interest loans for veterans to purchase homes and to attend college.

The Growth of Suburbia

An important postwar trend was the growth of suburbs. Suburbs were not a new phenomenon in the postwar period—indeed, the earliest residential suburbs were built around commuter railroad stations in the late nineteenth century. But a series of factors contributed to the unprecedented growth of these communities. New suburban communities were built just outside of major American cities to meet the housing crunch created by all the returning World War II soldiers. Huge numbers of these soldiers quickly married, had children, and looked for affordable housing. Race also played a factor in the development of suburbia. Many white people did not want to live in the urban neighborhoods that had become integrated after many southern, rural African Americans had moved north to work in war industries.

Levittown and Suburban Development

Developers facilitated the move to the suburbs. An innovative developer was William Levitt, who took large tracts of land outside of major cities (often farm land) and built huge developments of nearly identical, modest houses. He applied the techniques of mass production to these houses, building them rapidly and cheaply. Levittown, on Long Island, New York, became synonymous with these mass produced communities. These developments were not without their critics. Songwriter Malvina Reynolds skewered the monotony of life in these developments in the song "Little Boxes" (1962).

The Baby Boom

For several years before 1946, birth rates in the United States had remained relatively low. Couples tended to have fewer children during the lean years of the Great Depression; further, the dislocation and physical separation caused by World War II kept the birthrate low. However, when the war ended, returning veterans quickly got down to the business of starting families. The spike in birthrates from 1946 through the early 1960s produced a baby boom that would have lasting repercussions in American society. The baby boom required states to spend more money on public education in the 1950s and 1960s, and expanded college enrollment in the 1960s and 1970s.

Childrearing in the 1950s

The parents of the baby-boom generation were enthusiastic readers of child-rearing guides. The most influential was Benjamin Spock's *Baby and Child Care* (1946). Spock urged parents to treat their children as individuals, to let them develop at their own pace, and to focus less on discipline and more on affection. When baby boomers joined the counterculture in the 1960s, conservative critics cited Spock's book as part of the problem.

The Interstate Highway Act

Federal and local highway initiatives also made suburbia attractive. One could now drive into cities from the suburbs quickly and easily. With the National Interstate Highway and Defense

Act (1956), the federal government initiated a massive highway-building project that resulted in the interstate highway system. The act was also promoted as a defense measure, allowing for the rapid movement of military equipment and personnel. Americans could now feasibly leave cities and enjoy a small piece of land to call their own.

"White Flight" and the Decline of Older Cities

Not everyone shared equally in the abundance of the 1950s. As middle-class families left urban centers to move to the suburbs, they took with them their ability to pay local taxes. Cities saw their tax bases shrink dramatically. With funds scarce, cities had to cut back on basic services like policing and education. Crime became an unavoidable urban reality and city schools deteriorated. This decline in city services put more pressure on middle-class people to make the move to the suburbs. By the 1960s, entire sections of cities had become slums.

Urban Renewal

To address the decline of older cities, the federal government initiated a set of initiatives known as the urban renewal program. A central piece of the program was the Housing Act of 1949, which represented a dramatic expansion of federal money and power in the area of urban housing. Title I of the act provided federal financing for slum clearance programs, encouraging city administration to declare areas blighted and then to demolish vast swaths of inner cities. The program displaced thousands of urban residents. In Boston, almost a third of the old city was demolished. Frequently, nothing was built to replace the demolished neighborhoods. Low-income urban housing projects, built with funds from the federal government, often proved to be soulless structures that bred crime and unsanitary conditions. Title I was often used to clear land to build highways rather than additional housing. Urban renewal programs often left cities in worse shape than before the programs were initiated.

B. CONFORMITY AND ITS DISCONTENTS

American culture moved in distinctly different directions in the postwar period. On the one hand, an increasingly homogenous mass culture developed; on the other hand, many artists, intellectuals, and rebellious youth challenged the press toward conformity that marked postwar culture.

Conformity in a Conservative Decade

Several commentators noted the societal pressures toward conformity in the 1950s. Part of this push toward conformity can be attributed to the domestic Cold War and the dictates of McCarthyism. Many Americans felt intimidated from appearing non-conformist in the 1950s. Sociologists David Riesman, Nathan Glazer, and Reuel Denney, in their book *The Lonely Crowd* (1950), noted that Americans were more eager to mold their ideas to societal standards than they were to think independently. William H. Whyte's book, *The Organization Man* (1956), described the stultifying atmosphere of the modern corporation in which employees were pressured to think like the group. The novel, *The Man in the Gray Flannel Suit* (1955), by Sloan Wilson, depicted a man trapped in the materialistic business world of the 1950s. J. D. Salinger's best-selling novel, *The Catcher in the Rye* (1951), railed at the "phonies" who had achieved success in mainstream 1950s society.

Television

Television became an extremely popular medium in the 1950s. By the end of the decade nearly 90 percent of American homes owned a television set. After an initial burst of creativity in the late 1940s and early 1950s, television programming settled into safe, predictable genres. The most emblematic genre of the 1950s was the suburban situation comedy (sitcom), complete with a stay-at-home mother, such as *Leave It to Beaver* and *Father Knows Best*. Westerns, such as *Bonanza* and *Gunsmoke*, daytime dramas (labeled "soap operas" because of sponsorship by soap manufacturers) such as *The Guiding Light* and *Search for Tomorrow*, dominated the airwaves. Many of these genres were carryovers from radio. The *Ed Sullivan Show*, a variety show, was extremely popular, airing from 1948 to 1971.

Rock and Roll Music

Rock and roll music became extremely popular among young people in the 1950s. Rock and roll developed primarily in the African-American community. It was dubbed "race music" and was deemed dangerous by mainstream white commentators. Elvis Presley, a white singer from Memphis, Tennessee, became a huge cultural force in America. He followed in the footsteps of numerous African-American performers, some famous (Chuck Berry) and some largely forgotten ("Big Mama" Thornton). Rock 'n' roll music was part of a distinct youth culture ushering in a generational divide in American society.

> ### COUNTERCULTURES
>
> Do not confuse the timeframe for countercultural movements. The Beats were in the 1950s; hippies were in the 1960s; and punks were in the 1970s.

Beat Generation Literature

The beat literary movement represented a subversive undercurrent in the 1950s. The beats represented a rejection of mainstream social values—the suburban lifestyle, the consumer society, patriotism. The most important text of the beat movement is *On the Road*, by Jack Kerouac (1957). Initially written on a scroll—a stream of consciousness screed—the book depicts a life of spontaneity and freedom. Also important is Allen Ginsberg's book of poems, *Howl* (1956), which ripped apart the foundations of Cold War, materialistic American society.

Abstract Expressionism

An important artistic movement of the 1950s came to be called "abstract expressionism." Centered in New York City, the movement elevated the process of painting—emphasizing spontaneity, emotion, and intensity over studied, realistic reproductions of the visible world. The most well known practitioner of abstract expressionism is Jackson Pollock, who poured and dripped paint on his canvasses.

C. THE CONSERVATIVE RESPONSE TO RAPID SOCIAL AND ECONOMIC CHANGE

Conservatives perceived that society was under threat by many of the transformations that occurred in the postwar period. They challenged many of the trends they saw in the postwar period—urban unrest, a perceived increase in juvenile delinquency, and new ideas about family structures.

The Origins of the Conservative Movement

The modern conservative movement came of age and became a powerful force with the victory of Ronald Reagan in the presidential election of 1980 (see more on the modern conservative movement in Period 9). However, the origins of this movement can be seen in the 1960s. Many Americans were dismayed by the street protests against the Vietnam War and the permissive attitudes of the counterculture. They also reacted negatively to the changing nature of the American family and the rise in divorce rates. In addition, many white southerners grew hostile toward the tactics and the gains of the civil rights movement.

As early as the 1960s, we begin to see divisions within the conservative movement that have persisted within the movement down to the present. On the one hand, we see the growth of an angry, paranoid conservatism, evident in the "massive resistance" movement in the South, the John Birch Society, and the 1968 candidacy of George Wallace for president. On the other hand we see the growth of a more mainstream conservatism, evident in the influential magazine, *National Review*, edited by William F. Buckley and the candidacy of Barry Goldwater for president in 1964.

Barry Goldwater and the Origins of the New Right

President Johnson won reelection handily in 1964, capturing 61 percent of the popular vote. Although Johnson's opponent, Republican Senator Barry Goldwater, lost, he generated a great deal of grassroots enthusiasm. In many ways, Goldwater's campaign represented the beginning of the ascendency of a conservative movement that would become a force to reckon with later in the twentieth century (see Period 9).

II. Concern About Natural Resources in an Age of Economic Growth and Migration

The American economy expanded dramatically in the postwar period. Migrations of people, both within the United States and into the United States, occurred as more people sought to gain access to the growing prosperity of the United States. At the same time, critics began to question the growing exploitation of the country's natural resources.

A. MOVEMENTS OF PEOPLE AND ECONOMIC GROWTH

Large-scale migrations occurred in postwar America. Migrations from abroad increased dramatically after the passage of the Immigration Reform Act of 1965.

Immigration and Nationality Act of 1965

The Immigration and Nationality Act of 1965 (also known as the Hart-Celler Act) changed American immigration policy that had been in place since the 1920s. It abolished the national quota system and replaced it with overall limits on immigration into the United States. There was, for the first time, a limitation placed on Western Hemisphere immigration (of 120,000 per year); the limit for immigration from the Eastern Hemisphere was set at 170,000. There were exemptions set for those who had family members already in the United States, allowing for "chain immigration," outside of the limits established by the act. Preference was also given to immigrants with particular skills that were needed in the United States. The act opened the door to increased immigration into the United States, and has altered the demographic composition of the United States (see more on the impact of the act in Period 9).

B. THE GROWTH OF THE ENVIRONMENTAL MOVEMENT

Writers and activists began to call attention to the abuse of the natural environment in the 1960s. These writers and activists spearheaded an environmental movement that was able to successfully push for measures intended to address these problems.

The Environmental Movement

Another important movement for change in the 1960s and 1970s was the environmental movement. The movement became a national phenomenon and led to some important changes in laws and consciousness. Environmental issues were brought to the public's attention by Rachel Carson's 1962 book *Silent Spring*, which vividly described how modern society was poisoning the earth. She described the impact of the agricultural chemical DDT on the environment. Many participants in the environmental movement were veterans of the New Left and of the movement to end the Vietnam War. Many of these New Left activists had developed a critique of corporate power and influence. Finally, the environmental movement was connected to the counterculture of the 1960s. The so-called hippies of the 1960s encouraged people to rid themselves of material possessions and live a more simple life. The movement gained national exposure when the first Earth Day occurred in April 1970. That same year, the Nixon Administration created the Environmental Protection Agency (EPA) and approved the Clean Air Act to set standards for air quality.

III. A Nation Divided

A variety of political, moral, economic, cultural, and demographic issues led to bitter debates in America in the 1960s and 1970s and divided many Americans.

A. CHALLENGES TO THE TRADITIONAL FAMILY STRUCTURE

A variety of factors led to a questioning and rethinking of the traditional family structure in America. Although popular culture continued to portray idealized nuclear families, the increase in the number of working women and new social attitudes eroded the reality of this image.

The Sexual Revolution

The 1960s also witnessed the development of more tolerant attitudes toward sexual behavior. In 1960, the birth control "pill" was introduced to the market, allowing women more control over reproduction and over their sexual lives. Many states impeded the distribution of information and products related to birth control. The Supreme Court invalidated such laws in the case of *Griswold v. Connecticut* (1965), in which the Court ruled that laws forbidding the use of birth control devices were unconstitutional because they violated the privacy rights of individuals.

Roe v. Wade (1973)

One of the major issues of the women's rights movement was a woman's right to control reproduction, including the choice of whether to have an abortion. One of the major successes of the women's liberation movement was the Supreme Court decision in the case of *Roe v. Wade* (1973). The Court declared that states shall not prohibit women from having an abortion during the first two trimesters of pregnancy. Previously the decision had been left to the states, and many states forbade abortions. The Supreme Court reasoned that the Constitution guaranteed people the right to privacy. Abortion, they argued, was a decision that should be left to the woman with the advice of her physician. This decision echoed the reasoning of an earlier decision, *Griswold v. Connecticut* (1965), in affirming an individual's right to privacy. The issue of abortion has proved to be one of the most contentious issues in America in the late-twentieth and early twenty-first centuries.

The "Quiet Revolution"

From the 1970s to the present, the percentage of women engaged in the workforce has grown. There are several reasons for this. The women's liberation movement challenged traditional gender expectations—many women felt less pressure to marry at a young age, have children, and work at home. Also, the availability of the birth control pill and of abortions allowed women to have greater control over their reproductive lives. Many women made the decision to focus on a career first, putting off decisions about whether to have children or not into the future. Historians note a "quiet revolution" of women entering the work place from the late 1970s until the present. The percentage of households in which women are the sole or the primary breadwinner rose from 15 percent in 1970 to over 40 percent by 2011.

B. THE COUNTERCULTURE OF THE 1960s

A vibrant counterculture developed among young people in the 1960s. It rejected many of the mainstream values that characterized their parents' generation. As the baby-boom generation came of age in the 1960s, it grew increasingly weary of the cultural products of the previous generation. Mainstream culture seemed inauthentic, shallow, and corporate-controlled. This counterculture initiated a sexual revolution in American society and greater informality in everyday life.

> ## THE COUNTERCULTURE AND PUBLIC OPINION
>
> Nixon's victory in 1968 reveals that even at its height, the antiwar movement and the counterculture did not reach large segments of the electorate. This becomes even more evident in the sweeping reelection of Nixon in 1972.

Bob Dylan and the Folk Revival

Despite his protests to the contrary, Bob Dylan was able to verbalize many of the fears and hopes of the younger generation in the 1960s. Even his musical choices—simple, acoustic instrumentation—seemed a welcome break from the bland, overproduced products of the record industry. He cultivated a vocal approach that paid homage to the untrained, indigenous music of rural America, rather than to the smooth crooners of his parents' generation.

The British Invasion

In the 1960s, a series of British bands, most notably the Beatles and the Rolling Stones, transformed American culture. These bands took inspiration from the rich tradition of African-American music—from rhythm and blues to rock and roll—and infused it with a youthful energy. The Beatles inspired a manic following in the United States, known as "Beatlemania." If one event symbolized the beginning of the British invasion it was the first appearance by the Beatles on the Ed Sullivan Show in February 1964. The Beatles also generated a backlash in the United States. Conservative Americans were troubled by their long hair, veiled allusions to drug use, interest in Eastern religions, and challenges to traditional notions of propriety. A comment by one of the Beatles, that the band had become more popular than Jesus Christ, added to the backlash.

The Hippie Movement and Haight-Ashbury

The "hippie" movement became visible in the late 1960s in neighborhoods such as San Francisco's Haight-Ashbury and New York's Lower East Side. In many ways, this counterculture represented a complete rejection of the materialistic conformity that many young people grew up with in the 1950s. A variety of activities came to be associated with the hippie movement—urban and rural communal living, a "do-it-yourself" approach to the varied tasks of life, mystic spiritual experiences, drug use, experimental music, and avant-garde art. Taking inspiration from sit-ins of the civil rights movement, the counterculture organized be-ins—gatherings of young people in San Francisco's Golden Gate Park or New York's Central Park.

Woodstock and Altamont

The counterculture reached its peak and showed its limits in two important events, months apart from each other, in 1969. The Woodstock Festival, in August, attracted half a million people to a farm in upstate New York and seemed to provide a glimpse of a utopian future for many participants. In December, promoters tried to duplicate the success of Woodstock with a giant music festival at the Altamont Speedway in California. However, the Altamont event was marred by incidents of violence; one concertgoer, armed and apparently crazed, was stopped and stabbed to death by a member of the Hell's Angels Motorcycle Club security detail as the Rolling Stones performed.

C. CLASHING POLITICAL VALUES

The postwar period was marked by a number of political and social clashes between conservatives and liberals about the power of the presidency and the federal government, and about movements that sought to expand individual rights.

Watergate, the Undoing of President Nixon, and the Limits of Presidential Power

A major effect of the Watergate scandal was that it reduced people's trust in government. The scandal began in June 1972, when five men were caught breaking in to the headquarters of the Democratic Party at the Watergate Hotel in Washington, DC. Persistent reporting by Carl Bernstein and Bob Woodward of the *Washington Post* drew connections between the burglars and Nixon's reelection committee and ultimately the White House. When it became known that Nixon taped conversations in the White House Oval Office, investigators demanded that the tapes be turned over. Nixon argued that executive privilege allowed him to keep the tapes. In *United States v. Nixon*, the Supreme Court ordered Nixon to turn over the tapes. Also in 1974, the House Judiciary Committee voted in favor of articles of impeachment against President Nixon. Before the question of impeachment could be addressed by the entire House of Representatives, Nixon resigned. Since the 1970s, the percentage of people voting has declined and opinion polls have shown an erosion of trust in the government.

Clashes over Equal Rights

The culture clashes that would come to epitomize the last decades of the twentieth century could be seen in the push to add an Equal Rights Amendment to the Constitution in 1972. The Equal Rights Amendment would have prohibited the abridgement of "equality of rights under the law . . . on account of sex" either by the federal government or by the state governments. The movement galvanized the women's liberation movement. It also led to a conservative backlash against the proposal. Conservatives argued that passage of the amendment would destroy the American family. The movement against the proposal was led by Phyllis Schlafly. She organized a strong coalition, urging "positive women" to embrace femininity. The amendment was approved by both the House and the Senate in 1972 but failed to get the required thirty-eight states to ratify it, even after the deadline for ratification had been moved forward to 1982. It therefore did not become part of the Constitution.

Clashing Views of Affirmative Action

The movement for affirmative action was part of the civil rights movement. Activists hoped to not only end segregation, but to take affirmative action to rectify past discrimination by taking race into consideration in hiring, college admissions, and other areas. In 1961, President Kennedy issued an executive order mandating that projects using federal funds take "affirmative action" to make sure that employers did not discriminate based on race. In 1965, President Johnson went further, mandating that federal contractors and subcontractors make efforts to hire "protected class, underutilized" candidates. Many public universities began taking race into consideration when looking at applicants. Some schools set aside a certain number of seats for underrepresented groups.

Affirmative action policies generated a great deal of resentment among some white applicants for university admission and for jobs, who felt that they were being punished for wrongs done by others. The issue came to a head when an applicant to the U.C.-Davis Medical School named Allan Bakke, a white student, was denied admission. The University of California, Davis Medical School had set aside 16 percent of the seats in each entering class for minority applicants. Bakke, arguing that he was discriminated against, sued and took the case to the Supreme Court. In *Bakke v. University of California* (1978), the Court decided that specific quotas for underrepresented minorities violated the equal protection clause of the Fourteenth Amendment. However, Justice Lewis Powell's decision asserted that race could be one of the many factors that universities may look at in the admissions process, since diversity in higher education was a "compelling interest."

SUBJECT TO DEBATE

Many of our understandings of the Cold War were developed by American historians during the height of the Cold War. As might be expected, these historians saw American actions in a positive light and Soviet actions in a negative light. "Our" side stood for democracy, freedom, and progress; "their" side stood for repression, aggression, and coercion. Since the fall of the Soviet Union, historians have reevaluated this standard narrative. Some historians have put renewed emphasis on covert operations by the United States during the Cold War, such as the 1954 CIA-backed coup in Iraq that toppled Mohammed Mosaddegh and installed the Shah. These covert operations complicate the story. In addition, historians have also looked at Soviet moves in a slightly different light. Stalin's occupation of Eastern Europe following

World War II is still seen as an unfortunate move, but some historians have begun to put Stalin's actions in a larger historical context. After all, perhaps the moves are less reprehensible when looked at in the context of the history of attacks on Russia that had come through Eastern Europe.

On the other side of the political spectrum, historians of the Cold War period have revisited debates about the nature of the American communist movement in the 1940s and 1950s. For many years, historians looked at Communist Party members as victims of an irrational witch-hunt. More recently, since the fall of the Soviet Union, a group of historians, led by Harvey Klehr and John Earl Haynes, have scoured old Soviet archives and found some damning evidence against the Communist Party. Klehr and Haynes have found, for instance, transcriptions that seem to implicate Julius Rosenberg in spying for the Soviet Union.[1] Their findings have forced a reevaluation of the assumption that members of the Communist Party were innocent victims.

When writing history, beware of clichés. Mainstream media and popular memory often reduce a complex time period to a phrase or an image. When many of us hear, "the nineteen twenties," the first thing that pops into our head might be "the jazz age." We think of *The Great Gatsby*, martinis, flappers, and speakeasies. But this image has become a cliché, obscuring the complex tensions of the 1920s. Yes, people went to speakeasies, but they also joined Ku Klux Klan rallies. The more we read about the 1920s, the harder it becomes to reduce it to a catchphrase.

The same is true of the 1950s. For many Americans, the image of the 1950s can be reduced to the word "conformity." We look condescendingly at the naïve suburbanites of the decade, blithely watching bland television programs. However, as students of history, we should be weary of such easy clichés. As in the 1920s, there were complex social factors at work. There were many trends in the 1950s that flew in the face of conformity—the most obvious one being the civil rights movement. The 1950s also saw the birth of the beat movement, the popularity of rock 'n' roll, and the beginnings of the folk revival.

On a related note, be careful about identifying the decade too closely with one individual—Joseph McCarthy. Yes, he was a powerful figure. However, his power was brief; by 1954, he was largely discredited. Also, even at his height, he was not the entire anticommunist movement. By focusing on McCarthy we forget that there was a liberal anticommunist movement, one that was critical of the excesses of McCarthy. Historians are moving away from using the term "McCarthyism" to describe the entire anticommunist movement.

There has been much historical discussion about the origins of the civil rights movement. One key division in the discussion is between those who stress grassroots activism and those who focus on the actions of the government. Historians who take a more "top-down" approach elevate the importance of powerful institutions—the courts, the police, elected officials—in shaping events. This is the more traditional approach. Revisionist historians, many of whom come out of a "New Left" tradition, focus on the agency of ordinary people in shaping historical change. Of late, historians have looked at the interaction between the grassroots level and the halls of power. We see this at play with the Birmingham campaign in 1963. The campaign, which ignited a violent reaction from police (broadcast on the evening news), prompted the Kennedy and Johnson administrations to take action and to push for the 1964 Civil Rights Act. This act might not have been passed were it not for the events in Birmingham.

---

1 John Earl Haynes and Harvey Klehr, *Venona: Decoding Soviet Espionage in America* (New Haven: Yale University Press, 1999).

The legacy of the war in Vietnam has been hotly debated. Historians have argued about whether the conflict in Vietnam was essentially a civil war or an international Cold War struggle. Should the focus be on the rebellion by the indigenous Vietcong and its peasant supporters against an oppressive regime? Or should the focus be on North Vietnam and China fomenting chaos in South Vietnam? If we accept the first scenario, then American intervention seems misguided and bound for failure. If we accept the second scenario, then American intervention seems entirely reasonable. A related question is whether the war was winnable. To some, the United States was fighting a hopeless war—additional years of extensive bombing would simply steel the resolve of the populace to resist the American occupation. To others, victory was both possible and within sight; President Nixon abandoned the fight at just the wrong moment. Domestic political considerations and the Watergate scandal caused Nixon to make a hasty exit from Southeast Asia.

Historians have also debated the overall legacy of the Nixon presidency. In the popular imagination, the Watergate scandal looms large. However, historians point out, the scandal should not overshadow some of Nixon's real accomplishments, including promoting détente with China and the Soviet Union. Historians have also praised Nixon for avoiding the divisive social and religious issues that characterized subsequent Republican administrations. Other historians insist that Nixon's legacy is irreparably tarnished by the bombing of civilians in Southeast Asia.

Practice Multiple-Choice Questions

Directions: Pick the letter that best answers the following questions.

QUESTIONS 1–3 REFER TO THE FOLLOWING CARTOON

"HAVE A CARE, SIR"

—Herblock, *Washington Post*, 1954

1. The 1954 cartoon shown above makes the point that

   (A) Senator Joseph McCarthy and President Dwight D. Eisenhower successfully worked in tandem in the 1950s to slow the spread of communism in the United States.
   (B) Senator Joseph McCarthy went too far when he accused President Dwight D. Eisenhower of sympathizing with the communist movement.
   (C) Senator Joseph McCarthy had the foresight to guard America's borders from communist aggression, but President Dwight D. Eisenhower failed to perceive threats to national security.
   (D) President Dwight D. Eisenhower's criticisms of Senator Joseph McCarthy's anticommunist crusade were weak and ineffective.

2. The height of Senator Joseph McCarthy's power and influence coincided with

   (A) the wave of labor strikes immediately following World War II.
   (B) the Korean War.
   (C) the "massive resistance" campaign among white southerners.
   (D) the Cuban missile crisis.

3. The ideas expressed in the cartoon most directly reflect which of the following continuities in twentieth-century United States history?

   (A) Debates about the proper role of political parties
   (B) Debates about acceptable means for pursing domestic goals
   (C) Debates about the relationship between the executive branch and the legislative branch
   (D) Debates about the role of the federal government in economic regulation

Answers and Explanations to Multiple-Choice Questions

1. **(D)** The cartoon is suggesting that President Dwight Eisenhower did not take a strong enough stand in opposition to the tactics of Senator Joseph McCarthy. "McCarthyism" is the name given to the extreme anticommunist movement in the early 1950s. Senator Joseph McCarthy became the central figure in this movement. In 1950 he announced that he had a list of "known communists" who had infiltrated the State Department. This and similar claims, mostly baseless, created a name for McCarthy and set the stage for a host of measures to halt this perceived threat. Congress established committees to investigate Communist Party infiltration in different sectors of society. Finally McCarthy went too far, accusing members of the military establishment of being communists. The Senate voted to censure him in 1954, thus ending the worst excesses of what many people referred to as a witch-hunt. Eisenhower walked a fine line in regard to McCarthy. On the one hand, he found McCarthy's tactics reprehensible. He once said of McCarthy, "I just won't get down in the gutter with that man." However, he also welcomed the benefits that McCarthyism brought to the Republican Party. The cartoon notes Eisenhower's reluctance to publicly challenge McCarthy.

2. **(B)** Senator Joseph McCarthy had the greatest influence during the period of the Cold War. Often in American history, periods of war opened up political space for more extreme, jingoistic political movements. This can be seen in the anti-German sentiment that accompanied World War I. In 1950, the year the Korean War began, McCarthy gained a great deal of publicity for himself by announcing that he had a list of employees in the State Department who were also members of the Communist Party. The war ended in 1953; by 1954, political leaders were publicly challenging Senator McCarthy.

3. **(B)** The differences between McCarthy and Eisenhower reflect an ongoing debate about the acceptable means of pursuing domestic goals. These debates can be seen in differences over the tactics of the "Red Scare" of the 1920s, in debates over President Franklin Roosevelt's "court packing scheme" in the 1930s, and in debates about the Patriot Act in the 2000s. In many cases, political leaders might agree about broad goals—challenging the influence of radical groups, advancing the New Deal agenda, eliminating domestic terrorism—but might disagree on whether specific means are acceptable.

Period 9: 1980–Present Political and Foreign Policy Adjustments in a Globalized World

11

TIMELINE

1976	Election of Jimmy Carter
1978	Panama Canal Treaty
	Camp David Accords
1979	Three Mile Island nuclear accident
	Formation of the Moral Majority
	Soviet invasion of Afghanistan
	Iranian students seize U.S. embassy; hold hostages for over a year
1980	United States boycotts Olympic games held in Moscow
	Election of Ronald Reagan
1981	Release of American hostages held in Iran
	Reagan fires striking air traffic controllers
1984	Reelection of Ronald Reagan
1985	Founding of the Democratic Leadership Council
1987	Iran-Contra hearings
1988	Election of George H. W. Bush
1989	Collapse of communism in Eastern Europe
1991	Operation Desert Storm
	Collapse of the Soviet Union
1993	Fighting in Mogadishu, Somalia
	Ratification of the North American Free Trade Agreement (NAFTA)
1994	House Republicans issue the "Contract With America"
	Both houses of Congress shift from Democratic to Republican control
1995	Peace treaty signed in Ohio between Serbian, Bosnian, and Croatian leaders
1998	Impeachment of President Clinton
1999	NATO Bombing of Serbia in response to violence in Kosovo
2001	Terrorist attacks on the World Trade Center and the Pentagon

INTRODUCTION

The United States has had to adapt to a changing world in the late twentieth and early twenty-first centuries. The world of the recent past has been filled with challenges and possibilities. The United States has faced divisions along ideological and cultural lines at home and has had to adjust its foreign policy to changing global dynamics. The United States has also had to adapt to new technological and scientific advances, and to economic globalization.

The late twentieth century saw the growth of a powerful conservative movement. There had been signs of a growing conservative movement in the United States since the 1964 campaign of Barry Goldwater. This movement celebrated the election of Ronald Reagan in 1980 and has been successful in redefining the terms of political debate in the late twentieth and early twenty-first centuries. Recent decades have seen an intensification of partisan divisions—from the "Contract With America" in the 1990s to the Tea Party Movement in the wake of the election of the nation's first African-American president, Barack Obama. The era has also seen a series of adjustments, in both domestic and foreign policy, in the aftermath of the terrorist attacks of 2001.

KEY CONCEPT 9.1
THE RESURGENCE OF CONSERVATISM

A renewed conservative movement rose in importance and shaped political and cultural debates. This movement rejected liberal views on the role of the government and embraced traditional social values.

I. Factors in the Growth of the New Right

There are several factors that help explain the growth of the New Right at the end of the twentieth century. Notably, there was a marked decline in the public's confidence and trust in the government. Also, these decades experienced a significant growth in Christian fundamentalism and the rise of neoconservative ideas in public discourse.

A. THE DECLINE OF PUBLIC TRUST IN THE 1970s

A series of events and trends in the 1970s—economic decline and dislocation, major political scandals, a sense of moral decay, and a perception of misguided foreign policy priorities—contributed to a decline in public trust and confidence in the government.

"Stagflation"

The economy of the United States had remained strong throughout the 1960s, despite the costs of the war in Vietnam. As the 1970s began, however, the economy began to contract. By the early 1970s, economists noted an unusual set of phenomena—both unemployment and inflation were at high levels (both over 6 percent). High unemployment is a sign of a stagnant economy; but high inflation is usually a sign of an active economy. After all, it is consumer demand that pushes prices up. The incidence of both occurring simultaneously was dubbed "stagflation." Stagflation continued throughout the 1970s.

"Whip Inflation Now"

President Gerald Ford attempted to address the economic malaise of the 1970s, but his solutions struck the public as inadequate. Ford's most public initiative was the promotion of the Whip Inflation Now (WIN) campaign. The campaign encouraged people to be more disciplined with their money. Supporters were encouraged to wear "WIN" buttons.

The OPEC Oil Embargo and the Energy Crisis of the 1970s

Starting with the OPEC oil embargo in 1973, fuel prices rose dramatically in the 1970s. America had to confront a stark reality—there are limits to the amount of fossil fuels, particularly petroleum, available in the world, and much of it comes from the volatile Middle East. Up until the 1970s, Americans assumed that petroleum was a cheap, inexhaustible commodity. The 1970s saw a dramatic spike in petroleum prices and long lines as gas pumps.

Nuclear Energy and Three Mile Island

Some Americans put faith in nuclear energy as an alternative to fossil fuels. Electricity is generated by the spinning of turbines. In power plants, steam spins the turbines. The problem is generating energy to boil water to produce steam. In a nuclear power plant, a nuclear reaction generates that energy, rather than the burning of coal or oil. The material needed for nuclear power, such as uranium, is relatively cheap and plentiful, and the reaction does not produce the greenhouse gas, carbon dioxide. However, there are problems associated with the nuclear power. The waste product of a nuclear reaction is radioactive and must be safely disposed of. Also, accidents can occur that can have devastating effects on the environment. The worst nuclear accident in world history was in Chernobyl, Ukraine (formerly part of the Soviet Union) in 1986. The worst accident in United States history occurred at the Three Mile Island power plant in Pennsylvania (1979). These accidents raised significant concerns among Americans about the safety of nuclear power and the government's ability to effectively regulate it. Currently, nearly 20 percent of electricity is generated by nuclear power in the United States.

Foreign Policy "Failures" of the 1970s

President Jimmy Carter (1977–1981) faced a number of foreign policy challenges with mixed results. In one area, pursuing peace in the Middle East, Carter achieved a major victory. In regard to the Panama Canal Zone and the Iran hostage crisis (1979–1981), the results of Carter's foreign policy were more mixed and provided an opening for Republicans to assert that Carter had left the United States in a weaker position.

The Camp David Accords (1978)

President Carter succeeded in providing a foundation for a peace treaty between Egypt and Israel. The Camp David Accords are considered one of the few triumphs for President Carter's troubled presidency. Since the founding of Israel in 1948, tensions have existed in the Middle East. The Arab nations refused to recognize Israel's right to exist. Four wars occurred between Israel and its neighbors between 1948 and 1973. In 1977 Egyptian President Anwar Sadat broke with the other leaders of the Arab world and flew to Israel to meet with Israeli Prime Minister Menachem Begin. Negotiations ensued between the two leaders but they were unable to come up with a peace treaty. President Carter invited the two leaders to the Camp David presidential retreat in Maryland. The three men met for thirteen days and emerged with the basis for a peace treaty. The treaty resulted in an end to hostilities between Israel and Egypt, but tensions continued to exist between Israel and its other neighbors.

The Iran Hostage Crisis

In 1979, the U.S.–supported leader of Iran, Shah Pahlavi, was ousted by a revolution led by the Muslim religious leader, the Ayatollah Khomeini. The United States supported the Shah to the end. Later in 1979, when the United States admitted the deposed Shah to the United States for medical treatment, angry Iranian students took over the U.S. embassy and kept the personnel there hostage. Carter finally secured their release after the election in late 1980 but they were not actually released until thirty-three minutes into the administration of President Reagan in January 1981.

The Panama Canal (1977)

President Carter negotiated two treaties with Panama in 1977, the Torrijos-Carter Treaties, which turned the Panama Canal Zone over to Panama. One agreement, known as the Panama Canal Treaty, called for the United States to turn over control of the canal to Panama by December 31, 1999. The other agreement asserted that the canal shall remain neutral and open to shipping of all nations; if any country challenged this neutrality, the United States reserved the right to intervene. The treaties were ratified by the Senate in 1978. Many conservatives, notably Senators Strom Thurmond and Jesse Helms, were harshly critical of the treaty for surrendering direct control of a major strategic asset.

B. THE ANATOMY OF THE NEW RIGHT

The rapid growth of the Christian fundamentalist movement fueled the resurgence of the New Right. This fundamentalist movement started in churches but soon entered the political sphere, organizing opposition to liberal and social trends.

Competing Tendencies Within the New Right

The conservative movement has always had three distinct tendencies within it that have sometimes worked in unison and have sometimes been in conflict. First, there are Cold War conservatives, focused on containing or rolling back communist regimes abroad. In the post–Cold War era, interventionists have argued for continued U.S. actions abroad, notably in the Middle East. Second, are the economic conservatives. These conservatives argue for lower corporate taxes, deregulation, less government, and an economic atmosphere friendly to the priorities of big business. Economic conservatives might use the language of laissez-faire economics in regard to rolling back environmental regulations, but they are ready to use the power of the government to, say, extend military contracts to large corporations.

The third tendency within the conservative movement is the religious and cultural wing. It is this wing that has had the greatest grassroots support, fueling electoral victories for Ronald Reagan (twice), George H. W. Bush (once), and George W. Bush (twice). This movement gained steam as traditional-minded people grew frustrated with what they saw as the excesses of the counterculture of the 1960s. They railed against the women's liberation movement for challenging traditional gender roles, and the gay liberation movement. Many were troubled by the assertiveness of African Americans in the 1960s, and pined for an early time, in which everyone "knew their place." The public nature of drug-consumption in the 1960s also angered cultural conservatives.

Opposition to *Roe v. Wade*

The issue that propelled the cultural conservatives from the margins to prominence was abortion. In the wake of the 1973 decision, religious conservatives found their voice. The issue propelled evangelical Protestants to put aside their long-held suspicions of Catholicism, and create a broad Christian conservative movement.

The Moral Majority and Focus on the Family

The religious and cultural wing of the New Right found voice in several grassroots organizations. The Moral Majority was founded by the Reverend Jerry Falwell, a Southern Baptist pastor, in 1979. In the mid-1970s he embarked on a series of "I Love America" rallies. These rallies broke a traditional Baptist principle of separating religion from politics. Falwell asserted that this separation was at the heart of the moral decay that was afflicting America.

Focus on the Family was founded in 1977 by psychologist James Dobson. The organization is interdenominational, bridging the traditional divide between Catholics and Protestants. The organization promotes an abstinence-only approach to sexual education, the reintroduction of prayer into the schools, and reinforcement of traditional gender roles. The organization has stood against the expansion of rights for gay, lesbian, bisexual, and transgendered people; it has been vocal in its opposition to same-sex marriage. The organization is one of the leading voices in the movement against abortion.

II. The Achievements and Limits of the Conservative Domestic Agenda

The conservative movement achieved electoral successes in the 1980s, 1990s, and 2000s and witnessed the implementation of some of its policy and political goals. However, this period also made evident the limits of conservative reform—many of the government programs it sought to curtail or eliminate enjoyed broad public support.

A. REFORM IN THE ECONOMIC REALM; RESISTANCE IN THE SOCIAL REALM

The New Right achieved remarkable victories in terms of lowering taxes and deregulating business. The movement was less successful is implementing its moral agenda, meeting inertia and resistance.

The New Right and the Election of Ronald Reagan

The New Right achieved a remarkable victory in the nomination and election of Ronald Reagan in 1980. Reagan had been a well-known actor in B-movies from the 1930s to the 1960s. He was president of the Screen Actors Guild in the 1940s and 1950s. He became increasingly interested in politics, first as a New Deal Democrat. By the 1950s, he became increasingly anticommunist, and became an active Republican in the 1960s. He served as governor of California from 1967 to 1975.

The election of the conservative Ronald Reagan in 1980 has been seen by many historians as a repudiation of the political and social movements of the 1960s. Reagan's victory can, in part, be attributed to more immediate causes. President Jimmy Carter was seen as ineffective in not securing the quick release of hostages held at the American embassy in Tehran by Iranian militants. However, Reagan projected a sense of hope and optimism that promised to move the United States beyond the scandals and doubts of the 1970s. He promised a new "morning in America," and Americans listened. Reagan's tenure as president saw a tremendous military build-up and the beginning of the end for the Soviet Union and the communist bloc. He also gave voice to the rising New Right movement.

Reaganomics

President Reagan advanced a series of economic initiatives that bear the name "Reaganomics." He was not the first conservative politician to advance such policies—Reaganomics bears a striking similarity to Herbert Hoover's approach to the Great Depression. Reagan supported economic policies that favored big business. He based this on a belief in supply-side economics. This approach to the economy stressed stimulating the supply side of the economy—manufacturing firms, banks, insurance corporations. The idea is that if there is growth in the supply side, there will be general economic growth and the benefits of that growth will reach everyone. The alternative approach is to stimulate the demand side—consumers. Demand side economics would emphasize government policies designed to increase workers' wages and expand social programs such as welfare and unemployment benefits. As a believer in supply-side economics, Reagan implemented policies that he thought would stimulate business. Reagan cut taxes for corporations and greatly reduced regulations on industry. Reagan was a staunch proponent of deregulation. He and his secretary of the interior James Watt were criticized by environmental advocates for dismantling or weakening much of the environmental legislation of the 1970s.

HOOVER AND REAGAN

Be familiar with the similarities between Presidents Reagan and Hoover in regard to economics. Both promoted a supply-side approach to economic policy.

"Contract with America" (1994)

The Republican Party made significant gains in both the House of Representatives and the Senate in the midterm elections of 1994. The opposition party traditionally does well in the congressional elections that occur between presidential elections. In this case, the Republican Party gained control of both the House and the Senate. The Republicans had not controlled the House since 1954. House Republicans, led by minority leader Newt Gingrich, had signed and publicly issued the Contract with America six weeks before the 1994 election. It was a call to arms for Republicans and a specific blueprint for legislative action. The document called for action on a number of fronts, such as tougher anti-crime measures, tort reform, and welfare reform. Many of the House's initiatives died in the Senate, some were vetoed by President Bill Clinton, some were implemented, and some were reworked by both parties before being implemented. The success of the Republican Party in 1994 put President Clinton on the defensive in regard to his dealings with Congress.

Impeachment Proceedings

An important turning point in the deterioration of relations between the two main political parties was the impeachment proceedings against President Bill Clinton. The proceedings demonstrated the growing strength of the more conservative elements within the Republican Party. Republicans doggedly pursued evidence of scandal relating to President Clinton. During his first term, Kenneth Starr was appointed as an independent council to investigate the Clintons' participation in a failed and fraudulent real estate project in Arkansas that dated back to 1978, when Bill Clinton was governor. Starr pursued the Whitewater case relentlessly, but never tied the Clintons to the fraud.

President Clinton, however, was not able to avoid implication in a more salacious scandal. Clinton was publicly accused of having a sexual affair with a White House intern named Monica Lewinsky. Clinton denied the accusations publicly and also before a federal grand jury. When Clinton was later forced to admit the affair, Congressional Republicans felt they had evidence of impeachable crimes—lying to a grand jury and obstructing justice. Clinton was impeached by the House of Representatives in 1998. Impeachment is the act of bringing charges against a federal official; it is parallel to indictment in the criminal court system. After impeachment by the House, the Senate conducts a trial, based on the charges listed in the "articles of impeachment." Clinton was found "not guilty" by the Senate (two-thirds are needed for conviction). The entire incident reflected the tense relationship between the two major political parties. Clinton emerged from the affair largely unscathed. Many Americans disapproved of his personal misconduct, but resented the attempt by Republicans to remove him from office.

IMPEACHMENT

Impeachment is not synonymous with removal from office. Impeachment is the act of bringing charges against the president (or other federal official). It is parallel to indictment in the criminal court system. After impeachment by the House, the Senate conducts a trial, based on the charges listed in the "articles of impeachment." If found guilty of these charges, the president is removed from office.

The Presidency of George W. Bush

The New Right achieved a major victory with the election of George W. Bush in 2000. Bush, the son of the forty-first president, George H. W. Bush, was governor of Texas and had little national exposure. He ushered the country through the aftermath of one of the most tumultuous events on American soil since the Civil War—the terrorist attacks of 2001 (see page 313). By the end of his second term, public approval of his presidency was at an historic low, hampering the chances of the Republicans to hold on to the White House.

The Election of 2000

The 2000 election for president reflected political divisions in the United States and was one of the most contentious elections in American history. The voting in Florida was split almost evenly between the Democratic candidate, Vice President Al Gore, and Republican candidate George W. Bush. This would not have been such a problem beyond Florida, but, based on the electoral votes of the other 49 states, neither candidate had 270 electoral votes, the number needed to be declared the winner. After several weeks of legal wrangling in Florida, the U.S.

Supreme Court reversed an order by the Florida Supreme Court to do a hand recount of several counties in Florida. The decision by the U.S. Supreme Court in *Bush v. Gore* ended the dispute, with Bush slightly ahead of Gore in Florida, securing the presidency for Bush.

> ## A DIVIDED COURT
>
> The Supreme Court has been fairly evenly divided between its liberal wing and its conservative wing. Justice David Souter could have solidified a conservative court that would have overturned *Roe v. Wade*. Unfortunately, for conservatives, Souter joined the liberal wing of the Court despite the fact that he was chosen by a Republican president.

"No Child Left Behind"

The No Child Left Behind Act was signed into law in 2002 by President George W. Bush. As a program designed to reform public education, the law extended the reach of the federal government into education—traditionally a state responsibility. The law mandated that states set learning standards, that students attain "proficiency" in reading and math by 2014, and that teachers be "highly qualified" in the subject area. The law allowed students to transfer to other schools if they were attending a school that fell short of meeting new guidelines. The law also allowed the state to take over schools and school districts that did not meet new guidelines. The program was criticized by many states for its lack of funding to help schools reach these new goals. Also, many educators questioned the increased reliance on standardized exams in judging schools and school districts.

The Tea Party Movement and the Reaction to the Election of President Obama

The election of 2008 resulted in a profound milestone in American history—the election of the first African American to the presidency. Such an event was virtually unthinkable a generation earlier. As late as the 1960s, Jim Crow segregation was still the law of the land throughout the South and informal, de facto, segregation existed throughout the nation. The civil rights movement challenged and altered many of these practices, but racist attitudes persisted among large segments of the population.

Barack Obama's victory was the result of a series of factors. First, his campaign successfully held off a strong challenge to the Democratic nomination by Senator Hillary Clinton. Clinton's bid for the nomination, if successful, could have resulted in a different historic milestone—the first female president in the United States. The Obama campaign was able to harness the power of the Internet, as well as the candidate's abundant charisma, to build a large base. Clinton subsequently threw her support behind the Obama campaign in the general election. She was later named secretary of state.

In the general election, the Democratic Party was aided by an unpopular sitting Republican president, George W. Bush, and by an unfocused campaign by Republican Senator John McCain. The McCain campaign failed to articulate a consistent message. McCain's selection of the relatively unknown candidate, Sarah Palin, for vice president failed to propel the campaign forward. Palin energized the more conservative elements of the Republican Party, but failed to broaden the party's appeal.

The election of President Obama has generated a vocal opposition movement known as the Tea Party, harkening back to the American colonists' action against perceived British tyranny. To some extent the movement is a creation of the media—heavily promoted by the Fox News channel, and to some extent it represents a grassroots sense of discontent with big government. The movement often exhibits hyperbolic language, predicting the onset of "tyranny," "fascism," and "communism."

B. REDUCING "BIG GOVERNMENT": RHETORIC AND REALITY

Republicans repeatedly declared the era of "big government" was coming to an end. However, Republican administrations witnessed an increase in the size and scope of the government, as it became evident that eliminating or reducing popular programs would be politically dangerous.

The Expansion of Medicare and Medicaid

Since the creation of Medicare and Medicaid in 1965, as part of President Lyndon Johnson's "Great Society" (see Period 8), both programs have expanded. Medicare provides health insurance to those over sixty-five, who have worked and paid into the system, and to those with disabilities. Medicaid is a government insurance program for low-income people. Both programs have, over the years, added conditions and situations that would qualify for coverage. In addition, as people live longer—the "graying of America"—the costs to the Medicare program increase. Despite Reagan's promise's to end "big government," he led the effort to pass a Social Security reform bill designed to ensure the long-term solvency of the program and supported the expansion of the Medicare program to protect the elderly and disabled against "catastrophic" health costs.

Growth of the Federal Deficit

President Reagan's pro-business economic policies had mixed results. By cutting corporate taxes and taxes on wealthy individuals he cut government revenues. But, at the same time, he increased spending on armaments. This combination of increased spending and decreased revenues led to a doubling of the national debt from around $900 billion in 1980 to over $2 trillion in 1986. A large debt is a problem because it requires large interest payments. By 1988, the interest on the national debt had reached 14 percent of total annual government expenditures. This huge debt has hindered economic growth to some degree since and forced future administrations to make difficult decisions in regard to keeping the debt under control.

KEY CONCEPT 9.2
THE END OF THE COLD WAR AND THE REDEFINITION
OF FOREIGN POLICY GOALS

The United States redefined its role in the world in the 1990s and 2000s and had to redefine its foreign policy as well. This change was a response to the ending of the Cold War and growing importance of global terrorism.

I. The End of the Cold War

President Reagan had gained prominence earlier in his career as a strong anticommunist. He brought this rhetoric to the White House, and pursued an aggressive anticommunist agenda. His interventionist approach to foreign policy set the tone for the following administrations.

A. A WORSENING OF UNITED STATES-SOVIET RELATIONS IN THE LATE 1970s AND EARLY 1980s

Relations between the Soviet Union and the United States, which had been improving since Nixon's détente overtures earlier in the 1970s, soured after the Soviet Union invaded Afghanistan (1979). President Carter suspended grain sales to the Soviet Union in protest of the Soviet invasion. He also pushed for a U.S. boycott of the 1980 Summer Olympics in Moscow.

Increased Military Spending

President Reagan was determined to challenge the Soviet "evil empire." He initiated several weapons programs, vowing to close what he called a "window of vulnerability"—the ability of Soviet missiles to attack and decimate American missile locations before the United States could adequately respond. He began research on the Strategic Defense Initiative, dubbed "Star Wars" by critics, and initiated the costly MX missile program.

The Fall of the Soviet Union and the Collapse of Communism

President Reagan is often given credit for precipitating the fall of the Eastern bloc. In 1989, communist governments began to collapse in Eastern Europe. It was clear that Soviet leader Mikhail Gorbachev would not try to halt this development as previous Soviet leaders had. The iconic image of this movement was the collapse of the Berlin Wall in November 1989. The wall, separating West Berlin from East Berlin, had become a symbol of the rift between the Communist bloc countries and the Western democratic countries. By 1991, the Soviet Union itself had collapsed, ending communism in Europe. It is true that an accelerated arms race taxed the Soviet economy more than it did the American economy, but one must also look at the internal dynamics of Soviet society to understand this major development.

B. THE UNITED STATES AND THE WORLD, FROM REAGAN INTO THE TWENTY-FIRST CENTURY

In the post–Vietnam War years, debates ensued about the proper role of the United States in the world. These debates continued into the post–Cold War world, as the United States engaged in a host of military and peacekeeping interventions.

The Reagan Doctrine

The Reagan administration supported regimes that were anticommunist, even if they were undemocratic, or even repressive. This foreign policy came to be known as the Reagan Doctrine. Reagan sent troops to the island of Grenada in 1983 to topple the Marxist leaders of the country. Reagan continued to support the dictatorial regime of the Philippines led by Ferdinand Marcos despite reports of electoral fraud. The regime was finally toppled in 1986, with Corazon Aquino replacing Marcos.

Central America and the Iran-Contra Scandal

As part of the Reagan Doctrine, the Reagan administration consistently tried to undermine the left-wing Sandinista government in Nicaragua. The Sandinistas took power in 1979, after toppling the United States–backed dictatorship of Anastasio Somoza. The United States funded and trained an anti-Sandinista military group known as the Contras. In 1982, Congress, alarmed at reports of human rights abuses by the Contras, passed the Boland Amendment, to halt U.S. aid to the group.

Congressional action did not deter members of the Reagan administration from funding the Contras. An elaborate scheme was developed by members of the administration to secretly sell weapons to Iran and use funds from these sales to fund the Contras. In 1986, details of the Iran-Contra affair became public. Ultimately fourteen members of the Reagan administration were tried for violating U.S. law, and eleven were convicted. Among the convicted was Secretary of Defense Caspar Weinberger. Oliver North of the National Security Council, an architect of the program, was also initially convicted, but the convictions were overturned on appeal. Reagan himself claimed to not have direct knowledge of the program. Critics labeled him the "Teflon president," because accusations of wrongdoing did not stick to him.

President George Bush and the Persian Gulf War

President George H. W. Bush's main accomplishments were in the field of foreign affairs. It was during Bush's presidency that the Berlin Wall came down and the Soviet Union collapsed. After Iraq, under the leadership of Saddam Hussein, invaded neighboring Kuwait in an attempt to gain more control over the region's oil reserves, President Bush organized a United Nations military coalition to challenge the move. The Persian Gulf War involved Operation Desert Storm successfully removing Iraqi forces from Kuwait in 1991. During the Persian Gulf War significant numbers of women served in combat roles for the first time.

Chaos in Somalia

President Bill Clinton deployed U.S. forces to aid a United Nations humanitarian mission in Somalia in 1993. Troubles in Somalia began earlier, in 1991, after the government was toppled and fighting broke out between competing factions. The fighting in Somalia resulted in widespread famine, with more than half a million people dying. The United Nations took the initiative to deliver food to Somalia, but much of it was stolen by the warring factions and sold for weapons. In December 1992, President Bush had approved the use of United States troops to aid U.N. relief activities. By 1993, these U.S. troops had come under attack, resulting in intense fighting in the capital, Mogadishu. American forces suffered nineteen deaths. The mission soon ended.

Democracy in Haiti

President Clinton took the lead in insuring a transition to democracy in Haiti in 1994. After decades of dictatorship, a democratic election brought Jean-Bertrand Aristide to power in 1990. Subsequently, a Haitian army general ousted him. Clinton announced American intentions to use force, if necessary, to return Aristide to power. The United Nations authorized such a move, but former President Jimmy Carter was dispatched to Haiti to try to negotiate an end to military rule. He was successful, and Aristide returned to power in 1995.

Intervention in the Former Yugoslavia

The Clinton administration, like previous Democratic administrations, set out broad domestic reform goals but became enmeshed in foreign policy matters. Clinton became increasingly concerned about violence in the former Yugoslavia. Under communism, Yugoslavia had been a patchwork of different ethnicities. After communism fell in 1989, the country split into several smaller nations. Ethnic violence developed as Serbian forces attempted to gain control of areas of Bosnia with large Serbian populations. In the process, Serbian forces initiated a campaign to remove Bosnians, by force if necessary, from these areas. This "ethnic cleansing" campaign resulted in atrocities against the civilian population and became a focus of concern in the media and among foreign countries. The United States and other countries decided to take action as reports of Serbian brutality became known. President Clinton brought leaders from Bosnia, Serbia, and Croatia together in 1995 in Dayton, Ohio. A peace treaty, known as the Dayton Agreement, was signed and 60,000 NATO troops were dispatched to enforce it.

The United States again became concerned about violence in the region in 1998 when reports emerged of Serbian attacks against ethnic Albanians in the Serbian province of Kosovo. President Clinton approved the use of U.S. forces, under NATO auspices, to engage in a bombing campaign against Serbia in 1999.

Clinton and the Conflict in the Middle East

Toward the end of his second term, Clinton put a great deal of effort in attempting to broker a peace agreement between Israel and the Palestinians. Since the founding of Israel in 1948, tensions have existed in the Middle East. The Arab nations refused to recognize Israel's right to exist. Four wars occurred between Israel and its neighbors between 1948 and 1973. Since the Six-Day War in 1967, Israel has occupied adjacent lands where large numbers of Palestinians live. These lands currently include the West Bank, the Gaza Strip, and eastern Jerusalem. Palestinians have insisted that these lands should comprise a Palestinian state. Israel has resisted agreeing to the formation of a Palestinian state as long as Palestinians launch attacks on Israel. The continued growth of Jewish settlements in the West Bank complicates the situation. In 2000, President Clinton invited Palestinian leaders Yasser Arafat and Israeli Prime Minister Ehud Barak to Camp David. The goal was to work out a "final status settlement" to the Israeli-Palestinian conflict. The discussions at Camp David in 2000 did not resolve the conflict, which still remains unresolved.

President George W. Bush and the Withdrawal from the International Community

The debate over the role of the United States in the world continued during the administration of President George W. Bush. Although President Bush worked with a coalition of nations in the invasion of Iraq in the aftermath of the terrorist attacks of 2001 (see page 313), he distrusted many of the multilateral entities that the United States had previously participated in. Bush withdrew the United States from the Kyoto Protocol, an international agreement on environmental goals. Also, the administration violated international guidelines about the treatment of military prisoners. Bush withdrew from the Anti-ballistic Missile Treaty, in effect since 1972, in late 2001 so that the United States could develop a space-based missile-defense system. In 2002, the United States withdrew from the treaty creating the United Nations' International Criminal Court, which went into effect later that year.

The Bush Doctrine

Debates about military interventions continued during the presidency of George W. Bush. These debates took on added urgency in the aftermath of the terrorist attacks of 2001. President Bush shifted American foreign policy away from its traditional reliance on deterrence and containment. Bush put forth a more aggressive approach in the fall of 2002 that called for preemptive strikes against nations perceived as threats to the United States. In a speech at West Point, Bush identified an "axis of evil" consisting of Iraq, Iran, and North Korea. This reliance on preemptive warfare is known as the Bush Doctrine.

President Obama and the Muslim World

President Obama has taken a variety of steps in regard to the Muslim world. Soon after coming into office, Obama made a major speech in Cairo, Egypt, pledging to mend relations with the Muslim world. He has committed additional forces to Afghanistan while beginning a withdrawal of troops from Iraq. During the 2008 campaign, Obama repeatedly pledged to commit United States forces to finding and killing Osama Bin Laden. That pledge was fulfilled in the spring of 2011.

In 2011, Obama spoke favorably of the changes brought about by the "Arab Spring" protests in the Middle East and North Africa. He committed United States forces, working with European allies, to challenge forces loyal to Libyan leader Muhammar Qadaffi. Qadaffi was ousted and killed in 2011.

II. The United States in the Age of Global Terrorism

The terrorist attacks on the United States in 2001 caused the United States to focus its foreign policy on the war on terrorism. The actions taken by the United States, both at home and abroad, have generated debate about security and civil liberties.

A. THE TERRORIST ATTACKS OF 2001 AND THE UNITED STATES RESPONSE

Following the terrorist attacks on the World Trade Center and the Pentagon, a series of foreign policy and military initiatives began aimed at preventing future terrorist attacks. These initiatives included prolonged and controversial military campaigns in Afghanistan and Iraq.

Terrorist Attacks Against the United States

On the morning of September 11, 2001, nineteen terrorists working with the al-Qaeda network hijacked four domestic airplanes. The idea was to turn the airplanes into missiles that would destroy symbols of American power. One plane was flown into the Pentagon, inflicting heavy damage, and one plane crashed in a field after the hijackers were overtaken by passengers. The other two airplanes did the most damage, crashing into the two towers of the World Trade Center in New York City. The damage inflicted on each building weakened their structures so that both buildings collapsed within two hours. Approximately 3,000 people died in the four incidents, the vast majority of the deaths occurring at the World Trade Center.

War with Iraq

The terrorist attacks of 2001 were soon followed by President Bush initiating military action on two fronts—Iraq and Afghanistan. Operation Iraqi Freedom, begun in 2003, was the attempt by the United States to remove Saddam Hussein from office and create a less belligerent and more democratic government in Iraq. President Bush insisted that Hussein was developing weapons of mass destruction that could be used against the United States and its allies. U.S. forces failed to find evidence of such weapons. The administration also suggested that there was a connection between Hussein and the terrorist attacks of 2001. No evidence of such a link has been uncovered, and the administration moved away from that rationale. This operation proved to be more difficult and costly than Operation Desert Storm. Defeating the Iraqi army and removing Saddam Hussein from office was relatively easy. After these goals were accomplished, President Bush declared "mission accomplished" in May 2003. However, creating stability in Iraq proved to be an elusive goal for the Bush administration. Attacks by insurgents continued, both against U.S. forces and between different factions within Iraq. Operation Iraqi Freedom hurt President Bush's approval ratings in the United States and created tension between the United States and some European nations.

War in Afghanistan

The United States also initiated military actions in Afghanistan in 2001, less than a month after the September 11 terrorist attacks. American forces overthrew the Taliban, the government that had given refuge to al-Qaeda. The United States hoped to find the leader of al-Qaeda, Osama bin Laden, who was still at large at the end of President Bush's presidency.

B. LIBERTY, SECURITY, AND HUMAN RIGHTS IN THE WAR ON TERRORISM

The war on terrorism has fostered a series of intense debates among the American people about the proper methods of carrying out a global war on terrorism. Many Americans became increasingly concerned about issues of human rights and civil liberties in this campaign against terrorism.

The Patriot Act

The Patriot Act was passed in 2001, six weeks after the September 11 terrorist attacks. It greatly expanded the government's authority in the fight against terrorism. Some critics have said that it impinges on people's civil liberties. Perhaps one of the biggest controversies around the Patriot Act is the use of National Security Letters, or NSLs, by the FBI. These NSLs allow the FBI to search telephone, e-mail, and financial records without a court order, raising constitutional concerns for many people.

Department of Homeland Security

The creation of the Department of Homeland Security was a result of the September 11, 2001, terrorist attacks. It was created in 2003, absorbing the Immigration and Naturalization Service. It is a cabinet level department, with the responsibility of protecting the United States from terrorist attacks and natural disasters.

Tactics in the War on Terrorism

In 2004, the release of photographs of United States Army personnel humiliating and, apparently, abusing prisoners at the Abu Ghraib prison in Iraq cast light on new tactics used by the United States in its handling of prisoners in the aftermath of the 2001 terrorist attacks. Army personnel at detention camps in Iraq, Afghanistan, and Guantanamo Bay, Cuba, were given permission to use "enhanced interrogation" techniques. Critics said that these techniques, which include "waterboarding," amounted to torture. The government also began to hold suspects at these facilities indefinitely, denying them due process rights. The Supreme Court, in *Hamdan v. Rumsfeld* (2006), ruled that the Bush administration could not hold detainees indefinitely without due process and without the protection of the Geneva Accords.

President Obama and the War on Terrorism

Some of the concerns about the way the war on terrorism was being carried out under the administration of President George W. Bush helped elevate Barack Obama to the White House in 2008, over Republican John McCain. In 2011, the Obama administration was able to report that a Navy "SEAL Team Six" had killed Osama bin Laden. However, to the disappointment of many of Obama's supporters in 2008, President Obama has continued many of the controversial antiterrorism policies begun during the Bush administration and has pursued some new programs. The Patriot Act, for instance, is still in effect. In 2011, Obama allowed for the extension of three controversial measures within the Patriot Act that were set to expire. During the election campaign in 2008, he called the reports of prisoner abuse at the Guantanamo Bay detention camp "a sad chapter in American history" and promised to close it down by 2009. As of 2014, he has not closed it down.

In addition, President Obama has generated a great deal of debate over the increased use of unmanned drone attacks on suspected terrorist targets. The program, begun under President George W. Bush, has been greatly expanded under the Obama administration, despite it being criticized as "extrajudicial killings," and "summary justice" by the United Nations. Finally, President Obama renewed a clandestine program known as PRISM, which allows the National Security Agency to conduct mass data mining of phone, Internet, and other communications—including, under certain circumstances, those of United States citizens. The clandestine program was exposed by a computer specialist and former NSA contractor, Edward Snowden, in 2013. The revelations revived the ongoing debate among Americans around the protection of civil liberties in the age of global terrorism.

KEY CONCEPT 9.3
CHALLENGES FACING THE UNITED STATES
AT THE TURN OF THE CENTURY

At the turn of the twenty-first century, the United States faced a series of challenges related to a variety of social, economic, and demographic changes.

I. The United States, the Global Economy, and Public Policy

In the late twentieth and early twenty-first century the United States moved toward greater integration into the world economy. This move toward increased participation in globalization has been accompanied by economic instability and a series of challenges around ecological and social change, and around public policy.

A. THE PERSISTENCE OF ECONOMIC INEQUALITY

At the close of the twentieth century, the gap between the wealthy and the rest of the population widened in the United States. Workers in the United States experienced stagnation in terms of real wages as union membership declined and manufacturing jobs were eliminated.

The Growth of the Income Gap

Since the 1970s, economists have noted that the income gap between the wealthy and the middle class has grown increasingly wide. The income for the top earning 1 percent of households increased by about 275 percent between 1979 and 2007, while the middle 60 percent of wage-earners saw their income rise by just under 40 percent during the same period. The flattening of wages for the middle class and the poor has meant an increase in debt for many Americans and, for many population groups, a decrease in consumer spending.

The Deindustrialization of America

From the 1960s onward, large numbers of factories in northeastern cities such as New York and Philadelphia, as well as Midwestern "rust belt" cities such as Pittsburgh, Cleveland, Detroit, and Chicago, have closed. Some firms have relocated to the South and other areas within the United States where they can take advantage of lower wage expectations and a weak labor movement. Since the 1980s, there has been a rapid shift of the manufacturing sector from the United States and other developed countries to the less developed parts of the world. Free trade agreements have accelerated this trend. The rise of the private manufacturing sector in communist China has also played a major role. Because firms in China are able to produce goods at lower costs—because of considerably lower labor costs and an exchange rate that is favorable to China—the United States imports from China grew dramatically in the late twentieth and early twenty-first century. In 2012, the United States trade deficit with China was $315 billion.

Decline of Union Membership

The decline of manufacturing jobs in the United States has contributed to a drop in union membership. Union membership (as a percentage of the total workforce) peaked in the United States in 1954 at 35 percent; currently it is about 12 percent. Another contributing factor in the decline of unionized workers was the ability of the New Right to press an agenda that values deregulation and free market economics. A major turning point in government policy toward unionized workers came in 1981 under President Reagan. When air traffic controllers went on strike in 1981, he had them all fired. This action broke their union, the Professional Air Traffic Controllers' Organization, and was consistent with helping the supply side (the airline industry), rather than the demand side (the unionized air traffic controllers). The destruction of PATCO was a major blow to organized labor in the late twentieth century. In such an environment, and with a falling membership, there has been a marked decline in the militancy of the union movement. In 1970, there were more than 380 major strikes or lockouts in the United States; by 1980, that figure dropped to under 200. In 2010, there were 11 major strikes or lockouts.

B. DEBATES AROUND ECONOMIC TRANSFORMATIONS AND INTERNATIONAL TRADE

A number of heated policy debates have occurred during the period from 1980 to the present in regard to the role of government, regulation of the financial system, and international trade.

NAFTA and the Push Toward Free Trade

A heated debate occurred in the 1990s over free trade and the globalization of the world economy. President Bill Clinton broke with organized labor and environmental groups by embracing the North American Free Trade Agreement (NAFTA). NAFTA, ratified by Congress in 1993, eliminated all trade barriers and tariffs among the United States, Canada, and Mexico. NAFTA was the subject of much controversy when it was promoted by President Clinton. Free trade supporters promised global prosperity as more nations participated in the global economy. Opponents worried that nations would no longer be able to implement environmental regulations, ensure workers rights, or protect fledging industries from foreign competition. Clinton's championing of NAFTA represents a conscious decision by Clinton to try to move the Democratic Party away from its liberal traditions and toward a more centrist approach.

> ## CLINTON MOVES RIGHT
>
> Clinton frustrated Republicans, especially his opponent in the 1996 election, Bob Dole, by moving in a rightward direction. His embrace of NAFTA and welfare reform stole Republican thunder and assured his reelection.

The General Agreement on Tariffs and Trade (GATT)

The General Agreement on Tariffs and Trade has existed since 1948 but a controversial 1994 agreement was far-reaching in its commitment to free trade. The 1994 GATT agreement called into being the World Trade Organization (1995), which has served as a global trade referee committed to reducing barriers to trade. The issues of globalization and free trade have inspired vocal protests.

Opponents of the World Trade Organization have noted that the wealthy countries of the world have benefitted from new trade rules far more than the developing countries have. Some cite the inclusion of intellectual property in WTO rules as damaging to the developing world. The Agreement on Trade Related Aspects of Intellectual Property Rights (TRIPs) (1994), critics argue, made it more difficult for developing countries to gain access to new medicines and technologies. Subsequent WTO talks at Doha, Qatar (2001), called for a loosening of patent regulations so that developing countries could gain access to essential medicines.

Challenges to Globalization

President Clinton's embrace of NAFTA was part of a broader push toward the removal of trade barriers. Proponents of globalization argue that the elimination of trade barriers will lower prices of products and stimulate the global economy. However, the movement toward free trade has generated much debate. Labor organizations argue that eliminating trade barriers will lead to the loss of American manufacturing jobs as jobs gravitate toward countries where the going wages are the lowest. Also, environmentalists worry that free trade treaties will prevent the participating countries from enacting strong environmental protections. These opponents came together in Seattle, Washington, in November 1999 to protest at a meeting of the World Trade Organization, an international body charged with reducing trade barriers.

Changes in the Welfare System

In 1996, Bill Clinton adopted one of the planks of the Republican "Contract with America" by ending welfare as a federal program and shifting its administration to the state level. Clinton's embrace of welfare reform shocked many liberal Democrats. The Democratic Party had pushed for federal entitlement programs since the New Deal of President Roosevelt in the 1930s. Clinton perceived that many Americans were growing weary of programs that cost taxpayers money and did not seem to lessen poverty. Some Americans argued that welfare fostered a sense of dependency among recipients of welfare payments and stifled individual initiative. The reform required welfare recipients to begin work after two years—a stipulation known as "workfare."

Toward Health Care Reform

One of President Bill Clinton's first major domestic policy initiatives was reform of the country's health care system. Clinton put forth the idea of a federal health insurance plan that would provide subsidized insurance to many of the 39 million uncovered Americans, and would, according to the plan, bring down health insurance costs for everyone. The president's wife, Hillary Clinton, chaired a task force on the issue. The idea of a federal health insurance plan had been proposed as early as the 1930s. It came to the fore again in the late-twentieth century as health care costs spiraled out of control and more and more people could not afford insurance. The plan was vigorously opposed by the pharmaceutical and insurance industries, and was ultimately shot down by a Republican filibuster in the Senate.

President Obama and Health Care Reform

Like President Clinton, President Barack Obama chose health care reform as one of his first major domestic initiatives. The issues that motivated Clinton in 1993—spiraling health care costs, large numbers of uninsured Americans—had become more pronounced in the ensuing years. Proposals for creating a "public option" in regard to health insurance generated enthusiasm among many Democrats, but fierce opposition from the pharmaceutical and insurance industries, and from the Republican Party. Many Republicans likened such a proposal to "socialism." In 2009, both houses of Congress passed versions of health care reform. In early 2010, a special election to fill the late Senator Edward Kennedy's seat was won by a Republican, ending the Democrats' sixty-seat filibuster-proof majority in the Senate. Democrats were able to pass a watered-down version of health care reform in March 2010.

The Patient Protection and Affordable Care Act was challenged in several federal courts. Three upheld the act; two deemed provisions of it unconstitutional. Finally, in 2012, the Supreme Court upheld the major aspects of the Affordable Care Act; specifically, it upheld the constitutionality of the act's individual mandate as an exercise of Congress's taxing power. Still, the act has faced both legal and political challenges, even as Americans have begun participating in the health insurance exchanges established by the act.

Debates over Social Security Reform

With the percentage of Americans over the age of sixty-five growing, there will, by 2030, be a substantial increase in the number of people receiving Social Security. The "graying of America," and its impact on the Social Security system, has been a concern of politicians recently. One reason for the growing percentage of senior citizens is the large number of "baby boomers," born in the period after World War II, reaching retirement age. When such a large percentage of the American public is retired, many people worry that programs extending benefits to the elderly, notably Medicare and Social Security, will be unable to stay financially solvent. The issue of reforming the Social Security system has divided Democrats and Republicans, with Republicans pushing for some degree of privatization of the program, and Democrats pushing for increased funding streams to ensure its viability in the future. President George W. Bush, for example, pushed unsuccessfully for a combination of a government-funded program and personal accounts.

Reform of the Financial Sector

Heated debates have occurred from the 1980s to the present about the role of the government in regard to regulating the United States financial system. Republicans have generally argued for deregulation of major industries, including financial firms, and have resisted calls for increased government oversight. Republicans have argued that excessive regulation impedes risk-taking, competition, and economic growth. Democrats, on the other hand, argue that regulation is necessary to check reckless behavior on the part of the financial industry and to protect the economy from rapid fluctuations that can result from crises in the financial sector.

The Savings and Loan Crisis and Bailout

The issue of deregulation of the financial sector came into stark relief in the 1980s with the near collapse of the savings and loan industry. In the 1980s, the nation's savings and loans associations suffered from a spate of irresponsible and risky investments and a downturn in the housing market. Their situation was made worse by the deregulation of the industry in 1980. Legislation widened the options for S&Ls to invest their financial holdings, paving the way for riskier speculative investments. By 1989, more than 700 S&Ls had become insolvent. In response to this crisis, President George H. W. Bush signed a bailout bill that extended billions of dollars to the industry. Taxpayers ultimately paid more than $120 billion for the bailout. Some economists believe that the bailout of the S&L industry created a moral hazard for other lenders—that is, it created a situation in which actors are more willing to take risks knowing that the potential costs of such risks will be borne by others. Thus, these economists see a connection between the S&L crisis and the subprime mortgage crisis of 2007.

C. ENERGY POLICY, CONSUMPTION, AND THE LIMITS TO GROWTH

A series of developments have generated debates in the United States around energy use and policy. Ongoing conflicts in the Middle East and overwhelming evidence of long-term climate change have generated concern about continued reliance on fossil fuels. In addition, many Americans have become increasingly concerned about the overall impact on the environment of mass consumption.

Climate Change and Energy Policy

Americans are by far the largest consumers of energy. In the aftermath of the Arab oil embargo of 1973 and the energy crisis that followed the 1979 Iranian Revolution, some American policymakers began to look for ways for the United States to reduce its consumption of energy (see Period 8). This push toward a reduction in energy consumption has been augmented in recent decades by growing concerns over climate change.

Since the early 1980s, scientists have become aware of a trend toward warmer global temperatures. Some became convinced that this warming trend was caused by trapped greenhouse gasses, which, in turn were caused by human activities, primarily the burning of fossil fuels. In the 1990s and 2000s, a virtual consensus emerged in the scientific community around the connection between global warming and the emissions generated by the burning of fossil fuels. Calls were made to limit the human activities that were linked to global warming. The 1992 "Earth Summit" in Brazil led to the adoption by most of the counties in the world of the United Nations Framework Convention on Climate Change. The 1997 Kyoto Protocol sets binding obligations on industrialized countries to reduce the emission of greenhouse gasses. The United States signed, but did not ratify the protocol. Global climate change has generated debate in the United States between those who would like to see limits placed on the emissions of greenhouse gases and those who emphasize economic growth. To some degree, American society is making changes. California passed legislation in 2006 that would reduce greenhouse gas emissions from all sources, including automobiles. Other communities are taking steps that include encouraging bicycling and mass transit. Scientists and many observers wonder if the small steps being taken in the United States and elsewhere will be able to slow down the process of global warning.

D. NEW TECHNOLOGIES, NEW BEHAVIORS

The late twentieth and early twenty-first centuries have witnessed the spread of computer technology. The Internet has dramatically altered daily life, increasing access to information and fostering new social behaviors.

The Development and Spread of the Internet

The origins of the Internet date from the 1960s as the Department of Defense sought to create a computer system that would allow far-flung military installations to exchange computer information. In the late 1980s, universities in the United States created a computer network to facilitate the sharing of research, while in Switzerland, engineers developed the World Wide Web—a system of interlinked hypertext documents that organizes electronic information transmitted and accessed via the Internet.

Internet use grew rapidly in the 1990s, and has reshaped many aspects of daily life in the twenty-first century. E-mail communications quickly rendered letter writing obsolete. File sharing of music and video have forced the entertainment industry to rethink its business model. Traditional news outlets—newspapers, magazines, and even television—have been forced to compete with the instantaneous information available on the Internet. The Internet has changed practices in the workplace, allowing for virtual business meetings and telecommuting (working from home or a cafe). The Internet has also altered the world of commerce, allowing users to shop and purchase items with a few clicks on their personal computer. This has made shopping easier in many ways, but has driven many brick-and-mortar stores out of business. Bookstores have been hard hit by online booksellers and by the increased use of electronic books.

Although the Internet had become a popular fixture in American life by the mid-1990s, it was not fully utilized by political campaigns until the 2000s. In 2004, the unsuccessful campaign of Howard Dean demonstrated the potential of the Internet to raise money through donations. The 2008 campaign of Barack Obama fully embraced the Internet, building a grassroots movement of activists and contributors that helped carry Obama to victory. Today, websites and social media are central to political campaigns.

The Internet became more mobile with the introduction of smart phones in the early 2000s. Critics note the tendency of smart phones to distract users from tasks (such as driving) and social interactions in front of them, while enthusiasts marvel that the world of information on the Internet is now accessible in the palm of the hand.

II. Demographic and Social Changes

The United States experienced major demographic shifts in the late twentieth and early twenty-first centuries, contributing to significant cultural and political consequences.

A. IMMIGRATION AND THE GROWTH OF THE "SUN BELT"

Since 1980, there has been a significant shift in the population toward the states of the South and the West. The growth of these regions was partly the result of increased immigration from Latin America and Asia.

Changing Demographics in the United States

An important factor in the growth of the Southwestern states has been increased immigration from Latin America. After passage of the Immigration and Nationality Act of 1965, immigration, especially from Asia, Latin America, Africa, and the Middle East, increased significantly. Although the act added limits for migration from the Western Hemisphere for the first time, overall the impact of the act and of illegal immigration into the United States from within the Western Hemisphere have dramatically altered the demographics of the United States. Before the act, immigration accounted for less than 10 percent of population growth into the United States. Currently it accounts for approximately a third of population growth. For the thirty-five years before the act was passed, approximately 5 million immigrants came into the United States; in the 1970s alone, that number was 4.5 million, rising to more than 7 million in the 1980s, and more than 9 million in the 1990s.

Growth of the "Sun Belt"

The states of the "sun belt"—notably California, Texas, Arizona, Nevada, and Florida—have seen remarkable growth. This trend can be seen as early as World War II when defense-related industries attracted large numbers of workers. Affordable air conditioning also played a role in attracting migrants from within the United States. Florida has become a prime destination for retirees from colder parts of the United States. Immigration from Latin America accounts for much of the growth of the region. Many immigrants have been drawn to agricultural work in California and to the cities of the sun belt. The political power of the South and the West has grown significantly since 1980. This has generally augured well for the Republican Party as national politics have come to reflect the more conservative views of those in the West and South. As a result of the most recent census (2010), Arizona, Nevada, South Carolina, Georgia, and Utah, each gained one member of Congress; Texas added four seats; and Florida added two. By contrast, some of the more liberal states of the Midwest and Northeast lost power in Congress. Pennsylvania, Illinois, Michigan, Massachusetts, and New Jersey, each lost a House seat; New York and Ohio lost two seats each.

B. DEBATES AROUND IMMIGRATION REFORM

From the 1970s to the present, immigration into the United States has increased dramatically, increasing the size of the United States workforce, while also leading to intense political, economic, and social debates.

The Changing Ethnic Makeup of the United States

As the percentage of the American population composed of Asian, African, Middle Eastern, and Latin American immigrants and their children has grown, the percentage of the American population composed of non-Hispanic whites has declined—from 75 percent of the overall U.S. population in 1990 to just over 63 percent in 2011. It is estimated that by the year 2042, non-Hispanic whites will no longer constitute a majority of the population of the United States.

Debates Around Immigration

The changing profile of the American population has raised concern among some Americans and has generated a broad debate around immigration policy. Many Americans argue that immigration should be restricted because it hurts the country economically; others focus on stopping illegal immigration. Members of the New Right expressed concern about the cultural impact of large-scale immigration into the United States. Will America, they wonder, fragment into ethnic enclaves? The Republican Party has generally embraced and courted the anti-immigrant sentiment in the United States. Republican politicians have argued for a more secure border with Mexico and for deportations of immigrants without proper immigration papers. The Immigration Reform and Control Act of 1986 reflected some of these concerns. Although the act enabled some immigrants without proper papers to achieve legal status, it also forced employers to ensure that their workforce was composed only of legal immigrants. Further reform of immigration policy has been a priority of the Obama administration in the 2010s.

C. DEBATES AROUND IDENTITY

In the late twentieth and early twenty-first century a number of social and political issues have divided Americans and have led to debates around American identity. Specifically, debates have occurred around immigration policy, the status of gays and lesbians, and gender roles.

Redefining Family Structures

The last decades of the twentieth century witnessed major changes in family structures in the United States. These changes, in turn, generated intense debate about the identity of the American family. An important trend was the growth of non-traditional families. In 1972, non-married households (either with or without children) stood at 26 percent of all families; that figure rose to 47 percent by 1998. This trend has divided liberals and conservatives in the United States, with liberals pushing for measures to extend rights and services to such households, and conservatives calling for a return to traditional family values.

Women in Professions

The "quiet revolution," beginning in the 1970s, of women entering the workplace in larger numbers continued through the end of the twentieth century (see Period 8). Though women have made advances in the workplace, many note that disparities still exist. In the 1970s women, on average, earned 59 cents for each dollar that men earned doing comparable work. That gap has closed somewhat (to approximately 70 cents for each dollar earned by men) but still exists. In addition, women argued that they were often barred from higher positions in the corporate world. They argued that a "glass ceiling" existed that prevented them from climbing higher. The women's movement has also pushed for government–funded day care, so that women could work outside the home.

The Gay Rights Movements and Changing Public Perceptions

The gay rights movement grew in intensity after the Stonewall riots of 1969 (see Period 8). The growth and development of the movement, coupled with a strong conservative backlash against gay rights and public acceptance of homosexuality, has shaped debates around gay, lesbian, bisexual, and transgender identity, acceptance, and rights.

The AIDS Crisis

The gay community faced a major health crisis in the 1980s that brought into stark relief the public divide around homosexuality. Starting in 1981, news reports began to appear about a mysterious disease that seemed to disproportionately affect gay men, causing anxiety and sorrow in the gay community, but also resolve and action. The Centers for Disease Control and Prevention (CDC) identified the disease that would become known as acquired immunodeficiency syndrome (AIDS) in 1981. Soon it also found that the cause of the disease was infection by the human immunodeficiency virus (HIV), present in bodily fluids such as semen and blood. The National Institutes of Health (NIH), a government body within the United States Department of Health and Human Services, was slow to acknowledge and address the crisis. It was not until 1987 that NIH established a committee to research the impact of HIV.

AIDS swept through gay communities in New York, San Francisco, Los Angeles, and elsewhere. On the one hand, AIDS became a lightning rod in the culture wars of the 1980s and beyond. Many Christian fundamentalists saw AIDS as God's punishment for those who practiced sinful behavior. On the other hand, the crisis galvanized the gay community and led to an outpouring of both grief and activism. The group ACT-UP popularized the slogan "silence = death," and staged militant protests in New York and San Francisco. In 1987, ACT-UP staged a "funeral" on Wall Street in New York, with participants lying in the street as deceased persons with AIDS—suggesting that this would be the rapid fate of millions of people if more resources were not devoted to research and treatment.

"Don't Ask, Don't Tell"

The armed forces of the United States have historically discriminated against gays serving in the military. In 1982, the Department of Defense issued a policy which stated that, "Homosexuality is incompatible with military service." In the following years, gay and lesbian members of the military, and those excluded from the military, began a campaign to change the military's policy. The Gay and Lesbian Military Freedom Project was founded in 1988. Finally, in 1994, the military implemented a policy that allowed gay and lesbian members of the military to serve, as long as they remained "closeted," keeping their sexual identity hidden from public view. Advocates for gays and lesbians insisted that the policy, called "Don't Ask, Don't Tell," was discriminatory and that it limited the freedom of speech and expression of gay and lesbian members of the military. The policy was repealed by an act of Congress, signed by President Obama in 2011.

Same-sex Marriage

Perhaps the clearest indicator of the rapid changes in societal attitudes toward homosexuality can be seen in the changing legal status of marriage between same-sex couples. Although gay rights proponents have long demanded that the right to legally marry be extended to same-sex couples, the issue became part of the national dialogue in 1993, when the Hawaii

Supreme Court, in the case of *Baehr v. Lewin*, ruled that the state ban on same-sex marriage was discriminatory under the state constitution. Though the Court did not mandate that the state begin issuing licenses to gay couples, it had the effect of galvanizing social conservatives to mobilize against same-sex marriage and to defend "traditional" marriage. Hawaii ratified an amendment to its constitution allowing the state legislature to ban same-sex marriage. Many states followed in Hawaii's footsteps by amending their constitutions so as to prevent the legalization of same-sex marriage. These amendments usually defined marriage as an act between a man and a woman. Further, Congress passed the Defense of Marriage Act in 1996, which allowed states to not recognize same-sex marriages performed in other states and defined, for federal purposes, marriage as an act between one man and one woman.

The tide against same-sex marriage began to turn in 2003, when the Massachusetts Supreme Judicial Court ruled that the state may not forbid same-sex couples from legally marrying; it asserted that "the Massachusetts Constitution affirms the dignity and equality of all individuals. It forbids the creation of second-class citizens." Several other state high courts followed suit in the 2000s. In 2009, Vermont became the first state in the United States to legalize same-sex marriage through legislative means rather than through the court system. In 2013, the Supreme Court, in *United States v. Windsor*, struck down the section of DOMA that defined marriage, for federal purposes, as an act between a man and a woman. The Court however, did not mandate that states allow same-sex couples to marry. Public opinion has moved rapidly on this issue. According to the Gallup organization, the aggregate of polls taken in 1996 showed 68 percent of Americans opposed extending legal recognition to same-sex-couples, with only 27 percent supporting such a move. By 2013, the aggregate of polls showed that a majority of Americans favored legalized same-sex marriage.

SUBJECT TO DEBATE

With Ronald Reagan's passing away (in 2004), his legacy has increasingly been the subject of historical work. Much of that work is highly partisan. On the one side, critics cite Reagan's background in B-movies, such as *Bedtime for Bonzo*, and his seeming disinterest in matters of intellect, as evidence of incompetency as president. These critics note that Reagan napped during meetings while important policy matters were discussed. He seemed aloof from issues, and claimed ignorance of the complicated schemes that comprised the Iran-Contra scandal. Reagan's defenders focus on one of the major events of the Reagan-Bush years—the fall of communism in Europe. Reagan initiated a massive military build-up that the Soviet Union could not keep up with. The Soviets' attempt to keep pace broke their bank and led to the opening of the floodgates of change. In much of the recent work on Reagan's legacy, these poles dominate discussion.

Historians of social movements have tried to understand the rise of the "New Right." Some historians have drawn comparisons to previous conservative movements—the "Red Scare" of the 1920s or McCarthyism in the 1950s. Others have connected it to religious movements of the past, such as the Second Great Awakening of the early nineteenth century. Historians have also looked at the movement in the context of a backlash against the social movements and protest culture of the 1960s. If the legacy of the 1960s is "free love," protest, and multi-culturalism, the "New Right" stands for its opposites—conservative approaches to sexuality, respect for authority and discipline, and a unifying patriotism. The persistence of this movement into the age of President Barack Obama ensures that it will remain a topic of debate.

It is very difficult to debate the legacy of the very recent past. One topic that historians have begun to wrestle with is the origins of the toxic partisan atmosphere in Washington, DC. Some historians look to the impeachment process against President Clinton as a turning point in recent political history. The Republican-initiated inquest went beyond the usual jockeying between parties and made compromise between the parties increasingly difficult. Historians also note the unusual closeness of the two major parties in recent elections and in opinion polls. Both parties always feel like victory is in reach and seek to press any advantage they can to win points with the electorate. Future historians will have to put the election of the nation's first African-American president in a larger context.

Practice Multiple-Choice Questions

Directions: Pick the letter that best answers the following questions.

QUESTIONS 1–2 REFER TO THE FOLLOWING PASSAGE:

"[As] Members of the House of Representatives and as citizens seeking to join that body we propose not just to change its policies, but even more important, to restore the bonds of trust between the people and their elected representatives.

"That is why in this era of official evasion and posturing, we offer instead a detailed agenda for national renewal, a written commitment with no fine print.

"This year's election offers the chance, after four decades of one-party control, to bring to the House a new majority that will transform the way Congress works. That historic change would be the end of government that is too big, to intrusive, and too easy with the public's money. It can be the beginning of a Congress that respects the values and shares the faith of the American family.

"To restore accountability to Congress. To end its cycle of scandal and disgrace. To make us all proud again of the way free people govern themselves."

—"Contract With America" (excerpt), 1994

1. The writing of the "Contract With America," excerpted above, demonstrates which of the following?
   (A) The growth and influence of the conservative movement in the United States in the 1980s and 1990s
   (B) The ability of the Democratic Party and the Republican Party to forge alliances in the 1980s and 1990s
   (C) The importance of "third party" movements in terms of shaping political debates in the United States in the 1980s and 1990s
   (D) The growing importance of social and religious issues, such as gay marriage and abortion, in public discourse

2. Which of the following generalizations is illustrated by the impact of the Contract with America?

(A) The Republican Party experienced electoral setbacks, being shut out from control of the House of Representatives, the Senate, and the White House for the decade after the Contract with America appeared.

(B) The Republican Party was able to roll back or eliminate key elements of the Great Society agenda of President Lyndon Johnson.

(C) Although Republicans continued to denounce "big government," the size and scope of the federal government continued to grow in the 1990s, as many programs remained popular with voters and difficult to reform or eliminate.

(D) Many Congressional Republicans quit the Republican Party and joined the Democratic Party in protest of the divisive tone of the Contract with America.

Answers and Explanations to Multiple-Choice Questions

1. **(A)** The "Contract with America" demonstrates the growth and influence of the conservative movement in the United States in the 1980s and 1990s. By 1994, the Republicans had not controlled the House in more than four decades. In an effort to create a national campaign in the congressional elections of 1994, House Republicans, led by minority leader Newt Gingrich, had signed and publicly issued the Contract with America six weeks before the election. The document called for action on a number of fronts, such as tougher anti-crime measures, tort reform, and welfare reform. The Republican Party made significant gains in the Senate and gained control of the House of Representatives. Many of the House's initiatives died in the Senate, some were vetoed by President Bill Clinton, some were implemented, and some were reworked by both parties before being implemented.

2. **(C)** Although Republicans gained control of the House in 1994, Republican legislative successes were limited. The party continued to denounce "big government," but the size and scope of the federal government continued to grow in the 1990s and even grew in the first decade of the twenty-first century with a Republican president, George W. Bush, in the White House.

PRACTICE EXAMS

ANSWER SHEET
Practice Exam 1

1. Ⓐ Ⓑ Ⓒ Ⓓ
2. Ⓐ Ⓑ Ⓒ Ⓓ
3. Ⓐ Ⓑ Ⓒ Ⓓ
4. Ⓐ Ⓑ Ⓒ Ⓓ
5. Ⓐ Ⓑ Ⓒ Ⓓ
6. Ⓐ Ⓑ Ⓒ Ⓓ
7. Ⓐ Ⓑ Ⓒ Ⓓ
8. Ⓐ Ⓑ Ⓒ Ⓓ
9. Ⓐ Ⓑ Ⓒ Ⓓ
10. Ⓐ Ⓑ Ⓒ Ⓓ
11. Ⓐ Ⓑ Ⓒ Ⓓ
12. Ⓐ Ⓑ Ⓒ Ⓓ
13. Ⓐ Ⓑ Ⓒ Ⓓ
14. Ⓐ Ⓑ Ⓒ Ⓓ
15. Ⓐ Ⓑ Ⓒ Ⓓ
16. Ⓐ Ⓑ Ⓒ Ⓓ
17. Ⓐ Ⓑ Ⓒ Ⓓ
18. Ⓐ Ⓑ Ⓒ Ⓓ
19. Ⓐ Ⓑ Ⓒ Ⓓ
20. Ⓐ Ⓑ Ⓒ Ⓓ

21. Ⓐ Ⓑ Ⓒ Ⓓ
22. Ⓐ Ⓑ Ⓒ Ⓓ
23. Ⓐ Ⓑ Ⓒ Ⓓ
24. Ⓐ Ⓑ Ⓒ Ⓓ
25. Ⓐ Ⓑ Ⓒ Ⓓ
26. Ⓐ Ⓑ Ⓒ Ⓓ
27. Ⓐ Ⓑ Ⓒ Ⓓ
28. Ⓐ Ⓑ Ⓒ Ⓓ
29. Ⓐ Ⓑ Ⓒ Ⓓ
30. Ⓐ Ⓑ Ⓒ Ⓓ
31. Ⓐ Ⓑ Ⓒ Ⓓ
32. Ⓐ Ⓑ Ⓒ Ⓓ
33. Ⓐ Ⓑ Ⓒ Ⓓ
34. Ⓐ Ⓑ Ⓒ Ⓓ
35. Ⓐ Ⓑ Ⓒ Ⓓ
36. Ⓐ Ⓑ Ⓒ Ⓓ
37. Ⓐ Ⓑ Ⓒ Ⓓ
38. Ⓐ Ⓑ Ⓒ Ⓓ
39. Ⓐ Ⓑ Ⓒ Ⓓ
40. Ⓐ Ⓑ Ⓒ Ⓓ

41. Ⓐ Ⓑ Ⓒ Ⓓ
42. Ⓐ Ⓑ Ⓒ Ⓓ
43. Ⓐ Ⓑ Ⓒ Ⓓ
44. Ⓐ Ⓑ Ⓒ Ⓓ
45. Ⓐ Ⓑ Ⓒ Ⓓ
46. Ⓐ Ⓑ Ⓒ Ⓓ
47. Ⓐ Ⓑ Ⓒ Ⓓ
48. Ⓐ Ⓑ Ⓒ Ⓓ
49. Ⓐ Ⓑ Ⓒ Ⓓ
50. Ⓐ Ⓑ Ⓒ Ⓓ
51. Ⓐ Ⓑ Ⓒ Ⓓ
52. Ⓐ Ⓑ Ⓒ Ⓓ
53. Ⓐ Ⓑ Ⓒ Ⓓ
54. Ⓐ Ⓑ Ⓒ Ⓓ
55. Ⓐ Ⓑ Ⓒ Ⓓ

Practice Exam 1

SECTION I

Part A: 55 Multiple-Choice Questions

Directions: The questions in the section are grouped in sets of 2–4 questions. Each set is organized around a primary source, secondary source, or other historical issue. Select the best answer for each of the questions in this section. (55 minutes)

QUESTIONS 1–3 REFER TO THE FOLLOWING QUOTATION:

"The question, therefore, should be quickly settled, whether free colored persons, born and naturalized in this country, are not American citizens, and justly entitled to all the rights, privileges and immunities of citizens of the several states; and whether the Constitution of the United States makes or authorizes any invidious distinction with regard to the color or condition of free inhabitants.

"For myself, I have not the shadow of doubt on the subject. I believe that the rights of the free colored persons need only to be vindicated before the U.S. Supreme Court, to be obtained; that no prejudice or sophistry . . . can prevent their acknowledgement . . . and that the present laws, affecting your condition, are clearly unconstitutional. The fact that you have been treated, by common consent and common usage, as aliens and brutes, is not proof that such treatment is legal, but only shows the strength, the bitterness, and the blindness of prejudice."

—William Lloyd Garrison, "To the Free People of Color of the United States,"
The Liberator, January 15, 1831

1.   The approach of William Lloyd Garrison and *The Liberator* can be seen as directly challenging the approach of

   (A) David Walker in his book, *An Appeal to the Colored Citizens of the World*.

   (B) Elijah P. Lovejoy in the newspaper he edited, *The Alton Observer*.

   (C) Charles Fenton Mercer, Henry Clay, and other activists in the American Colonization Society.

   (D) Benjamin Lundy in the newspaper he edited, *Genius of Universal Emancipation*.

2. The argument put forth by William Lloyd Garrison in the passage was later contradicted in which of the following Supreme Court decisions?

(A) *Dred Scott v. Sanford* (1857)
(B) *Ex parte Milligan* (1866)
(C) *Pace v. Alabama* (1883)
(D) *Plessy v. Ferguson* (1896)

3. The reform that William Lloyd Garrison is advocating in the passage was later enacted as a result of the

(A) issuing of the Emancipation Proclamation (1863).
(B) passage of the Reconstruction Act of 1867.
(C) ratification of the Fourteenth Amendment (1868).
(D) passage of the Civil Rights Act of 1875.

QUESTIONS 4–5 REFER TO THE FOLLOWING IMAGE:

4. The differences in the two maps shown above illustrate which of the following?

(A) The result of the Articles of Confederation government successfully handling the question of western lands.
(B) Territorial transfers that were brought about by the treaty ending the French and Indian War
(C) The evolving status of slavery in the newly acquired territories of the United States
(D) The impact of the "Quasi-war" with France on competing land claims in the American West

5. The establishment of the Northwest Territory (visible in the second map) by the Northwest Ordinance of 1787 contributed to problems in the subsequent decades of American history because the ordinance

   (A) ignored the earlier designation of that land as an "Indian Reserve" by the British, setting the stage for violent conflict in the region.

   (B) failed to address the issue of slavery in the Northwest Territory, leading to violence between proslavery and antislavery forces.

   (C) called for any political entities carved out of the Northwest Territory to be treated as inferior bodies to the original thirteen states, leading to a constitutional conflict that was eventually resolved by the Supreme Court.

   (D) made no provisions for individuals to gain title to land in the Northwest Territory, setting off a series of violent skirmishes among people with competing land claims.

QUESTIONS 6–8 REFER TO THE FOLLOWING IMAGE:

UNCLE SAM'S NEW CLASS IN THE ART OF SELF-GOVERNMENT.

6. The circumstances depicted in the cartoon suggest that the cartoon was published in the immediate aftermath of

   (A) the War of 1812.
   (B) the Mexican-American War.
   (C) the Spanish-American War.
   (D) World War I.

7. Which of the following reflects a main point of the political cartoon?

    (A) The United States used excessive violence in suppressing independence movements in its recently acquired territories.
    (B) The inhabitants of America's newly acquired colonial holdings might not initially be able to handle self-government and would require some degree of long-term American control.
    (C) American expansionistic efforts were misguided and costly; the United States would be well-advised to abandon its experiment in imperialism.
    (D) The United States should extend citizenship rights to inhabitants of its newly acquired colonies; the Constitution should follow the flag.

8. In the period following the events depicted in the cartoon the United States

    (A) formed multilateral agreements and regional alliances with developing nations.
    (B) withdrew from global affairs in the face of opposition at home and abroad to imperialistic ventures.
    (C) expanded its economic and military presence in the Caribbean, Latin America, and Asia.
    (D) insisted that the countries referred to in the cartoon improve their human rights records or suffer a reduction of foreign aid.

QUESTIONS 9–10 REFER TO THE FOLLOWING QUOTATION:

"The power . . . given to the commanding officer over all the people of each district is that of an absolute monarch. His mere will is to take the place of all law. . . . It reduces the whole population of the ten states—all persons, of every color, sex, and condition, and every stranger within their limits—to the most abject and degrading slavery."

9. The excerpt from the presidential veto message above is from

    (A) President Thomas Jefferson's veto of the Alien and Sedition Acts.
    (B) President James Monroe's veto of an act for the preservation and repair of the Cumberland Road.
    (C) President Andrew Jackson's veto of the bill rechartering the Second Bank of the United States.
    (D) President Andrew Johnson's veto of one of the Reconstruction Acts of 1867.

10. The political sentiment of the veto message above is most similar to which of the following political positions taken in the twentieth century?

    (A) Justice Frank Murphy's dissent in the Supreme Court case, *Korematsu v.* the *United States* in 1944
    (B) United States Army lawyer Joseph Welsh's opposition to Senator Joseph McCarthy in the Army-McCarthy hearings in 1954
    (C) Governor Orval Faubus's response to the steps taken by President Dwight Eisenhower to resolve the Little Rock crisis in 1957
    (D) John Lewis's endorsement of the Voting Right's Act in 1965

JUST AS DANGEROUS NOW AS THEN.

11. The 1883 cartoon above makes the point that

(A) the "new" immigrants from eastern and southern Europe, with their different customs and religious beliefs, were just as dangerous to the American way of life as the American Indians were to the Pilgrims in the seventeenth century.

(B) the United States was getting filled up with people; additional immigrants would displace native born Americans, just as the seventeenth century Pilgrims displaced the American Indians.

(C) among the "new immigrants" were many hard working men and women, but also many radicals, anarchists, revolutionaries, criminals and other "dangerous" elements.

(D) incoming immigrants faced a gauntlet of dangers when they arrived in America, just as the Pilgrims did when they arrived in the seventeenth century.

12. Which of the following best represents a continuity with the political sentiments expressed in the cartoon above?

(A) Jane Addams and Ellen Gates Starr founding Hull House in 1889

(B) Madison Grant writing the book, *The Passing of the Great Race* (1916)

(C) Attorney General A. Mitchell Palmer carrying out deportation hearings during the "Red Scare" of the 1920s

(D) Congressmen Albert Johnson and David Reed proposing the Immigration Act of 1924

13.   The 1936 cartoon above, from the *New York Daily News*, is making the point that

(A)   although European individuals and countries might be seduced into waging another major war, the United States would be wise to avoid participating.

(B)   the policy of appeasement is a bankrupt policy that can only lead to more death and destruction.

(C)   munitions manufacturers, the so-called merchants of death, were pushing the world toward war in the name of profits.

(D)   the weaponry of modern warfare had advanced to such a degree that future military engagements would result in unprecedented carnage.

14.   Which of the following political positions most closely parallels the political position reflected in the cartoon?

(A)   Newspaper publisher William Randolph Hearst's position on declaring war on Spain in 1898

(B)   The Abraham Lincoln Brigade position on American intervention in the Spanish Civil War in 1937

(C)   Secretary of State Dean Acheson's position on United States intervention in the Korean War in 1950

(D)   Martin Luther King, Jr.'s, position on the Vietnam War in 1967

"The seeds of totalitarian regimes are nurtured by misery and want. They spread and grow in the evil soil of poverty and strife. They reach their full growth when the hope of a people for a better life has died. We must keep that hope alive. . . . Great responsibilities have been placed upon us by the swift movement of events. . . . I am confident that the Congress will face these responsibilities squarely."

—President Harry S. Truman, 1947

15. The passage above is part of President Truman's argument to Congress in favor of

   (A) the Servicemen's Readjustment Act (G.I. Bill).
   (B) development of the hydrogen bomb.
   (C) the McCarran Internal Security Act.
   (D) an extension of aid to Greece and Turkey.

16. The passage above can best be seen as providing a rationale for

   (A) the policy of containment.
   (B) the principle of "massive retaliation."
   (C) participation in the Atlantic Charter.
   (D) embarking on a "roll back" of communism.

17. The ideas expressed in the passage above most directly reflect which of the following continuities in United States history?

   (A) Debates about the relationship between Congress and the president
   (B) Debates about the use of military force in volatile situations
   (C) Debates about the role of the United States in world affairs
   (D) Debates about the proper role of political parties

QUESTIONS 18–19 REFER TO THE FOLLOWING IMAGE:

—"Your Honor, this woman gave birth to a naked child" (the figure speaking is
Anthony Comstock, United States Postal Inspector), *The Masses*, September 1915

18.   The political cartoon above is making the point that

(A)   government officials were taking their crusade against immoral behavior to
      extreme lengths.
(B)   unregulated immigration was leading to an increase in crime among men and
      women in urban centers.
(C)   "flappers" were imposing their standards of moral behavior on an unsuspecting
      public.
(D)   the court system was bogged down with insignificant complaints while
      perpetrators of major crimes were left untouched by the law.

19.   The cartoon reflects a point of view about which of the following continuities in
      United States history?

(A)   Debates about immigration policy
(B)   Debates about the role of the federal government in regulating morality
(C)   Debates about access to healthcare for working-class women
(D)   Debates about the rights of the individuals accused of crimes

QUESTIONS 20–22 REFER TO THE FOLLOWING PASSAGE:

"If it be conceded, as it must be by every one who is the least conversant with our institutions, that the sovereign powers delegated are divided between the General and State Governments, and that the latter hold their portion by the same tenure as the former, it would seem impossible to deny to the States the right of deciding on the infractions of their powers, and the proper remedy to be applied for their correction. The right of judging, in such cases, is an essential attribute of sovereignty, of which the States cannot be divested without losing their sovereignty itself, and being reduced to a subordinate corporate condition. In fact, to divide power, and to give to one of the parties the exclusive right of judging of the portion allotted to each, is, in reality, not to divide it at all; and to reserve such exclusive right to the General Government (it matters not by what department to be exercised), is to convert it, in fact, into a great consolidated government, with unlimited powers, and to divest the States, in reality, of all their rights, It is impossible to understand the force of terms, and to deny so plain a conclusion."

—John C. Calhoun, "South Carolina Exposition and Protest," 1828

20. The issue that precipitated the passage excerpted above was

(A) the removal of American Indians from the South.
(B) the rechartering of the Second Bank of the United States.
(C) the passage of an act creating higher tariff rates.
(D) the funding of "internal improvements."

21. The argument put forth by John C. Calhoun in the passage above states a position in a debate that is most similar to which of the following debates from earlier in United States history?

(A) The debate over whether to count slaves in the census for purposes of representation
(B) The debate over the Constitutionality of purchasing the Louisiana Purchase
(C) The debate over disestablishment of the Episcopal Church in several states
(D) The debate over replacing the Articles of Confederation with the Constitution

22. The language of "protest" that Calhoun used in his "Exposition and Protest" was similar to the language of which of the following political positions?

(A) The response of supporters of Andrew Jackson to the "corrupt bargain" of 1824
(B) The response of New England Federalists to the War of 1812
(C) The response of the Jefferson administration to the actions of the "Barbary pirates"
(D) The response of Daniel Shays to fiscal policies of the Massachusetts legislature in the 1780s

QUESTIONS 23–25 REFER TO THE FOLLOWING IMAGE:

23. The 1933 political cartoon shown above makes the point that

(A) the New Deal's proposals for open immigration would threaten American democracy.

(B) the New Deal would be ineffective in addressing the problems of the Great Depression.

(C) the Supreme Court acted in a tyrannical way in declaring certain New Deal measures unconstitutional.

(D) New Deal programs would usher in unconstitutional restrictions on American freedoms and liberties.

24. The sentiment expressed in the cartoon above most directly reflects which of the following continuities in United States history?

(A) Debates about the proper role of the federal government in the economy

(B) Debates about the power of the Supreme Court to "legislate from the bench"

(C) Debates about the proper relationship between the federal government and the states

(D) Debates about individual liberties during time of war

25. The sentiment reflected in the cartoon above was similar to which of the following political expressions?

(A) Support by the feminists for the Equal Rights Amendment in 1972
(B) Opposition by the Republican Party to the creation of Great Society programs in the 1960s
(C) Opposition by environmentalists to passage of the North American Free Trade Agreement in 1994
(D) Opposition by Korean War veterans to the firing of General Douglas MacArthur by President Dwight D. Eisenhower in 1951

QUESTIONS 26–27 REFER TO THE FOLLOWING PASSAGE:

"A drunkard in the gutter is just where he ought to be. . . . The law of survival of the fittest was not made by man, and it cannot be abrogated by man. We can only, by interfering with it, produce the survival of the unfittest. . . . The millionaires are a product of natural selection, acting on the whole body of men to pick out those who can meet the requirement of certain work to be done. In this respect they are just like the great statesmen, or scientific men, or military men. It is because they are thus selected that wealth—both their own and that entrusted to them—aggregates under their hands. Let one of them make a mistake and see how quickly the concentration gives way to dispersion."

—William Graham Sumner, *What Social Classes Owe to Each Other*, 1883

26. During the late 1800s, those who followed the ideas of William Graham Sumner in his book, *What Social Classes Owe to Each Other* (excerpted above), would most likely have advocated

(A) government ownership of major banks and railroad companies.
(B) a social welfare "safety net" to help people get through difficult economic times.
(C) government efforts to curb alcohol consumption.
(D) a laissez-faire approach to the economy.

27. The sociological ideas of William Graham Sumner reflect the idea that during the late 1800s

(A) cultural and intellectual arguments justified the success of those at the top of the socioeconomic structure as both appropriate and inevitable.
(B) popular writers rejected ideas from the sciences, and based their arguments on faith.
(C) intellectuals were critical of the cut-throat competition of the ages, and proposed radical alternatives based on creating a cooperative economy.
(D) cultural products of the era tended to ignore the economic direction of society and looked back wistfully to the past.

QUESTIONS 28–30 REFER TO THE FOLLOWING PASSAGE:

"If any person or persons shall, from and after the passing of this act, by force and violence, take and carry away, or cause to be taken or carried away, and shall, by fraud or false pretense, seduce, or cause to be seduced, or shall attempt so to take, carry away or seduce, any negro or mulatto, from any part or parts of this commonwealth, to any other place or places whatsoever, out of this commonwealth, with a design and intention of selling and disposing of, or of causing to be sold, or of keeping and detaining, or of causing to be kept and detained, such negro or mulatto, as a slave or servant for life, or for any term whatsoever, every such person or persons, his or their aiders or abettors, shall on conviction thereof, in any court of this commonwealth having competent jurisdiction, be deemed guilty of a felony."

—Excerpt from Pennsylvania law, 1826

28. This law was challenged in a Supreme Court case, *Prigg v. Pennsylvania* (1842), on the grounds that it

    (A) violated the Constitutional injunction against bills of attainder.
    (B) undermined the intent of the fugitive slave clause of the Constitution.
    (C) circumvented the three-fifths clause of the Constitution.
    (D) was inconsistent with the "eminent domain" clause of the Fifth Amendment of the Constitution.

29. The passage and implementation of this Pennsylvania law reflected an ongoing conflict between

    (A) rural and urban interests.
    (B) federal law and state law.
    (C) those who favored gradual emancipation and those who favored immediate emancipation.
    (D) supporters and opponents of government regulation of commerce.

30. Debate and conflict over the Pennsylvania law, excerpted above, reflected the fact that the framers of the Constitution

    (A) specifically declared that the institution of slavery would be protected "in perpetuity" in the original thirteen states.
    (B) allowed for a state to be exempt from federal laws that went against that state's constitution.
    (C) postponed a solution to the problems of slavery.
    (D) declared that slaves could be both citizens and property.

QUESTIONS 31–32 REFER TO THE FOLLOWING PASSAGE:

"I come to present the strong claims of suffering humanity. I come to place before the Legislature of Massachusetts the condition of the miserable, the desolate, the outcast. I come as the advocate of helpless, forgotten, insane and idiotic men and women; of beings, sunk to a condition from which the most unconcerned would start with real horror; of beings wretched in our Prisons, and more wretched in our Alms-Houses. . . .

"I must confine myself to few examples, but am ready to furnish other and more complete details, if required. If my pictures are displeasing, coarse, and severe, my subjects, it must be recollected, offer no tranquil, refined, or composing features. The condition of human beings, reduced to the extremest states of degradation and misery, cannot be exhibited in softened language, or adorn a polished page.

"I proceed, Gentlemen, briefly to call your attention to the present state of Insane Persons confined within this Commonwealth, *in cages, closets, cellars, stalls, pens! Chained, naked, beaten with rods,* and *lashed* into obedience!"

> —Dorothea Dix, "Memorial to the Massachusetts Legislature" (1843)

31. Dorothea Dix's testimony to the Massachusetts legislature reflects the influence of which of the following?

    (A) Social Darwinism
    (B) The Second Great Awakening
    (C) Second-wave feminism
    (D) The Christian Science movement

32. Dorothea Dix's research and testimony is best understood in the context of

    (A) women gaining the right to vote in many states.
    (B) an economic downturn that was responsible for the closure of many state institutions.
    (C) an evolving relationship between the federal government and issues of health and poverty.
    (D) the rise of voluntary organizations to promote religious and secular reforms.

QUESTIONS 33–35 REFER TO THE FOLLOWING PASSAGE:

"I was once a tool of oppression
And as green as a sucker could be
And monopolies banded together
To beat a poor hayseed like me.

"The railroads and old party bosses
Together did sweetly agree;
And they thought there would be little trouble
In working a hayseed like me. . . ."

> —"The Hayseed"

33. The song lyrics would most likely have appeared in

(A) an abolitionist newspaper in the 1830s.
(B) a Republican leaflet in the 1870s.
(C) a populist newspaper in the 1890s.
(D) a civil rights pamphlet in the 1950s.

34. Which of the following is an accomplishment of the political movement that was organized around sentiments similar to the one in the song lyrics?

(A) Establishment of the minimum wage law
(B) Enactment of laws regulating railroads
(C) Shift in United States currency from the gold standard to the silver standard
(D) Creation of a price support system for small-scale farmers

35. The song, and the movement that it was connected to, highlights which of the following developments in the broader society in the late 1800s?

(A) Corruption in government—especially as it related to big business—energized the public to demand increased popular control and reform of local, state, and national governments.
(B) A large-scale movement of struggling African American and white farmers, as well as urban factory workers, was able to exert a great deal of leverage over federal legislation.
(C) The two-party system of the era broke down, and led to the emergence of an additional major party that was able to win control of Congress within ten years of its founding.
(D) Continued skirmishes on the frontier in the 1890s with American Indians created a sense of fear and bitterness among western farmers.

QUESTIONS 36–37 REFER TO THE FOLLOWING PASSAGE:

"We are men; we have souls, we have passions, we have feelings, we have hopes, we have desires, like any other race in the world. The cry is raised all over the world today of Canada for the Canadians, of America for the Americans, of England for the English, of France for the French, of Germany for the Germans—do you think it is unreasonable that we, the Blacks of the world, should raise the cry of Africa for the Africans?"

—Marcus Garvey, 1920

36. The passage could best be understood as

(A) an argument in favor of restrictions on immigration into the United States.
(B) an attempt to unite working-class African American and white men and women.
(C) an expression of black nationalism.
(D) a pamphlet designed to promote the advancement of African Americans in industry.

37. The passage above presents a position in which of the following ongoing debates in American history?

   (A) The debate between interventionism and isolationism in regard to foreign policy
   (B) The debate between separatism and integration in regard to the place of African Americans in American society
   (C) The debate between exclusion and inclusion in regard to immigration policy
   (D) The debate between laissez-faire policies and government intervention in economic affairs

QUESTIONS 38–39 REFER TO THE FOLLOWING PASSAGE:

"But even if southern progressivism included women, was it reserved for whites? The answer is that whites intended for it to be, and it would have been even more racist, more exclusive, and more oppressive it there had been no black women progressives. . . . . As much as southern whites plotted to reserve progressivism for themselves, and as much as they schemed to alter the ill-fitting northern version accordingly, they failed. African-American women embraced southern white progressivism, reshaped it, and sent back a new model that included black power brokers and grass roots activists. Evidence of southern African-American progressivism is not to be found in public laws, electoral politics, or the establishment of mothers' aid programs at the state level. It rarely appears in documents that white progressives, male or female, left behind. Since black men could not speak out in politics and black women did not want to be seen, it has remained invisible in virtually every discussion of southern progressivism. Nonetheless, southern black women initiated every progressive reform that southern white women initiated, a feat they accomplished without financial resources, without the civic protection of their husbands, and without publicity."

> —Glenda Elizabeth Gilmore, "Diplomatic Women," from *Gender and Jim Crow: Women and the Politics of White Supremacy in North Carolina, 1896–1920* (Chapel Hill: University of North Carolina Press, 1996), 147–75.

38. The excerpt above, from the essay by Glenda Elizabeth Gilmore, implies that historians of the Progressive movement have

   (A) failed to adequately explain why the agenda and goals of the Progressive movement never resonated with the African-American community.
   (B) ignored the latent racism and white supremacy inherent in the Progressive movement.
   (C) not written extensively on the contributions of black women to progressivism in the South because of a scarcity of documentary evidence.
   (D) overemphasized the extent of African-American participation in the Progressive movement in order to improve the public perception of the movement.

39. The efforts described in the reading above occurred in the context of

(A) increased federal support for civil rights measures in the United States, as American political leaders sought to bolster the democratic image of the United States on a global stage.

(B) rapid industrialization in the South, which brought African-American working-class activists in closer contact with whites.

(C) successful efforts by the United States military to segregate units fighting in the Spanish-American War and World War I, but resistance by state governments to follow the lead of the military.

(D) a nadir in race relations in the United States as "scientific" ideas about race, inaction by the federal government, and rigid segregation in the South relegated African Americans to a second-class status in the United States.

QUESTIONS 40–42 REFER TO THE FOLLOWING PASSAGE:

"Your sentiments, that our affairs are drawing rapidly to a crisis, accord with my own. What the event will be is also beyond the reach of my foresight. We have errors to correct. We have probably had too good an opinion of human nature in forming our confederation. Experience has taught us that men will not adopt and carry into execution measures the best calculated for their own good without the intervention of a coercive power. I do not conceive that we can exist long as a nation without having lodged somewhere a power which will pervade the whole Union in as energetic a manner as the authority of the state governments extends over the several states. . . .

What astonishing changes a few years are capable of producing. I am told that even respectable characters speak of a monarchical form of government without horror. . . . What a triumph for our enemies to verify their predictions! What a triumph for the advocates of despotism to find that we are incapable of governing ourselves, and that systems founded on the basis of equal liberty are merely ideal and fallacious. . . ."

—George Washington, letter to John Jay, August 1, 1786

40. The sentiments in the letter by George Washington, above, reflect which of the following continuities in American history?

(A) Debates about the proper balance between liberty and order

(B) Debates about reconciling republicanism with the institution of slavery

(C) Debates about the relationship among the three branches of government

(D) Debates about the use of the military in subduing domestic disturbances

41. Based on the context of the letter, which of the following most closely describes the meaning of Washington's phrase, "We have probably had too good an opinion of human nature"?

(A) Contemporary Deist spiritual beliefs were misguided in that they abandoned the Calvinist notions of "original sin."

(B) The United States had overestimated the good will and honor of Great Britain in terms of following the stipulations of the Treaty of Paris (1783).

(C) The United States army misread the willingness of American Indians in the Ohio Valley and Great Lakes regions to live side-by-side with white settlers.

(D) The framers of the Articles of Confederation made a mistake in allowing for too great a degree of democracy in the new republic.

42. In subsequent United States history, those who shared the sentiments George Washington expressed in the letter, above, would most likely have taken which of the following positions?

(A) Support for joining France in its war with Great Britain in 1793 in honor of the 1778 Treaty of Alliance with France

(B) Opposition to the chartering of a national bank in 1791

(C) Support for ratification of the Constitution in 1789

(D) Opposition to the Alien and Sedition Acts of 1798

QUESTIONS 43–44 REFER TO THE FOLLOWING PASSAGE:

"As our late Conduct at the Conestoga Manor and Lancaster have occasioned much Speculation & a great diversity of Sentiments in this and neighboring Governments; some vindicating & others condemning it; some charitably alleviating the Crime, & others maliciously painting it in the most odious & detestable Colours, we think it our duty to lay before the Publick, the whole Matter as it appeared, & still appears, to us. . . .

"If these things are not sufficient to prove an unjustifiable Attachment in the Quakers to the Indians Savages, a fixed Resolution to befriend them & an utter insensibility to human Distresses, let us consider a few more recent Facts. When we found the last Summer that we were likely to get no Assistance from the Government, some Volunteers went out at our own Expense, determined to drive our Enemies from our Borders; & when we came near to the great Island, we understood that a Number of their Warriors had gone out against our Frontiers. Upon this we returned and came up with them and fought with them at the Munfey Hill where we lost some of our Men & killed some of their Warriors & thereby saved our Frontiers from this Story in another Expedition. But no sooner had we destroyed their Provisions on the great Island, & ruined their trade with the good People at Bethlehem, but these very Indians, who were justly suspected of having murdered our Friends in Northampton County, were by the Influence of some Quakers taken under the Protection of the Government to screen them from the Resentments of the Friends and Relations of the Murdered, & to support them thro the Winter."

—"Apology of the Paxton Boys" (pamphlet), 1764. (Note: "apology" in this context should be read as an explanation, not an admission of guilt or regret)

43. The sentiments expressed in the explanation reflect which of the ongoing tensions during the colonial period of American history?

    (A) Tensions between British policies and the aspirations of North American colonists

    (B) Tensions between American Indians allied with the French and those allied with the British

    (C) Tensions between freed African Americans and white planters

    (D) Tensions between backcountry settlers and elites within colonial America

44. Which of the following events from either earlier or later in the colonial period can best be seen as being part of a continuity with the events described in the passage?

    (A) The expulsion of Anne Hutchinson from Massachusetts Bay Colony

    (B) Bacon's Rebellion in colonial Virginia

    (C) The Boston Tea Party

    (D) The trial of John Peter Zenger

QUESTIONS 45–48 REFER TO THE FOLLOWING PASSAGE:

"When we were kids the United States was the wealthiest and strongest country in the world; the only one with the atom bomb, the least scarred by modern war, an initiator of the United Nations that we thought would distribute Western influence throughout the world. Freedom and equality for each individual, government of, by, and for the people—these American values we found good, principles by which we could live as men. Many of us began maturing in complacency.

"As we grew, however, our comfort was penetrated by events too troubling to dismiss. First, the permeating and victimizing fact of human degradation, symbolized by the Southern struggle against racial bigotry, compelled most of us from silence to activism. Second, the enclosing fact of the Cold War, symbolized by the presence of the Bomb, brought awareness that we ourselves, and our friends, and millions of abstract 'others' we knew more directly because of our common peril, might die at any time. . . ."

—Port Huron Statement, 1962

45. The Port Huron Statement, excerpted above, can most clearly be seen as an important document in which of the following movements?

    (A) The labor union movement

    (B) The civil rights movement

    (C) The New Right

    (D) The New Left

46. The language of this document can be seen as a repudiation of which of the following policies or actions from the Eisenhower years?

    (A) The "New Look" foreign policy

    (B) Increases in funding for the United Nations

    (C) Intervention in the Little Rock, Arkansas, crisis

    (D) Renewed focus on education

47. The primary intended audience for the Port Huron Statement was

(A) African Americans in the South
(B) Government officials
(C) Middle-class college students
(D) Factory workers

48. The growth of the organization, through the remainder of the 1960s, that published the Port Huron Statement can best be understood in the context of

(A) rapid industrialization, urban growth and congestion, and corporate consolidation.
(B) the baby boom, economic growth, and a rapid expansion of higher education.
(C) economic polarization, supply-side economic policies, and the disappearance of the middle class.
(D) the proliferation of personal computer technologies, the rise of Christian fundamentalism, and an increase in student apathy.

QUESTIONS 49–51 ARE BASED ON THE FOLLOWING PASSAGE:

"An act for the more effectual protection of the property of married women:

"§1. The real property of any female who may hereafter marry, and which she shall own at the time of marriage, and the rents, issues, and profits thereof, shall not be subject to the sole disposal of her husband, nor be liable for his debts, and shall continue her sole and separate property, as if she were a single female.

"§2. The real and personal property, and the rents, issues, and profits thereof, of any female now married, shall not be subject to the disposal of her husband; but shall be her sole and separate property, as if she were a single female, except so far as the same may be liable for the debts of her husband heretofore contracted.

"§3. Any married female may take by inheritance, or by gift, grant, devise, or bequest, from any person other than her husband, and hold to her sole and separate use, and convey and devise real and personal property, and any interest or estate therein, and the rents, issues, and profits thereof, in the same manner and with like effect as if she were unmarried, and the same shall not be subject to the disposal of her husband nor be liable for his debts."

—Married Women's Property Act, New York State (1848)

49. The Married Women's Property Act was significant in that it

(A) expanded women's participation in the political sphere.
(B) challenged traditional understandings of women and property embodied in the legal concept of *femme covert*.
(C) codified the cultural assumptions implicit in the concept of "Republican motherhood."
(D) relegated women to a second-class status in regard to citizenship.

50. Which of the following groups would be most likely to support the perspective of the Married Women's Property Act?

    (A) Participants in the Seneca Falls Convention
    (B) Southern supporters of the concept of "female virtue"
    (C) Proponents of the "cult of domesticity" value system
    (D) Congregational ministers

51. The ideas expressed in the passage most directly reflect which of the following continuities in United States history?

    (A) Debates about access to voting rights
    (B) Debates about the role of federal government in marriage law
    (C) Debates about discrimination in employment
    (D) Debates about the legal status of women

QUESTIONS 52–53 REFER TO THE FOLLOWING QUOTATION:

"The law of love, peace and liberty in the states extending to Jews, Turks and Egyptians, as they are considered sonnes of Adam, which is the glory of the outward state of Holland, soe love, peace and liberty, extending to all in Christ Jesus, condemns hatred, war and bondage. And because our Saviour sayeth it is impossible but that offences will come, but woe unto him by whom they cometh, our desire is not to offend one of his little ones, in whatsoever form, name or title hee appears in, whether Presbyterian, Independent, Baptist or Quaker, but shall be glad to see anything of God in any of them, desiring to doe unto all men as we desire all men should doe unto us, which is the true law both of Church and State; for our Saviour sayeth this is the law and the prophets.

"Therefore if any of these said persons come in love unto us, we cannot in conscience lay violent hands upon them, but give them free egresse and regresse unto our Town, and houses, as God shall persuade our consciences, for we are bounde by the law of God and man to doe good unto all men and evil to noe man. And this is according to the patent and charter of our Towne, given unto us in the name of the States General, which we are not willing to infringe, and violate, but shall houlde to our patent and shall remaine, your humble subjects, the inhabitants of Vlishing (Flushing, part of the colony of New Netherlands)."

—*The Flushing Remonstrance*, 1657

52. Which of the following most accurately describes the context in which the document, above, was written?

(A) The Dutch West India Company had sought to establish a model community in the New World, based on Enlightenment principles; the document grew out of this mandate.

(B) The policies of the Dutch West Indian company had discouraged non-Dutch immigrants from settling in New Netherlands; the document was an attempt to diversify the colony.

(C) Religious toleration had become the norm in the neighboring New England colonies in the seventeenth century; the document was an attempt to bring New Amsterdam to the same levels of toleration.

(D) The director-general of the colony of New Netherlands, Peter Stuyvesant, was attempting to enforce conformity in New Netherlands despite the multi-ethnic makeup of the colony; the document was an attempt to accommodate the diverse population.

53. Which of the following was most significant in enshrining into the United States legal structure the ideas contained in the Flushing Remonstrance?

(A) The preamble of the Declaration of Independence
(B) The enumeration of congressional powers in the Constitution
(C) The "Free Exercise Clause" of the First Amendment
(D) The "Establishment Clause" of the First Amendment

QUESTIONS 54–55 REFER TO THE FOLLOWING PASSAGE:

"The petition of several poor negroes and mulattoes, who are inhabitants of the town of Dartmouth, humbly showeth,—

"That we being chiefly of the African extract, and by reason of long bondage and hard slavery, we have been deprived of enjoying the profits of our labor or the advantage of inheriting estates from our parents, as our neighbors the white people do, having some of us not long enjoyed our own freedom; yet of late, contrary to the invariable custom and practice of the country, we have been, and now are, taxed both in our polls and that small pittance of estate which, through much hard labor and industry, we have got together to sustain ourselves and families withall. We apprehend it, therefore, to be hard usage, and will doubtless (if continued) reduce us to a state of beggary, whereby we shall become a burthen to others, if not timely prevented by the interposition of your justice and your power.

"Your petitioners further show, that we apprehend ourselves to be aggrieved, in that, while we are not allowed the privilege of freemen of the State, having no vote or influence in the election of those that tax us, yet many of our colour (as is well known) have cheerfully entered the field of battle in the defence of the common cause, and that (as we conceive) against a similar exertion of power (in regard to taxation), too well known to need a recital in this place."

—Paul Cuffe's Petition, Massachusetts, 1780

54. The main purpose of the petition by Paul Cuffe was to demand

(A) that the petitioners be released from slavery because slavery was incompatible with the Massachusetts constitution.

(B) that the Massachusetts legislature extend reparations to the petitioners as compensation for their time in slavery.

(C) that the petitioners receive land that had been expropriated from loyalists in order to reward them for their service to the Continental Army during the American Revolution.

(D) that the Massachusetts legislature either grant the petitioners the right to vote or that it excuse them from paying taxes.

55. The petition by Paul Cuffe best illustrates which of the following developments?

(A) The rhetoric of the American Revolution raised awareness of social inequalities and inspired groups and individuals to call for greater political democracy.

(B) Slave rebellions, such as the Stono Rebellion, inspired enslaved Americans throughout North America to engage in similar behavior.

(C) African Americans who had fought with the British during the American Revolution felt doubly vulnerable—as African Americans and as traitors to the patriot cause—after the British defeat.

(D) African Americans received worse treatment under the state government of Massachusetts than they had under British law during the colonial period.

Part B: Short-Answer Questions

Directions: The following section contains four questions. Answer each of the questions, using the source material and your knowledge of American history. Note—students are not required to develop and support a thesis statement in responding to these questions. (45 minutes)

QUESTION 1 IS BASED ON THE FOLLOWING PASSAGE:

DECLARATION OF RIGHTS

"The members of this congress, sincerely devoted, with the warmest sentiments of affection and duty to His Majesty's person and government . . ., and with minds deeply impressed by a sense of the present and impending misfortunes of the British colonies on this continent; having considered as maturely as time would permit, the circumstances of said colonies, esteem it our indispensable duty to make the following declarations, of our humble opinions, respecting the most essential rights and liberties of the colonists, and of the grievances under which they labor, by reason of several late acts of Parliament.

"1st. That His Majesty's subjects in these colonies owe the same allegiance to the crown of Great Britain that is owing from his subjects born within the realm, and all due subordination to that august body, the Parliament of Great Britain.

"2d. That His Majesty's liege subjects in these colonies are entitled to all the inherent rights and privileges of his natural born subjects within the kingdom of Great Britain.

"3d. That it is inseparably essential to the freedom of a people, and the undoubted rights of Englishmen, that no taxes should be imposed on them, but with their own consent, given personally, or by their representatives.

"4th. That the people of these colonies are not, and from their local circumstances cannot be, represented in the House of Commons in Great Britain.

"5th. That the only representatives of the people of these colonies are persons chosen therein, by themselves; and that no taxes ever have been or can be constitutionally imposed on them but by their respective legislatures.

"6th. That all supplies to the crown, being free gifts of the people, it is unreasonable and Inconsistent With The Principles And Spirit Of The British Constitution For The People Of Great Britain To Grant To His Majesty The Property Of The Colonists. . . ."

—*The Declaration of Rights of the Stamp Act Congress*, 1765

1. Use the excerpt from "The Declaration of Rights of the Stamp Act Congress" above and your knowledge of United States history to answer parts A, B, and C.

    (A) How did British political leaders, most notably Prime Minister George Grenville, respond to the arguments put forth by the Stamp Act Congress in the labeled points "3rd," "4th," and "5th"?

    (B) How does the tone of this declaration differ from Thomas Paine's pamphlet, *Common Sense*, published in January 1776? Use evidence from this declaration to support your answer.

    (C) Describe the context of the meeting of the Stamp Act Declaration in terms of relations between Great Britain and its thirteen North American colonies.

"The Tournament of To-Day.—A Set-To Between Labor and Monopoly," *Puck,* 1883

2. Use the image above and your knowledge of United States history to answer parts A, B, and C.

    (A) Explain the point of view of the above cartoon, published in 1883.

    (B) Discuss specific events from the era that the cartoon was published that would support the point of view of the cartoon (1865–1900).

    (C) Discuss the continuities and changes between the period the cartoon was published and the period of the New Deal of the 1930s in regard to the position of labor in society, as depicted in the cartoon above.

"It is too true that there are public journals who try to dignify this mob by some respectable appellation. The Herald characterizes it as the people, and the World as the laboring men of the City. These are libels that ought to have paralyzed the fingers that penned them. It is ineffably infamous to attribute to the people, or to the laboring men of this metropolis, such hideous barbarism as this horde has been displaying. The people of New-York and the laboring men of New-York are not incendiaries, nor robbers, nor assassins. They do not hunt down men whose only offence is the color God gave them; they do not chase, and insult; and beat women; they do not pillage an asylum for orphan children, and burn the very roof over those orphans' heads. They are civilized beings, valuing law and respecting decency; and they regard with unqualified abhorrence the doings of the tribe of savages that have sought to bear rule in their midst."

—Editorial, *New York Times*, July 15, 1863

"To the Editor of the New-York Times:

"You will, no doubt, be hard on us rioters tomorrow morning, but that 300-dollar law has made us nobodies, vagabonds and cast-outs of society, for whom nobody cares when we must go to war and be shot down. We are the poor rabble, and the rich rabble is our enemy by this law. Therefore we will give our enemy battle right here, and ask no quarter. Although we got hard fists, and are dirty without, we have soft hearts, and have clean consciences within, and that's the reason we love our wives and children more than the rich, because we got not much besides them, and we will not go and leave them at home for to starve. Until that draft law is repealed, I for one am willing to knock down more such rum-hole politicians as Kennedy. Why don't they let the nigger kill the slave-driving race and take possession of the South, as it belongs to them."

—Letter to the editor of the *New York Times,* signed
"A poor man, but a man for all that," July 15, 1863

3. Use the two documents above and your knowledge of United States history to answer parts A, B, and C.

    (A) Explain the source of the anger of the participants of the riot described in both documents.

    (B) Explain how the point of view of the letter to the editor of the *New York Times* differs from the point of view of the paper's editorial.

    (C) Compare the event described in the documents with one of the three following events in United States history:

    Shays' Rebellion (1786–1787)
    March of Coxey's Army (1894)
    Tulsa race riot (1921)

QUESTION 4 IS BASED ON THE FOLLOWING IMAGE:

THE NEGRO IN HIS OWN COUNTRY.

THE NEGRO IN AMERICA.

—Josiah Priest, 1852

4. Use the image above and your knowledge of United States history to answer parts A, B, and C.

(A) Explain the point of view reflected in the image above regarding slavery.

(B) Explain how the point of view reflected in the image represents a shift in thinking among southern planters in regard to slavery from earlier (before 1830) ideas about slavery.

(C) Explain how the point of view in the image above reflects the context in which the image was produced (with attention to the period 1830–1852).

SECTION II

Part A: Document-Based Question

> **Directions:** The following question is based on the accompanying Documents 1–7. This question is designed to test your ability to apply several historical thinking skills simultaneously, including historical argumentation, use of relevant historical evidence, and contextualization. Your response should be based on your analysis of the documents and your knowledge of the topic. (60 minutes)

WRITE A WELL-INTEGRATED ESSAY THAT DOES THE FOLLOWING:

- States an appropriate thesis that directly addresses all parts of the question.
- Supports the thesis or an appropriate argument with evidence from all or all but one of the documents AND your knowledge of United States history beyond/outside the documents.
- Analyzes a majority of the documents in terms of such features as their intended audience, purpose, point of view, format, argumentation, and/or social context as appropriate to the argument.
- Places the argument in the context of broader regional, national, or global processes.

Question 1.

What was the economic, political, and social context of the conflict between congressional Republicans and President Andrew Johnson in regard to plans for Reconstruction in the South? Use the documents and your knowledge of the years 1864–1877 in your answer.

Document 1

Source: Abraham Lincoln, Second Inaugural Address, March 4, 1865.

   With malice toward none, with charity for all, with firmness in the right as God gives us to see the right, let us strive on to finish the work we are in, to bind up the nation's wounds, to care for him who shall have borne the battle and for his widow and his orphan, to do all which may achieve and cherish a just and lasting peace among our-selves and with all nations.

Document 2

Source: Mississippi legal codes, "An Act to Confer Civil Rights on Freedmen, and for other Purposes," 1865.

An Act to Amend the Vagrant Laws of the State

Section 1. All rogues and vagabonds, idle and dissipated persons, beggars, jugglers, or persons practicing unlawful games or plays, runaways, common drunkards, common night—walkers, pilferers, lewd, wanton, or lascivious persons, in speech or behavior, common railers and brawlers, persons who neglect their calling or employment, misspend what they earn, or do not provide for the support of themselves or their families, or dependents, and all other idle and disorderly persons, including all who neglect all lawful business, habitually misspend their time by frequenting houses of ill—fame, gaming—houses, or tippling shops, shall be deemed and considered vagrants, under the provisions of this act, and upon conviction thereof shall be fined not exceeding one hundred dollars, with all accruing costs, and be imprisoned, at the discretion of the court, not exceeding ten days.

Section 2. All freedmen, free negroes and mulattoes in this State, over the age of eighteen years, found on the second Monday in January, 1866, or thereafter, with no lawful employment or business, or found unlawful assembling themselves together, either in the day or night time, and all white persons assembling themselves with freedmen, Free negroes or mulattoes, or usually associating with freedmen, free negroes or mulattoes, on terms of equality, or living in adultery or fornication with a freed woman, freed negro or mulatto, shall be deemed vagrants, and on conviction thereof shall be fined in a sum not exceeding, in the case of a freedman, free negro or mulatto, fifty dollars, and a white man two hundred dollars, and imprisonment at the discretion of the court, the free negro not exceeding ten days, and the white man not exceeding six months.

Document 3

Source: "Acts of the General Assembly of Louisiana Regulating Labor, Extra Session," 1865.

[Each laborer] shall not be allowed to leave his place of employment, until the fulfillment of his contract, unless by consent of his employer, or on account of harsh treatment, or breach of contraction the part of the employer; and if they do so leave, without cause of permission, they shall forfeit all wages earned to the time of abandonment. . . .

In cases of sickness of the laborer, wages for the time lost shall be deducted, and where the sickness is feigned for purpose of idleness, . . . and also should refusal to work be continued beyond three days, the offender shall be reported to a justice of the peace, and shall be forced to labor on roads, levee, and other public works, without pay, until the offender consents to return to his labor.

When in health, the laborer shall work ten hours during the day in the summer, and nine hours during the day in winter, unless otherwise stipulated in the labor contract; he shall obey all proper orders of his employer or his agent. . . . Failure to obey reasonable orders, neglect of duty, and leaving home without permission will be deemed disobedience; impudence, swearing, or indecent language to or in the presence of the employer, his family or agent . . . shall be deemed disobedience. . . . For all absence from home without leave, the laborer will be fined at the rate of two dollars per day.

Document 4

Source: "Selling a Freeman to Pay His Fine at Monticello, Florida," *Frank Leslie's Illustrated Newspaper*, January 19, 1867.

—American Social History Project

Document 5

Source: Petition to United States Congress, South Carolina Colored People's Convention, November 1865.

We simply desire that we shall be recognized as men; that we have no obstructions placed in our way; that the same laws which govern white men shall direct colored men; that we have the right of trial by a jury of our peers, that schools be opened or established for our children; that we be permitted to acquire homesteads for ourselves and children; that we be dealt with as others, in equity and justice.

We claim the confidence and good-will of all classes of men; we ask that the same chances be extended to us that freemen should demand at the hands of their fellow-citizens. We desire the prosperity and growth of this State and the well-being of all men, and shall be found ever struggling to elevate ourselves and add to the national character; and we trust the day will not be distant when you will acknowledge that by our rapid progress in moral, social, religious and intellectual development that you will cheerfully accord to us the high commendation that we are worthy, with you, to enjoy all political emoluments—when we shall realize the truth that "all men are endowed by their Creator with inalienable rights," and that on the American continent this is the right of all, whether he come from east, west, north or south; and, although complexions may differ, "a man's a man for that."

Document 6

Sources: Speech, Samuel J. Tilden, leader of the Democratic Party, New York, 1868.

[The Republican Party] resolved to make the black race the governing power in those States, and by means of them to bring into Congress twenty senators and fifty representatives practically appointed by itself in Washington. . . .

The effect of a gain to the Republican party of twenty senators and fifty representatives is to strengthen its hold on the Federal Government. . . . Nor is there the slightest doubt that the paramount object and motive of the Republican party is by these means to secure itself against a reaction of opinion adverse to it in our great populous Northern commonwealths. The effect of its system and its own real purpose is to establish a domination over us of the Northern states.

Document 7

Source: Thaddeus Stevens, speech in Congress, January 3, 1867.

Since the surrender of the armies of the confederate States of America a little has been done toward establishing this Government upon the true principles of liberty and justice; and but a little if we stop here. We have broken the material shackles of four million slaves. We have unchained them from the stake so as to allow them locomotion, provided they do not walk in paths which are trod by white men. We have allowed them the privilege of attending church, if they can do so without offending the sight of their former masters. We have imposed on them the privilege of fighting our battles, of dying in defense of freedom, and of bearing their equal portion of taxes; but where have we given them the privilege of ever participating in the formation of the laws for the government of their native land?

What is negro equality, about which so much is said by knaves and some of which is believed by men who are not fools? It means, as understood by honest Republicans, just this much, and no more: every man, no matter what his race or colour; every earthly being who has an immortal soul, has an equal right to justice, honesty, and fair play with every other man; and the law should secure him those rights. The same law, which condemns or acquits an African, should condemn or acquit a white man.

Part B: Long Essay Questions

Choose ONE of the following questions and write an analytical essay that uses specific, relevant evidence to support your thesis and to demonstrate the specified historical thinking skill. *Historical Thinking Skill: Historical Causation. Thematic Learning Objectives: America in the World, #5 (for question 1) and #7 (for question 2).* (35 minutes)

1. Historians debate the long-term and short-term causes of the Mexican-American War. Analyze the relative importance of the different causes of the war.

2. Historians debate the long-term and short-term causes of the Spanish-American War. Analyze the relative importance of the different causes of the war.

ANSWER KEY
Practice Exam 1

1. **(C)**	11. **(D)**	21. **(D)**	31. **(B)**	41. **(D)**	51. **(D)**
2. **(A)**	12. **(A)**	22. **(B)**	32. **(D)**	42. **(C)**	52. **(D)**
3. **(C)**	13. **(A)**	23. **(D)**	33. **(C)**	43. **(D)**	53. **(C)**
4. **(A)**	14. **(D)**	24. **(A)**	34. **(B)**	44. **(B)**	54. **(D)**
5. **(A)**	15. **(D)**	25. **(B)**	35. **(A)**	45. **(D)**	55. **(A)**
6. **(C)**	16. **(A)**	26. **(D)**	36. **(C)**	46. **(A)**	
7. **(B)**	17. **(C)**	27. **(A)**	37. **(B)**	47. **(C)**	
8. **(C)**	18. **(A)**	28. **(B)**	38. **(C)**	48. **(B)**	
9. **(D)**	19. **(B)**	29. **(B)**	39. **(D)**	49. **(B)**	
10. **(C)**	20. **(C)**	30. **(C)**	40. **(A)**	50. **(A)**	

PRACTICE EXAM 1
Answers and Explanations to Multiple-Choice Questions

1. **(C)** Garrison is arguing that free African Americans should be granted citizenship and equality in the United States. Advocates of colonization believed that slaves either could not or should not receive treatment as equals in the United States, and should therefore go to Africa. Garrison broke with the colonization movement. He said all slaves should be immediately freed, that there should be no compensation to their owners, and that freed slaves were entitled to the same rights as white people. Garrison was one of the leading white figures in the abolitionist movement that grew in strength after 1830. He is in general agreement with the men in the other three choices about the need for immediate abolition of slavery.

2. **(A)** Garrison is specifically calling for equality and citizenship for free African Americans in the United States. The decision in the *Dred Scott* case asserted the exact opposite; it stipulated that African Americans, whether slave or free, could not be American citizens and therefore had no standing to sue in federal court. *Ex parte Milligan* (1866) (B) held that military tribunals, used on occasion during the Civil War, were unconstitutional when civilian courts were functioning. *Pace v. Alabama* (1883) ruled that Alabama's anti-miscegenation statute was constitutional. *Plessy v. Ferguson* (1896) (D) allowed for segregated facilities, using the principle, "separate but equal."

3. **(C)** With ratification of the Fourteenth Amendment (1868), African Americans were granted citizenship in the United States. This amendment, ratified during Reconstruction, also stated that no person shall be denied "equal protection of the laws." This was a vindication of the position that Garrison took a generation earlier. Garrisonians would have endorsed the developments in the other three choices, but those choices did not specifically bestow citizenship on African Americans.

4. **(A)** The differences in the two maps illustrate the result of the Articles of Confederation government successfully handling the question of western lands. After the United States victory in the American Revolution, there was a great deal of debate about status area between the Appalachian Mountains and the Mississippi River. Some states

insisted that western land claims from the colonial period should be honored, while other states had no claims on this land. Maryland, a state with no western land claims, insisted that it would not ratify the Articles until all states gave up their land claims and the western lands became part of a national domain. Congress persuaded the states with claims to do just that. The handling of western lands was considered one of the major successes of the Articles of Confederation government. The maps do not indicate any French land claims (B), nor do they refer to slavery (C). By the time of the "Quasi-war" (1798–1800) (D), western land claims by the various states had long been settled.

5. **(A)** The Northwest Ordinance did not recognize the land claims of the American Indians in the region that dated from the period of British rule. The act encouraged fair treatment of native peoples, but it did recognize their earlier claims to the land, setting the stage for a series of clashes between whites and American Indians during the 1780s and 1790s in the Ohio River Valley and Great Lakes region. In general the Northwest Ordinance is considered an important piece of legislation from the "critical period." It divided up the land and provided a plot in every town for public schools. The Northwest Ordinance spelled out the steps that these areas would have to go through in order to become states, on equal footing with the original thirteen states (C). In addition, the Northwest Ordinance banned slavery in the Northwest Territory (B).

6. **(C)** In many ways the Spanish-American War can be seen as a turning point in American history. After the war, the United States became a colonial power like Britain, the nation Americans had defeated in order to establish their own independence. The United States and Spain negotiated the Treaty of Paris (1898) following the war. In the treaty, Spain agreed to cede the Philippines, Puerto Rico, and Guam to the United States; the United States agreed to pay Spain $20 million for these possessions. The cartoon is depicting problems that ensued in these newly acquired lands. However, the cartoon does not question the wisdom of American policy, nor does it display empathy for residents of the newly acquired lands. Rather, it portrays them as unruly children that the United States needs to discipline.

7. **(B)** Following the Spanish-American War in 1898, the United States gained control of the Philippines, Puerto Rico, and Cuba. The acquisition of new territories generated a great deal of debate in the United States. Many Americans wondered aloud what do to with these newly acquired territories. The cartoon reflects contemporary racist notions about the inhabitants of the Philippines, Puerto Rico, and Cuba—asserting that they are childlike, unruly, and violent. The cartoon suggests that only the strong hand of the United States could steady these peoples and prepare them for self-government at some point in the future.

8. **(C)** In the period following the Spanish-American War (1898), the United States expanded its economic and military presence in the Caribbean and Latin America, and increased its involvement in Asia. America's more active role in the world was due, in large part, to the aggressive foreign policy of President Theodore Roosevelt (1901–1909). He envisioned the United States acting as the world's policeman, punishing wrongdoers. He claimed that the United States had the right to militarily intervene in the nations of Latin America. This assertion of American might is known as the Roosevelt Corollary to the Monroe Doctrine. Roosevelt's aggressive approach to Latin America is clearly evident in regard to Panama. Panama had been part of Colombia. With the backing of

President Roosevelt and the United States military, pro-American Panamanians instigated a "rebellion" against Colombia. Panama became an independent country and immediately reached a deal with the United States to build a canal. With the acquisition of Pacific territories and with an increased interest in trade with China, American policymakers became interested in a shortcut to the Pacific.

9. **(D)** The excerpt from the presidential veto message is from President Andrew Johnson's veto of one of the Reconstruction Acts of 1867. The message alludes to treating the ten former Confederate states (excluding Tennessee) as military districts. This was a central aspect of the acts. These sweeping acts divided the South into five military districts. These areas could only rejoin the United States if they guaranteed basic rights to African Americans. The radicals were not able to fully carry out their program. They were not able to extend land ownership to African Americans, nor did they carry out mass arrests of former Confederates.

10. **(C)** Governor Orval Faubus's response to the steps taken by President Dwight Eisenhower to resolve the Little Rock crisis in 1957 echoes the sentiment of President Andrew Johnson in 1867. Faubus knew that alluding to the Reconstruction period would resonate among white southerners; bitterness over that period was still present in the collective memory of white southerners almost a hundred years later. The conflict began when local authorities had decided to allow nine African-American students to enroll in Central High School at the beginning of the school year in 1957. Governor Orville Faubus refused to cooperate with the plan, leading to mob action and violence outside of the high school. The violence and the national news coverage of the flaunting of federal authority convinced Eisenhower to send federal troops. The use of federal troops in a southern state provided Faubus with a metaphor that aroused bitterness almost a century after Reconstruction.

11. **(D)** The 1883 cartoon makes the point that incoming immigrants faced a myriad of dangers when they arrived in America, just as the Pilgrims did when they arrived in the seventeenth century. The dangers immigrants faced in the late nineteenth century included crooked money-changers, baggage handlers who stole all of the immigrant's worldly possessions, landlords renting out substandard housing, and employers looking to exploit cheap labor. This is a rare pro-immigrant cartoon. Most cartoons of the period saw immigrants as a threat to the United States in one way or another (A), (B), and (C).

12. **(A)** The founding of Hull House in Chicago (1889) by Jane Addams and Ellen Gates Starr represents a continuity with the political sentiments expressed in the cartoon above. Both the cartoon and the settlement house movement demonstrate empathy for the predicament that recent immigrants often found themselves in. Settlement houses, such as Hull House, were established to aid immigrants, especially immigrant women. By 1911 more than 400 settlement houses existed in the United States, usually run by women. The other choices all reflect aspects of the nativist, or anti-immigrant, movement.

13. **(A)** The 1936 cartoon is making the point that although European individuals and countries might be seduced into waging another major war, the United States would be wise to avoid participating. The cartoon is an expression of isolationism, which became

a common sentiment among many Americans between the two world wars. The cartoon is implying that war may be seductive, but it is also brutal and deadly. Many Americans had vivid memories of World War I, and many had lost friends and loved-ones. Ultimately, many asked, was it worth it? In addition, the Senate's Nye committee (1934–1937) uncovered evidence that certain American corporations greatly profited from World War I. Americans wondered if the so-called merchants of death had pushed the country into World War I.

14. **(D)** The position of Martin Luther King, Jr., in 1967 paralleled, in many ways, the sentiment of the cartoon in the question. Both argued against military involvement in foreign conflicts, and both held that the conflicts in question—World War I and the Vietnam War—did not have the potential to significantly advance American interests in the world. Initially, King did not take a position on the Vietnam War, focusing instead on domestic civil rights issues. However, King began to see the disproportionate role that African Americans played on the front lines of Vietnam, and he began to see the war as a question of morality and justice. In 1965 King began to publicly express doubts about the Vietnam War. In a 1967 appearance at the Riverside Church in New York City King delivered a speech titled "Beyond Vietnam: A Time to Break Silence."

15. **(D)** The passage is part of President Truman's argument to Congress in favor of an extension of aid to Greece and Turkey. As part of the policy of containment, the United States extended military aid to Greece and Turkey in 1947. The aid was successful. It helped the Greek monarchy put down a communist-influenced rebel movement. Further, the move quieted Republican criticism of Truman and improved Truman's standing in public opinion polls; he won reelection the following year.

16. **(A)** The passage can best be seen as providing a rationale for the policy of containment. In order to block any further aggression by the Soviet Union, Truman issued the Truman Doctrine (1947), in which he said that the goal of the United States would be to contain communism. The containment approach to the Soviet Union had been spelled out in an article entitled "Sources of Soviet Conduct," published in *Foreign Affairs* (1947). Containment remained the cornerstone of American foreign policy for decades to come.

17. **(C)** The ideas expressed in the passage most directly reflect a continuity with debates about the role of the United States in world affairs. This debate emerged as early as President George Washington's Proclamation of Neutrality (1793), as war broke out between France and Great Britain. It can be seen in the aftermath of the American victory in the Spanish-American War (1898) and in the lead-up to both World Wars.

18. **(A)** The political cartoon is making the point that government officials were taking their crusade against immoral behavior to extreme lengths. The cartoon is depicting Anthony Comstock, a former United States postal inspector and the public face of the moral reform movement, dragging a woman into court and, absurdly, accusing her of giving birth to a "naked child." Although the cartoon is satirical, Comstock's actual actions were only slightly less outrageous. For example, he prohibited certain anatomy textbooks from being sent to medical students. The 1873 Comstock Law outlawed the distribution of information or devices related to contraception. Comstock repeatedly clashed with birth-control advocate Margaret Sanger.

19. **(B)** The cartoon reflects a point of view in the ongoing debate about the role of the federal government in regulating morality. This debate can be seen in the lead-up to the ratification of the Eighteenth Amendment in 1919. The Eighteenth Amendment called for a ban on the manufacture, sale, and transportation of alcoholic beverages. The movement to ban alcohol from American society was one of the largest movements in the nineteenth and early twentieth centuries. The debate can also be seen in 1960s in discussions of various forms of birth control, including "the pill," as well as in recent debates around gay marriage and marijuana policy.

20. **(C)** The issue that precipitated the speech was the passage of an act creating higher tariff rates. The act, known by its critics as the "Tariff of Abominations," dramatically raised tariff rates on many items, and led to a general reduction in trade between the United States and Europe. This decline in trade hit South Carolina's cotton plantations especially hard. By 1832, John C. Calhoun and other South Carolina political leaders asserted the right of states to nullify federal legislation. Under the theory of nullification, a state could declare an objectionable law null and void within that state. President Jackson, a defender of states' rights, was, nonetheless, alarmed at this blatant flouting of federal authority. He pushed for passage of the Force Bill, which authorized military force against South Carolina for committing treason. At the same time, Congress revised tariff rates, providing relief for South Carolina. The Force Bill and the new tariff rates, passed by Congress on the same day, amounted to a face-saving compromise.

21. **(D)** The debate over nullification and the debate over ratifying the Constitution are similar in that in both the issue of the power of the states was at stake. Under the Articles of Confederation, the states had a great deal more power. Those who defended the Articles—the Antifederalists—used language strikingly similar to Calhoun's. In the excerpt above, Calhoun argues, "to reserve such exclusive right to the General Government . . . is to convert it, in fact, into a great consolidated government, with unlimited powers, and to divest the States, in reality, of all their rights. . . ." Such an argument echoes the arguments of the Antifederalists against the Constitution.

22. **(B)** Calhoun's protest included the threat of state nullification of federal decisions. He even threatened to consider secession if other measures did not work. This form of protest can also be seen in the response of New England Federalists to the War of 1812. The Hartford Convention (1814) raised the very real possibility that New England would secede from the United States in order to protect its economic and maritime trade interests. Although talk of nullification and secession is more associated with southern political leaders, it was also uttered in the intense debates about the War of 1812. The war ended before the Federalists could follow through on their threat.

23. **(D)** The main point of the cartoon is that President Franklin D. Roosevelt has a secret agenda. He claims that he is creating programs to help people, but secretly he is attempting to create some sort of dictatorship that would take away people's freedom. The cartoon reflects conservative criticisms of the New Deal. Note that the presence of a "Trojan horse" in a political cartoon implies that someone has a sinister agenda different from his stated agenda.

24. **(A)** This cartoon is taking a position in the debate about the proper role of the federal government in the economy. This debate first became part of the national agenda during the Progressive era of the early decades of the twentieth century, when reformers insisted that the federal government should play a greater role in regulating economic activity in the United States. The debate continued through the New Deal, the Great Society, and into the debates in recent decades about the federal government playing a role in reforming the health care system. Some conservatives accused the Supreme Court of legislating from the bench in the 1950s and 1960s, under Chief Justice Earl Warren (B). Conservative opposition to the New Deal did not center on issues of states' rights or the power of the states (C). The country was not at war in 1933 (D).

25. **(B)** The sentiment reflected in the cartoon was similar to opposition by the Republican Party to the creation of Great Society programs in the 1960s. Johnson's Great Society programs included Medicare and Medicaid. The Medicare program provides health care for every American reaching the age of sixty-five. The main components of Johnson's Great Society were landmark civil rights acts as well as a comprehensive "war on poverty." Many aspects of Johnson's Great Society were underfunded as the federal government spent more and more on the Vietnam War. In both the 1930s and the 1960s, conservatives argued that the federal government's reach was extending beyond its traditional limits and threatening individual liberty and the Constitution.

26. **(D)** William Graham Sumner is associated with the intellectual movement, social Darwinism. Followers of Sumner and his book, *What Social Classes Owe to Each Other*, would most likely have advocated a laissez-faire approach to the economy. The French phrase *laissez-faire* means "to let alone." It describes a government policy that would take a hands-off approach in regard to economic activities. Social Darwinism was an attempt to apply Charles Darwin's ideas about the natural world to social relations. Sumner was attracted to Darwin's ideas about competition and "survival of the fittest." He argued against any attempt at government intervention into the economic and social spheres. Interference, he argued, would hinder the evolution of the human species. The inequalities of wealth that characterized the late 1800s were part of the process of "survival of the fittest." Social Darwinism appealed to owners of large corporations, because it both justified their wealth and power and warned against any type of regulation or reform.

27. **(A)** The ideas of social Darwinism justified the success of those at the top of the socio-economic structure as both appropriate and inevitable. Sumner argues that we should let nature run its course; to do otherwise could lead to disaster. He argues, "We can only, by interfering with [the natural order], produce the survival of the unfittest. . . ." He therefore was against government regulations of economic activity.

28. **(B)** The law, excerpted in the question, mandated that citizens in Pennsylvania do not cooperate with slave-catchers, seeking to capture fugitive slaves. The fugitive slave clause of the Constitution was present from the drafting of the Constitution, but it was given teeth later in history, with the passage of the Fugitive Slave Act, as part of the Compromise of 1850. Even before that act was passed, states were not allowed to pass laws that went directly against return slaves to their owners. The Supreme Court declared the Pennsylvania law invalid in 1842.

29. **(B)** The existence of the Pennsylvania law, excerpted in the question, demonstrates an ongoing tension between federal and state law. The Supremacy Clause of the Constitution states that the Constitution and federal laws and treaties are the "supreme law of the land." Therefore, state laws must operate within the bounds of the Constitution, as defined by the Supreme Court. However, states repeatedly asserted their right to do as they pleased in the antebellum period, hoping the federal government would not try to enforce the Constitution. This tension persisted into the twentieth century, with many white southerners vowing "massive resistance" to federal edicts against segregation.

30. **(C)** The conflict around the Pennsylvania law reflected the ambiguous nature of slavery in the Constitution. The framers of the Constitution were, to some degree, uneasy with the institution. This uneasiness is reflected in the fact that the word "slavery" is not mentioned in the entire document. Slaves are often referred to as "other persons." Although the framers of the Constitution did not mention the word slavery, they were willing to compromise on the issue and postpone any final decision about slavery to the future. This postponement led to decades of debate and conflict over the issue.

31. **(B)** Dorothea Dix's testimony to the Massachusetts legislature reflects the influence of the Second Great Awakening. The movement spoke to many of the men who were brought into the larger society by the "market revolution." The Second Great Awakening told the individual that salvation was also in his or her hands. Righteous living, self-control, and a strong moral compass would lead to salvation. This idea that one could determine his or her eternal life was very different from the old Puritan notion of predestination, which held that one's eternal life was planned out by God. The Second Great Awakening not only encouraged individual redemption, but also societal reformation. Not only could one become perfect in the eyes of God, but one could work to perfect society as well. In this respect the Second Great Awakening acted as a springboard for a variety of reform movements.

32. **(D)** Dorothea Dix's research and testimony is best understood in the context of the rise of voluntary organizations to promote religious and secular reforms. This activism was inspired in part by the Second Great Awakening. The era also saw the rise of the abolitionist movement, the women's rights movement, and the temperance movement. Women did not gain the right to vote in several states until the late 1800s (A). Dix's activism was not motivated by an economic downturn (B); on the contrary, many historians note that the Second Great Awakening and the market revolution went hand in hand, suggesting such activism occurred in an expanding economy. Dix was making her argument to the Massachusetts states government, not the federal government (C). It is not until the twentieth century that the federal government begins to play a role in issues of health and poverty.

33. **(C)** The song lyrics appeared in a populist newspaper in the 1890s. The allusions to monopolies, railroads, and party bosses indicate that this song was meant to publicize the plight of farmers in the late 1800s. The populist movement tapped into growing discontent among farmers in the West about the economic bind they found themselves in and became a formidable force in the 1890s. The populists grew angry at the concentration of wealth and power by eastern industrialists. They supported a national income tax so that those with higher incomes would pay more than the poor. They also supported free and unlimited coinage of silver. Populists wanted the United States to get

off the gold standard and to issue money backed by silver as well. This would increase the amount of money in circulation and would lead to inflation. Farmers supported inflationary policies so that the prices they received for their produce would increase.

34. **(B)** The farmers' movement pushed state governments to pass laws regulating railroad rates and practices. These laws, known as Granger laws, had limited effectiveness. In the 1886 *Wabash* case, the Supreme Court limited the ability of states to regulate railroads. In response, the federal government created the Interstate Commerce Commission (1887) to regulate railroads. However, the ICC was chronically underfunded and was, therefore, ineffective.

35. **(A)** The era saw widespread corruption in government; this is hinted at in the allusion to old party bosses. As the extent of corruption in government became more widely known, from the Grant Administration in Washington to Tammany Hall in New York City, activists demanded reform of local, state, and national governments. Some activists hoped that the broad coalition described in choice B could form, but differences in race, ethnicity, and location made such a coalition untenable. The farmers did create a third party, the Populist Party, but it remained just that—a third party; it did not rise in prominence on a national level to compete with the two main political parties (C). The "Indian Wars" of the West were over by the 1890s (D).

36. **(C)** The passage from Marcus Garvey is best understood as an expression of black nationalism. Garvey is best known for urging African Americans to return to their ancestral homelands in Africa. Not many African Americans made the journey, but Garvey instilled a sense of pride among many African Americans; in this he is seen as an important figure in the movement for black nationalism.

37. **(B)** Marcus Garvey argued for African Americans to build separate institutions to demand greater power. His activism highlights the ongoing debate between separatism and integration in regard to the place of African Americans in American society. There are echoes of this tension in the 1960s between King's call for integration and the rise of the "Black Power" movement.

38. **(C)** The excerpt above, from the essay by Glenda Elizabeth Gilmore, implies that historians of the Progressive movement have not written extensively on the contributions of black women to progressivism in the South because of a scarcity of documentary evidence. She argues that African-American women "remained invisible in virtually every discussion of southern progressivism" because they did not have access to the public expressions of activism that white women did. She implies that it is the job of the historian to recognize this limitation, and to figure out other ways of studying the activities of black women in the Progressive movement.

39. **(D)** The efforts by black women to participate in the southern Progressive movement occurred in the context of a nadir in race relations in the United States as "scientific" ideas about race, inaction by the federal government, and rigid segregation in the South relegated African Americans to a second-class status in the United States. The year 1896, the beginning of Gilmore's study, was also the year the Supreme Court issued the *Plessy v. Ferguson* decision, giving sanction to segregation, on a "separate but equal" basis.

40. **(A)** The letter by Washington reflects his position in the ongoing debate about the proper balance between liberty and order. This is the debate that also occurred around President Abraham Lincoln's suspension of habeas corpus during the Civil War, around the Espionage and Sedition Acts during World War I, around the Japanese internment during World War II, and around the McCarran Internal Security Act of 1950. It is occurring today around the 2001 Patriot Act.

41. **(D)** Washington came to believe that the Articles of Confederation government erred in allowing for too great a degree of democracy. There was a heated debate in the 1780s about the appropriate degree of democratic participation in society and about the nature of the public. Many of the political leaders who coalesced around the Federalist point of view on the Constitution came to believe that too much democracy was dangerous. There fears would be borne out in the coming weeks when Shays' Rebellion began in Massachusetts. This was a central reason that Washington, Hamilton, and other Federalists wanted to replace the Articles of Confederation with the Constitution.

42. **(C)** George Washington is expressing great unease with the ability of the government under the Articles of Confederation to maintain order in the United States. He was worried about the lack of strong authority in the United States. People who shared this view would have supported the ratification of the Constitution, as Washington himself did. People who favored order over democracy would certainly not have supported the revolutionary French government in 1793 (A). Supporters of increasing the power and authority of the central government generally supported the chartering of a national government (B). The Alien and Sedition Acts imposed greater order and restraints on the people (D); therefore, someone who shared Washington's sentiments would have supported it, not opposed it.

43. **(D)** The actions of the Paxton Boys represent ongoing tensions between backcountry settlers and elites within colonial America. In the aftermath of the French and Indian War and of Pontiac's Rebellion, a vigilante group of these Scots-Irish immigrants organized raids against American Indians on the Pennsylvania frontier. These raids included an attack on Conestoga Indians in 1763 that resulted in twenty deaths. After the attacks on the Conestoga, in January 1764, about 250 Paxton Boys marched to Philadelphia to present their grievances to the Pennsylvania legislature. Tensions began to develop around this time between colonists and British authorities (A), but the Paxton boys are citing resentment at local elites, not British authorities. Tensions did exist among Indian groups allied with different European powers (B); this was evident in the Beaver Wars of the 1600s. Tensions existed in colonial America between freed African Americans and white planters (C), as evidenced in court proceedings, changing attitudes of whites, and legislative acts, but this was not central to the grievances of the Paxton Boys.

44. **(B)** Bacon's Rebellion and the March of the Paxton Boys form a clear continuity in colonial American history in that both events were precipitated by tensions on the frontier between backcountry settlers and American Indians; both events reflected resentment by the western backcountry settlers against the eastern colonial elites; both events reflect differing opinions around policies in regard to American Indians: and both involved extralegal violence. The other events reflected tensions in colonial America, but do not represent as clear a continuity as Bacon's Rebellion does.

45. **(D)** The Port Huron Statement, written and approved by Students for a Democratic Society, was an important foundational document of the emerging New Left of the 1960s. It raises a host of concerns that shaped the New Left of the 1960s—poverty, racism, the misguided priorities of an affluent society, the proliferation of nuclear bombs, the paranoia of the anticommunist crusade. The New Left was supportive of the civil rights movement (B); however, this document reflects the concerns of middle-class students, "bred in at least modest comfort." The New Left was generally supportive of workers' rights and just wages for working-class people, but it was often at odds with some of the more conservative political positions of large unions (including anticommunism and support for the war in Vietnam) (A). The concerns in the Port Huron Statement are far different from the agenda of the New Right (D). In some ways, the New Right can be seen as a reaction to the rise of the New Left.

46. **(A)** The "New Look" foreign policy shifted American military priorities away from conventional forces and toward increased reliance on nuclear weapons. The Port Huron Statement expressed concern about the proliferation of nuclear weapons that occurred, in part, as a result of the "New Look" foreign policy. United States funding for the United Nations increased in the 1950s (B); however, the sentiments in the Port Huron Statement are not critical of the United Nations. The Port Huron Statement expressly embraces the "southern struggle" for racial justice; as such, it would have supported Eisenhower's intervention in the Little Rock crisis (C). The United States devoted additional resources to education, especially in math and science, in the wake of the Sputnik launch (D); the Port Huron Statement contains no repudiation of funding for education.

47. **(C)** The primary intended audience for the Port Huron Statement was middle-class college students. The statement was written at the founding convention of Students for a Democratic Society, and was intended to be a recruiting tool as SDS tried to attract support on college campuses. The statement refers to having grown up in "comfort," not poverty. The statement expressed solidarity with African Americans in the South, but it was not meant as a recruiting tool for African Americans (A). SDS made many appeals and petitions to government officials (B), but this is not one of them. The "old left" of the 1930s attempted to recruit factory workers (D); the "new left" focused more on recruiting college students.

48. **(B)** The growth of Students for a Democratic Society—the organization that published the Port Huron Statement—can best be understood in the context of the baby boom, economic growth, and a rapid expansion of higher education. The campus-based organization thrived at a time when the size of the college-aged demographic ballooned as baby boomers reached their upper teens. In addition, the growth of the middle class contributed to a large increase in the number of students enrolled in four-year universities in the 1960s.

49. **(B)** The New York law, cited in the question, allowed married women to own their own property and to keep money they might inherit. This challenged traditional understandings of women and property embodied in the legal concept of *femme covert*. Under the legal doctrine of *femme covert*, wives had no independent legal or political standing.

50. **(A)** Participants in the Seneca Falls Convention, which occurred in New York State, just weeks after the New York legislature passed the Married Women's Property Act (1848), would certainly have supported the act as a step forward for the women's rights movement. The Seneca Falls Declaration, which was written at the Convention, specifically sites unequal property rights as an injustice to be rectified.

51. **(D)** The passage of the Married Women's Property Act directly reflects the ongoing debate around the legal status of women. From the colonial period until the contemporary period, the legal status of women has changed so that women currently enjoy virtually the same legal rights and responsibilities as men. These debates have involved divorce, custody, property, voting, serving on juries, serving in the military, and other issues.

52. **(D)** The Flushing Remonstrance (1657) was written by English residents of the village of Flushing in the Dutch colony of New Netherlands. The director-general of the colony of New Netherlands, Peter Stuyvesant, was attempting to enforce conformity in New Netherlands despite the multi-ethnic makeup of the colony. The authors were protesting a ban on Quaker worship in New Netherlands, even though the authors themselves were not Quaker. A similar controversy occurred with members of the Jewish community of New Netherlands.

53. **(C)** The main idea of the Flushing Remonstrance—that government should not interfere or limit different religious practices—was enshrined into the United States legal structure by the "Free Exercise Clause" of the First Amendment. The First Amendment mentions religion in two contexts. The "Establishment Clause" (D) prohibits the establishment of an official religion in the United States. The "Free Exercise Clause" asserts that Congress shall make no laws limiting the right to worship freely.

54. **(D)** The main purpose of the petition by Paul Cuffe was to demand that the Massachusetts legislature either grant the petitioners the right to vote or that it excuse them from paying taxes. Cuffe and his brother were free African Americans. They paid taxes, but they were not permitted to vote. The petition was based on the oft-repeated principle of the Patriot cause—no taxation without representation.

55. **(A)** The petition by Paul Cuffe illustrates the fact that the rhetoric of the American Revolution raised awareness of social inequalities and inspired groups and individuals to call for greater political democracy. The documents and publications of the Revolutionary era are filled with the language of inequality, injustice, and enslavement. The Declaration of Independence contains the idea that all men have certain basic rights, in the phrase "life, liberty, and the pursuit of happiness." Many groups—African Americans (free and enslaved), indentured servants, women, American Indians—were inspired by this language and insisted that the new government abide by its principles.

ANSWER SHEET
Practice Exam 2

1. (A) (B) (C) (D)
2. (A) (B) (C) (D)
3. (A) (B) (C) (D)
4. (A) (B) (C) (D)
5. (A) (B) (C) (D)
6. (A) (B) (C) (D)
7. (A) (B) (C) (D)
8. (A) (B) (C) (D)
9. (A) (B) (C) (D)
10. (A) (B) (C) (D)
11. (A) (B) (C) (D)
12. (A) (B) (C) (D)
13. (A) (B) (C) (D)
14. (A) (B) (C) (D)
15. (A) (B) (C) (D)
16. (A) (B) (C) (D)
17. (A) (B) (C) (D)
18. (A) (B) (C) (D)
19. (A) (B) (C) (D)
20. (A) (B) (C) (D)

21. (A) (B) (C) (D)
22. (A) (B) (C) (D)
23. (A) (B) (C) (D)
24. (A) (B) (C) (D)
25. (A) (B) (C) (D)
26. (A) (B) (C) (D)
27. (A) (B) (C) (D)
28. (A) (B) (C) (D)
29. (A) (B) (C) (D)
30. (A) (B) (C) (D)
31. (A) (B) (C) (D)
32. (A) (B) (C) (D)
33. (A) (B) (C) (D)
34. (A) (B) (C) (D)
35. (A) (B) (C) (D)
36. (A) (B) (C) (D)
37. (A) (B) (C) (D)
38. (A) (B) (C) (D)
39. (A) (B) (C) (D)
40. (A) (B) (C) (D)

41. (A) (B) (C) (D)
42. (A) (B) (C) (D)
43. (A) (B) (C) (D)
44. (A) (B) (C) (D)
45. (A) (B) (C) (D)
46. (A) (B) (C) (D)
47. (A) (B) (C) (D)
48. (A) (B) (C) (D)
49. (A) (B) (C) (D)
50. (A) (B) (C) (D)
51. (A) (B) (C) (D)
52. (A) (B) (C) (D)
53. (A) (B) (C) (D)
54. (A) (B) (C) (D)
55. (A) (B) (C) (D)

Practice Exam 2

SECTION I

Part A: 55 Multiple-Choice Questions

Directions: The questions in the section are grouped in sets of 2–4 questions. Each set is organized around a primary source, secondary source, or other historical issue. Select the best answer for each of the questions in this section. (55 minutes)

QUESTIONS 1–3 REFER TO THE FOLLOWING POLITICAL CARTOON:

"FIRE!"

—Herblock, *Washington Post*, 1949

1. Which of the following statements most accurately describes the main point of this cartoon?

   (A) The need to extinguish the communist threat justified swift and severe government action.

   (B) The freedoms of Americans were at risk because of an overreaction to the perceived threat of communism after World War II.

   (C) The existence of communists in the United States was a simple problem to solve.

   (D) There was no need to panic in the face of the communist threat.

2. Which other historical time period could have elicited a similar political cartoon?

   (A) The Panic of 1873
   (B) The era of the New Deal
   (C) The Great Awakening
   (D) The Quasi-War with France in 1798

3. Which of the following actions would this cartoonist most likely have criticized?

   (A) Congressional passage of the McCarran Internal Security Act
   (B) President Eisenhower's Farewell Address
   (C) Vice President Nixon's "Kitchen Debate" with Soviet Premier Khrushchev
   (D) The implementation of the containment policy

QUESTIONS 4–6 REFER TO THE FOLLOWING PASSAGE:

"I know that whenever the subject has occurred in conversation where I have been present, it has appeared to be the opinion of every one that we could not be taxed by a Parliament wherein we were not represented. But the payment of duties laid by an act of Parliament as regulations of commerce was never disputed. . . . An *external* tax is a duty laid on commodities imported; that duty is added to the first cost and other charges on the commodity, and, when it is offered for sale, makes a part of the price. If the people do not like it at that price, they refuse it; they are not obliged to pay it. But an *internal* tax is forced from the people without their consent if not laid by their own representatives. The Stamp Act says we shall have no commerce, make no exchange of property with each other, neither purchase nor grant, nor recover debts; we shall neither marry nor make our wills, unless we pay such and such sums; and thus it is intended to extort our money from us or ruin us by the consequence of refusing to pay it."

—Benjamin Franklin, *Examination before Parliament*, 1766

4. Which Enlightenment political ideal is best represented in this passage?

   (A) Governments derive their powers from the consent of the governed.
   (B) Governmental power should be divided among three branches.
   (C) The general will, or majority, should determine the rules of society.
   (D) The free market is the best way to determine the economic course of a society.

5. Prime Minister George Grenville later challenged Benjamin Franklin's statements that the American colonists should have representation in Parliament by claiming that

   (A) the colonists had virtual representation in Parliament, meaning that Parliament represented all subjects of the British king.
   (B) the Stamp Act would be only the first of many internal taxes that the Americans would be expected to pay.
   (C) no subject of the king had the right to challenge Parliament's authority.
   (D) by refusing to pay the taxes imposed by Parliament, the Americans were committing treason.

6. Which of the following actions most closely mirrors the arguments presented in this quotation by Benjamin Franklin?

(A) Antifederalist arguments in favor of adding a Bill of Rights to the United States Constitution

(B) Representatives of the colonies convening the Stamp Act Congress to protest the laws of Parliament

(C) South Carolina implementing the doctrine of nullification in the 1830s

(D) The business-friendly policies of Presidents Calvin Coolidge and Herbert Hoover in the 1930s

QUESTIONS 7–9 REFER TO THE FOLLOWING QUOTATION:

"As a means of effecting this end I suggest for your consideration the propriety of setting apart an ample district west of the Mississippi, and without the limit of any State or Territory now formed, to be guaranteed to the Indian tribes as long as they shall occupy it. . . . There they may be secured in the enjoyment of governments of their own choice, subject to no other control from the United States than such as may be necessary to preserve peace on the frontier and between the several tribes. There the benevolent may endeavor to teach them the arts of civilization. . . .

"This emigration would be voluntary, for it would be as cruel and unjust to compel the aborigines to abandon the graves of their fathers and seek a home in a distant land. But they should be distinctly informed that if they remain within the limits of the States they must be subject to their laws. . . ."

—President Andrew Jackson, 1829

7. Which author was most critical of the policy being described here by President Jackson?

(A) Rachel Carson in *Silent Spring*

(B) Ralph Ellison in *Invisible Man*

(C) Helen Hunt Jackson in *A Century of Dishonor*

(D) William Lloyd Garrison in *The Liberator*

8. The policy described above most immediately led to

(A) peace between Indian tribes and white settlers.

(B) the forced removal of the Cherokee tribe from their homelands.

(C) the first Treaty of Fort Laramie, which guaranteed Indian possession of lands west of the Mississippi River.

(D) a negotiated settlement between the tribes of the Southeast and the United States government in which the tribes were allowed to remain on their lands for ten years.

9. President Jackson's policy was later altered by the

(A) Homestead Act of 1862.

(B) Immigration Act of 1921.

(C) Supreme Court decision in *Plessy v. Ferguson*.

(D) Dawes Act of 1887.

QUESTIONS 10–12 REFER TO THE FOLLOWING QUOTATION:

"I am in Birmingham because injustice is here. . . . Moreover, I am cognizant of the interrelatedness of all communities and states. I cannot sit idly by in Atlanta and not be concerned about what happens in Birmingham. Injustice anywhere is a threat to justice everywhere. We are caught in an inescapable network of mutuality, tied in a single garment of destiny. Whatever affects one directly affects all indirectly. Never again can we afford to live with the narrow, provincial "outside agitator" idea. Anyone who lives inside the United States can never be considered an outsider anywhere in this country. . . ."

—Martin Luther King, Jr., "Letter from a Birmingham Jail," April 16, 1963

10. Based on this quotation, what can you infer about the efforts of Martin Luther King, Jr., and others in the civil rights movement of the 1950s?

(A) The civil rights movement was not finding success through nonviolent methods.

(B) Advocates for civil rights were coordinating their efforts to raise awareness of racial segregation across the country.

(C) Martin Luther King, Jr., was focused on ending segregation in Birmingham only.

(D) Martin Luther King, Jr., was willing to compromise his principles and would be a violent agitator if necessary.

11. Which of the following Supreme Court decisions provided the legal basis for the system of segregation that Martin Luther King, Jr., and others were trying to end?

(A) *Dred Scott v. Sanford* (1857)

(B) *Brown v. Board of Education of Topeka, Kansas* (1954)

(C) *Worcester v. Georgia* (1831)

(D) *Plessy v. Ferguson* (1896)

12. Martin Luther King, Jr., was in jail in Birmingham, Alabama, because of his belief in protesting injustice through the use of

(A) targeted assassinations of segregationist public officials.

(B) massive letter-writing campaigns denouncing segregated businesses.

(C) violent self-defense.

(D) nonviolent direct action.

"One-half of the people of this nation to-day are utterly powerless to blot from the statute books an unjust law, or to write there a new and a just one. The women, dissatisfied as they are with this form of government, that enforces taxation without representation,—that compels them to obey laws to which they have never given their consent,—that imprisons and hangs them without a trial by a jury of their peers, that robs them, in marriage, of the custody of their own persons, wages and children,—are this half of the people left wholly at the mercy of the other half, in direct violation of the spirit and letter of the declarations of the framers of this government, every one of which was based on the immutable principle of equal rights to all."

—Susan B. Anthony, 1872

13. On which of these documents is Susan B. Anthony basing her appeal for women's equality?

    (A) Articles of Confederation
    (B) Proclamation of Amnesty and Reconstruction
    (C) Compromise of 1850
    (D) Declaration of Independence

14. Which other nineteenth century reform movement made similar arguments to those written here by Susan B. Anthony?

    (A) The temperance movement
    (B) Utopian communities
    (C) The abolition movement
    (D) Public school advocates

15. Susan B. Anthony and others in the women's rights movement had a major influence on the ratification of which of the following?

    (A) The Nineteenth Amendment
    (B) The Equal Rights Amendment
    (C) The Fifteenth Amendment
    (D) The Twenty-sixth Amendment

16. The language of this passage by Susan B. Anthony demonstrates which of the following continuities in United States history?

    (A) Debates over free speech
    (B) Debates over voting rights
    (C) Debates over federal power and states' rights
    (D) Debates over the procedures of amending the Constitution

FORTY-MILLIONAIRE CARNEGIE IN HIS GREAT DOUBLE ROLE.

AS THE TIGHT-FISTED EMPLOYER HE REDUCES WAGES THAT HE MAY PLAY PHILANTHROPIST AND GIVE AWAY LIBRARIES, ETC.

—American Social History Project

17. Which of the following statements best represents the criticism of Andrew Carnegie found in this cartoon?

(A) Carnegie was able to give away a great deal of money only because he abused his workers' rights.

(B) Carnegie did not give enough of his considerable fortune to charity.

(C) Carnegie was dividing his attention and was therefore not as successful in either of his main endeavors.

(D) Carnegie's ruthless business practices were causing him to lose touch with his working-class origins.

18. Which of the following was another common criticism of Andrew Carnegie?

(A) As an immigrant, Carnegie has no right to own a controlling interest in major American industries.

(B) Carnegie did nothing to prevent the use of violence against his workers when they asked for better wages and working conditions.

(C) Carnegie was seen as the epitome of American success, but he was not even the richest man in America.

(D) Too much of Carnegie's philanthropic efforts were concentrated on his homeland of Scotland, denying Americans the benefits of his charity.

19. Which of the following federal laws was NOT designed to empower the government to regulate the increasing wealth and power of the industrialists in the late nineteenth and early twentieth centuries?

(A) Sherman Anti-Trust Act (1890)
(B) Interstate Commerce Act (1887)
(C) Federal Trade Commission Act (1914)
(D) Newlands Reclamation Act (1902)

20. During the Pennsylvania anthracite coal miner strike in 1902, President Theodore Roosevelt altered governmental policy toward striking workers by

(A) using the United States Army to take over the administration of the coal mines.
(B) helping the coal miners keep their jobs but preventing them from collecting a higher salary.
(C) mediating negotiations between the miners and the mine owners.
(D) declaring the use of collective bargaining to be unconstitutional and using the United States Army to bar the workers from entering the mining facilities.

QUESTIONS 21–23 REFER TO THE FOLLOWING QUOTATION:

"Wherever I go—the street, the shop, the house, or the steamboat—I hear the people talk in such a way as to indicate that they are yet unable to conceive of the Negro as possessing any rights at all. Men who are honorable in their dealings with their white neighbors will cheat a Negro without feeling a single twinge of their honor. To kill a Negro they do not deem murder; to debauch a Negro woman they do not think fornication; to take the property away from a Negro they do not consider robbery. The people boast that when they get freedmen affairs in their own hands, to use their own classic expression, 'the niggers will catch hell.'

"The reason of all this is simple and manifest. The whites esteem the blacks their property by natural right, and however much they may admit that the individual relations of masters and slaves have been destroyed by the war and the President's emancipation proclamation, they still have an ingrained feeling that the blacks at large belong to the whites at large, and whenever opportunity serves they treat the colored people just as their profit, caprice or passion may dictate."

—Congressional testimony of Col. Samuel Thomas, Assistant Commissioner, Bureau of Refugees, Freedmen and Abandoned Lands, 1865

21. According to this official from the Freedman's Bureau, how has southern society reacted to the end of the Civil War?

(A) Blacks were able to freely travel around the country without fear of reprisal.
(B) The only way for southern whites to demonstrate their manhood was to mistreat freed slaves.
(C) Southern whites were willing to accept the freedom of slaves as long as the slaves did not ask for voting rights.
(D) The freed slaves were experiencing discrimination and limitations on their rights similar to their treatment under slavery.

22. The Fourteenth Amendment attempted to eliminate the societal conditions described in this passage by

(A) revoking the voting rights of all known members of the Confederate government and soldiers of the Confederate Army.
(B) granting citizenship and guaranteeing equal protection under the law to former slaves.
(C) creating a special appeals process that expedited civil rights claims directly to the Supreme Court.
(D) ensuring that former slaves received the forty acres of land promised to them by General William Sherman and the Freedman's Bureau Bill of 1866.

23. Which of the following events of the twentieth century reflects a continuation of the attitudes of southern whites as described in this passage?

(A) The Great Migration
(B) Jim Crow legislation
(C) The Civil Rights Act of 1957
(D) The March on Washington for Jobs and Freedom

QUESTIONS 24–26 REFER TO THE FOLLOWING QUOTATION:

"For we live in fear of the enemy every hour, yet we have had a combat with them on the Sunday before Shrovetide. And we took two alive and made slaves of them. But it was by policy, for we are in great danger, for our plantation is very weak, by reason of death and sickness of our company. For we came but twenty, for the merchants, and they are half dead just. And we look every hour when two or more should go. . . .

"And I have nothing to comfort me, nor is there nothing to be gotten here but sickness and death, except one had money to lay out in some things for profit. But I have nothing at all, no, not a shirt on my back, but two rags, nor no clothes, but one poor suit, nor but one pair of shoes, but one pair of stockings, but one cap. My cloak was stolen by one of my own fellows, and to his dying hour he would not tell me what he did with it. But some of my fellows saw him have butter and beef out of a ship, which my cloak I [don't] doubt paid for. So that I have not a penny, nor a penny worth to help me to either spice, or sugar, or strong waters [alcohol, probably rum], without the which one cannot live here. For as strong beer in England doth fatten and strengthen thee, so water doth wash and weaken here, only keeps life and soul together."

—Indentured servant Richard Frethorne, in Virginia, 1623

24. The conditions described in this passage contributed to

(A) the Virginia Company's decision to abandon the colony and try to establish a new colony farther to the south.
(B) a successful rebellion by the white indentured servants who were brought to the colony to work on tobacco plantations.
(C) the importation of African slaves as a labor force.
(D) an aggressive war over resources with the local Indian tribe.

25. Which of these is the most likely effect of declining mortality rates of indentured servants in the Chesapeake region in the seventeenth century?

   (A) Indentured servants outlived their contracts and gained freedom, but discovered that freedom did not equate to land ownership.
   (B) Most indentured servants were able to purchase plots of land that guaranteed them economic security.
   (C) Cash crop planters were eager to help indentured servants acquire land so that the colony as a whole would be more economically viable.
   (D) There was an increased demand for cooperation with the Indian tribes on the frontier of the colonies.

26. Which of the following best describes a yeoman farmer in the Chesapeake region in the seventeenth century?

   (A) A farmer who was only in the colony until he earned enough money to purchase land in England
   (B) A farmer who owned a small, family-farmed plot of land and possibly had a few servants to help work the land
   (C) A farmer who lived a subsistence life in the wilderness
   (D) A farmer who was unwilling to cede political control to the growing population of indentured servants

QUESTIONS 27–29 REFER TO THE FOLLOWING PASSAGE:

"Lincoln was strongly anti-slavery, but he was not an abolitionist or a Radical Republican and never claimed to be one. He made a sharp distinction between his frequently reiterated personal wish that 'all men everywhere could be free' and his official duties as a legislator, congressman, and president in a legal and constitutional system that recognized the South's right to property in slaves. Even after issuing the Emancipation Proclamation he continued to declare his preference for gradual abolition. While his racial views changed during the Civil War, he never became a principled egalitarian in the manner of abolitionists such as Frederick Douglass or Wendell Phillips or Radical Republicans like Charles Sumner."

—Eric Foner, *The Fiery Trial*, 2010

27. Which of the following statements best describes Eric Foner's argument in regard to President Abraham Lincoln's views on slavery?

   (A) President Lincoln was a consistent supporter of the abolitionist cause.
   (B) President Lincoln was reluctant to be ideologically associated with advocates like Frederick Douglass.
   (C) In his ambition to become president, Abraham Lincoln declared his desire to use his constitutional powers to end slavery.
   (D) President Lincoln had continually changing views on slavery and abolition that did not always fit into the prevailing political categories.

28. How did President Lincoln's issuance of the Emancipation Proclamation alter the course of the Civil War?

(A) The war came to a swift conclusion because the Proclamation made the Confederacy realize the futility of their cause.

(B) The war grew in scope because the Proclamation caused Great Britain to join the fight on the side of the Union.

(C) President Jefferson Davis of the Confederacy vowed massive resistance to any Union effort to free the slaves.

(D) The war aims of the United States were no longer exclusive to the preservation of the Union.

29. Which of these statements best describes the Emancipation Proclamation?

(A) It guaranteed the freedom of all slaves living within the boundaries of the United States at the conclusion of the Civil War.

(B) It freed only the slaves in states and portions of states in rebellion against the United States at the time it was issued.

(C) It declared that the freedom of the slaves was conditional upon the agreement of individual southern states to sign a peace treaty with the United States government.

(D) It prohibited the use of slaves in combat in both the Union and Confederate Armies.

QUESTIONS 30–31 REFER TO THE FOLLOWING QUOTATION:

"The only force which is strong enough to break down social convention is economic necessity. . . .The economic necessity which has forced women out of the home and into the world of business has completely annihilated the old idea that a woman should eat only in the privacy of her household or in the homes of her friends, has created the absolutely new social phenomenon of women eating in public, unescorted by men, by the tens of thousands, and has given rise to a wholly new phase of the restaurant business."

—*New York Times*, October 15, 1905.

30. Which of the following groups would have most likely supported the scenario described in this passage?

(A) Ku Klux Klan

(B) American Temperance Union

(C) National Woman Suffrage Association

(D) Southern Christian Leadership Conference

31. The scenario described in the passage above is most directly reflected in the ideas of which of the following?

(A) Voting Rights Act of 1965

(B) Equal Rights Amendment

(C) Pure Food and Drug Act

(D) Interstate Commerce Act

—The Granger Collection

"Pull away, pull away my Son. Don't fear. I'll give you all my assistance."
"Oh! I fear it is stronger rooted than I expected but with the assistance of my old friend and a little more brandy I will bring it down."

"Mad Tom in a Rage" unknown cartoonist circa 1802

32. The above cartoon illustrates which of the following?

(A) The growing political partisanship after the election of Thomas Jefferson as president
(B) A governmental effort to regulate excessive drinking
(C) An effort on the part of the British government to subvert American democracy
(D) The pessimistic outlook of many Americans concerning the ability of the nation to survive its formative years

33. The development of political parties led to which of the following amendments to the Constitution of the United States?

(A) The elected president would appoint the vice president after the election to ensure that members of the same political party filled both positions.
(B) The majority party in Congress would have the authority to choose the vice president.
(C) Distinct ballots would be cast for president and vice president, avoiding a situation in which one person from each political party would serve in those posts.
(D) The electoral college was abolished and the winner of the popular vote would be declared president, with the vice president being chosen by the officials of the president's political party.

34. How does this cartoon demonstrate the political viewpoint of the Federalist Party?

(A) Thomas Jefferson is portrayed as the Devil and is helping to tear down the federal government.

(B) Thomas Paine is attempting to hold back the efforts of the Devil to destroy the national government.

(C) Alexander Hamilton is working with the Devil to dismantle the Constitutional principle of federalism.

(D) John Adams and George Washington were unable to successfully argue against the negative attitudes of the Republican press.

QUESTIONS 35–38 REFER TO THE FOLLOWING QUOTATION:

"The economic ills we suffer have come upon us over several decades. They will not go away in days, weeks, or months, but they will go away. They will go away because we as Americans have the capacity now, as we've had in the past, to do whatever needs to be done to preserve this last and greatest bastion of freedom. In this present crisis, government is not the solution to our problem; government is the problem. . . .

It is my intention to curb the size and influence of the Federal establishment and to demand recognition of the distinction between the powers granted to the Federal Government and those reserved to the States or to the people. All of us need to be reminded that the Federal Government did not create the States; the States created the Federal Government."

—Ronald Reagan, First Inaugural Address, January 21, 1981

35. The conservative political revival that led to President Ronald Reagan's election in 1980 was most directly a reaction to

(A) President Franklin Roosevelt's New Deal.
(B) the Supreme Court's decision in *Loving v. Virginia.*
(C) President John F. Kennedy's close electoral victory over Richard Nixon.
(D) President Lyndon Johnson's Great Society.

36. Which of the following would have most likely agreed with President Reagan's statement that the federal government was created by the states and the federal government's role should be limited?

(A) The Antifederalists
(B) The Whig Party
(C) The Mugwumps
(D) The Progressives

37. Which of the following issues found across eras in United States history is expressed in the quotation?

   (A) Debates over the powers of the president
   (B) Debates over participation in elections
   (C) Debates over federal power over the economy
   (D) Debates over federal power over international affairs

38. One way in which President Reagan acted on his rhetoric in the passage was to

   (A) increase the military budget.
   (B) work with Congress to cut taxes and government spending.
   (C) eliminate the Department of Housing and Urban Development.
   (D) prohibit pay increases for government workers.

QUESTIONS 39–40 REFER TO THE FOLLOWING QUOTATION:

"Our energy plan will also include a number of specific goals, to measure our progress toward a stable energy system. These are the goals we set for 1985:

   – Reduce the annual growth rate in our energy demand to less than two percent.
   – Reduce gasoline consumption by ten percent below its current level.
   – Cut in half the portion of United States oil which is imported, from a potential level of 16 million barrels to six million barrels a day.
   – Establish a strategic petroleum reserve of one billion barrels, more than six months' supply.
   – Increase our coal production by about two thirds to more than 1 billion tons a year.
   – Insulate 90 percent of American homes and all new buildings.
   – Use solar energy in more than two and one-half million houses."

   —President Jimmy Carter, speech on April 18, 1977

39. The quote above reflects which of the following continuities of United States history?

   (A) Concern for working-class Americans
   (B) The shifting role of the federal government
   (C) Concern for natural resources and their environmental impact
   (D) The role of the United States in world diplomacy

40. President Jimmy Carter's speech quoted above was primarily a reaction to which of the following events?

   (A) The Soviet Union's invasion of Afghanistan
   (B) The Iran hostage crisis
   (C) A series of embargos enacted by the Middle East-dominated organization known as OPEC
   (D) Terrorist bombings that targeted United States military personnel

A BIGGER JOB THAN HE THOUGHT FOR.
UNCLE SAM—Behave, You Fool! Durn Me, If I Ain't Most Sorry I Undertook to Rescue You.

—William Carson, "A Bigger Job Than He Thought For,"
Sunday Globe (Utica, NY), 1899

41. The 1899 cartoon shown above makes the point that

(A) insurgents in Cuba were being manipulated by Spain into resisting the presence of American troops.
(B) native Hawaiians behaved in a childlike manner when the Hawaiian islands were annexed by the United States.
(C) the United States misread the reaction of the Filipino people when it acquired the Philippines following the Spanish-American War.
(D) the task of completing the Panama Canal was more time consuming, and more costly, than the United States had originally anticipated.

42. The cartoon reflects which of the following continuities in United States history?

(A) Debates over extending constitutional rights to people's in territories acquired by the United States
(B) Debates over the wisdom of asserting American control over foreign possessions
(C) Debates over the morality of tactics used by the United States in wars of colonial independence
(D) Debates over allowing the Central Intelligence Agency to engage in covert operations in foreign countries

43. The event depicted in the cartoon represents which of the following?

   (A) A shift in American foreign policy from "gun boat diplomacy" to "dollar diplomacy"
   (B) The beginning of a period of isolation from world affairs
   (C) A shift from "brinksmanship" to détente
   (D) The beginning of a period of imperialistic activities by the United States

QUESTIONS 44–45 ARE BASED ON THE FOLLOWING QUOTATION:

"I marvel not a little, right worshipful, that since the first discovery of America (which is now full four score and ten years), after so great conquests and plantings of the Spaniards and Portuguese there, that we of England could never have the grace to set fast footing in such fertile and temperate places as are left as yet unpossessed of them. But . . . I conceive great hope that the time approacheth and now is that we of England may share and part stakes [divide the prize] (if we will ourselves) both with the Spaniard and the Portuguese in part of America and other regions as yet undiscovered.

   "And surely if there were in us that desire to advance the honor of our country which ought to be in every good man, we would not all this while have [neglected] the possessing of these lands which of equity and right appertain unto us, as by the discourses that follow shall appear most plainly."

—Richard Hakluyt, *Divers Voyages Touching the Discovery of America and the Islands Adjacent*, 1582

44. The ideas expressed in the quotation above most closely reflect the influence of which of the following?

   (A) The Enlightenment philosophy of natural rights
   (B) The economic policy of mercantilism
   (C) The religious philosophy of predestination
   (D) The social contract theory

45. By following the ideas of Richard Hakluyt, England was eventually able to

   (A) drive the French and Portuguese governments into bankruptcy.
   (B) conquer large parts of Africa in the eighteenth century.
   (C) establish several colonies along the Atlantic coastline of North America.
   (D) destroy the Dutch commercial empire.

"The God that holds you over the pit of hell, much as one holds a spider, or some loathsome insect, over the fire, abhors you, and is dreadfully provoked; his wrath towards you burns like fire; he looks upon you as worthy of nothing else, but to be cast into the fire; he is of purer eyes than to bear to have you in his sight; you are ten thousand times so abominable in his eyes as the most hateful venomous serpent is in ours. You have offended him infinitely more than ever a stubborn rebel did his prince: and yet 'tis nothing but his hand that holds you from falling into the fire every moment: 'tis to be ascribed to nothing else, that you did not go to hell the last night; that you was suffered to awake again in this world, after you closed your eyes to sleep: and there is no other reason to be given why you have not dropped into hell since you arose in the morning, but that God's hand has held you up: there is no other reason to be given why you ha[ve] n't gone to hell since you have sat here in the house of God, provoking his pure eyes by your sinful wicked manner of attending his solemn worship: yea, there is nothing else that is to be given as a reason why you don't this very moment drop down into hell."

—Jonathan Edwards, "Sinners in the Hands of an Angry God," 1741 (excerpt).

46. An important point that Jonathan Edwards is making in the sermon, excerpted above, is that

(A) despite the sinful nature of humanity, God has given individuals a chance to rectify their sins.
(B) human beings are born inherently good, but are corrupted by the evils of society.
(C) God is merciless, allowing sinners and saints alike to suffer in the fires of hell.
(D) it is not important what you believe in life, just as long as you live your life in a moral and ethical manner.

47. The sermon by Jonathan Edwards was a central text of

(A) Transcendentalism
(B) Mormonism
(C) the Great Awakening
(D) the Social Gospel

48. Which of the following describes the context that Jonathan Edwards was preaching in?

(A) There had been a marked decline in piety in Puritan New England; Edwards hoped to rekindle the fires of New England church members.
(B) The government of Massachusetts had disestablished the Congregational Church forcing preachers like Edwards to travel from town to town in search of adherents.
(C) New England had experienced a wave of immigrants from all over Europe, including many Catholics, Jews, Protestants of a variety of sects, and non-believers; Edwards hoped to convert them to teachings of the Congregational Church.
(D) New England was recently devastated by war with American Indians; Edwards sought to reassure the survivors that God did, indeed, exist.

49. Jonathan Edwards was part of a broader religious movement that impacted colonial American society by

(A) encouraging colonists to question and challenge the legitimacy of British authorities.

(B) citing the immorality of slavery and stressing the importance of ending the institution.

(C) asserting the importance of developing amicable relations with American Indians.

(D) fostering changes in colonists' understandings of God, themselves, and the world around them.

QUESTIONS 50–52 REFER TO THE FOLLOWING IMAGE:

50. What does the above image tell you about the decade of the 1920s?

(A) Consumer safety was the primary concern of leading manufacturing companies.

(B) Automobiles were a rare commodity and therefore extremely expensive.

(C) New technologies such as automobiles were unproven and unsafe, requiring extensive propaganda in order to make consumers interested in them.

(D) Consumer products were increasingly affordable and highly desired by the public as a sign of status.

51. Like other consumer products such as radios and home electric appliances, automobiles were often offered to consumers through

(A) credit buying plans, which allowed consumers to defer full payment over time.
(B) self-manufacturing kits, which reduced the costs for the companies selling the products.
(C) exclusive retail stores, which prevented consumers from buying products at the lowest possible price.
(D) incentives such as rebates, which consumers could acquire by agreeing to sell products for the manufacturer.

52. The consumer economy of the 1920s most directly shows the influence of which of the following?

(A) Manifest Destiny and territorial expansion
(B) The Industrial Revolution and entrepreneurial spirit
(C) Reconstruction and the "Redemption" of the South
(D) World War I and international cooperation

QUESTIONS 53–55 ARE BASED ON THE FOLLOWING TABLE:

Wholesale Price Index of Farm Products
(Based on 1910–1914 = 100)

1866	140
1870	112
1876	89
1880	80
1882	99
1886	68
1890	71
1896	56
1900	71

53. Which of the following describes an important reason for the trend reflected in the figures in the table above?

(A) The number of family farms increased in the 1870s and 1880s, as thousands of "new immigrant" families settled in the rural Midwest.
(B) Population stagnated as the spread of birth control and the growth of the middle class led to falling birthrates.
(C) Mechanization of agriculture, improved techniques, and an increase in acres under cultivation created agricultural surpluses.
(D) American expansion into Latin America resulted in surplus agricultural products from Central and South America flooding American markets.

54. Which of the following was a demand of the Populist Party in the 1880s and 1890s to address the situation reflected in the figures in the table?

(A) A national sales tax

(B) Government funding for the purchase of agricultural machinery

(C) "Internal improvements" in the West, including railroads and canals

(D) An end to the gold standard and a shift to currency backed by silver as well as gold

55. Which of the following describes developments in the 1870s, 1880s, and 1890s that occurred, in part, as a result of the trend indicated in the chart?

(A) The federal government established agencies that oversaw agricultural production in the United States, limiting production of certain products.

(B) The United States lowered import tariffs in order to stimulate international trade and reduce surpluses of agricultural products.

(C) Farmers created local and regional networks to challenge and resist corporate control of agricultural markets.

(D) Major agricultural producers invested in the establishment of a transcontinental railroad network to more effectively transport agricultural goods to urban markets.

Part B: Short-Answer Questions

Directions: The following section contains four questions. Answer each of the questions, using the source material and your knowledge of American history. Note—students are not required to develop and support a thesis statement in responding to these questions. (45 minutes)

QUESTION 1 IS BASED ON THE FOLLOWING TWO PASSAGES:

"Our greatest danger is that in the great leap from slavery to freedom we may overlook the fact that the masses of us are to live by the productions of our hands, and fail to keep in mind that we shall prosper in proportion as we learn to dignify and glorify common labour, and put brains and skill into the common occupations of life; shall prosper in proportion as we learn to draw the line between the superficial and the substantial, the ornamental gewgaws of life and the useful. No race can prosper till it learns that there is as much dignity in tilling a field as in writing a poem. It is at the bottom of life we must begin, and not at the top. Nor should we permit our grievances to overshadow our opportunities. . . . The opportunity to earn a dollar in a factory just now is worth infinitely more than the opportunity to spend a dollar in an opera-house."

—Booker T. Washington, "Atlanta Compromise Speech," 1895

"The Negro race, like all races, is going to be saved by its exceptional men. The problem of education, then, among Negroes must first of all deal with the Talented Tenth; it is the problem of developing the Best of this race that they may guide the Mass away from the contamination and death of the Worst, in their own and other races. Now the training of men is a difficult and intricate task. Its technique is a matter for educational experts, but its object is for the vision of seers. If we make money the object of man-training, we shall develop money-makers but not necessarily men; if we make technical skill the object of education, we may possess artisans but not, in nature, men. Men we shall have only as we make manhood the object of the work of the schools—intelligence, broad sympathy, knowledge of the world that was and is, and of the relation of men to it—this is the curriculum of that Higher Education which must underlie true life. On this foundation we may build bread winning, skill of hand and quickness of brain, with never a fear lest the child and man mistake the means of living for the object of life. . . . Education and work are the levers to uplift a people. Work alone will not do it unless inspired by the right ideals and guided by intelligence. Education must not simply teach work—it must teach Life. . . ."

—W.E.B. DuBois, "The Talented Tenth," 1903

1. Use the excerpt above and your knowledge of United States history to answer parts A, B, and C.

   (A) Briefly explain the main idea of the first passage.

   (B) Briefly explain the main idea of the second passage.

   (C) Using ONE specific example from United States history, explain how it supports the argument of ONE of the passages.

2. The governmental response to the Great Depression known as the New Deal has been subject to historical and popular debate ever since its implementation. Use your knowledge of United States history to answer parts A, B, and C.

   (A) Explain one criticism of a specific New Deal program that was put forth during the 1930s.

   (B) Provide evidence from the 1930s of public support for New Deal programs or opposition to these programs.

   (C) In the decades since the 1930s, discuss the place of the New Deal either among historians or among members of the public.

QUESTION 3 IS BASED ON THE FOLLOWING TWO PASSAGES:

"The first requirement for the acquisition of power by the Positive Woman is to understand the differences between men and women. . . . She understands that men and women are different, and that those very differences provide the key to her success as a person and fulfillment as a woman. . . . The Positive Woman looks upon her female-ness and her fertility as part of her purpose, her potential, and her power. She rejoices that she has a capability for creativity that men can never have. . . .

The overriding psychological need of a woman is to love something alive. A baby fulfills this need in the lives of most women. If a baby is not available to fill that need, women search for a baby-substitute. This is the reason why women have traditionally gone into teaching and nursing careers. They are doing what comes naturally to the female psyche."

—Phyllis Schlafly, *The Power of the Positive Woman*, 1977.

"I don't think most women want to pick up briefcases and march off to meaningless, depersonalized jobs. . . . We want to liberate men from those inhuman roles as well. We want to share the work and the responsibility, and to have men share equal responsibility for the children. Probably the ultimate myth is that children must have fulltime mothers, and that liberated women make bad ones. The truth is that most American children seem to be suffering from too much mother and too little father. . . . [W]e need free universal daycare. With that aid, as in Scandinavian countries, and with laws that permit women equal work and equal pay, man will be relieved of his role as sole breadwinner and stranger to his own children. . . . Women's Liberation really is Men's Liberation too. . . .

The point is that Women's Liberation is not destroying the American family. It is trying to build a human compassionate alternative out of its ruins."

—Gloria Steinem, 1972

3. Use the excerpt above and your knowledge of United States history to answer parts A, B, and C.

   (A) Explain the point of view of the first quotation.

   (B) Explain the point of view of the second quotation.

   (C) Choose a specific person or event from United States history and explain how that person or event exemplifies the point of view of ONE of the quotations.

QUESTION 4 IS BASED ON THE FOLLOWING QUOTATION:

"I would like to talk on behalf of all those veterans. . . . In our opinion and from our experience, there is nothing in South Vietnam which could happen that realistically threatens the United States of America. And to attempt to justify the loss of one American life in Vietnam, Cambodia or Laos by linking such loss to the preservation of freedom . . . is to us the height of criminal hypocrisy, and it is that kind of hypocrisy which we feel has torn this country apart. . . .

"Each day . . . someone has to give up his life so that the United States doesn't have to admit something that the entire world already knows, so that we can't say that we have made a mistake. Someone has to die so that President Nixon won't be, and these are his words, "the first President to lose a war."

"We are asking Americans to think about that because how do you ask a man to be the last man to die in Vietnam? How do you ask a man to be the last man to die for a mistake?..."

—John Kerry, testimony before the Senate Foreign Relations Committee,
April 23, 1971

4. Use the excerpt above and your knowledge of United States history to answer parts A, B, and C.

(A) Explain the criticism of United States political power found in this quotation.

(B) Provide evidence, not included in the passage, that could be used to support Kerry's point of view.

(C) Choose ONE of the following conflicts from United States history and explain how the quotation's argument could also be used in relationship to that conflict. Cite at least one piece of specific information about your chosen conflict to support your argument.

War of 1812
Mexican-American War
World War I

SECTION II
Part A: Document-Based Question

> **Directions:** The following question is based on the accompanying Documents 1–8. This question is designed to test your ability to apply several historical thinking skills simultaneously, including historical argumentation, use of relevant historical evidence, and contextualization. Your response should be based on your analysis of the documents and your knowledge of the topic. (60 minutes)

WRITE A WELL-INTEGRATED ESSAY THAT DOES THE FOLLOWING:

- States an appropriate thesis that directly addresses all parts of the question
- Supports the thesis or an appropriate argument with evidence from all or all but one of the documents AND your knowledge of United States history beyond/outside the documents
- Analyzes a majority of the documents in terms of such features as their intended audience, purpose, point of view, format, argument, limitations, and/or social context as appropriate to the argument
- Places the argument in the context of broader regional, national, or global processes

Question 1.

Analyze the ways in which immigration to the United States was addressed by American citizens in the period 1750–1915.

Document 1

Source: Benjamin Franklin, *Observations Concerning the Increase of Mankind, Peopling of Countries, etc.,*1753.

Why should the [*Germans*] be suffered to swarm into our Settlements, and by herding together establish their Language and Manners to the Exclusion of ours? Why should *Pennsylvania*, founded by the *English*, become a Colony of *Aliens*, who will shortly be so numerous as to Germanize us instead of our Anglifying them, and will never adopt our Language or Customs, any more than they can acquire our Complexion.

Document 2

Source: J. Hector St. John De Crevecoeur, *Letters From An American Farmer*, Letter III, 1782.

What then is the American, this new man? He is either an European, or the descendant of an European, hence that strange mixture of blood, which you will find in no other country. I could point out to you a family whose grandfather was an Englishman, whose wife was Dutch, whose son married a French woman, and whose present four sons have now four wives of different nations. *He* is an American, who leaving behind him all his ancient prejudices and manners, receives new ones from the new mode of life he has embraced, the new government he obeys, and the new rank he holds. He becomes an American by being received in the broad lap of our great *Alma Mater*. Here individuals of all nations are melted into a new race of men, whose labours and posterity will one day cause great changes in the world. Americans are the western pilgrims, who are carrying along with them that great mass of arts, sciences, vigour, and industry which began long since in the east; they will finish the great circle. The Americans were once scattered all over Europe; here they are incorporated into one of the finest systems of population which has ever appeared, and which will hereafter become distinct by the power of the different climates they inhabit. The American ought therefore to love this country much better than that wherein either he or his forefathers were born.

Source: Joseph Keppler, "Welcome to All!," *Puck*, 1880.
Credit: The Granger Collection

WELCOME TO ALL!

"We may safely say that the present influx of immigration to the United States is something unprecedented in our generation."—*N. Y. Statistical Review.*

Source: Billy Ireland, "We Can't Digest the Scum, *Columbus Dispatch*, 1919.
Credit: Billy Ireland Cartoon Library and Museum, Ohio State University

WE CAN'T DIGEST THE SCUM

Source: Robert Ernst, *Immigrant Life in New York City, 1825–1863* and *NY State Census of 1855.*

Occupations of Gainfully Employed Irish Immigrants in New York, 1855	Occupation # Irish-born and % of total
SKILLED	
Bakers	861 (23%)
Blacksmiths	1,339 (50)
Brewers/Distillers	52 (14)
Carpenters	2,230 (30)
Dressmaker/Seamstress	4,559 (46)
Ironworkers	150 (56)
Machinists	398 (23)
Mason/Bricklayer	2,203 (61)
Merchants	278 (4)
Policemen	292 (25)
Printers	519 (25)
Retail shopkeepers	916 (35)
Shoemakers	2,121 (31)
Tailors	4,171 (33)
Wine and liquor dealers	891 (55)

PROFESSIONALS	
Doctors	113 (8)
Lawyers	40 (4)

UNSKILLED	
Domestic Servants	23,386 (74)
Laundresses	1,758 (69)
Laborers	17,426 (86)
Drivers/Hackmen/Coachmen	805 (46)

Source, Theodore Roosevelt, Address to the Knights of Columbus,
New York City, 1915.

There is no room in this country for hyphenated Americanism. When I refer to hyphenated Americans, I do not refer to naturalized Americans. Some of the very best Americans I have ever known were naturalized Americans, Americans born abroad. But a hyphenated American is not an American at all. . . . The one absolutely certain way of bringing this nation to ruin, of preventing all possibility of its continuing to be a nation at all, would be to permit it to become a tangle of squabbling nationalities, an intricate knot of German-Americans, Irish-Americans, English-Americans, French-Americans, Scandinavian-Americans or Italian-Americans, each preserving its separate nationality, each at heart feeling more sympathy with Europeans of that nationality, than with the other citizens of the American Republic. . . . There is no such thing as a hyphenated American who is a good American. The only man who is a good American is the man who is an American and nothing else.

Source: Norman Assing, *Daily Alta California*, 1852.

To His Excellence Gov. Bigler

"Sir:—I am a Chinaman, a republican, and a lover of free institutions; am much attached to the principles of the Government and the United States; and therefore take the liberty of addressing you as the chief of the government of the state. Your official position gives you a great opportunity of good or evil. . . . The effect of your late message has been . . . to prejudice the public mind against my people, to enable those wait the opportunity to hunt them down, and rob them of the rewards of their toil. . . .

"We would beg to remind you that when your nation was a wilderness, and the nation from who you sprung barbarous, we exercised most of the arts and virtues of civilized life; that we are possessed of a language and literature, and that men skilled in science and the arts are numerous amongst us; that the producers of our manufactories, our sail and work-shops, form no small share of the commerce of the world; and that for centuries colleges, schools, charitable institutions, asylums and hospitals, have been as common as in your own land. . . . We came amongst you as mechanics or traders, and following every honorable business of life. You do not find us as pursuing occupations of a degrading character, except you consider labor degrading, which I am sure you do not. . . . As far as the aristocracy of skin is concerned, ours might compare with many of the European races; nor do we . . . believe that the framers of your declaration of rights ever suggested the propriety of establishing an aristocracy of skin."

Source: Joseph McDonnell, *Labor Standard,* June 30, 1878.

The cry that the "Chinese must go" is both narrow and unjust. It represents no broad or universal principle. It is merely a repetition of the cry that was raised years ago by American Indians against the immigration of Irishmen, Englishmen, Germans and others from European nations. It now ill becomes those, or the descendants of those, against whom this cry was raised in past years, to raise a similar tocsin against a class of foreigners who have been degraded by ages of oppression. . . .

The feeling at the bottom of the "Know Nothing" movement IN ITS EARLY DAYS was certainly a general one against low wages, and if it had raised the cry:

No low wages

No cheap labor!

Instead of sounding the intolerant, silly, and shameful cry against Irishmen, Englishmen, Germans and all other "foreigners," it would have accomplished incalculable good. As it was it fell into the hands of infamous, scheming politicians, who pandered to the worst prejudices of the masses by raising a cry against men of various religious faiths and foreign nationalities. This policy suited them; it raised them to prominence and office and allowed what they IN THEIR HEARTS desired, the onward march of low wages."

Part B: Long Essay Questions

Choose ONE of the following questions and write an analytical essay that uses specific, relevant evidence to support your thesis and to demonstrate the specified historical thinking skill. *Historical Thinking Skill: Contextualization. Thematic Learning Objective: Politics and Power, #3.* (35 minutes)

1. Historians debate the impact of the reform movements of the antebellum period of 1820–1860. Assess the extent to which the reforms of that period changed American society.

2. Historians debate the impact of the reform efforts of the Progressive era of 1890–1920. Assess the extent to which the reforms of that period changed American society.

ANSWER KEY

Practice Exam 2

1. **(B)**	11. **(D)**	21. **(D)**	31. **(B)**	41. **(C)**	51. **(A)**
2. **(D)**	12. **(D)**	22. **(B)**	32. **(A)**	42. **(B)**	52. **(B)**
3. **(A)**	13. **(D)**	23. **(B)**	33. **(C)**	43. **(D)**	53. **(C)**
4. **(A)**	14. **(C)**	24. **(C)**	34. **(A)**	44. **(B)**	54. **(D)**
5. **(A)**	15. **(A)**	25. **(A)**	35. **(D)**	45. **(C)**	55. **(C)**
6. **(B)**	16. **(B)**	26. **(B)**	36. **(A)**	46. **(A)**	
7. **(C)**	17. **(A)**	27. **(D)**	37. **(C)**	47. **(C)**	
8. **(B)**	18. **(B)**	28. **(D)**	38. **(B)**	48. **(A)**	
9. **(D)**	19. **(D)**	29. **(B)**	39. **(C)**	49. **(D)**	
10. **(B)**	20. **(C)**	30. **(C)**	40. **(C)**	50. **(D)**	

PRACTICE EXAM 2

Answers and Explanations to Multiple-Choice Questions

1. **(B)** The cartoonist Herblock was pointing out that the growing anticommunist sentiment in the United States following World War II could become a threat to the civil liberties of Americans. The hysterical figure climbing the ladder is about to extinguish the torch of liberty.

2. **(D)** In 1798, President John Adams and the Federalist Party in Congress were concerned that Americans supportive of France and French immigrants in America were working to undermine the U.S. government. This led to the passage of the Alien and Sedition Acts, which were criticized as violations of the liberties guaranteed by the Bill of Rights.

3. **(A)** Congress passed, over President Truman's veto, the McCarran Act in 1950, requiring groups deemed to be "subversive" to register with the federal government, prohibited some members of these groups from becoming American citizens, created an investigatory agency to find people suspected of engaging in subversive activities, and gave the president the power to detain suspected subversive people in the event of an emergency.

4. **(A)** John Locke's contract theory was well-known among the American colonial elites such as Franklin and was a foundational principle of American democracy. The concept is integral to both the Declaration of Independence and the Constitution of the United States.

5. **(A)** Grenville's argument that the colonies of the British Empire had virtual representation was criticized in both Parliament and the American colonies as illogical and not at all founded in British law. The backlash against Grenville's policies led to the repeal of the Stamp Act later in 1766.

6. **(B)** Benjamin Franklin was an early proponent of colonial unity, often arguing that the thirteen British colonies in America should work together for the betterment of all. A prime example of this type of advocacy was Franklin's famous "Join or Die" political cartoon from the French and Indian War era. His testimony to British officials in 1766

was directly related to the Stamp Act and colonial actions to protest against the stamp tax, such as the Stamp Act Congress. Franklin and other colonial leaders argued that the colonies should be given representation in Parliament if Parliament was going to tax the colonies.

7. **(C)** Published in 1881, Helen Hunt Jackson's book *A Century of Dishonor* was a scathing indictment of United States policy toward Indian tribes over the previous century. Jackson sent the book to every member of Congress, but it did not have as immediate an impact as she had hoped.

8. **(B)** The Indian Removal Act put Jackson's policy request into law in 1830. It took several years of political and legal maneuvering, but the Indian Removal act was eventually implemented during the presidency of Jackson's successor, Martin Van Buren. The Cherokee tribe, unlike the other affected tribes, resisted the pressure to sign a treaty that would cede their ancestral lands. The result of their resistance was their forcible removal, leading to the deaths of thousands of Cherokee.

9. **(D)** The Dawes Act established a system of land allotments to Indian tribes, granting 160 acres to the head of a family, and allowed for a method by which Indians could receive United States citizenship. The Dawes Act ended the reservation system of community ownership of land for Indian tribes and made the assimilation of Indians into American culture a matter of national policy.

10. **(B)** Martin Luther King, Jr., was only one of many civil rights leaders across the country, but he was probably the most prominent by the end of the 1950s. King coordinated his activist effort for civil rights with many of those civil rights leaders, culminating with the March on Washington for Jobs and Freedom in August 1963, which was organized by King, labor leader A. Phillip Randolph, and various other activist groups.

11. **(D)** Racial segregation was given the endorsement of the Supreme Court with the 1896 *Plessy v. Ferguson* decision, which established the "separate but equal" doctrine. Using that allowance, many states continued and expanded the Jim Crow laws that disenfranchised and discriminated against African Americans.

12. **(D)** Martin Luther King, Jr., followed the precedent set by Henry David Thoreau and Mohandas Gandhi and practiced nonviolent protest methods. King knew that in order to win the struggle for civil rights, advocates for racial equality must occupy the moral high ground. That meant that he did not support the use of violence as a means to achieve the end of segregation or to acquire voting rights.

13. **(D)** Susan B. Anthony and other advocates for women's rights often appealed to America's founding documents in their arguments for equality. In this quote, she echoes the list of grievances against the king of England found in the Declaration of Independence—taxation without representation, withholding trial by jury, depriving them of property without due process—as a way to connect the women's rights movement to the leaders of the Revolution and their struggle for freedom.

14. **(C)** Abolitionists sought freedom for slaves and felt that the promises outlined in the Declaration of Independence, namely that "all men are created equal," should and did apply to all people. Those promises could not be fulfilled until slaves were granted their freedom.

15. **(A)** The Nineteenth Amendment, ratified in 1920, gave women the right to vote on a nationwide basis. It was the result of at least seventy-two years of effort on the part of women's rights advocates, who had been arguing for equal suffrage since the adoption of the Declaration of Rights and Sentiments at the Seneca Falls Convention in 1848.

16. **(B)** Susan B. Anthony was, along with Elizabeth Cady Stanton, a founder of the National Woman Suffrage Association in 1869. Anthony was arrested for voting in the 1872 presidential election and refused to pay the fine imposed on her by a judge. In addition to women like Susan B. Anthony, other groups that have fought for voting rights include African Americans (Fifteenth Amendment) and young people (Twenty-sixth Amendment).

17. **(A)** Andrew Carnegie made sizable philanthropic contributions in both the United States and his homeland of Scotland. The cartoonist draws attention to Carnegie's cash donations and his monetary grants to build libraries while he was simultaneously cutting the wages of the workers in his steel plants. The dichotomous nature of Carnegie's wealth has often been used as a symbol of the "Gilded Age" of the late nineteenth century.

18. **(B)** Workers went on strike at Andrew Carnegie's Homestead Steel plant near Pittsburgh in 1892. Carnegie and his operations manager Henry Clay Frick hired the Pinkerton Detective Agency to defend the plant and the newly hired non-union workers. The strikers and the Pinkertons clashed violently, with the striking workers winning the battle. Pennsylvania state militia later arrived to restore order, allowing Frick to reopen the plant with the non-union workers.

19. **(D)** The Newlands Reclamation Act was part of the environmental legislation of the Progressive era. The law gave the federal government authority over water rights in much of the nation, which paved the way for federal construction of dams and irrigation projects. All of the other choices were federal attempts to regulate or limit the abusive practices of big businesses.

20. **(C)** President Theodore Roosevelt abandoned the policy of previous administrations, which saw federal troops used to quell strikes. Often, states employed state militias for the same purpose. Instead, Roosevelt gave the coal miners a voice at the negotiating table, brokering a compromise deal between the two groups in which the workers got a raise and promises of better safety conditions in exchange for a promise from the workers to not strike for ten years.

21. **(D)** Despite the freedom former slaves obtained via the Thirteenth Amendment, this representative of the Freedman's Bureau said that southern whites were slow to accept the new social conditions brought about by the amendment. Many southern states began to pass restrictive laws in an attempt to continue their dominance.

22. **(B)** In an effort to integrate the freed slaves into American political and social life, and to deny individual states the ability to legally discriminate against blacks, the Fourteenth Amendment declared, "No state shall make or enforce any law which shall abridge the privileges or immunities of citizens of the United States; nor shall any state deprive any person of life, liberty, or property, without due process of law; nor deny to any person within its jurisdiction the equal protection of the laws."

23. **(B)** Jim Crow legislation was a term used to describe laws passed to disenfranchise blacks and to systematize racial segregation. Some examples of Jim Crow laws include the poll tax, literacy tests, and separate facilities, including schools, for whites and blacks. The Jim Crow system was eroded by several Supreme Court decisions in the 1950s, most famously *Brown v. Board of Education* in 1954, and Congressional legislation in the 1960s such as the Civil Rights Act of 1964. Additionally, the Twenty-fourth Amendment prohibited the poll tax.

24. **(C)** The difficult living conditions that early settlers in Virginia endured led to a high mortality rate and a demand for laborers. The Virginia Company first implemented the headright system to encourage immigration from England. Under this system, settlers were granted an additional fifty acres for each servent they brought to Virginia. Subsequently, beginning in 1619, the company turned to the importation of African slaves in order to meet the increasing demand for unskilled labor in the burgeoning tobacco fields. By 1700, the slave population in Virginia had risen to approximately 8,000.

25. **(A)** As the large population of indentured servants earned their freedom by fulfilling their contracts, they had expected to receive land grants of their own with which they could support themselves and their families. Instead, most of the formerly indentured servants were held landless and grew increasingly restless under the political control of elite planters.

26. **(B)** Yeomen were a small part of the Chesapeake population, occupying a space in society between the elite planters and the indentured servants and slaves. Yeomen had little social and economic power in the Chesapeake colonies, but Thomas Jefferson would later advocate for the yeomen farmers as the basis for the American economic and democratic systems.

27. **(D)** Historian Eric Foner's 2010 Pulitzer Prize-winning book, *The Fiery Trial*, traces Abraham Lincoln's changing perspectives on slavery and abolition from his youth in Kentucky and Illinois all the way through his assassination in 1865. Foner's book argues that it is difficult to place labels on Lincoln's beliefs on these subjects because Lincoln did not hold a consistent belief throughout his life. Instead, Lincoln's thoughts on slavery changed as he gathered more information on the subject, met new people in his public and private life, and gained power as a politician.

28. **(D)** Up until the summer of 1862, when President Abraham Lincoln began contemplating the way he could legally emancipate slaves in the South, he had been repeatedly stating publicly that his whole goal in the war was to save the Union. President Lincoln used the Emancipation Proclamation to marry the freedom of the slaves to the plan of preserving the Union, declaring that the Proclamation was a "military necessity," and allowed for black men to serve in the United States Army through the Proclamation.

29. **(B)** The Emancipation Proclamation, despite being a groundbreaking document in United States history, was intentionally limited in its scope. President Abraham Lincoln was careful to stay within what he believed to be his Constitutional powers in issuing the document. He did so by only applying the document to the emancipation of slaves who were in states that were in rebellion on the date the Proclamation went into effect—January 1, 1863. President Lincoln had been stating, even before he was president, that he did not believe that the federal government had the authority to abolish

slavery. But the Civil War was a special circumstance, and President Lincoln believed that his interpretation of the Constitution allowed him special powers in the event of an insurrection. There were also political considerations that President Lincoln needed to take into account, especially the need to keep the slaveholding "Border States" of Delaware, Maryland, Kentucky, and Missouri in the Union. As such, the Emancipation Proclamation exempted those states from its decrees.

30. **(C)** The National Woman Suffrage Association (NWSA) was formed in 1869 and was active in women's rights causes until its merger with the American Woman Suffrage Association in 1890; among its leaders were Elizabeth Cady Stanton and Susan B. Anthony. NWSA advocated an amendment to the United States Constitution that would grant women the right to vote on a national basis. In addition to suffrage, NWSA campaigned for a broad-based platform of women's equality including political, social, and cultural issues.

31. **(B)** Women's suffrage activist Alice Paul first wrote the Equal Rights Amendment in 1923, when it was also first introduced in Congress. The proposed amendment's language guaranteed that the "Equality of rights under the law shall not be denied or abridged by the United States or by any State on account of sex." It was re-introduced in Congress every year until it finally passed in 1970. Congress imposed a time limit for ratification on the Amendment, originally 1979 but later extended until 1982. The Equal Rights Amendment fell short of ratification by eight states (or three, if the rescission of ratification of five states is not counted).

32. **(A)** This cartoon, drawn by an unknown artist sometime in 1801 or 1802, shows two Revolutionary leaders, Thomas Jefferson and Thomas Paine, coordinating their efforts to pull down the federal government that had been led by Jefferson's predecessors as president, George Washington and John Adams. Paine is shown with radical writings in his pockets and is depicted as a heavy drinker, while Jefferson, the new president, was shown as the Devil. The Federalist Party, led by Alexander Hamilton, had been in nominal control of the national government ever since the adoption of the Constitution in 1788 and escalated its written and verbal attacks on Thomas Jefferson's Republican (or Democratic-Republican) Party.

33. **(C)** The Twelfth Amendment altered the procedure by which the Electoral College voted for president and vice president. Previous to the amendment's ratification, the winner of the electoral vote became president and the second-place candidate became vice president. With the advent of the party system, it was obvious that having the top two executive branch officials come from different political parties would cause problems of governance. The Twelfth Amendment says, "[the Electors] shall name in their ballots the person voted for as President, and in distinct ballots the person voted for as Vice-President. . . ." This change meant that members of the Electoral College would now be voting for party tickets for the two high offices, not just voting for first and second choices for the office of president.

34. **(A)** The Federalist Party, led by Alexander Hamilton, had long been suspicious of Thomas Jefferson's political viewpoints and often characterized Jefferson as a radical and an atheist. The political press in the period of the early Republic was not shy about outright attacks on the characters of public officials, and being the author of the Decla-

ration of Independence did not in any way shield Jefferson from those attacks. Thomas Paine, the pamphleteer responsible for *Common Sense*, was also the subject of Federalist attacks because of his support for the radical revolutionaries in France.

35. **(D)** There were many factors that led to the election of Ronald Reagan as president, but one of the largest factors was the conservative reaction to the growth of government spending on social welfare programs under President Lyndon B. Johnson in the 1960s. President Johnson's "Great Society" agenda included new or expanded government spending to combat poverty, housing shortages, and nutritional needs for millions of Americans. Conservatives like President Reagan believed that issues such as those were not under the purview of the federal government, but rather should be handled by the individual states.

36. **(A)** During the debate over the ratification of the Constitution of the United States in 1787 and 1788, many people, generally categorized as the Antifederalists, argued that the new nation would be best served by a limited national government, with a larger role for the individual states, which would allow for the states to respond to the needs of their people on a local level. The Antifederalists were satisfied with the structure of the United States government under the Articles of Confederation, which had limited the powers of Congress and guaranteed the equality and sovereignty of each state.

37. **(C)** President Ronald Reagan ran on a platform of shrinking the size and spending of the federal government, and his inaugural address takes on that issue directly. President Reagan and the Republican Party had vowed to change the way the federal government interacted with the economic system of the United States, primarily promising to cut taxes, cut spending, and to reduce or eliminate regulations on businesses. This was a reversal of policy from much of the twentieth century, where presidents such as Franklin Roosevelt, Dwight Eisenhower, and Lyndon Johnson had used the federal government to shape a changing United States economy.

38. **(B)** President Ronald Reagan's economic policies, commonly called supply-side or "trickle-down" economics were intended to cut taxes and regulations while also cutting government spending in order to reduce the growing national debt. The theory behind much of President Reagan's economic plans was that the wealthy and business owners, with their taxes lowered and restrictions loosened, would be able to invest more money and spur job growth, thereby allowing working-class Americans to have more earning potential.

39. **(C)** President Jimmy Carter's 1977 speech on the energy crisis was part of an ongoing debate in the United States about how best to use natural resources such as petroleum and natural gas. President Carter urged Americans to change their energy consumption habits and advocated for national policies that would protect the environment, help the economy, and promote national defense.

40. **(C)** Starting with the presidential administration of Richard Nixon, the United States had been subjected to several oil embargoes enacted by the Organization of Petroleum Exporting Countries (OPEC). The embargoes had resulted in gasoline shortages, higher fuel prices, and other economic consequences. President Jimmy Carter was hoping to ease some of the threat of those embargoes by enacting a new national energy policy that would make the United States less reliant on imported petroleum.

41. **(C)** The 1899 cartoon makes the point that the United States misread the situation in the Philippines following the Spanish-American War (1898). Under the provisions of the Treaty of Paris (1898), the United States assumed several of Spain's possessions following the war, including the Philippines, Guam, and Puerto Rico. The United States stated that it would grant the Philippines independence sometime in the future, but for the time being, it held on to the Philippines. Many Filipinos were deeply disappointed in this outcome, hoping to attain independence, as Cuba had following the war. A resistance movement developed in the Philippines and a bloody three-year war, known as the Philippine-American War ensued. Filipino forces were led by Emilio Aguinaldo. The infantilization of the Filipino people in the image can be read on two levels. It serves as a visual pun, comparing Uncle Sam to a parent coming to the realization that a baby is more work than he or she thought. Also, it reflects racist attitudes toward the Filipino people.

42. **(B)** The cartoon questions the wisdom of American involvement in the Philippines. It does not reject the morality of such involvement. After all, the portrayal of Filipino rebel leader Emilio Aguinaldo as an infant seems to imply that the Philippines was not ready for self-rule. However, the cartoon wonders if the effort is worth it. Similar questions were raised during the war in Vietnam and during other American interventions.

43. **(D)** The cartoon depicts the war in the Philippines with rebels following the American victory in the Spanish-American War. Many Filipino people expected to gain independence after Spain's defeat. They were deeply disappointed that the United States decided to hold on to the Philippines. This move by the United States marks a turn toward a more imperialistic direction.

44. **(B)** Mercantilism, as practiced by European nations in the sixteenth through eighteenth centuries, was an economic system by which nations attempted to accumulate wealth by creating a trade surplus, especially by founding colonies on other continents. Mercantilism served to strengthen the power of monarchs and led to intense competition for land and resources between the European nations. Here, the Englishman Richard Hakluyt advocated for English participation in that competition by striving to establish colonies on the Atlantic coast of America.

45. **(C)** Richard Hakluyt wrote extensively on the benefits of establishing colonies in the New World. The arguments he presented in favor of doing so included economic, spiritual, political, and nationalistic benefits for England. England's first permanent colony was established at Jamestown in Virginia in 1607 and by 1732 there were thirteen colonies along the Atlantic Coast of North America, as well as an English foothold in Canada and island possessions in the Caribbean Sea.

46. **(A)** Edwards is asserting that God gives individuals a chance to rectify their sins because he is merciful. The sermon presents a dark view of humanity, but Edwards offers hope to those who find their way to Jesus. This sermon is one of the central texts of the Great Awakening. The idea that human beings are inherently good, but are corrupted by the evils of society (B) is associated with Jean-Jacques Rousseau, one of the great philosophers of the French enlightenment. Edwards has a dimmer view of human nature. In Edwards's view, God is angry, but he is not merciless (C). It is his action, after all, that is preventing us from descending into the fires of hell. Choice D describes a

more modern view of ethics and morality; Edwards certainly argued that it is important that you believe in the saving grace of Jesus.

47. **(C)** Edwards was a central figure in the Great Awakening. In the face of declining membership in the Congregational Church of New England, preachers such as Edwards attempted to revive flagging piety. By the 1730s, we see several charismatic ministers attempting to infuse a new passion into religious practice. These ministers, and their followers, were part of a religious resurgence known as the Great Awakening. The movement took a more emotional, and less cerebral, approach to religion. The other choices identify nineteenth-century religious movement.

48. **(A)** By the early 1700s, the white-hot piety of Puritanism had dimmed considerably. The succeeding generations of New England became increasingly interested in commerce and matters of this world, rather than spiritual things. They had not endured religious suppression in England, nor had they suffered through the difficulties of settling in the New World. The Great Awakening hoped to revive the intense religious feeling of the previous century. Disestablishment—the severing of links between the church and the state—occurred in many states in the early nineteenth century (B). New England remained fairly homogeneous throughout the colonial period. It failed to attract immigrants from outside of England (C). There were devastating wars with American Indians in New England, such as King Philip's War, but those wars occurred in the seventeenth century (D).

49. **(D)** Edwards was part of the Great Awakening, and the Great Awakening contributed to changes in colonists' understanding of God, themselves, and the world around them. Specifically, it led to questioning of traditional authorities and encouraged colonists to see themselves as agents for change. It did not specifically encourage a questioning of British policies (A); this did not occur until after the French and Indian War, well after the height of the Great Awakening. Great Awakening ministers did not, for the most part, condemn slavery (C), nor did they encourage better treatment of American Indians (D).

50. **(D)** The Ford Motor Company was known for the policy of its chairman, Henry Ford, to pay his workers well enough to be able to afford the product they were making. American consumers of the 1920s were able to buy more products at affordable prices, but were also subjected to a great deal of advertising that attempted to convince them of the necessity of those purchases in order to increase or maintain their status in society.

51. **(A)** Credit-buying plans offered by companies like the Ford Motor Company allowed consumers to purchase products that they otherwise may not have been able to afford if they had been required to pay the entire purchase price up front. Many consumers were willing to use credit to buy the new products as a way to demonstrate their status in an increasingly status-centered culture. However, the growth of consumer debt was a significant harbinger of the approaching economic calamity of the Great Depression.

52. **(B)** The Industrial Revolution in the United States began in the late 1700s and grew along with the nation throughout the 1800s. American manufacturing had become one of the world's leading exporters of manufactured goods, in no small part because of the contributions of numerous inventors and entrepreneurs like Eli Whitney, Charles Goodyear, John Deere, Cyrus McCormick, and Henry Ford himself.

53. **(C)** The numbers in the table illustrate a major problem for farmers in the post–Civil War period. Commodity prices for agricultural products were falling; in other words, farmers were getting less and less for their produce. It reached a point where it was hardly worth growing crops. The costs of production were almost more than the price they received for their goods. A primary culprit in this situation was mechanization and improved agricultural techniques. These created surpluses which pushed down prices. Another important culprit was the tight money supply, which contributed to deflation. An important demand of the movement was to base currency on silver as will as gold.

54. **(D)** Farmers' organizations, such as the Grange and the Populist Party, wanted more money in circulation so that there would be inflation. Inflation would lead to higher prices for agricultural commodities. The populists demanded an end to the gold standard and a shift to currency backed by silver as well as gold.

55. **(C)** In the last decades of the nineteenth century, farmers organized groups to challenge the corporate-driven policies that were putting them in a bind. The Populist Party became a formidable force in the 1890s. The movement challenged the concentration of wealth and power among eastern industrialists and bankers. It supported a national income tax so that those with higher incomes would pay more than the poor. It also supported free and unlimited coinage of silver. The Populist Party wanted the United States to get off the gold standard and to issue money backed by silver as well. This would increase the amount of money in circulation and would lead to inflation. Farmers supported inflationary policies so that the prices they received for their produce would increase.

Index

Washington, George, 86, 88, 97–98, 105

Washington Conference, 251

Watergate, 294

Webster-Ashburton Treaty, 140

Wesley, John, 126

West Bank, 312

Western Hemisphere, 136–140

West Indies, 61, 63–64, 106

Westward expansion, 131, 142–143, 150–153, 183–187, 192–193

Whigs, 116

Whiskey Rebellion, 103

"White Man's Burden, The," 235

White superiority, 42

White supremacy, 227

Whitney, Eli, 129

Wilderness protection, 183–184, 187

Williams, Roger, 58

Wilmot Proviso, 140–141

Wilson, Woodrow, 216–217, 227, 239–241, 243–244

Women
in antebellum society, 133
domesticity of, 125, 133–134, 199
Equal Rights Amendment, 295
in Great Depression, 225
liberation movement by, 282
Progressive movement and, 210–211
rights movement by, 121, 171
"Rosie the Riveter," 248–249
in twentieth century, 208

Women's Army Auxiliary Corps, 249

Wool Act, 65

Worcester v. Georgia, 117, 143

Work, exchange, and technology, 9–10

Working class, 179, 188

Works Progress Administration, 222

World Trade Organization, 317

World War I, 206, 241–247, 255, 264

World War II, 206, 233, 247–253, 255, 264, 278

Wounded Knee massacre, 193

X

XYZ affair, 88

Y

Yalta Conference, 253

"Yellow Journalism," 236

Yom Kippur War, 271

Yugoslavia, 311–312

Z

Zenger, John Peter, 73–74

Zimmermann note, 243

 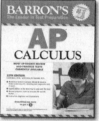

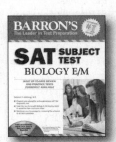

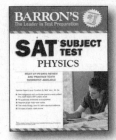

How to Use the CD-ROM

The software is not installed on your computer; it runs directly from the CD-ROM. Barron's CD-ROM includes an "autorun" feature that automatically launches the application when the CD is inserted into the CD-ROM drive. In the unlikely event that the autorun feature is disabled, follow the manual launching instructions below.

Windows®

1. Click on the Start button and choose "My Computer."
2. Double-click on the CD-ROM drive, which will be named **AP_US_History.exe**.
3. Double-click **AP_US_History.exe** to launch the program.

Mac®

1. Double-click the CD-ROM icon.
2. Double-click the **AP_US_History** icon to start the program.

SYSTEM REQUIREMENTS

(Flash Player 10.2 is recommended)

Microsoft® Windows®	**MAC® OS X**
Processor: 2.33GHz or faster x86-compatible processor, or Intel Atom™ 1.6Hz or faster processor for netbook class devices.	Processor: Intel Core™ Duo 1.83GHz or faster processor.
Memory: 512MB of RAM.	Memory: 512MB of RAM.
Graphics Memory: 128MB.	Graphics Memory: 128MB.
Platforms:	Platforms:
Windows 7, Windows Vista® Home Premium, Business, Ultimate, or Enterprise (including 64 bit editions) with Service Pack 2, Windows XP, Windows Server® 2008, Windows 8 Classic.	Mac OS X v10.6, v10.7, v10.8, or v10.9